THE DEVELOPING PERSON

The Developing Person

KATHLEEN STASSEN BERGER

BRONX COMMUNITY COLLEGE

CITY UNIVERSITY OF NEW YORK

WORTH PUBLISHERS, INC.

The Developing Person

Library of Congress Catalog Card Number: 80-80298
ISBN: 0-87901-117-3
Sixth Printing, June 1985

Editors: June Fox
         Peter Deane
Illustrator: Angie Lloyd
Picture Editor: June Lundborg
Production: Kenneth R. Ekkens
Design: Malcolm Grear Designers
Composition: Graphic Arts Composition, Philadelphia
Printing and Binding: R. R. Donnelley & Sons

Cover: *Children's Games* (Detail), Pieter Bruegel, The Elder
       Kunsthistorisches Museum, Vienna

Worth Publishers, Inc.
444 Park Avenue South
New York, New York 10016

Preface

I wrote this book because throughout my eight years of teaching I have longed for a text that was accurate and current, that reflected the best theories and research in developmental psychology, and, at the same time, seemed to care about the student's interests and motivation. The present book represents my attempt to achieve these goals.

At its most useful and exciting level, developmental psychology employs the scientific tradition to address both practical and urgent human questions. For me, it is precisely the combination of rigorous ongoing research and its necessary, often surprising, application that makes developmental psychology a fascinating field to study and teach.

In writing this book, then, I have naturally combined discussions of theory and research with examples of practical application and unique personal events. The laws of genetics, for example, are discussed not only in terms of their broad implications for human development, but also with regard to such things as the treatment and prevention of genetic disorders. The nature of parent-infant bonding is viewed in several theoretical aspects, and at the same time is seen in terms of the potential impact of a mother's holding or not holding her baby in the hours after birth. The universal playfulness of children not only is explained in terms of its reflection of physical, cognitive, and psychosocial development, but is illustrated with dozens of examples of play patterns in different cultures, communities, and age groups. Likewise, the processes of adolescent cognition are treated from a theoretical perspective and at the same time are applied to the many personal questions that teenagers must confront, including contraception, drug use, and career choice. Other problems of personal and social importance, such as infant day care, child abuse, reading readiness, and mainstreaming, are also discussed within both a scientific and a practical framework. Throughout, my hope has been to encourage students to relate developmental psychology to the events of their own lives, and in so doing to share my enthusiasm for this exciting subject.

The Organization of the Book

Two introductory chapters, one on definitions and methodology, the other on theoretical perspectives, are followed by five parts that correspond to major chronological periods of child development—the prenatal period, infancy, early childhood, middle childhood, and adolescence. With the exception of the prenatal section, each part consists of a trio of chapters dealing with physical development, cognitive development, and psychosocial development, respectively. I believe this topical organization within a chronological frame provides the clearest way for readers to realize that the various aspects of development are interrelated—and that body, mind, and personality develop together, rather than separately.

In keeping with the emphasis on research, the book highlights the first years of life, although I do not believe that this period is necessarily more "critical" than later years. However, I do think that the basic aspects of development, such as the interaction between heredity and environment, the importance of social, cultural, and economic influences, and the nature of the learning process, are best explained carefully in relation to their initial occurrences.

Finally, the adult years are briefly discussed in an epilogue, not because I believe development stops at age 21, but simply because to do justice to the early years as well as the adult years would demand a much longer book—one probably too long for a one-semester course.

The Book as a Teaching Tool

To help students apply concepts rather than merely memorize them, I have used two special devices, the Research Report and the Closer Look. The Research Reports include details of relevant studies and explore the strengths and weaknesses of the methodology, as well as the conclusions of the research. Closer Looks provide a personal examination of some aspect of development and are intended to be thought-provoking. In addition, each chapter opens with a series of deceptively simple true-false questions intended to spark the reader's interest; and each closes with a numbered summary of the chapter's central concepts and a list of recommended paperback readings for the student's personal use. (For students doing research papers, the bibliography at the end of the book should provide ample source material.)

A final note about this book should probably say something about the author, since any author's theoretical perspective, values, and assumptions will influence what is included in, or left out of, any text. My training has been chiefly behaviorist and cognitive, and I particularly admire Jean Piaget's work, although I wish he had as much to say about learning as he does about the process of thinking. At the same time, I have great respect for Erik Erikson, despite the fact that his work is more art than science. Also appealing and convincing to me is Urie Bronfenbrenner's emphasis on the ecological approach to developmental psychology.

Equally important in shaping my viewpoint have been my students and my own children. My students have come from dozens of ethnic, economic, and educational backgrounds, and have broadened my understanding of human development through the questions they ask and the answers they give. My children—the oldest is in early adolescence; the youngest, now a preschooler, was an infant during most of the writing of the book; and my middle child is, appropriately, in middle childhood—have provided immediate, and sometimes stunning, insights into the process of development. (They have also provided me with rich material for some of the anecdotal examples in the text.) All told, my theoretical orientation and my experience as a teacher and a parent have led me to believe that a broad, eclectic approach to human development is the best one.

**Supplementary
Materials**

A *Study Guide* is available to aid students in their understanding of the key concepts and terms in the text, as well as to help them review the material. Each chapter includes a list of learning objectives, a detailed summary, and an extensive battery of self-tests including matching, true-false, and multiple-choice questions and a final quiz. Along with the answers to these tests, page numbers are given indicating where in the text the concept is explained.

For the instructor, there is a comprehensive *Instructor's Resource Book,* which includes ideas for lectures, class discussions, essay tests, and research papers, and a *Test Bank* with over a thousand four-choice multiple-choice questions.

Thanks

Every textbook is the work of many people. This is especially true for *The Developing Person,* in part because the editors and sales staff of Worth Publishers are devoted to excellence, and the company provides consistent help in meeting their high standards. I am particularly grateful to June Fox, for her tireless efforts, from the signing of the contract through the many months of development and production, and to Peter Deane, for his countless valuable contributions.

Many academic reviewers provided suggestions, criticism, references, and encouragement. Each of them made the book a better one, and I thank them all:

Linda Acredolo, University of California, Davis
Barbara L. Blum, Herbert H. Lehman College
Joseph J. Campos, University of Denver
Catherine Cooper, University of Texas, Austin
D. R. Devers, North Virginia Community College
Robert Dennehy, Pace University
Richard Elardo, University of Iowa
Gregory Fautz, University of Calgary
Larry Fenson, San Diego State University
Harold Grotevant, University of Texas
Calvin Hall, University of California, Santa Cruz
Ann Dell Duncan-Hively, Spaulding Youth Center, Tilton, N.H.
John C. Johnson, Weatherford College
Paul S. Kaplan, Suffolk County Community College
Sandra Kreeger, Suffolk County Community College
Charles LaBounty, Hamline University
Asenath LaRue, University of California, Los Angeles
Judith Lindfors, University of Texas, Austin
Eric Mash, University of Calgary
Cecil Nichols, Miami-Dade Community College
Ardis Peterson, Contra Costa College
J. M. Pirone, Rockland Community College
Harriette Ritchie, American River College
Judy F. Rosenblith, Wheaton College
John Sempowski, Monroe Community College
Maria Taranto, Nassau Community College
Diana S. Trenary, Eastern Kentucky University
Trude Unger, Brookdale Community College

I am particularly grateful to five reviewers who read virtually the entire manuscript in several drafts. Joseph Campos was one of the first reviewers to see the original outline and draft chapters in 1976, and over the last three years he has read drafts, revisions, and the final manuscript. The combination of his perceptive criticism and his support and encouragement at every stage has been invaluable. Eric Mash and John Sempowksi also read several versions of many chapters. Their suggestions were particularly useful in the most difficult chapter of all to write—the first one. Paul Kaplan, a most conscientious reviewer, has been helpful in shaping the book as a whole, for he has a clear view of the need for a developmental psychology text that maintains accuracy and integrity while being interesting and readable. Finally, a special thanks to Asenath LaRue, who not only read and reread the entire manuscript but who also gave special help with the Epilogue.

I am very grateful to my husband and children for providing the steady support that has allowed me to juggle the many demands of teaching, writing, and family life. And my students have provided inspiration throughout. Without them, the book could not have been written; to them, the book is dedicated.

New York City   Kathleen Stassen Berger
January, 1980

The Developing Person

…"Because, after all,
A person's a person no matter how small."

Horton

THE DEVELOPING PERSON

Introduction

To be what we are, and to become what we are capable of becoming, is the only end of life.

Robert Louis Stevenson

All cases are unique, and very similar to others.

T. S. Eliot
The Cocktail Party

True or False?

The average teenage boy shows higher math achievement than the average teenage girl, even though boys and girls in elementary school show equal math aptitude.

Keeping an infant confined to a small, dark living space during the first year of life, with little communication or stimulation from others, is bound to cause irreversible retardation.

If your intelligence test scores are in the top 1 percent, you are probably more likely than your less brilliant contemporaries to avoid divorce or being placed in a mental institution.

As seemed to be the case fifty years ago, "only" children today are often destined to become loners.

Research showing that people in late adulthood scored lower on intelligence tests than people in middle adulthood and lower still than people in early adulthood proves that intelligence declines with age.

The aim of developmental psychology is to understand the processes of human growth and change. When confronted with a person at any moment of his or her life, developmental psychologists try to determine what events and circumstances shaped that individual; they also try to predict what that person's future might hold. Developmental psychologists are not unique in this interest. We all try to interpret past experiences and speculate about our future accomplishments and those of the people we know. Of course, none of us, no matter how perceptive or highly trained, can understand or predict anyone's life with complete accuracy. Yet, as you will discover in this book, decades of research in developmental psychology have yielded a wealth of information about usual and unusual development, information that helps us understand and predict with increasing insight.

Two Infants Named Cynthia

To show how the process of explanation and prediction operates, this chapter begins and ends with an account of two babies named Cynthia who captured newspaper headlines in New York City early in 1979.

Cynthia Callow

Ten-month-old Cynthia Callow was admitted to a hospital on New Year's Day, dehydrated and losing weight. A normal 10-month-old weighs about 20 pounds (9 kilograms), but Cynthia was down to 9.3 pounds, 2 pounds less than her weight two months earlier.

When doctors thoroughly examined her digestive system and found nothing wrong, they tried to learn about her family background. Cynthia had been born an unwanted, sickly, 3-pound baby in Colombia, South America. Her mother had given her to a convent, where she stayed until she was placed with her adoptive parents, Pat and John Callow. The Callows knew very little about her medical history; they knew only that their long-awaited baby was wasting away.

Cynthia was fed every common and uncommon infant formula, including those based on cow's milk, goat's milk, and soybean concentrate. To each one, she responded with diarrhea and vomiting, losing precious ounces. Finally, Cynthia was given human breast milk, and it worked. As one member of the hospital staff described it: "Mother's milk is like magic. It's the only thing she can keep down."

However, Cynthia needed almost a quart of milk a day, more than the hospital or the local chapter of the La Leche League (a group of breast-feeding mothers) could supply. Her parents appealed to the public (*Newsday*, January 11, 1979). The response was overwhelming (*Newsday*, January 12, 1979). More than a thousand breast-feeding women offered their milk. The reaction of Diane Ryan, whose 1-year-old son weighed 23 pounds, was typical: "I know if I didn't have any milk I'd want someone to help me . . . I have plenty to share." Three weeks later Cynthia was discharged from the hospital, well on her way to recovery.

Cynthia Feliccea

Nine-month-old Cynthia Feliccea was found frozen to death in her home, which had been without heat for about a year (*The New York Times*, February 7, 1979). Cynthia had lived with seventeen relatives, including her parents, grandparents, a great-grandmother, and six other children. Despite the frigid weather and the lack of heat, apparently none of them had thought about keeping her warm: she froze while lying in her carriage, clad in only a diaper. It seems they had also forgotten to feed her sometimes, because she was malnourished, dehydrated, and weighed only 9 pounds when she died, half the normal weight for her age (*The New York Times*, February 8, 1979).

Public officials already knew about this family. In August 1974, an anonymous caller had reported them for child neglect. A social worker investigated and concluded that the charges were unfounded. In May 1978, a judge of the Family Court had put the family "on probation," although what this meant in practical terms is unclear. In addition, the household's monthly income of $1400 came from the government in Social Security, pension, and welfare checks, which suggests that several government agencies might have known about various family members.

Cynthia's death brought renewed official attention to the plight of the other children in the household. All of them were hospitalized for exposure to the cold; one of them, Cynthia's 2-year-old brother, Thomas, was suffering from frostbite.

Questions Raised by the Two Cynthias

What insight can developmental psychology offer about the two Cynthias? Could developmental psychologists explain the biological, psychological, or sociological factors that caused the vomiting of one baby and the death of another? If so, could they then predict what the future is likely to be for both families? For instance, what are the chances that Cynthia Callow's malnutrition might have hindered her brain development, causing her to become a mentally retarded child? Will her hospitalization affect her later development? Will her illness affect the way her parents interact with her? And what is the outlook for Cynthia Feliccea's brothers and sisters?

The answers to these questions have practical implications for other children and their families. In fact, research on nutrition, adoption, hospitalization, child neglect, and foster care is changing our understanding of, and our attitudes about, many of these topics. At the end of this chapter, we will try to answer these questions and discuss the implications. But first, let us explore the nature and methods of developmental psychology, to help put those answers into context.

Definitions

Briefly, *developmental psychology is the branch of psychology that studies how people change with time*. Like most areas of psychology, it is *rooted in the scientific study of behavior*, and *nourished by a practical concern for human needs*. Developmental psychologists study *all* aspects of development, at every period of life, from conception until death.

The Three Domains

To make it easier to study, human development often is somewhat arbitrarily separated into three domains: the physical, including body changes and motor skills; the cognitive, including thought and language; and the psychosocial, including emotions, personality, and relationships with other people (see Figure 1.1).

All three domains are important at every age. For instance, studying infant nutrition, memory, and affection is part of understanding the first year of life, as are dozens of other aspects of physical, cognitive, and psychosocial development. To understand adolescence, developmental psychologists study changes in such things as body size, shape, and function; in the ability to think about abstract ideas; and in emotions, values, and goals.

Many of the behaviors that developmental psychologists study may at first seem to be in only one of these domains. For example, the study of the first words babies speak is now an active area of research in language development, which logically seems part of mental, or cognitive, development. When psychologists focus on one behavior, however, they recognize that it cannot be divorced from other aspects of development. The child's first words depend not only on the child's mental development but also on his or her physiological maturity and social exposure. Indeed, research on infant language has led to cross-cultural analyses of baby talk, and an appreciation of the way babies elicit baby talk from their parents, as well as the way

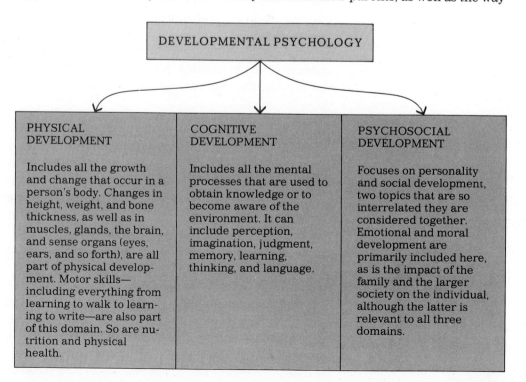

Figure 1.1 *The division of development into three domains makes it easier to study, but we must remember that very few factors belong exclusively to one domain or another. Development is not piecemeal but holistic: each aspect of development is related to all three domains.*

DEVELOPMENTAL PSYCHOLOGY

PHYSICAL DEVELOPMENT

Includes all the growth and change that occur in a person's body. Changes in height, weight, and bone thickness, as well as in muscles, glands, the brain, and sense organs (eyes, ears, and so forth), are all part of physical development. Motor skills—including everything from learning to walk to learning to write—are also part of this domain. So are nutrition and physical health.

COGNITIVE DEVELOPMENT

Includes all the mental processes that are used to obtain knowledge or to become aware of the environment. It can include perception, imagination, judgment, memory, learning, thinking, and language.

PSYCHOSOCIAL DEVELOPMENT

Focuses on personality and social development, two topics that are so interrelated they are considered together. Emotional and moral development are primarily included here, as is the impact of the family and the larger society on the individual, although the latter is relevant to all three domains.

parents elicit language from their children. It seems that parents all over the world speak to their babies with a certain inflection, pronunciation, and vocabulary, a way of speaking that has been dubbed "Motherese" (Snow and Ferguson, 1977). For instance, "choo-choo" and "tummy" are words created by parents trying to communicate with babies who find "train" and "stomach" too hard to pronounce.

Understanding when, why, and how a child talks is thus related to all three domains, not just to cognitive development. Developmental psychologists agree that development is holistic, that is, whole, or unified. Although they may focus on a particular domain in their research, they realize that each aspect of development relates to the others, creating a unified whole. In addition, this holistic view often leads them to study research outside the traditional areas of psychology. If you glance at the bibliography at the end of this book, you will notice references to work in medicine, education, history, linguistics, anthropology, and sociology, as well as psychology. All these disciplines contribute to our understanding of human development.

Old Controversies and New Directions

Most developmental psychologists agree that all aspects of development, at all periods in the life span, are important. However, controversies rage about which aspects should be emphasized and to what degree. Here we will look briefly at five particularly significant controversies.

Nature and Nurture

Some psychological research focuses on "nature," the inborn capacities and limitations of each person. Other studies emphasize "nurture," the way a person is raised—the influence of family, school, neighborhood, and culture. The continuing debate over whether inherited or acquired traits are greater determinants of human behavior is called the nature-nurture controversy.

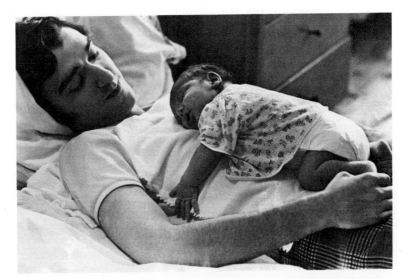

Figure 1.2 *Even in the first days of life, nature and nurture interact. Inborn characteristics (such as a placid temperament) and environmental factors (such as a loving father) affect each infant's development.*

All psychologists agree that both nature *and* nurture are essential to development, and that the *interaction* between nature and nurture is the crucial influence on any particular individual. They point out, for example, that intelligence is determined by the interplay of heredity and such aspects of the social and physical environment as schooling and nutrition. Despite their acknowledgment of the interaction between nature and nurture, however, psychologists sometimes get into heated arguments about the relative importance of each. When Arthur Jensen published a report (1969) stating that most of a child's intelligence is inherited, for instance, hundreds of psychologists wrote papers either criticizing or defending his ideas. (We shall learn more about this particular controversy in Chapter 3.)

Maturation and Learning

maturation- aging process
Learning-experience

Maturation and learning are two distinct processes that bring about changes in the course of every individual's development. Maturation results from the aging process, while learning is produced by experience. Specifically, maturation is an autonomous internal process that results from biochemical information transmitted by the individual's genes. (A key word in that definition is *autonomous,* which means self-regulating, or unaffected by learning.) The genetic mechanisms that control maturation determine the traits that typify a species and the sequence in which those traits emerge. The maturation pattern of the human jaw, for example, determines when baby teeth will appear, when they will be lost, and how the permanent teeth will arrange themselves in the mouth, just as maturation determines when a child will be able to pronounce correctly words beginning with triple consonants, such as "street" or "spring."

Learning, by contrast, refers to changes within the individual that occur because of specific experiences. Some learning experiences are obvious, as in a math lesson, with 8-year-old children learning to do division with the help of their teacher, a workbook, a set of math blocks, and the promise of a gold star. Others are less obvious, as in the efforts of a baby trying to walk, in imitation of others and in an attempt to get at attractive objects that cannot be reached by crawling.

Gesell and Watson   Is either process—maturation or learning—more important than the other? Some psychologists have thought so. Arnold Gesell, a leader of child study in the first half of the twentieth century, emphasized maturation. He believed that the biological processes of growth within each child are much more powerful than family and culture. According to Gesell, "Environmental factors support, inflect, and modify but they do not generate the progression of development . . . . The glove goes on the hand; the hand determines the glove" (Gesell, 1954).

The opposite point of view was articulated by John B. Watson, another dominant figure in the early decades of this century. He believed that "babies are made, not born." Almost everything, according to Watson, is learned:

> Give me a dozen healthy infants, well-formed, and my own specified world to bring them up in and I'll guarantee to take any one at random and train him to become any type of specialist I might select—doctor, lawyer, merchant, chief, and yes, even beggar-man and thief, regardless of his talents, penchants, abilities, vocations, and the race of his ancestors. [Watson, 1930]

Most psychologists today would agree that both Gesell and Watson overstated their cases. However, while few contemporary researchers would go to the ex-

Figure 1.3 *In practice, it is impossible to separate the effects of maturation and learning in the acquisition of any skill, such as this rascal's ability to balance on the edge of the sink.*

tremes that Gesell and Watson did, this controversy is still very much alive, for two reasons. First, it is difficult to prove whether maturation or learning is more responsible for a particular developmental change; second, the practical implications involved are enormous.

For example, although boys and girls in elementary school show the same math aptitude, the mathematical achievement of the average teenage boy is higher than that of the average teenage girl. Is this discrepancy a result of maturation? Does something develop within the male brain at puberty that permits young men to grasp math concepts more easily? Or is it the result of learning? Do young women learn that mathematical ability is not considered feminine? Do their parents or teachers have the same view and therefore discourage them from taking advanced math? If the difference in the math ability of adolescent males and females is maturational, it is foolish and frustrating to expect young women to do as well in math as young men. On the other hand, if the difference is the result of learning, we are wasting half our mathematical talent by not encouraging girls to develop their full math potential.

The controversy over the relative importance of maturation and learning is not easy to settle because both maturation and learning account for many developmental changes. And, of course, individual differences make the issue even more complex, because genetic factors might play a major role in the level of achievement of one person, while learning is primarily responsible for the same ability in another. One girl simply might not have the mental ability to master trigonometry as fast as her brother can; her younger sister, on the other hand, may have more aptitude than the brother, yet might shy away from advanced math because she has been taught that it is "masculine."

Figure 1.4 *Development can be envisioned (a) as a continuous, steady progression or (b) as a series of distinct stages, separated by transitional periods during which rapid change occurs.*

(a)

Continuity and Discontinuity

How would you describe human growth? Would you say we gradually grow older and more mature, as a seedling becomes a tree? Or do you think we undergo sudden changes, like a caterpillar becoming a butterfly?

Many psychologists emphasize the continuity of development. They believe there is a continual progression from the beginning of life to the end. Accomplishments that seem abrupt, such as a baby's first step, can be viewed as the final event in weeks of practice and growth. In the same way, these psychologists see learning to

Figure 1.5 *Learning to walk can be seen as a series of points along a continuum, beginning with reflexive kicking in the first days after birth and ending with the effortless stride of a typical 4-year-old. This infant is about halfway there.*

(b)

talk or read, or the entering of adolescence or adulthood, as a gradual process rather than an abrupt change.

Many other psychologists, called discontinuity theorists, think that growth occurs in stages, with distinct abilities and problems typical at each stage. They believe that, at certain times during life, a person moves from one level to another, as though climbing a flight of stairs. As you will see in Chapter 2, this view has been held by two of the most famous psychologists, Sigmund Freud and Erik Erikson.

According to discontinuity theorists, development occurs more quickly during periods of transition from one stage to another. After each phase of rapid change, the person is notably different in some way. For example, according to Erikson (1963), the new mobility gained by babies when they begin to walk and run changes the way they respond to other people and think about themselves. They become independent, proud, and stubborn—much different from their former dependent and pliable selves.

Childhood and Adulthood

Are children essentially different from adults? Are they unique? Or are they simply small adults? Today, childhood is regarded as a distinct phase of development, but it was not always so. As historian Philippe Ariès (1962) has shown, children in earlier centuries have been variously ignored, exploited, coddled, or treated as adults. His historical survey of art, literature, clothing, and sexual habits led him to the conclusion that there was no concept of childhood in Europe before 1600. Children were cared for until they could take care of themselves—at about age 6—and then they entered the adult world. During the Middle Ages, for example, children dressed as adults, drank with them, and worked beside them at home and in the fields. Children could be husbands and wives, kings and queens—or hung as thieves.

Figure 1.6 *Louis XIV became king of France in 1643, at age 5, ruling until his death in 1715. This portrait shows him at age 10 astride a kingly stallion, wearing a heavy helmet and ornate clothes, precisely as if he were an adult. Historians have discovered that the day-to-day life of the child king, in fact, included many activities we normally reserve for adults: little Louis drank wine, partied until the wee hours of the morning, and played sexual games with his nursemaids.*

Children continued to be without a separate role or status for centuries. Although children of the rich usually received special care and tutoring, it was not until the late 1800s that laws providing universal education and prohibiting child labor began to appear. At the same time, psychologists came to believe that the events of childhood shape a person's entire adult life, and they began to stress the importance of early experiences. They undertook the scientific study of early development, distinguishing the sequences of biological and psychological growth.

Figure 1.7 *Before society recognized the child's right to special care and protection, labor was an accepted way of life for children. They were especially employable in the coal mines because they could crawl into shafts too narrow for adults to squeeze through. These boys worked in Appalachia in 1908.*

The emphasis on early childhood is still strong in developmental psychology. Some authorities hold that the first few minutes after birth are critical in the formation of the parent-infant bond, or that intelligence and personality are determined in the first five years. Recently another point of view has emerged. Psychologists who study development in the later years have come to realize that some individuals change dramatically in middle childhood, adolescence, and adulthood. Many developmental psychologists now believe that the first years of life have been overemphasized, while the later years have been neglected.

Children in Guatemala Jerome Kagan is one psychologist who thinks we have overstressed the early years (Kagan et al., 1978). In an isolated village in Guatemala, Kagan found that "infants typically spend their first year confined to a small dark hut. They are not played with, rarely spoken to, poorly nourished . . . . When compared to American babies of the same age, the Guatemalan infants are retarded" (Kagan, 1978). This retardation is apparent in what they can remember, how they play with toys, and when they learn to talk. For example, they begin to speak at 3 years, a year and a half later than the typical North American baby.

By 4 or 5, the social world of these children expands as they play together and help their parents with work. These additional experiences apparently advance the learning process. Tests of older children from this village show that at around age 10 they begin to overcome their early retardation. By adolescence, they do almost as well on tests of memory and reasoning as North American teenagers do, leading Kagan to conclude that their early deprivation had little, if any, long-term effect.

Although the importance of the later years is being acknowledged increasingly, most developmental psychologists still specialize in childhood and adolescence. Ninety percent of the articles in *Developmental Psychology* (a journal published by the American Psychological Association) are about the first twenty years of life. And most textbooks in developmental psychology, like this one, focus on childhood.

Wide and Narrow Focus: The Ecological Approach

Recently, several developmental psychologists have emphasized that in order to understand human growth and change more fully, we should pay more attention to the overall environment in which development occurs. This ecological approach (Barker, 1968; Bronfenbrenner, 1977) takes its name from the ecological perspective in biology, which considers the interaction between living things and the physical environment, as well as the relationship of one living thing to another. To use the ecological approach in developmental psychology requires looking at the physical, social, and cultural environments in which people develop.

The scope and implications of the ecological approach are best seen by Urie Bronfenbrenner's (1977) explanation of the four levels of environmental structures that the ecological approach considers:

1. *The microsystem.* The interaction between the person and the environment in the immediate setting. For instance, how and when a child interacts with other family members at home, and how the size and design of the home affects this interaction, would be a topic for the ecological study of the microsystem.

2. *The mesosystem.* The interrelationships among the various settings in which the person is developing. For a 12-year-old, for instance, the mesosystem would include the relationship between home and school, or school and peer group. For some children church, camp, and the world of work would also be included.

3. *The exosystem.*   The major social structures that impinge on the individual. These include formal and informal institutions of society, such as neighborhood, the mass media, agencies of the government, transportation facilities, and informal social networks.

4. *The macrosystem.*   The "overarching institutional patterns of the culture or subculture, such as the economic, social, educational, legal, and political systems, of which the micro-, meso-, and exosystems are concrete manifestations." The macrosystem is the source and carrier of the ideologies that affect everyone's development. For instance, how much value a particular culture places on children will influence how each child is treated in every setting.

The practical implication of this approach is that the psychologist is more likely to study the interactions among individuals and more likely to consider the overall context of development, rather than studying one individual performing one behavior. For instance, Bronfenbrenner (1973) compared child development in the Soviet Union and the United States. Instead of comparing levels of achievement of Soviet and American children at various ages, as a more conventional psychologist might do, he first compared the value systems of the two nations, then looked at the curriculum and design of the two educational systems, the interactions among students and teachers in various day-care centers and schools, and at the ways that mothers discipline and play with their children. He noted that Soviet children are taught to care for themselves and help each other at an early age. Even in nursery schools, group games are emphasized, and special toys are designed to work only when two or three children cooperate in using them. Bronfenbrenner discussed the implications of this mode of upbringing on the future adults, suggesting that Americans have gone too far in emphasizing individual autonomy.

Figure 1.8 *The ecological approach attempts to consider all the familial, social, and cultural influences that affect each person's development. For instance, this boy's daily life is affected by economic and political factors, as well as by the more obvious characteristics of his social world.*

Figure 1.9 *Five-year-olds in Kirovabad, U.S.S.R., learn to wait their turn and to obey traffic rules in this "auto-town," complete with traffic lanes, directional signs, traffic lights, and railway crossings. Compare this ecological milieu with the demolition-derby approach of bumper cars in American amusement parks.*

Even critics of the ecological approach agree that, ideally, the entire context of development should be considered. However, some psychologists think that this approach is impractical; they prefer to study individuals performing specific behaviors in controlled environments, so that the scientist can avoid drawing conclusions based on so many variables that most of the rigor and objectivity of the scientific method is lost.

The Scientific Method

Although psychologists disagree on what to emphasize in the study of development, they agree on the importance of the scientific method—even though they interpret and apply this method in different ways. As our initial definition of developmental psychology states, the discipline is *rooted in the scientific study of behavior.*

The scientific method involves four steps:

1. *Observe carefully.*   Look, analyze, talk to others, read other research, and formulate a question.
2. *Develop a hypothesis.*   To answer the question, begin with a theory or a hunch, and then form it into a hypothesis (a specific prediction of behavior) that can be tested.
3. *Test the hypothesis.*   Use a particular procedure, such as a laboratory experiment or naturalistic observation, that will prove or disprove the hypothesis.
4. *Draw conclusions.*   Base your conclusions on the results of the test.

A fifth step is often added:

5. *Make your findings available.*   Describe the methods and data in sufficient detail so that other scientists can appraise the conclusions or try to *replicate* the experiment (repeat it and obtain the same results).

Research Design

Developmental psychology offers many opportunities to use the scientific method. Usually, a theory of development is the starting point. From one of the theories, as well as from other research and observation, the psychologist develops a hypothesis, then systematically tests it, records the results, and draws conclusions. Each of the specific methods used to test a hypothesis has advantages and disadvantages.

Naturalistic Observation   A scientist can test a hypothesis by using naturalistic observation, observing people in their usual habitat. When observing children, this usually means going to a home, a school, or a playground, and carefully recording what occurs.

Figure 1.10 *Many developmental psychologists begin their research with the careful observation of children in natural settings, as Jean Piaget is doing here.*

Mary Ainsworth (1967), for example, studied emotional attachment between mothers and their children by observing twenty-eight mother-infant pairs in a village in Uganda. She recorded each instance when a baby clung to its mother, called her name, cried when she left, and so on, and noted the mother's reaction. Ainsworth concluded that the babies whose emotional attachment to their mothers is strongest are those whose mothers are most responsive to their needs.

Naturalistic observation is an excellent method, but it has two main disadvantages. First, it does not differentiate among several possible explanations for a particular behavior. If a child cries when the mother leaves, it may mean that the mother spends too much time away from the baby and the baby is crying in protest at yet another separation; or it may mean that the mother rarely leaves and the baby is crying in confusion at this unexpected event. Or perhaps a babysitter's presence, not the mother's departure, is the crucial variable.

Second, naturalistic observation does not usually indicate cause and effect. We may assume that a responsive mother produces a happy baby, but perhaps we are wrong; maybe a happy baby produces a responsive mother. Because the variables in a natural setting are numerous and uncontrolled, it is difficult to pinpoint precisely which of them could explain a particular event.

Laboratory Experiment   In a laboratory experiment, the scientist brings people together in a controlled environment and records their responses to specific actions or conditions. When Mary Ainsworth returned from Uganda, she studied mother-child attachment in a laboratory playroom equipped with many toys. In one experiment (Ainsworth and Wittig, 1969), a number of babies were observed individually through a one-way mirror in seven successive episodes: with mother, with mother and a stranger, with a stranger, with mother again, all alone, with a stranger again, and finally reunited with mother. As expected, the babies usually played happily with their mothers present and protested when they left, especially for the second time. They cried more when their mothers left them alone at the beginning of the fifth episode than when the stranger entered at the beginning of the sixth. Sometimes the stranger even succeeded in quieting their protests. When their mothers returned in the final episode, most of the babies clung tightly to them and would no longer play. Experiments like this led Ainsworth (1973) to suggest that repeated separation from the mother, rather than repeated experiences with strangers, causes insecure attachment, which in turn hinders natural curiosity. (We will examine the Ainsworth research in more depth in later chapters.)

The advantage of the laboratory experiment is that the scientist can manipulate the environment to provide a precise test of the hypothesis. Consequently, the link between cause and effect is much clearer than it is in naturalistic observation. The

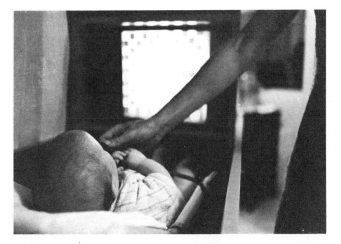

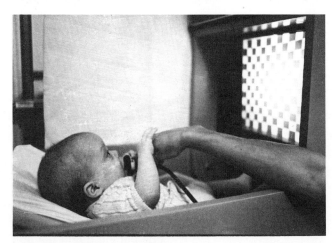

Figure 1.11 *In this laboratory experiment on infant perception, various pictures come into focus on a screen when the infant sucks on a pacifier. By sucking on the pacifier, this infant is bringing the checkerboard pattern shown on the screen into greater focus. By recording the intensity and duration of the infant's sucking response to each picture, psychologists can study infant visual abilities and preferences.*

disadvantage is that almost everyone behaves differently in the artificial environment of the laboratory than in a more natural setting, and this fact is often reflected in the results of the experiment. For this reason, conclusions drawn from laboratory experiments will not always apply to the real world.

Psychologists who take the ecological approach are particularly aware of the limitations of manipulating one variable at a time in an artificial setting. Robert McCall (1977) puts the case strongly. He wants developmental psychology to become more naturalistic and relevant and insists that we must "alter a value system that excludes or disparages questions that cannot be studied experimentally."

Naturalistic observation and laboratory experiments can be used to complement each other. The lack of precision in naturalistic observation is balanced by the control of the laboratory experiment; the artificiality of the laboratory is balanced by the realism of naturalistic observation. Psychologists usually prefer to consider results from both methods before drawing any firm conclusions. They also try to combine the methods; for example, by doing an experiment in a natural setting, or by observing, rather than experimenting, in a laboratory.

Interview Method   Another means psychologists use to gather their information is the interview method. Instead of observing behavior, in either a natural or laboratory setting, they ask people questions about a particular topic and tabulate the results. This method is especially helpful when it is difficult to observe behavior directly. Robert Sorensen used this method in his 1973 study of adolescent sexual behavior and attitudes, asking young people aged 13 to 19 about their sexual experiences and values.

As might be expected, the main disadvantage of the interview method is that people may not answer the questions with complete honesty. Although Sorensen took care to assure the teenagers that their participation was confidential and that the results would be anonymous, some of them may have stretched the truth. Besides, even when people answer as honestly and completely as they can, their answers can still be inaccurate. For instance, parents are notoriously unreliable in remembering even such simple and "memorable" facts as when their children first began to walk or talk.

Case-Study Method   Psychologists sometimes prepare a case study, a description of one particular person, and then analyze it to draw conclusions. Case studies often contain the following kinds of information about a person: physical characteristics, family background, critical events in the life history, education, medical history, expressed feelings and attitudes, and the results of psychological testing. Occasionally, the scientist's own children are the subjects of such studies. In fact, one of the earliest case studies was written in 1877 by Charles Darwin about his son. Clinical psychologists, who work directly with people having psychological problems, sometimes write case studies of their patients, following the historical model set by Sigmund Freud, who reported his patients' dreams, memories, and fantasies. Psychologists sometimes also examine historical figures in similar fashion, as Erik Erikson did with Martin Luther, Gandhi, and others.

The advantage of a case study is that the complexity and uniqueness of an individual can be reported, something not possible in group studies, where individual differences are usually obscured. The disadvantage is that the experience of one person might not apply to others.

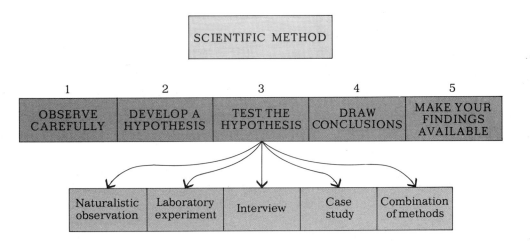

Figure 1.12 *The steps of the scientific method are the same in all the natural and social sciences, but the particular methods used to test hypotheses vary from science to science.*

Problems and Solutions

An important factor in any research project is the objectivity and/or subjectivity of the research. Objective means impersonal and impartial; subjective means personal, that is, reflecting one's own ideas, feelings, and perspectives. Even the most objective research and experiments have a subjective component, because someone must decide what questions to investigate, how to conduct the investigation, and how to interpret the results.

Subjectivity affects research in all the sciences, but plays a particularly important role in psychology, simply because the subjects of psychological investigation as well as the investigators are diverse and complex human beings. Given the seemingly infinite number of interacting variables, it is not surprising that no specific way to examine and interpret human behavior is acceptable to all psychologists. To determine how heavy a child is, is one thing; any number of people reading the scale should arrive at the same answer. To determine how creative a child is, is quite another; various psychologists might reach considerably different conclusions, depending on their definition of creativity, their way of measuring it, and their interpretation of their findings.

Statistics   Scientists have found many ways to minimize the effects of their own subjectivity. One is to use statistical methods to analyze data so that experimental results can be expressed in numbers as well as words. Complex statistical techniques help to lessen the chance that a scientist will believe results are conclusive when in fact they are not.

For example, when researchers find a difference between the averages of two related sets of data (such as how frequently a group of fathers talk to their sons, compared with how often they talk to their daughters), they usually report whether the difference was significant or not. This use of the word "significant" implies nothing about the importance of the results. Instead, "significant" here is a specialized term meaning that the difference between the averages is unlikely to have occurred by chance. In general, the more people studied and the larger the difference found between the two sets of data, the more likely it is that the difference is significant.

Statistics are an important tool in psychology. However, one reason for the extensive research that exists on certain topics, such as the toddler's vocabulary, the schoolchild's reading ability, and the adolescent's arrest record, is simply that the research results are easy to quantify—to measure and express numerically. Other topics, such as a toddler's happiness, a child's creativity, or an adolescent's dreams about the future, are equally important. But research on such topics is often neglected, because the findings are harder to assess with numbers.

"Blind" Experimenters and Control Groups   Another way to minimize the impact of subjective factors is to design the experiment so that data are collected by researchers who do not know what results to expect. Such researchers are called blind experimenters. A psychologist measuring the differences between the intelligence test scores of children who attended a preschool program and those who did not might employ a "blind" tester who would not know which children attended the program. In this way, even if the psychologist hoped to prove that preschool education is beneficial, that hope could not inadvertently bias the results.

This example demonstrates another important technique. Researchers often use two groups of people in a study rather than just one. Both groups are chosen to be as similar as possible in any characteristics that might be important; for example, in studying the effect of preschool education, one would want both groups to be similar in learning ability, achievement, family background, age, and in the number of boys and girls. The researchers begin by testing both groups for some factor, say, the ability to perform a certain task. Next, one of the groups, the experimental group, is subjected to the variable being tested; the other group, the control group, is not. Then both groups are again tested.

If there are test-score differences between the two groups at the end of the experiment that were not present at the beginning, it can be concluded that the variable being tested caused them. Suppose it is found that, after a year of preschool, the experimental group of 4-year-olds showed marked improvement at recognizing letters, copying shapes, and speaking grammatically. That fact alone would prove nothing about the effects of the preschool program, for the children might have learned these skills from their parents, or from television. However, if the children in the control group, who did not participate in the preschool program, showed no similar progress, the preschool program was probably responsible for the improvement.

Just as the psychologist's expectations can affect how information is collected and how conclusions are drawn, the research subjects' expectations also can make a difference. This is especially true in a laboratory experiment if the subjects know the hypothesis on which the experiment is based. But it also can happen in naturalistic observation, since the mere presence of an observer usually affects how people behave. Ideally, the subjects should be blind as well, unaware that they are involved in research until it is over. However, this is often difficult or impossible, for both practical and ethical reasons.

Representative Sampling   Another way to make an experiment more reliable is to choose participants who will be a representative sample of a larger group. Usually this means selecting people who reflect the racial, ethnic, religious, sexual, and economic distribution of the general population, or a particular segment of it. Age, intelligence, schooling, and birth order (whether the child was born first, last, or in between) are often important as well. When psychologists describe their research, they usually include a statement about the subjects' characteristics, pointing out the ways in which they were or were not representative of the total population.

In his research on American adolescent sexuality, for example, Sorensen reported that his subjects came from two hundred areas across the nation, including urban, suburban, and rural communities. They included adolescents at every age from 13 to 19, married and unmarried, living at home and living in institutions (jails and schools), and of all major religions and races. Even runaways were part of the sample. Sorensen had tried to get the same proportion of subjects from each category as exists in the total teenage population. Nevertheless, as he took care to note, there was one way in which his sample was not representative. He had sought parental permission before interviewing any adolescents who lived at home, and had been refused 40 percent of the time, most often by the more conservative parents of younger teenagers.

Emphasis on Behavior In some kinds of research, such as the case study, being blind to one's own expectations is impossible, and describing the case with statistics is inadequate. Especially in such situations, scientists try to report the subject's behavior before they present interpretations of that behavior.

The following is a portion of Jean Piaget's report on the behavior of one preschool child:

> A little girl, who while on vacation had asked various questions about the mechanics of the bells observed on an old village church steeple, now stood stiff as a ramrod beside her father's desk, making a deafening noise. "You're bothering me, you know. Can't you see I'm working?" "Don't talk to me," replied the little girl, "I'm a church." Similarly, the child was deeply impressed by a plucked duck she'd seen on the butcher table, and that evening was found lying on the sofa, so still that she was thought to be sick. At first she did not answer questions; then in a faraway voice she said, "I'm the dead duck!" [Piaget and Inhelder, 1969]

Piaget uses this example to demonstrate the beginning of symbolic thinking, but he provides enough detail to allow readers to draw their own conclusions.

Longitudinal Studies Developmental psychologists face additional obstacles in designing their research, because they want to study, not just how people behave in

"I don't know what I'm going to be when I grow up.
Probably just a watered-down version of what I am now."
Drawing by Norment; © 1978. The New Yorker Magazine, Inc.

a particular situation, but also how behavior changes with time. An excellent way to study development is longitudinal research, in which the scientist studies the same people over a period of time. This kind of research enables us to learn, for example, the various ways people cope with the aftereffects of their early experiences; or which human characteristics are stable and which are likely to change.

Some of the most interesting findings in developmental psychology come from longitudinal research on the relationship between intelligence test scores in early childhood and achievement in later life. In general, these studies have challenged the old idea that intelligence is a fixed characteristic (Bayley, 1968). These studies also cast doubt on the folk wisdom that it is not good to be "too" smart. One longitudinal study of children with intelligence test scores in the top 1 percent traced them through adulthood and found that they generally became happier adults than their more average peers (Terman and Oden, 1959). They were less likely to be divorced or to be institutionalized for emotional problems.

Longitudinal research can present problems, however. The first is that we do not know whether children of today will follow the same paths of development that previous generations did, because social conditions are constantly changing. For instance, based on the life histories of adults born fifty years ago, we could conclude that "only" children often grow up to become loners, with fewer social skills than children who grow up in large families. But this probably happens less often today, since parents now are generally more aware of an only child's social needs and tend to provide playmates even in early childhood. In addition, many contemporary couples who have only one child do so by choice, while years ago the parents of a single child usually wanted more children but could not have them. Certainly, the quality of the interaction between parents and their only child might be affected by this difference.

A second problem with longitudinal research is that many questions that interested psychologists when the earlier longitudinal studies were undertaken interest them much less today, while today's research questions were rarely asked in previous decades. Forty years ago psychologists were much more likely to rely on IQ (intelligence quotient) tests as a measure of cognitive development than they would be today. There was more faith then in the accuracy of a single test score, and less awareness of the ways in which such a score can be altered by the interactions among child, school, and home. Consequently, we have excellent longitudinal data relating childhood IQ scores to various aspects of adult achievement. Unfortunately, the degree of relevance of much of this research, as well as its practical usefulness, is much in question. Equally unfortunate is the fact that we do

Figure 1.13 *In doing longitudinal research, the psychologist follows the same individuals over a long time period. This is probably the best way to study the process of development, for the scientist can see which characteristics change and which remain stable as each person responds to individual experiences and general maturation.*

not have information we would value more—a moment-by-moment description, for example, of the behavior of these children at home and in the classroom. It would be fascinating to see how various teacher-student relationships might relate to later achievement and happiness in adulthood.

Finally, longitudinal research is difficult, time-consuming, and expensive. Many people move from one neighborhood to another, or even from one country to another, so it is difficult for the psychologist not to lose track of some subjects. Some people tire of repeated testing, year after year, and drop out of the study; others may be in the hospital or on vacation when the psychologist is ready to interview them. Good longitudinal research is a testimony to the psychologist's persistence and the participants' cooperation.

Cross-Sectional Studies   An alternative to longitudinal research is cross-sectional research. In this kind of study, groups of people who are different in age but similar in other important ways (the proportion of males to females, of blacks to whites, and so on) are compared. Carol Eckerman, Judith Whatley, and Stuart Kutz (1975) used this method when they observed the play patterns of a group of 12-month-olds, a group of 18-month-olds, and a group of 24-month-olds. One of the things they found was that the 2-year-olds were almost four times as likely to play together as the 1-year-olds.

Although we can assume in this case that the differences in play patterns are the result of age, not all differences found in cross-sectional research are. Consider an example from adulthood, where cross-sectional research is often used because longitudinal research is particularly difficult, since changes in adult patterns occur slowly, taking decades, not months. In this instance, cross-sectional research showed that people in early adulthood scored higher on intelligence tests than people in middle adulthood, who, in turn, scored higher than people in late adulthood. These results seemed to indicate that intelligence decreased significantly with age. But when psychologists later combined both research tools, obtaining longitudinal and cross-sectional data, they learned that the test scores of most adults remain stable over the years (Baltes, 1968). The previous cross-sectional research that seemed to show a correlation between aging and a decline in intelligence was really measuring the difference in average education levels of the groups studied. In earlier decades, most people did not attend school for as long as people who have grown up more recently, and this difference was reflected when the test scores of people born in 1900, for example, were compared with the scores of those born in later decades.

Figure 1.14 *In cross-sectional research, subjects are carefully selected so that age is the only significant difference between members of one group and members of others. This kind of research reveals the steps of development much more quickly, and almost as well, as longitudinal research.*

**Advantages of the
Scientific Method**

Given all these difficulties with the methods of conducting scientific research in psychology, you might wonder if the results justify the effort involved. Almost all psychologists agree that they do.

By far the greatest advantage of the scientific method is that it encourages people to test their ideas and base their conclusions on evidence rather than on guesses, prejudices, or inadequate information. This can be clearly seen with regard to research on temperament. Psychologists used to think that all babies were born essentially alike, and that personality developed as a result of the way their parents treated them. The mothers of babies who cried a great deal were blamed for their infants' behavior. Then research on temperament and other newborn characteristics showed that from the moment of birth infants differ in many ways. Some are placid and inactive; others are irritable and active. Some babies enjoy a great deal of touching and cuddling; others do not. Once this fact was established, it led to the

---

RESEARCH REPORT **Wayne Dennis and the Scientific Method**

The advantages of the scientific method are evident in the lifework of one developmental psychologist, Wayne Dennis.

When Dennis was a student at Clark University in the 1920s, he "learned and agreed that behavioral development comes automatically with maturation, which is essentially predetermined by heredity" (Hunt, 1977). This conviction led him to try to prove conclusively that maturation was much more important than experience. He studied the effects of keeping an infant strapped to a cradle board, a practice common among the Hopi Indians, and found that it had little or no effect on the age of walking (Dennis and Dennis, 1940).

Dennis also set out to show that a baby deprived of all normal motor experiences would nevertheless develop motor skills based purely on maturation. As Dennis explained: "One can deprive the infant of all objects for which he may reach, or one may refuse to place him in a sitting or standing position, and one may find the results of such deprivation of normal activities . . . . The present paper reports such a study. Mrs. Dennis and I reared two infants from end of the first to end of the fourteenth calendar months of life under conditions of full experimental control" (Dennis, 1935).

The twin baby girls in this experiment (not the Dennises' own children) lived in a special room in the Dennis home. They were given no toys until they were 11 months old, and were kept on their backs in their cribs. Until the babies were 6 months old, the adults kept impassive faces when caring for them, "neither smiling, nor frowning, and never played with them, petted them, tickled them . . . nor spoke."

Dennis was surprised to see how slowly the babies developed the normal motor skills, such as reaching, sitting, and standing. One child did not walk without holding on until her 17th month, the other not until her 26th month. Dennis then gave the twins special training. He reported that they soon overcame their retardation, without as much practice as a younger infant ordinarily gets. Dennis concluded that maturation was indeed important, but that maturation alone is not sufficient to develop normal skills. Experience is also vital.

As time went on, Dennis himself wondered whether the twins' training had actually erased all of their early retardation (Hunt, 1977). He read a report by René Spitz that motherless infants raised in a foundling home developed motor skills slowly, and he suspected that lack of experience had caused this retardation. Later, while in Iran, Dennis sought out an orphanage where all the babies got very little stimulation. He found that the children in this institution were even more retarded than the twin girls he had raised; some did not stand or talk at all by age 2 (Dennis and Najarian, 1957). Following the development of these Iranian orphans as they grew older, Dennis learned that, unless they were adopted in the first two years, they were still somewhat retarded as adolescents. Girls were more retarded than the boys, because during childhood the girls received even less attention (Dennis, 1973).

Thus Dennis' research shows how the scientific method encourages people to test their hypotheses, base their conclusions on evidence, and develop new tests to explore ideas raised in previous research. It also demonstrates the practical applications of developmental research: Dennis' studies on orphanages in Iran, as well as other research that confirmed his basic conclusions, have revolutionized the care of parentless children. Most large, impersonal orphanages have closed their doors forever, to be replaced by foster homes and smaller, more personal institutions.

idea that personality was innate, and that parents could do little except adjust to their child's personality. We now know, thanks to longitudinal research, that this, too, is an oversimplification. Personalities change and develop as people mature (Thomas and Chess, 1977). Parents and children continually affect each other, so it is as inaccurate to attribute all a child's characteristics to inborn temperament as it is to blame them all on mother and father.

A second advantage of the scientific method is that it helps scientists to learn from each other. By reporting hypotheses, experiments, and results, scientists provide the raw material for their colleagues to reanalyze the data, repeat the experiment, or build on the results.

Finally, new knowledge in science often leads to new applications; basic science becomes applied science. For instance, research showing that abused children often grow up to be abusing parents has helped to identify new parents who might become violent with their children. These parents can be taught better ways to interact with their children before it's too late.

Ethics

Questions of ethics arise in all the sciences. However, experiments with people raise ethical questions that do not occur when a scientist is experimenting with atoms or amoebas. Dennis' experiment with the twins is an obvious example. Questions could also be raised about Sorensen's asking teenagers about their sex lives, or Ainsworth's putting 1-year-olds in a situation that made them cry and cling to their mothers.

Today, psychologists are very concerned about the ethics of scientific research, especially when children are involved. Among the precautions that are urged by the Society for Research in Child Development are the following:

> No matter how young the child, he has rights that supersede the rights of the investigator . . .

> The investigator should respect the child's freedom to choose to participate in research or not, as well as to discontinue participation at any time . . .

> The informed consent of the parents . . . should be obtained, preferably in writing. Informed consent requires that the parent or other responsible adult be told all features of the research that may affect his willingness to allow the child to participate . . .

> The investigator uses no research operation that may harm the child either physically or psychologically. . . . [Society for Research in Child Development, 1973]

If these standards had been adopted at the turn of this century, much of the early research in child development might not have occurred, including Wayne Dennis' experiment in raising twin girls without stimulation. Dennis tried to design his research in an ethical manner. He did not expect the girls to be harmed by their deprivation, and he obtained the permission of the twins' mother, who consented because she knew they would get good food and adequate shelter, which she was too poor to provide. Nevertheless, many people feel Dennis did not sufficiently respect the children's rights or assess the possibilities of harm.

Ethics and John B. Watson

The ethical standards set by a society often change over time. Research scientists usually conform to the society's current standards in their experiments, but not always. Consider two series of experiments done in the beginning of this century by John B. Watson. The first series was not considered unethical then, but certainly would be criticized if it were done today. The second created a scandal.

Watson wanted to find out if children's fears are learned. Accordingly, he showed a gentle white rat to an 11-month-old baby named Albert (Watson and Rayner, 1920). Albert eagerly crawled toward the rat and played with it, as he had earlier with a dog and a rabbit. Then Watson hit a steel bar with a hammer, making a loud noise to frighten the little boy. After several such experiences, as soon as he saw the rat, Albert cried, fell over, and tried to crawl away. According to Watson, Albert's fear then became generalized, making him frightened of many white and fuzzy objects, including the rabbit, the dog, a fur coat, and even a Santa Claus mask.

At this point, Albert left the hospital where the experiment had taken place—without being taught by Watson that white furry things are not always frightening. The possible ramifications of this did not seem to bother Watson very much; he had known for at least a month that Albert was going to leave, but he still did not alter his experiment (Harris, 1979).

Psychologists today consider this experiment unethical. Albert's mother does not seem to have given her "informed consent," and Albert, who had been a happy child, became a frightened one. Even if his fear was temporary, causing such

harm is unethical. But in this case, the damage may have been long-lasting, a problem made even worse by the fact that Albert was adopted by a family that did not know about the experiment and its consequences.

In Watson's day, such ethical considerations were overridden by the needs of science. As Watson put it, "We were rather loathe at first to conduct experiments in this field, but the need of study was so great that we finally decided to attempt to build up fears in the infant and then later to study practical methods for removing them" (Watson, 1926).

There is no doubt, however, that Watson violated the moral standards of his day with another series of experiments (McConnell, 1977). Having become interested in the physiological responses during sexual intercourse, he began to observe animals copulating. Then he decided to study human subjects. Enlisting the help of his female laboratory assistant, he attached several monitoring instruments to her as well as to himself. Then they made love. Unfortunately for Watson, his wife, who earlier had refused to participate as his experimental partner, discovered his ongoing project. She destroyed the data and sued for divorce.

At the divorce trial, the judge called Watson a "specialist in misbehavior," and newspapers printed all the shocking and titillating details they could find or imagine. Watson lost his professorship at Johns Hopkins University and most of his friends. He eventually married his assistant and went to work on Madison Avenue, applying his knowledge of psychology to a new profession—advertising.

Today, most universities and other research institutions have committees that review proposals to make sure experiments are ethical before the researcher is allowed to begin. Dennis' experiment would almost certainly have been turned down. He would have been told to use naturalistic observation rather than a controlled experiment.

Applications

At this point, it is time to recall that according to our original definition, developmental psychology is *nourished by a practical concern for human needs*.

Psychology is a practical as well as an experimental profession. According to a survey of 35,361 members of the American Psychological Association, much of the typical psychologist's time (39 percent) is spent in applying psychology, and only 18 percent in research (teaching rated 24 percent, management, 19 percent) (Boneau and Cuca, 1974). For psychologists working with children and adolescents, the proportions are probably even more heavily weighted toward the practical task of helping young people become happy and successful adults.

A Ph.D. in developmental psychology is a research degree, not a clinical degree, but the research of the developmental psychologist is often designed for, or put to, practical use by parents, as well as by professionals in education, health, and public policy.

Let us see, for example, what developmental psychology can offer to explain what happened to Cynthia Callow and Cynthia Feliccea, and to forecast the future of the Callow and Feliccea families.

The Two Cynthias Revisited

Confronted with the case of Cynthia Callow, a psychologist might think first of "failure-to-thrive," a condition in which an infant vomits rather than digests food for no apparent medical reason. This condition can arise when parents are either extremely neglectful or extremely overstimulating, so the balanced needs of the infant for some affection and some quiet are not met. Some babies respond to such treatment by losing weight and even dying, unless they get better care. But Cynthia Callow's adoptive parents seemed caring and emotionally stable, and she did not vomit everything, just everything but breast milk. This means that the cause of her problem was primarily physiological, not emotional.

A more plausible explanation is that Cynthia has a genetic intolerance for cow's milk and to certain of the other ingredients found in infant formulas. The fact that Cynthia was born in Colombia, where many people have Native American* ancestors, fits this hypothesis, for milk and sugar allergies are much more common among Native Americans than among most other Americans.

Since Cynthia's problem is in the physical domain, it will not reoccur as long as her parents attend to her diet. However, a serious problem in one domain usually affects development in all the other domains. In this case, what chance does Cynthia have of becoming a normal, healthy child, despite her low birth weight, malnutrition, and hospitalization? Will these factors slow down her cognitive development, or impair her psychological growth?

Considering the first of these questions, a developmental psychologist would note that Cynthia's birth weight of 3 pounds suggests that she was born about two months early. This means her weight at 10 months should be compared with the weight of an average baby two months younger than she is. Even by this standard Cynthia was underweight, but she was not as severely malnourished as she had first appeared to be.

Most developmental psychologists would therefore be optimistic, because recent research has shown that malnutrition must be extreme to affect mental development in a significant way. According to one large study in the Netherlands, even babies who began life in a severe famine showed no intelligence deficits at age 19 (Stein et al., 1975). Other malnourished children who were adopted by caring and intelligent parents have done very well. Indeed, one study of ninety-four mal-

---

*Native Americans are those groups of people who were already in America when Columbus arrived. He called them Indians, because he thought he had reached India, but "Native American" is a more accurate term, and will be used throughout this book.

nourished Korean girls who were adopted before age 3 by middle-class American families showed that their average scores on intelligence and achievement tests in elementary school were higher than those of the average American child (Winick et al., 1975).

Will Cynthia's weeks in the hospital impair her emotional development? Developmental psychologists used to think that children 6 months old or older who were hospitalized were likely to be emotionally bruised in ways that would affect their future personalities (Bowlby, 1966; originally published 1952). But according to a more recent review of the research, hospitalization is not usually injurious, if the hospital staff gives the child good personal care and the parents visit often (Rutter, 1974). That was certainly true for Cynthia.

Other research has shown that a child's cognitive and personality development can be harmed by malnutrition or hospitalization, *if* the child receives little love and stimulation at home. But problems like Cynthia's do not produce permanent damage if the child has a stimulating, responsive, and loving home. From the evidence given by the newspaper stories, we can predict that Pat and John Callow will be fine parents. They had not only the enterprise to find an adoptable infant— no easy task today when people wanting to adopt babies far outnumber the babies available—but also the concern and coping skills to obtain the necessary nourishment for her despite many obstacles.

The one problem psychologists would anticipate is that Cynthia's parents might be overprotective, as are many parents of children who come close to death in infancy, especially if the child is adopted and/or an only child. But this tendency is also widely recognized—by parents as well as psychologists—and the Callows can take deliberate steps to restrain their impulse to be overcautious.

Figure 1.15 *While her parents look on, Cynthia Callow plays with a list of breast-feeding mothers who have offered to donate some of their milk so she can survive.*

Confronted with the sad story of Cynthia Feliccea, developmental psychologists would be puzzled and pessimistic. Cynthia's problem itself, of course, is all too clear: a 9-month-old baby, unclad and underweight in a freezing building, is the obvious victim of neglect. The puzzle is in understanding how this happened in a household of eleven adult family members. Cynthia's basic needs—food and warmth—would have been easy to provide. Merely letting Cynthia sleep with one of the adults would probably have kept her warm enough.

Figure 1.16 *Cynthia Felic-cea's parents remove the clothes that belonged to their daughter.*

In this case, the immediate cause of the infant's death is physical, but the root causes are cognitive and psychosocial. The most likely explanation for Cynthia's neglect is that the family members did not recognize the basic needs of an infant and could not imagine how to solve even the simplest problems of daily living. After Cynthia's death, officials noted that the adults "seemed slow, and appeared to have difficulty in reading, writing and coping with everyday life" (*The New York Times*, February 8, 1979). If that is true, the next question is obvious: Why didn't the social worker, the children's teachers, the judge, or the neighbors notice the family's poor coping skills and their inadequate child care? Why did no one do something more effective than making an anonymous complaint or issuing a warning? It is not easy to understand why Cynthia had to die.

The future of the family's remaining members is not difficult to predict, but it is discouraging. Developmental psychologists believe that anyone can change at any age, so we could hope that the remaining six children and eleven adults have already lived through the worst days of their lives. But these hopes are not likely to be realized, especially for the adults, since the two factors that make it easier to change, youth and social support, are beyond them. Given the community's inability or unwillingness to intervene, even when an infant was dying, it seems unlikely that anyone will provide the massive support needed for these adults to better understand and cope with their world.

For the children, the picture is not necessarily so grim, especially if they can be removed to a better environment. Young children, even from very neglectful homes, often become competent adults if they are placed with loving and skilled families (Fanshel and Shinn, 1978). Older children also show surprising resilience, although much depends on the extent of their deprivation (Kadushin, 1970).

**Preventing Future
Problems**

Our two Cynthias illustrate an important goal of developmental psychology: to understand the interactions among the physical, cognitive, and psychosocial influences on each person, so future problems can be anticipated and prevented. The future we predict for the Feliccea family is discouraging partly because their problems have continued for years. But research has shown that other families can be helped sooner, before destructive patterns of behavior are firmly established. By analyzing family background and observing the first moments of interaction between parents and their newborn, Ruth and Henry Kempe (1978) have been able to anticipate which families might maltreat their children, and to prevent some of the abuse. Other research has made us realize that finding a new permanent home for a child can reverse many of the cognitive and emotional problems caused by abuse, neglect, or malnutrition, a fact that gives us at least some hope about the future of Cynthia Feliccea's brothers and sisters.

The importance of parent-child interaction is a major theme of developmental psychology, for we have found that a child's development depends more on the home than on complications in infancy. In Arnold Sameroff's words: "Supportive, compensatory, and normalizing environments appear to be able to eliminate the effects of early complications. On the other end of the continuum, caretaking by deprived, stressed, or poorly educated parents tends to exacerbate early difficulties" (Sameroff, 1978).

The research also shows that there are dozens of factors that affect the development of any individual; so to make useful recommendations and accurate predictions for either family, we need to know more information than the newspapers provide. But the two Cynthias show how the practical applications of developmental psychology follow naturally from what developmental psychologists study. They observe human development when it falters, such as when poor nutrition, inadequate care, misguided teachers, or social stress hinder growth. They also watch development when all goes well, as when an infant becomes a happy child, a proud adolescent, a successful and loving adult. As the developmental psychologist compares the many paths development can take, and learns the reasons why one child thrives while another languishes, the ultimate goal of all this study and research becomes clear: to help each human realize his or her full potential.

SUMMARY

Definitions

1. Developmental psychology is the branch of psychology that studies how people change with time. It is rooted in the scientific study of behavior and nourished by a practical concern for human needs.

2. Developmental psychologists study all aspects of development, at all stages of life. This includes the physical, cognitive, and psychosocial domains. Development is perceived as holistic, although for reasons of convenience it is usually studied part by part.

Old Controversies and New Directions

3. Psychologists disagree about the relative impact of nature and nurture, and of maturation and learning, on development. Neither do they agree on whether development is more continuous or discontinuous.

4. New directions in developmental psychology include more attention to the adult years of life, and more interest in the ecological approach, including setting, community, and human interaction.

The Scientific Method

5. The scientific method is used, in some form, by most psychologists. They observe, develop hypotheses, test the hypotheses, and draw conclusions based on their results. This can be done through naturalistic observation, laboratory experiments, case studies, and interviews.

6. To check their conclusions, and to be as objective as possible, psychologists use various experimental designs and statistical methods. "Blind" experimenters,

representative samples, longitudinal and cross-sectional research, all help developmental psychologists to produce more accurate studies.

7. The advantages of the scientific method are that it is objective, cumulative, and practical. In psychology, however, since humans are usually the subjects of research, care must be taken to respect the rights of individuals. Ethics are particularly important when children are studied.

Applications

8. Developmental psychologists hope that their work will have practical applications. When confronted with an individual who needs help, they try to learn why that person's problem occurred, how they can keep it from harming his or her future, and how similar problems in other people can be avoided.

KEY QUESTIONS

What is developmental psychology?

What is included in the study of developmental psychology?

Why is the maturation-learning controversy hard to settle?

Why do some psychologists think that the early years of life have been overemphasized?

What are the steps of the scientific method?

What are some of the problems in conducting scientific research in psychology?

What are the advantages of the scientific method?

What ethical precautions should developmental psychologists take?

KEY TERMS

physical development	interview method
cognitive development	case study
psychosocial development	objective
holistic	subjective
nature-nurture controversy	significant
	blind experimenters
maturation	control group
learning	experimental group
continuity	representative sample
discontinuity	longitudinal research
ecological approach	cross-sectional research
naturalistic observation	
laboratory experiment	

RECOMMENDED READINGS*

Bronfenbrenner, Urie. *Two worlds of childhood.* New York: Pocket Books, 1973.

This book combines fascinating descriptions of child-rearing in the U.S.S.R. and the United States with an exploration of the psychological consequences of each culture's methods. Bronfenbrenner believes in the application of ideas from cross-cultural research.

Ariès, Philippe. *Centuries of childhood.* New York: Vintage Books, 1962.

A provocative account of the contrast between childhood in the Middle Ages and today. For instance, the variability in sexual information given to young children, from bawdy jokes and sexual experience offered the child king of France to the strictest puritanism for later children in England, is enough to make one rethink contemporary practices. This book is a masterful example of using nonconventional sources for research.

DeMause, L. (ed.). *The history of childhood.* New York: Psychohistory Press, 1974.

Ten psychohistorians discuss the last 200 years of childhood. The editor concludes that each generation of children receives better care than the previous one—an encouraging, if not universally held, conclusion.

Lorenz, Konrad. *On aggression.* New York: Harcourt, Brace, Jovanovich, 1966. (Harvest edition, 1974.)

Lorenz is an ethologist, a scientist who studies animals in their natural environments searching for patterns of behavior. In this book, he discusses aggression among fish, birds, and higher animals, including people. The book is recommended, not only because it is good reading, but because it raises questions about applying animal research to people.

Watson, J. D. *The double helix.* New York: Signet, 1968.

A fascinating description of the scientific method at work, including the wrong assumptions, interpersonal jealousy, luck, care, and the excitement involved in scientific discovery. In this case, the discovery was the structure of DNA, the molecule that carries genetic information in cells.

*All books listed in the Recommended Readings are paperbacks, selected with a concern for readability. Students who want to do further research should consult the bibliography at the back of the book.

Theories

It is a capital mistake to theorize before one has data.

Sherlock Holmes

True or False?

One nineteenth-century cure for women suffering from "hysteria" was surgical removal of the uterus.

According to at least one psychoanalytic perspective, how a society in general respects law and order is related to its toilet-training practices.

Not only do behaviorists dismiss Freudian notions like the importance of toilet training, but they attach very little significance to the idea that much human behavior is determined by unconscious motives.

People who can't quit smoking are hooked less on nicotine than on habit.

Up until about age 7, most children will say that a tall, thin quart bottle holds more than a short, wide one.

According to Piaget, most children under 9 do not understand what a brother or a sister is.

"Tell that boy to bring you home by midnight," a father tells his 14-year-old daughter, on her way out the door to meet her date.

"Don't drink anything stronger than coffee," her mother calls after her.

The daughter turns angrily and yells, "I'll come home when the party's over."

"Then don't bother to come at all," her father shouts.

The daughter slams the door, and her mother bursts into tears.

How would you explain what happened in this scene? Let us speculate for a moment. Would you say that the father provoked the entire drama, by setting a curfew without consulting his daughter and then overreacting to her defiance? Or would you blame the mother, with her old-fashioned advice and ineffectual tears? Or is this scene the fault of the daughter, for showing anger instead of respect toward her parents? Or do you believe that social pressures and/or biological impulses make conflict between adolescents and their parents inevitable?

What Theories Do

Each of these speculations may have some truth, but a moment's thought makes it apparent that all of them are superficial. In order to analyze this scene, or any situation in real life, we need some way to clarify what we see: a way that takes us deeper than our first (probably biased) speculations and organizes our guesses into hypotheses that can be tested.

For example, one of the major perspectives in psychology is psychoanalytic theory, which holds that emotions and behavior are governed by unconscious, or hidden, impulses. If we were to consider this family scene in terms of psychoanalytic theory, we would search for the underlying emotions of these family members. The father may have unrecognized sexual feelings for his daughter, which makes him jealous of her boyfriend and resentful of her independence. The mother may be distressed because her daughter's sexual blossoming evokes memories of her own sexual fears during adolescence. And the daughter may feel guilty about her relationship with her boyfriend because she knows her parents would disapprove if they knew more, and she expresses this guilt with anger whenever her parents seem suspicious. In fact, most psychoanalytic theorists conclude that outbursts like this one are inevitable in adolescence, when the young person's sexual urges conflict with the parents' desire to prolong their child's dependence.

Other theories in psychology are founded on different general laws or principles and would lead to different ways of interpreting this scene. However, every theory performs the same function: it takes us beyond one isolated incident and away from trying to find a single cause of a problem. Theories give us a framework that helps us to have some insight into general rules of behavior and the complex interactions that cause people to act as they do.

Theories are made to be tested. The test can be on a grand scale, as was Margaret Mead's (1928) extensive naturalistic observation of adolescent girls in Samoa, from which she concluded that stormy parent-child relationships are not inevitable in adolescence. The test can also be on a very small scale, as when a father asks himself if he objects to his daughter's first boyfriend because of something about that particular boy, or simply because he would object to any boy his daughter dated.

In either case, the value of a theory can be measured by how useful it is (Lee, 1976). In everyday speech, we sometimes treat theory and practice as opposites—as though we had to choose between them. In fact, theories arise from practical experiences, and once a theory is formulated, it leads to practical applications.

This will be clear as we discuss psychoanalytic, behaviorist, and cognitive theories—the three theories that are the most comprehensive, influential, and useful in developmental psychology.

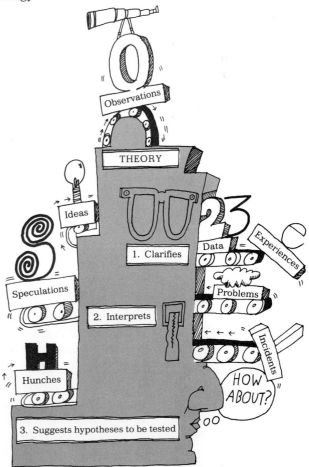

Figure 2.1 *A theory provides a frame of reference that organizes particular experiences, observations, ideas, and guesses about given phenomena.*

Psychoanalytic Theory

As we have seen, psychoanalytic theory understands human development in terms of unconscious drives and motives. These unconscious impulses are viewed as governing everything a person thinks and does, influencing not only the crucial decisions of a lifetime, including whom to love or hate, and whether to live or die, but also the smallest of daily decisions, such as what to wear, eat, or say.

To understand the impact of this theory, it is helpful to know something about the intellectual climate in which it arose. In the Europe of the 1870s, when Sigmund Freud was a medical student, men were thought to be completely rational, children were believed to be too innocent to have any sexual feelings, and women with ''nervous diseases'' were called hysterics, from the Greek word *hustera,* meaning ''womb.'' Physicians believed that the uterus caused hysteria, so they sometimes performed hysterectomies (surgical removal of the uterus) on women with severe emotional problems.

Freud suspected that the cause of these emotional problems was in the mind, not in the uterus. Following the lead of a French physician, Jean Martin Charcot, in 1886 Freud hypnotized his first patients. Sometimes these treatments were successful: the patients responded under hypnosis to Freud's suggestion that they talk about events and feelings related to their hysteria, until eventually they revealed the events which had precipitated their illness. When this occurred, their symptoms would disappear or be much relieved.

Figure 2.2 *Many of Freud's students and patients spoke about his penetrating gaze, which, they said, helped them uncover their hidden thoughts and fantasies.*

Freud was not satisfied with hypnosis, however. Some patients did not know what troubled them; others did not respond to hypnotic suggestion. Gradually Freud developed an ingenious new way to uncover the hidden thoughts of his patients. He would have them recline on his office couch and talk about anything and everything that came into their minds—events, dreams, memories, fears, desires—no matter how seemingly trivial or unpleasant. From such things as dream incidents, slips of the tongue, unexpected associations between one word and another, and memories from childhood, Freud was able to discover the deep conflicts that paralyzed one person or terrified another.

The medical establishment ridiculed Freud's "talking cure," especially when he reported that many emotional problems were caused by unconscious sexual desires, some of which originated in infancy. But patients flocked to Freud's door; he cured them when other doctors failed. As they revealed their problems and fantasies, Freud listened, interpreted, and formulated a theory of the human psyche that still influences psychiatry and psychology today.

Freud's Ideas

One of Freud's most famous studies involved a 4-year-old named Hans who had recently become very worried about his penis (his "widdler," as he called it), especially with regard to masturbation. Hans' father wrote to Freud:

> My dear Professor: I am sending you a little more about Hans—but this time, I am sorry to say, material for a case history . . . . He is afraid that a horse will bite him in the street, and this fear seems somehow to be connected with his having been frightened by a large penis. As you know from a former report, he had noticed at a very early age what large penises horses have, and at that time inferred that as his mother was so large she must have a widdler like a horse . . . .

Freud analyzed the problem in this way:

> Where did the material for this phobia come from? Probably from the complexes, as yet unknown to us, which had contributed to the repression . . . [of his] feelings towards his mother . . . .

> I arranged with Hans' father that he should tell the boy that all this business about horses was a piece of nonsense and nothing more. The truth was, his father was to say, that he was very fond of his mother and wanted to be taken into her bed. The reason he was afraid of horses now was that he had taken so much interest in their widdlers. He himself had noticed that it was not right to be so very much preoccupied with widdlers, even with his own, and he was quite right in thinking this. I further suggested to his father that he should begin giving Hans some enlightenment in the matter of sex knowledge . . . . [Freud, 1909]

This passage illustrates one of Freud's basic ideas, that children have sexual pleasures and fantasies long before they reach adolescence. According to this theory of infantile sexuality, each stage of development is characterized by the focusing of sexual interest and pleasure in a particular part of the body, specifically the mouth, the anus, the penis, or the genitals. For this reason, Freud's stages are called stages of psychosexual development. At Hans' age, the penis is the most pleasure-providing part of a boy's body.

Although few psychologists today would agree with Freud's specific suggestions, Freud's response to Hans' father contains two ideas later accepted by most psychologists. First, it is better to recognize one's wishes, ideas, and fears for what they are, rather than to deny them. In this case, Freud wants Hans to be told he wants to join his mother in bed, and that he is afraid of horses because he is anxious about penises, including his own. The second widely accepted idea is that the parents' influence is crucial for developing a healthy personality.

Id, Ego, and Superego   The father and mother are especially influential as the child learns to regulate the interplay of what Freud saw as the three theoretical components of personality: the id, ego, and superego. The id is the source of our unconscious impulses toward gratification of our needs. It operates according to the *pleasure principle,* which means that it wants whatever seems satisfying and enjoyable—and wants it *now.* The impatient, greedy infant, screaming for food in the middle of the night, with no awareness of the half-asleep parents' difficulty in heating a bottle, is all id.

Gradually, as the ego begins to develop, babies learn that other people exist and that gratification must sometimes wait. The ego operates according to the *reality principle,* dealing with life as it is, not as the id wants it to be.

According to Freud, whether the conflict between the ego and the id is relatively peaceful or troubled depends on the way the parents manage weaning and toilet training. For instance, psychoanalytic theorists note that some children have no problems giving up their bottle at the appropriate age. Others feel cheated and deprived because their parents limited their sucking or weaned them too abruptly. These children will always try to return to the oral pleasures of infancy. They will suck their thumbs and chew on pencils, and even in adulthood they will eat, drink, smoke, or talk too much.

At about 4 or 5, the superego starts to develop, as children begin to identify with their parents' moral standards. The superego is like a *relentless conscience* that distinguishes right from wrong in no uncertain terms. According to Freud, Hans' superego caused his worry about being bitten by a horse. Hans felt guilty for thinking so much about his penis, especially for the impulse from the id to masturbate, and this guilt made him fascinated and terrified when he saw a horse with a

Figure 2.3 *Freud developed this model of human mental processes to explain why people have conflicting ideas of what to do or think. The id, ego, and superego are not actually parts of the mind, but they represent the conscious and unconscious forces within the human psyche.*

Suppose someone invites you to a ''wild'' party on Saturday night. You say you will try to come, but as Saturday night approaches, you are torn in two directions. Your id wants you to go; you have fantasies of sexual promise—of drinking until you lose all your inhibitions, of dancing to loud rhythmic music in a crowded room, of exciting strangers and intimate conversations in dark corners.

Your superego meanwhile is horrified by all this, and prefers that you avoid places where you might lose control. Besides, your superego has other plans for Saturday night: it wants you to study for a math exam, organize your closet, and write a letter home.

Your ego must now mediate the conflict. But the fantasies of the id and the strict judgments of the superego make the choice difficult, interrupting your sleep with nightmares of parties gone wrong and tests flunked. And if you can't come to a definite decision, you may suddenly find yourself using a defense mechanism: you may get sick on the afternoon of the party, or lose the address, or take so long to get ready that it's too late to go.

To pick a more immediate example, your ego is telling you to read this chapter carefully and remember all the concepts, to figure out the best way to study, and to judge realistically what terms you need to learn. Meanwhile, your id may be interfering. You may be having aggressive thoughts about your teacher or sexual fantasies about the student next to you, making you misread words or think thoughts that are irrelevant to the text, although closely related to your hidden desires. At the same time, your superego expects you to master all these ideas perfectly, making you feel guilty whenever your mind wanders. It refuses to let you take a break, even though your ego knows that you study better if you stop to stretch your legs occasionally. How well you are able to concentrate on the task at hand depends on how well your ego copes with the demands of your id and superego.

large penis. His superego made him think he would be punished in some way for masturbating, and in this case the punishment was manifested in his phobia about horses.

By elementary school, many children have internalized the standards of right and wrong they learned from their parents. They no longer need someone to tell them that they have been bad, because they are already aware of their misdeeds and feel guilty and ashamed, imagining terrible punishments. A child who tells a lie might have nightmares about the fires of hell; another child who steals a candy bar might shudder every time a policeman comes into view.

Defense Mechanisms   When the superego becomes so overbearing, or the id so insistent, that the ego cannot bear it, people involuntarily defend themselves against the superego's attack and against the frightening impulses of the id by using one of dozens of defense mechanisms. Three common defense mechanisms are *regression, repression,* and *displacement.*

Regression occurs when someone returns, or retreats, to a form of behavior typical of a younger person. An 18-year-old might become overly dependent on his or her parents; a 10-year-old might start wetting the bed again; a 3-year-old might talk baby talk and want to sleep with a bottle. Repression occurs when an idea or memory is pushed from someone's conscious mind because it is too difficult to deal with. Adolescents who are not interested in sex, or abused and neglected children who insist that their parents love and care for them, are probably using repression. Displacement is the shifting of a drive from a threatening or unavailable object to a substitute object. A baby displaces the need to suck on a nipple and sucks on a thumb instead. As the child grows older, the same need is displaced to chewing on fingernails or pencil erasers, or, in adulthood, to smoking cigarettes or a pipe.

According to psychoanalytic theory, psychologically healthy children gradually develop a strong ego, able to cope with the demands of the id and superego. Defense mechanisms help regulate this process throughout life. At any point, however, defense mechanisms can be overused. We must grow up, not regress; we must face reality, not repress it. Many emotional problems arise because defense mechanisms become too rigid, never allowing the ego to confront the unconscious drives of the id directly. According to psychoanalytic theory, each person inherits a legacy of problems, and ways to cope with them, from childhood. Depending on our early experiences, some of us are more able to cope with the stresses of daily life than others.

Erikson's Ideas

Dozens of Freud's students became famous theorists in their own right. They acknowledged the importance of the unconscious, of sexual urges, and of early childhood. At the same time, they expanded and modified Freud's ideas. Many of them, including Karen Horney, Otto Rank, Margaret Mahler, Helene Deutsch, and Anna Freud, are mentioned later in this book. One of them, Erik Erikson (1902–   ) formulated his own comprehensive theory of development.

Eight Crises of Life Erikson was born in Denmark. He spent his childhood in Germany, his adolescence wandering throughout Europe, his young adulthood in Vienna as Freud's student and patient, and finally his adulthood in the United States. As an American citizen. he has studied students at Harvard, soldiers who

Figure 2.4 *Erik Erikson, who is approaching his eightieth birthday, continues to write and lecture on psychosocial development. His most recent book,* Toys and Reasons, *discusses the significance of play throughout the life span.*

TABLE 2.1 **Stages in Psychoanalytic Theory**

Approximate Age	Freud	Erikson*
Birth to 1 year	*Oral Stage* The mouth is the focus of pleasurable sensations in the baby's body, and feeding is the most stimulating activity.	*Trust vs. Mistrust* Babies learn either to trust or mistrust that others will care for their basic needs, including nourishment, sucking, warmth, cleanliness, and physical contact.
1–3 years	*Anal Stage* The anus is the focus of pleasurable sensations in the baby's body, and toilet training is the most important activity.	*Autonomy vs. Shame and Doubt* Children learn to be self-sufficient in many activities, including toileting, feeding, walking, and talking, or to doubt their own abilities.
3–6 years	*Phallic Stage* The phallus, or penis, is the most important body part. Boys are proud of their penis but ashamed when they masturbate, and girls are envious and wonder why they don't have one. Children of both sexes have sexual fantasies about their parents, for which they feel guilty.	*Initiative vs. Guilt* Children want to undertake many adultlike activities, sometimes overstepping the limits set by parents and feeling guilty.
7–11 years	*Latency* Not a stage but an interlude, when sexual needs are relatively quiet and children can put psychic energy into learning skills.	*Industry vs. Inferiority* Children are busy learning to be competent and productive, or feel inferior and unable to do anything well.
Adolescence	*Genital Stage* The genitals are the focus of pleasurable sensations, as the young person seeks sexual stimulation and sexual satisfaction.	*Identity vs. Role Confusion* Adolescents try to figure out "Who am I?" They establish sexual, ethnic, and career identities or are confused about what future roles to play.
Adulthood	Freud believed that the genital stage lasts throughout adulthood. He also said that the goal of a healthy life is "to love and to work."	*Intimacy vs. Isolation* Young adults seek companionship and love with another person or become isolated from other people. *Generativity vs. Stagnation* Adults are productive, performing meaningful work and raising a family, or become stagnant and inactive. *Integrity vs. Despair* People try to make sense out of their lives, either seeing life as a meaningful whole or despairing at goals never reached and questions never answered.

*Although Erikson describes two extreme resolutions to each crisis, he recognizes that there is a wide range of solutions between these extremes and that most people probably arrive at some middle course.

broke down during World War II, civil rights workers in the South, and Sioux and Yurok Indians. With this diversity of personal experience, it is not surprising that Erikson came to think that Freud's stages of development are too limited and too few. He proposed instead eight stages, each with a particular conflict, or *crisis,* to be resolved (see Table 2.1). As you can see, Erikson's first stages are related to Freud's stages. But Freud's last stage occurs at adolescence, whereas Erikson sees adulthood as having three stages. Each of these specific stages in Freudian and Eriksonian theory is explained in detail later in this book.

Psychosocial Development   All of Erikson's stages share one general characteristic that is different from Freud's stages. They are centered, not on a body part, but on each person's relationship to the social environment. To highlight this emphasis on social and cultural influences, Erikson calls his theory the psychosocial theory of human development.

Figure 2.5 *Erikson believes that in the last crisis of development, integrity versus despair, each person must decide if life is worthwhile. The senior citizen who volunteered to teach a retarded boy to swim appears to have resolved this crisis more successfully than the man with the glass in his hand.*

According to Erikson, there are three major aspects in the study of development:

Somatic. Physical strengths and weaknesses
Personal. Life history and current developmental stages
Social. Cultural, historical, and social forces

He believes that psychologists should study these areas, not to find cause and effect, but to find relationships and interdependence. His use of this theoretical framework is shown in the research report on the next page.

Cultural Differences Central to Erikson's theory is his conviction that each culture promotes different paths of development, in part because each society functions best with adults who have a particular character structure. He suggests that the traditional German stress on early toilet training and cleanliness prepared adults for a society where law and order were paramount, just as the stress on independence and self-assertion in pioneer America prepared adults to explore new territory and ignore traditional laws and conventions—precisely what that society needed at the time (Erikson, 1963).

A problem arises when a society's traditional customs no longer prepare its children to cope with the demands they face as adults. As in the case of the marine in the research report that follows, a strict moral code probably helps some people meet the crises of their lives, giving them temporary security, *under certain conditions.* But when those conditions change dramatically, as when the young man had to confront the situation on the Pacific beachhead, the same code can be crippling.

No culture anticipates the future so well that each child is prepared to live in it without problems. Each society handles the eight crises differently and is more successful with some than others. Erikson believes that our society makes the identity crisis the most difficult to weather successfully.

"Combat Crisis" in a Marine

A young patient at the veteran's clinic where Erikson worked as a therapist suffered such severe headaches that he couldn't work. Erikson described the origins of the problem:

A group of marines, just ashore, lay in the pitch darkness of a Pacific beachhead within close range of enemy fire. Somehow it had always contradicted the essential spirit of their corps to have "to take it lying down." Yet it had happened in this war. And when it happened, it exposed them not only to damnable sniping from nowhere, but also to a strange mixture of disgust, rage, and fear—down in their stomachs.

Here they were again. The "supporting" fire from the Navy had not been much of a support . . . . Among these men lay our patient . . . a medical soldier . . . .

Our medical soldier never quite remembered what happened that night. . . . He claims that the medical corps were ordered to unload ammunition instead of setting up a hospital; that the medical officer, somehow, became very angry and abusive, and that sometime during the night somebody pressed a sub-machine gun into his hands. Here his memory becomes a blank.

The following morning the patient . . . found himself in the finally improvised hospital. Overnight he had developed a severe intestinal fever. He spent the day in the twilight of sedatives. At nightfall the enemy attacked from the air. All the able bodied men found shelter or helped the sick to find one. He was immobilized, unable to move, and, much worse, unable to help . . .

From then on his life was made miserable by raging headaches. His fever (or whatever had caused it) was cured; but his headaches and his jumpiness made it necessary for him to be returned home to the States and to be discharged.

Where was the seat of his neurosis? For a "war neurosis" it was, if we accept his doctors' diagnosis . . . .

He had not seen his mother, it appeared, since he was fourteen years old. His family had then been on an economic and moral decline. He had left home abruptly when his mother, in a drunken rage, had pointed a gun at him. He had grabbed the gun, broken it, and thrown it out of the window. Then he had left for good. He secured the secret help of a fatherly man—in fact, his [high-school] principal. In exchange for protection and guidance, he had promised never to drink, or swear, or to indulge himself sexually—and then, never to touch a gun. He had become a good student and teacher, and an exceptionally even tempered man, at least on the surface, until that night on the Pacific beachhead.

Several factors combined to cause a real crisis and make it a lasting one. [Erikson, 1963]

According to Erikson, a combination of somatic, personal, and social factors caused the crisis. Without the fever (somatic) or the family problems in adolescence (personal) or the war (social), he might never have become sick.

The marine had resolved the crisis of adolescence (trying to find an identity of one's own) by adopting a rigid code of behavior, usually not the best solution. Then he temporarily solved the crisis of young adulthood—intimacy versus isolation—by joining the marines. When his troop could no longer attack and he could no longer help the wounded, he felt isolated, cut off from the security of a joint enterprise. Then when his officer cursed him and someone put a gun in his hands, his identity was shattered and he fell apart. This breakdown would not have happened if his identity had been less rigid and his attachment to the marines less strong.

Erikson thinks that at every stage people experience both sides of each crisis—a negative as well as a positive side. Every toddler sometimes feels shame; every adolescent experiences role confusion; all mature people know despair. The critical question is how to resolve each developmental crisis, not how to avoid it.

Contributions of Psychoanalytic Theory

All psychologists owe a debt of gratitude to Freud, and to the neo-Freudians who extended and refined his concepts. Many of Freud's ideas are so widely accepted today that they are no longer credited to him—for example, that unconscious motives affect our behavior, that we use defense mechanisms to avoid conflicts, and that sexuality is a potent drive in humans and in other animals as well. While few clinical psychologists accept his ideas completely, most have learned from his insights.

Developmental psychologists have been particularly influenced by three psychoanalytic ideas. Stage theory is one of them. Although poets and playwrights had previously written about the "ages" of man, Freud was the first to construct a coherent theory regarding our different needs and problems at various ages.

Another influential idea concerns the importance of certain parts of the life span. Freud centered our attention on the critical first five years, a time previously neglected in education and psychology. Erikson led us to recognize that adolescents and adults also experience developmental changes.

Finally, psychoanalytic theory has helped us to realize that human thoughts and actions are likely to be far more complicated than might at first be apparent. The forces of impulse and fantasy, and the pressures of parents and society, shape and direct our behavior throughout our lives. It is hard to imagine a society before Freud, when adults were always supposed to be rational and children always innocent. Because of psychoanalytic theory, we are much more understanding and sympathetic to irrational thoughts and behaviors.

Criticism of Psychoanalytic Theory

In some ways psychoanalytic theory is a model of what a theory should be, clarifying and interpreting our observation, and suggesting new hypotheses to be tested. But we have learned a great deal since the time of Freud's great insights, and it is hardly surprising that contemporary psychologists find many of his ideas to be inadequate or wrong.

For instance, Freud's idea that the child's experiences during weaning and toilet training form the basis for character structure and personality problems in adulthood has found little support in studies of normal children. It seems that the nature of the parent-child relationship, rather than any specific event of early childhood, is the primary factor in later emotional development.

Another of Freud's concerns was that the superego was too repressive in dealing with aggressive and sexual impulses. This idea may have reflected the mores of nineteenth-century Vienna and the problems of Freud's patients, but it no longer seems true about the universal human condition.

Erikson's interpretation of the stages of development has fared better with developmental psychologists than Freud's, perhaps because Erikson's experiences are more recent and varied than Freud's were, and because he had the benefit of

Figure 2.6 *Freud believed that the timing and intensity of toilet-training profoundly and permanently affected personality structure. However, subsequent research has shown that the psychological effects of the toilet-training experience are, on the whole, temporary.*

Freud's insights to build on. However most of the sources for Erikson's theory are subjective, as were Freud's—his own experiences, the recollections of patients in therapy, and the wisdom from classic literature. This makes psychoanalytic theory hard to test in a laboratory, under controlled conditions, and leads to the accusation that this theory is more myth than science.

Since scientific proof is hard to find for psychoanalytic theory, we are left with personal evaluation. Some psychologists today find psychoanalytic theory illuminating and insightful; others find it provocative nonsense; most think it a combination of both. Many try to see if it helps them understand their own lives, with mixed results. Calvin Hall's words probably strike a responsive chord in a number of psychologists:

> I have lived through nearly all of Erikson's stages and I must confess that I can find little in my memory that agrees with what Erikson says I should have experienced . . . I did not have any concerns about identity during adolescence . . . nor did I know anything about intimacy and love until I was well into my 50's. . . . as for integrity and wisdom, I had more of both when I was younger. Integrity is a luxury only the young can afford. [Hall, 1977]

Behaviorism

Early in the twentieth century, John B. Watson (1878–1958) decided that if psychology was to be a true science, psychologists should study only what they could see and measure. In Watson's words: "Why don't we make what we can *observe* the real field of psychology? Let us limit ourselves to things that can be observed, and formulate laws concerned with only those things . . . We can observe behavior— what the organism does or says" (Watson, 1967; originally published 1930). Many American psychologists agreed with Watson. Thus began a major theory of American psychology, behaviorism.

Emphasis on Behavior

Behaviorists focus on what people do, and what particular circumstances make people likely to behave the same way again. Consider the following example:

> . . . a three-year-old girl had regressed to an excessive amount of crawling . . . By "excessive" is meant that after three weeks of school she was spending most of her morning crawling or in a crouched position with her face hidden. Her parents reported that for some months the behavior had been occurring whenever they took her to visit or when friends came to their home . . .
>
> Observations recorded in the third week at school showed . . . that more than 80 percent of the child's time was spent in the off-feet positions. The records also showed that the crawling behavior frequently drew the attention of the teachers. On-feet behaviors, such as standing and walking, . . . seldom drew such notice. [Harris, et al., 1964]

The emphasis in this description is on the girl's crawling and on the teachers' response to this odd behavior, not on the thoughts of either child or teachers. Nowhere in their report do the authors try to analyze the unconscious forces that might have caused this regression, because behaviorists think that unconscious urges are either irrelevant or nonexistent.

Instead, when trying to account for a given behavior, behaviorists try to figure out the immediate causes and consequences of that behavior. Behavior therapists want to know what can be done in the immediate environment to change problem behavior. In the little girl's case

> a program was instituted in which the teachers no longer attended to the child whenever she was crawling or crouching, but gave her continuous warm attention as long as she was . . . standing, running, or walking. Initially the only upright behavior . . . occurred when the child pulled herself almost to her feet in order to hang up or take down her coat from her locker, and when she pulled herself up to wash her hands in the wash basin. Within a week of the initiation of the new attention-giving procedure, the child acquired a close-to-normal pattern of on-feet behavior. [Harris, et al., 1964]

Laws of Behavior

Unlike the other theorists in this chapter, behaviorists have not developed a stage theory of human development. Instead, they have formulated laws of behavior that can be applied to any individual at any age, from fetus to octogenarian.

The basic laws of behaviorism (sometimes called *learning theory*) explore the relationship between one event and another, or, in behaviorist terms, between the stimulus and the response.

Some responses are automatic, like reflexes. If someone suddenly waves a hand in your face (stimulus), you will blink (response); if a hungry dog smells food, it will salivate. But most responses are not innate; they are learned. Behaviorists consider life a continual learning process, as new responses appear and old ones fade away. This learning process, which behaviorists call conditioning, occurs in two basic ways: classical and operant.

Classical Conditioning   More than sixty years ago, a Russian scientist named Ivan Pavlov (1849–1936) began to study the link between stimulus and response. In one experiment, he taught a dog to salivate at the sound of a bell. Pavlov began by ringing the bell just before feeding the dog. After several repetitions, the dog began to associate the bell with the food. Eventually he salivated upon hearing the bell, even if there was no food. This simple experiment in learning was one of the first scientific demonstrations of classical conditioning (also called *respondent conditioning*), in which an animal or person learns to *associate* a neutral stimulus with a meaningful one, and then responds to the former stimulus as if it were the latter. In this case, the dog associated the bell with food. This part of the conditioning process is called learning by association.

Behaviorists find many everyday examples of classical conditioning: imagining a lemon might make your mouth pucker; reading the final-exam schedule might make your palms sweat; seeing a sexy photograph might make your heart beat faster. In each instance, the stimulus is connected, or associated, with another

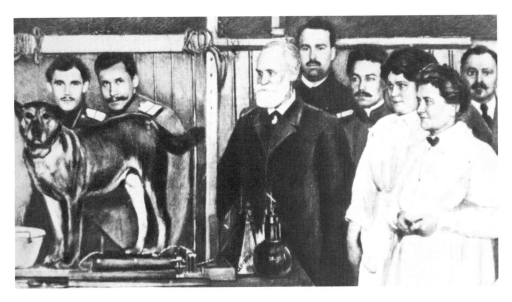

Figure 2.7 *Pavlov, his assistants, and one of his famous dogs are shown in this photo taken in Czarist Russia in 1911. Despite the war, revolution, and the purges of the next two decades, Pavlov's laboratory continued to receive government support.*

stimulus that produced the physiological response in the past. Reading the exam schedule might make you sweat if actually taking tests has made you anxious on earlier occasions.

Operant Conditioning   B. F. Skinner (1904–   ) is contemporary behaviorism's most influential theorist. Skinner agrees with Pavlov that the processes of classical conditioning help to explain much of human behavior, but he believes that another type of conditioning, called operant conditioning, plays a greater role in complex learning.

Figure 2.8 *B. F. Skinner is best known for his experiments with rats and pigeons, but he has also applied his knowledge to a wide range of human problems. For his daughter, he designed a special glass-enclosed crib in which temperature, humidity, and perceptual stimulation could be controlled to make time spent in the crib as enjoyable and educational as possible. In the realm of theoretical speculation, he has envisioned and written about an ideal society where, for example, workers at the less desirable jobs earn greater rewards.*

"Operant" comes from the Latin word meaning work, the same root as in "opus" and "operate." The emphasis is on the work done to get a particular response. To be specific, operant conditioning is any learning process in which the person or animal is more likely to do or not do a certain act because of having been reinforced or punished for it in the past.

Reinforcement is a process whereby a particular behavior is strengthened, making it likely that the behavior will occur more frequently (Skinner, 1953). The stimulus that strengthens the behavior is called a reinforcer, and may be either positive or negative. A positive reinforcer is something pleasant—a piece of candy, perhaps, or a word of praise. A negative reinforcer is an unpleasant stimulus that is removed when a particular behavior is performed, making it likely that the behavior will be repeated. A child who learns to clean up her room in order to stop her parents' nagging is responding to a negative reinforcer—the nagging. Note that a negative reinforcer is clearly not a *punishment*—an unpleasant event which makes a behavior *less* likely to recur.

Laws of Reinforcement. Behaviorists have learned to judge how effective a reinforcer is by how well it strengthens or changes behavior, not by how rewarding one would think it is. For instance, some children would work very hard to earn a quarter; others wouldn't care about money but would be eager to earn a chance to read a book with an adult. Unless we keep this in mind, we might tend to assume that all children would react to a particular promise or threat in the same way. Many parents are indeed puzzled when a child doesn't want to finish his dinner in order to get dessert, or another child seems to enjoy being sent to her room.

Behaviorists interested in developmental psychology have shown that basic reinforcers (food, physical comfort) are usually more effective with young children, while more complex and symbolic reinforcers (a college degree, an antique car) are very effective for adults. At every age, social reinforcers, such as a word of praise or time spent with a favorite person, are powerful.

Figure 2.9 *For many people, close contact with another human body is a powerful reinforcer.*

Figure 2.10 *Behaviorists take individual differences into account when the laws of behavior are applied to people. Primary reinforcers, such as food, secondary reinforcers, such as money, and social reinforcers, such as a smile or a token of affection, are important to almost everyone. Each person finds different particular experiences reinforcing.*

Timing is important when reinforcement is being used to promote learning (Ferster and Skinner, 1957). Immediate reinforcement for each step in the right direction is usually best at first, especially for children. Later, occasional reinforcement for larger accomplishments is better. For example, an 8-year-old boy learning to read might get a small piece of candy for sounding out each letter; later he might sometimes be allowed to buy a new book when he finishes an old one. Still later, an occasional word of praise for his reading ability will be enough. Eventually, the act of reading becomes reinforcing in itself, and he will read everything, from cereal boxes to textbooks, without external reinforcers.

To create lasting changes, behaviorists prefer reinforcers to punishments (Skinner, 1953). Hitting a child or jailing an adult might work for a short while, but research has shown these are not the best ways to alter behavior permanently. They also have destructive side effects: someone who is punished frequently can become an apathetic or aggressive person.

Social Learning Theory

Traditionally, in both classical and operant conditioning, behaviorists focus on one's direct personal experience, for they believe that each individual's current behavior is a result of past conditioning.

However, behaviorists also acknowledge that people learn from watching other people, even if they have not personally experienced the same reinforcers that they see others getting. Social learning theory explains how this occurs, for behavioral laws govern social learning just as they do the more traditional forms of conditioning. For one thing, we do not learn equally well from everyone; it's not just "monkey see, monkey do." We are more likely to imitate the behavior of others if we see them reinforced for what they do (Miller and Dollard, 1941) or if we particularly admire and identify with them (Bandura, 1977).

Learning from Parents   Social learning theory has become especially important in developmental psychology, because it helps explain how people acquire complicated ideals and characteristics. For example, parents are crucial to a child's learning, partly because they reinforce and punish the child's behavior, and partly because they are the most important people in the child's life. The child identifies with them and tries to imitate their behavior. When children become adults they probably still follow the patterns acquired in childhood, either because new patterns were never learned or because the old patterns became rewarding in themselves (Sears, 1965). This explains why many adults find themselves thinking and acting as their parents did, even to the point of repeating their parents' mistakes.

Choosing a Model   Social learning is sometimes called modeling, because people model their behavior after that of others. Children follow models for undesirable as well as desirable behavior, as research with aggression shows. Children often choose sports heroes and movie stars as models, sometimes even trying to dress

---

RESEARCH REPORT   **Learning from a Movie**

Children also learn from other children, from strangers, and even from television, according to social learning theory. In a classic experiment, Albert Bandura and his colleagues (1963) demonstrated the power of example. Bandura divided 96 children, ages 3 to 5¾, into four groups. Each group had 12 boys and 12 girls, and each group had the same proportion of children who had been rated aggressive by their nursery-school teachers. Then the children, one by one, experienced one of four possible conditions.

Children from the first group saw an adult (half saw a man, half saw a woman) playing with a 3-foot-high rubber clown by hitting it with a hammer, sitting on it, and punching it in the nose with appropriate verbal aggression ("Sock him!"). Another group saw a movie of the same adult behaving the same way. A third group saw a "cartoon"—actually a film of a woman dressed in a cat costume, in a fantasy-land setting, attacking the same doll the same way. The fourth and last group saw no film or real-life model of aggressive behavior.

After viewing or not viewing the model, the children were deliberately frustrated. Each was allowed to play with some fascinating toys for a few moments and then told that he or she could not continue playing with them.

In the final part of the experiment, each child was allowed to play for 20 minutes with several other toys, including dolls, crayons, trucks, dart guns—and a rubber clown just like the one the adult had attacked. An observer watched each child, unobtrusively, and rated the child's behavior every 5 seconds, giving a total of 240 time samples for each child.

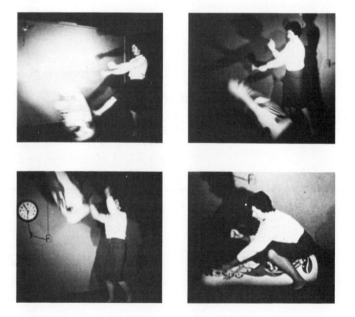

The results were clearcut. The children who had seen the model played much more aggressively than the children who had not; many duplicated almost every detail of the attack on the clown. They also played more aggressively with the other toys, for instance, choosing to shoot the dart gun rather than draw with the crayons.

The average number of times a child behaved aggressively, as rated every 5 seconds, was 83 for those who saw the real-life adult, 92 for those who saw the realistic movie, 99 for those who saw the cartoon, and 54 for those who saw no

Figure 2.11 *In real life, children model their behavior
after people they admire
most. In the left picture, a
daughter tries to sketch
along with mother. In the
right picture, the little girl
observes intently as her
mother lights a cigarette. We
know that the first child is
now studying to be an artist
at Cooper Union, a college
that specializes in the arts.
We do not know if the second
child is now lighting up on
her own, but statistically
speaking, she probably is:
children of smoking parents
are more likely to become
smokers themselves.*

and talk like them. As people grow older, they usually become more selective and
realistic, following the example of their best friend instead of a distant idol. But social
learning, like other forms of conditioning, remains important throughout life.

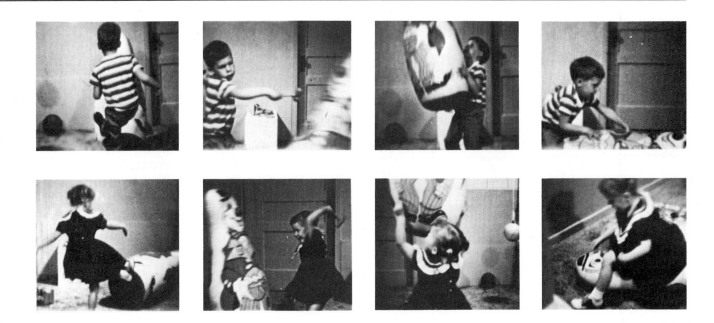

model of aggression. The results were subdivided by sex, to
see whether boys or girls were more influenced by seeing a
model of their own sex.

**Average Number of Times Children Behaved
Aggressively, Rated Every 5 Seconds**

	Real-Life Woman	Real-Life Man	Film Woman	Film Man	Cartoon	Control Group
Girls	65.8	57.3	87.0	79.5	80.9	36.4
Boys	76.8	131.8	114.5	85.0	117.2	72.2

When all 24 children who saw a model of their own sex are
compared with the 24 children who saw a model of the
opposite sex, the trend to imitate the behavior of someone of
the same sex is significant. (The 12 boys who saw the film
seem to contradict this, but the difference in their scores is
too small to be significant, and when they are averaged with
the other 36 children, the trend is reversed.) The basic
conclusions of this experiment have been proven many
times in other research. Children imitate the behavior they
see, especially if they identify with the model, whether in
real life, in a realistic movie, or in a cartoon.

AN AGGRESSIVE CHILD: Victim and architect of his family.

Inconsistent and coercive parenting sets poor example.

Child follows parents' example with parents, siblings, and friends.

Sibling of aggressive child reacts to what he sees, adding to the problem.

All family members intensify anger and punishment.

Family members avoid communication and escalate conflict. The children become increasingly aggressive and develop poor self-concepts, never learning positive social skills.

Figure 2.12 *According to social learning theory, a parent's poor example can begin a chain of events that makes it difficult for any family member to cope with problems constructively. An angry child with a poor self-image is not likely to make friends or encourage adults to be helpful.*

The Social Network   Social learning theory has led behaviorists to conclude that in order to change behavior, the entire social network should be analyzed. For example, Gerald Patterson (1976) found that aggressive boys are both the victims and the creators of the type of family they belong to. (This pattern is depicted in Figure 2.12.) In order to change this pattern, Patterson reports, the boys' parents and teachers had to change their response to the boys and to other family members or classmates. In this project, most of the boys did change—when their parents and teachers changed.

A CLOSER LOOK   Habit

Do you know anyone who seems to be intelligent and self-controlled, yet can't stop smoking cigarettes? Does this seem paradoxical to you? It doesn't to a behaviorist, who knows how deeply conditioned a habit can be.

It probably all began with social learning, when the smoker was young. Statistics show that children whose parents smoke are much more likely to become smokers than are children of nonsmokers. Even if Mom and Dad didn't smoke, most children saw many smoking role models, from magazine advertisements to the "cool" teenagers around the corner.

The smoker probably lit up for the first time in adolescence, and found that smoking cigarettes was a way of attaining recognition within the social group (positive reinforcement) and of relieving tension and anxiety in social situations (negative reinforcement). As the habit developed, smoking relieved the growing craving for nicotine and reduced the smoker's nervousness—more reinforcement. Smoking became an example of operant behavior; it was done to stop unpleasant feelings and increase positive feelings.

Classical conditioning also occurred. As smoking became part of the daily routine, it became linked with dozens of events—work breaks, answering the telephone, after-dinner coffee, the lull after lovemaking. Cigarettes became associated with daily living, and the smoking ritual became the usual way of keeping one's hands and mouth occupied.

After a long history of conditioning, as in this example, a habit is very hard to break. The specific nicotine craving is not easy to overcome, but it lasts only a few days. Much more difficult to alter is the heritage of social learning and conditioning.

Psychologists who help people break the smoking habit have found that it is best to use the principles of all three forms of behaviorism. The conditioned association between smoking and other activities is broken by giving smokers other things to do with their mouth and hands and new ways to handle other routines, perhaps a hard candy to suck while talking on the phone. New reinforcements (imagining how much farther one will be able to jog without puffing desperately, or buying a present with the money saved by not smoking) and new social pressure (joining a group of people who are quitting smoking) are also helpful. A smoker has a much better chance of quitting by using measures like these than by relying on logic or willpower alone.

Contributions of Behaviorism

Developmental psychologists have benefited from behaviorist theory in at least two ways. First, the emphasis on the causes and consequences of a specific behavior has led psychologists to see that many actions that children and adults perform are the result of the immediate environment rather than of deeply rooted problems or immutable inborn characteristics. This has encouraged psychologists to try to change the reinforcement for particular problem behaviors, such as temper tantrums, fear of school, or reluctance to study. The success achieved in eliminating such behaviors has astonished many psychologists who had accepted the psychoanalytic viewpoint. Behaviorists today work in classrooms, with families, and in institutions, helping people to change their behavior patterns.

Second, behaviorism has provided a model for psychologists of all theoretical backgrounds. It encourages them to define terms precisely, test hypotheses, and publish supporting data as well as conclusions. Because of behaviorism, psychology has become more of a science.

Criticism of Behaviorism　　Behaviorists have faced very different criticisms from those leveled at psychoanalytic theorists. Instead of being called unscientific, they are accused of ignoring any human emotions or ideas that don't fit neatly into controlled experiments. They do not accept the existence of the unconscious, and this, their critics believe, limits their understanding of behavior, particularly abnormal behavior. Many psychologists think that focusing on laws of observable behavior is such a narrow approach that behaviorists cannot really grasp the human condition. This complaint is heard particularly often among developmental psychologists, who see human development as a complex process with a great many individual and cultural differences.

Some psychologists think behaviorists underestimate the inner motivation and potential within each human being. In Maslow's words (1968), "Healthy children enjoy growing and moving forward, gaining new skills, capacities and powers. . . . In the normal development of the healthy child, . . . if he is given a really free choice, he will choose what is good for his growth." This conflicts with the behaviorists' idea that what we do is the result of past conditioning. In behaviorism, a "really free choice" does not exist (Skinner, 1971).

Cognitive Theory

Instead of seeing the human being as a creature governed by unconscious internal forces, or as a mere reactor to impinging external forces, cognitive theory emphasizes that individuals think and choose, and that their thoughts and interpretations are a powerful influence on their future actions and ideas. The Swiss psychologist Jean Piaget (1896—　　) reports this example of his daughter's cognitive development:

> At one year, four months, twelve days, Jacqueline has just been wrested from a game she wants to continue and placed in her playpen from which she wants to get out. She calls, but in vain. Then she clearly expresses a certain need [to go to the bathroom], although the events of the last ten minutes prove that she no longer experiences it. No sooner has she left the playpen than she indicates the game she wishes to resume! [Piaget, 1951]

Cognitive theorists are fascinated by such instances in which clever thinking produces new behavior. Other psychologists might be more interested in other aspects of this incident. Psychoanalysts would note that Jacqueline is using the most significant event of toddlerhood, toilet training, to get what she wants. Behaviorists would observe the sequence of events: her game was interrupted; she was not taken out when she declared her true wishes, but was when she pretended she had to go to the bathroom. In other words, she was punished for playing, ignored for telling the truth, and rewarded for lying.

But cognitive theorists are not so involved in analyzing motives or consequences. What absorbs their interest is the active thought process within each person, for according to cognitive theory, thinking is an active process whereby people organize their perceptions of the world. As Piaget concluded in his observation, "Jacqueline, knowing that a mere appeal would not free her from her confinement, had imagined a more efficacious means, foreseeing more or less clearly the sequence of actions that would result from it." This mental activity, say cognitive theorists, is more powerful than unconscious motives or stimulus-response chains.

Piaget's Ideas

Piaget, the most famous of cognitive theorists, was interested in observing natural processes even as a boy. At age 10 he published his first scientific paper, a description of an unusual sparrow he had seen at a park. In his first job as a psychologist, Piaget asked children questions that were being considered for a standard intelligence test. He was supposed to find the age at which most children could answer each question correctly. But he became more interested in the children's wrong answers, partly because he saw that children who were the same age made similar types of mistakes. He began to believe that *how* children think is much more revealing of their mental ability than *what* they know (Flavell, 1963).

Figure 2.13 *Piaget's legendary warmth and friendliness may be one reason children have readily told him their ideas.*

Basic Cognitive Processes   When Piaget's own three children were born, he began taking meticulous notes on their intellectual development—watching the process as much as the results. From these observations, Piaget developed his ideas about what intelligence is and how it should be measured.

In Piaget's view, intelligence consists of two interrelated processes, organization and adaptation. People *organize* their thoughts so that they make sense, separating the more important thoughts from the less important ones as well as connecting one idea to another. At the same time, people *adapt* their thinking to include new ideas, as new experiences provide additional information. This adaptation occurs in two ways, through assimilation and accommodation. In the former process, new information is simply added to the cognitive organization already there. In the latter, the intellectual organization has to change somewhat to adjust to the new idea.

Figure 2.14 *Piaget believes intelligence is an active process, involving the organization and adaptation of ideas.*

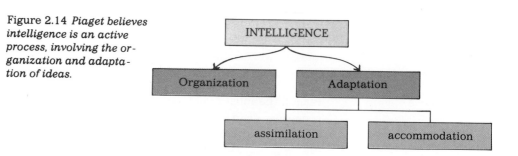

According to Piaget, the basic cognitive processes are similar to basic biological processes (Piaget, 1952). In digestion, for example, the stomach constantly *organizes* whatever food it receives, separating wastes from essential nourishment, depending on the physical needs of the body at the moment. At the same time, the digestive system *adapts* itself to whatever new food the person eats. It *assimilates* food by chewing it and breaking it down into basic nutrients, and *accommodates* food by adding acids and working faster or slower.

Piaget sees the basic cognitive processes at work even in the first weeks of life. Babies are born with a sucking reflex. They automatically suck everything that touches their lips. But by the time they are 3 months old, they have organized their world into objects to be sucked for nourishment (breasts or bottles), objects to be sucked for pleasure (fingers or pacifiers), and objects not to be sucked at all (fuzzy blankets and large balls). They have adapted to their environment, first by assimilation (sucking everything they could get their mouth on), and then by accommodation (adjusting the sucking reflex so that milk-giving nipples are sucked one way, pacifiers another, and fingers a third—Figure 2.15). In the same way, the ideas of a preschool child show assimilation and accommodation.

Figure 2.15 *The sucking reflex is quickly adapted to the various objects the infant sucks. In breast-feeding, the lips are rounder, the gums and tongue exert more pressure, and the sucking rhythm is steadier than in finger-sucking.*

When one 3-year-old, named Elissa, tripped over her toybox, spilling its contents, she acknowledged her responsibility when questioned. But when she came across some scattered toys in another part of her room, Elissa had only one explanation— "Charlie did it." Charlie, her best friend, did sometimes mess up her toys, but not as often as she herself or her siblings did. Rather than considering the complexity or responsibility, however, Elissa used assimilation to explain every new disruption. Her world view was simple: Charlie makes a mess.

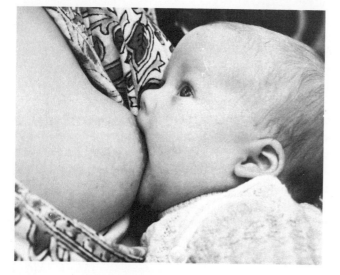

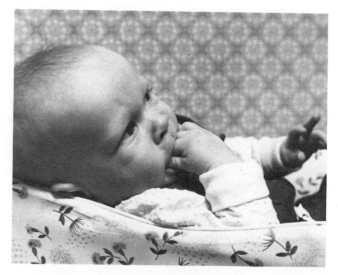

One windy day Elissa was playing by herself with some doll clothes she had arranged on a picnic table. When she noticed a dress that had fallen to the ground, she again resorted to "Charlie did it." Just at that moment, a gust of wind blew several additional articles of clothing off the table. Confronted by this direct evidence that Charlie did not do it, Elissa adapted her thinking by accommodating: "The breezes did it." The next time she saw her blocks strewn across the floor of her room, she was back to assimilation, but of a more sophisticated sort: "Charlie did it, or maybe the breezes did it."

A CLOSER LOOK

Dancing: A Metaphor of Adaptation

What makes someone a good dancer? If you were going to measure dancing ability, would you give a DQ (dancing quotient) test with questions about names of dances and sequences of steps, and add up the score? Probably not. If good dancing can be measured at all, it would have to be through watching people dance. One criterion you could use would be Piaget's concept of adaptation, assimilation, and accommodation.

It is easy to spot very poor dancers, who don't adapt their movements to the music at all. They always do the same old step at the same old pace, so they miss the beat. But it's harder to differentiate the good dancers. Some people dance well because they assimilate well. They don't need to adjust, or accommodate, their usual dancing style very much because it fits almost any music and almost every beat. If their partner says, "I don't know that dance," they reply, "Don't worry, just follow me." They are good leaders, but if you watch them long enough you realize they aren't creative, just skilled.

By contrast, other people dance well because they accommodate well. They quickly change their movements to adjust to their partner, to the music, to the current fad. They are good followers and more enjoyable to watch, but they don't seem to have a style of their own.

The best dancers of all assimilate and accommodate. Sometimes they lead; sometimes they follow. Sometimes they do traditional dances; sometimes they invent new ones. They change steps smoothly, no matter what the dance. The particular steps they choose depend on the music, their partner, what's "in," their mood, their energy, and even the space on the floor. When you watch a pair of these dancers, you can't tell who is leading because they move as one, adapting to each other and to the music. They are flexible and creative dancers, just as, according to Piaget, the most intelligent people are flexible and creative thinkers.

How Cognitive Development Occurs Piaget holds that there are four major stages of cognitive development. He believes that just as infants crawl whereas older children walk, infants think one way (sensorimotor thought), preschool children another (preoperational thought), school-age children another (concrete operational thought), and adolescents and adults yet another (formal operational thought). Each of these ways of thinking is explained later in this book.

The way children progress from one phase of cognitive development to another, or from one concept to another within a given phase, is the same throughout the life span. Piaget believes that everyone seeks mental equilibrium, that is, a balance of opposing forces. What he means by this is that each person needs to make sense out of conflicting experiences and perceptions. People need a mental concept, or to use another of Piaget's terms, a scheme, that will strike a harmony between their ideas and their experiences. A scheme is a general way of thinking about, or interacting with, ideas and objects in the environment. The infant has a sucking scheme and a grasping scheme; an adult might have the scheme that a human life is more valuable than any material thing. When traditional schemes do not seem to fit present experiences, people are put into a state of disequilibrium

TABLE 2.2   **Piaget's Periods of Cognitive Development**

Approximate Age	Name	Characteristics	Major Acquisitions
Birth–2 years	Sensorimotor	Infant uses senses and motor abilities to understand the world. This period begins with reflexes, and ends with complex coordinations of sensorimotor skills.	The infant learns that an object still exists when it is out of sight (*object permanence*) and begins to remember and imagine ideas and experiences (*mental representation*).
2–6 years	Preoperational	The child uses *symbolic thinking*, including language, to understand the world. Most thinking is *egocentric*, which means that children understand the world from only one perspective, their own.	The imagination flourishes. Children gradually begin to *decenter*, or become less egocentric, and to understand other points of view.
7–11 years	Concrete Operational	The child understands and applies logical operations, or principles, to help interpret specific experiences or perceptions.	By applying logical abilities, children learn to understand the basic ideas of conservation, number, classification, and many other specific, or concrete, ideas.
From 12 on	Formal Operational	The adolescent or adult is able to think about abstractions and hypothetical concepts. During adolescence, this glimpse of the vastness and complexity of knowledge leads some people to believe they understand nothing and others to believe they are on the verge of understanding everything.	There evolves the idea that there are many answers to every question, and many questions about every answer. Ethics, politics, and all the social sciences become more interesting and involving.

These ideas become clearer with an example. In one of Piaget's experiments, a child is shown two identical glasses, each containing the same quantity of liquid. Next, the child pours the liquid from one of these glasses into a third glass, which is taller and thinner than the other two. The experimenter then asks the child which glass contains more. Almost every child younger than 6 says the taller glass contains more, because preschool children have the scheme that taller things are bigger. They are unshakable in this conviction, even when the experimenter points out that the taller glass is thinner, and the amount of water in each of the identical glasses was obviously the same.

Children older than 7, on the other hand, almost always realize that pouring the liquid into a taller glass does not change the amount of liquid. They have the scheme that Piaget calls conservation of liquids. They remain steadfast in this conviction despite the experimenter's attempts to convince them otherwise.

In both these cases, the children are in a state of equilibrium. They have managed to construct a mental structure that enables them to interpret what they see. However, at some point between ages 5 and 8, children enter a transitional period and begin to be able to consider two conflicting facts. In the tall-glass experiment, for instance, they remember that the identical glasses originally contained the same amount of liquid, but they do not yet know how to reconcile that fact with the apparent quantity in the tall glass. They resolve this dilemma in a variety of ways. Some imagine that water was magically added to the tall glass. Some even say that the tall glass contains less because it is thinner, reversing their previous scheme in their confusion. Some are puzzled, some are distressed, some say the question is impossible. All these reactions are evidence of disequilibrium caused by the failure of the children's existing scheme to satisfy their new ability to perceive and remember.

Thirst for Knowledge Periods of disequilibrium can be disquieting to a child or an adult, who realizes that the old ideas no longer hold true. But they are also exciting periods of mental growth. Children seek out new experiences to challenge their traditional ideas. Babies poke, pull, and taste everything they get their hands on; preschool children ask thousands of questions; school-age children read literature and trash; and adolescents try out roles and experiences their parents would not condone—all because people at every age want cognitive challenges. Recognition of this active searching for knowledge is the essence of the cognitive theory of human development.

RESEARCH REPORT **The Clinical Method**

Piaget developed a new way to measure a child's mental development. It is called *the clinical method* because, like a doctor with a patient, the psychologist follows the child's lead. Experimenters using the clinical method observe children in their daily life in order to design an experiment that uses the words and problems of the children themselves. The researcher then asks questions or presents problems to individual children. All children are asked the same questions at first, but follow-up questions depend partly on each child's responses to the initial questions.

For example, Piaget decided to investigate children's understanding of family relationships (Piaget, 1962; originally published 1928). He asked 140 boys, age 4 to 12, six questions about brothers. Almost every 4- and 5-year-old knew whether or not he was a brother, but few understood what a brother is. Most young children think that all girls are sisters and all boys are brothers. Often children think the size of the person determines brother or sister status.

Boy, age 7: All boys are brothers.
Piaget: Is your father a brother?
Yes, when he was little.
Why was your father a brother?
Because he was a boy.
Do you know your father's brother?
He doesn't have a brother.

Boy, only child, age 6: A brother is a boy. (He has just said

that he himself is not a brother.)
Piaget: Are all boys brothers?
[No] because some of them are little.
If anyone is little, isn't he a brother?
No, you can only be a brother if you are big.

Even older children often make mistakes:

Boy, age 9: When there is a boy and another boy, when there are two of them.
Piaget: Has your father got a brother?
Yes.
Why?
Because he was born second.
Then what is a brother?
It is the second brother that comes.
Then the first is not a brother?
Oh no. The second brother that comes is called a brother.

Similar results were obtained with 100 girls who were asked about sisters. Not until age 9 did 75 percent of the children define "brother" or "sister" correctly.

Some psychologists have declared Piaget's method unscientific because the experimenter varies the questions according to the child's responses. However, as Philip Cowan (1978) explains, "Piaget intends the clinical method to support a fully scientific study of the child: it is public and repeatable across observers. The key word describing the clinical method is systematic, replacing the previous emphasis on 'objectivity'."

Contributions of Cognitive Theory

Cognitive theory has revolutionized developmental psychology by focusing attention on the child's active mental processes. The attempt to understand the mental structures of the child's thought, and to appreciate the child's internal need for new mental structures when the old ones appear outmoded, has led to a new understanding of why children act as they do. It has also profoundly affected education throughout England and North America, allowing teachers and students to become partners in the educational process once the child's own capacities and needs are recognized. For instance, elementary school math is now taught with objects the child can manipulate, because we now know children learn more when they work out solutions by measuring blocks or counting pennies than when they memorize a table of mathematical facts.

Piaget's formulations have also helped us know how to communicate with children. Say, for example, that a preschool girl tells you she saw a lion on the sidewalk. If you realize that the 4-year-old has trouble distinguishing reality and fantasy, you will undoubtedly be more inclined to ask her about her adventure than to lecture her about lying or worry about her sanity.

Criticism of Cognitive Theory

Piaget's theories at first met with indifference and criticism in North America. He seemed too uninterested in emotions for Freud's followers and too unscientific for the behaviorists. But his ideas have gradually won over many professionals, especially educators.

At the same time, however, many people think Piaget is so absorbed by the child's active search for knowledge that he ignores external motivation or teaching. While it is comforting to think that children develop their own schemes when they are ready, this concept implies that teachers should not intervene when a child seems uninterested in learning to add or spell. To some extent, the "back to basics" movement in American education is a reaction against Piagetian ideas carried to their logical extreme. And even some of those who most admire Piaget believe that he underestimates the role of society and home in fostering cognitive development. Partly for this reason, Jerome Kagan (1971) has called Piaget "a developmental idealist." Many psychologists believe that culture and education can be crucial in providing the proper mix of equilibrium and disequilibrium to help the child develop. In Bruner's (1973) words, "Some environments push cognitive growth better, earlier, and longer than others . . . it makes a huge difference to the intellectual life of a child simply that he was in school."

Comparison of Theories

Each of the three theories presented here has contributed a great deal to developmental psychology. Psychoanalytic theory has made us aware of the complex effects of early childhood experiences; behaviorists have taught us to look at the sequence of events that lead to the behavior patterns we see; cognitive theorists have reminded us to respect each person's thoughts about his or her experiences. Each has also been criticized: psychoanalytic theory for being too subjective; the behaviorist viewpoint for being too narrow; and cognitive theory for ignoring the power of direct instruction.

Despite these criticisms, the three theories share many common characteristics. They all deal with children as they actually are, so the same behaviors and ideas encountered in children are described by all three. As explained in Chapter 11, for instance, they all see the child developing a stronger sense of moral rules at about age 6, in a process called *identification* by Freud, *modeling* by Bandura, and *decentering* by Piaget.

They also share similar goals: that all the emotional needs of children will be met, that their intellectual potential will be realized, and that all children will grow up to be adults who are happy with themselves and helpful to others.

In some ways, these three theoretical perspectives complement rather than contradict each other, because they emphasize different aspects of development. For this reason, most developmental psychologists describe themselves as eclectic, meaning that rather than adopting any one of these theories exclusively, they make use of parts of all of them.

Whatever the similarities of these theories, however, at the heart of each is a different view of the nature of the child. Psychoanalytic theory describes the child as a collection of hidden impulses that need to be expressed, understood, and controlled. Behaviorist theory envisions the child as a lump of clay, to be molded by the environment for good or ill. Cognitive theory sees the child as a thinker, organizing and adapting experiences so they make sense. Consequently, on many specific issues, such as how important the mother is, or why a child learns to talk, or where moral standards originate, proponents of one theory clash with advocates of another. These debates are described later in this book.

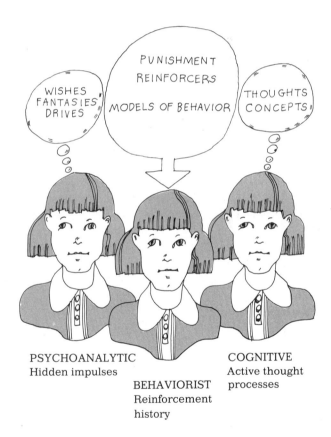

Figure 2.16 *The three major theoretical perspectives each view human nature differently. But most developmental psychologists believe that all three perspectives should be considered in order to fully understand development.*

PSYCHOANALYTIC
Hidden impulses

BEHAVIORIST
Reinforcement
history

COGNITIVE
Active thought
processes

The theories also differ in their deference to scientific experiment. It would be exaggerating to say that psychoanalysts spurn experimental science, behaviorists worship it, and cognitive theorists manipulate it, but this overstatement highlights a lingering disagreement among theorists from the three camps. The three research reports in this chapter—Erikson's case study, Bandura's laboratory experiment, and Piaget's clinical interview—typify the methodologies preferred by psychologists of each of the three perspectives. Psychologists from every background use and respect all three methods, but they tend to believe the most valid research is acquired through the method favored by their own theoretical perspective.

**How Useful Are
These Theories?**

Given these similarities and differences, it is time to ask again what purpose theories serve. A good theory provides a framework, clarifies and organizes existing observations, and indicates new directions to be tested. All the theories presented here have been illuminating to developmental psychologists. In subsequent chapters, as echoes and elaborations of psychoanalytic, behaviorist, and cognitive theories appear, you can form your own opinion on the validity of each theory.

SUMMARY

What Theories Do

1. A theory is a coherent set of general principles that attempts to explain what we observe. Theories help us to interpret what we experience, and to suggest new hypotheses to be tested.

Psychoanalytic Theory

2. Psychoanalytic theory emphasizes the hidden forces within each person—the unconscious memories and instincts that make us think and act as we do.

3. Freud, the founder of psychoanalytic theory, developed the theory of infantile sexuality to explain how unconscious impulses are shaped and directed during the psychosexual development of the child. Freud saw the basic personality in terms of three theoretical constructs: the id operates according to the pleasure principle; the ego operates according to the reality principle; and the superego acts like a conscience.

4. Erikson's theory of psychosocial development stresses the interaction between somatic, personal, and social forces at each stage of development. Each person's experience with the eight crises of psychological development depends a great deal on the culture in which one lives.

Behaviorism

5. Behaviorists believe that psychologists must study only behavior that can be observed and measured. They emphasize the relationship between one observable event and another, that is, stimulus and response.

6. Behaviorists think people are conditioned to behave as they do, either through classical conditioning (Pavlov), in which the association between one stimulus and another is the essential factor, or operant conditioning (Skinner), in which reinforcement is crucial.

7. Social learning theory recognizes that much of human behavior is modeled after the behavior of others. For children, models of behavior include parents, peers, and sports, movie, literary, and historical figures.

Cognitive Theory

8. Cognitive theorists believe that human thinking is an active and creative process. The most famous cognitive theorist, Jean Piaget, believes intelligence is a process of organization and adaptation. Children and adults develop schemes that help them organize their perceptions and experiences.

9. According to Piaget, a mental balance, or equilibrium, lasts until the person becomes aware of discrepant perceptions or experiences. Then disequilibrium leads to a new period of growth.

Comparison of Theories

10. All three theories have been useful, although all have met considerable criticism. Their central concern is human development, but they focus on different aspects, hold different assumptions, and often use different methods.

KEY QUESTIONS

What functions does a good theory perform?

Why are developmental psychologists, in particular, interested in psychoanalytic theory?

How does culture affect human development, according to Erikson?

How is Erikson's theory similar to Freud's?

How is Erikson's theory different from Freud's?

What are the differences between classical and operant conditioning?

What factors should be considered in choosing a reinforcement?

How can children learn from example?

What is intelligence, according to Piaget?

What is the difference between assimilation and accommodation?

What are the main differences between psychoanalytic theory, behaviorism, and cognitive theory?

KEY TERMS

psychoanalytic theory	operant conditioning
infantile sexuality	reinforcement
psychosexual development	positive reinforcer
id	negative reinforcer
ego	social reinforcers
superego	social learning theory
defense mechanisms	modeling
regression	cognitive theory
repression	organization
displacement	adaptation
psychosocial theory	assimilation
behaviorism	accommodation
stimulus	equilibrium
response	scheme
conditioning	disequilibrium
classical conditioning	eclectic
learning by association	

RECOMMENDED READINGS

Freud, Sigmund. *The sexual enlightenment of children.* New York: Collier Books, 1963.

This book contains several essays by Freud, including the complete case history of Hans. In one essay, Freud advocates that children should be told the truth when they ask questions about sexual matters, stating, "I do not think there is even one good reason for denying children the information which their thirst for knowledge demands." In other essays, he analyzes the sexual implications of some of the fantasies that children have and some of the lies they tell.

Hall, Calvin S. *A primer of Freudian psychology.* New York: World, 1973.

A straightforward explanation of Freud's theory that includes discussion of the id, ego, and superego, defense mechanisms, and stages of development.

Erikson, Erik. *Childhood and society* (2nd ed.). New York: Norton, 1963.

Erikson's beautifully written classic, which explains his theory of psychosocial development, including the eight stages, and his reinterpretation of Freud. The discussion of several American subcultures, as well as the childhoods of Hitler in Germany and Gorky in Russia, is fascinating.

Bijou, S. W., and Baer, D. M. *Child development.* New York: Appleton, 1961.

The behaviorist view of child development, clearly written by two famous behaviorists.

Skinner, B. F. *About behaviorism.* New York: Knopf, 1974.

The most famous American behaviorist defends behaviorism in clear and definite terms. Skinner lists and rebuts twenty criticisms of behaviorism which he thinks are "an extraordinary misunderstanding of the achievements of a scientific enterprise."

Piaget, Jean, and **Inhelder, Barbel.** *The psychology of the child.* New York: Basic Books, 1969.

Relatively brief, yet comprehensive, which is why it is recommended. However, it is also quite difficult (as is all of Piaget), so you might prefer to look at the next book on the list.

Cowan, Philip A. *Piaget with feeling.* New York: Holt, Rinehart and Winston, 1978.

A description of Piaget's theory that is both accurate and readable. Cowan spells out the educational implications of Piaget's ideas, and describes the link between cognitive and emotional development.

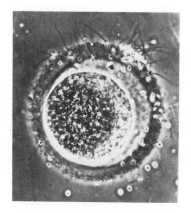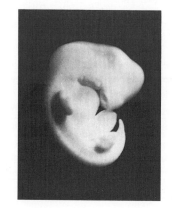

The Beginnings

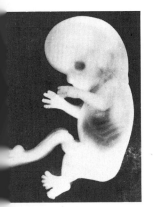 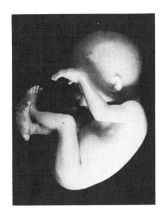 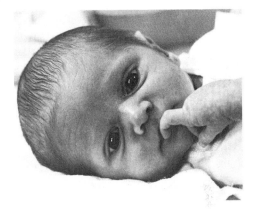

PART I

When considering the human life span, most people ignore or take for granted the time from conception through birth. Indeed, among all the cultures of the world, China seems to have been the only one to have ever included the prenatal period when reckoning age. Yet, these 266 or so days could not be more crucial. On the very first day, for instance, our entire genetic heritage is set, affecting not only what we see when we look in the mirror but also many of the abilities, talents, and disabilities that characterize each of us. Survival is much more doubtful and growth much more rapid during the prenatal period than at any other time in our lives. Finally, each child's day of birth usually provides the occasion for more anticipation, worry, excitement, and joy on the part of parents than any other day of childhood. Indeed, the impact of the physiological and emotional events of that day can be felt for weeks, months, even years.

These early days, usually uncounted and underemphasized, are the focus of the next three chapters.

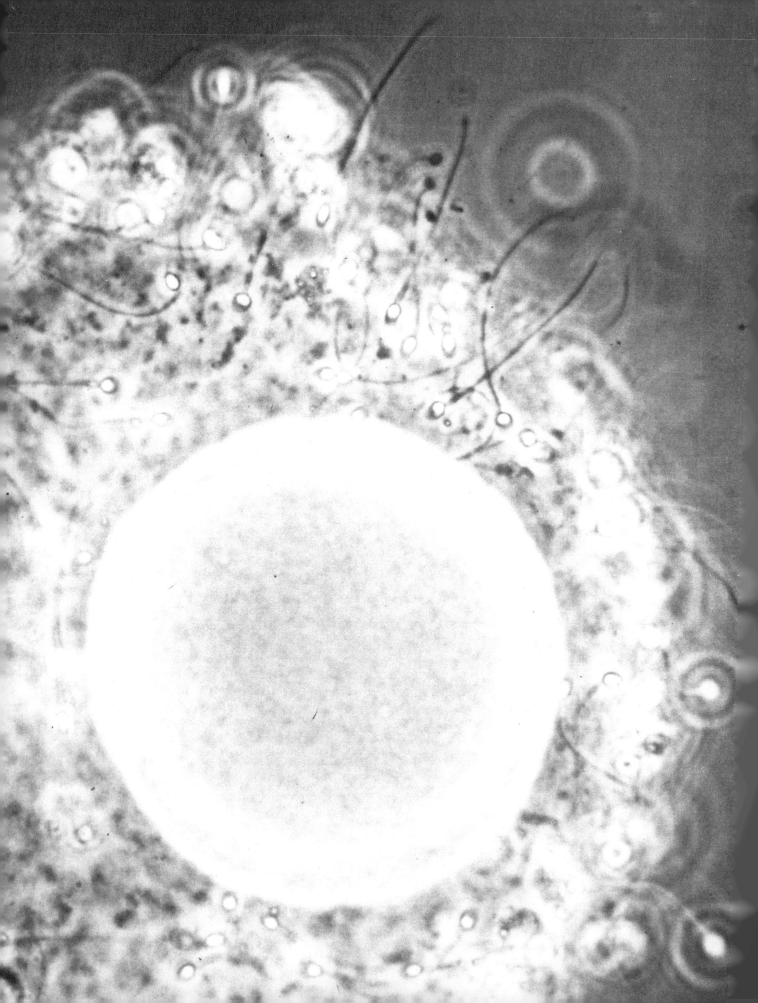

Conception and Heredity

A million, million spermatozoa,
All of them alive
Out of their cataclysm but one poor Noah
Dare hope to survive
And among that billion minus one
might have chanced to be
Shakespeare, another Newton, a new Donne
But the One was Me.

Aldous Huxley
"Fifth Philosopher's Song"

CHAPTER 3

True or False?

At the present rate of population growth, the United States will be standing-room-only by the year 2050.

Research has shown that Freud was correct in his assertion that parenthood is a prerequisite for psychological fulfillment.

Every individual is 1 of 64 trillion possible genetic combinations his or her parents might have produced.

A woman's chances of having twins is affected by her ethnic origin.

If a brown-eyed, dark-haired man married to a brown-eyed, dark-haired woman is presented with a blue-eyed, blond offspring, he had better start asking some hard questions.

Long-term studies show that temperament remains fairly constant from birth: newborns who are restless, cranky, and difficult to please will most likely be the same way as adults.

Conception—that moment when a sperm and ovum join to begin a new human being—might seem a simple topic in developmental psychology, a miracle to be briefly mentioned. But much depends on that moment, for within a very short time the genes contained in the sperm and ovum combine to influence virtually everything about the person-to-be, not only physical attributes, such as gender and appearance, but every intellectual and personality characteristic as well.

Many environmental influences are also set at conception. Some of these, such as the mother's health, age, and previous childbearing history, have a direct impact on the uterine environment where the embryo will live or die. Other environmental factors, such as the parents' education, income, and social class, also have a powerful, although indirect, impact.

Beyond that, like a stone tossed into a quiet pond, the beginning of each life alters the future for those who are closest to the prospective baby, and sends ripples that may eventually be felt by a vastly larger circle of people. One couple may be delighted with the addition to their lives, another may find a child to be just one more source of stress and anger, a thing to be ignored or even abused.

Thus, conception is much more than a brief miracle; it is the foundation upon which a life is built.

Planning Conception

If developmental psychologists had their way, every baby would be planned for and every child wanted. Psychologists have seen too many unplanned and unwanted babies become unloved and neglected children who grow up to be unloving and troubled adults. Of course, this does not mean that every unplanned baby is unloved nor that every planned baby gets good care. But planning for children is the first step toward raising well-nurtured children.

Contraception in History

For most of human history, married couples did not plan their family's size; they simply had as many babies as chance allowed (Rudel et al., 1973). Until about a hundred years ago, this unchecked reproduction did not produce a world-wide population explosion (see Figure 3.1), because the death rate of children and childbearing women was high enough to keep the total population almost steady (Berelson, 1974). In addition, poor nutrition often reduced the woman's years of fertility (Frisch, 1978).

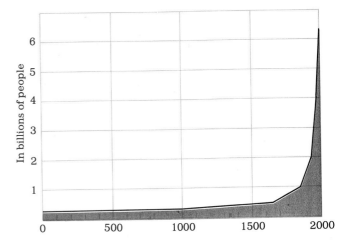

Figure 3.1 *The population explosion is a recent phenomenon: more people have lived in the twentieth century than have lived from the beginning of human history until 1900. Although earlier projections for world population in the year 2000 have been scaled downward as the world birth rate has slowed, experts estimate that at least 2 billion children will be born in the last two decades of the twentieth century.*

When a population increased beyond what the land could support, cultural values tended to change to encourage later marriage or more frequent abstinence (Rudel et al., 1973). Abortion and contraception were not unknown (there is evidence of their use 3000 years ago in Egypt), but the methods involved were unreliable—swallowing fourteen live tadpoles three days after menstruation was, for example, a Chinese form of contraception—and, in the case of abortion, very dangerous. If all else failed during times of famine, infanticide (killing newborn babies) solved the problem of too many mouths to feed (Langer, 1972).

Recently there have been important refinements in contraceptive methods, from pinpointing the time of ovulation so that the rhythm method (the forgoing of sexual intercourse during ovulation) can be more effective, to surgical advances that make sterilization safer. Now almost every North American adult agrees that some form of family planning is advisable (Ryder and Westoff, 1971; Jaffe, 1973). Proof of this is seen in the birth rate, which reached an all-time low in the mid-1970s in the United States and Canada, and in many other countries as well.

The Pros and Cons of Having Children

Not many years ago, parenthood was considered absolutely essential to a full life. Little girls automatically expected to be mothers; little boys planned to be breadwinners; everyone pitied childless couples.

Today, according to several surveys, many young people plan smaller families than the ones they grew up in (Nobbe and Okraku, 1974; Stolzenberg and Waite, 1977; Haskell, 1977). And the number who plan to have only one child, or even no children, is increasing.

Psychologists' attitudes on this matter have also changed. Until recently, most psychologists followed Freud in thinking that parenthood was necessary for psychological fulfillment, especially for women. For instance, Helene Deutsch (1945)

A CLOSER LOOK   **Birth Control Around the World**

Medical advances over the last hundred years have increased fertility and reduced mortality rates so rapidly that overpopulation is now a world-wide problem. Curbing the birth rate is especially critical in poorer countries. Without it, economic growth is virtually impossible. Controlling the birth rate depends on two interrelated factors: the availability of contraception and the values of the society (Reed, 1978). Making contraceptive techniques available is pointless if people cannot be persuaded to use them (Rudel et al., 1973).

China provides its estimated 1 billion people with both the means and the motive. Premarital sex and youthful marriages are forbidden. Large families are criticized; and contraception, abortion, and sterilization are provided free by "barefoot doctors," medically trained men and women who live in the same rural villages as their patients. In the last ten years, the Chinese birth rate has dropped at least 15 percent, which means that the number of babies born in China *per thousand members of the population* was 15 percent less in 1979 than it was ten years before.

No other developing nation has a record as good as China's. However, several have made impressive strides. India, Colombia, Sri Lanka, and the Philippines have reduced their birth rate at least 10 percent in the last decade. From 1975 to 1977, the Indian government pushed a controversial program of *compulsory* sterilization, stipulating that Indian families with two or more children could receive welfare benefits or public housing only if the parents had been sterilized. In addition, men were provided with incentives (in

some cases, transistor radios) to get vasectomies, even if they had not fathered two children. Distress at these birth-control policies was one reason for the ouster of Indira Gandhi's government.

India is the only country that has attempted widespread sterilization. Most countries use family-planning publicity and make contraception freely available. (A United Nations survey of 144 countries found only 8—Saudi Arabia, Burma, Chad, Equatorial Guinea, Gabon, Laos, Syria, and Malawi—that restrict access to modern birth-control methods, such as the pill and the IUD [*The New York Times,* June 28, 1978]). In Japan, England, and most of the countries of Scandinavia and Eastern Europe, abortion is an important birth-control method (there are more abortions per year in Rumania, Hungary, and the Soviet Union than there are live births).

North Americans are now reproducing at the ZPG (zero population growth) level, about 2.1 children for every woman of childbearing age. If the ZPG birth rate continues, by the year 2050 the total number of Americans will level off at about 335 million, assuming the rate of immigration does not change (Cetron and Sugarek, 1977). The number of births and deaths each year will then be the same. At the moment, however, births outnumber deaths each year because there are far more people under 40 than over 40. When today's young adults become senior citizens, the proportion of those under 40 to those over 40 will be about the same—unless today's children create a new "baby boom."

Figure 3.2 *Most industrialized nations have followed similar patterns of birth rate increases and decreases in this century—low during the depression years, high in the 1950s. The specific numbers given here show how many babies are born in the United States each year per thousand women of childbearing age. Canadian rates are almost identical; most European countries are similar in pattern but lower in actual rates each year.*

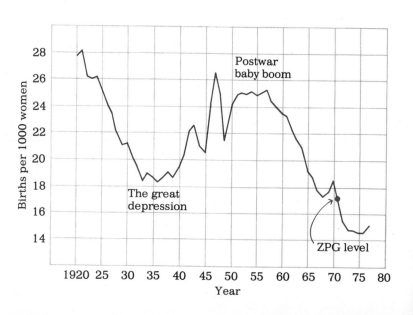

(a) *Subway riders in New York City are asked to think about family planning.* (b) *Happiness is a family with two children, according to this billboard in Benares, one of the most crowded cities of India.* (c) *Insertion of an IUD is explained to Egyptian women in this family-planning class in Cairo.* (d) *The People's Park in Shanghai is a favorite place for an evening stroll, especially on hot summer nights. The Chinese government has installed educational exhibits along one side of the park, including this one describing various birth-control methods.*

(a)

(c)

(d)

Many European nations are actually below the ZPG rate. In both East Germany and West Germany, the average couple has only one child. German officials are concerned that voluntary birth control has gone too far, for each year more Germans die than are born.

When the entire world is considered, however, it is much too soon to worry that contraception might be too successful: the world population is now about 4 billion, double what it was forty years ago, and growing by about 80 million per year. Current contraceptive methods are imperfect; even careful couples have unwanted pregnancies. Sterilization procedures are quite safe and effective, but they are hard to reverse, which limits their desirability. What is needed is a safe alternative to the pill and the IUD, better male contraception, and reversible sterilization.

said that pregnancy is a woman's deepest and most powerful wish, and Erikson wrote that the usual solution to the crisis of adulthood—generativity versus stagnation—is parenthood.

Today, however, psychologists and lay people agree that many nonparents are well adjusted and happy, sometimes envied rather than pitied. One study of 590 professional women who chose to remain childless found that almost all of them led active and satisfying lives, a far cry from the stagnation that Erikson might have predicted (Welds, 1977). Another study revealed that infertile couples were more likely to discuss ideas and share opinions on a wide range of issues than were couples with children (Humphrey, 1975).

When they do have children, for instance, young women tend to be happier with one child than with two, according to one study (Knox and Wilson, 1978). Many of the mothers reported that a second child meant more work and more noise, with less time for oneself and less enjoyment of marriage. Another study found that teenage mothers are less likely to graduate from high school, find a job, or feel proud of themselves than their classmates who, either by luck or forethought, have avoided pregnancy (Furstenberg, 1976). A review of the literature on marital satisfaction reports that happiness in the typical marriage follows a U-shaped curve; it begins relatively high, dips when the children are young, and gradually rises as the children become more independent (Goldman, 1979).

The Cost of Children   A century ago, unrestricted childbearing made economic sense, since each child in the family could be looked upon as an investment. In the first place, the cost of raising children was very small, especially in rural areas, where most people lived. And since few children attended school and most jobs were simple, each child became an unpaid helper at home, on the farm, or in the shop. Most important, before the era of Social Security, pension funds, and nursing homes, elderly parents were financially supported, and cared for, by their grown children. An older childless couple had good reason to worry about their future.

Today each new baby is a long-term financial liability rather than an investment. It costs $115,000 to raise a child from birth through high school, at 1980 prices (Figure 3.4).* This estimate is for an average child who attends public school, wears clothes until they are outgrown, shares a room with a sibling, and has no unusual medical or dental problems. It does not include lost income if one parent quits work to care for the child, or child-care expenses if both parents work.

Figure 3.3 *When this photograph was taken in 1880, a family with nine children was the envy of the neighborhood.*

---

*Based on a 1976 estimate, adjusted for inflation (*The New York Times,* September 20, 1976).

Figure 3.4 *The $115,000 price tag seems high until one totals up all the food, clothing, shelter, medical, and play costs of raising an average child. Not only does each child personally consume many items, but each child also increases the amount needed for family expenses, such as rent, electricity, paper goods, telephone, vacations, laundry, and so forth. When a child has special medical or educational needs, the cost is much higher than this estimate.*

Children cost much more than money. They take time, patience, energy, and a daily commitment. All costs considered, it is no wonder that many young people wonder if parenthood is for them.

How Many Children?   Nonetheless, more than nine out of ten couples do decide to have children if they can. Most people simply feel that the delight and pride in watching their children grow will outweigh the cost and effort of caring for them. For most couples, the question is not whether to have children but how many to have. Although happy families obviously come in all sizes, psychologists have found that, in general, the smaller the family, the brighter and more successful the children. Parents benefit from smaller families too. They are usually more satisfied with their lives and less likely to be divorced than parents with many children (Thornton, 1977). This is true for American groups that traditionally have emphasized large families, such as Mexican-Americans, as well as for those that have favored small families for generations, such as white Protestants (Bean et al., 1977).

Planning a Healthy Baby   After choosing to have children and deciding on family size, a couple should consider a third question: What can be done *before* conception to ensure the birth of a healthy infant?

Some precautions are simple. Dr. Virginia Apgar, who directed research on birth defects for the March of Dimes, has recommended spacing pregnancies at least two years apart, as well as limiting total family size, because later-born children are slightly more likely to have birth defects, especially if less than twenty-four months have elapsed between their conception and a previous birth, miscarriage, or abortion. Apgar also suggested that women should bear their children between the ages of 20 and 35, and that men should father their children before age 45. Both future parents should avoid exposure to x-rays and other radiation during the years they are trying to conceive a child, and the woman should try to avoid unnecessary drugs, including alcohol and cigarettes (Apgar and Beck, 1973).

Another recommendation is more complicated: The couple should find out if they are likely to have a child with a genetic disease or handicap. Before discussing this recommendation, we need to understand the biological process of conception and the mechanisms of heredity.

The Biology of Conception

Human reproductive cells are called gametes. Female gametes are ova (singular, ovum). Sometimes they are called eggs. An ovum is the largest cell in the human body, about one-quarter the size of the period at the end of this sentence. Male gametes are *spermatozoa* (singular, *spermatozoon*), usually abbreviated to sperm A spermatozoon is only about one twenty-fifth the size of an ovum.

Before Conception

A baby girl is born with about 2 million immature ova contained in her two tiny ovaries. The ova remain inactive and undeveloped until sometime during puberty, when the first ovum ripens, leaves the ovary, and enters one of the Fallopian tubes. This process, called ovulation (see Figure 3.5), usually occurs about fourteen days after the beginning of each menstrual period. Most of the time the ovum travels uneventfully through a Fallopian tube and into the uterus (womb), whereupon, not having encountered a sperm, it dissolves. The average woman ovulates 300 to 400 times during her thirty or more years of fertility, from puberty until menopause.

A baby boy, on the other hand, is not born with spermatozoa. But once he reaches adolescence, his testicles produce the hormones that stimulate sperm production, about 200 million a day for as long as he lives.

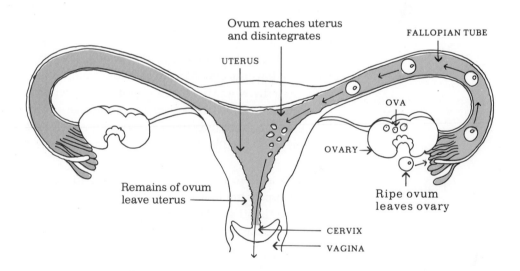

Figure 3.5 *Most of the approximately 400 times a woman ovulates, the ovum does not become fertilized; consequently, it passes through the Fallopian tube, into the uterus, and then, within a day or two, it disintegrates and passes out the vagina.*

The Moment of Conception

At his climax during sexual intercourse, a man ejaculates about 350 million sperm into the vagina. Some of these sperm make their way to the Fallopian tubes. If intercourse occurs a few days before or after ovulation, the few thousand sperm that actually survive the journey to the Fallopian tubes might meet an ovum, and one sperm might penetrate the egg's lining. When this happens, a chemical reaction begins within seconds that prevents the other nearby sperm from fertilizing the ovum. Within hours, the sperm and ovum fuse to form a new cell, called a zygote (see Figure 3.6). A human life has begun.

A CLOSER LOOK   Infertility

About 15 percent of all American married couples are physically unable to have children, and an additional 10 percent would like to have more children than they are able to have, according to the American Medical Association. Men and women are equally likely to have fertility problems. In fact, in many infertile couples, neither spouse is fully fertile (Kolata, 1978a).

One common type of infertility in men is a low sperm count, meaning that the total number of sperm per ejaculation is below the minimum (estimated at 60 million to 200 million) necessary for it to be likely that one spermatozoon will survive the journey from the vagina to one of the Fallopian tubes and fertilize the ovum. A solution to this problem is *artificial insemination,* in which the man's sperm are collected artificially and then injected into the woman's uterus. Providing this shortcut to the Fallopian tubes ensures the survival of sperm that otherwise would have died en route, and thereby increases the odds that the egg will be fertilized.

The two major fertility problems in women are failure to ovulate (the egg never leaves the ovaries) or blocked Fallopian tubes (the egg never reaches the uterus). The first problem can be remedied, in many cases, with drugs that stimulate ovulation. Sometimes, however, the drugs work too well, and the woman ovulates several ova at a time rather than just one. As a result, many couples who were childless for years find themselves the proud parents of twins, triplets, quadruplets, or even quintuplets. The second problem, blocked Fallopian tubes, is harder to solve. Microsurgery (surgery so delicate that it requires the use of a special microscope viewer) can be used to remove the obstruction, but, unfortunately, this method is successful in less than half of all cases.

Many people have become parents with the help of artificial insemination, fertility drugs, and microsurgery. However, there are a great many more who want children but cannot

According to all reports, Louise Brown is a normal and adorable baby, despite the fact that she spent the first days of her life in a glass petri dish rather than in her mother's Fallopian tube. This photo shows her at 7 months, arriving in Osaka to appear on a Japanese television program.

conceive them. On July 25, 1978, many of these couples rejoiced when Louise Brown, the first "test tube" baby, was born in England. Her mother's ovum, which ordinarily would have been blocked from reaching the uterus, was surgically extracted and fertilized by her father's sperm in the laboratory. Approximately three days after conception, the resulting zygote was implanted into her mother's uterus.

The process of fertilization outside the uterus is a theoretically simple one (Kolata, 1978b). After taking a drug that induces the ovaries to prepare ova for release, the woman is given general anesthesia, and a small incision is made in her abdomen. The doctor inserts a long metal tube that allows the ova to be viewed and the ripe ones removed. These ova are placed in a solution with sperm from the husband. Within a few hours, fertilization occurs. Within two days, the zygote has divided repeatedly to become an eight-celled organism. Two to four days after the ovum was removed from the ovary, the tiny mass of cells is inserted into the woman's uterus. If all goes well, a healthy normal baby is born nine months later.

Unfortunately, this simple process is very difficult to perform successfully. While it is relatively easy to insert a mass of cells into the uterus, there is no way to guarantee that those cells will implant themselves and grow. Hundreds of couples have undergone this procedure without success.

Figure 3.6 *One of the millions of sperm that entered the uterus has found and fertilized the ovum in the Fallopian tube, about an hour after intercourse. This union produces a zygote, a single cell which contains all the genes and chromosomes of the person-to-be.*

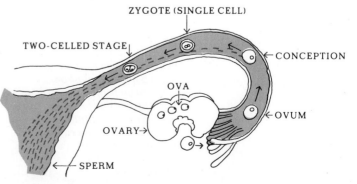

Genes and Chromosomes

All our internal and external physical characteristics, from our blood type to our hair texture, from the size of our kidneys to the shape of our feet, are inherited from our parents. The vehicle for this inheritance is the genetic material, the genes, contained in the sperm and the ovum. A gene is a segment of a DNA (deoxyribonucleic acid) molecule that provides all of the biochemical information needed to enable a cell to make one of the many kinds of molecules it needs to function. Genes are arranged in specific locations like, to put it loosely, beads on a string, the string being the long, exquisitely thin DNA molecule that, together with other materials, makes up a chromosome Since each chromosome has on it about 20,000 genes and the sperm and the ovum have twenty-three chromosomes apiece, there are, in round numbers, almost a million sources of information that come together when the father's and mother's chromosomes pair up during the fusion of the sperm and ovum.

Shortly after the zygote has been formed, it begins to grow by a process of duplication and division known as mitosis. The single cell first divides into two cells; then the two cells divide into four, the four into eight, and so on. Just before each cell division, the twenty-three pairs of chromosomes (forty-six chromosomes in all) duplicate themselves and separate, with each forty-six–chromosome set going to opposite sides of the cell. The cell then divides in the middle. Each new cell thus has the same twenty-three pairs of chromosomes, and therefore the same genetic information, as the "parent cell." Mitosis continues throughout the development of the individual, creating new cells and replacing old ones. At birth, a baby is made up of about 10 trillion cells. By adulthood, the number has increased to between 300 and 500 trillion, each with the same forty-six chromosomes.

The Twenty-third Pair

Twenty-two of the twenty-three pairs of chromosomes found in the human being are similar in both males and females. The twenty-third pair, the one that determines gender, is, as you might guess, a very special case. In the male, the pair members are X and Y, the X chromosome being three times larger than the Y. In the female, both pair members are X.

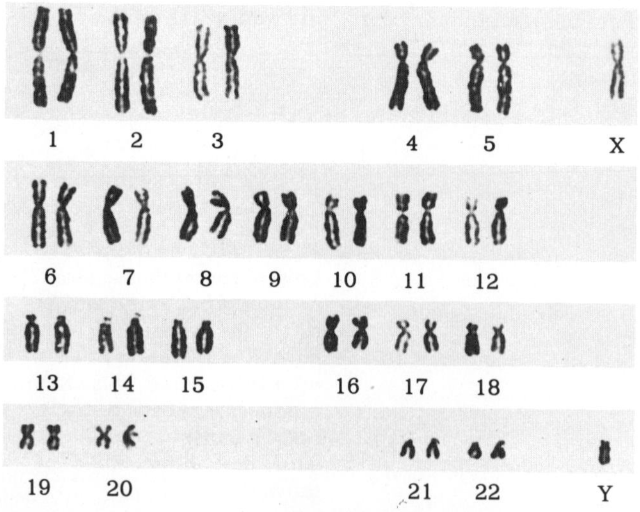

Figure 3.7 *A picture of the forty-six chromosomes from one individual, in this case a normal male. In order to produce a chromosomal portrait such as this one, a cell is removed from the person's body (usually from inside the mouth), processed so that the chromosomes become visible, magnified many times, photographed, and then arranged in pairs according to length of the upper "arms."*

Now, when the male germ cells in the testes and the female germ cells in the ovaries divide to produce gametes (sperm and ova, respectively), they do so in a way different from that of body cells, that is, the chromosomes do not merely duplicate themselves as they do in mitosis. Instead, through a complex process called meiosis, the chromosomes duplicate, exchange segments with each other, divide, and then divide again. As a result of this second division, each sperm or ovum has only twenty-three chromosomes, half as many as the original cell. Since the twenty-third pair of all female cells is XX, each ovum carries one X chromosome, one of the two X chromosomes in that pair. However, since the twenty-third pair of all male cells is XY, some sperm will have an X chromosome and some a Y. If an ovum is fertilized by a sperm bearing a Y chromosome (XY zygote), a male will develop. If it is fertilized by a sperm bearing an X chromosome (XX zygote), a female will develop (see Figure 3.8). And to think that throughout history, women have gotten the blame, the boot, or even the ax for failing to produce male offspring!

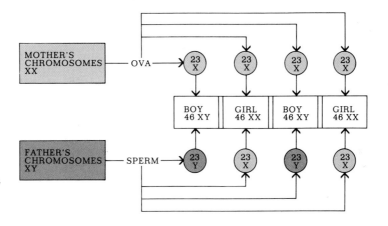

Figure 3.8 *Whether a fertilized ovum will develop into a male or female depends on whether the ovum, which always has an X chromosome, is fertilized by a sperm carrying an X chromosome (a female will result) or a sperm carrying a Y chromosome (a male will result).*

As an aside, it should be noted that while the sex of the zygote is determined by the father's sperm, other factors play a role in determining the ratio between the number of male and female babies that are born (and the ratio between males and females throughout the life span as well). For instance, male embryos are more likely to be miscarried or spontaneously aborted (see Table 3.1), which means maternal health may be even more important for the survival of the male fetus than the female.

TABLE 3.1 **Approximate Sex Ratio for the Human Species**

This table shows changes in the sex ratio as life develops. Far more male than female zygotes are conceived, slightly more boy than girl babies are born, about the same number of men and women reach adulthood, and many more women than men live to old age.

Conception	120 to 150 males for every 100 females
Birth	105 males for every 100 females
Age 15	100 males for every 100 females
Age 50	90 males for every 100 females
Age 60	70 males for every 100 females
Age 70	60 males for every 100 females
Age 80	50 males for every 100 females
Age 100	20 males for every 100 females

Source: Data from Nagle, 1979; McMillen, 1979.

Genetic Uniqueness

On the basis of what you have been told so far, you might well wonder why, except with regard to gender, all children in a given family do not look exactly alike, inasmuch as they each have twenty-three chromosomes from their father and twenty-three from their mother. The reason is that during meiosis, when the chromosome pairs divide, which of the two pair members will wind up in a particular gamete is pretty much a matter of chance. The laws of probability show that there are 2^{23} (two to the twenty-third power), or about 8 million, possible outcomes. In other words, approximately 8 million different gametes can be produced by a single individual. In addition, corresponding segments of chromosome pairs are sometimes exchanged in the first stages of meiosis. And finally, when the genes of the ovum and the sperm combine, they interact to form combinations not present in either parent. All things considered, any given couple can form over 64 trillion different combinations (Scheinfeld, 1972).

Since each person has a unique combination of genes, no two people look exactly alike. Nor do they have the same voice pattern or identical fingerprints. This means we can identify lost babies, suspected criminals, and amnesia victims. But genetic uniqueness does have one major drawback. In organ transplants and skin grafts, the human body often recognizes the transplanted organ or skin as foreign matter and tries to destroy it.

Twins   Identical twins are the exception to the rule of genetic uniqueness. Occasionally a zygote splits, and the two identical halves begin to develop independently, becoming identical twins. They are called monozygotic twins because they come from one (mono) zygote. They look alike, are the same sex, and share all other inherited characteristics (see Figure 3.9).

Figure 3.9 *From their heart-shaped hairlines to their long, supple toes, these twins seem to be identical. However, absolute proof of monozygoticity comes from fingerprinting or biochemical analysis, not from similarity of physical appearance.*

Not all twins are identical. Dizygotic, or fraternal, twins develop when a woman ovulates two ova at the same time and each is fertilized by different sperm. Dizygotic twins are about twice as common as monozygotic twins.

Dizygotic twins share no more genes than any other two offspring of the same parents. They may be of opposite sexes and very different in appearance (see Figure 3.10). Or they may look a great deal alike, just as two brothers or sisters sometimes do. Other multiple births, such as triplets and quadruplets, follow the same pattern. They can be monozygotic, dizygotic, trizygotic, and so forth.

Figure 3.10 *These brothers are twins—obviously dizygotic. They have inherited distinct coloring, facial structure, and body type. Even the onset of puberty was different for each, with one beginning his adolescent growth spurt about two years before the other.*

Incidence of Twinning   A woman's chances of having twins depend primarily on her genetic tendency to ovulate more than one ovum at a time (Pritchard and MacDonald, 1976). The highest twinning rate in the world occurs among the women of western Nigeria, who have twins once in every 22 births (Scheinfeld, 1967). The Japanese have one of the lowest rates, about one pair in every 155 births. Among white Americans, the average rate is one pair of twins in every 93 births; the rate is higher for black Americans (about 1 in every 75) and lower for Chinese-Americans, Japanese-Americans, and Native Americans (less than 1 in 150).* The chance of having twins also rises with the mother's age and parity (how many babies she has had). A 40-year-old woman in her eighth pregnancy is three times more likely to have twins than a 20-year-old in her first pregnancy (Pritchard and MacDonald, 1976).

---

*These statistics are for spontaneous twinning, without fertility drugs.

Dominant and Recessive Genes

Usually at least one pair of genes—one gene from each parent—interact to influence each characteristic. This interaction is not always 50–50. Sometimes one gene "dominates" the other gene, so a particular characteristic is controlled by one gene more than the other. When this happens, the more influential gene is called dominant, and the weaker gene is called recessive. Hundreds of physical characteristics follow the dominant-recessive pattern, including hair color (black and brown are dominant, red and blond are recessive), eye color (brown is dominant, blue and green are recessive), blood type (Rh positive is dominant, Rh negative is recessive), and hair curliness (dominant).

Let us consider eye color. To simplify somewhat, the gene for brown eyes is dominant; the gene for blue eyes is recessive. Each person has at least two eye-color genes, one from each parent. If both your genes are for blue eyes, your eyes are blue. If one gene is for brown eyes and the other for blue, your eyes will be brown, since the brown-eye gene is dominant.

The sum total of what a person inherits genetically—that is, his or her genetic potential—is called the person's genotype. The end result of the interaction of the genes with each other and with the environment—that is, a person's actual appearance and behavior—is called the phenotype. As you can see in the example of brown eyes, although two people have the same phenotype with respect to eye color, they may have different genotypes: one brown-eye gene and one blue-eye gene producing the same eye-color phenotype as two brown-eye genes—brown eyes. It is also possible for parents to have offspring whose phenotype for a particular characteristic is completely different from theirs, if the parents both have the necessary recessive genes (see Figure 3.11). Let us consider how this works in practice.

Figure 3.11 *Phenotype and genotype are not always the same. Since both parents here have curly black hair, a dominant characteristic, we know from looking at their phenotype that they both have the genotype for this characteristic. But we know that they also have the genotype for straight red hair, a recessive characteristic, only because they have a child who has this phenotype. She must have inherited the necessary recessive genes from both parents.*

Since both a man and a woman have at least one pair of eye-color genes, there are four possible combinations that a child could inherit. One way to calculate the odds that a child with a particular genotype will be born to parents with particular genotypes is to draw a table with the father's two genes on the top and the mother's two genes on the left:

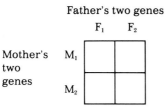

Father's two genes

The table is filled in very simply. The letters at the top of each column are written into the boxes reading down, and then the letters at the side are written into the boxes reading across:

	F_1	F_2
M_1	F_1M_1	F_2M_1
M_2	F_1M_2	F_2M_2

As you can see by looking in the boxes, there are four possible combinations a child could inherit from the parents' two pairs of genes.

Consider how this works in practice. When both parents have two brown-eye genes, all the children will have brown eyes, as well as two brown-eye genes.

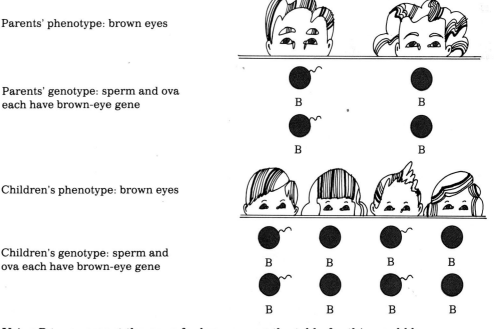

Parents' phenotype: brown eyes

Parents' genotype: sperm and ova each have brown-eye gene

Children's phenotype: brown eyes

Children's genotype: sperm and ova each have brown-eye gene

Using B to represent the gene for brown eyes, the table for this would be

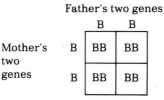

Father's two genes

	B	B
Mother's B	BB	BB
two genes B	BB	BB

The same pattern holds true if both parents have two blue-eye genes. Here, we use b to represent the blue-eye gene.

Parents' phenotype: blue eyes

Parents' genotype: sperm and ova each have blue-eye gene

Children's phenotype: blue eyes

Children's genotype: sperm and ova each have blue-eye gene

And the table for this would be

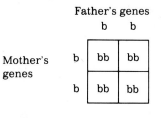

		Father's genes	
		b	b
Mother's genes	b	bb	bb
	b	bb	bb

It gets more complicated if one parent, for example, the father, has two brown-eye genes (B) and the other, the mother, has two blue-eye genes (b). All the children will inherit one brown-eye gene and one blue-eye gene. This means they will all have brown eyes, because the brown-eye gene is dominant over the blue-eye gene. Half the sperm or ova of these children will have the dominant brown-eye gene, while the other half will carry the recessive blue-eye gene. They are called carriers of the recessive gene, even though the gene does not affect their appearance (their phenotype).

		Father's genes	
		B	B
Mother's genes	b	Bb	Bb
	b	Bb	Bb

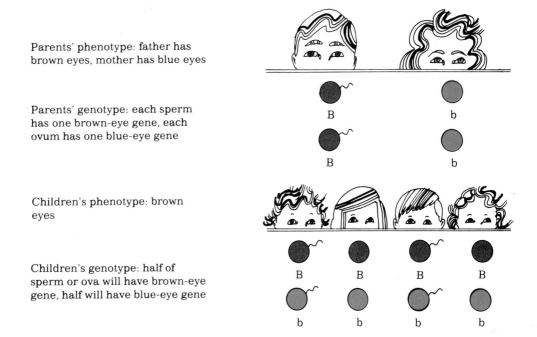

Parents' phenotype: father has brown eyes, mother has blue eyes

Parents' genotype: each sperm has one brown-eye gene, each ovum has one blue-eye gene

Children's phenotype: brown eyes

Children's genotype: half of sperm or ova will have brown-eye gene, half will have blue-eye gene

Now, what if one parent, let's say the father, has one brown-eye gene (B) and one blue-eye gene (b), and both of the mother's eye-color genes are for the same color? If the mother's eyes are blue, approximately half the children will have blue eyes and the other half will have brown eyes, but they will carry the recessive blue-eye gene.

	Father's genes	
	B	b
b	Bb	bb
b	Bb	bb

Mother's genes

Parents' phenotype: father has brown eyes, mother has blue eyes

Parents' genotype: half of sperm have brown-eye gene, half have blue-eye gene; each ovum has blue-eye gene

Children's phenotype: approximately half the children will have brown eyes, half will have blue eyes

Children's genotype: for brown-eyed children, half of sperm and ova will have brown-eye gene, half will have blue-eye gene; for blue-eyed children, sperm and ova will each have blue-eye gene

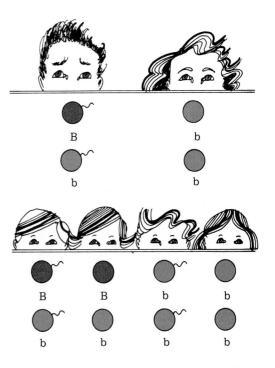

If, in the preceding case, the mother's eyes are brown (we will assume this is because she has two brown-eye genes), all the children will have brown eyes. Approximately half of them will carry the blue-eye gene, just like their father.

Father's genes

		B	b
Mother's genes	B	BB	Bb
	B	BB	Bb

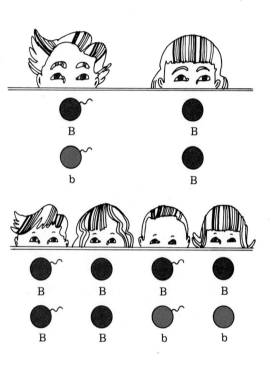

Parents' phenotype: brown eyes

Parents' genotype: half of sperm have brown-eye gene, half have blue-eye gene; each ovum has brown-eye gene

Children's phenotype: brown eyes

Children's genotype: for children carrying the blue-eye gene, half their sperm or ova will have the brown-eye gene and half will have the blue-eye gene; for those with only brown-eye genes, all sperm and ova will each have only the brown-eye gene

The following possibility is the most surprising: Two brown-eyed parents can produce blue-eyed children if each parent has one brown-eye gene and one blue-eye gene. As you can see from the following table, there is one chance in four that each child of such parents will have blue eyes.

Father's genes

		B	b
Mother's genes	B	BB	Bb
	b	Bb	bb

This explanation of eye-color determination is greatly oversimplified. The examples show only statistical probabilities; the children of any particular family often do not follow the predicted pattern precisely. It's similar to picking four cards from a full deck. Chances are, you will get one club, one diamond, one heart, and one spade; then again, you might get four hearts, or none. In addition, most dominant genes are not completely dominant. A bit of the recessive gene may appear in the phenotype, as in the brown-eyed boy whose eyes are light brown because one of his parents is blue-eyed, or the curly-haired girl whose hair would be even curlier if she had inherited curly-hair genes from both parents instead of just one.

Sex-Linked Recessive Genes   Some recessive genes are sex-linked because they are located only on the X chromosome or, in a few rare instances, only on the Y chromosome. For example, the recessive genes for baldness, most forms of color blindness, certain allergies, several diseases, and perhaps some perceptual skills are carried only by the X chromosome. This means that a female (XX) who has a recessive gene on only one X chromosome will not show the recessive characteristic, for the other X chromosome has the controlling dominant gene. A woman will not become bald, for instance, unless she inherits the baldness genes on both her X chromosomes. A male, however, has only one X chromosome, the one he inherits from his mother. If that chromosome carries the baldness gene, he will become bald, for his Y chromosome has no corresponding gene to countermand the instructions of the recessive gene.

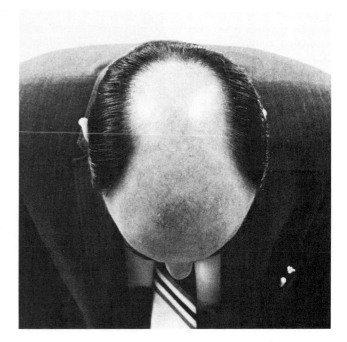

Figure 3.12 *Men develop "male pattern" baldness because they inherit a particular recessive gene from their mothers. The extent of the baldness is also affected by the level of androgens, or male hormones, produced by the man's body.*

Polygenic Inheritance

Most human characteristics are affected by many genes, rather than by a single pair. Eye color can be green, hazel, or flecked, depending on various genes. Another example is skin color, which can be hundreds of shades and tones, depending on which genes are inherited. A light-skinned person and a dark-skinned person will usually have children whose skin is some shade between light and dark, because each child will have half the light-skin genes from one parent and half the dark-skin genes from the other. A couple could also have a child who is lighter or darker than either of them, depending on whether the child happened to inherit each parent's lighter or darker skin genes.

Almost all complex human characteristics such as intelligence, behavioral patterns, and special talents are influenced by *many* genes; so they are called polygenic. Artistic talent, for example, is partially inherited, and insofar as it is, depends on a great number of genes, not on a few "artistic" genes. Master painters usually have, among other things, good eye-hand coordination, good spatial perception, and a strong sense of color.

Heredity and Environment

Most important human characteristics, especially complex ones such as personality, intelligence, temperament, and talent, are not solely the result of genes, acting either singly or in combination. Although nearly every human quality is affected by genes, the environment, which includes specific experiences as well as the overall milieu where development occurs, is almost always crucial. Another way of saying this is that most characteristics are multifactorial, that is, caused by the interaction of many genetic and environmental factors.

Figure 3.13 *When talent runs in a family, we cannot separate the impact of heredity from that of environment. Henry Fonda's genes and his example both contributed to Jane's and Peter's acting success.*

Even physical characteristics are often multifactorial rather than purely genetic. Height, for example, might seem to be a simple case of the influence of genes. We are as tall as our genes allow, right? Not exactly.

There definitely *is* a relationship between genes and height: maximum possible growth is genetically determined. But not everyone grows as tall as their genes would permit, because adequate nutrition and medical care are needed for maximum growth. For instance, Americans were about six inches shorter, on average, in the nineteenth century than they are today. Throughout most of the twentieth century, each succeeding generation was slightly taller than the previous one, not because genes changed from decade to decade, but because the environment—specifically nutrition and medical care—improved. Apparently most Americans are now sufficiently nourished to reach their maximum height, for today's young people are no taller on average than the adolescents of the 1960s.

The effects of better nutrition have been even more apparent in Japan, where babies born after World War II grew up to be several inches taller than their parents (*The New York Times*, May 17, 1970). Consequently, the Japanese had to enlarge everything that had been designed for the "traditional" Japanese body size—bathtubs, clothes, shoes, and even the seats on the railroad trains. This last

Figure 3.14 *The newspaper story accompanying this photo reported: "Many young girls have complained that they have been 'forced' to give up their seats and stand in the aisles to save themselves from the 'disgrace' of being 'invaded' by the knees of male passengers . . ." (Mainichi Daily News, July 4, 1974).*

item was a matter of some urgency, because adolescent boys and girls who sat in facing seats had found that they were obliged to touch knees—a physical contact that social custom forbids between strangers of the opposite sex (*Mainichi Daily News,* 1974).

Psychological characteristics such as intelligence or personality are much more complicated and controversial instances of multifactorial inheritance. Psychologists agree that certain intellectual abilities, such as memory for numbers, and certain personality characteristics, such as activity level, are primarily influenced by genes. Environment plays some role in determining these traits as well. Whether genetic or environmental factors are the more powerful influence in the determination of almost any given human behavior is a subject of great debate.

Intelligence

Many psychologists believe that intelligence is a collection of a number of specific abilities, such as memory, visual perception, and skill with numbers or words. Most IQ (intelligence quotient) tests are based on this assumption. However, as we will see later in this book, many other psychologists are critical of this notion of intelligence and of IQ tests (see Chapter 13). Nevertheless, even though psychologists disagree about precisely what IQ tests measure, they are still interested in the extent to which aptitude at these tests is determined by heredity.

Correlation The usual way to study the impact of genes and environment on IQ scores is to compare the IQ scores of relatives. But before we try to understand the results of such research, we need to know what correlation means. A correlation indicates whether two variables are related. Any characteristic that can vary—from time to time, place to place, individual to individual, group to group—is called a *variable.* If a change in one variable occurs together with a change in another in the same direction, the correlation is said to be *positive.* For instance, there is a positive correlation between height and weight, because, usually, the taller a person is, the more he or she weighs. There is also a positive correlation between wealth and education, and perhaps even between springtime and falling in love.

Don't misunderstand. A positive correlation does not mean that two variables are related in every instance. Some tall people weigh less than people of average height; some people are more likely to fall in love in summer than in spring. Nor does correlation indicate cause and effect. The positive correlation between education and wealth does not necessarily imply that more education leads to greater wealth. It may be that wealthy people are usually better educated because their families had the money to send them to college; or it may be that a third variable, perhaps intelligence or family background, is the underlying cause of the high level of both income and education.

When a correlation is *negative,* the two variables are inversely related. Snow and summertime, maleness and motherhood, and blue eyes and black hair are negatively correlated. When a correlation is *zero,* there is no statistical relationship between two variables. There is a zero correlation between the color of your eyes and your age, and between how much milk you drank yesterday and whether it is raining today.

When correlations are expressed numerically, they range from +1.0 (the highest positive correlation) to −1.0 (the most negative correlation). The number halfway between +1.0 and −1.0 is 0, which means no correlation.

Research on IQ   Now let's look at some of the research on IQ scores. The correlation between IQ scores of siblings is about .45, as is the correlation between the IQ of parent and child (Erlenmeyer-Kimling and Jarvik, 1963). This means that a child who scores high on an intelligence test usually has parents and siblings who are also above average in IQ score. Since siblings have about half their genes in common, as do a parent and child, this positive correlation can be used as evidence that genes affect IQ.

Further evidence for the heritability of IQ comes from the study of twins. Monozygotic twins, who have identical genes, often have IQ scores within a few points of each other; dizygotic twins, on the other hand, have scores that are only slightly closer than those of siblings who were not born at the same time. In addition, the pattern of performance on subtest scores is very similar for monozygotic twins (see Figure 3.15). Both twins might score much higher on vocabulary than on geometric design, and both might show an increase or decrease in IQ score at the same age (Wilson, 1975).

Figure 3.15   *This chart shows the ten subtest scores of the Wechsler Preschool-Primary Scale of Intelligence (WPPSI) for a pair of twins. An average score on a subtest is 10, so, as you can see, these twins are amazingly similar in their patterns, scoring above average on some tests and below on others. Wilson (1975) found that subtest patterns are much more similar in monozygotic twins than in dizygotic twins, although not all pairs in his study were as similar as the two represented here.*

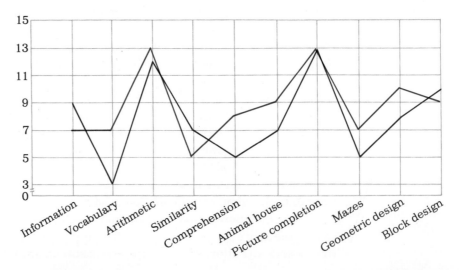

But evidence like this does not distinguish the influence of genes from the influence of environment. Parents and children may have similar scores because parents with higher IQs may provide more stimulating environments for their children than parents with lower IQs. Identical twins could be more similar in IQ than dizygotic twins because they get identical treatment from parents and teachers, who cannot always tell them apart.

The best way to distinguish genetic and environmental influences is to study children who have the same genes but different environments, and children who have the same environments but different genes. In practice, this means comparing IQ scores of monozygotic twins who grew up in separate homes, or comparing the IQ scores of adopted children with those of both their biological and their adoptive parents. Such studies have found strong evidence for both heredity and environment.

James Shields (1962) managed to find forty-four pairs of identical twins who were raised in separate homes. Most of them showed similar patterns of IQ scoring in adulthood; thirty-four pairs were within 15 IQ points of each other, which led Shields to conclude that genes are the dominant influence on intelligence. However, most of his pairs were raised in similar economic and cultural environments; and in thirty cases, both twins were raised by relatives. Shields also found three pairs who showed substantial IQ difference. One pair differed by 23 IQ points; another by 24; and the third by 30 points, which is enough of a point spread to make the difference between average IQ (100) and superior IQ (130), or between average and mentally retarded (70).

Sandra Scarr and Richard Weinberg (1977) studied adopted children and found the following correlations between the IQs of the adopted children and their parents:

Education* of biological mother	.32
Education of biological father	.52
IQ of adoptive mother	.23
IQ of adoptive father	.15

These data show a strong genetic influence in IQ scores, for the children's IQs can be predicted more accurately by knowing the biological parents' educational achievements than by knowing the adoptive parents' IQs.

The same researchers studied white families who had adopted black children, comparing the IQ scores of the adopted children with those of the children born into these families. For instance, one such family might have had two white children (biological) and two black adopted children who were not biologically related to each other. The correlations between IQ scores of sibling pairs were as follows:

Adopted child and biological child in same family (black and white)	.30
Biological sibling pairs (both white)	.37
Two unrelated adopted children in same family (both black)	.49

---

*Actual IQ scores are not available; but education is often used as a rough measure of intellectual ability, since there is a strong positive correlation between IQ and adult educational attainment.

These results show the impact of the specific environment on IQ scores. First of all, the .30 correlation between adopted children and biological children raised in the same family is significantly higher than the zero correlation ordinarily found between genetically unrelated children. The home environment has already had an impact on the adopted children, bringing their scores close to that of their siblings born into that family.

The second correlation, .37 between biological siblings, is somewhat higher than .30, as one would expect for children who share many of the same genes as well as the same home. However, the third correlation, .49 for adopted children who are unrelated by blood but who grow up in the same adoptive home, is both surprising and intriguing. It means that two unrelated black children adopted by one white family might both have high IQ scores, but if adopted by a different family, they might both have low scores. Even though they share no genes, the general impact of adoption by a family of another race, combined with their specific experience within a particular home, would appear to make genetically unrelated children closer in IQ than siblings who share the same home and half the same genes!

Regarding performance on IQ tests, environment in this situation seems to have been more important than heredity. However, one can think of specific cases— certain forms of severe mental retardation, for example—where genes play a dominant role. It is very difficult—some would say impossible—to establish a hard and fast rule about the relative importance between heredity and environment in determining performance on IQ tests.

Controversy and Conclusions.   Depending upon how they interpret IQ data, scholars are able to argue alternately that intelligence is almost entirely inherited (about 80 percent), or that genes play a minor role. This disagreement became a heated controversy when Arthur Jensen (1969) suggested that the explanation for the fact that black Americans' IQ scores are, on average, lower than whites' is primarily genetic. Most psychologists disagree with Jensen, maintaining that differences between the environments experienced by black and white children in the United States are much more powerful than genetic differences in determining performance on IQ tests. Hundreds of environmental influences can affect scores on IQ tests, including social class, parents' education, number of children in the family, nutrition, medical care, neighborhood stimulation, and preschool education. For the most part, the average black child is disadvantaged with regard to all these factors.

Many psychologists now think that there is no good reason, as well as no perfect way, to figure out precisely how much of a person's intelligence is genetic and how much is learned. The interaction between genes and environment is always more important than either one alone when complex characteristics like intelligence are involved. Just as in the case of height and nutrition, that portion of intelligence that is genetic depends on a stimulating environment to develop fully. Instead of trying to unravel the components of the interaction between heredity and environment, we should probably direct our attention to finding out what we can do to make sure each child has the best possible learning environment.

Personality   Are emotions inherited? When we say "She has her father's temper" or "She cries as easily as her mother," are we talking about genetic characteristics? Probably not. There is no specific gene for temper or crying that one child could inherit and another not. On the contrary, psychologists have shown that children *learn* how to express anger or sadness by watching others and trying to copy them.

To some extent, however, personality characteristics are inborn. Newborn babies are not all alike in personality. It is possible, of course, that prenatal environment and the circumstances of birth might help to make one baby more placid than the next. However, Daniel Freedman (1979) found ethnic differences in infant personality, even though all the mothers he studied received the same prenatal care and all the birth processes were similar. He discovered that in the first days of life, Chinese-American babies are more adaptable, easier to console, and harder to annoy than other American babies.

For example, one standard way to test newborn reflexes is to let a cloth rest gently on the baby's nose. Most white and black American newborns immediately turn aside or try to push the cloth away with their hands. Pediatricians, accustomed to testing white and black babies, consider this the normal, healthy reaction. But twenty-four Chinese-American newborns, who were similar to a group of Caucasian babies in health, sex, family background, socioeconomic status, and birth history, usually did not try to remove the cloth as the Caucasian babies did. The Chinese-American infants just lay back quietly and breathed through their mouths. Some Native American babies are even more calm and adaptable than Chinese-Americans, according to tests of Navajo infants (Freedman, 1979).

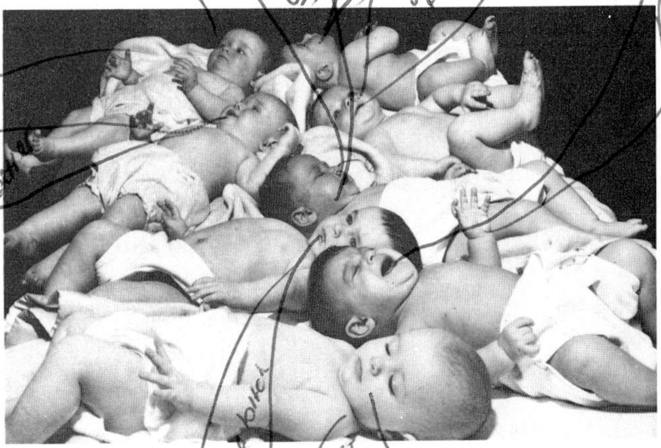

Figure 3.16 *Pleasure and distress, curiosity and indifference, placidness and irritability, are among the reactions of these infants when placed on a bed with seven contemporaries. Temperamental differences such as these are apparent in the first days after birth.*

Alexander Thomas, Stella Chess, and Herbert Birch (1963) also studied innate temperamental differences. They used parent interviews, trying to compensate for the unreliability of this method by asking the parents how the infant reacted to the first bath or first mouthful of Pablum within weeks after the event occurred, rather than asking more general questions months or years later. According to their findings, babies in the first weeks and months of life differ in nine personality characteristics:

1. *Activity level.* Some babies are active. They kick a lot in the uterus before they are born, they move around in their basinettes, and as soon as they are old enough, they always climb or run. Other babies are much less active.

2. *Rhythmicity.* Some babies have regular cycles of activity. They eat, sleep, and defecate on schedule almost from birth. Other babies are much less predictable.

3. *Approach-withdrawal.* Some babies delight in everything new; others withdraw

from every new situation. The first bath makes some babies laugh and others cry; the first spoonful of cereal is gobbled up by one baby and spit out by the next.

4. *Adaptability*. Some babies adjust quickly to change; others are unhappy at every disruption.

5. *Intensity of reaction*. Some babies chortle when they laugh and howl when they cry. Others are much calmer; they respond with a smile or a whimper.

6. *Threshold of responsiveness*. Some babies seem aware of every sight, sound, and touch. Others seem unaware of bright lights, street noises, or wet diapers.

7. *Quality of mood*. Some babies are happy little people: almost anything makes them smile. Others are unhappy: they are ready to complain at any moment.

8. *Distractibility*. Some babies forget that their diapers are being changed if someone hands them a rattle, or suck happily on a pacifier even though they would prefer a bottle. Others are more single-minded.

9. *Attention span*. Some babies play happily with one toy for a long time. Others move quickly from one activity to the next.

Inborn characteristics are not necessarily permanent, however. Thomas and Chess (1977) found that many babies' characteristics changed as they grew older, depending partly on their parents' child-rearing methods. Babies who are not adaptable may become adaptable adults, especially if the parents allow them to have many new experiences without pushing them along too quickly.

By adolescence, many of the young people in this study had characteristics quite different from those they had as infants. Genes probably are part of the explanation of temperament, but the rest of the story depends on how the environment and those genes interact.

Mental Illness   Many forms of mental illness are partially inherited. Some people, for example, are born with a predisposition toward schizophrenia or manic-depression (Rosenthal, 1970). Schizophrenia is a mental illness that disorganizes the personality, making it hard for the person to think, speak, or behave appropriately or realistically. Manic-depression is an illness that leads to exaggerated moods, such as extreme elation or deep depression. Between 10 and 20 percent of the children born to schizophrenic parents become schizophrenic themselves. For both illnesses, the interaction between heredity and environment is crucial.

Proof of the genetic predisposition to mental illness comes from studies of monozygotic twins (Cohen et al., 1972; Gottesman and Shields, 1972). If one twin becomes schizophrenic or manic-depressive, chances are (estimates range from 80 percent to 20 percent depending on definition) the other twin will have serious psychological problems too. (If a dizygotic twin becomes schizophrenic or manic-depressive, the likelihood of the other twin's becoming emotionally disturbed is much lower than with monozygotic twins.) But since there are many cases where one identical twin is schizophrenic and the other is not mentally disturbed, and since, furthermore, monozygotic twins have identical genes and usually very similar environments, apparently some specific environmental differences (perhaps a teacher or a career choice) can have a large impact. In a family where one parent is schizophrenic, for instance, the other parent can often maintain family stability and help the children to understand why one of their parents sometimes seems out of touch with reality (Garmezy et al., 1979). For almost all mental illnesses, genes make some people more vulnerable than others, but personal experiences determine whether a person becomes ill or not.

Abnormal Genes and Chromosomes

Half or more of all zygotes have abnormal genes or chromosomes. Almost all of these are aborted spontaneously, usually so early that the woman never knows she was pregnant. Others die later in pregnancy.

But as many as one baby in seven is born with a congenital problem (Apgar and Beck, 1973). Although congenital problems are, by definition, present at birth, only about half of them are *apparent* at birth. The other half appear later in life. For instance, genes are responsible for some types of diabetes and muscular dystrophy even though babies are not born with either disease.

Congenital problems are discussed in some detail in this book for several reasons. The first is that most physical problems can create psychological difficulties for the child and the child's family. Psychologists interested in child development need to understand something of the origins of these problems. A second is that developmental psychologists are always concerned with ways to prevent physical and emotional problems, and many of these congenital problems can be prevented. Finally, interested students might consider a career in working with children (and their families) who have special needs because of mental or physical handicaps, or in counseling couples who might have genetic problems. More well-trained psychologists are needed in both fields.

Some congenital problems originate during the formation of the sperm or ova; others, during conception, when the sperm and ovum join, or in the prenatal period, or at birth. Here we will concentrate on those caused primarily by genes and chromosomes.

Chromosomal Abnormalities

Sometimes when sperm or ova are formed, the forty-six chromosomes do not split up evenly as the germ cell divides. Instead, the split is uneven, so a gamete has too few or too many chromosomes. Most such abnormal sperm and ova never create a zygote; or, if they do, the organism usually destroys itself in the first days or weeks after conception. But sometimes, about once in every 200 births, a baby is born with one chromosome too many or one too few (Goad et al., 1976).

Abnormal Sex Chromosomes Several chromosomal abnormalities involve the sex chromosomes. Males (normally XY) are sometimes born with two or three Y chromosomes (XYY or XYYY), or two or three X chromosomes (XXY or XXXY), or two of each (XXYY). Females (normally XX) are sometimes born with only one X chromosome (XO) or three, four, or five (XXX, XXXX, XXXXX) (Roberts, 1973).

Klinefelter's syndrome, in which a male is born with an extra X chromosome (XXY), is the most common of these abnormalities, occurring about once in every 200 males (Goad et al., 1976). (Klinefelter's syndrome usually involves more than one defect and so is referred to as a *syndrome*, a group of disorders that occur together.) These males seem normal until secondary sex characteristics do not appear in adolescence. Their penises and testicles do not grow, their faces remain hairless, their voices do not change. Sometimes they develop breasts.

Males with the XYY pattern sometimes develop into men who are taller, more prone to acne, and more likely to have intellectual and social problems than the average man. Several studies of prison populations have found a higher percentage of XYYs than is found in the general population. At first it was believed that the extra Y made antisocial behavior unavoidable. But we now know that many XYY men are normal, law-abiding citizens. Obviously, environment affects the eventual behavior of the baby born with two Y chromosomes (Borgaonkar and Shah, 1974).

Occurring about once in every 3000 female infants, Turner's syndrome (XO) is the most common abnormality in the sex chromosomes of girls. Females having this abnormality are often shorter than average, and they usually have a thick neck with folds of extra skin that make it look webbed. At adolescence, their breasts do not develop, nor do their ovaries release ova.

Other Chromosomal Abnormalities   Not all chromosomal abnormalities involve the sex chromosomes. Sometimes part of a chromosome breaks off. Occasionally a chromosome gets misplaced, attaching itself to another pair of chromosomes. Sometimes an abnormal sperm or ovum containing twenty-three autosomes (non-sex chromosomes), in addition to the one sex chromosome, is involved in the formation of a zygote. The extra autosome attaches itself as a third chromosome to either the eighth, thirteenth, fourteenth, fifteenth, eighteenth, twenty-first, or twenty-second pair of chromosomes, forming syndromes known as trisomy-8, trisomy-13, and so forth (Yunis, 1977).

The most common of these extra chromosomal problems is trisomy-21, or Down's syndrome, which occurs in about 1 baby out of every 600. People having this abnormality are sometimes called mongoloids because of the very superficial resemblance between their eyelids and those of people from Mongolia. Down's syndrome children usually have rounder faces and shorter limbs than normal children and suffer heart, eye, or ear problems. They are usually less developed, physically and intellectually, than other children. How well they function as adults seems to depend a great deal on early experience, especially on whether they were raised at home or in an institution (Edgerton, 1979).

Figure 3.17 *Twenty years ago, most Down's syndrome children died of heart ailments before adolescence. With today's better medical care, and with sufficient love and education, many Down's syndrome children can become self-sufficient adults.*

Causes of Chromosomal Abnormalities   How do such chromosomal abnormalities occur? Some forms seem to be inherited, especially if either parent has some cells with an extra or a missing chromosome, even though most of their cells have the usual forty-six chromosomes. This condition is known as *mosaicism* because the person's cells are like a mosaic of different patterns. Other abnormalities are more common when the parents have been exposed to radiation, either from the atmosphere or from x-rays, or to certain drugs or chemicals.

Walter Goad and his colleagues (1976), in an extensive screening program for chromosomal abnormalities, tested all 40,371 babies born in two hospitals in Denver between 1964 and 1974. They found seasonal variations: most babies with abnormalities were born between May and October. They also found that whereas only 8 babies with abnormal sex chromosomes were born in the three years from 1968 to 1970, 30 such babies were born between 1971 and 1973. Something must have caused this difference—perhaps a virus, or a chemical the women had eaten or breathed—but what it could have been remains a mystery.

Finally, some babies with chromosomal abnormalities, especially trisomy-21, are more often born to older parents.

TABLE 3.2   **Age of Mother and Down's Syndrome**

Age of Mother When Baby is Born	Chance of Down's Syndrome
Younger than 30	1 in 1500
30–34	1 in 750
35–39	1 in 280
40–44	1 in 130
Older than 45	1 in 65

Source: U.S. Department of Health, Education, and Welfare.

One possible explanation for this is the aging of the ova. Since ova are formed during prenatal development, a 45-year-old woman has ova that are, obviously, more than 45 years old. Perhaps ova tend to degenerate as they age. This explanation makes logical sense, but in about 25 percent of the instances of Down's syndrome, the sperm, not the ovum, carried the abnormality (Magenis et al., 1977). Probably Down's syndrome can be caused by one or several of the following factors: mosaicism in either parent, aging ovum, malformed sperm, and perhaps infrequency of intercourse (the infrequency would make it more likely that a relatively "old" sperm or an ovum that had been in the Fallopian tube for several days might be involved in the formation of the zygote).

Genetic Problems

It is estimated that everyone carries between four and eight genes related to serious diseases and handicaps (Milunsky, 1977) (see Table 3.3). Many of these conditions are recessive, so a child cannot have the condition unless both parents carry the same gene. (Cultural prohibitions against incest lessen the incidence of such problems.) Others are polygenic, so several specific genes must be inherited before the problem appears. Still others are multifactorial and do not manifest themselves unless certain conditions occur in the prenatal environment. Most babies are born without apparent genetic problems, although most are carriers like their parents. However, according to a leading geneticist, about one baby in every thirty is born with a serious genetic problem (Roberts, 1973).

TABLE 3.3 **Common Genetic Diseases and Conditions**

Name	Description	Prognosis	Method of Inheritance	Incidence*	Carrier Detection?†	Prenatal Detection?
Cleft palate, cleft lip	The two sides of the upper lip or palate are not joined.	Correctable by surgery.	Multifactorial. Drugs taken during pregnancy or stress may be involved.	One baby in every 700. More common in Japanese and Native Americans; rare in blacks.	No.	No.
Club foot	The foot and ankle are twisted, making it impossible to walk normally.	Correctable by surgery.	Multifactorial.	One baby in every 300. More common in boys.	No.	Possible in near future.
Cystic fibrosis	Lack of an enzyme. Mucous obstructions in body, especially lungs and digestion.	Few victims survive to adulthood.	Recessive gene.	One baby in every 1000. One in 20 or 25 white Americans is a carrier.	No.	Possible in near future.
Diabetes	Abnormal metabolism of sugar because body does not produce enough insulin.	Usually fatal if untreated. Controllable by insulin and diet.	Recessive gene, but exact pattern hard to predict because environment is crucial.	About 7 million Americans. Most develop it in late adulthood. One child in 2500 is diabetic. More common in Native Americans.	No.	No.
Hemophilia	Absence of clotting factor in blood. Called "bleeder's disease."	Crippling and death from internal bleeding. Now transfusions can lessen or even prevent damage.	X-linked. Also spontaneous mutations.	One in 1000 males. Royal families of England, Russia, and Germany had it.	Yes.	Yes.
Huntington's chorea	Deterioration of body and brain in middle age.	Death.	Dominant gene.	Rare.	No.	No.
Hydrocephalus	Obstruction causes excess water in brain.	Can produce brain damage and death. Surgery can make survival and normal intelligence possible.	Multifactorial.	One baby in every 100.	No.	Yes, in severe cases.
Marfan's syndrome	Long bony limbs, heart malformation, hearing loss, eye weakness.	Depends on severity; possibly death.	Dominant gene of varying strength.	Rare.	Yes.	Yes.

*Incidence statistics vary from country to country; those given here are for the United States. All these diseases can occur in any ethnic group of Americans. When certain groups have a higher incidence, it is noted here.

†Studying the family tree can help geneticists spot a possible carrier of many genetic diseases or, in some cases, a definite carrier. However, here "Yes" means that a carrier can be detected even without knowledge of family history.

Name	Description	Prognosis	Method of Inheritance	Incidence*	Carrier Detection?†	Prenatal Detection?
Muscular dystrophy (13 separate diseases)	Weakening of muscles. Some forms begin in childhood, others in adulthood.	Inability to walk, move; wasting away and sometimes death.	Duchenne's is X-linked; other forms are autosomal recessive or multifactorial.	One in every 4000 males will develop Duchenne's (about 600 per year). About 100,000 Americans have some form of MD.	Yes, for some forms.	No.
Neural tube defects (open spine)	Two main forms: anencephaly (part of the brain and skull is missing) and spina bifida (the lower portion of the spine is not closed over).	Babies with anencephaly die within days after birth. Babies with spina bifida die, or survive with surgery. Trouble with walking; poor bowel and bladder control.	Multifactorial; defect occurs in first weeks of pregnancy.	Anencephaly: 1 in 1000 births; spina bifida: 3 in 1000.	No.	Yes, usually.
Phenylke-tonuria (PKU)	Abnormal digestion of protein.	Mental retardation, hyperactivity. Preventable by diet.	Recessive gene.	One in 15,000 births; one in 80 whites is a carrier.	No.	Yes.
Pyloric stenosis	Overgrowth of muscle in intestine.	Vomiting, loss of weight, eventual death; correctable by surgery.	Multifactorial.	One male in 200; one female in 1000.	No.	No.
Sickle-cell anemia	Abnormal blood cells.	Possible painful "crises" (see page 102), heart and kidney failure.	Recessive gene.	One in 400 black babies is affected. One in 10 black Americans is a carrier; one in 20 Latin Americans is a carrier.	Yes.	Yes.
Tay-Sachs disease	Enzyme disease.	Apparently healthy baby dies by age 3.	Recessive gene.	One in 30 American Jews is a carrier.	Yes.	Yes.
Thalassemia (Cooley's anemia)	Abnormal blood cells.	Paleness and listlessness, low resistance to infection; treatment by blood transfusion.	Recessive gene.	One in 10 Greek- or Italian-Americans is a carrier; one in 400 of their babies is affected.	Yes.	Yes.

Sources: Apgar and Beck, 1973; Nyhan, 1976; Milunsky, 1977; Motulsky et al., 1974; Moss, 1979; Omenn, 1978.

Genetic Counseling

Many genetic problems can be avoided with genetic testing and counseling. Some doctors recommend this precaution for everyone who plans to become a parent. But it is particularly important in four situations: when the couple already has a child with a condition that might be genetic; when relatives have genetic problems; when both prospective parents are from the same genetic stock, either because they are relatives or because, in cases involving certain ethnic groups, their ancestors came from particular places in the world; and when several earlier pregnancies ended in spontaneous abortion.

A CLOSER LOOK   **Tay-Sachs Disease**

About a hundred years ago, many people in a small region in northeastern Poland carried an unusual recessive gene. When two carriers married, each of their children had one chance in four of inheriting the gene from both parents. A newborn with the double recessive gene often seemed perfectly healthy. The infant would smile, lift its head, and grow and gain weight like any other baby. But as the weeks went by, the infant's muscles would weaken and the baby would not roll over or sit up when normal babies do; gradually even the ability to smile would disappear. What had seemingly been a normal newborn would become a helpless child, unable to move or, eventually, even eat. Death would come, usually before the third birthday.

As it happened, many of the people from that part of Poland were Jewish, and war and persecution drove most of them to Western Europe or America, where they were more likely to marry people without the gene. But some of their descendants still give birth to babies doomed to die of the disease.

Today, a blood test can tell future parents if they both carry the recessive gene for this disease, now labelled Tay-Sachs. Jewish groups recommend that all Jews with eastern European ancestors have the test, for about one in every thirty of them is a carrier. One screening program found the rate to be even higher—one in twenty-four. In addition, it found eleven couples in which both husband and wife had the recessive gene. Before the testing, neither knew they could have had a Tay-Sachs baby (Kaback et al., 1974). (Non-Jewish Americans and Jews from Spanish, North African, or Oriental Jewish communities have only about 1 chance in 300 of carrying the gene [Goodman, 1974]).

The personal tragedy of Tay-Sachs becomes clear when we look at the case of Marsha and Gary, a young couple from Queens, New York (Stockton, 1979). Like most new parents, they were thrilled at the birth of their firstborn, a daughter named Jennifer, and proudly watched her development: like a normal baby, she smiled, reached for a rattle, held a bottle, tried to turn over. But by eight months, their joy turned to

It is no accident that Joshua and his younger brother, David, are free of genetic disease. Following the tragic discovery that her first child was a victim of Tay-Sachs, the boys' mother had amniocentesis performed each time she become pregnant, to be sure that the fetus had not inherited a recessive gene for the disease from both her and her husband.

worry, for she did not sit up or crawl. Although their pediatrician assured them that many normal babies develop motor skills slowly, Marsha was convinced that something was wrong.

Then, when Jennifer was 11 months old, her eyes began to cross. Gary took her to the pediatrician, who suggested that they go to an eye doctor. After a quick exam, the ophthalmologist said, "I see a grave situation. I think you should go back to your pediatrician."

The process of genetic counseling varies from couple to couple, depending on the genetic background of each prospective parent. First the counselor tries to figure out how likely the couple is to have a child with a genetic problem and then tells the couple what, if anything, they can do to decrease the odds.

Testing for Genetic Conditions

Detecting some genetic conditions is relatively simple. A blood test can detect the recessive genes for sickle-cell anemia, Tay-Sachs disease, phenylketonuria (PKU), hemophilia, and thalassemia (Cooley's anemia). Analyzing a cell from the prospective parents' bodies can indicate the possibility of some chromosomal abnormalities. Minor physical abnormalities, even an oddly shaped finger or unusual

---

Furious, Gary refused to leave the office until the doctor told him what the "grave situation" was. The doctor finally said that he saw a "cherry red spot" in the fundus of the eye, a sign of Tay-Sachs. In Gary's words, "We left his office and went right back to the pediatrician, and he just looked at us as if he couldn't do anything. And then we knew that he had known all along."

The next day, Marsha and Gary went to a genetic counselor, to try to understand what had happened to their daughter and why. The genetic counselor described their reaction to the information:

Very often, even though other physicians are fairly sure, they will push off on the geneticist the problems of telling the family. I've learned to watch the couple when they are told. They do one of two things. They either move together, physically reach for each other. Or they move apart. One man jumped up and ran out of the room. Gary and Marsha came together.

Ironically, a Tay-Sachs screening program had been conducted in Gary and Marsha's neighborhood eighteen months before, but the couple did not even hear of Tay-Sachs until Jennifer was 8 months old. Gary wondered angrily why no one—not the rabbi who married them, the obstetrician who provided prenatal care, nor the pediatrician who had suspected Tay-Sachs months before the diagnosis was made—told them about the disease earlier.

Now Marsha and Gary had to make two difficult decisions: whether to put Jennifer in an institution, and whether to try to have another child. They decided to keep Jennifer at home as long as they could and to conceive another baby as quickly as possible. Within six months, Marsha became pregnant, and in her sixteenth week, underwent amniocentesis (see p. 101)—a test to determine if their second baby had inherited two Tay-Sachs genes, one from each of them. Fortunately, this fetus was fine, and in fact, had not inherited a Tay-Sachs gene from either parent. This child was one of the lucky one-in-four offspring from such a couple who are neither diseased nor a carrier.

After their son, Joshua, was born, Gary and Marsha were forced to pay much more attention to Jennifer than to him. As Marsha described it:

We would sleep downstairs with her. We did that for two years because I had a fear that she would choke and I wouldn't be in the room. You just couldn't leave her alone. We practically lived in her room. During the day, we would bring Josh in and play with him on the floor.

Jenny just lay there with her eyes open, no movement, no brain activity to speak of. As for the daily routine, she was being fed by a nasogastric tube [a tube from the nose to the stomach]. With a Tay-Sachs child all you can do is make them comfortable. They require little, if anything. Her care was never difficult at all, other than the constant moving her so she wouldn't lie in one spot and get bedsores, and the feeding. She had to be moved every hour. We had a suction machine in the house. She did have trouble with her saliva and choking. So we had to constantly suction her if she needed it . . . .

There came a point when I felt it wasn't a healthy family situation any more . . . . Any activity, such as family holidays, either Gary would go or I would go. One of us stayed home. Jenny had a very low resistance to infection, so we didn't have any children of our friends in the house for more than a year, and the reactions of our friends is another whole story. It was difficult for them to be with us . . . . I wasn't fair to Josh. He was cooped up at home with us—tied to Jenny's room too. It wasn't healthy for any of us. [Stockton, 1979.]

Reluctantly, they finally decided to admit Jennifer to the hospital. Several times a week the couple went to the Tay-Sachs ward to hold, cuddle, kiss, bathe, and talk to Jennifer, although she had not responded to such attention in two years. Marsha explained, "Somehow I feel better after I bathe her and fix her hair. She looks so . . . pretty, terrific."

At age 4½, Jennifer died, one of the few Tay-Sachs children to have survived so long. The ordeal her family went through is one shared by thousands of families living with the stress of a child suffering a serious genetic disease, such as Tay-Sachs, sickle-cell anemia, muscular dystrophy, cystic fibrosis, or phenylketonuria. The heartbreaking fact is that many of these tragedies could have been prevented through genetic counseling.

ears, may sometimes signal the presence of recessive genes for a more serious defect. Family history or already-born children can sometimes provide clues. Even knowing where one's ancestors came from can be helpful. Tay-Sachs disease is most common among Jews whose ancestors came from eastern Europe; sickle-cell anemia, among blacks whose ancestors came from central Africa; thalassemia, among Greek- and Italian-Americans; phenylketonuria, among Scandinavian-Americans, and so on.

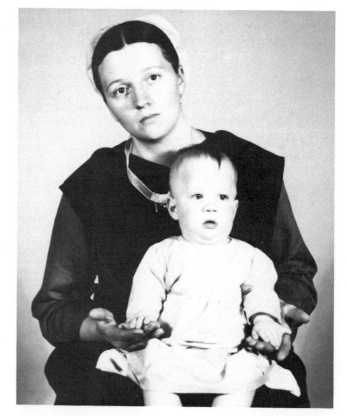

Figure 3.18 *Rare genetic conditions become more common when blood relatives marry, because the chance of a child's inheriting the same recessive genes from both parents increases. This child is a six-fingered dwarf, a condition extremely rare in the general population. However, at least sixty-one cases have occurred among the Old Order Amish, a religious group founded by three couples over 200 years ago. Members of this group are forbidden to marry outsiders, despite the fact that approximately one out of every eight members is a carrier of this gene.*

Prediction Once a genetic counselor knows that a problem may be present, the next step is calculating the odds that a child could inherit the condition. Sometimes the prediction is simple. If two carriers of the same recessive gene marry, each of their children has one chance in four of inheriting the recessive gene from both parents.

Of course, knowing the odds does not mean that the predictions will necessarily come true for the children of particular marriages. The chances of having a girl are about 50 percent for each birth, but we all know families of four boys and no girls. In the same way, it is possible for none of the children of two carriers of a recessive gene to inherit the gene, or for all of them to inherit the recessive gene from both parents and have the disease.

In sex-linked conditions, such as color blindness, Duchenne's muscular dystrophy, or hemophilia, a male who inherits the recessive gene on his X chromosome will always have the disease. A woman who is a carrier will transmit the gene to about half of her ova, so about half of her sons will be likely to have the disease, and half of her daughters will probably be carriers like their mother. Since daughters cannot inherit the condition unless both parents have the recessive gene, it is extremely rare for females to have serious X-linked genetic diseases: males with such diseases as hemophilia or certain forms of muscular dystrophy either do not survive until adulthood or decide not to become fathers. However, it is less rare for females to have minor sex-linked conditions such as color blindness.

Some genetic diseases are carried by dominant rather than recessive genes. This means that half the children of each carrier are likely to have the disease even though their other parent is not a carrier. Deadly dominant diseases are rare, because carriers always have the disease as well as the gene, and therefore usually die before they are old enough to have children. Huntington's chorea, a dominant disease that causes gradual deterioration of the nervous system, leading to physical weakness, emotional disturbance, mental retardation, and eventually death, is an exception. The symptoms of the disease do not appear until the person is over 30. Woody Guthrie, the folk singer who wrote "This Land Is Your Land," and the father of Arlo Guthrie, died of Huntington's chorea.

There are some other dominant diseases that can be passed from one generation to another because they vary in severity. For example, Abraham Lincoln probably had Marfan's syndrome, which usually produces abnormally long limbs, eye problems, and heart defects. Lincoln had only the first two symptoms, but his son, Tad, most likely died of the third.

Many genetic conditions follow neither the recessive nor the dominant gene pattern. Some are caused by mutation, that is, a spontaneous change in a gene's form. In this case, the genetic problem is not in the overall genotype of either parent. In other cases, dominance is partial, or the problem is polygenic or multifactorial. Cleft palate and cleft lip, club feet, spina bifida (a malformation at the end of the spinal column), diabetes, and high blood pressure are probably among this group of genetic diseases (Dronamraju, 1974). They are hard to predict, because they depend on genes and environment for their appearance.

What Are the Choices?   Until recently, couples who knew they had a high risk of having a baby with a serious genetic condition had only two options: (1) Decide to have a baby and hope that the baby will be one of the lucky ones. (2) Decide to avoid the risk of giving birth to a handicapped baby by seeking permanent sterilization; and perhaps consider adoption.

Prenatal Diagnosis   Now there is a third option. New methods have been discovered to detect many genetic conditions prenatally (Emery, 1974), making it possible for a woman to abort a defective fetus rather than give birth to an abnormal baby.

The main technique for prenatal diagnosis is amniocentesis. In this procedure, a bit of the amniotic fluid is withdrawn through the abdominal wall by means of a syringe (see Figure 3.19). The fluid can be analyzed to detect chromosomal abnormalities, as well as several other genetic conditions. If the possibility of a sex-linked disease is detected, the chromosomes can be analyzed to learn if the fetus is male or female.

Amniocentesis is almost painless and virtually risk-free. Complications occur in less than one case in a thousand. Emotionally, however, it can be difficult, partly because it is best to do the procedure in mid-pregnancy (after the thirteenth week), when there is sufficient amniotic fluid. It can be upsetting to carry a fetus for several months not knowing whether it is going to be aborted or carried full term. However, many women prefer three months of uncertainty to the other two options—not becoming pregnant or bearing an abnormal baby.

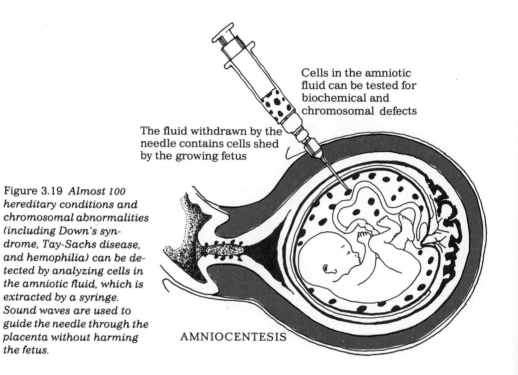

Cells in the amniotic fluid can be tested for biochemical and chromosomal defects

The fluid withdrawn by the needle contains cells shed by the growing fetus

Figure 3.19 *Almost 100 hereditary conditions and chromosomal abnormalities (including Down's syndrome, Tay-Sachs disease, and hemophilia) can be detected by analyzing cells in the amniotic fluid, which is extracted by a syringe. Sound waves are used to guide the needle through the placenta without harming the fetus.*

AMNIOCENTESIS

Early Treatment   Finally, for some genetic or chromosomal problems, there is a fourth possibility: early diagnosis and treatment, which can minimize or prevent many serious problems. Properly treated, newborns with diagnosed cystic fibrosis sustain less lung damage, and children with known hemophilia are unlikely to bleed to death. Adolescents with abnormal sex chromosomes (XXY or XO) can be given hormones to make them more normal in appearance.

Phenylketonuria.   The most dramatic example of early diagnosis and treatment is in the story of phenylketonuria, abbreviated PKU. PKU is a genetic disease caused by a recessive gene carried by 1 in every 80 white Americans. About 1 in every 10,000 American babies has PKU. If there were no treatment, these babies would become hyperactive, irritable, and severely retarded children.

However, nearly fifty years ago in Norway, a mother who had two such children traveled from doctor to doctor to find out what the problem was. In 1934, a physician discovered that her children could not metabolize protein normally: their blood accumulated too much of the chemical phenylalanine. Twenty years after this discovery, a diet was developed that prevents the buildup of phenylalanine. The diet cannot reverse damage already done, but it does prevent further retardation and controls the PKU child's hyperactive behavior.

Then in 1961, Robert Guthrie discovered that a drop of blood from the heel of a baby a few days old can be analyzed to detect PKU *before* any damage is done. Today this serious genetic problem need not affect children at all, if the environment—in the form of an early blood test, and diet—counteracts it. According to the laws in forty-six of the fifty states, the PKU test must be performed on all newborns.

Whose Responsibility?

The laws concerning testing for PKU raise an important question. Whose responsibility is it to prevent genetic and chromosomal problems? At the moment, most couples who seek genetic counseling have already borne a defective child, or have close relatives with genetic diseases, or have had a series of spontaneous abortions or stillborn babies. Obviously, they need genetic testing and counseling.

But should couples wait until they know they have a problem? Should someone advise or even compel people to learn about their genes before they have a baby? Many obstetricians recommend amniocentesis for every pregnant woman over 35. (In a legal first, the court recently agreed to hear the case of a 37-year-old mother of a Down's-syndrome newborn who wished to sue her doctor for not suggesting this test.)

Some psychologists (e.g., McIntire, 1973) and physicians (Milunsky, 1973) suggest that all people about to be married or to become parents should be required to have simple genetic tests, just as applicants for a marriage license must now be tested for syphilis. Others believe that genetic testing should be completely voluntary. However, many high-risk couples do not know what the risks are. One authority (Milunsky, 1977) estimates that 90 percent of the couples who need genetic counseling do not get it.

Sickle-Cell Anemia Before you decide which side is right, consider the controversy surrounding sickle-cell anemia, which is a serious, often fatal, blood disorder caused by inheriting two recessive genes, one from each parent. About 2.5 million, or 1 in every 100, Americans carry the recessive gene. This gene, sometimes called the sickle-cell trait, can be detected by a simple blood test. Since the disease is serious, the recessive gene common, and the genetic test easy, you might expect everyone to endorse mass screening for the sickle-cell trait.

In 1972, almost everyone did. Congress appropriated $115 million for a nationwide testing program, to last three years, from 1973 through 1975. Several states passed laws requiring testing for all high-risk people (Nyhan, 1976).

But two facts make mass testing for the sickle-cell trait controversial. The first is that some people are more likely to be carriers than others. The sickle-cell trait gives some protection against malaria, so people in malaria-prone areas (Africa, Central America, and parts of the Caribbean) have had a better chance of survival if they had the recessive gene. As a result, the gene is very common in these areas. In Sierra Leone (West Africa), more than half the population has the sickle-cell trait.

One out of every ten black Americans has the sickle-cell trait, as does one out of every twenty Hispanic-Americans. This statistic led some black people to suspect that mass screening for the sickle-cell trait was a subtle form of genocide; that is, a means of psychologically coercing the 2 million black Americans who have the trait to remain childless (Linde, 1972). In addition, there is concern that the sickle-cell gene might be used as a new excuse for discrimination. A black stewardess lost her job when the airline discovered she had the sickle-cell trait; the grounds for her firing were that some people with this trait are very sensitive to lack of oxygen.

Another factor that made the mass testing controversial was the tendency of people to panic if they learned they had the trait, an understandable reaction when testing is not accompanied by good counseling. However, sickle-cell anemia varies in intensity. In serious cases, people have periodic "crises," during which their joints swell and they experience intense pain. Victims of severe sickle-cell anemia often die of complications of the heart or kidney. Even in its mildest form, which may involve little more than fatigue and shortness of breath, sickle-cell anemia can cause complications that result in death during pregnancy or during surgery with general anesthesia. Nevertheless, many people with sickle-cell anemia live almost normal lives. This means that people who have the sickle-cell trait must consider many options when they plan their families.

Many Alternatives

In a careful testing and counseling program, couples "at risk" for bearing a child with a genetic condition learn that they have many alternatives (see Figure 3.21). Not only can counselors explain the odds of having a normal child; they can sometimes also predict how severe the disease would be if the child inherited it. The counselor also knows which genetic problems might soon be solved by medical research. A couple might postpone both pregnancy and adoption for a few years until the outcome of this research is known.

Rh Disease   Waiting proved to be the wisest strategy for women with Rh negative blood married to Rh positive men. Since about 14 percent of all Americans are Rh negative (15 percent of whites, 6 percent of blacks, and less than 1 percent of Asian- or Native Americans), about 12 percent of all American marriages are this combination. The gene for Rh positive blood is dominant, so most children from those marriages inherit the father's blood type. During childbirth, some of their positive

Figure 3.20 *If he had been born forty years earlier, this hemophilic boy would have had little chance of surviving until adulthood. Today he can live the life of a normal boy, with one exception: he must regularly receive transfusions of the clotting factor that is missing from his blood. Like many child diabetics, he has learned to give himself the necessary transfusions.*

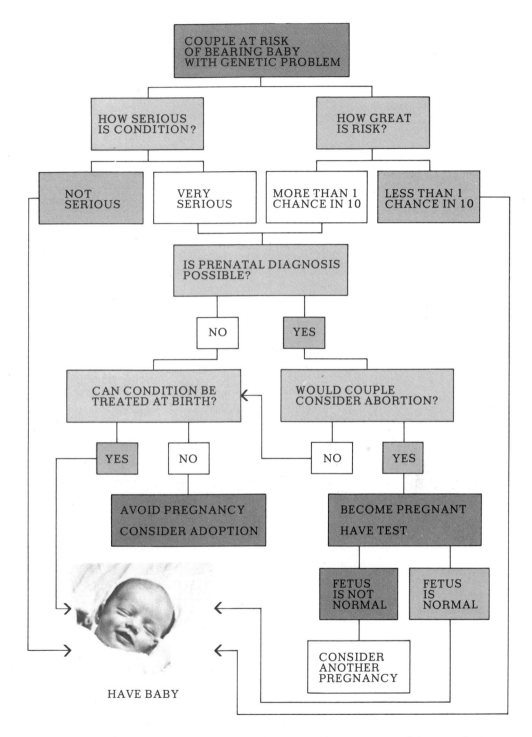

COUPLE AT RISK
OF BEARING BABY
WITH GENETIC PROBLEM

HOW SERIOUS
IS CONDITION?

HOW GREAT
IS RISK?

NOT
SERIOUS

VERY
SERIOUS

MORE THAN 1
CHANCE IN 10

LESS THAN 1
CHANCE IN 10

IS PRENATAL DIAGNOSIS
POSSIBLE?

NO

YES

CAN CONDITION BE
TREATED AT BIRTH?

WOULD COUPLE
CONSIDER ABORTION?

YES

NO

NO

YES

AVOID PREGNANCY

CONSIDER ADOPTION

BECOME PREGNANT

HAVE TEST

FETUS
IS NOT
NORMAL

FETUS
IS
NORMAL

CONSIDER
ANOTHER
PREGNANCY

HAVE BABY

Figure 3.21 *With the help of a genetic counselor, even couples who know they run a risk of having a baby with a genetic defect might decide to have a child. Although the process of making that decision is more complicated for them than it is for a couple with no family genetic illness and no posi-* *tive tests for harmful recessive genes, the outcome is usually a healthy baby. In each case, the genetic counselor provides facts and alternatives; every couple must make their own decision. In fact, two couples who have the same potential for producing a child with a genetic defect, and are* *aware of the same facts regarding the situation, sometimes make opposite decisions because they differ in their attitudes about abortion, in their willingness to raise a child with a genetic abnormality, or in their desire to have their own child rather than an adopted one.*

blood, which has been circulating in the placenta, might enter the mother's bloodstream, especially if the birth is a difficult one. This causes the mother to develop antibodies to the positive blood, in much the same way a vaccination causes someone to develop antibodies against a disease.

In any subsequent pregnancy, these antibodies cross the placenta, attacking and destroying some of the fetus' blood. The more antibodies the mother has, the stronger the attack. Twenty years ago, an Rh negative woman married to an Rh positive man could usually count on having at least one normal child (unless she had mistakenly been given a blood transfusion of Rh positive blood). But if her second baby showed signs of the illness, for instance, jaundice for a few days following birth, it was fairly certain that later newborns would be critically sick and might even die.

In the most severe cases, antibodies destroyed the fetus months before the baby would have been born. Until 1968, 10,000 Rh positive babies born to Rh negative women died each year in the United States, and 20,000 had serious birth defects, including deafness, cerebral palsy, and mental retardation (Apgar and Beck, 1973). The cause was *erythroblastosis,* or Rh disease

But recent medical advances have made this disease rare. Since the beginning of the 1960s, doctors have been able to give ill newborns a series of blood transfusions, removing all the blood with its destructive antibodies and replacing it with new blood. Most impressive of all, if the fetal blood supply is attacked, even months before birth, the fetus can be given a blood transfusion in the uterus.

Since 1968, there has been a way to avoid the formation of Rh antibodies. In the first days after giving birth, women are given Rhogam (Rh negative blood that already contains antibodies), which stops their bodies from forming additional antibodies. The injected antibodies disappear within a few weeks. When the woman becomes pregnant again, she has no antibodies to destroy the blood cells of the new fetus.

Difficult Choices Unfortunately, few genetic conditions have been controlled as well as Rh disease. Most couples who know they might give birth to a baby with genetic or chromosomal problems must make a difficult choice. Counselors believe their role is to explain facts, probabilities, and alternatives (Lebel, 1978). They hope that people will make the best choice for themselves—even if their decision is not the one the counselor would advise.

Figure 3.22 *For some couples, adoption or foster-parenting is a viable alternative to having their own child. When Betty Pollock learned she could not have children of her own, she and her husband took in their first foster child. In the sixteen years since then, more than thirty foster children have "graduated" from the Pollock farm at age 19. At this moment, another eighteen children—all previously rejected from other adoptive or foster homes—are living with the Pollocks.*

SUMMARY

Planning Conception

1. The birth rate is dropping in many countries; in some, it is already at the ZPG level. Small families have become much more common, partly because better contraceptive methods have been developed, and partly because raising a child is so expensive.

The Biology of Conception

2. Conception occurs when one of the millions of sperm from an ejaculation penetrates an ovum that has just left the ovary, creating a single-celled organism called a zygote.

Genes and Chromosomes

3. Each sperm and each ovum carries thousands of genes, which carry biochemical information about the characteristics of the person who might develop from them.

4. Genes are organized into groups and are contained in a larger particle, called a chromosome. Each ovum and each sperm contain twenty-three chromosomes, together forming forty-six chromosomes, the normal number each human has. Genes interact with the environment to determine the heritage of the individual. A zygote with two X chromosomes will become a girl; a zygote with one X and one Y will become a boy.

5. Each person has a unique combination of genes, with one important exception. Identical, or monozygotic, twins are formed from one zygote that splits in two, creating two zygotes with identical genes.

6. Genes can interact in many ways. In dominant-recessive pairs, the person develops the phenotype of the dominant gene, although he or she still carries the genotype of the recessive gene. In sex-linked inheritance, males are more likely to exhibit the characteristics they inherit from their mothers.

7. Many inherited characteristics are polygenic, the result of many genes rather than a single pair.

Heredity and Environment

8. Most important psychological characteristics are multifactorial, the result of the interaction of many genetic and environmental influences. Intelligence, temperament, and mental illness are all multifactorial.

Abnormal Genes and Chromosomes

9. Chromosomal abnormalities occur when the zygote has too many or too few chromosomes. Most of these involve the sex chromosomes. The most common chromosomal abnormality that does not involve the sex chromosomes occurs when there is an extra chromosome at the twenty-first pair. This causes Down's syndrome.

10. Most people are carriers for several of the thousands of genetic handicaps or diseases. Unless they have a child with another carrier of the same disease, and the child inherits the problem from both parents, they are usually unaware that they are carriers.

Genetic Counseling

11. Genetic testing and studying the family background can help predict whether a couple will have a child with a genetic problem. If it seems possible that they will, they can consider several options, such as remaining childless, obtaining prenatal diagnosis and abortion, if necessary, or administering immediate postnatal treatment. The option a couple chooses depends on their own values, the odds, and the seriousness of the potential problem.

KEY QUESTIONS

What are the main differences between family planning in earlier centuries and family planning today?

How is the sex of a baby determined?

How do multiple births occur?

What does the research on intelligence tell us about the interaction between heredity and environment?

What are the causes and consequences of Down's syndrome?

How does a genetic counselor predict the chances of a baby's inheriting a genetic disease?

Who should receive genetic counseling?

What are the arguments for and against mandatory genetic testing?

KEY TERMS

gamete	phenotype
ovum, ova	carrier
sperm	sex-linked gene
ovulation	polygenic inheritance
zygote	multifactorial characteristic
artificial insemination	correlation
gene	congenital
chromosome	XXY (Klinefelter's syndrome)
mitosis	
meiosis	XYY
XY	XO (Turner's syndrome)
XX	Down's syndrome
monozygotic twins	amniocentesis
dizygotic twins	phenylketonuria (PKU)
dominant gene	sickle-cell anemia
recessive gene	Rh disease
genotype	

RECOMMENDED READINGS

Whelan, Elizabeth. *A baby ... maybe.* New York: Bobbs Merrill, 1975.

An enjoyable book on the pros and cons of parenthood, including what to tell your parents if you decide not to have children. The book gives all the wrong reasons to have children, and good reasons for remaining childless. Whelan leaves the decision up to the reader.

Boston Women's Health Collective. *Our bodies, ourselves.* Rev. ed. New York: Simon and Schuster, 1976.

Discusses many aspects of female physiology and psychology, and includes comments by many women on contraception, sex, pregnancy, birth, and motherhood.

Environment, Heredity, and Intelligence. Reprint series #2. Harvard Educational Review, Cambridge, Mass., 1969.

Includes Jensen's original article and many scholarly responses to it. A bit technical at times, but the authors' passion will evoke responses that will help you when the concepts and statistics get difficult.

Richardson, Ken, and Spears, David. *Race and intelligence.* Baltimore: Penguin, 1972.

A series of essays by scholars from many disciplines. Overall, the essays are easier to read, and cover a broader range of issues, than the Harvard reprint.

Etzioni, Amitai. *Genetic fix.* New York: Harper & Row, 1975.

Ostensibly this book is a review of an international conference on the social and ethical implications of new developments in biology and medicine. Actually, it is an engaging account of the potential, for good or ill, of genetic engineering. It includes fascinating discussions of the implications of being able to choose the sex of future offspring.

Apgar, Virginia, and Beck, Joan. *Is my baby all right?* New York: Pocket Books, 1974.

A masterful discussion of the cause, prevention, and treatment of birth defects. Includes twenty-five chapters, each on one type of congenital problem, with case histories to help the reader understand the personal impact of each defect.

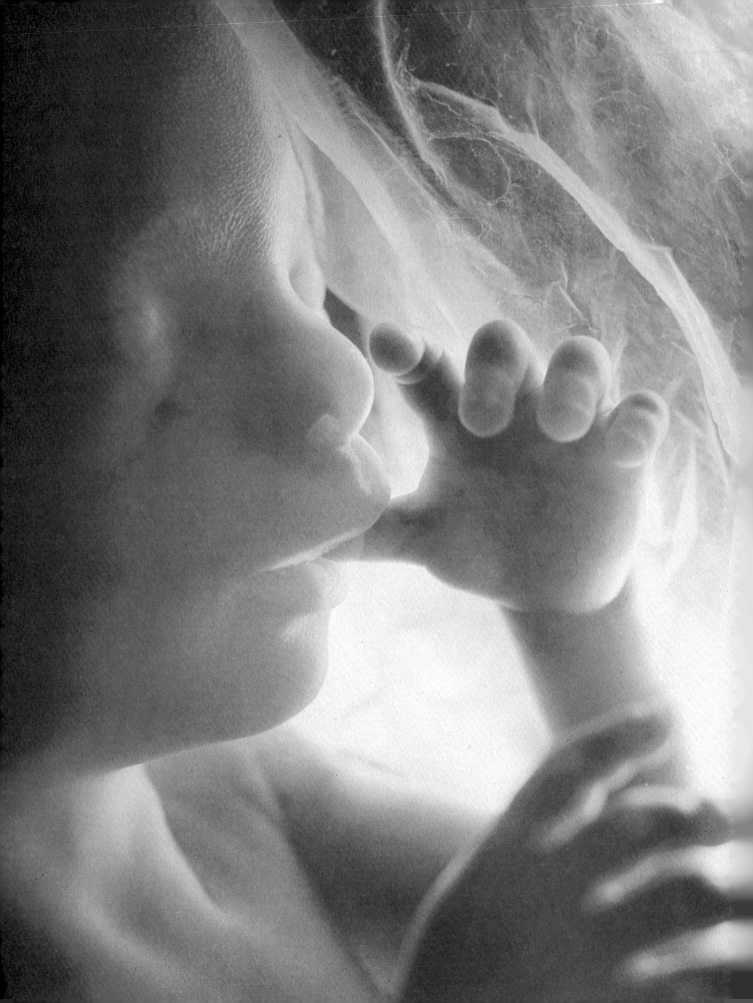

Prenatal Development

"I don't care whether it's a boy or a girl; I just want it to be healthy."

Every pregnant woman says that. Or thinks it. Or prays it. Or incants it like a charm in the secret core of her soul. So does every prospective father, every grandparent-to-be.

Virginia Apgar and Joan Beck
Is My Baby All Right?

Yes, the history of a man for the nine months preceding his birth would, probably, be far more interesting, and contain events of greater moment, than all three score and ten years that follow it.

Samuel Taylor Coleridge

True or False?

From the moment of your conception, your chances of surviving the first two weeks of pregnancy were less than 50–50.

By the eighth week after conception the fetus is only about an inch long, yet it has almost all the organs and features of an adult.

It is impossible for an XY (male) baby to be born with female genitals, and equally impossible for an XX (female) baby to be born with male genitals.

Pregnant women who like to listen to music at high volume should probably use headphones: loud noises can startle a fetus.

As long as a pregnant woman drinks no more than 3 ounces of alcohol a day, there is no risk to the fetus.

Fathers-to-be sometimes exhibit symptoms of pregnancy (vomiting, abdominal pains), and in some cultures may even appear to experience labor pains.

Figure 4.1 *A seventeenth-century scientist's conception of the human sperm is shown in this engraving, originally published in 1694. The future baby is already formed and in the birth position; all it needs now is an ovum to grow in for nine months until it reaches full size.*

People have always wondered how a fetus develops. About 300 years ago, the first crude microscopes were invented and living sperm were seen for the first time. Some scientists believed they saw within each human sperm a homunculus, or "little man," which was the future human being in miniature (see Figure 4.1). During the same decade (the 1670s), the ovarian follicle, the structure in which the human egg cell forms, was also described for the first time. This discovery led to another school of thought, proposing that the female egg, not the male sperm, held the tiny future human being. These "ovists," as they were called, believed that the sperm merely stimulated the human being within the egg to grow larger, emerging nine months later as a full-sized baby.

Both ovists and spermists carried the argument a logical step further. Each homunculus had within it another perfectly formed homunculus, and in that was still another one, and so on—children, grandchildren, great-grandchildren—all stored away for future use. Some ovists even went so far as to say that Eve had contained within her body all the unborn generations yet to come.

Today we know that each person begins life as a single cell formed equally by two parent cells. The developing organism does not resemble a human until eight weeks after conception, and the brain and lung maturation necessary for survival takes at least six months to develop. We also know that many circumstances during prenatal development affect the growing organism. As we will see, the facts of prenatal development are much more complicated, though no less miraculous, than the seventeenth-century natural scientists imagined.

From Zygote to Newborn

Each newborn begins life as a zygote, a tiny speck barely visible to the human eye. The growth of this single-cell organism into a fully developed baby has been divided into three main periods. The first two weeks are called the period of the ovum (also called the germinal period); from the third week through the seventh week is the period of the embryo; and from the eighth week until birth is the period of the fetus. Each period must go well if a healthy infant is to develop.

The Period of the Ovum

About twenty-four hours after conception, the one-celled zygote suddenly divides into two separate cells. These two cells soon become four, then eight, then sixteen. This is the most rapid growth of the entire life span. One week after conception, the organism, now called a blastula, contains more than a hundred cells. These cells separate into two groups: a mass of inner cells, called the blastocyst, and a surrounding circle of cells, called the trophoblast (from the Greek *trophe*, "to nourish").

Implantation The blastula travels down the Fallopian tube and arrives at the uterus just at the time in the woman's menstrual cycle when the lining of the uterus is covered with tiny blood vessels. The blastula burrows into this lining, rupturing the blood vessels to obtain nourishment and to create a safe haven where it can grow undisturbed. This process, called implantation, is difficult. Half or more of the blastulas never become implanted (Roberts and Lowe, 1975), usually because they are abnormal. If implantation is successful, growth continues, with the trophoblast forming four membranes that make it possible for the blastocyst to develop.

Four Protective Membranes One membrane, the *yolk sac,* produces blood cells for the embryo until the embryo can produce its own, whereupon the yolk sac disappears (see Figure 4.2). Another membrane, the *allantosis,* forms the umbilical cord and the blood vessels in the placenta. A third membrane, the *amnion,* holds the amniotic fluid (also called the "bag of waters") that cushions the organism against sudden movement or shock, like a warm, comfortable water bed surrounding the future baby. The fourth membrane is the *chorion,* which becomes the lining of the placenta.

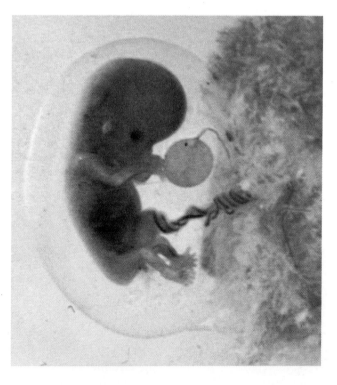

Figure 4.2 *The developing embryo is encased in the amnion, which holds the amniotic fluid. The yolk sac, visible at the upper right of the embryo, will soon disappear, and the tiny blood vessels of the placenta will grow.*

The Placenta. The placenta is the amazing organ that makes it possible for the embryo (and later the fetus) to have its own independent blood supply and at the same time make use of the mother's blood. In the placenta, blood vessels from the mother are interwoven with blood vessels from the embryo, but are separated by membranes that prevent mixture of the two bloodstreams. Oxygen and nourishment from the mother pass through these membranes into the embryo's bloodstream, and carbon dioxide and other waste products from the embryo are transferred to the mother's blood supply. She removes these wastes with her lungs and kidneys as if they were her own. The pregnant woman is literally breathing, eating, and urinating for two.

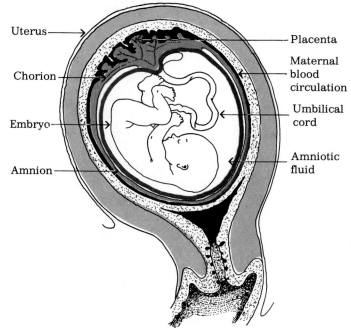

Uterus — Placenta

Chorion — Maternal blood circulation

Embryo — Umbilical cord

Amnion — Amniotic fluid

Figure 4.3 *The fetus in its protective prenatal environment.*

The embryo is connected to the placenta by the umbilical cord, which contains three blood vessels—a vein to carry nourishment and two arteries to remove waste products [see Figure 4.4(d)]. The movement of blood keeps the umbilical cord taut, like water at high pressure in a hose, making it almost impossible for the cord to become knotted or squeezed during prenatal development, no matter how many somersaults the developing baby or its mother does.

The placenta grows even more rapidly than the embryo in the first weeks of pregnancy, but gradually its growth slows. At birth, the placenta weighs about a pound. When the baby is born and begins to breathe through its own lungs, the umbilical cord is cut and tied. A few minutes later the placenta is expelled, its work complete.

The Blastocyst Develops While the outer cells of the organism are forming the placenta, the inner cells separate into layers; an outer layer (*ectoderm*), which will become the skin and the nervous system, and an inner layer (*endoderm*), which will become the digestive system and lungs. There soon appears a middle layer (*mesoderm*), which becomes muscles, bones, blood vessels, and kidneys, forming the circulatory, excretory, and reproductive systems.

About fourteen days after conception, two ridges appear. These fold to make the neural tube, the future head and backbone. At this point the organism is no longer called a blastocyst. It is now an embryo.

The Period of the Embryo

The embryo's growth is rapid and orderly. It proceeds in two directions: from the head downward, called cephalo-caudal development (from the Latin words for head and tail); and from the center (spine) toward the extremities, called proximo-distal development (from the Latin words for near and far).

Following this pattern, in the third week after conception, the head and blood vessels begin to form. In the fourth week, the heart begins to beat. Ears, nose, and mouth start to form, and buds that will become arms and legs appear. The embryo is 5 millimeters long (1/5 inch), about 7000 times the size of the zygote it was twenty-eight days before.

In the second month, the embryo develops what appears to be a primitive tail, which will soon be enclosed by skin and protective tissue at the tip of the backbone (the coccyx). The upper arms, then forearms, then hands, then fingers appear. Legs, feet, and toes follow in that sequence a few days later, each with the beginnings of the skeletal structure.

By the eighth week after conception, the embryo weighs about 1/30 of an ounce (1 gram), and is about 1 inch (2.5 centimeters) long, almost half the total length the head. The embryo has almost all the basic organs (except the sex organs), skeleton, and features of a human being, including elbows and knees, fingers and toes, and even buds for the first baby teeth. It is ready for a new name, the fetus.

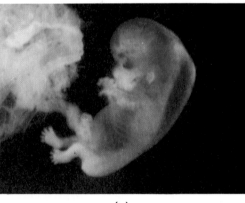

(a)　　　　　　(b)　　　　　　　　　　　(c)

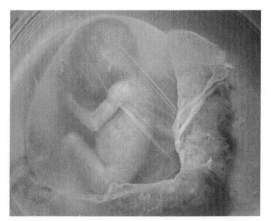

(d)

Figure 4.4 (a) *Growth of the embryo is rapid and orderly. At 40 days, the head is as large as the rest of the body, and the spine is fully outlined, while arms and legs are just beginning to grow.* (b) *At 45 days, the proportions of the body have changed: the lower half has grown and the arms and legs are longer.* (c) *Only three weeks later, as the fetal period begins, hands, feet, and facial features are* formed. *While the head is still large, the overall proportions are close enough to those of a full-term baby that we can recognize this as a well-formed human fetus, even though it is only about an inch and a half long (4 centimeters).* (d) *At 3 months, the tiny fetus weighs only 3 ounces. The umbilical cord will bring nourishment for the next 6 months. At full term, the average fetus will weigh more than 7 pounds.*

The Period of the Fetus   During the third month, muscles develop and bones begin to harden. All the major organs complete their formation, including stomach, heart, lungs, kidneys. Finally the sex organs take shape, as the gender, or biological maleness or femaleness, is set.

Beginning in the third month, the fetus moves almost every part of its body, kicking its legs, sucking its thumb, making fists, and even squinting and frowning. The 3-month-old fetus also swallows amniotic fluid, digests it, and urinates. By the end of the third month, fingerprints can be seen with a magnifying glass. The eyelids close, not to reopen for several months. This active, perfectly formed little creature weighs only 3 ounces and is about 3 inches long.

The Second Trimester   In the fourth, fifth, and sixth months—the second *trimester* of pregnancy—hair, including eyebrows and eyelashes, begins to grow. Fingernails, toenails, and buds for adult teeth form. A stethoscope can now pick up the heartbeat; an x-ray or sonograph can detect the hardening skeleton. The woman can feel the flutter, and later the thump, of fetal arms and legs.

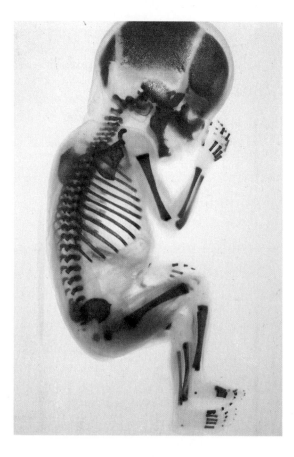

Figure 4.5 *During the fetal period, cartilage becomes bone, as can be seen by this x-ray of a fetus at 18 weeks. Although the skull and the spine are most clearly developed, the bones of the fingers and toes are also visible. Even buds for the teeth will soon begin to harden, although the first "baby" tooth will not emerge until 6 months after birth.*

During these three months, the brain cells of the fetus mature and multiply. This brain development is the critical factor in attaining the age of viability (sometime between the twenty-fourth and the twenty-sixth weeks), at which point the fetus has developed enough to survive outside the uterus. This does not mean that babies born this early usually live; on the contrary, almost all of them die. However, it does mean that sometime toward the end of the sixth month of pregnancy a prematurely born fetus *might* survive, although the average 27-week-old fetus weighs only 2

A CLOSER LOOK   **The Development of Sex Organs**

Maleness and femaleness appear surprisingly late in prenatal life. Of course the sex chromosomes are set at the moment of conception: the embryo is either an XX (female) or XY (male). But not until about six weeks after conception does actual sex differentiation begin to occur. The first stage is the appearance of a genital ridge—a cluster of cells called the *indifferent gonad,* because it can develop into male or female organs (Jirasek, 1976).

In male embryos, a gene attached to the Y chromosome sends a biochemical signal to the indifferent gonad, triggering development of male organs—first the testes at about seven weeks after conception and later the other male organs. If the embryo has no Y chromosome, the indifferent gonad receives no signal. Without specific instructions to become male, the embryo develops female organs—first the ovaries at about ten weeks and then the other female organs.

Very rarely, the indifferent gonad develops both ovaries and testes, due to some genetic error. In such a case, the person will be a *hermaphrodite,* that is, someone who has functioning male and female organs. There are less than a hundred documented cases of true hermaphroditism (Katchadourian and Lunde, 1975). However, about once in every 10,000 births, a *pseudohermaphrodite* is born. Pseudohermaphrodites can be XY babies who have the genitals of a female, XX babies who have the genitals of a male, or babies with ambiguous genitals. If a pregnant woman takes hormones such as progesterone or androgen, this sometimes causes female embryos to develop external sex organs that appear to be male. Rare genetic abnormalities also cause pseudohermaphroditism (Simpson, 1976).

When a newborn's sex is ambiguous, laboratory tests (usually of chromosomal structure) can determine whether the infant is male or female. Then surgery in the first year of life and hormones during adolescence can give the person a normal male or female appearance, although he or she will probably be unable to reproduce.

Such medical procedures to clarify sexual identity are usually successful, because, as psychologists have learned, gender is probably less important in determining sexual identity than are external physical appearance and childhood experiences. John Money and his colleagues (1968) studied ten young adults who had XY (male) chromosomes but, because of genetic problems, had female external sex organs. They had all been raised as females. Their attitudes, behavior, and plans for the future followed traditional female sex-role patterns. For instance, they had played with dolls when they were little, and now that they were older, they hoped to be wives and mothers. They thought of themselves as women, and except for their male chromosomes and absent ovaries, they were.

Figure 4.6 *Muntaha Ibrahim is a survivor. She was three months premature and weighed only 1½ pounds (679 grams) at birth. Pictured here at the end of the first month of life after her birth, she weighs 2 pounds, 5 ounces.*

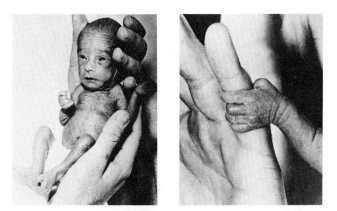

pounds (900 grams). Babies born before the twenty-fourth week or weighing less than 21 ounces (600 grams) have never lived, even with excellent medical care (Pritchard and MacDonald, 1976).*

---

*On August 2, 1979, in Albert Einstein Hospital in New York City, Chaya Snyder was born twenty-four weeks after conception, weighing only 15 ounces (425 grams). She made medical history, for she survived her first two months, doubling in weight. As of this writing, doctors predict that she will continue to thrive.

The Third Trimester In the last three months, the fetus gains about 5½ pounds (2500 grams). Someone who rests a hand on the woman's abdomen when the fetus shifts position will feel movement. By the ninth month, the surface of the mother's abdomen can be seen rippling and bulging with the movement of the fetal head, elbows, knees, and feet.

The fetus is now so large that the mother is almost constantly aware of its presence, day and night. At the same time, it becomes more aware of her. When she is walking, the fetus is quiet, lulled by the rhythmic rocking movement. When she sits or lies down in a way that causes the fetus to rest against a bone, it squirms to find a more comfortable position. Abrupt loud noises startle the fetus, and internal noises, such as the mother's heartbeat, soothe it (Macfarlane, 1977).

During the last trimester, brain cells multiply rapidly. The fetus gains an insulating layer of fat that will protect it in the cooler world outside the uterus. The lungs and heart become able to sustain life without the placenta. Every day of prenatal life makes postnatal survival more likely.

Nutrition

Some babies are born after nine full months of prenatal development; they weigh at least 5½ pounds (2500 grams) and are ready to thrive outside the uterus. Others are born early, small, or feeble. Nutrition is probably the main reason for these differences (Winick, 1976).

Twenty years ago, many women tried to keep their weight down during pregnancy. Folk wisdom encouraged them to believe that the fetus would get nourishment from their bodies even if it was absent from their diets. One old saying, "A tooth for every baby born," meant that each fetus would take calcium for its bones from the mother's teeth, causing the mother to lose a tooth but the fetus to grow strong. Doctors used to scold pregnant patients who gained more than 2 pounds a month. Now they worry more if a pregnant woman gains too little, because they are aware of the possible complications of prenatal malnutrition (Pritchard and Mac-Donald, 1976).

Immediate Effects of Malnutrition

Many studies have shown that virtually every complication of prenatal development and birth—from premature and deformed infants, or long labor and medical complications in the birth process, to maternal postnatal depression and inability to breast feed—is more common when the woman is not well nourished. Good diet may be especially important in the last trimester of pregnancy, when the fetus gains almost three-fourths of its birth weight and when the brain cells increase most rapidly. Giving malnourished women additional calories and protein in the last half of pregnancy has reduced prematurity and other problems dramatically (Habicht et al., 1974; Stein and Susser, 1976). In addition, if the mother is well nourished, the fetus is able to store extra iron and other nutrients during the last weeks before birth to use during its first postnatal weeks.

This emphasis on nutrition does not mean that pregnant women should overeat or take dozens of vitamins. According to the Committee on Maternal Nutrition of the National Academy of Sciences, only iron and folic acid are routinely needed as supplements for the well-nourished pregnant woman. Excessive quantities of other vitamins may even be harmful to the fetus (Pritchard and MacDonald, 1976). For instance, excess doses of vitamin A cause deformities in the fetuses of virtually every nonhuman animal tested (Schardein, 1976). Eating a balanced diet is far better than relying on multivitamins for prenatal nutrition.

Long-term Effects of Malnutrition

The possible long-term effects of prenatal malnutrition are hard to demonstrate. We do know that babies born to severely malnourished women have fewer brain cells than babies born to women who are better nourished. Autopsies of malnourished newborns who died within the first few weeks have proven this (Winick, 1976).

It seems reasonable to assume that malnutrition leads to loss of brain cells, even when the infant survives, and that fewer cells would mean a slightly less intelligent child. But the results of one study (Stein et al., 1975) cast doubt on this assumption. In 1945, while still under Nazi occupation, half of the Netherlands was deprived of virtually all food. The other half had been liberated; and while they had little food, the inhabitants were not starving. Psychologists predicted that the babies born to the starving women would show some impairment of intelligence when they grew up. However, this forecast seemed to be contradicted by a study of the IQ scores of virtually all the Dutch men who reached 19 years of age between 1963 and 1965. Although there were clear differences in IQ among men from different social classes, there were none in terms of which half of the nation the men were born in.

This does not prove that malnutrition never affects mental development. In fact, because the infant mortality was higher in the starving part of the Netherlands, it may well have been that those children most severely affected during the prenatal period did not participate in the study because they did not survive. But the results do suggest that family and school influences can help a surviving child overcome whatever learning deficits malnutrition might cause. This conclusion has been confirmed by other research (Butler, 1974).

Hazards to Normal Prenatal Development

The development of a healthy human infant from a zygote in nine months is so awe-inspiring a feat, it is easy to think that the uterus, placenta, and amniotic fluid must protect the developing organism from all external hazards while this miracle occurs. Until recently, that was precisely what most people believed, including scientists. They thought any abnormalities were genetically caused. Now we know that there are hundreds of teratogens*—viruses, drugs, chemicals, and radiation— that sometimes cross the barrier of the placenta and harm the embryo.

---

*The root word, *tera*, comes from the Greek word for monster. Hence, teratology is the study of abnormalities, and a teratogen is anything that causes birth defects.

Difficulty with Research in Teratology

Teratology, the scientific study of birth defects, is a fairly new field of research. No one yet knows what all the teratogens are, or precisely how they do their damage. One problem in this research is that there rarely seems to be a consistent relationship between specific teratogens and particular birth defects. Almost no substance harms every fetus exposed to it, and many teratogens cause different defects in different babies. Another problem is that the list of possible teratogens includes so many drugs, chemicals, and diseases that almost every fetus is probably exposed to several of them. Consequently, it is often impossible to pinpoint which factor (or factors) might have been the cause of any given deformity in any given baby.

Finally, it sometimes takes a long time before the effects of prenatal hazards are apparent. Approximately half of all congenital problems are obvious at birth; the others appear later. This is especially true in the case of learning difficulties or emotional problems (Apgar and Beck, 1973).

A CLOSER LOOK   **Long-term Effects: DES**

The effects of one teratogen, the hormone called DES (diethylstilbestrol), were not discovered until fifteen years after the first affected baby was born. Between 1948 and 1969, DES was given to pregnant women to prevent miscarriages. Between 500,000 and 2,000,000 women took the hormone over the twenty-one-year period.* The drug seemed to work well, for most of these women gave birth to healthy full-term boys and girls. (Later studies suggested, however, that they would have had normal pregnancies without the hormone.)

Then in 1965, doctors discovered several cases of vaginal cancer in teenage girls, a disease almost unheard of in females so young. The cancer was traced to the DES given to their mothers during pregnancy. Males whose mothers had taken DES were apparently unaffected, or so it was thought. Now it seems that a surprisingly high number of them have

abnormalities of the genital tract, sometimes causing sterility (Cosgrove and Henderson, 1977).

Although most DES daughters have minor abnormalities of the cervix, only about 1 in 500 has developed cancer thus far (Shapiro, 1977). And many DES sons are not sterile. Nevertheless, even if their bodies are not affected, DES children live with the fear and anxiety that they might be affected eventually. They often blame their mothers, who often blame themselves. Self-help groups for DES victims focus as much on the psychological consequences of DES as on the physiological problems.

---

*The reason for the wide difference in estimates of how many women took DES is that many doctors' records are missing or inaccurate, and it is virtually impossible to collect and read what records there are. Many women do not remember what drugs they were given in pregnancy ten or more years ago.

What Is Known

However, we do know some specific teratogens and at what stage of prenatal development their damage is most likely to occur. We also know why certain babies are more susceptible to them than others are. We will first discuss timing and risk factors and then consider some of the most harmful teratogens.

Critical Periods Each part of the developing embryo and fetus has a critical period, a time when that particular organ or body part is most vulnerable. In general, the critical period occurs while that part of the body is forming. Malformations of the head and spinal column are most likely to occur in the third week; of the eyes and heart, in the fourth week; of most of the other organs and the skeleton, in the second month. Because the body forms during the period of the embryo, the first two months are sometimes called the "critical period of pregnancy."

But, in fact, all nine months of pregnancy are critical (see Figure 4.8). One careful study of 50,282 pregnancies found structural malformations in 6 percent of the babies born (Heinonen et al., 1976). According to these researchers, two-thirds of

Figure 4.7 *These photographs show three stages in finger development: (a) notches appear in the hand at day 44; (b) fingers are growing but webbed together at day 50; and (c) fingers have separated and lengthened at day 52. By day 56, fingers are completely* *formed, and the critical period for hand development is over. Other parts of the body, especially the eyes, heart, and central nervous system, take much longer to complete development, so they are vulnerable to teratogens for months rather than days.*

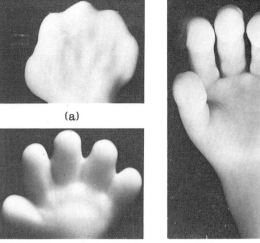

(a)

(b)   (c)

Figure 4.8 *As this chart shows, the most serious damage from teratogens is likely to occur in the first eight weeks after conception. However, damage to many vital parts of the body, including brain, eyes, and genitals, can occur during the last months of pregnancy as well.*

the defects were probably caused in the first trimester by genes or teratogens. The remaining one-third were dubbed anytime malformations because they could have originated anytime during the nine months of pregnancy. There were thirty-seven different anytime malformations, affecting 911 children.

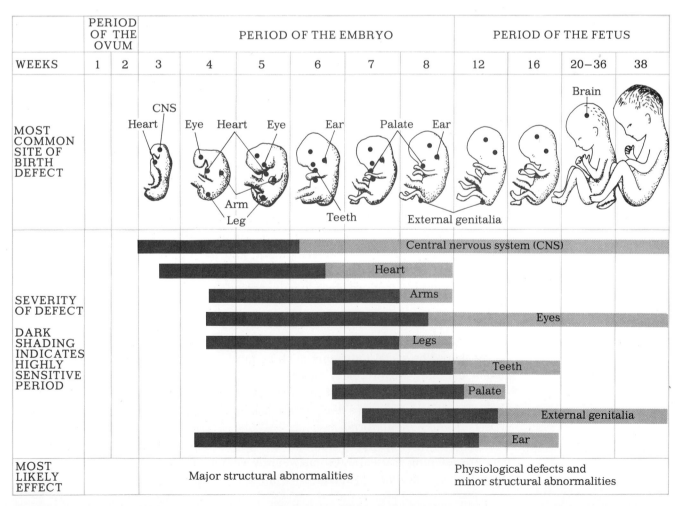

Risk Factors   Many factors make some babies more likely to have serious congenital problems than others (see Table 4.1). Among these are the baby's genetic structure (for instance, some seem especially vulnerable to cleft palate) and gender (males are more vulnerable), and the mother's age, health, social class, and nutrition. Birth order is also a factor: later-borns are more vulnerable.

TABLE 4.1   **Risk Factors**

	A specific teratogen is more likely to harm a particular embryo or fetus if several of the following conditions prevail.
Family Background	Several children already born to the family.
	Low socioeconomic status.
Inborn Characteristics	Genetic predisposition to certain problems.
	The fetus is XY (male).
Mother's Characteristics	Undernourished.
	Over 40 or under 18.
Nature of Teratogen	Occurs early in pregnancy.
	High dose or exposure.
	Occurs over a period of several days or weeks.
	Other teratogens also present.
Nature of Prenatal Care	Woman is several months pregnant before prenatal care begins.
	Prenatal visits to doctor are more than four weeks apart.

The *interaction* among factors is crucial. An analogy can be made to a football team that wins almost all its games. Many things are responsible for each victory— the training and condition of the individual players, the wisdom of the coaches, the encouragement of the fans, the favorableness of the weather. And when the team wins, it wins in spite of several things going wrong; perhaps some of the players are injured, some of the coaching is foolish, and some of the opponents are tough.

Even when the team is defeated, the same analysis applies. Defeat is rarely caused by only one factor. Instead a combination of problems—perhaps a key player on the injured list, an unlucky series of passes, a particular play at just the wrong moment—loses the game.

In the same way, most pregnant women experience some of the potential hazards to normal prenatal development, and have healthy babies nonetheless. Most of the hazards—malnutrition, diseases, drugs, pollution, chemicals—probably affect only fetuses that are already vulnerable for some other reason.

Social Class   One crucial factor that influences the likelihood of congenital problems is socioeconomic status (Illsley, 1967). This may seem puzzling, for social class is measured by social indicators such as income, occupation, and education, not biological ones. Nevertheless many biological influences, among them malnutrition, disease, excessive drug use, poor medical care, unwanted pregnancies, and large family size, are more likely to occur in families of lower socioeconomic status (Osofsky and Kendall, 1973).

Of course, some very poor women provide an excellent prenatal environment for their developing fetuses, and some wealthy women do not. It is also true that babies who had an excellent prenatal environment can develop learning problems or psychological difficulties. A complex interaction among genetic, prenatal, and postnatal influences makes us who we are. To return to the football analogy, prenatal development rarely determines the whole ball game. More often the nine months before birth simply give some newborns a few points advantage, and others a handicap of a few points.

Specific Teratogens

We shall now look at some of the specific teratogens, because the more we know about them, the better we can prevent the damage they cause. This topic is as important to psychologists as to physicians, for learning and emotional problems often accompany physical ones.

Diseases

Throughout history, many pregnant women have had infections, viruses, and even major illnesses and still given birth to normal babies. The idea that the placenta screened out all diseases was widely accepted. But about forty years ago, this belief had to be revised due to the findings of medical research.

Rubella In 1941 an Australian physician named McAllister Gregg noticed a sudden increase in the number of babies born blind (1941; reprinted in Persaud, 1977). He remembered an epidemic of rubella (German measles) in July and August of 1940, and interviewed the blind babies' mothers. Many of them recalled having had rubella symptoms (a pink rash on the stomach, a sore throat, swollen glands) during early pregnancy. Gregg's suspicions alerted other doctors throughout the world, and they began to keep track of pregnant patients who had rubella. They were amazed to discover that many of them gave birth to babies with birth defects, including deafness, heart abnormalities, and mental retardation, as well as blindness.

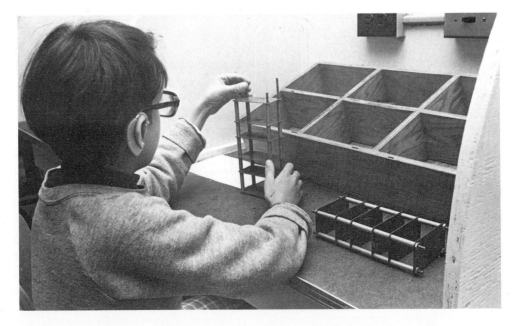

Figure 4.9 *Rubella syndrome children often have a number of handicaps, but with proper attention, many of these children can live relatively full lives. This rubella boy, who must wear glasses and a hearing aid, is assembling machine components in an educational workshop.*

About 80 percent of all babies born to mothers who had rubella during early pregnancy show some effects (Hardy, 1973). The rubella virus attacks whatever part of the embryo or fetus is developing at the onset of the disease. Damage to the central nervous system, causing emotional and behavioral disturbances, is especially likely to occur in the first four months (Chess et al., 1971).

In the second trimester, after the fetus is completely formed, rubella almost never causes obvious physical defects, but it can cause hearing problems and language retardation. One study of twenty-four women who had rubella later than the third month of pregnancy found that only seven had normal children (Hardy et al., 1969). Two had spontaneous abortions, and the other fifteen had children with handicaps, especially in hearing and speech.

Severe rubella epidemics have occurred every twenty-five years. The most recent one, 1964–1965, resulted in the birth of about 20,000 handicapped babies in the United States. But two subsequent developments should make the birth of a rubella baby a rare event. The first is a blood test that a woman can have before she becomes pregnant to see if she is immune to rubella (about 85 percent of American women are). The second is a rubella vaccine which nonimmune women should get at least six months before they become pregnant. The vaccine is also recommended for all preschool children. If this recommendation is followed, the rubella epidemic due in 1980–1981 should not appear.

Other Diseases   Once the link between rubella and birth defects was established, scientists began searching for other viruses that might affect unborn babies. They found dozens, including mumps, chickenpox, polio, measles, and some strains of flu. Again, the woman need not be very ill for the fetus to be affected. One virus, called cytomegalovirus, usually produces no symptoms in the adult, but can cause fetal brain damage. Even certain vaccines (smallpox, rubella, mumps, diphtheria, and rabies) cause serious problems to some embryos (O'Brien and McManus, 1978).

Recently, doctors discovered that another mild disease, toxoplasmosis, can cause prenatal eye and brain damage. Toxoplasmosis is caused by a parasite often present in uncooked meat and in cat feces. Many women already have antibodies against toxoplasmosis. However, if a blood test indicates no immunity, pregnant women should not eat rare or uncooked meat; and if they have a cat, someone else should attend to the litter box.

One of the most serious diseases that affects the fetus, syphilis, has been known for a long time. If a pregnant woman has syphilis, her baby can be born with congenital syphilis, which causes serious bone, liver, or brain damage. Luckily, syphilis cannot cross the placenta in the first months of pregnancy, so the disease can be diagnosed with a blood test and cured with antibiotics before the fetus is affected (Pritchard and MacDonald, 1976). But if a woman does not get early prenatal care (and many, especially teenagers, do not), her fetus may die or be severely handicapped.

One disease, preeclampsia (toxemia), is never present in nonpregnant women but occurs during the last trimester in about 6 percent of all pregnancies (Pritchard and MacDonald, 1976). Early symptoms are high blood pressure, sudden weight gain due to retention of water, and protein in the urine. If preeclampsia is not controlled promptly, it can become eclampsia, which can cause fetal brain damage. If left untreated, it can cause brain damage in the mother as well; eventually it kills both fetus and mother.

Drugs

Not long ago, if a drug seemed safe when tested on pregnant rats, it was assumed to be safe for people. Scientists no longer make this assumption, because one drug proved it false.

Thalidomide Thousands of pregnant women in 1960 were pleased to find a new mild tranquilizer, supposedly effective against nausea and insomnia, that had been tested on pregnant rats with no side effects. Many women took this tranquilizer in early pregnancy, especially in England and Germany, where they could buy it without a prescription.

The drug was thalidomide. The women who took it gave birth to 8000 deformed babies, born in twenty-eight countries (Schardein, 1976). If a pregnant woman took thalidomide between the thirty-fourth and thirty-eighth day after conception, her baby had no ears; if she used it between the thirty-eighth and forty-sixth days, her infant had deformed arms or no arms; if she took it between the fortieth and forty-sixth days, her baby had deformed legs or no legs. If she waited until fifty days after conception, the critical periods during which thalidomide could be harmful were over. Her baby was not affected (Saxen and Rapola, 1969).

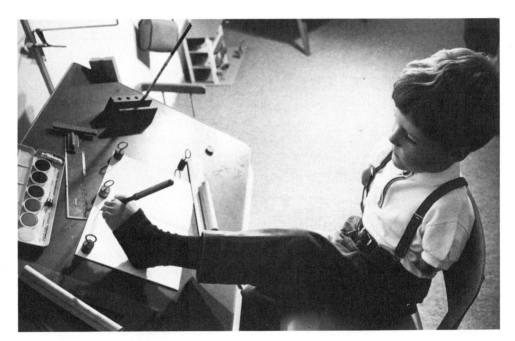

Figure 4.10 *This German boy has deformed arms, one of the three specific effects of thalidomide, but his ears and legs are normal. He is learning to write and draw with his toes.*

Other Medicines The thalidomide tragedy has made physicians more cautious in prescribing drugs for pregnant women. They now assume that all drugs enter the fetal bloodstream, and try to make sure that the benefits of an indicated drug outweigh the risks (Pritchard and MacDonald, 1976). Pregnant women should avoid unnecessary over-the-counter drugs, as well. Drugs with proven harmful effects on the human fetus include streptomycin, tetracycline, anticoagulants, bromides, Thorazine, Valium, iodine, and most hormones (O'Brien and McManus, 1978).

Drug Consumption in Pregnancy Given this situation, how many drugs do you think the average pregnant woman takes? If you think the answer is none, except life-saving drugs such as insulin for the diabetic or anticonvulsive medicine for the epileptic, think again. Every study shows that most pregnant women take several drugs during pregnancy (Degenhardt et al., 1972; Heinonen et al., 1976).

One study of 156 pregnant women in Houston, Texas, found that the average woman ingested more than ten drugs during pregnancy, *excluding* vitamins, iron supplements, caffeine, nicotine, and alcohol: 64 percent took analgesics, such as aspirin, 57 percent took diuretics (water-reducing pills), 52 percent, antihistamines, 33 percent, sedatives, and 20 percent hormones (Hill, 1973). Animal studies have put drugs in all these categories on the suspicious list.

Social Drugs   Many of the drugs that pregnant women take are not purchased at the drugstore. They are bought at the supermarket, candy store, liquor store, or on the street. Usually it does not occur to them that these drugs can affect the fetus; in fact, they often do not even think of them as drugs.

Cigarettes.   A few years ago, a pregnant woman lighting up an after-dinner cigarette never thought that she might be about to harm her fetus. Although scientists had known for decades that the fetal heart beats faster when the mother smokes (Sontag and Wallace, 1935) and that smoking increases the level of carbon monoxide in the mother's blood, they did not see the likelihood of any long-term harm being done to babies born to women who smoked. In the last ten years, however, two large studies have proved that cigarette smoking sometimes harms the fetus.

British researchers have followed the development of virtually every baby born between March 3 and March 8, 1958, in England, Scotland, and Wales—a total of 17,000 infants. Comparing babies of mothers from the same social class and with the same medical and childbearing history, they found that babies whose mothers smoked were about 7 ounces (180 grams) lighter, on average, than babies born to nonsmokers. In addition, babies born to smoking mothers were twice as likely to have heart abnormalities.

Figure 4.11 *If this moment is typical of this woman's daily routine, she may be inhibiting her baby's growth and setting the stage for a complicated birth.*

Following the British babies throughout childhood, the researchers found that the children of smoking mothers had more problems with social adjustment, behavior, and reading in elementary school than did the children born to nonsmoking mothers from the same background. The smokers' children on the average were almost six months behind the children of nonsmokers in reading (Butler, 1974).

A recent analysis of the Collaborative Prenatal Project, a study of 53,000 American infants, confirmed that smoking mothers are more likely than nonsmokers to have babies who are underweight and who have medical complications during labor, delivery, and the first months of life. This study found that the risks were higher even if the women stopped smoking as soon as they knew they were pregnant. However, the study did not find any differences in learning ability between siblings whose mother smoked in one pregnancy but not in the other (*The New York Times*, January 17, 1979).

Although the studies on maternal smoking do not agree on the specifics of how, why, or in what way fetuses are affected, Julius Richmond, the surgeon general of the United States, was able to summarize the results of thousands of studies with this conclusion: "The children of women who smoke are more likely to have measurable deficiencies in physical growth and development" (U.S. Department of Health, Education, and Welfare, 1979). This conclusion is, if anything, an understatement.

Alcohol.   Another addiction can have serious teratogenic consequences. For years doctors have known that alcoholic mothers often have small, retarded babies, but they thought that nutrition, rather than alcohol, was the probable cause. After all, they reasoned, if a woman drinks a pint of vodka (about 1200 calories) or a quart of wine (between 700 to 1300 calories) each day, she will be less likely to consume enough milk, juice, fruit, vegetables, grains, eggs, meat, and fish for the fetus.

But we now know that even well-nourished alcoholics put their unborn babies in jeopardy (see Figure 4.12). According to the Department of Health, Education, and

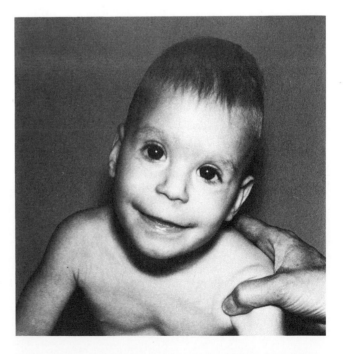

Figure 4.12 *This boy's widely spaced eyes, underdeveloped upper jaw, and flattened nose are three of the typical facial characteristics of children with fetal alcohol syndrome. Many babies born to women who drank alcohol during pregnancy show no signs of FAS; others have more obvious deformities of the eyes and head.*

Welfare, each year in the United States about 1500 babies are born physically deformed or mentally retarded because their mothers drank too much alcohol during pregnancy (Smith, 1978). One study found that 43 percent of the babies born to severe alcoholics have the distinctive symptoms of the fetal alcohol syndrome, including small heads, abnormal eyes, and malproportioned faces (Jones, 1975). They are also relatively short for their weight, and throughout childhood and adolescence, their physical and mental growth is retarded (Streissguth et al., 1978).

Even moderate drinking may affect embryos. One group of fifty-four mothers who consumed between one and two ounces of absolute alchohol (that is, about three or four cocktails) per day during the month before they knew they were pregnant gave birth to nine babies with at least two of the half dozen or so facial characteristics typically associated with the fetal alcohol syndrome (Hanson et al., 1978). None of these women were considered alcoholics; in fact, many of them said they took only an occasional drink once they knew they were pregnant. As a result of such studies as this, The March of Dimes, the national organization that tries to prevent birth defects, recommends that pregnant women, and women trying to become pregnant, stop drinking entirely.

Heroin and Methadone. Experts disagree about whether heroin or methadone is worse for the fetus (Harbison, 1975). Babies whose mothers are addicted to either drug are born addicted themselves. They must get the drug soon after birth; otherwise they may die of severe withdrawal symptoms. Babies born to mothers addicted to either drug are also more likely to be premature, underweight, jaundiced, and malformed than other babies. Compared to babies born to nonaddicted mothers from the same socioeconomic class, they are twice as likely to die within days after birth, primarily because they have trouble breathing (Ostrea and Chavez, 1979).

To make matters worse, addicted babies that survive are difficult to care for. They are restless, irritable, and hard to comfort or cuddle; and they have irregular sleeping habits that last for a year or more. These characteristics make it hard for their mothers, or anyone else, to establish a loving relationship with them. Without someone who loves them and provides good care, it is much more difficult for them to overcome the handicaps they were born with.

Figure 4.13 *Many infants are born addicted to heroin or methadone. These two preschoolers are ex-drug addicts living in Odyssey House, an institution in New York City dedicated to fighting drug addiction. If they lived at home with addicted parents, it is likely they would be abused and neglected.*

Other Common Drugs. Other common drugs, such as marijuana and caffeine, have not been proven harmful to human embryos, although they have produced some harmful effects in animal studies. Many other drugs, including LSD, have been proven harmful by some studies but not by others. However, since so many other substances have been implicated in birth defects, many women who are determined to have healthy babies are cautious about these as well. They hesitate before drinking a cup of coffee or a glass of Coke, and try to avoid smoking anything, with or without nicotine.

Environmental Hazards

Pregnant women who are sufficiently cautious can avoid taking drugs. With a little luck and planning, they can even avoid getting sick. But without adopting a very different lifestyle, it would be virtually impossible for most of them to avoid all cosmetics, food additives, and pollutants in the air and water. Could these be harmful as well? The answer is yes, sometimes. A few are known to cause serious damage. Most of the rest are probably harmless, but no one knows for certain.

Radiation Massive doses of radiation from the atmosphere can cause many congenital problems. The best evidence of this, unfortunately, comes from the results of the atom-bomb explosions in Hiroshima and Nagasaki in 1945; none of the surviving pregnant women who were within a mile of the center of the explosion gave birth to live babies. Three-fourths of the pregnant women who were between one and four miles of the center had spontaneous abortions, stillborn babies, or severely handicapped infants (Apgar and Beck, 1973).

Another source of radiation is x-rays, which twenty years ago were routinely used to diagnose twins and to check on the position of the fetus. Today physicians are much more cautious and check on the fetus by means of the *sonogram,* which uses sound waves instead of radiation to outline the fetal skeleton.

Figure 4.14 *This sonogram reveals the outline of two fetal heads—proof that twins are on the way.*

Small amounts of radition are natural in the environment. The testing of nuclear weapons has added to this, as have such appliances as color televisions and microwave ovens. Most experts believe that the level of radiation that each of us experiences each day is harmless to us and to our unborn children. A marked increase in this radiation level could have serious consequences, however, particularly in terms of chromosomal abnormalities and cancers.

Pollution   Several pollutants in the atmosphere have been proven teratogenic when taken in large doses, among them carbon monoxide and lead. Some studies have shown higher rates of birth defects in populations living in areas that have excessive levels of air pollution. However, a direct cause-and-effect relationship is difficult to prove, partly because women living in areas with high air pollution tend to be poorer than women living away from (or above) the smog. Poverty, rather than pollution, could cause the higher incidence of problems.

Tracking down the source of teratogenic pollution is often difficult. For example, many severely deformed and retarded babies were born to the women of Minamata Bay in Japan over a seven-year period. No one could figure out why. Finally, doctors realized that a nearby industrial plant was discharging mercury into the water. By way of the food chain, the mercury was passed in increasingly concentrated amounts from fish to the women to their babies. Since then, *Minamata disease* has become a synonym for mercury poisoning (Milunsky, 1977).

Figure 4.15 *A woman who ate too much mercury-contaminated fish during pregnancy now cares for the result, her deformed and retarded daughter. She is one of 181 known victims of Minamata disease.*

Pesticides   If inhaled or absorbed through the skin in sufficient amounts, certain pesticides can cause illness. Some can be fatal if swallowed. One agricultural pesticide, DBCP, has been banned because many of the men who used it became sterile. Another, *Agent Orange,* used to defoliate Vietnamese forests, has been blamed by veterans of the Vietnam war for a wide range of birth defects, although the evidence is not definitive because the events occurred too recently and alter-nate interpretations have not been ruled out. With regard to most pesticides, we do not know if doses that are too small to affect adults might still be harmful to the human embryo or fetus. Animal evidence gives cause for concern: many pesticides are harmful or even fatal to unborn rats, rabbits, hamsters, chicks, cats, and dogs, if given to their mothers in large doses (Streitfeld, 1978).

Chemicals in Food and Cosmetics   Most of the thousands of chemicals used in food and cosmetics have never been tested for their possible harmful effects on the embryo or fetus, either in humans or in lower animals (Ames, 1979). Of those tested and held in suspicion, very few have been removed from the market, and those that have been banned are suspected primarily of causing cancer rather than birth defects. Among these are artificial sweeteners, used by millions of pregnant women attempting to keep their weight down, and red dye #2, once used in hundreds of cosmetics and foodstuffs. Both these products can harm the embryo, according to research reports (Streitfeld, 1978).

Pamela Streitfeld's review of the literature (1978) concludes on a plaintive note: "It is unsettling to find that so few [chemicals in the food supply] have been tested for adverse effects, including teratogenicity and mutagenicity." This conclusion can be applied to much of teratology, for many substances need to be tested a great deal more carefully before we know what their effects might be. Psychologists have another complaint about teratogenic testing: most tests look only for physical defects in the victims. Only very rarely are attempts made to discover possible teratogenic links to emotional and learning problems. Yet in recent years it has become increasingly evident that psychological difficulties can be caused by teratogens and that such problems are more widespread and often just as hard to cure as the physical defects. Nevertheless, given the interaction between inborn characteristics and the social environment, many teratogenic problems, whether they involve physical and/or psychological handicaps, can be ameliorated by families, teachers, and members of the community.

The Expectant Parents

Thus far, we have discussed prenatal development in terms of how the mother's health, habits, and environment can affect that development. Now we will look at the other side of the coin: how the prenatal period affects the expectant parents.

The Psychological Impact of Pregnancy

Pregnancy is an enormous emotional experience for most parents-to-be. One study that measured expectant couples' attitudes toward pregnancy found that husbands and wives usually shared the same feelings about an impending birth. Both partners in one marriage might be thrilled; both partners in another marriage might be terrified (Soule, 1974).

For almost every woman, pregnancy is a time of stress and tension (Grimm, 1967), as it is for expectant fathers as well. This is especially true, of course, if the baby is unplanned and unwanted. But any change, even a joyous one, brings stress and readjustment.

The Expectant Mother's Emotions   The moods of a pregnant woman often change from day to day (Colman and Colman, 1977). Certainly, physical and hormonal changes account for some of this fluctuation. But just thinking about the implications of the pregnancy itself is probably as responsible for her emotional variations as physical factors are. On the one side, there is the joy of creating a new life, and the anticipation of holding and loving her baby. On the other side, there is the distress of additional responsibilities and the fear that something might go wrong.

Many pregnant women become unduly concerned about their own physical safety and that of their husband. They have nightmares about death, or cannot ride in a car without imagining a crash. Excessive fear that the fetus is sick or deformed is so common that it has a name, *teratophobia*.

Arthur and Libby Colman (1977), a physician-psychologist team who studied the psychological experience of pregnancy, found that women in each trimester have distinctive emotions:

RESEARCH REPORT   **Stress and Pregnancy**

Some psychologists have developed a scale that attempts to quantify the amount of stress people experience. Each stressful experience is assigned a point value; the more points, the greater the stress. Here is one version, called the Social Readjustment Rating Scale:

Death of a husband or wife	100
Divorce	73
Marital separation	65
Jail term	63
Death of close family member	63
Personal injury or illness	53
Marriage	50
Fired at work	47
Marital reconciliation	45
Retirement	45
Change in the health of family member	44
Pregnancy	40
*Sex difficulties	39
*Gain new family member	39
Business readjustment	39
*Change in financial state	38
Death of a close friend	37
Change to different line of work	36
More or fewer arguments with spouse	35
Mortgage over $10,000	31
Foreclosure of mortgage or loan	30
Change of responsibilities at work	29
Son or daughter leaving home	29
Trouble with in-laws	29
Outstanding personal achievement	28
*Wife begins or stops work	26
Begin or end school	26
*Change in living conditions	25
*Revision of personal habits	24
Trouble with boss	23
Change in work hours or conditions	20
*Change in residence	20
Change in schools	20
Change in recreation	19
Change in church activities	18
Change in social activities	18
Mortgage or loan less than $10,000	17
*Change in sleeping habits	16
More or fewer family gatherings	15
*Change in eating habits	15
Vacation	13
Christmas	12
Minor violations of the law	11

More than 300 points within six months is considered very stressful. A person who experiences this much stress is likely to have a major illness within a year or so (Holmes and Masuda, 1974). Minor problems, such as skin rashes and stomach upsets, also occur frequently when people experience high levels of stress (Holmes and Holmes, 1970).

Pregnancy itself is rated at 40. In addition, several other changes often precede or follow pregnancy by a few months. If all the changes that are asterisked on the list above are experienced during pregnancy, the total score is 327, much higher than most people can easily adjust to.

More recent research has led psychologists to be cautious in using the stress scale. Each person's particular situation and coping skills affect how stressful any life event is (Bieliauskas and Strugar, 1976). A careful review of the literature concluded that, as we would expect, stress associated with threatening events—events that jeopardize or destroy something a person values—is more closely related to mental and physical illness than stress associated with nonthreatening events (Brown et al., 1973a and b). According to these studies, pregnancy, for example, is always stressful, but some pregnancies are much more difficult than others. Some pregnancies mean a loss of freedom and a threat to financial stability; others do not.

Another study found that when a person has few close friends, threatening experiences are much more likely to produce physical and psychological symptoms (Miller et al., 1976). Social support is probably the decisive factor in determining whether pregnancy, birth, and any other complex life experience is too stressful (Cobb, 1976).

---

*The asterisks added here indicate events that often occur during pregnancy.
Source: Holmes and Holmes, 1970

In the first trimester, many women are ambivalent about pregnancy. Even those who wanted the baby sometimes consider abortion; they seem to feel that they may have entered a new stage of life without being ready. At the same time, many women worry about miscarriage, or cannot believe they really are pregnant, despite the positive test results.

Many women also become more involved in their relationship with their own mothers, and temporarily less interested in their husbands. Perhaps they feel that the minor discomforts of early pregnancy, such as nausea and tiredness, and the thrill of carrying new life, are easier for a mother to understand. Also, Masters and Johnson (1966) found that the sexual relationship between husband and wife often ebbs in early pregnancy.

In the second trimester, women usually feel well and the fetus begins to move, two developments that quiet the woman's fears (and sometimes hopes) of miscarriage. At this point, many women become more interested in their husbands. Sexual relationships often improve, not only over the previous few months, but over the months before conception. Many women become concerned with their husband's safety, and want him to be as involved with the pregnancy as they are.

In the third trimester, women become intrigued by the baby. Preparing the baby's room, choosing the best name, and talking to the fetus can take up an amazing amount of time. This is also the period when the simple everyday tasks are difficult to do. Nonetheless, most women are glad they are having a baby, in marked contrast to their mixed reactions in the first trimester.

For both husband and wife, worries and excitement about birth reach a peak during this period. Especially with first babies, almost every couple experiences a "false alarm," thinking that birth is imminent when actually it is still weeks away.

Figure 4.16 *The beginning of the last trimester is probably the easiest and most enjoyable period of pregnancy. The fetus is large enough that others can feel it move, and perhaps even hear the heartbeat, but not yet so large that such simple chores as getting up out of a chair or tying shoes take considerable effort.*

Mother's Emotions and the Fetus   Emotional stress produces physical changes in the mother—such as tension in the muscles and less oxygen and more adrenalin in the bloodstream—that affect the fetus. Some studies show a relationship between the mother's stress during pregnancy and the baby's temperament at birth (Ferreira, 1965). Psychological tension seems related to spontaneous abortion early in pregnancy, and to high blood pressure late in pregnancy.

A direct cause-and-effect relationship between the woman's psychological state and the newborn's mood or health is hard to prove (Sameroff and Chandler, 1975). To attempt to measure emotional stress is difficult enough; to prove that particular consequences were caused by stress rather than by some other factor is virtually impossible. Nervous, worried women may digest food less well or smoke more than relaxed, confident women do—and these factors may affect the fetus more than the adrenalin or other physiological changes associated directly with stress. On the other hand, it may be that it is an abnormal pregnancy or a very active fetus that is making the mother tense and nervous. Or it may be that both conditions exist and are influencing each other in circular fashion. For whatever reason, however, it is safe to conclude that a relaxed and easy pregnancy is good for both mother and child, so factors that increase stress should be avoided (see Table 4.2). While few of these factors are completely under a woman's control, most women can help to make their own pregnancy a less stressful experience. Some women feel happier and healthier during pregnancy than at any other time.

TABLE 4.2   **Some Factors Affecting Expectant Mothers' Stress During Pregnancy**

Less Stress	More Stress
Planned and wanted baby	Unplanned, unwanted baby
Entire family wants baby	Not everyone in family wants baby
Sufficient income for baby	Insufficient income for baby
Sufficient space for baby	Insufficient space for baby
No other children under 3	Has another infant
Good nutrition	Poor nutrition
Good prenatal care	Poor prenatal care
No physical complications	Physical complications (nausea, swelling, high blood pressure, etc.)
Not afraid of birth process	Afraid of birth process
Birth will not mean change of plans or lifestyle	Birth will mean loss of job, schooling, or personal freedom
Assured that there is a very low risk of problem birth or diseased infant	Knows or believes high risk of problem birth or diseased infant
Age is between 18 and 35	Younger than 18, older than 35
Second or third child	First baby, or fourth or more

The Expectant Father's Emotions   Many non-Western cultures assign special status to husbands of pregnant women. Sometimes the expectant father must eat specific foods, or must refrain from certain activities. Anthropologists studying various South American cultures in the first half of the twentieth century were astonished to note the custom of couvade (from the French word for hatching), in which fathers-to-be showed physical symptoms of pregnancy and even shouted and writhed with labor pains during childbirth. The father's efforts were supposed to help the baby to be born (Mead and Newton, 1967).

Social scientists have since learned that many Western fathers experience some form of couvade. One British study found that 11 percent of expectant fathers had symptoms of pregnancy and birth, such as vomiting and abdominal pains, while their wives were pregnant (Trethowan and Conlon, 1965). Other research has found that more than half of all expectant fathers have some sympathetic physical responses to pregnancy (Tanzer and Block, 1976).

Figure 4.17 *One practical way for husbands to show their support for their pregnant wives is to perform birth-preparation exercises along with them. This has an added benefit: it helps work off the extra few pounds that many men gain when their wives become visibly pregnant.*

A man's response to pregnancy is not always sympathetic, however. The Colmans write:

> The most common behavioral problem for the expectant father is simply that of "running away." But it is rarely recognized as such by the man himself or by the people around him. There always seems to be an explanation: business trips, new casual acquaintances, ball games; the pattern develops gradually and extends itself into long absences from home or sexual affairs with other women. [Colman and Colman, 1977]

Some men react in even more destructive ways. Wife-beating is surprisingly common during pregnancy (Gelles, 1975). Richard Gelles lists five possible reasons:

1. *Sexual frustration,* if the husband or wife mistakenly thinks intercourse is wrong during pregnancy.*

2. *Stress,* especially from anticipated economic burdens.

3. *Biochemical changes in the woman,* that make her harder to live with. She might be unusually tired, or she might cry more easily.

4. *An attempt to get rid of the fetus,* by causing an "accidental" miscarriage.

5. *The increased defenselessness* of the pregnant woman.

Clinical psychologists would probably add a sixth, jealousy. According to Karen Horney (1967), men are as likely to experience "womb envy" as women are to experience "penis envy."

---

*Recent medical research now suggests that intercourse in the last month before delivery may increase the risk of infections in the amniotic fluid and of other harmful effects on the baby, such as jaundice and respiratory distress (Naeye, 1979).

Father's Emotions and the Fetus   A man's attitude toward his wife's pregnancy can indirectly affect prenatal development, in that how well the expectant mother takes care of her body may depend on how concerned and supportive her husband is. Psychologists have frequently demonstrated that other people (especially significant others) are crucial in helping someone to change or maintain their behavior (Bandura, 1977; Mischel, 1973). When it comes to husbands and pregnancy, however, this basic fact seems to get overlooked. Husbands are not usually included in conversations between obstetrician and patient, nor are they usually informed about hazards to healthy prenatal growth. Unfortunately, the assumption is often made that the woman is solely responsible for her behavior during pregnancy.

Figure 4.18 *As this father-to-be supports his wife while she does her natural-childbirth exercises, he is preparing for his role in the birth process. Many men hold their wives upright during contractions, which alleviates back pain and makes it easier for the woman to push the baby through the birth canal.*

For instance, when the Food and Drug Administration proposed putting a label on liquor bottles warning of the dangers of excessive drinking during pregnancy, a representative of the liquor industry ridiculed the idea. He said it would be "the breakthrough of the century" if a pregnant alcoholic reduced her drinking because of a printed warning (*The New York Times,* November 23, 1977). But many drinkers can stop, or at least cut down, when they are given sufficient encouragement, as Alcoholics Anonymous has shown. A warning label would be read by expectant fathers as well as expectant mothers; together they might well be able to change their drinking habits.

Preparation for Parenthood

The nine months of pregnancy provide the couple with time to get ready for parenthood. During this period they can develop their relationship with each other by exploring their worries and hopes and disagreements concerning the coming child—before experiencing all the stress of actually having a new infant. At least one childbirth instructor thinks such sharing of feelings is just as important to the new family as is learning about the birth process and practicing breathing techniques (Kitzinger, 1971).

Figure 4.19 *Couples who do all they can to care for their baby-to-be, and who share their fears and hopes during pregnancy, are most likely to weather the stresses of the birth process and of early infancy.*

This prenatal period also gives the couple a chance to learn how to care for an infant, before the nurse hands them one of their own. Some expectant fathers are as eager to learn the how-tos of parenthood as their wives are, but they often have a harder time getting the information and experience they want. One man said that, judging from the books on parenthood he had read, the world was composed only of mothers and sons (Fein, 1976). But obtaining information is important. Fathers with the least knowledge about raising children have the greatest adjustment difficulties after the baby is born (Wente and Crockenberg, 1976).

There is another, more obvious, benefit of sharing information. Prospective parents who understand their feelings about their unborn child and know what they can do to make things go well are more likely to have a healthy, alert baby. By preparing themselves as fully as possible for their new roles, as well as doing all they can to ensure healthy prenatal development, expectant parents are giving their infant a good start in life, even before it is born. Most likely, the baby will return the favor. Healthy, active newborns are much easier to care for.

SUMMARY

From Zygote to Newborn

1. The first two weeks of prenatal growth are the period of the ovum. During this period, the single-celled zygote becomes a multicelled blastula. The blastula consists of a mass of inner cells called the blastocyst, and a surrounding circle of cells, called the trophoblast.

2. The blastula travels down the Fallopian tube, implants itself in the uterine lining, and begins to grow. The trophoblast forms the placenta; the blastocyst becomes the embryo.

3. The period from two to eight weeks after conception is the period of the embryo. The development of the embryo is cephalo-caudal (from the head downward) and proximo-distal (from the inner organs outward).

4. At eight weeks after conception, the future baby is only about an inch long. Yet it already has the organs and features of a human baby, with the exception of the sex organs, which take a few more weeks to develop.

5. From the eighth week after conception until birth is the fetal period. The fetus grows rapidly; muscles develop and bones begin to harden. The sex organs take shape, and the

other organs complete their formation. The fetus attains viability when the brain is sufficiently mature, between the twenty-fourth and twenty-sixth week after conception.

6. The average fetus weighs 2 pounds at the beginning of the third trimester and 7½ pounds at the end. The additional pounds, plus maturation of brain, lungs, and heart, ensure survival for more than 99 percent of all full-term babies.

Nutrition

7. Virtually every complication of prenatal development and birth, including premature and deformed infants, long labor and medical complications, and postnatal depression, occurs more frequently when the pregnant woman is malnourished. We are uncertain of the long-term effects of maternal malnutrition, but babies born to severely malnourished women have fewer brain cells than those born to women who are better nourished.

Hazards to Normal Prenatal Development

8. The identification of teratogens (substances that cause birth defects) is hindered by three facts. First, substances that are teratogenic in animals are not always teratogenic in humans, and vice versa. Second, most pregnant women are exposed to so many teratogens that it is hard to pinpoint which one is responsible for any given defect. Finally, few teratogens harm every fetus who is exposed to them, and most teratogens cause different defects in different babies.

9. Teratogens can affect fetal development throughout pregnancy, but are especially likely to do so in the first eight weeks, the critical period. Some babies, such as males born to malnourished women of low socioeconomic status, are more vulnerable to teratogens than others.

Specific Teratogens

10. Certain diseases and a large number of drugs are teratogenic. For instance, rubella and thalidomide are teratogenic to almost every fetus exposed to them. Recently, two of the most commonly used drugs, cigarettes and alcohol, have been shown to be harmful. Radiation and certain pollutants can also prove harmful in large doses.

The Expectant Parents

11. Pregnancy is stressful for both expectant parents. How they react to that stress affects their baby's future, as well as their relationship to each other.

12. Prospective parents who understand their feelings about their unborn child and are well-informed about prenatal development are more likely to have an alert, healthy baby.

KEY QUESTIONS

What parts of the body develop during the period of the embryo?

What parts of the body develop during the period of the fetus?

How does prenatal nutrition affect development?

What problems complicate research on teratogens?

Why are some fetuses more likely to be affected by teratogens than others?

How do cigarettes and alcohol affect prenatal development?

What is the relationship between stress, pregnancy, and prenatal development?

How do expectant fathers react to pregnancy?

KEY TERMS

period of the ovum	age of viability
period of the embryo	teratogens
period of the fetus	teratology
blastula	critical period
blastocyst	anytime malformations
trophoblast	rubella
implantation	toxoplasmosis
amniotic fluid	congenital syphilis
placenta	preeclampsia
umbilical cord	eclampsia
neural tube	thalidomide
cephalo-caudal development	fetal alcohol syndrome
proximo-distal development	couvade
gender	

RECOMMENDED READINGS

Guttmacher, Alan F. *Pregnancy, birth, and family planning:* New York: Viking, 1973.

Written for expectant parents by a famous obstetrician, this book is filled with facts and reassurance. It emphasizes the pregnant woman's physical condition and problems, but includes material on the father, the fetus, the newborn, and the infertile couple as well.

Null, Gary, Null, Steve, and the staff of the Nutrition Institute of America. *Successful pregnancy.* New York: Pyramid Publications, 1977.

This book describes many hazards to the prenatal development of the baby and suggests how a woman can increase her chances of having a healthy baby. Nutrition is especially emphasized. The book includes charts, tables, and references to specific research.

Seaman, Barbara, and Seaman, Gideon. *Women and the crisis in sex hormones.* New York: Bantam, 1978.

This book discusses the effects of taking sex hormones, forms of contraception, and treatments for menopause. It includes a thorough discussion of DES and oral contraceptives. Although the tone of this book is sometimes strident, the facts and ideas may warrant the anger and concern that the Seamans express.

Colman, Arthur, and Colman, Libby. *Pregnancy: The psychological experience.* New York: Bantam, 1977.

An account of various reactions to pregnancy, this book is based primarily on clinical observations and experiences with discussion groups for expectant parents. The authors psychoanalytic background is apparent in the discussion of dreams and childhood memories.

Price, Jane. *You're not too old to have a baby.* New York: Penguin, 1977.

This book discusses the risks and delights of having a baby after age 30, 35, or even 40. The basic message is that the possible medical problems involved can be controlled with good prenatal care, and that the potential psychological joys outweigh the risks.

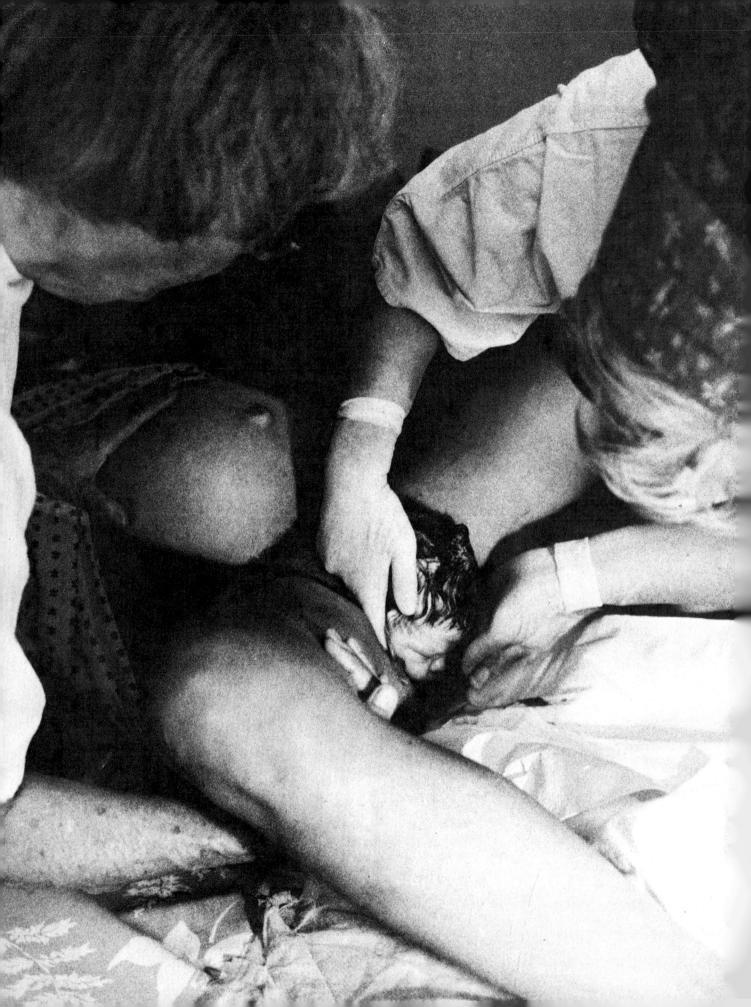

Birth

*We must behave with the most enormous respect
    toward this instant of birth, this fragile moment.
The baby is between two worlds. On a threshold.
    Hesitating.
Do not hurry. Do not press. Allow this child to enter.
What an extraordinary thing: this little creature, no
    longer a fetus, not yet a newborn baby.
This little creature is no longer inside his mother, yet
    she's still breathing for them both.
An elusive, ephemeral moment.
Leave this child. Alone.
Because this child is free—and frightened.
Don't intrude: stay back. Let time pass.
Grant this moment its slowness, and its gravity.*

Frederick Leboyer
Birth Without Violence

CHAPTER 5

True or False?

The common practice of administering pure oxygen to premature infants was discovered to cause blindness.

Medication given to mothers during the birth process seems to have a calming effect on their babies as well, making them peaceful and amenable for several days after birth.

Because 98 percent of the births in the United States take place in hospitals, this country has the lowest infant mortality rate in the world.

Maternal depression soon after the birth of a child is almost always a sign that the newborn was unwanted.

A mother's nurturing response to her newborn is automatic, triggered by maternal instinct.

In the animal kingdom, where there is no question of "unwanted" babies, mothers will go to any lengths to care for their young.

Parents of premature children often have difficulty feeling love for their babies.

Birth can be simple or complicated, brief or prolonged, a "natural" event or a medical emergency. Some describe it as fulfilling; others as traumatic. Some speak of ecstasy and rapture, others of terror and pain.

No matter how smooth the course of the birth process itself, the moment of birth marks the most dramatic transition of the entire life span. No longer insulated from the harsh conditions of the outside world, abruptly deprived of the nourishment and oxygen that have been provided through the umbilical cord, the fetus is thrust into the world, totally dependent upon others.

Birth is a transforming experience for parents as well. For people having their first child, the event is marked by the sudden realization "I am a mother" or "I am a father" and by a more immediate sense of the responsibilities, worries, sorrows, and joys that go with being a parent. If there are already one or more children in the family, their lives, too, may be dramatically altered by the new arrival. We will now look more closely at this moment of transition, and at the first days of life for newborns and their families.

The Normal Birth

As you read the following account of the birth process, bear in mind that each birth is unique. What we describe here as "normal birth" is really an approximation of an overall average that takes into account many unusual and abnormal experiences.

Preparation

In the last months of pregnancy, the fetus and the uterus prepare for the birth process. The muscles of the uterus contract and relax at irregular intervals, gaining tone and widening the cervix a centimeter or two. Sometime during the last month, most fetuses change position for the last time, moving so that their heads are in the mother's pelvic cavity. They are now in position to be born in the usual way, headfirst.

Waiting   For many parents, waiting for birth is the hardest aspect of the entire pregnancy. As one expectant father reported:

> Sharon was getting bored with her big belly. She was at the stage where she was getting food stains on her clothing, as if this immense protuberance wasn't really part of her. Her attitude was "Come on Baby, hurry up." But we were both very anxious. Not about the birth itself . . . [about] the change in our lives. We were beginning to snap at each other. [Quoted in Bing, 1970]

Many women have trouble sleeping, walking, or even standing during the last days of pregnancy, and this adds to their impatience. One woman writes:

> When I couldn't see my feet or walk up to the counter close, I'd have this sensation of "Wait a minute, where is how it used to be?" The baby was late, and every morning past the due date I'd wake up, look down at that mound and say "Hey, kid, there is one too many of us in this body." [Boston Women's Health Book Collective, 1978]

Finally, about 266 days after conception, the birth process begins when the uterus contracts at regular intervals to push the fetus out.

The Birth Process

The period from the first regular contraction until the cervix is fully open, so that the baby's head can squeeze through, is called the first stage of labor. This stage usually lasts about eight hours for a first-born child and four to six hours in subsequent births (Danforth, 1977), although there is much variation—from a few minutes to a few days (Guttmacher, 1973).

Once the cervix is dilated enough for the baby's head to pass through, a process called transition begins: the baby's head moves from the uterus to the vaginal opening (see Figure 5.1). This is the most difficult stage for the woman to control

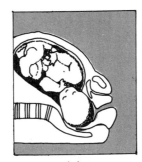
(a)

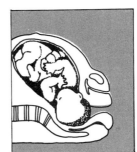
(b)

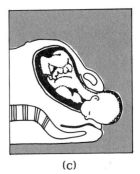
(c)

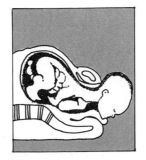
(d)

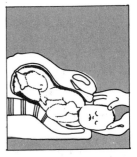
(e)

Figure 5.1 (a) *End of the first stage of labor. Baby's head is moving through the cervix.* (b) *Transition. The baby's head is moving through the "birth canal," the vagina.* (c–e) *The second stage of labor. The baby's head is moving through the opening of the vagina* (c), *it emerges completely* (d), *and then the head is turned so the rest of the body slides out* (e).

with breathing or relaxation techniques. Luckily, it usually lasts only a few minutes before the start of the second stage of labor, in which the baby's head moves through the vagina. Soon the skin surrounding the opening of the vagina stretches as the head emerges. Moments later, the rest of the body follows. The second stage of labor is over, often less than an hour after it began.

The birth process, however, is not quite finished. Minutes after the baby is born, the third stage of labor occurs when contractions quickly expel the placenta. Except in first births, the entire birth process usually lasts less than six hours.

The Newborn's First Minutes

Newborns, or *neonates,* usually breathe and cry as soon as they are born. The neonate's heart rate, breathing, muscle tone, circulation, and reflexes are noted at one minute and five minutes after birth, and rated according to a ten-point system called the Apgar scale. The umbilical cord is cut, and silver nitrate is put into the newborn's eyes to prevent blindness in case the mother has gonorrhea, a type of venereal disease. Then the baby is weighed, measured, and examined for any abnormalities.

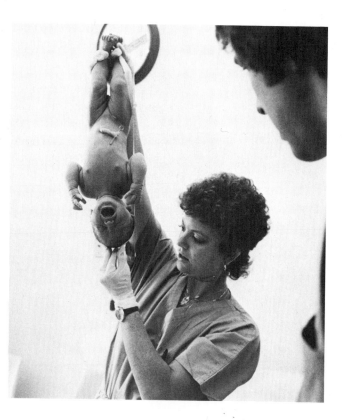

Figure 5.2 *Measuring the neonate is one of the standard procedures of a hospital birth.*

The Newborn's Appearance   Many normal neonates look abnormal to someone whose image of a newborn comes from baby-food advertisements. Infants are frequently born with misshapen heads, flattened noses, and body bruises acquired in birth. Often the head will appear abnormal because the bones of the skull overlapped during the birth process, in order to make the baby's head narrow enough to squeeze through. There is no lasting damage when this happens, because the infant's skull is flexible; its bones do not fuse until the *fontanelle* ("soft spot") on the baby's head has closed several months after birth.

A CLOSER LOOK   **The Apgar Scale**

Dr. Virginia Apgar worked in the delivery room of a large hospital. She saw many newborns who needed immediate medical aid but did not get it, partly because the medical personnel who specialize in obstetrics are trained to care for pregnant women rather than newborn babies. Before a pediatrician could examine a baby, precious minutes might be lost.

Apgar subsequently developed a method of diagnosing newborn distress that is simple enough and quick enough to be used even when the mother's condition demands full attention. Someone need only look at the five standard characteristics, rate each from 0 to 2, and add up the total. If the score is 7 or better, the newborn is not in danger; if the score is below 7, the infant needs help establishing normal breathing; if the total is below 4, the baby is in critical condition and needs immediate expert attention (Danforth, 1977).

In many hospitals, "Paging Dr. Apgar" is the code used to summon the pediatrician on duty to the delivery room because of a pediatric emergency. The Apgar scale, now used in almost every American hospital, helps to save thousands of new lives each year.

The Apgar Scale

Characteristic	0	1	2
Heart rate	absent	slow (below 100)	rapid (over 100)
Respiratory effort (breathing)	absent	irregular, slow	good, baby is crying
Muscle tone	flaccid, limp	weak, inactive	strong, active
Color	blue, pale	body pink, extremities blue	entirely pink
Reflex irritability	no response	grimace	coughing, sneezing, crying

Source: Apgar, 1953.

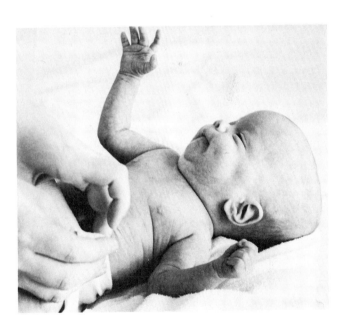

Figure 5.3 *This hairless and virtually chinless infant still has the pointed head that resulted when his skull bones squeezed together to allow the head to pass through the mother's pelvic cavity.*

Often the newborn's skin is red, splotchy, or wrinkled. Some newborns have no hair; others have hair on their faces and bodies as well as their heads. All these characteristics are temporary; the Apgar score is a much more accurate indication of neonatal health than the newborn's external appearance.

The Brazelton Scale   Another scale, the Brazelton Neonatal Behavior Assessment Scale, is designed to assess the maturation of the central nervous system and the way the infant responds to people (Brazelton, 1974). It lists twenty-six items of behavior (such as reaction to cuddling, orientation to the examiner's voice and face, trembling, startling, and irritability) that are rated on a nine-point scale. In addition, the strength of twenty reflexes is rated on a four-point scale. (A reflex, such as an eye blink, is an automatic response involving only one part of the body.)

The Brazelton scale can be used to assess the effects of birth problems and of any anesthesia given to the mother. It is also used to spot babies who are likely to have certain psychological difficulties in the years ahead. For instance, a baby who appears not to react to people might, as a result, receive insufficient parental attention and therefore develop emotional problems. Once babies "at risk" are spotted, their parents can learn how to provide stimulation and comfort that may prevent the difficulties predicted by the scale (Als and Brazelton, 1975).

Reflexes in the Newborn

Babies are born with dozens of reflexes, some indicative of brain maturity, and some essential for life itself (Kessen et al., 1970). Testing the strength of a newborn's reflexes is part of every standard medical and psychological measure of neonatal health, including the Apgar and Brazelton scales.

For example, the following five reflexes are present in normal, full-term new-borns. (1) When their feet are stroked, their toes fan upward (Babinski reflex). (2) When their feet touch a flat surface, they move as if to walk (stepping reflex). (3) When they are held horizontally on their stomachs, their arms and legs stretch out (swimming reflex). (4) When something touches their palms, their hands grip tightly (grasping reflex). (5) When someone bangs on the table they are lying on, newborns usually fling their arms outward and then bring them together on their chests, as if to hold on to something, and they may cry and open their eyes wide (the Moro reflex). The presence of all these reflexes is a sign that the baby's brain and body are functioning normally. Many reflexes, including these five, disappear in the first months of life. Premature babies usually develop these reflexes weeks after birth, and lose them later.

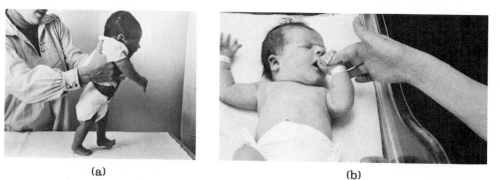

(a)   (b)

Figure 5.4 (a) *At 3 weeks, this infant's tiny legs are much too small to support his body, but the stepping reflex occurs nonetheless.* (b) *This newborn demonstrates two reflexes as she holds on to her mother's finger (grasping reflex) and turns toward whatever brushed her cheek (rooting reflex).* (c) *With startled expression and limbs flung outward, this 3-month-old illustrates the Moro reflex. In two months, this reflex will disappear.* (d) *One of the breathing reflexes is the yawn, which is triggered by a low concentration of oxygen in the blood and forces the person to take a deep breath.*

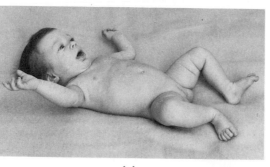

(c)   (d)

Three sets of reflexes are critical for survival and become stronger as the newborn matures. One set helps the newborn maintain constant body temperature: when infants are cold, they cry, shiver, and tuck their legs close to their bodies. A second set of reflexes ensures adequate nourishment. One of these is the sucking reflex, which causes newborns to suck anything that touches their lips—fingers, toes, blankets, and rattles, as well as nipples of various shapes. Another is the rooting reflex, which helps babies find a nipple by causing them to turn their heads and start to suck whenever something brushes against their cheek. *Swallowing* is another important reflex that aids feeding, as is *crying* when the stomach is empty.

The third set of reflexes maintains an adequate supply of oxygen. The most obvious is the breathing reflex. Normal newborns take their first breath even before the umbilical cord, with its supply of oxygen, is cut. For the first few days, breathing is somewhat irregular, and reflexive *hiccups, sneezes,* and *spit-ups* are common, as the newborn tries to coordinate breathing, sucking, and swallowing.

Variations and Problems

Unfortunately, the birth process is not always as short and simple as it is in the foregoing description. Variations in the position of the fetus, the timing of the birth, and the use of medical assistance can create immediate complications and, occasionally, lifelong handicaps.

Position of the Fetus

About 96 percent of the time, the fetus is born headfirst. However, about one fetus in twenty-five positions itself for birth by sitting upright, with the buttocks resting on the mother's pelvis, and comes out bottom first. This is called a breech birth. Most breech babies are completely healthy, but some suffer brain damage caused by the complications of such deliveries. For example, about one breech baby in fifty has cerebral palsy (Apgar and Beck, 1973).

Much rarer is the baby who is positioned crossways; when babies are in such a transverse presentation, they must be turned around in the uterus before they can be born, or must be delivered by a Cesarean section.

Anoxia

Another birth complication is anoxia, a temporary lack of oxygen. There are many causes of anoxia, including mucus in the baby's throat after birth, or an overreaction to anesthesia used during birth. Anoxia also occurs when the umbilical cord becomes squeezed or tangled in the birth process, cutting off this source of oxygen before the head has emerged and the baby can breathe air. This occasionally happens in headfirst births, but it is more frequent in breech births, in which several minutes elapse between the time the baby's body, including the umbilical cord, is born, and the time the head emerges. Whether a particular newborn is damaged by a temporary lack of oxygen depends on the severity and duration of anoxia, the maturity and health of the fetus, and the presence of anesthesia in the fetal bloodstream.

According to a review of the literature by Sameroff and Chandler (1975), what seems most important for the long-term development of babies who have experienced anoxia is the environment they grow up in. In one study they cite, several hundred children who were without oxygen in the minutes before or after birth were tested repeatedly (Corah et al., 1965). In the first days of life, they scored poorly on tests of cognitive development. By age 3, however, many of them performed normally, especially if the oxygen deprivation occurred before rather than after birth. By age 7, virtually all of them did as well as another group of children from the same socioeconomic background who had not experienced anoxia. It was Corah's conclusion that whatever retardation anoxia may have caused in the early months was reversed by the stimulation of the home environment.

Timing of the Birth

The usual way to calculate when a baby is due is to count 280 days from the first day of the woman's last menstrual period. Such a calculation assumes that ovulation occurs fourteen days after the beginning of a period, an assumption that can be off by several days or weeks, especially if the woman's menstrual periods are irregular. Actually, only one baby in twenty-five is born exactly on the due date, and babies born within three weeks of the due date are considered "timely" (Guttmacher, 1973).

TABLE 5.1 **When Will the Baby Be Born?**

Week after Last Menstrual Period	Chance of Baby Being Born that Week*
28	1:625
29	1:625
30	1:525
31	1:240
32	1:240
33	1:135
34	1:115
35	1:58
36	1:39
37	1:22
38	1:11
39	1:5
40	1:3.5
41	1:5.67
42	1:12
43	1:34
44	1:74
45	1:140
46	1:140

*Based on more than 17,000 pregnancies carried at least twenty-eight weeks after the woman's last menstrual period.
Source: Guttmacher, 1973.

Low-Birth-Weight Babies Normally, babies born more than three weeks before the due date are considered premature. Partly because errors in calculating the time of conception are common, the World Health Organization of the United Nations uses weight, rather than due date, to define prematurity. All newborns who weigh less than 2500 grams (5½ pounds) are considered premature. By this definition, about 8 percent of all North American babies are premature.

Actually, there are two types of newborns who weigh less than 2500 grams. Although both are labeled "premature," the infants in one case are in fact born close to the due date, but they weigh less than a usual full-term neonate. They are called small-for-dates.

The second type of low-birth-weight baby, the one born early, is more common. Such babies show many signs of immaturity, in addition to low birth weight. Often they have fine, downy hair (*lanugo*) and a thick waxy coating (*vernix*) on their faces or bodies. If born more than six weeks early, their nipples are not yet visible, and if they are boys, their testicles have not descended into the scrotum. Their reflexes are immature, as well.

Most of these characteristics pose no serious problem. Vernix and lanugo disappear, and nipples and testicles emerge naturally within a few days or weeks. However, the immaturity of the reflexes can be critical.

Even full-term babies sometimes need a few days to coordinate all their reflexes and to suck and breathe without experiencing such difficulties as spitting up or hiccupping. But premature babies need more than a few days. They need special equipment and skilled care to sustain life until their reflexes mature. They must be placed in heated isolettes to maintain their body heat and to keep them free from infection. ("Isolette" is a more accurate term than the traditional "incubator," since the device serves to isolate and protect, rather than incubate or hatch, the neonate.) If they are more than six weeks early, they must be fed intravenously.

The most critical problem for premature babies, however, is oxygen. Babies born more than five weeks prematurely usually do not produce enough surfactin, a substance that coats the lungs and aids normal reflexive breathing. Because of this, premature babies often breathe irregularly, or even stop breathing for no apparent reason. This problem is called the respiratory distress syndrome or *hyaline membrane disease,* and is the leading cause of death for North American premature babies (Evans and Glass, 1976).

Causes of Low Birth Weight Prematurity can result from many factors. One common cause is multiple pregnancies. Twins usually gain weight normally until eight weeks before the due date, then gain more slowly than the single fetus does. The average twin is born three weeks early, and weighs less than 5½ pounds. Triplets are usually born even earlier and weigh even less.

Figure 5.5 *This fifteenth-century painting of a mother presented with her alert quadruplets shortly after they were born is a charming fantasy. Until the twentieth century, quadruplets always died in the first days after birth. Even today, multiple-birth infants are less likely to survive than single-born infants are.*

Often a "small-for-dates" baby is small because the mother was malnourished, or because the placenta and the umbilical cord did not function properly. Prenatal infections and genetic handicaps can also cause small or immature neonates.

The incidence of low-birth-weight babies follows socioeconomic patterns, with a rate of prematurity among lower-class mothers twice that of upper-class mothers, primarily because poor women are more likely to be malnourished, ill, or have inadequate prenatal care. Age is also a factor: teenage mothers are twice as likely to give birth to babies weighing under 1500 grams (3 pounds, 4 ounces) as women between the ages of 25 and 30. However, neither wealth nor maturity can guarantee the delivery of a full-term infant or the survival of a premature one. While Jacqueline Kennedy was First Lady, she gave birth to her third child, a son named Patrick. He was five and a half weeks premature, suffered respiratory distress syndrome, and died.

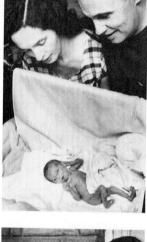

Figure 5.6 *The survival of 28-ounce Stella Waltz, whose breech birth was two and a half months premature, was doubtful at first. However, as this photo of her at 18 months shows, once she lived through her first weeks and came home from the hospital, she developed normally. Most children who survive birth complications do likewise.*

Consequences of Low Birth Weight Babies who weigh less than 2500 grams have more medical problems than full-term babies. One reason is that many of the same conditions that cause low birth weight, such as an ill mother or a genetically handicapped fetus, also cause other complications that impair the health of the newborn. In addition, the birth process itself is more likely to harm a premature baby than a full-term infant. Medication given to the mother during birth usually causes no serious damage to a full-term baby, nor is the normal newborn harmed by a few moments without oxygen. However, premature babies are more likely to be damaged by drugs or anoxia. Too much oxygen can harm them as well.

This last fact was discovered when the number of children suffering a kind of blindness known as *retrolental fibroplasia* rose alarmingly in the 1940s, especially among babies who weighed less than 3½ pounds . Researchers realized that many of these children had been placed in isolettes supplied with concentrated oxygen to help them breathe. This excess of oxygen had caused a growth of fibrous tissue that detached the retina of the eye, causing blindness. By 1957, most hospitals had taken measures to protect premature babies from this problem, and the number of blind children dramatically declined.

For very small babies, life itself may be uncertain. Since they are less resistant to infection, a mild cold can make them seriously ill. Almost all premature babies who weigh between 5 and 5½ pounds survive, but most of the infants who weigh under 3 pounds die. A few hospitals have highly specialized nurseries and are sometimes able to save the lives of even 2-pound (900-gram) babies. For babies this small, the number of weeks of gestation is more crucial than birth weight (Stewart and Reynolds, 1974).

Experts used to believe that premature babies were more likely to have learning difficulties than full-term babies (Drillien, 1964). However, recent research has found that unless they are brain-damaged, premature babies are just as capable as their full-term contemporaries from the same social class who are the same *conceptual age,* that is, the same number of weeks past conception (Tilford, 1976; Goldstein et al., 1976; Hunt and Rhodes, 1977). Even premature babies who weigh less than 3 pounds (1360 grams) at birth usually develop normally in height, weight, and intelligence, although one in ten of these tiny babies is handicapped (Stewart and Reynolds, 1974). Even if they began life in an isolette, fighting for each breath, children who are given a good education by a loving family usually develop well (Sameroff and Chandler, 1975).

Postmature Babies About 10 percent of all babies are called postmature because they are born two or more weeks after the due date. Postmature babies sometimes weigh less than they would have if they had been born at term, because the placenta often becomes less efficient after the full nine months of pregnancy. The main concern for postmature fetuses is that the inefficiency of the aging placenta might make the baby severely malnourished. This would affect the brain development as well as body size (Evans and Glass, 1976). However, obstetricians hesitate to induce labor for postmature babies, unless tests show that the fetus is losing weight or manifesting other signs of distress (Danforth, 1977). Many "late" babies are completely healthy and develop normally.

Medical Procedures

In every developed country, thousands of babies are saved each year because of the special procedures and facilities that hospitals have available for newborns. Because hospitals are better prepared for medical emergencies than any home could be, most American women choose to have their babies there: 98 percent of all American births occur in hospitals.

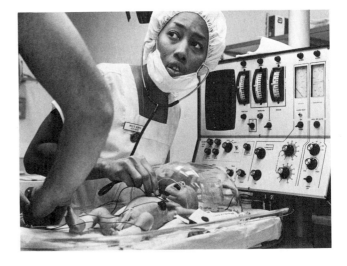

Figure 5.7 *Prenatal monitoring can determine if antibodies in the maternal blood supply are destroying fetal blood cells. When this happens, early delivery and immediate blood transfusions can save the baby's life. In this photo, a nurse checks a newborn's heartbeat while a doctor prepares the baby's first blood transfusion.*

Several medical practices save maternal and neonatal lives, including induced labor, forceps delivery, Cesarean section, fetal monitoring, and the use of drugs during the birth process. However, each of these practices can also cause problems.

Induced Labor If continuing the pregnancy endangers the health of the mother or the fetus, or if the fetus is several weeks postmature, the obstetrician may decide to use a procedure known as induced labor. In this procedure, uterine contractions are initiated either by giving the mother a hormone (called oxytocin) or by breaking the membranes of the placenta.

Labor is also sometimes induced for convenience, for example, when the obstetrician is scheduled to go on vacation, or when the parents want to be sure their older child's babysitter is available. This is unwise, for babies born after induction of labor have a higher rate of medical problems (Macfarlane, 1977).

Forceps Delivery   A pair of *forceps* consists of two pieces of metal, shaped like two large flat spoons. They are designed to hold the fetal head so that it can be pulled down and out of the birth canal during the second stage of labor (see Figure 5.7). A forceps delivery can be very helpful if the fetus is getting too little oxygen or experiencing too much pressure on its head, which is sometimes the case in a breech birth, or in a headfirst birth if the head is wide and the pelvis narrow. Great care is needed, however, for brain damage can result from misapplied forceps.

Figure 5.8 *Obstetrical forceps are two large, spoon-shaped blades that are gently placed around the baby's head to help pull it out of the birth canal. Forceps applied relatively late in the birth process, called "low forceps" and illustrated here, are much less hazardous than "high forceps," used before the fetal head has begun to emerge.*

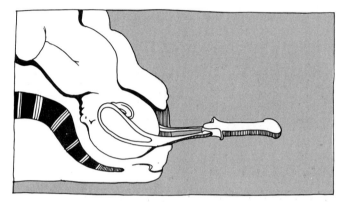

Cesarean Section   A Cesarean section is a surgical operation whereby a doctor cuts open the abdomen and uterus to remove the baby. Thirty years ago this operation was unusual because it was associated with many complications. Today medical techniques have made the Cesarean section almost as safe as vaginal delivery. By using this procedure, doctors can often deliver the baby less than five minutes after beginning general anesthesia, thus preventing the hazards of too much medication.

Consequently, Cesareans have become more common. In the United States today, 16 percent of all babies are delivered by this method (Hausknecht and Heilman, 1978), compared to 5 percent in 1968 (Donovan, 1977). Breech babies, twins, large babies born to small women, and babies who show distress during the last weeks of pregnancy or the first stage of labor are often delivered by Cesarean. Hospitals that specialize in high-risk pregnancies deliver 20 to 25 percent of all babies this way.

Fetal Monitoring   New methods for monitoring the growth and health of the fetus have allowed doctors to know when to use induction, or forceps, or Cesareans. One device of fetal monitoring, the sonogram, is similar to an x-ray but uses sound waves rather than radiation to measure the size and position of the fetus. Amniocentesis, discussed in Chapter 3 as a way to learn in mid-pregnancy if the fetus is normal, is also used to assess fetal health in the last weeks of pregnancy. The extracted amniotic fluid can be analyzed for the presence of surfactin (determining if the lungs are sufficiently mature to sustain normal breathing once the baby is born), for meconium (fecal matter, a sign of distress if the fetus expels it before birth), or for sensitivity to the mother's blood type (which could eventually cause fetal death). Information from these techniques helps answer two important questions: whether the fetus is mature enough to survive outside the uterus and whether the condition of the fetus dictates that birth should occur quickly, before spontaneous contractions begin.

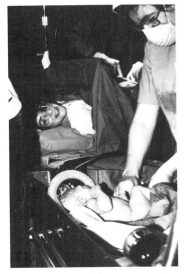
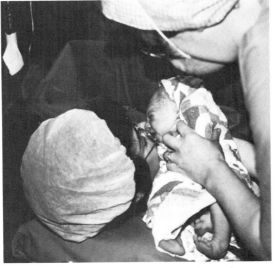
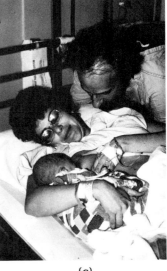

(a)   (b)   (c)

Figure 5.9 (a) *Moments after giving birth by Cesarean, this mother watches her infant receive oxygen and identifying arm and leg bands, while the doctor begins the process of sewing up her incision.* (b) *After the five-minute Apgar score is totaled and the newborn is found not to be in danger, his mother holds and kisses him for the first time.* (c) *In the recovery room, the infant receives his first meal from his mother, as the father looks on. This family is fortunate: many hospitals ban fathers not only from the delivery room but from the recovery room as well.*

Other monitoring methods allow doctors to keep track of the birth process itself. The woman can wear a special belt that measures how long and how strong the contractions are. Once the amniotic sac has broken and the head is in the birth position, an electrode placed on the scalp of the fetus provides a continuous record of the heartbeat. If the fetal heart rate slows down, indicating that oxygen is inadequate, an emergency Cesarean or forceps delivery can be performed; if contractions are too weak, oxytocin can be given to the mother to make them stronger and more frequent.

These monitoring techniques not only signal the need for medical assistance but also help doctors avoid unnecessary intervention (McCleary, 1974). However, fetal-monitoring equipment should not always be used, because the special techniques can make the pregnant woman tense. Tension slows down contractions, prolonging labor. In this way, fetal monitoring can cause, rather than prevent, fetal distress.

Medication In fact, none of the medical procedures just described is risk-free. All are criticized by advocates of natural childbirth, and none is used routinely by good obstetricians. However, the sharpest criticism is directed at a procedure that *is* done routinely—the use of medication during labor. Less than one North American woman in ten has a baby without drugs to speed up contractions or lessen pain.

Most of the problems that researchers have linked to obstetric medication in healthy, full-term babies are not life-threatening. But they do affect the relationship between newborns and the world around them. It appears, for example, that the more anesthesia mothers are given, the more difficulty their babies have getting used to noises (Vander Maelen et al., 1975) and the more irritable they are in the days after birth (Standley et al., 1974).

One study that covered the first month of life reported on the development of forty-four normal infants whose mothers had all received some medication during labor. In the first few days after birth, the babies born to the more heavily medicated mothers were less responsive to their surroundings and harder to cuddle. Although these problems decreased during the first month, some other effects were more apparent at the end of the month than at the beginning. For example, these same babies smiled least (Aleksandrowicz and Aleksandrowicz, 1974).

Similar results were found by Yvonne Brackbill and her colleagues (Conway and Brackbill, 1970; Brackbill, 1977; Brackbill and Broman, 1979). Babies whose mothers had been given relatively potent medication showed slower muscle development, poorer vision, and less mature nervous systems than babies whose mothers had had mild medication. These problems were still apparent at retesting, one, four, eight, and twelve months after birth. Inhaled anesthetics, such as nitrous oxide, were most likely to affect development.

A CLOSER LOOK   ## Drugs Used During Birth

Many drugs are commonly used during childbirth: *anesthetics* inhibit sensation; *analgesics* reduce pain; *sedatives* induce relaxation; and a fourth group, *stimulants*, start or strengthen contractions.

This four-part classification makes obstetric medicine seem simpler than it actually is, for there are thousands of specific drugs and many ways to use them. For instance, all anesthetics produce *anesthesia*, which is a loss of feeling. But a woman might be given *general anesthesia* (perhaps by inhaling nitrous oxide to make her unconscious during the entire birth process), or *local anesthesia* (such as an injection of novocaine) to numb the skin around the vagina while an incision or tear is being sewn up. Both are anesthetics, but the reason for their use, the amount administered, and when they are given are quite different.

The effects of various drugs also differ. Large doses given early in labor are more likely to harm the mother and fetus than small doses administered just before birth. Then, too, women often receive a combination of drugs: If labor is

speeded up by stimulants, contractions become more painful, increasing the need for analgesics.

The effects of a combination of drugs are generally less predictable and more harmful than the effects of a single drug.

Virtually all obstetrical medication enters the mother's bloodstream and rapidly crosses the placenta into the baby's blood supply (Bowes, 1970). Several studies have shown that babies born to mothers who received relatively large doses of obstetrical medication are more likely to have problems at birth and in the first days of life. The most serious of these is breathing difficulties, a problem more common among premature infants than among full-term babies. However, other studies show no such harmful effects when the drugs are carefully administered (Bowes, 1970; Aleksandrowicz, 1974).

How can birth medication have a greater effect several days or weeks after birth than in the first hours? Newborns are slow in ridding their bodies of wastes. Consequently, a drug that passes from the mother's body in a matter of hours might stay with the baby for days. The drug becomes concentrated in the newborn's tissues, dissipating gradually over several weeks as the baby's circulation and kidneys function more efficiently (Caldwell, 1976). Even when the drug is out of the system, babies may continue to be affected because of the slow start they had in responding to the environment or in establishing a relationship with their parents.

Conclusions.   Specific conclusions about drug use in labor are often controversial (Federman and Yang, 1976; Yang et al., 1976; Kolata, 1979). Obviously, some drugs are more beneficial than harmful, and some babies show no harmful effects from drugs given to their mothers in labor (Horowitz et al., 1977). However, most psychologists would agree with three general conclusions.

1. To determine the effects of any drug, infant intellectual and emotional development in the weeks after birth should be studied as much as physical health at birth.

2. Until more is known about the specific effects of particular drugs, all medication should be used sparingly.

3. To minimize the need for medication, pregnant women should learn psychological methods of pain relief.

Many psychologists stress the emotional advantage of giving birth without unnecessary medical intervention (e.g., Sugarman, 1977). If the mother participates actively in the birth process, and feels well immediately after the birth, she is more likely to feel pleased with herself and with her newborn. If she does not have to overcome the aftereffects of medication or the pain of healing incisions, she is more able to feed and care for her infant, who in turn will be more responsive. Such a beginning helps the establishment of the mother-infant bond.

Birth Problems and Later Handicaps

All the birth problems discussed in this section have been linked to later intellectual and emotional difficulties in the babies who experience them. However, as you now realize, a correlation between two factors does not prove that one causes the other. A difficult birth may make a child more vulnerable, but later intellectual and emotional difficulties are likely to result only if the prenatal and postnatal circumstances add to the vulnerability.

According to two careful reviews of the research, most children overcome birth problems and develop normally as long as two important criteria are met: there must be no demonstrable brain damage in the days after birth, and the home environment must be good (Sameroff and Chandler, 1975; Balow et al., 1975–1976).

Many of the early studies that showed a direct link between temporary birth problems and permanent learning disabilities did not control for multiple birth problems or for socioeconomic class. For instance, some studies show that premature babies are more likely than full-term babies to have reading problems to age 6; but they are also more likely to experience other birth complications, more likely to be male, and more likely to have low socioeconomic status, all correlates of early reading problems. It would be foolish to decide that prematurity caused the problem without first taking into account all the other variables.

For some children, the parents' attitude about birth complications may serve to perpetuate the problem. Arnold Sameroff (1975) points out that when an infant is considered abnormal in birth history, appearance, or behavior, the parents may treat that baby differently than they would a normal newborn. The result may be a self-fulfilling prophecy, for children raised as if they are abnormal are likely to reflect that fact in their development.

Alternatives A growing recognition of the importance of parental attitudes toward birth and the newborn is one reason many North American communities now have alternatives to the traditional hospital setting, either a special maternity center that has been designed to be homelike, or facilities such as the Santa Cruz birth center, which helps couples have their babies at home (Lang, 1972). Obviously, having a baby at home seems hazardous to most Americans, since only 2 percent of American births occur there. However, complications necessitating medical assistance occur only about once in every ten births.

Birth in the Netherlands

In some countries where many babies are born at home, the rate of maternal and infant mortality is lower than in the United States. The Netherlands is an outstanding example. The overall infant mortality rate in Holland is one of the lowest in the world: in 1973 the death rate for babies under 28 days was 10.3 per thousand live births, significantly lower than the 1973 rate of 13.0 per thousand in the United States.

In that year, 99,000 Dutch babies were born at home and 98,000 babies were born in hospitals (Macfarlane, 1977). The Dutch do not hesitate to use hospitals when necessary: women in high-risk categories (for example, diabetics, or women over 40 or under 17) are discouraged from giving birth at home. And when complications do appear in the process of home birth, a special ambulance with emergency obstetrical equipment speeds the mother and baby to the hospital, treating them en route.

The 1973 death rate in Holland for home-born babies was 4.5 per thousand, compared to 16.3 per thousand for hospital births. Of course, the main reason the death rate was higher for hospital births is that women with prenatal complications are usually taken to the hospital to have their babies. Nonetheless, the remarkably low mortality rate for home births shows that home births need not always be risky.

Advocates of home births believe that the Netherlands' overall record is so good precisely because so many deliveries occur at home, free of medical intervention and many of the infections or diseases that are common in hospitals. Another advantage of home birth is that the mother is often more relaxed than she would be in a hospital, making labor quicker and easier on both mother and child.

However, the Dutch statistics do not necessarily prove that home births are better, for there are other explanations for the low death rate. For one thing, the Dutch are healthier in general than Americans. Mortality statistics show that even after age 1, the Dutch citizen is somewhat more likely to survive than the American citizen of the same age and sex (United Nations Demographic Yearbook, 1977).

Another reason for the low death rate in Dutch births may be the attitude of Dutch obstetricians. As G. J. Kloosterman, Professor of Obstetrics at the University of Amsterdam, put it: "Childbirth in itself is a natural phenomenon and, in the large majority of cases, needs no interference whatsoever . . . only close observation, moral support, and protection against human meddling" (quoted in Macfarlane, 1977). An attitude like this is difficult to export: most American doctors, hospitals, and parents-to-be *expect* some "interference" when a baby is born.

The Birth Experience

The moment of birth changes or expands the identity of every person in the family. How each one's identity is modified may be profoundly influenced by the first minutes and days after birth.

The Baby's Experience

How does it feel to be born? Buddha called birth one of the inevitable great sufferings of human existence. Otto Rank, a psychoanalyst, believed that the experience of leaving the uterus, where food, warmth, quiet, and oxygen are abundant, and entering a harsh world of hunger, cold, noise, and breathing difficulties causes a birth trauma that results in lifelong fear and anxiety (Rank, 1929). Although on the face of it Rank's theory might seem probable, there is no scientific proof for it—and, in fact, it seems to be contradicted by a number of observations.

For one thing, many medical procedures that are very painful for older children, such as circumcision or the setting of a broken bone, produce very few cries from newborns. This suggests that newborns are much less sensitive to pain. In addition, if newborns are held securely next to their mother's body or wrapped snugly in a soft blanket immediately after birth, they quickly become peaceful and curious— not the usual reaction after a traumatic experience. It just may be that newborns are too immature to feel much pain.

Gentle Birth   Nevertheless, there are many who feel that the first moments of life are often made unnecessarily difficult. Indeed, the French obstetrician Frederick Leboyer describes many common obstetrical practices as the "torture of the innocents" (Leboyer, 1975). Such rituals as holding newborns upside down by their heels, slapping or spanking them, setting them on a cold metal scale, putting silver nitrate in their eyes, separating them from their mothers immediately, and startling them with the bright lights and loud noises of the typical delivery room are only some of the procedures he condemns.

Leboyer is particularly critical of the usual habit of cutting the umbilical cord the moment the baby is born. This practice makes newborns instantly dependent on air ("the burning sensation of air entering the lungs") for oxygen, rather than allowing them a few minutes to adjust to the new method of obtaining oxygen.

Leboyer believes there are many ways the birth experience can be made joyful rather than agonizing for the newborn. The delivery room can be quiet and dimly lit. The baby can be placed on the mother's abdomen immediately after birth, so that she can caress the newborn until the umbilical cord stops pulsating. Then the baby can be placed in warm water to relax and play. According to Leboyer, newborns who experience a gentle birth cry only once or twice, and then seem blissful. There is some evidence that Leboyer's method of delivery results in babies who are more alert in the first thirty hours after birth (Salter, 1978).

Figure 5.10 *This newborn is being held in warm water reminiscent of the amniotic fluid that used to surround him. Leboyer believes that this relaxing moment eases the transition from the uterus to the outside world. Leboyer believes that the blissful smile on this neonate would be much more common if "gentle" birth techniques were used more often.*

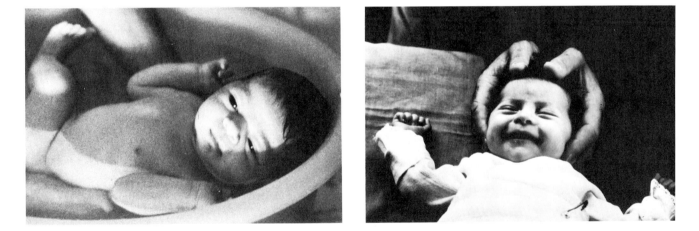

Although many obstetricians worry that attempts to make the neonate's first moments comfortable might divert attention from the medical needs of the mother and child, Leboyer's concerns have affected some hospital routines. Certainly it would seem that most doctors and nurses have had their consciousness raised regarding the gentle treatment of newborns. And while not many American hospitals have instituted soft lighting and warm baths for newborns, mothers are now usually permitted to hold and comfort their babies minutes after they are born.

The Mother's Experience   Biological factors (such as the size of the baby's head and the mother's pelvis) affect the length of labor. So does the mother's age and her childbearing experience; older women having their first babies usually have longer labors than younger women who have given birth before. However, psychological factors may be much more important than biological ones in determining a woman's overall experience. They can make a long labor exhilarating or a short labor terrifying.

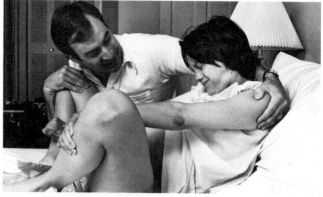

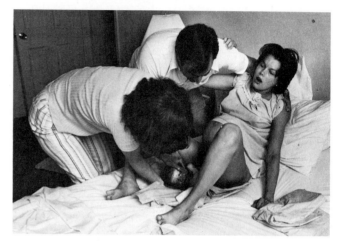

Figure 5.11 *The Simons decided to have their baby at home, attended by a nurse-midwife. In the first photo (above), the midwife confirms that the transition is over and the second stage of labor is about to begin. It is now time for Lee Simon to begin pushing. In the third photo (top left on page 159),* *an area of the fetus's skull has become visible. After each push by the mother, a wider circle of the head comes into view (from the size of dime, to a quarter, to a half-dollar, and so on). The last three photos (lower row) show the moment of birth and an obviously ecstatic mother.*

Childbirth Classes   Two psychological factors are especially important: preparation for childbirth and support from other people. Women who attend childbirth classes and whose husbands help them in labor and delivery feel less pain, use less anesthesia, and have more positive feelings about birth. Studies of the effects of attending childbirth classes, even when attendance was ordered by the doctor rather than requested by the women themselves, have shown psychological benefits for mothers, such as delight in their babies and themselves (Tanzer and Block, 1976). Other research has found additional benefits, including shorter labors (Fisher et al., 1972), less medical intervention, and healthier babies (Enkin et al., 1972).

Prepared Childbirth Forty years ago, most women who gave birth in hospitals were unconscious when their babies were born, because general anesthesia was routinely given during childbirth. Today, general anesthesia is rarely used in normal childbirth. One reason for this change is that women have learned to use psychological techniques to relieve pain. Two pioneering obstetricians, Grantly Dick-Read, from England, and Fernand Lamaze, from France, are credited with the rediscovery of natural childbirth—"natural" in the sense that medical assistance is minimized, although psychological assistance and preparation are used.

Dick-Read believed that women who are afraid of childbirth will tighten their muscles, making birth painful. He maintained that if women know what to expect, and can relax during contractions (which he insisted should *not* be called labor pains), they will not be afraid, and birth will be easier (Dick-Read, 1972; originally published in 1933).

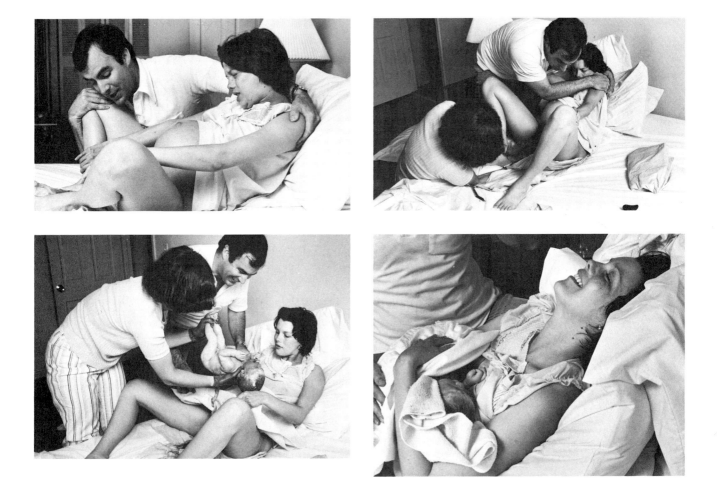

About thirty years later, in 1951, Fernand Lamaze traveled to the Soviet Union and saw many women giving birth without medication, and without the screams of agony which he had assumed were inevitable. He learned that Soviet doctors had applied Pavlov's theory of classical conditioning to childbirth, teaching women to associate childbirth with pleasant feelings and to lessen the discomfort of their contractions by using specific breathing techniques. Women concentrated on the work, rather than the pain, of giving birth.

Lamaze returned to Paris and changed his way of delivering babies. With breathing, massage, and exercise, he taught women to participate actively in childbirth. By chance, one of his early patients was Marjorie Karmel, an American. Early in pregnancy she "was not interested in natural childbirth—not even if they were giving it away." Later she decided to "string along for a week or two," and joined a class in the Lamaze method. Finally, she felt "exhilarated and excited" after delivering her first baby with the help of her husband, her Lamaze teacher, and Dr. Lamaze.

In the past twenty years, millions of Americans have read either Karmel's book, *Painless Childbirth: Thank you Doctor Lamaze* (1959), or Dick-Read's *Childbirth Without Fear: The Original Approach to Natural Childbirth* (1972). Classes to prepare for childbirth are now common. Some teachers stress education and relaxation, as in Dick-Read's method of natural childbirth; others stress active control and participation in the birth process, as Lamaze taught.

Support from Other People All advocates of "prepared childbirth" agree that women should never be left alone during labor or birth. Someone—nurse, doctor, husband, mother, or friend—should give constant encouragement and help. In the case of hospital births, the attitude of the staff is often crucial. Many women who remember childbirth as a joy also praise their doctors or midwives.* The reverse is also true: many women are more upset by the attitudes of doctors and nurses than by the physical discomfort of birth.

On the whole, it also seems that the less education and income women have, the more likely they are to experience pain, loneliness, and confusion during childbirth (Nettlebladt et al., 1976; Rosengren, 1961; Davenport-Slack and Boylan, 1974). One reason for this is that many doctors appear wealthy, educated, and aloof, making it especially hard for poor women to ask questions. Hence, these women often begin labor in bewilderment and fear, still considering the doctor an unfriendly stranger. This almost guarantees a painful delivery (Hubert, 1974).

Some husbands ensure the success of the prepared childbirth by providing essential support and encouragement. Fathers time contractions, help regulate the breathing patterns, massage sore muscles, and hold their wives in a sitting position when it is time to push the baby through the birth canal. Apart from such practical help, the presence of the father makes it more likely that the woman will enjoy the birth and feel pleased with herself afterward (Tanzer and Block, 1976; Davenport-Slack and Boylan, 1974).

Disappointment and Depression Sometimes women who have prepared for childbirth anticipate the pleasure of birth so much that they are disappointed if they feel pain, need medication, or lose control in labor.

In fact, no matter how well a woman prepares, some medication is often helpful to prevent fetal distress or to allow the mother to control her contractions. Indeed, birth complications are difficult to predict, so a woman can be as proud of having an emergency Cesarean which helped her baby avoid serious problems as she would be of having a vaginal delivery without medication.

A few days after birth, many women find themselves overreacting to minor annoyances, crying for no apparent reason, and resenting their babies. These emotions are so common that they have the household name "baby blues," as well as a formal label, post-partum depression. "Post partum," literally, "after separation," refers to the first days and weeks after birth.

Most researchers believe that a majority of new mothers experience some form of the blues (Nott et al., 1976; Asch and Rubin, 1974), and that about one-sixth of all new mothers show clinical signs of depression. Their symptoms include withdrawal, inability to cope with simple demands, and feelings of hopelessness (Meares et al., 1976).

The Father's Experience How a man experiences the birth of his child depends on many of the same factors that influence his wife's experience, such as preparation for the birth and support from other people. If the baby is the couple's first child, both of them must go through a period of readjustment while they learn to care for the new family member.

---

*Traditionally, midwives were women who helped other women have babies at home when doctors were scarce. Today most midwives are specially trained nurses, who deliver babies in hospitals. They usually spend more time with each mother, and use fewer drugs and other medical procedures than most obstetricians. When surgery or other emergency measures are needed, they call the physician on duty (Brennan and Heilman, 1977).

Causes of Post-partum Depression

Like most other kinds of depression, post-partum depression is partly the result of physical, psychological, and social factors. Different researchers emphasize one factor or another.

Physical Causes

1. *Tiredness.* Labor is exhausting work. It is often performed under difficult conditions, with little sleep or nourishment. Physical weariness makes a person especially susceptible to pain and stress.

2. *Pain.* Post-partum contractions of the shrinking uterus, the pull of healing incisions, the tightness of overfull breasts, and the aches of weary muscles can be quite painful in the days after birth.

3. *Malnourishment.* Many women become malnourished in the last weeks of pregnancy, and may be especially lacking iron and folic acid. These deficiencies can cause depression (Tod, 1972).

4. *Hormonal changes.* As the woman's body shifts from pregnancy to lactation (milk production), hormonal changes can upset her equilibrium (Meares et al., 1976).

5. *Drugs.* Most drugs used during birth have side effects, from headaches to mood depression, which last several days.

Psychosocial Causes

1. *Hospital environment.* In a hospital, a woman must sleep in an unfamiliar bed, eat strange food, and follow hospital routines. She is surrounded by people she does not know. One British study found that 64 percent of the women who gave birth in hospitals were depressed after birth, compared to 19 percent of those who had their babies at home (Cone, 1972), although this contrast could have occurred because women with problem pregnancies are more likely to give birth in hospitals.

2. *Separation from the baby.* A common practice in many modern hospitals is for mothers to see their babies only at feeding time. Many women feel happier when close to their infants and feel incomplete when separated from them (Klaus and Kennell, 1976).

3. *Lack of support from other people.* Family members, friends, and hospital staff sometimes seem interested only in the new baby. The woman feels ignored. If the nurses act as if they know much more about taking care of babies and can do a better job of it than the new mother, the woman may feel she will never become an adequate mother.

In addition, many men experience a frustration that their wives do not—exclusion from the birth itself. One father watched his wife wheeled into the delivery room:

> Tears welled up in my eyes: I wanted so much to stay with her, to help her, to see my child born. For a moment I was dizzy with rage and despair; I felt like destroying the entire hospital in a fury of vengeance for denying my right to see my child born. [Quoted in Colman and Colman, 1977, originally published in 1971]

In many hospitals, fathers are not allowed in the delivery room, for fear that they might disrupt the birth process or bring harmful bacteria into the room. Other hospitals allow fathers to be with their wives during the entire birth. The latter policy is due partly to the recognition that prepared childbirth is more successful if the father helps, and partly to the fact that the father's role is getting more attention. Hospitals that allow fathers in the delivery room have also found that well-scrubbed fathers clad in hospital gowns add no more bacteria to the proceedings than well-scrubbed obstetricians, anesthesiologists, or nurses.

Some women prefer *not* to have their husbands with them during delivery, and some husbands prefer *not* to be there. But most researchers have found that the father's presence is a positive experience for the mother and the father. In one study of 544 fathers who had been present during the delivery, 542 were glad they had been there, one was not sure, and only one regretted it (Pawson and Morris, 1972). In another study, husbands who were with their wives during delivery were more likely to be "highly pleased and enthusiastic" about the birth process than were husbands who saw only the first stage of labor (Henneborn and Cogan, 1975). In addition, their wives felt less pain and used less medication.

One husband describes the birth of his son, Christopher:

> I administered oxygen to her [his wife] between contractions and coached her on pushing, holding her around the shoulders as support during each push. She was magnificent. Slowly I began to feel a kind of holiness about all of us there, performing an ageless human drama, a grand ritual of life. The trigger was probably the emergence of the baby's head—coughing, twisting, covered with blood, as purple as error, so eager for life—that set me into such intensities of joy and excitement that I cannot possibly adequately describe them. It was all so powerful I felt as though my head might come off, that I might simply explode with joy and a sense of participation in a profound mystery. I did explode, was literally reborn myself, saw how my birth, all births, the idea of birth, is profoundly right, good, joyous.
>
> Christopher was placed in my wife's arms even before the umbilicus was cut; shortly after it was cut he was wrapped (still dripping and wonderfully new like a chick out of an egg) and given to me to hold while my wife got her strength back.
>
> He was very alert, apparently able to focus his attention on me and on other objects in the room; as I held him he blossomed into pink, the various parts of his body turning from deep purple and almost blue, to pink, to rose. I was fascinated by the colors, time stopped; I thought my friends hooked on LSD should simply take a wife, have a baby, and watch it born! [Quoted by Tanzer and Block, 1976]

Not all husbands are so moved by watching their children born, of course, but there does seem to be a tendency for fathers who hold and care for their babies in the hours and days after birth to become engrossed with their infants. This is often true even if they have not witnessed the delivery.

The Older Sibling's Experience

The birth of a younger brother or sister is not necessarily a happy event. During the period of hospital confinement, a young child at home may feel that mother has disappeared, especially if this is the first time she has been away for any length of time. Further confusion may arise if a stranger is brought in to care for the child. The mother's hospitalization may be especially frightening if the young child associates hospitals with sickness and death.

When mother and baby come home, things often get worse rather than better. The parents are understandably busy and tired. They want the older children to be quiet and self-sufficient. Visitors come to admire the newborn, making older children feel slighted. To top it off, the baby is not like a doll or a friend. Instead, it cries and sleeps, and never plays.

No wonder many older siblings are disturbed by the birth of a baby. A child who asks "Isn't it time to take it back to the hospital?" or who is inclined to give the baby a bite instead of a kiss is not unusual. Some children revert to babyish behavior, crawling, whining, talking baby talk, or wetting the bed for the first time in months. These are all examples of the defense mechanism Freud called regression. Children who use regression to cope with stress are neither abnormal nor unhealthy, as long as they are able to return to age-appropriate behavior when they become accustomed to the stress.

RESEARCH REPORT   **Engrossment**

Thirty fathers who helped care for their babies in the hospital became fascinated with their newborns, according to one study (Greenberg and Morris, 1974). This engrossment included seven characteristics:

1. *Visual awareness of the baby.*   The men thought they could recognize their own infants among a crowd of newborns. The men who had been present at delivery thought they could spot their babies with 100 percent accuracy; some of those who had not seen their babies born were not that sure.

2. *Tactile awareness of the baby.*   One father wrote, "One hears the expression 'soft as a baby's backside' I suppose, but when I touched it, it seemed incredibly soft, like velvet."

3. *Awareness of the distinctive characteristics of the baby.*   Fathers seemed certain that this particular infant, rather than any of the dozens of others in the nursery, was theirs. This was especially true of the fathers present at delivery. One wrote, "The fact that you actually see it born—you *know* it's yours. I'm not suggesting that if you don't go into the delivery room they swap them. But you see your wife actually giving birth. And you know that this is something the two of you have produced."

4. *The infant is perceived as "perfect."*   One father wrote, "In the afternoon I walked up and down and looked at all the babies in that room up there and they all looked a bit ugly, a bit rubbery, and then when she came out she looked so beautiful, really, a little gem, so beautiful."

5. *Extreme elation.*   From a father who had been present at birth: "I took a look at it and I took a look at the face and I left the ground—I just left the ground. I thought, 'Oh, Jesus Christ! This is marvelous.'"

6. *Strong feeling of attraction.*   As one father said, "When she starts moving I go and pick her up and she starts moving in your hands and your arms and you can feel her moving up against you. It's like a magnet."

7. *Increased sense of self-esteem.*   These fathers were proud of themselves, as well as of their wives and babies.

The fathers in this study came from a broad range of social, economic, and national backgrounds, including English, French, Turkish, Greek, Arab, Israeli, and Chinese. However, since all the babies were first-borns, and all the deliveries were normal, a conclusion based on the reactions of these thirty fathers must be tentative. Despite this limitation, the authors of the study believe that engrossment is an inborn potential that is activated by a father's contact with his newborn. According to them, since infants are more alert and active in the minutes right after birth than they are in the next several days, engrossment is especially likely to occur if the father is present during the birth. Activity of any kind—grasping, sucking, kicking, looking—is interpreted by both mother and father as a response to them.

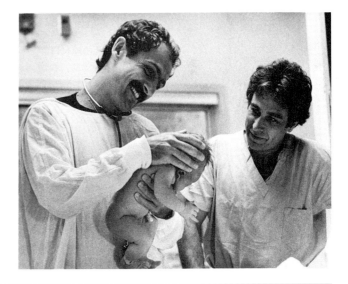

A fascinated father watches his newborn while a pediatrician examines her. Fathers who participate in their children's birth are usually as intrigued by their newborns and as tender with them as mothers are.

Some emotional upset and jealousy in older siblings is probably inevitable when a new baby is born. However, parents can make birth a little easier for the older children. A child can be brought to visit the mother in the hospital,* be given a present when a visitor arrives with a baby gift, and be encouraged to hold and care for the newborn. Paternity leave, which permits the father to be home, can allow one parent to care for the baby while the other does something special with the older children.

---

*Visitation is subject to hospital regulations, of course. Whether or not a hospital allows such visits might be an important factor in choosing where to give birth.

The Parent-Infant Bond

What the future holds for an infant probably depends more on the relationship between parent and child than on any other factor. This relationship, which usually begins to develop as parents and newborns gaze at each other in the first hours and days after birth, is often called the parent-infant bond, a term intended to emphasize the tangible, as well as metaphorical, fastening of each to the other. With older babies, the parent-infant bond is also called *attachment,* as explained in Chapter 8.

**Origin of the
Parent-Infant Bond**

The bond between parents and children does not develop automatically: contrary to popular belief, there is no maternal or paternal "instinct." How does the bond occur, then? In search of an answer, some psychologists have turned to ethologists and their studies of newborn animals, who are either protected and nurtured, or rejected and abandoned, by their parents.

Many factors seem to be involved in the reactions of animals to their offspring. One of them is the babies' appearance (see Figure 5.12): the large heads and eyes, fat cheeks, prominent foreheads, and small bodies characteristic of babies, whether kittens, puppies, monkeys, or humans, seem to trigger a nurturant response in adults of all species (Hess, 1970). This fact also helps explain why small adult dogs allow unfamiliar puppies of much larger breeds to sniff and paw them in ways that would trigger an attack if the puppy were an older dog. Puppylike appearance, rather than small size, is the key. Appearance is also the crucial factor explaining why many animal mothers reject their offspring who are malformed, especially if the newborn's head is smaller than normal.

For mothers, another factor may be that the same hormones that cause the uterus to shrink and the milk to flow right after birth may also cause a desire to

Figure 5.12 *In many species, the shape of the head, eyes and nose, and chin of infants follows the same distinctive pattern. Ethologists believe this babyish appearance is a determinant of the nurturing response in adults.*

care for an infant (Hinde, 1974). A third factor is "ownership." Most animals act as if they believe their own territory, possessions, and offspring are more worthy of protection than those that belong to others. Similarity is also important: animals and people are more helpful to others who are similar in appearance and behavior to themselves. Some animal mothers reject and even kill their newborns who appear different in any marked way.

Early Contact Between Parent and Baby For many birds and animals, *early contact* between mother and infant can be crucial to the establishment of the bond. For example, if a baby goat is removed from its mother immediately after birth, and returned a few hours later, the mother sometimes rejects it, kicking and butting it away. However, if the baby remains with her for the critical first five minutes, and is then separated from her, she welcomes it back. Many species of birds react in similar fashion.

Figure 5.13 *Under normal circumstances, goslings instinctually follow their mothers, but these seven are following the ethologist Konrad Lorenz instead. In the critical first days of their lives, he was the only moving creature they saw, so they became attached to him. And since their mother was not with them in the early hours of their lives, she now ignores them. Lorenz's research led to the realization that, for many animal species, the first hours of contact between mother and offspring serve to bond one to the other. This raised an important question: Does a similar critical period exist for humans?*

As part of their effort to see if a similar critical period exists for humans, researchers have tried to determine whether the amount of time mothers spend with their newborns in the hospital makes any difference in the mother-child bond. Their findings suggest that for most experienced mothers with healthy babies, immediate mother-infant contact does not seem to make any lasting difference in the relationship (Macfarlane, 1977). However, in certain cases, early contact is important.

For example, one study compared twenty-eight new mothers, all of whom had full-term, healthy, bottle-fed babies (Kennell et al., 1974). Most of these mothers were poor, uneducated, and unwed. Their average age was 18. Half these women followed the traditional hospital routine: a glance at their infants at birth, a short visit within the next twelve hours, and then about thirty minutes with their babies at feeding every four hours, except at night. The other half were permitted extended contact with their newborns, including an hour with their naked infants (warmed by a special heat panel) within three hours after birth, and five hours per day for each of the first three days in the hospital.

Figure 5.14 *During an hour of contact, one of the mothers in Kennell's study caresses her newborn, who is less than 3 hours old. If this pair is like the typical mother-infant pair who had extended contact in this research, then throughout infancy, the mother will be more nurturing, and the baby more responsive, than either would have been without such contact.*

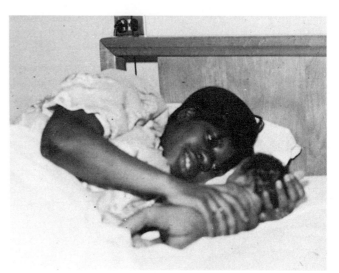

Many differences developed between these two groups of mothers. The mothers with extended contact were more involved with their infants throughout the first year of life. They soothed their babies, cuddled them, looked at them, picked them up when they cried, enjoyed them when they were present, and worried about them when they were not. The infants thrived under this attention, and scored better on tests of physical and mental development at 1 year than did the babies who did not have the extended contact (Kennell et al., 1974). Even when the babies were 2 years old, the mothers who had had more contact with them at birth spoke to them more and gave them fewer commands and more encouragement than the mothers who had had only routine contact with their newborns (Macfarlane, 1977).

Another study compared married, middle-class women who had premature babies. The mothers who had the most contact with their babies felt the most confident of themselves in the hospital (Seashore et al., 1973) and cuddled and smiled at their babies most at home (Leifer et al., 1972).

A study of premature infants in Sweden (Hansen and Bjerre, 1973) compared twenty-three premature infants separated from their mothers for several weeks after birth with twenty-one similar premature infants who were not separated. At age 7, eighteen of the separated group had at least one psychiatric symptom, while only seven from the not-separated group had psychiatric symptoms. In addition, eight of the twenty-three separated children were considered by their mothers to be "difficult to manage" at age 7, whereas only one mother of the not-separated group felt the same way (Hansen and Bjerre, 1977).

These studies are especially noteworthy because poor, young, uneducated, and unmarried mothers, like those in the first study, and infants in intensive care, like those in the second and third, are among the types of mothers and babies who often have difficulty establishing healthy mother-infant relationships. No one factor creates a poor relationship, but several factors such as poverty, prematurity, and mother-infant separation can interact to make a mother feel like rejecting her baby. Because of studies such as these, many psychologists have concluded that early contact helps establish the parent-infant bond, and most hospitals allow much more mother-infant contact than they did ten years ago. Even with normal babies, "rooming in" (allowing the newborn to stay in the mother's room) and extended contact may help strengthen the mother-infant relationship (Kontos, 1978).

Bonding and Premature Babies

The bond between parent and child is formed by their *mutual* interaction: it is affected as much by the characteristics of the baby as by those of the parent. In cases of premature birth, there are difficulties in the formation of this bond that seem almost inherent.

To begin with, premature babies are often forbiddingly scrawny ("about the size of a rat," as one father put it). Then, too, because their reflexes are immature, premature babies are less responsive—that is, they are less likely to turn to hear a voice or to stare with fascination at a face—than full-term babies are. They also need more care—special feedings and monitoring, and sometimes isolation—and are harder to satisfy than full-term babies. Consequently, parents are often either uninclined to, or unable to, hold and play with their premature baby.

Especially if there is any doubt about the baby's survival, friends and family are less likely to call with presents and congratulations. Also, the baby born too early often catches the parents unprepared—without the baby clothes and crib, and also without the emotional readiness for birth.

All things considered, parents can hardly be blamed if they find it harder to love a premature baby than to love a responsive, full-term child. It appears, unfortunately, that this absence or withholding of affection sometimes begins a sequence of events that leads to child neglect or abuse later on, for premature babies are more likely to be victims of such treatment than are full-term babies (Kempe and Kempe, 1978).

However, if hospital personnel recognize these problems, they can provide the special attention to parent-infant bonding that premature babies and their parents need. For instance, a parent who is permitted to change the premature baby's diapers, or to feel the strength of even a 3-pound baby's reflexive grasp, realizes that the baby is a person, who needs love and care just like any other infant. Even the simple act of discussing the medical procedures used and explaining the likelihood of the baby's survival has helped many parents feel more comfortable. Successful parent-child relationships can flourish even with the most vulnerable babies (Klaus and Kennell, 1976).

Adoption

Biological ties and early contact are important, but they should not be overemphasized. The crucial factor is that each child has someone, whether a biological parent or an unrelated care-giver, who provides loving, caring, individual attention and stimulation. Consider the experience of millions of children (an estimated one out of every ten Americans) who spend part of their childhood living in families with neither biological parent.

According to several reports, most adopted children have better childhoods than they would have had if they had not been adopted. As already mentioned in Chapter 4, researchers followed the development of all the babies born in Great Britain between March 3 and 8, 1958. Of those who were illegitimate, the ones who were adopted usually fared better on measures of physical, emotional, and intellectual development than did their contemporaries who stayed with their unwed mothers (Pringle, 1974).

Research like this does not mean that unwed mothers cannot provide good care for their children. Obviously, despite the social prejudice against them, some unwed mothers give their children all the love and stimulation a child needs to thrive. But this research does suggest that many adoptive parents give their children good care, and that many "natural" parents need help in learning how to raise their children.

Further evidence that biological relationships are not necessary to cement the parent-child bond comes from the thousands of instances of successful interracial adoptions, which demonstrate, in addition, that love is a lot more important than skin color.

As long as racial discrimination persists in the United States, *intra*racial adoptions are easier for parents and better for children than *inter*racial adoptions.

However, studies show that children adopted by families whose background is different from their own fare better than similar children who grow up without families, spending time in institutions or a series of foster homes (Kadushin, 1970). A survey of interracial adoptions showed that, despite society's racial attitudes, black children adopted by white families do well on tests of intelligence, school achievement, and on measures of social adjustment (Simon and Altstein, 1977).

Thus, the experience of thousands of adoptive families shows that successful parent-child bonds can be established without the usual advantages of blood relationships: post-partum hormones and early parent-infant contact are helpful but not essential. Even when the child taken in by a family no longer looks like a baby or does not "belong" to the parents (as is the case with a foster child) or has a different culture, history, or appearance from the parent (as in cross-cultural and interracial adoptions), excellent parent-child relationships can develop. In short, the bond between parent and child grows or atrophies for many reasons; the first days of life are significant, but circumstances and events before birth and throughout childhood are essential as well.

SUMMARY

The Normal Birth

1. Birth usually occurs about 266 days after conception. The three stages of labor begin with contractions that push the fetus, headfirst, out from the uterus through the vagina.

2. Many neonates appear misshapen or bruised from the birth process, but are usually quite healthy, as measured by the Apgar scale. This scale notes the neonate's heart rate, breathing, muscle tone, circulation, and reflexes at one minute and five minutes after birth and rates them according to a ten-point system.

3. The Brazelton Neonatal Behavior Assessment Scale measures the way the infant responds to the environment. It rates twenty-six items of behavior and twenty reflexes. It can be used to assess the effects of birth problems and anesthesia and to predict which babies are most likely to have psychological problems.

4. Testing the strength of the neonate's reflexes is part of every standard medical and psychological measure of neonatal health. Three groups of reflexes are critical for survival and become stronger as the newborn matures. One set helps the newborn maintain constant body temperature, a second set ensures adequate nourishment, and a third maintains an adequate supply of oxygen.

Variations and Problems

5. Variations in the birth process—such as breech births, prematurity, postmaturity, and anoxia—sometimes cause learning problems later in childhood. However, often a combination of complications and deprivations, rather than any one event, seems to create the difficulty.

6. Medical help for difficult births has saved many lives, and simultaneously given rise to much controversy. Among these measures are Cesarean sections, forceps delivery, induced labor, and fetal monitoring. None of these procedures are risk-free.

7. Less than one North American woman in ten has a baby without drugs, and many problems have been linked to obstetric medication. Most of these problems affect the relationship between newborns and their environment, making it, for example, difficult for them to get used to noises, increasing their irritability, and lowering their responsiveness to surroundings.

The Birth Experience

8. Some people believe that the fetus is insensitive to the birth process; others feel that the baby suffers during and after birth. Leboyer advocates "gentle birth," an idea accepted, in part, by many doctors, nurses, and parents today.

9. While biological factors are the primary determinants of birth complications and the length of labor, the woman's overall experience is affected primarily by psychological factors. Women who are prepared for birth—knowing what to expect and how to make labor easier—and who have the support of their husbands are most likely to find the birth experience exhilarating.

10. How much fathers participate in the birth process affects how they feel about it. Fathers who see their babies being born or who care for them in the first days of life are more likely to be thrilled by the birth process and engrossed with their infants. Women whose husbands are present throughout delivery feel less pain and use less medication.

The Parent-Infant Bond

11. Many factors affect the parent-infant bond, including the appearance of the baby and the hormones of the mother. Especially for inexperienced mothers, the amount of early contact between mother and newborn may be important.

12. Studies of adopted children show that good parent-child relationships can occur even when the physiological and the early psychological factors that promote parent-infant bonding are absent. Biological relationships are not necessary to cement the parent-child bond. Love, care, attention, and stimulation are the crucial factors.

KEY QUESTIONS

What are the differences between these ways of judging the health of a newborn: appearance, the Apgar scale, and the Brazelton scale?

How are the newborn's reflexes useful?

What is the relationship between birth problems and later emotional or intellectual problems?

What are the types and causes of low-birth-weight infants?

Which medical procedures used during the birth process are controversial and why?

What are the advantages and disadvantages of home births?

Why has prepared childbirth become so popular?

What are the advantages and disadvantages of the father's presence in the delivery room?

What factors promote the parent-child bond?

What is essential in establishing a good parent-child relationship?

KEY TERMS

first stage of labor	premature
transition	small-for-dates
second stage of labor	surfactin
third stage of labor	respiratory distress syndrome
Apgar scale	postmature
Brazelton scale	induced labor
reflex	oxytocin
Babinski reflex	forceps delivery
stepping reflex	Cesarean section
swimming reflex	fetal monitoring
grasping reflex	meconium
Moro reflex	birth trauma
sucking reflex	gentle birth
rooting reflex	natural childbirth
breathing reflex	Lamaze method
breech birth	post-partum depression
transverse presentation	engrossment
anoxia	parent-infant bond

RECOMMENDED READINGS

Macfarlane, Aidan. *The psychology of childbirth.* Cambridge, Mass.: Harvard University Press, 1977.

A British pediatrician reviews pregnancy, birth, and the first days of life, with special emphasis on the effects of many common practices on the health of the infant. Includes discussion of the mother-infant relationship.

McCleary, Elliot. *New miracles of childbirth.* New York: McKay, 1974.

Includes chapters on many medical procedures to make birth easier and safer and babies healthier. The description of fetal monitoring is especially detailed and intriguing, although not everyone will agree with McCleary's conclusions.

Kitzinger, Sheila. *Giving birth: The parents' emotions in childbirth.* New York: Taplinger, 1971.

A series of vivid, personal accounts of the birth of a baby, many from both the mother's and father's point of view. The book also includes a discussion of the parents' relationship to each other, to the birth, and their first impression of the baby, as well as informative notes and a glossary.

Karmel, Marjorie. *Painless childbirth: Thank you Dr. Lamaze.* Philadelphia: Lippincott, 1959.

The story of Karmel's birth experiences with Dr. Lamaze in Paris and her subsequent search for a similar obstetrician in New York. A warm, first-person account.

Klaus, Marshall, and Kennell, John H. *Maternal infant bonding.* St. Louis: Mosby, 1976.

Reports research on the importance of the first contact between a mother and her infant. Especially interesting is the discussion on the problems of parents who have premature, congenitally handicapped, or critically ill babies.

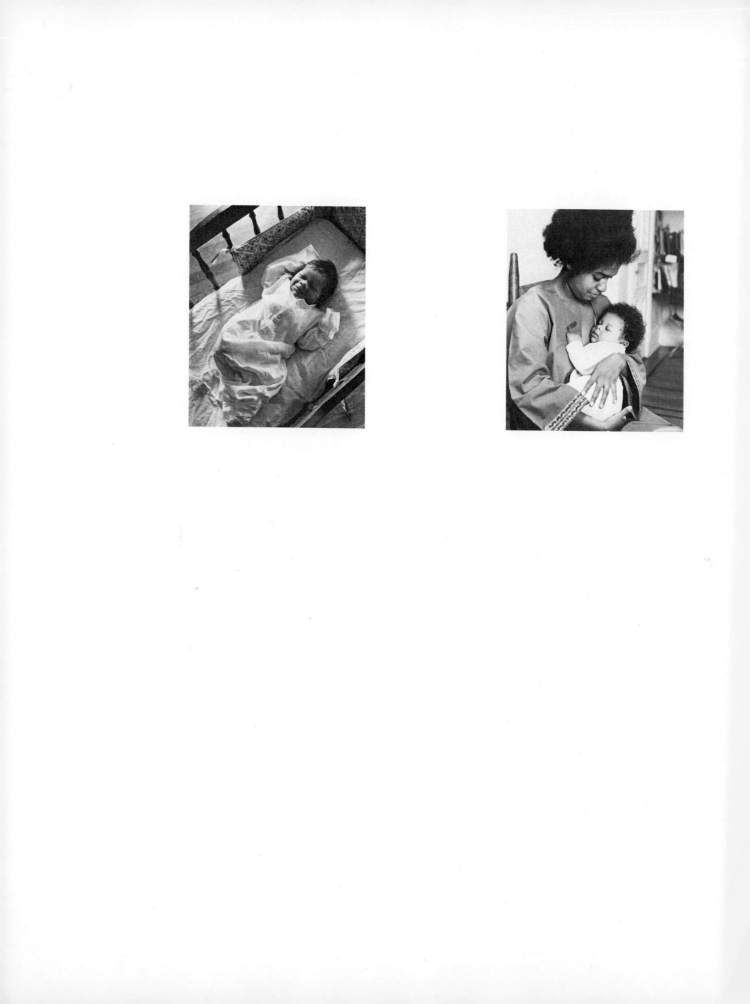

The First Two Years: Infants and Toddlers

PART II

Adults usually don't change much in a year or two. Sometimes their hair gets longer or grows thinner, or they gain or lose a few pounds, or they become a little wiser or more mature. But if you were to be reunited with some friends you hadn't seen for several years, you would recognize them immediately.

If, on the other hand, you were to care for a newborn, twenty-four hours a day for the first month, and when next you saw the baby it was a year or two later, the chances of your recognizing that child are similar to those of recognizing a best friend who had quadrupled in weight, grown 14 inches, and sprouted a new head of hair. Nor would you find the toddler's way of thinking, talking, or playing familiar. A hungry newborn just cries; a hungry toddler says "more food" or climbs up on the kitchen counter to reach the cookies.

While two years seem short compared to the more than seventy years of the average life span, children in their first two years reach half their adult height, complete the first of Piaget's four periods of cognitive growth, and have almost finished the second of both Freud's and Erikson's sequence of stages. Two of the most important human abilities, talking and loving, are already apparent. The next three chapters describe these radical and rapid changes.

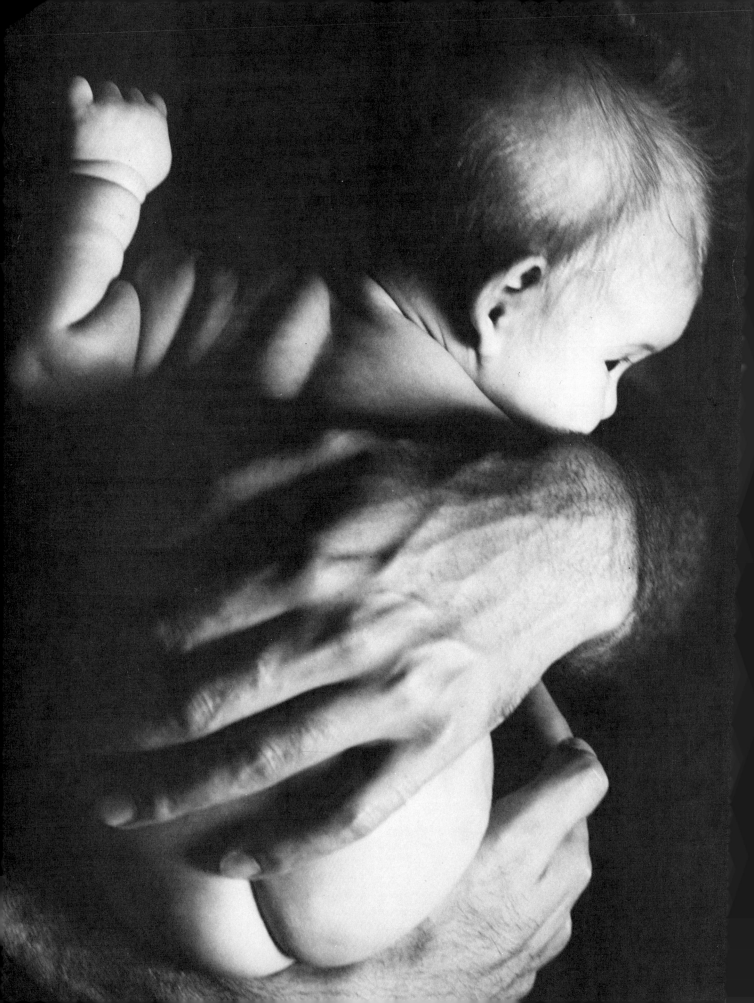

The First Two Years: Physical Development

. . . he co-operates
With a universe of large and noisy feeling states
  Without troubling to place
Them anywhere special, for, to his eyes, Funnyface
  Or Elephant as yet
Mean nothing. His distinction between Me and Us
Is a matter of taste; his seasons are Dry and Wet;
  He thinks as his mouth does.

W. H. Auden
"Mundus et Infans"

True or False?

Mastering the art of grasping objects leads infants to a new problem: letting-go.

Black Americans tend to walk two months earlier than white Americans.

A newborn can see an object at 20 feet about as well as an adult with normal vision can see it at 600 feet.

Infants cannot distinguish between very similar sounds at only 1 month of age.

Throughout the world, the oldest age at which weaning occurs is 3 years.

Most drugs consumed by a lactating mother (including nicotine and alcohol) turn up in her breast milk.

Children between 1 and 5 years old are among the least well nourished age groups in the United States.

A baby's physical development happens so rapidly that size, shape, and skills change daily. This is no exaggeration: pediatricians expect normal infants to gain an ounce a day for the first few months; and parents keeping a detailed baby diary record new achievements daily, such as, along about the twelfth month, the baby's taking one step on a Monday, two steps on Tuesday, and five steps by the weekend.

As we will soon see, this rapid physical growth follows the same orderly sequence as prenatal growth, from the head downward and the center outward, and it is affected by the interaction of genes, experience, diet, and the quality of care (Tanner, 1974).

Size and Shape

The easiest way to perceive both the speed and sequence of infant physical development is to look at the changes in body size and shape that occur between birth and age 2. The average North American newborn measures 20 inches (51 centimeters) and weighs 7½ pounds (about 3400 grams). This means that the average neonate is lighter than a gallon of milk, and about as long as the distance from a man's elbow to the tips of his fingers.

In the first days of life, most newborns lose a few ounces before their bodies adjust to sucking, swallowing, and digesting on their own. However, after the first week, infants grow rapidly, doubling their birth weight in four months. By 12 months, the average infant weighs three times the birth weight—about 22 pounds, or 10 kilograms—and measures almost 30 inches, or 75 centimeters.

By 24 months, most children weigh almost four times their birth weight, and measure between 32 and 36 inches (81 to 91 centimeters), with boys being slightly taller and heavier than girls. In other words, by their second birthday most boys have already reached about half their adult stature and most girls have passed the halfway mark by an inch or two (see Figure 6.1).

Much of the weight gained in the first months of life is fat, providing insulation for warmth and calories for nourishment in case teething or other problems cut down on food intake for a few days. By 9 months, most babies have enough fat, and the

Figure 6.1 *These figures show the range of height and weight of American children during the first two years. The lines labeled "50th" (the fiftieth percentile) show the average; the lines labeled "90th" (the ninetieth percentile) show the size of children taller and heavier than 90 percent of their contemporaries; and the lines labeled "10th" (the tenth percentile) show the size of the relatively small children, who are taller or heavier than only 10 percent of their peers. Note that girls (color lines) are slightly shorter and lighter, on the average, than boys (black lines).*

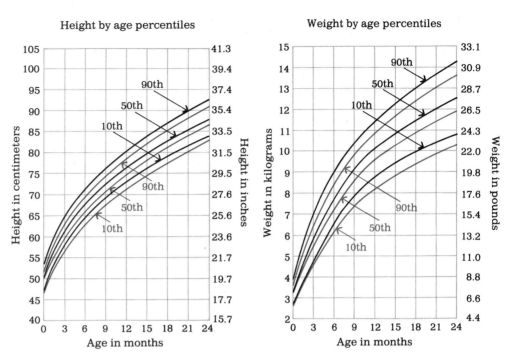

weight they gain thereafter is primarily bone and muscle. Indeed, once they start walking, most children lose fat rather than gain it. The toddler's dimples and pot-belly gradually disappear, and by first grade many healthy children look almost skinny, with no baby fat at all.

Proportions

The shape of the baby's body also changes in the first two years, following the head-downward (cephalo-caudal) and center-outward (proximo-distal) direction of development. Most newborns seem top-heavy because their heads comprise about one-fourth of their total length, compared to one-fifth at a year and one-eighth in adulthood. Newborns have short legs, not much longer than their heads; at adulthood, legs account for about half the total height (see Figure 6.2).

Figure 6.2 *As shown in this figure, the proportions of the human body change dramatically with maturation, especially in the first years of life. For instance, the percentage of total body length below the belly button is 25 percent two months past conception, about 45 percent at birth, 50 percent by age 2, and 60 percent by adulthood.*

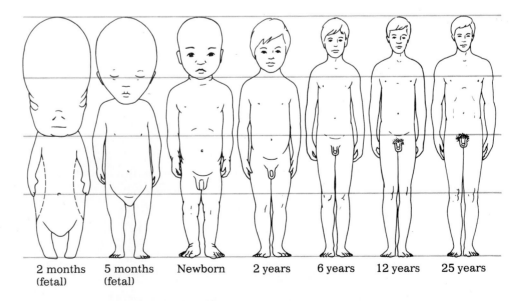

2 months (fetal)   5 months (fetal)   Newborn   2 years   6 years   12 years   25 years

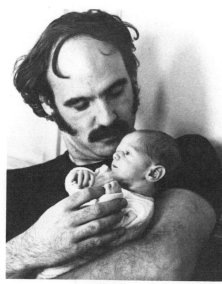

(a)   (b)   (c)

Figure 6.3 *Comparing the head size of each of these infants with their father's shows the rapid growth from approximately one week (a), to 5 months (b), to 2 years (c). (This sequence also shows infants' visual maturation: the newborn stares into space; the 5-month-old stares at the telephone; and the toddler watches the eyes and mouth of the speaker, just as an adult would.)*

Proportionally, the smallest part of a newborn's body is that part farthest from the head and most distant from the center—namely, the feet. By adulthood, the feet will be about five times as long as they were at birth, while the head will have only doubled in size.

Brain Growth   Even the head itself grows more at the bottom than at the top; the baby's chin is underdeveloped at birth compared to the skull (see Figure 6.4). One reason the skull is so large is to accommodate the brain, which already weighs 25 percent of its adult weight. By age 2, the brain is about 75 percent of the adult brain weight, while the 2-year-old's total body weight is only about 20 percent of adult weight (Tanner, 1970).

The areas of the brain that increase most rapidly in the first months are the primary motor areas of the cortex and primary sensory areas of the cortex—those that control the senses and simple motor abilities (e.g., waving the arms). By 6 months, the parts of the cortex that aid coordination between the senses (matching faces with voices) and that control more complicated motor skills (picking up an object, or later, kicking a ball) have shown rapid development.

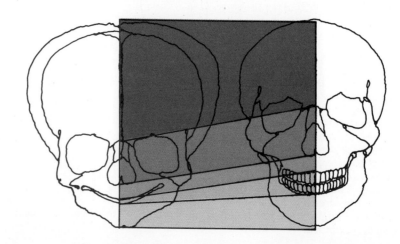

Figure 6.4 *Compared to the proportions of the head of a typical adult, the newborn's brain and cranium are much larger.*

Catch-up Growth

In the first weeks of life, very small babies often gain weight even more rapidly than bigger babies: a 4-pound baby might double in weight in two or three months rather than the usual four, and might weigh five times the birth weight at 1 year. This remarkable phase of growth in smaller babies is called the birth catch-up, because these babies seem to be racing to catch up to the average baby.

The birth catch-up is particularly common among infants born of small mothers and large fathers. This may be a biological adaptation that allows a person who is destined to become a large adult to develop in a small uterus and pass through a narrow pelvis (Tanner, 1963). A 230 pound (104 kilo) football fullback might have been a 6-pound (2.7 kilo) infant born to a woman who was 4' 11" (1.5 meters) and weighed 95 pounds (43 kilos).

Development of Motor Abilities

Imagine a family composed of an 11-month-old little girl, her older sister, her parents, and her grandparents, relaxing after dinner. As the rest of the family watches, the baby stands next to a chair, holding on for balance. Four feet away, Grandpa squats down, holds out his hands, and says "Come." This sequence of events may have happened many times before, but tonight is different. This time the infant lets go of the chair, takes a step, and another one, before Grandpa sweeps her up in his arms as the entire family applauds.

Later on, the grandfather may boast that he taught his granddaughter to walk, to which the mother might reply that, on the contrary, babies walk when they are ready, whereupon father and grandmother are likely to chime in that only a smart baby could have caught on so quickly. Older sister, meanwhile, might wonder why such a fuss is being made over a few steps. Even when the rest of infancy is forgotten, most families have special memories of the day a baby began to walk. Walking is the most dramatic of a long list of motor skills (skills that involve body movement) that normal infants master before age 2.

The Sequence of Motor Skills

Motor abilities follow the same cephalo-caudal–proximo-distal pattern as physical growth: infants can lift their heads before they can sit up, and can sit up steadily before they can stand. Most babies first learn to move from place to place by crawling, lying on their stomachs and pulling themselves ahead with their arms.

Figure 6.5 *The first motor skill newborns try is lifting up their heads, although, as shown here, many need help to accomplish this feat.*

Figure 6.6 *By 3 months, on the average, prone infants can lift their heads and chests; and by 5 months, as you can see here, they can lift the entire upper half of their bodies. The precise age at which a particular baby demonstrates these abilities varies, but the average black infant masters these early motor skills before the average white infant does.*

Creeping on hands and knees, which involves the coordination of arms and legs, comes later: for some babies, as early as 5 months; for others, as late as 12. Some babies do not creep at all, achieving mobility instead by scooting along on their buttocks, rolling over and over, doing the "bear walk" (on all fours, without letting their knees or elbows touch the ground), or even cruising unsteadily on two feet, moving from place to place by holding onto tables, chairs, or bystanders. However it is achieved, such mobility increases the world the infant can explore, giving the child new experiences, and the parents new problems.

Figure 6.7 *As long as the hands are needed for locomotion, carrying toys presents a challenge.*

With the first steps at about age 1, the infant's world expands again, for a walking baby can see and reach many objects that previously were inaccessible. In recognition of their accomplishment of walking, babies are given the name toddler, although, technically, children are *infants* until they begin to talk. Toddlers are named for the characteristic way they use their legs, toddling from side to side. Since their heads and stomachs are relatively heavy and large, they spread out their short little legs for stability, making them seem bowlegged, flatfooted, and unbalanced.

In fact, 1-year-olds *are* unbalanced, falling frequently. They trip on the edge of a rug, or slip on the grass, or topple over because their bodies get too far ahead of their legs when they try to run. But falling doesn't stop them, for they don't have far to fall and they are too excited by their new mobility to be stopped by a momentary setback. By age 2, most children can walk and run quite well, although they still place their feet wide apart for balance. They can even walk backward and climb stairs, using the two-footsteps-to-each-stair method.

Figure 6.8 *Adult help makes it easier to stand and walk without falling, but whether such help speeds up the learning process is debatable.*

Hand Skills   Arm, hand, and finally finger control develops, a sequence predictable by the law of proximo-distal growth. Newborns wave their arms and hands when they see dangling objects, but their aim is poor. Rarely do they succeed in grasping an object, except as a reflex when something touches their palm (Bower, 1977). By 3 months, babies hit dangling objects, but they still grab successfully only rarely, because they close their hands too soon or too late.

By 6 months, most babies can reach, grab, and hold onto a dangling object, but they have a new problem: they can't let go. A toy seems stuck in their hands until they lose interest in it; then their hands relax and the object, unnoticed, drops out.

After letting-go is mastered during the next month or so, babies work on another skill: picking up a small object with their fingers. At first, infants use their whole hand, especially the palm and the fourth and fifth fingers to grasp (the *ulnar grasp*).

Figure 6.9 *This infant's ulnar grasp on these bits of grass is the typical grasp of a 7-month-old. (At this age, most babies explore each new object they get a hold of by tasting it.)*

Then they use the middle fingers and center of the palm (*palmar grasp*) or the index finger and side of the palm (*radial grasp*) (Johnston, 1976). Finally, babies use thumb and forefinger together (*pincer grasp*), a skill mastered sometime between 9 and 14 months (Frankenberg and Dodds, 1967). At this point, infants delight in picking up every tiny object within sight, including bits of fuzz from the carpet and bugs from the lawn.

Variation

Table 6.1 shows the age at which half of all infants master each major motor skill, and the age at which 90 percent master each skill. These averages, or norms, are based on 1036 normal children in Denver, Colorado, who were tested in the 1960s.

TABLE 6.1 **Age Norms (in Months) for Motor Skills**

Skill	When 50% of All Babies Master the Skill (in Months)	When 90% of All Babies Master the Skill (in Months)
Lifts head 90° when lying on stomach	2.2	3.2
Rolls over	2.8	4.7
Sits propped up (head steady)	2.9	4.2
Sits without support	5.5	7.8
Stands holding on	5.8	10.0
Walks holding on	9.2	12.7
Stands momentarily	9.8	13.0
Stands alone well	11.5	13.9
Walks well	12.1	14.3
Walks backward	14.3	21.5
Walks up steps	17.0	22.0
Kicks ball forward	20.0	24.0

Source: From the Denver Developmental Screening Test (Frankenberg and Dodds, (1967).

Norms are statistics, not diagnoses: one need not worry when an alert, active, happy baby walks at 15 months rather than 12. However, extremely slow development can be a sign of serious deprivation or physical problems, which is one reason developmental psychologists are interested in physical norms. If an 18-month-old is not walking, someone should find out why.

Norms vary from place to place and from time to time. The average baby in Stockholm walks at 12½ months, more than a month earlier than the average baby in Paris (Hindley et al., 1966). The earliest walkers in the world seem to be from Uganda, in Central Africa, where, on average, babies walk at 10 months.

The norms of fifty years ago in the United States show babies progressing more slowly then. For example, Shirley (1933) found that, on average, babies did not walk alone until 15 months, the same age reported in the Gesell Developmental Schedules (Gesell and Amatruda, 1947), which are based on babies tested in the 1920s.

Reasons for Variation Why does this variation occur? To answer that, we would have to know how motor skills develop in the first place, and on this subject, psychologists have the same disagreements as the grandfather and mother of the little girl in our example. Some argue that motor skills not only can be taught but should be, because each new ability to use hands and legs enables an infant to learn more; others say that infants have their own timetables for maturation, and that rushing development is frustrating and pointless. As usual with the maturation-versus-learning controversy, there is evidence to support both sides.

On the one hand, cultural patterns of infant care are probably responsible for some of the variation among babies. For instance, Ugandan mothers often give their infants a chance to practice walking by holding them upright on their laps; Mary Ainsworth (1967) thinks this helps explain the precocious motor development of the Ugandan babies. In Kenya, lower-class rural babies are given daily practice in sitting and walking, so they are more advanced in these skills than middle-class urban Kenyan babies (Super, 1976). Obviously, culture affects which particular skills infants learn: North American toddlers can usually eat with a spoon, balance on a teeter-totter, and change stations on a television set, while in certain other cultures, 2-year-olds can eat with chopsticks, swim, and weave cloth. And, of course, within a culture or subculture, the emphasis placed on the development of particular motor skills varies from family to family.

But there is other evidence that shows that inherited factors, such as activity level, rate of physical maturation, and body type, are the primary cause of variation in the acquisition of motor skills. For instance, American babies whose ancestors came from Africa usually walk about two months earlier than babies whose ancestors came from Europe, even when they are raised in similar homes. Identical twins are more likely to sit up, and to walk, on the same day than fraternal twins are, a fact that suggests genes are more important than family encouragement of motor abilities (Wilson and Harpring, 1972).

Part of the reason norms show that babies today are mastering skills earlier than babies half a century ago is environmental: infants today receive better nourishment and medical care, and spend less time in playpens, than infants did fifty years ago. But genes may also be a factor, for the infants tested by both Shirley and Gesell were almost all descendants of western and northern Europeans. The Denver norms are based on a more representative sample, including 18 percent from two ethnic groups known to walk early, blacks and Hispanics.

Individuality Statements such as "The earliest walkers are from Uganda" or "Infants today progress more rapidly than infants fifty years ago" are generalities. The age at which a *particular* baby sits up and walks depends on the interaction between inherited and environmental factors. Each infant has a genetic inner timetable, which can be faster or slower than that of other infants from the same ethnic group and even from the same family; and each infant also has a family and culture that provide encouragement, nutrition, medical care, and opportunity to practice.

Figure 6.10 *Few 2-year-olds can stand steadily on one foot on the ground, let alone on someone's hand, as Alina Korkin is doing here. The hand in this case belongs to her father, a famous Soviet gymnastics coach. In addition to having different genetic and cultural backgrounds, each infant experiences different family encouragement and training, so the skills of 2-year-olds show great variation from child to child.*

When it comes to a particular infant such as the 11-month-old girl in our example, we do not know how much effect Grandpa's encouragement had, nor can we predict the child's future achievement based on her early development of one skill. But there is still good reason to applaud that first step, as well as the other motor skills of the infant, for each new skill mastered means more opportunities for the child to learn.

Sensation and Perception

Psychologists draw a distinction between sensation and perception. Sensation is the ability of the senses to detect a particular stimulus in the environment, for instance, the sound of running water filling the tub for your evening bath. Perception is the mind's processing, or interpreting, of those sensations. Your ears are now *sensing* sounds, but if you are concentrating on reading this book, you are not *perceiving* them, and in a few minutes your bathroom floor will be a mess.

During infancy, both sensory and perceptual abilities develop far more rapidly than scientists once thought. In the Middle Ages, it was believed that newborn senses were so poorly formed that infants were virtually deaf and blind. In the nineteenth century, William James (1950; originally published 1890) took the opposite approach, describing the newborn's universe as a perceptual nightmare—"one great, blooming, buzzing confusion." Neither view is true.

All the senses function at birth. Newborns see, hear, smell, and taste, and they respond to pressure, motion, temperature, and pain. Most of these sensory abilities are immature, becoming more acute as the infant develops.

Perception is also present at birth, although it is very selective. Neonates pay attention to bright lights, loud noises, and objects within a foot of their eyes and screen out almost everything else. Their perceived world is simple, and not confusing.

Research on Perception Charting the extent and progression of the infant's perceptual abilities has become one of the most exciting research areas in developmental psychology. In the last fifteen years, researchers have been tripping over each other in their haste to demonstrate capacities at younger and younger ages, and then backtracking to question each other's overenthusiastic conclusions, as well as their own.

The reason for this rash of new research has been a methodological breakthrough. Instead of waiting until children are old enough to indicate what they perceive, either with gestures or words, researchers can now figure out what infants perceive by recording precisely how long they look at something, or how hard they suck on a nipple, or how fast their hearts beat. Researchers might, for example, present two stimuli to an infant—perhaps the mother's voice and the voice of a stranger, or a circle with dots in it and a circle without dots—and then determine if the baby perceives the difference. If the baby sucks harder, or has a change in heart rate, upon hearing a particular voice, or stares significantly longer at one image than another, the indication is that the baby perceives some difference between the sounds and sights.

Curiosity and Habituation Underlying much of this research is the realization that even newborns are curious, interested in looking at or hearing something new. Researchers often show an infant a picture and wait until the baby becomes bored, or in more scientific terminology, habituated. Habituation refers to the process whereby a particular stimulus has become so familiar that physiological responses initially associated with it (e.g., slower heart rate, concentrated gazing) are no longer present. Once habituation occurs, researchers show the baby another picture, similar to the first one but different in some detail. If the baby's heart rate changes or the eyes focus more on the new picture, it is likely that the baby perceives the difference in the stimulus.

Vision Studies on infant vision provide the best example of the explosion of research on infant sense abilities. Psychologists have long known that newborns seem to look at things without focusing very well. The distance vision of a neonate is about 20/600, which means that the baby can see an object 20 feet (6.1 meters) away no better than an adult with 20/20 vision could see the same object 600 feet (183 meters) away. By 4 months, distance vision is 20/150, still far from 20/20 (Salapatek, 1977). Near vision is better; in the first weeks of life, babies seem to focus reasonably well on objects between 7 and 10 inches (20 centimeters) away.

Figure 6.11 *Although this newborn is not yet 1 week old, she already stares fixedly at anything within her range of focus.*

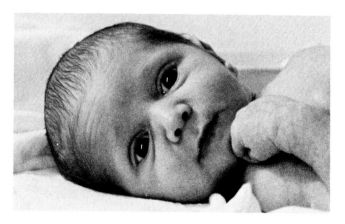

However, it is not easy to tell precisely what they perceive. Do they just stare mindlessly at whatever comes into focus? Or do they already prefer to look at particular things, perhaps a brightly colored rattle or their mother's face?

Looking at Faces   Robert Fantz (1961) set out to answer this question by showing 2-month-old infants six disks and measuring the duration of their gaze at each one. He found that babies looked longer at patterned disks than at plain red, white, or yellow ones, and looked longest of all at the disk of a smiling face (see Figure 6.12). This research led some psychologists to conclude, not only that 2-month-olds can see patterns, but also that by 2 months a baby already knows that people are the most interesting objects around, a conclusion that brought about much celebration of the social skills of the newborn.

Figure 6.12 *What do 2-month-olds like to look at? Fantz found that they liked faces best of all. He measured how long 2- and 3-month-olds stared at the six types of disks portrayed here, presented one by one. As this graph shows, the infants stared at the face disk more than twice as long as at the disk of newsprint or the bull's-eye, and more than four times as long as at the patternless disks.*

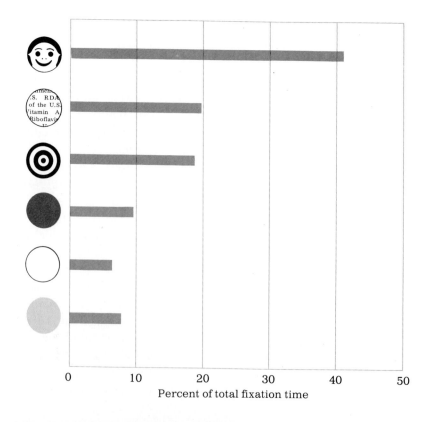

The celebration was unwarranted, however. It is true that infants are more interested in people than in most other objects they encounter. But further research found that babies look at faces, not because they belong to fellow humans, but because faces have an interesting pattern of dots (eyes) within an outlined circle (the face surrounded by hair) (Caron et al., 1973). There is even a developmental shift in precisely what part of a face is most interesting: 1-month-old babies look more at the hairline than the eyes (57 percent compared to 30 percent of total fixation time), but 2-month-old babies look more at eyes than hairline (49 percent compared to 33 percent) (Haith et al., 1977).

All told, infant vision is impressive—a far cry from the blindness that once was attributed to newborns. In the first weeks of life, babies are already focusing on interesting patterns and colors (Milewski and Siqueland, 1975) and prefer looking at moving objects rather than stationary ones. They see colors in much the same way adults do, and even have favorites, preferring reds and blues to greens and yellows (Bornstein, 1975).

RESEARCH REPORT   ## Depth Perception

Depth perception, the ability to see that one surface (such as the floor) is lower than another (such as the table) develops early. Eleanor Gibson and Richard Walk (1960) first learned this by placing babies beside a visual cliff, an apparent drop of several feet that actually was covered by a protective sheet of transparent glass (see photos below). Even when their mothers urged them to crawl onto the glass, 8- to 12-month-old babies hesitated to go over the "edge."

Joseph Campos and his colleagues (1970) decided to see if depth perception develops even before babies can crawl. To do this, they used a variant of the visual-cliff experiment, placing the infant not only on the "shallow" side of the visual cliff, as Gibson and Walk did, but also on the "deep" side (actually on the protective glass). They measured the infant's heart rate on both sides, theorizing that if the babies were old enough to realize that they were over a "cliff," their heart rates would speed up, but if they were too young to perceive the depth, heart rates would be the same on both sides.

Half of their prediction was correct: babies older than 8 months showed a rapid increase in heart rate on the "deep"

side of the cliff, compared to slightly younger babies who showed no significant heart-rate differences between the two sides. What the researchers had not foreseen was that very young babies—as young as 2-months-old—would show a *decrease* in heart rate on the "deep" side, showing that they perceived the difference, and were interested in it but not afraid of it. The younger babies were also much less likely to fuss or cry on the deep side than the older babies were.

Thus, depth perception develops in the first months of life, but fear of falling over an edge does not appear until about 8 months. Why is there this lag between perception and fear? Campos and his colleagues (1978) have several ideas. Perhaps perceptual and cognitive maturation are necessary before the baby realizes what the edge of a cliff means. Maybe babies under 6 months are essentially fearless. It may be that babies have to fall, or almost fall, once or twice before fear develops. Perhaps experience in crawling helps perception. In fact, probably several of these factors play a role.

These photos show the visual cliff used by Joseph Campos and his colleagues. Normally, babies older than 8 months old crawl happily toward their mothers to play, but when such crawling would take them over the apparent edge of a "cliff," almost all babies stay on the "shallow" side.

Hearing

Compared to the blurry vision of the newborn, hearing is well developed very early in life. Sudden noises startle newborns, making them cry; rhythmic sounds, such as a lullabye or a heartbeat, soothe them and put them to sleep. In fact, in one study of sixteen neonates, babies only a few hours old responded to conversation, opening their eyes, tensing their muscles, and moving their tongues, arms, and legs in reaction to the speech they heard (Condon and Sander, 1974). These responses were forthcoming for two very different languages, English and Chinese.

Some researchers are skeptical that newborns are so talented in the hours after birth, but there is no doubt that 1-month-old infants are adept, not only at hearing, but at perceiving what they hear (Eimas, 1975). In one experiment, 20-day-old infants showed that they preferred listening to their own mothers speaking certain words over listening to an unfamiliar woman saying the same words. This was demonstrated when they sucked much harder on artificial nipples that activated a recording of their own mother's voice than they sucked on nipples that activated a recording of the stranger's voice (Mills and Melhuish, 1974).

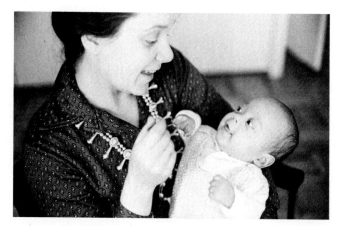

Figure 6.13 A "conversation" at 5 months is possible because the infant's hearing and vision are well developed.

Another experiment showed that infants can detect differences between very similar sounds. One-month-old babies sucked on a nipple that activated a recording of the "bah" sound, which was repeated whenever they sucked. At first, they sucked diligently; but as they became habituated to the sound, their sucking decreased. At this point, the experimenters changed the sound from "bah" to "pah." The babies immediately sucked harder, proving that they perceived the difference (Eimas et al., 1971).

Locating Sound   At least one auditory ability is not present at birth—using both ears to locate a specific sound (Bower, 1977). Accurate sound location depends on detecting the interval between one ear's perception of a sound and the other's, a tiny difference made particularly hard for infants to apprehend because the distance between their ears changes as their heads grow during the first year.

In one experiment, babies aged 1, 4, or 7 months faced their mother as she talked to them through a microphone (McGurk and Lewis, 1974). Sometimes the sound of the mother's voice was switched to loudspeakers in different parts of the room. Infants of all three ages looked for the source of the sound when it did not seem to come from their mothers, but only the 4- and 7-month-olds turned toward the correct side. One-month-olds were likely to look in the wrong direction for the noise.

Figure 6.14 *As cultures throughout the world recognize, infant carriers not only make it easier to hold a baby while working or shopping, they also keep babies happy. In the early months, front carriers allow infants to see the parent's face, hear the heartbeat, and feel the cradling movement of walking. In later months, back carriers allow babies to observe the sights and sounds of the world from a lofty perch. From the infant's perspective, the traditional baby carriage is a much less satisfying mode of transport, because it prevents constant contact with the parent and severely limits the view.*

The Other Senses

Of all their senses, infants' sense of touch seems to be the most developed: crying newborns usually can be soothed by being wrapped or swaddled in a blanket, or by being held snugly. The sense of motion is also present, as is demonstrated when an adult rocks a restless baby to sleep.

Two senses, taste and pain, seem to be poorly developed at birth. Newborns prefer to suck on a bottle of sweet rather than sour milk, and cry for a moment when their heel is pricked to obtain blood for a blood test, but these responses are much weaker than those of an older baby.

The sense of smell functions at a very young age. Not only do infants turn away from smells like vinegar or ammonia, but breast-fed babies are more quickly roused from sleep by the smell of a cloth that their mother has worn under her bra than by the smell of a cloth worn by another breast-feeding mother (Russell, 1976).

Careful research such as this, using the infant's preference for familiar people, has proven to psychologists that the senses develop early in life. By age 1, the senses are so acute, and preference for familiar people and objects is usually so strong, that some babies scream at the voice or sight of a stranger, require the feel of a special blanket before they sleep, and often refuse food that smells or tastes unfamiliar.

The Impact of Perceptual-Motor Skills

As you will learn in the next chapter, the infant's senses and motor skills provide the foundation for learning: the greater the baby's ability to focus visually and reach objects, the more experiences the baby accumulates. As Wayne Dennis found in his experimental raising of twin baby girls (see Chapter 1), without such experiences, skills develop very slowly.

The development of the infant's senses and motor abilities transforms not only the baby's world; it also affects the world of those around the baby. This is plainly obvious in toddlerhood, when, say, an older sister finds her school notebooks in tatters or all scribbled up with magic markers by the marauding toddler.

However, the impact of the infant's perceptual abilities is felt even in the first moments of life. The gaze of the newborn, which seems to focus on objects about 10 inches away—just the distance between the neonate's eyes and the face of an adult who is holding the infant in the usual feeding position—appears to call forth a response from the parents. In the minutes after birth, when their baby's eyes are closed, parents still talk *about* the baby; but once the baby's eyes are open, they talk *to* the infant (Macfarlane, 1977).

When a baby is blind, this mutually reinforcing system, of course, does not exist. Because the baby doesn't focus and track, many parents, even with the best intentions, find themselves responding less often to their baby than they would to a sighted infant (Fraiberg, 1974). In the same way, any abnormality or retardation in the infant might provoke an abnormal or hesitant response in the parents, setting up a poor parent-child interaction.

When we see an alert, active toddler with a responsive, stimulating parent, it is impossible to tell who started this happy partnership. Usually we take it for granted that the parent is the more important participant in the beginning of the relationship. But some evidence suggests not only that the partnership might be more equal but even that the infant's behavior may determine the parent's behavior more than the parent's determines the infant's (Bell and Harper, 1977).

Consider a longitudinal study of ninety-three infant-mother pairs (Bradley et al., 1979). When the babies were 6, 12, and 24 months old, their mental development was measured by the Bayley scales, primarily a test of perceptual-motor skills. At the same time, their mothers' involvement with them and stimulation of them were measured by the HOME scale, which indicates provision of appropriate toys and challenges. The scores were then compared over time to see which came first, a bright child or a stimulating mother.

The link between the infant's behavior at 6 months and the mother's behavior six months later was stronger than that between the infant's behavior at 1 and the mother's behavior six months earlier. In other words, a baby who was advanced in sitting up and reaching in the middle of the first year was likely to have an involved mother at the end of the year. This link approached significance (the .06 level) and was stronger than the link between the mother's involvement at 6 months and the baby's mental development at a year. In the second year of life, the authors of this study report, mother and child often develop "a mutually reinforcing 'steady state' relation. That is, brighter children continue to receive more advanced learning materials that continue to advance their capability."

Of course, as in any intimate relationship between two people, it is impossible in this case to attribute the eventual outcome of the interaction to one person or the other. But other researchers studying mother-infant relationships have reached similar conclusions (Sameroff, 1978). Certainly it is clear that the infant's contribution to the relationship, expressed in simple perceptual and motor skills, helps determine the parent's response. Indeed, it might be the child's most important contribution to establishing future relationships with the rest of the family.

Coordination of Perceptual and Motor Skills

We have already noted several instances in which two or more perceptual-motor skills are used together: by 4 months, infants look for the source of a sound and try to grasp objects dangled in front of them. As the infant matures, coordination sometimes reaches a point where skills used in isolation deteriorate. For instance, the grasping reflex that infants are born with becomes less automatic, as reaching and grasping come under better visual control. In one experiment, infants were shown a dangling object; then, just as they were about to reach for it, the lights were turned off so they could not see it (Bower and Wishart, 1972). Even in the dark, 5-month-old infants grabbed the object 50 percent of the time. On the other hand,

Figure 6.15 *Like many infants, when this 4-month-old coordinates two infant skills, looking and reaching, he adds a third skill, kicking.*

9-month-old infants, having learned to rely on visual information, were less skilled in the dark, grabbing successfully only once in every six tries.

Usually, the ability to coordinate senses is helpful, rather than handicapping, for it helps us to interpret our experiences. For example, as infants learn to distinguish one shape, sound, or tactile sense from another and to coordinate information from the various senses, they become able to recognize people and to mentally connect faces, voices, and hair texture. Mother and father become human beings, rather than simply isolated stimuli.

One experiment showed that 6-month-old infants are able to recognize the similarities and the differences between a photograph of a wooden object and the object itself (Rose, 1977). This finding suggests that "reading" a book to an infant by pointing to the pictures is an activity a 6-month-old could appreciate.

This coordination of perceptual skills raises the question of what kinds of experiences a child needs in order to develop as fully as possible. Are reaching for dangling objects, locating sound sources, and being "read" to necessary learning experiences, or do perceptual skills automatically coordinate as the baby grows older? Chapter 7 attempts to answer these questions.

Feeding Babies: Patterns and Problems

In order to thrive, infants must consume about 50 calories per day per pound, more than twice an adult's rate of consumption, and must be fed several times each day. Since babies have such an obviously essential need for food, one might imagine that when, how, and what babies are fed would be simple questions with standard answers, known to parents all over the world. The reverse is true: it is one of the most variable and controversial aspects of infant care. Feeding is discussed in some detail in the following pages, not only because nutrition is an important part of infant development, but also because variation in feeding patterns provides a good example of the fact that psychological and cultural patterns affect every aspect of infant development.

When to Feed: Schedule versus Demand

Forty years ago, American doctors told parents to feed their babies according to a strict schedule. Newborns should receive 4 ounces of formula every four hours, six times a day; older babies should get 6 or 8 ounces, four or five times a day. These doctors were influenced by many experts, including the psychologist John Watson (1928), who thought that scheduled feeding would produce an orderly and controlled child. Obedient parents woke up their sleeping infants to feed them, and tried to ignore their crying babies who got hungry "too early."

Figure 6.16 *A slave to scheduled feeding, this parent prepares for the 2 A.M. meal.*

The Decline of the Schedule This policy gradually changed, for at least four reasons. First, anthropologists reported that babies in many cultures are fed much more often than Watson advised. Second, Freud's theories became more popular, including his emphasis on the infant's need to suck. Third, doctors came to realize that infants themselves are usually the best judges of how much to eat, a conclusion influenced by an experiment in self-feeding, which indicated that when given a wide choice of healthy foods, babies would, over the long run, consume a balanced diet (Davis, 1928). When they went on occasional binges, overeating one food, they compensated by undereating that food for several days.

Finally, many parents and babies never adjusted to feeding on schedule. Because hunger is the most common cause of newborn crying, many parents would feed their babies before the scheduled hour for the sake of peace and quiet. On the other hand, since some very young babies sleep peacefully through the night, parents often woke up to give the 2 A.M. feeding only to find their infants sound asleep. Many of them gratefully went back to bed.

The Rise of Demand Feeding These four factors led to demand feeding, in which the timing of the feeding, and usually the amount of food, are determined by the baby's wants. Breast-feeding in particular is more successful on demand, because the total quantity of milk produced increases the more often the nipple is sucked and the breast emptied. Nursing whenever the baby is hungry thus stimulates milk production, and causes the supply of milk to adjust to the baby's needs.

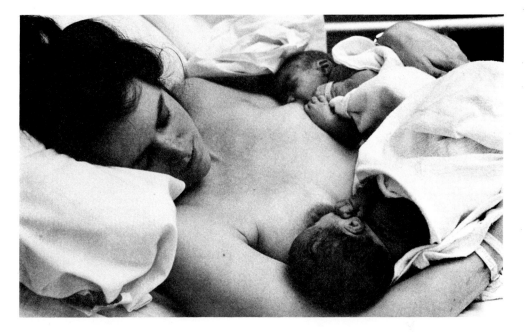

Figure 6.17 *In a well-nourished mother, production of breast milk follows the law of supply and demand: the greater the demand for milk, evidenced by strength and duration of sucking, as well as how often the breast is emptied, the greater the supply. Many mothers of twins have breast-fed them both, claiming that breast milk is not only the best nourishment, it also is the easiest to prepare.*

Weaning the baby from breast or bottle to the cup has been influenced by demand feeding. Babies used to be forced to give up sucking a nipple long before their first birthday, despite tears and protest. In the 1950s Robert Sears found that 69 percent of the families surveyed had weaned their babies completely by 16 months (Sears et al., 1957). Now babies usually are weaned more gradually, giving up breast and bottle when they and their families are ready—whether that means at 6 months or 3 years.

In some cultures, babies are still fed according to strict schedules; and in other cultures, babies are fed *before* demand. Konner (1972) studied child-rearing among the Zhun/twa (also called the !Kung) people of Namibia (South-West Africa). He writes:

> The mother, with the infant against her skin, or in her arms, can literally feel his state changes. She makes every effort to anticipate hunger. Waking up, moving, gurgling, the pucker face, the slightest fret, a change in the rate of breathing—any of these may result in nursing . . . Infants through at least the first year are nursed many times a day (twice an hour would be a conservative estimate) . . . It would be most sensible to describe the Zhun/twa as 'continual feeders'.

In some cultures, complete weaning from the breast does not occur until age 7, when school begins.

How to Feed: Breast versus Bottle

Should a newborn get milk from the mother's breasts or commercial formulas from a bottle? Most pediatricians recommend breast-feeding; most mothers choose bottle-feeding. Why?

Advantages of Breast Milk　Breast milk is always sterile and at body temperature. It contains more iron, vitamin C, and vitamin A than cow's milk (Bakwin, 1965) and has antibodies that increase the baby's resistance to disease. Breast-fed babies have fewer allergies and digestive upsets than bottle-fed babies, even when the bottle-fed babies are given well-prepared formulas and excellent care (Larsen and Homer, 1978).

Most doctors agree that breast milk from a well-nourished woman is the ideal infant food (Jelliffe and Jelliffe, 1977). Advocates of breast-feeding also believe that it strengthens the bond between mother and baby by bringing them into frequent close physical contact (Montagu, 1971). There is evidence that babies who are breast-fed on demand develop earlier and feel more secure (Newton, 1972).

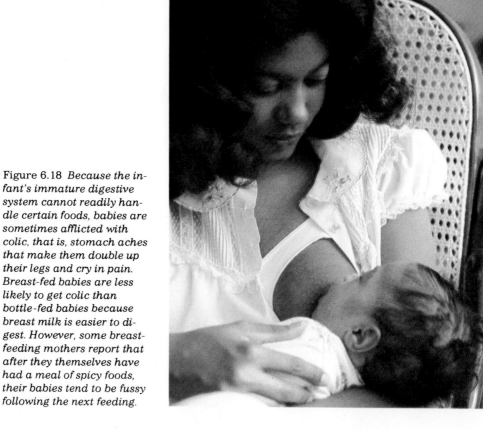

Figure 6.18 *Because the infant's immature digestive system cannot readily handle certain foods, babies are sometimes afflicted with colic, that is, stomach aches that make them double up their legs and cry in pain. Breast-fed babies are less likely to get colic than bottle-fed babies because breast milk is easier to digest. However, some breast-feeding mothers report that after they themselves have had a meal of spicy foods, their babies tend to be fussy following the next feeding.*

Prevalence of Bottle-Feeding　Despite the advantages of breast milk, about three out of four newborns, and nineteen out of twenty 6-month-olds, are bottle-fed (Fomon, 1974). In the first half of the twentieth century, the opposite was the case, because most formulas were difficult to prepare and very hard to digest. In the past thirty years, however, the convenience and digestibility of commercial formulas have improved. Most drugstores now sell formulas in six-packs: parents just screw a nipple onto the bottle and their baby's meal is ready.

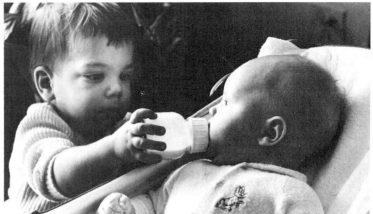

Figure 6.19 *Probably the greatest advantage of bottle-feeding is that anyone can do it. Some mothers decide to breast-feed in the early months and then switch to bottle-feeding at about 6 months, when digestive problems are less common and, incidentally, the first teeth usually appear.*

Convenience is only one of the reasons most women decide not to breast-feed. For one thing, most drugs (including alcohol, nicotine, and hormones in birth-control pills) turn up in breast milk, so many women decide to bottle-feed rather than limit their drug consumption. Social conditions that make it hard to have a job and breast-feed; family influences, such as the father's jealousy, and personal opinions about modesty, also play an important part in the decision. So does education. One nationwide survey found that 32 percent of college-educated women breast-fed their babies, compared with 8 percent of those who had not graduated from high school (Berg, 1973). Even babies have some involuntary influence over how they will be fed: once a woman starts breast-feeding her newborn in the hospital, the baby's characteristics (especially how much the baby consumes, how strongly the baby sucks, and how alert the baby is) are the most influential factors in determining how long breast-feeding continues (Hillenbrand, 1965; Newton and Newton, 1972).

For those who choose bottle-feeding, research on mother-child relationships is reassuring, for bottle-fed babies *can* be held and cuddled as much as breast-fed babies; and neither method guarantees good care. For instance, Escalona (1968) found that breast-feeding does not always result in maternal sensitivity; some breast-feeding mothers seemed oblivious to their infant's sucking or feeding problems. In addition, Bettye M. Caldwell's 1964 review of the research on specific child-care practices found that the mother's warmth and responsiveness to the infant's needs are much more important for the long-term development of the child than any specific mode of infant care or feeding.

However, before choosing bottle-feeding for convenience, there is one other argument for breast-feeding that should be considered. Breast-fed babies are less likely to die of sudden infant death syndrome (crib death), the leading cause of death in babies older than 1 month. Lewis Lipsitt (1978) suggests that this correlation may occur in part because breast-fed babies learn to breathe even when their noses are partly obstructed, and this learning helps them avoid crib death. His theory linking sudden infant death to learning is fascinating, but unproved. However, since breast-feeding in the early weeks lessens the chances of crib death (Jelliffe and Jelliffe, 1978), mothers of high-risk newborns have one more reason to consider breast-feeding. While there are some cases in which bottle-feeding is the wisest choice, most psychologists, like most pediatricians, think breast-feeding is generally preferable.

A CLOSER LOOK | **Sudden Infant Death**

Each year in the United States between 10,000 and 20,000 babies go to sleep and never wake up. They seem to be healthy, normal babies; then suddenly, inexplicably, they die. The cause is said to be sudden infant death syndrome (SIDS), although the term "sudden infant death" merely describes the event. The actual cause is still unknown. This uncertainty makes it especially hard for parents to accept the death of a SIDS victim, for they are completely unprepared for the possibility that their new baby might die, and often blame themselves.

Neighbors, relatives, and even the police sometimes blame the parents as well. In a small town in South Carolina in 1972, for example, a baby died of SIDS while his father was caring for him. Not knowing that a healthy infant can die suddenly for no known cause, the police arrested the father for murder. He was not released from jail until after his child's funeral, when analysis of the autopsy findings confirmed that the infant had died of SIDS (Raring, 1975).

Comparing infants who died of SIDS with other infants, some researchers have found that there are several characteristics that are more common among the victims, as summarized in the chart (Carpenter, 1974; Lipsitt, 1978).

High-risk babies can be identified from this list, and given special attention to prevent some cases of crib death (Carpenter, 1974). For example, often the babies who die of SIDS have a slight cold. Parents whose babies are at-risk can take special precautions, such as preventing contact between the baby and anyone who has a cold and using a humidifier in the baby's room. Mothers of high-risk babies might choose to breast-feed, even if it is not convenient.

However, identifying high-risk babies is not enough, for healthy low-risk babies also die of SIDS. Researchers are trying to pinpoint the causes of SIDS in order to prevent it completely, rather than simply minimizing the risk of its occurring. Botulism appears to be the cause of some cases of SIDS. If this bacteria is spotted in the digestive tract of an infant, medical care can prevent SIDS in that baby. One source of the botulism spores is raw honey, which, obviously,

Factors Correlated with SIDS

	SIDS More Likely	SIDS Less Likely
Characteristics of Mother		
Age	Under 20	Over 30
Blood type	O, B, or AB	A
Personal habits	Smoker	Nonsmoker
Characteristics of Infant		
Sex	Male	Female
Birth order	Later-born	First-born
Birth weight	Under 2500 grams (5½ lbs)	Over 2500 grams
Apgar score at 1 minute	7 or lower	8 or higher
Characteristics of Pregnancy		
Mother's health	Urinary infection	No complications
Length of pregnancy	Less than eight months	Full-term
Mother's nutrition	Anemia (not enough iron)	No anemia
Situation at Time of Death		
Time of year	Winter	Summer
Age of infant	2–4 mos.	Under 1 mo., more than 6 mos.
Infant health	Has a cold, with stuffy nose	Has no cold, nor runny nose
Feeding	Bottle-fed	Breast-fed

should not be given to infants (Marx, 1978). Researchers are also studying breathing patterns, lung structures, and blood chemistry, searching for small abnormalities that will forecast SIDS. Once doctors know which newborns will take the overlong pauses between breaths (called *apnea*) that occur prior to some sudden deaths, they can use the same monitoring equipment already used to keep premature babies breathing regularly. Then at least some cases of SIDS can be prevented.

What to Feed: Nutrition and Malnutrition

Deciding what to feed an infant may now seem a simple matter: you feed breast milk if possible, and formula based on cow's milk if not. Deciding how much to feed may seem simple too: you give as much as the baby wants. However, many babies are given the wrong diet, with malnourishment as a result.

Malnutrition takes two forms. The first, called *protein-calorie deficiency,* occurs when people do not get enough protein and calories to sustain their growth; the result can be starvation. The second form, *specific vitamin or mineral deficiencies,* occurs when people get enough food but from a diet that is not well-balanced.

Giving a child enough protein and calories would seem fairly easy to do in North America. Breast milk and commercial formulas are designed to meet the young infant's nutritional needs; and a peanut-butter sandwich, a pint of milk, and one egg provide more than the 23 grams of protein and almost half the 1300 calories recommended for 2-year-olds each day (Recommended Dietary Allowances, 1974). Yet protein-calorie deficiency does sometimes occur in North America, especially among Appalachian whites, inner-city blacks, Mexican-Americans, Native Americans on reservations, and Eskimos (Winick, 1976). In parts of South America, Asia, and Africa, most children suffer from protein-calorie malnutrition.

The second form of malnutrition is common in almost every country. For example, almost half of the American children between 1 and 5 do not get enough vitamin C or A, and 95 percent do not get enough iron. This makes them one of the least well-nourished groups in the nation (National Center for Health Statistics, 1974).

Results of Malnutrition   In the first years of life, severely malnourished babies are likely to suffer from marasmus, a disease that occurs when the baby does not digest enough food. Growth stops, body tissues waste away, and the infant dies. During toddlerhood, protein-calorie deficiency is more likely to cause kwashiorkor, a condition in which the child's hair becomes thin and loses color and the face, legs, and abdomen swell with water, sometimes making the child appear well fed to anyone who doesn't realize that the bloated stomach is empty. Malnutrition reduces a child's resistance to other diseases: when severely malnourished children get measles, for instance, about half of them die (Winick, 1976).

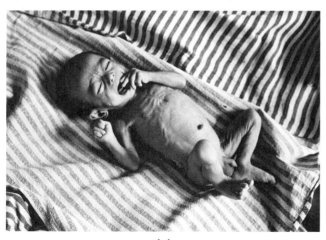

(a)

(b)

Figure 6.20 (a) *This Indonesian infant suffers from marasmus, the most common result of severe protein-calorie deficiency in the first months of life. If he survives, he will never fulfill his full physical or mental growth potential, for malnutrition has been too prolonged for catch-up growth to remedy the destruction of brain and body cells.*
(b) Unlike starvation in infancy, starvation in toddlerhood often creates the swollen stomach seen on this Angolan child, a symptom of kwashiorkor. If mother and child obtain immediate care, most of the ill effects of their malnutrition can be remedied.

Serious early malnutrition prevents brain growth and even destroys brain cells, according to animal research and autopsies of babies who die of marasmus (Scrimshaw and Gordon, 1968). Prolonged protein-calorie deficiency makes a child listless and mentally retarded. Research conducted by Joaquin Craviato in Central America found that severe malnutrition slows down some aspects of development more than others, among them language (Craviato and De Licardie, 1975), and the ability to coordinate information from the various senses (Craviato et al., 1966). These are two of the most important skills that should develop in the first years of life.

In North America, death from malnutrition is extremely rare, and few children show such physical signs of vitamin deficiency as hair loss or rickets (National Center for Health Statistics, 1974). Moderate malnutrition probably does not destroy necessary brain cells, but vitamin deficiencies can slow down learning nevertheless. Malnutrition makes many toddlers more tired, sick, or irritable—and consequently less curious—than they would be if they were well fed. It also affects their parents, for it is much easier to respond positively to a happy child than to a cranky one. The interaction of an impatient parent and an apathetic child is bound to slow down learning.

Causes of Malnutrition   The reasons for malnutrition vary from nation to nation and from child to child. In many developing countries, arable land and economic resources are insufficient to feed everyone. Social customs can make the problem worse. Sometimes, when food is scarce, the best food is saved for the men.

In developed countries, the situation is reversed. Social factors, rather than insufficient supply, are the primary cause of malnutrition. Chief among these is poor education about nutrition: many people simply do not know what the essential nutritional requirements are or what foods supply them best. For example, some parents who think of milk as the "basic" food rely too heavily on it for the toddler's diet, not realizing that although milk is high in protein, it is low in iron. (Iron deficiency makes a child listless and more vulnerable to disease; the best sources of iron are meat and green vegetables.) Many toddlers eat too much sugar, thanks partly to dozens of TV cartoon characters telling them how great sweetened cere-

Figure 6.21 *On a typical Saturday morning, each hour of children's television includes twelve minutes of commercials, advertising fifteen different kinds of sugary foods.*

als and candy are. When parents have personal problems, such as illness or depression, the above factors are even more likely to result in a malnourished child. Let us examine the interaction between poverty and custom more closely in two situations—a protein-poor country and a poverty-stricken American family.

Poverty and Malnutrition: Developing Nations.   In many poor countries, the only protein source available for infants and toddlers has been breast milk. Traditionally, children in such countries were weaned from the breast when the next baby was due. This custom usually prevented marasmus, but not kwashiorkor. Indeed, the word "kwashiorkor" is a combination of the words "kwashi," meaning first, and "orkor," meaning second, in the Ga language of Africa. It was so named because the first born children often got kwashiorkor when the second child arrived (Lloyd-Still, 1976).

According to a theory originally suggested by John Whiting (1964), some societies in protein-poor countries developed an interrelated set of customs to prolong breast-feeding and prevent kwashiorkor. In these cultures, children were breast-fed until age 3 or 4. To prevent a new pregnancy from interfering with the milk supply, women abstained from intercourse for several years after the birth of each child.

A society with such long periods of sexual abstinence might have an insufficient birth rate, as well as frustrated husbands. Interestingly enough, many of these same cultures practice polygamy. But then, it would seem, such an arrangement might produce lonely women. Again, it is notable that in most of these cultures, mothers are especially close to their children, not only breast-feeding them for years but sleeping beside them until puberty. Finally, for the boys of these cultures, living so close to the mother would seem a likely cause of problems with masculine identification. However, these cultures also have dramatic and painful puberty rites, usually including circumcision, which help the adolescent boy to put away childish ideas and desires and identify with the men of the tribe. One example was dramatized by Kunta Kinte in *Roots,* who no longer could live with, or even converse with, his mother after the ceremonies that marked the beginning of manhood (Haley, 1976).

WHITING'S THEORY

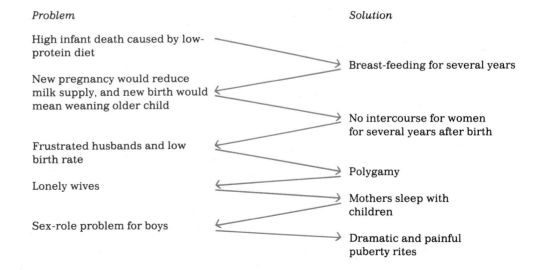

Problem	Solution
High infant death caused by low-protein diet	Breast-feeding for several years
New pregnancy would reduce milk supply, and new birth would mean weaning older child	No intercourse for women for several years after birth
Frustrated husbands and low birth rate	Polygamy
Lonely wives	Mothers sleep with children
Sex-role problem for boys	Dramatic and painful puberty rites

Critics have pointed out that many cultures with low-protein diets do not follow this pattern, and Whiting himself acknowledges that this is an oversimplification of a complicated process. In fact, most South American countries have a serious problem with infant nutrition, but none allow polygamy and few practice circumcision. However, no one disputes that a long period of breast-feeding is the best solution for a culture with inadequate protein (Wray, 1978).

Unfortunately, in many developing countries the trend is toward shorter rather than longer breast-feeding. In Chile, which had the highest rate of infant death in all South America during the early 1970s, nutritionists blamed the new custom of weaning babies from the breast at 3 months (Winick, 1976). The same "modern" custom affects babies elsewhere. As Maurice King writes: "In Zambia . . . it is the custom to put something belonging to a child on his grave when he dies. It is sad to see so many children with the feeding bottle that may well have killed them put on their graves" (King, 1973).

Figure 6.22 *Many infant deaths in developing countries are caused by the inevitable chronic diarrhea that results from bottle-feeding without proper refrigeration or sterilization. To prevent such deaths, some nations forbid the importation of baby formulas.*

As breast-feeding declines in poor countries, both the birth rate and the infant mortality rate rise (Knodel, 1977). Powdered commercial formulas are an adequate substitute for breast milk in countries with potable water and a high literacy rate (so the instructions can be read). But commercial formulas can be fatal where the water is contaminated and the mother doesn't know how to prepare them. They are also very expensive, so many parents add extra water to make them last longer (Ainsworth, 1967).

Poverty and Malnutrition: Developed Nations.   By contrast, in North America, the water for the most part is wholesome, and commercial formulas are available to impoverished families through a special federal program. But that still does not guarantee that all infants receive adequate nutrition. In order for the food to get to the baby, there must be a responsive bureaucracy and a responsible care-giver.

Consider one example. An 8-month-old girl was admitted to a Boston hospital. She was emaciated; she could not sit up; she did not respond when spoken to. In the hospital, the baby rapidly gained weight, started to smile and play with the nurses, and was discharged. Two months later she was readmitted, "a small, dirty, smelly infant, with restless movements of her hands, and again, underweight" (Newberger et al., 1976). Clearly, her malnutrition could not be cured without paying attention to the environment that caused the problem.

This time the hospital staff took an ecological approach. Treatment focused on the mother, who had four children, no husband, little money, and few friends or relatives. She received medical help for a chronic infection and dental help for aching teeth. A social worker helped place the two older children in a nursery school, and found a homemaker and a public health nurse to give the mother day-to-day support. These measures helped the baby as well as her mother. Four years later the little girl entered kindergarten, normal in her physical and psychological development.

Conclusions As the authors who described this case point out, treating both mother and child was necessary for a solution of this particular problem. For prevention of such problems, a broader ecological approach, combating social ills such as poverty and isolation, would be necessary.

A similar conclusion could be drawn for all aspects of physical development covered in this chapter. For the most part, babies grow and develop skills as rapidly as their genes allow, as long as their family and culture provide the opportunity. At the same time, when things go wrong, the cause is usually complex. Biological, familial, and cultural conditions all interact to affect the growth of the child.

SUMMARY

Size and Shape

1. In their first two years, most babies gain about 20 pounds (9 kilograms) and grow almost 15 inches (38 centimeters). The proportions of the body change. The newborn is top-heavy, for the head takes up one-fourth of the body length, partly because the growth of the brain during prenatal life is faster than that of any other part of the body. In adulthood, the head is about one-eighth of the body length.

Development of Motor Abilities

2. Motor skills follow the cephalo-caudal and proximo-distal sequences; the upper part of the body is controlled before the lower part is, and the arms are controlled before the hands and fingers are. Babies vary greatly in the ages at which they master specific skills, because the development of these skills depends on the interaction of cultural and genetic forces.

Sensation and Perception

3. Both sensation and perception are present at birth, and both become more developed with time. Some senses—notably hearing—seem very acute within the first months of life; others—notably vision—develop more slowly throughout the first year.

Feeding Babies: Patterns and Problems

4. Families and cultures choose different ways to feed babies, from strictly scheduled bottle-feeding to almost continuous breast-feeding. Breast milk is healthier for most babies, and breast-feeding may strengthen the mother-infant bond. However, commercial formulas are a nourishing substitute.

5. Protein-calorie malnutrition is the leading cause of death in many developing countries. Severe malnutrition causes two major diseases, marasmus and kwashiorkor, and lowers resistance to infections. Severe malnutrition is rare among North American infants, but vitamin deficiencies are common. Even moderate malnutrition can affect learning.

6. The specific causes of malnutrition vary from country to country, family to family, and child to child. The interaction between custom, poverty, and family problems underlies most instances of inadequate nourishment.

KEY QUESTIONS

How do the proportions of the body change as the infant grows?

What is the general sequence of the development of motor skills?

Why do norms vary from group to group and time to time?

Why has there been a sudden burst of research in infant sensation and perception?

How well can infants see?

How well can infants hear?

When and why does fear of falling from high places occur?

What are the advantages and disadvantages of demand feeding?

What are the advantages and disadvantages of breast-feeding?

What are the causes of malnutrition?

What are the consequences of malnutrition in infancy?

KEY TERMS

primary motor areas of the cortex

primary sensory areas of the cortex

birth catch-up

motor skills

crawling

creeping

toddler

norms

sensation

perception

habituation

depth perception

visual cliff

scheduled feeding

demand feeding

sudden infant death syndrome (SIDS)

malnutrition

marasmus

kwashiorkor

RECOMMENDED READINGS

Lewin, Roger (ed.). *Child alive.* New York: Doubleday, 1975.

Includes many readable short articles about the competence of young babies, written by leading researchers.

Bower, T. G. R. *A primer of infant development.* San Francisco: Freeman, 1977.

This is a review of infant development, including research examples from Bower's specialty, the perceptual skills of the very young infant. He relates these abilities to cognitive and social development.

Eiger, Marvin, and Olds, Sally. *Complete book of breastfeeding.* New York: Bantam, 1973.

This is one of the best books on breast-feeding, with practical suggestions for getting ready before birth, dealing with jealousy from older children, and responding to criticism from relatives and neighbors. There is also good coverage of the advantages of breast milk and of the process of feeding.

Raphael, Dana. *The tender gift.* New York: Schocken Books, 1976.

A survey of breast-feeding in many countries and cultures, including our own. Margaret Mead wrote the Introduction to this book.

Lappe, E. M. *Diet for a small planet.* New York: Ballantine, 1971.

This book gives practical suggestions for eating healthily without gobbling up the protein sources of the world. If you want a family of more than two children but would feel guilty about using more than your share of the world's resources, this book might help you have your family and still show your concern about your fellow humans. It will also save you money.

The First Two Years: Cognitive Development

The only language men ever speak perfectly is the one they learn in babyhood, when no one can teach them anything!

Maria Montessori

True or False?   Early development of sensorimotor skills, such as reaching or walking, is a good indicator of high intelligence in later life.

Motherese, the language of such utterances as "choo-choo," "bow-wow," and "tummy," is strictly a product of Western culture.

Most psychologists agree that language is acquired by first hearing speech and then being reinforced for using it.

From the psychologist's point of view, infants are capable of conversation long before they can actually speak words.

Until they are about 6 months old, deaf babies make the same babbling sounds that hearing babies do.

Whether children are beginning to speak Spanish, French, Syrian, Arabic, or Swahili, the word they use for "mother" is the same.

Infants begin life knowing nothing about the world around them. But the reflexes, senses, and curiosity that they are born with are soon put to good use. By age 1 they have already learned about many of the objects in their environment (that some make noises, that others move, that some are fun to play with, that some are not to be touched), about people (that some are familiar, that others are strangers), and about experiences (that playing in sandboxes is fun, that visiting the doctor can hurt). Most impressive of all, they have learned to communicate. They understand many of the gestures and words of other people and can make their own needs and emotions known, perhaps even saying a word or two themselves.

By age 2, the simple cognitive abilities of the 12-month-old baby have developed into the more complex talents of the child. Toddlers are what Dr. Spock (1976) calls "demon explorers," continually experimenting to find new ways to get what they want, at first by trial and error and later by reflection. By this time, they are not only saying dozens of words but sometimes even putting words together to make sentences.

Before we trace this rapid cognitive development in the first two years of life, it is only fair to warn you: There is probably more debate among developmental psychologists about the cognitive development of young children than about any other topic. Most of the controversy centers on how babies gain the ability to think. Is it maturation or learning that moves an infant from simple reflexes to complex skills? Do babies teach themselves, or must they be taught?

How Cognitive Development Occurs

Not so many years ago, developmental psychologists too often found themselves obliged to take sides in the controversy between those who thought that biological forces were the crucial factor in determining mental development and those who thought that social forces were more important. This debate took many forms and was given many names ("heredity versus environment," "maturation versus learning," and "nature versus nurture"), but the essential question was the same: Is a child's cognitive growth influenced more by internal forces such as genes and maturation or by external factors such as family and teachers, toys and neighborhood?

Those supporting the former view maintained that each child is genetically "programmed" to walk and talk after a certain period of maturation, just as a tadpole is destined to become a frog or a caterpillar, a butterfly. If a child is retarded, they held, the cause is biological—perhaps faulty genes or complications during birth.

Those on the other side of the argument, that is, those who believed the environment is crucial, emphasized the particular experiences a person needs to learn. In their view, if two identical twins were raised half a world apart, one in the slums of Calcutta and one in the middle-class suburbs of Dallas, they would differ, not only in language, values, and personality, but in intelligence and physique as well. An example like this one, according to the environmentalists, demonstrates that while genes set the stage for development, environment runs the show, because specific experiences and a general educational milieu make an enormous difference in the person a child becomes.

Interaction Between Maturation and Learning

In the last twenty years, research has brought a measure of calm to this controversy. Psychologists now recognize that *both* maturation and learning are essential. The development of sensorimotor skills—when the baby can focus well visually, or when the baby walks—seems to depend more on physiological maturity than on anything else. Indeed, maturation seems to be a prerequisite for almost everything, even, as we shall see later, for speaking in sentences and saying good-bye to Mom without crying.

At the same time, experience has also proven to be indispensable, even for perceptual skills. If an infant animal is prevented from using certain of its senses, those senses do not develop normally (Thompson and Grusec, 1970; Riesen, 1975). For example, if kittens are kept harnessed so that they cannot move but are carried around so they can explore the environment visually, when let free they initially bump into objects as though blind (Held and Hein, 1963). Chimpanzees who are prevented from moving with castlike restraints do not climb when they are released; dogs who are protected from pain actually burn their noses by sniffing a lit candle when they have free rein. Not only does the functioning of such animals become temporarily impaired; their brains sometimes deteriorate as well (Globus, 1975). With humans, such experiments are out of the question, but studies of enriched and deprived children (such as the experiment by Dennis discussed in Chapter 1) point in the same direction—experience can be crucial.

Difference in Emphasis Although almost all psychologists now agree that maturation and learning work together, they still debate over the relative importance of each. Specifically, they are at odds on the question of whether babies will learn on their own as long as there is sufficient environmental stimulation available or whether they need an organized environment and/or specific instruction.

Piaget emphasizes the baby's own search for equilibrium, a balance between new experiences and old ideas. He does not think a child's development should be accelerated with specific teaching techniques, structured experiences, or environmental enrichment. He believes that "pushing" a child is neither possible nor wise.

On the other hand, many psychologists in the United States and Canada share Jerome Bruner's belief that parents should feed an infant's curiosity by providing an enriched environment, because the infant's powerful desire to learn will benefit from well-organized experiences (Bruner, 1968).

Before we try to sort out these opinions, let us examine the actual phenomena that these psychologists argue about—the thought processes of the infant.

Sensorimotor Intelligence

All psychologists who study infant thinking begin by observing basic perceptual and motor skills, because very young babies, unlike adults, think exclusively with their senses and movements. Presented with a rattle, a typical adult might refer to it by name, classify it according to function, evaluate it aesthetically, and at the same time have thoughts of pregnancy, childhood, or the rising costs of petrochemicals. Give a rattle to a baby and he or she will stare at it, shake it, suck it, bang it on the floor. As Flavell (1977) explains, the infant "exhibits a wholly practical, perceiving-and-doing, action-bound kind of intellectual functioning: he does not exhibit the more contemplative, reflective, symbol-manipulating kind we usually think of in connection with cognition." For this reason, Piaget calls the first two years of cognitive development the sensorimotor period, focusing on senses and motor skills.

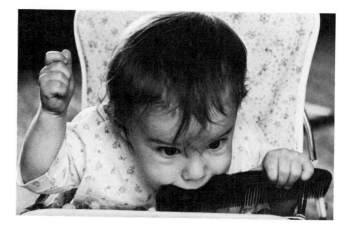

Figure 7.1 *In the sensorimotor stage of intelligence, infants understand their world through actions, grasping and mouthing almost everything within reach.*

In the 1920s, Piaget studied his own three children with the same fascinated care that had characterized his work as a natural scientist. His observations led to a step-by-step description of sensorimotor intelligence (Piaget, 1952), a description that was first ignored, then studied, challenged, tested, and finally accepted by most developmental psychologists throughout the world. Not everyone agrees with Piaget's theory of *how* a child moves from stage to stage, and even Piaget feels that the ages given for each stage are approximate, but his basic observations, and the overall sequence of development that he mapped out, have been confirmed by the studies of many researchers (Flavell, 1963, 1977). In infancy, Piaget's developmental sequence occurs in six stages.

The Six Stages of Sensorimotor Development

To get an overview of the stages of sensorimotor thought, it might help to group the six stages in pairs. The first two involve the infant's own body (*primary circular reactions*).

I. BIRTH TO 1 MONTH	*Reflexes*—sucking, grabbing, staring, listening.
II. 1–4 MONTHS	*The first acquired adaptations*—accommodation and coordination of reflexes—sucking a pacifier differently from a nipple; grabbing a bottle to suck it.

The next two involve objects and people (*secondary circular reactions*).

III. 4–8 MONTHS	*Procedures for making interesting sights last*—responding to people and objects.
IV. 8–12 MONTHS	*New adaptation and anticipation*—becoming more deliberate and purposeful in responding to people and objects.

The last two are the most creative, first with action (*tertiary circular reactions*) and then with ideas.

V. 12–18 MONTHS	*New means through active experimentation*— experimentation and creativity in actions of "the little scientist."
VI. 18–24 MONTHS	*New means through mental combinations*—thinking before doing makes the child experimental and creative in a new way.

Stage One: Reflexes (Birth to 1 Month)

Sensorimotor intelligence begins with newborns' reflexes, such as sucking, grasping, looking, and listening. Take sucking as an example: neonates suck everything that touches their lips, and sometimes even make sucking motions in their sleep. This repetition of the sucking motion gives them experience with a variety of objects and helps them to develop variations of the sucking scheme.

Stage Two: The First Acquired Adaptations (1 Month to 4 Months)

The second stage of sensorimotor intelligence begins when infants adapt their reflexes to the environment, for instance, sucking on various objects (bottles, breasts, pacifiers, and fingers) in different ways. By the time they are a few weeks old, many infants have learned to spit out a pacifier if they are hungry, although they will contentedly suck one if they are not.

Perceptual skills also show this adaptation. Instead of automatically reacting in the same way to every stimulus, as most newborns do, in the second stage of cognitive development infants show some judgment: they are more interested in looking at faces than at featureless circles, and they prefer their own mother's voice and smell to those of a stranger.

Even more impressive, between 1 and 4 months infants begin to coordinate two senses or actions. They hear a noise and turn to locate it (though not always in the right direction) (McGurk and Lewis, 1974), or they see an object and try to touch it (rarely successfully) (Bower, 1977). These behaviors are obviously not very well developed. In fact, according to Piaget, babies at this stage do not even try to reach for an object unless they can see both the object and their own hand. Nonetheless, such actions are clearly more advanced than simple reflexes. They show perception as well as sensation.

CIRCULAR REACTION

PRIMARY CIRCULAR REACTION

Primary Circular Reactions   Stages one and two also mark the beginning of what Piaget calls circular reactions, in which a baby's given action triggers a reaction, in the baby or in another, that in turn makes the baby repeat the action.

Piaget describes three types of circular reactions: primary, secondary, and tertiary. In the primary circular reaction, typical of stage two, the baby's own body is the source of the response: babies suck their thumbs, kick their legs, or stare at their hands again and again, seemingly for the pleasure of it.

The following selections from Piaget's observations of his son Laurent show the adaptation of the sucking reflex as well as the primary circular reaction:

> During the second half of the second month, after having learned to suck his thumb, Laurent continues to play with his tongue and to suck, but intermittently. On the other hand, his skill increases. Thus at 1 month, 20 days, I notice he grimaces while placing his tongue between gums and lips and in bulging his lips, as well as making a clapping sound when quickly closing his mouth after these exercises.
>
> During the third month he adds to the protrusion of his tongue and finger sucking new circular reactions involving the mouth. Thus from 2 months, 18 days Laurent plays with his saliva, letting it accumulate within his half-open lips and then abruptly swallowing it. About the same period he makes sucking-like movements, with or without putting out his tongue, changing in various ways the position of his lips; he bends and contracts his lower lips, etc. [Piaget, 1952]

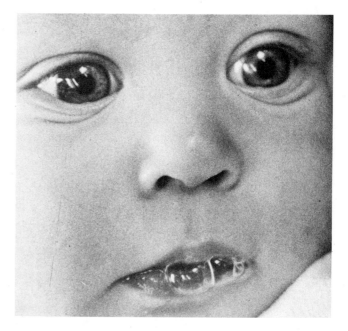

Figure 7.2 *An early adaptation of the sucking reflex is blowing bubbles, one of the first instances of the infant's learning to use simple body movements for pleasure.*

Stage Three: Procedures for Making Interesting Sights Last (4 Months to 8 Months)

In the third stage, babies become more aware of objects and other people, and they begin to recognize some of the specific characteristics of the things in their environment. This is the first step toward the baby's realization that he or she is an individual with independent ideas and desires.

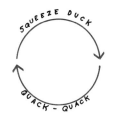

SECONDARY CIRCULAR REACTION

Secondary Circular Reactions Infants show this new perspective when they perform secondary circular reactions. Here, the response babies get from someone or something when they perform a specific action causes them to repeat the action in hopes of getting the same response. A baby might accidently squeeze a rubber duck, hear a quack, and squeeze the duck again. If the quack is repeated, the infant will probably laugh and give another squeeze, for most babies are delighted to realize that they can control the objects around them.

Piaget calls stage three "procedures for making interesting sights last," because babies interact diligently with people and objects to produce exciting experiences. Realizing that rattles make noise, babies at this stage shake their arms and laugh when someone puts a rattle in their hands. Vocalization increases a great deal, for now that babies realize that other people can respond, they love to make a noise, listen for a response, and answer back. Almost any form of imitation becomes fun, such as making noises, gestures, and expressions just like the ones other people make.

Another interesting reaction that develops at this time is ticklishness. What causes tickling movements to tickle is the awareness that another person is making them, which explains why younger babies do not laugh when they are "tickled." (It also explains why you can't tickle yourself.) However, stage-three babies often chortle gleefully when their stomachs are kissed or their feet lightly brushed (White, 1975).

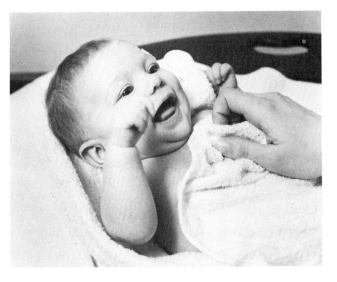

Figure 7.3 *Being tickled becomes exciting when the infant realizes that another person is doing the tickling. In the first 3 months of life, infant cognition is usually too immature to appreciate tickling.*

Object Permanence Begins The major intellectual accomplishment of stage three is the infant's awakening understanding that objects continue to exist even when they cannot be seen. This concept is called object permanence. For younger babies, "out of sight" is literally "out of mind," but toward the end of stage three, babies suspect that when objects disappear, they have not vanished forever. When a toy falls from the crib, for instance, a stage-three baby might look for it for a moment rather than immediately losing interest in it. Piaget interprets the baby's search for objects as the emergence of the concept of object permanence. However, another explanation holds that the increased memory abilities of 8-month-olds enables them to search for objects because they can remember where they were when they lost sight of them (Kagan et al., 1978).

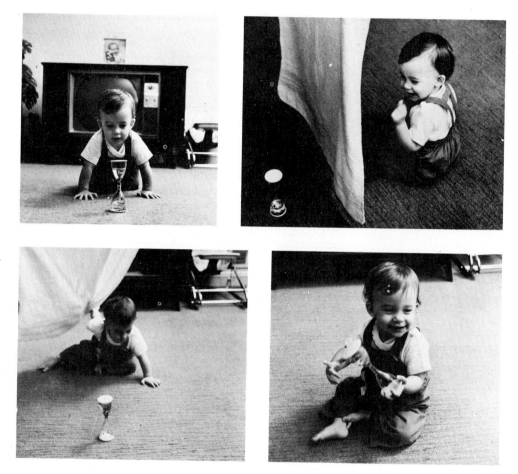

Figure 7.4 *Between 8 and 12 months, finding a toy that has been "hidden" is a cognitive challenge that leads to deliberate action, and to much delight if the challenge is met.*

No matter which explanation is correct, the test of this achievement is the same: show a baby an interesting toy and then cover it up. If the baby tries to uncover it, he or she must suspect that the toy still exists. Most stage-three infants do not try to uncover the toy unless part of it is left visible. At the end of this stage, they make an effort to find completely hidden objects, although they do not search very well or very long. Piaget calls this active searching "goal-directed behavior." When infants try to accomplish a goal, they enter the fourth stage of sensorimotor intelligence.

Stage Four: New Adaptation and Anticipation (8 Months to 12 Months)

Between 8 and 12 months, infants become more deliberate and purposeful in what they do. Whereas a younger infant is likely to treat all objects the same way, either sucking, or dropping, or shaking them, the 9-month-old is likely to pause to examine an object before doing something with it. It is as if the baby must decide what to do, knowing that some objects should be tasted, others shaken, and still others—like unfriendly cats—avoided. Imitation becomes a favorite activity. Babies try to join their parents and older siblings in almost anything, including dancing, fighting, and "reading" a book.

Babies at stage four develop definite ideas about what they want. They might see something clear across the room and crawl toward it, ignoring many interesting distractions along the way. Or they might grab a forbidden object—a box of matches, a thumbtack, a cigarette—and cry with rage when it is taken away, even if they are offered a substitute that is normally fascinating to them.

Figure 7.5 *Mother and stage-four child in a classic confrontation.*

Finally, stage-four babies anticipate events: they might cry when they see Mother putting on her coat, and might even hide the hat she usually wears with that coat; if they enjoy splashing in the bathtub, they might squeal with delight when the bath water is turned on. Younger babies often spit out distasteful food *after* they taste it; 12-month-olds are sufficiently wise to keep their mouths tightly shut when they see spinach on the spoon.

Stage Five: New Means Through Active Experimentation (12 Months to 18 Months)

Through persistent practice, toddlers learn to coordinate arms, legs, hands, feet. However, the toddler's practice is quite different from that of the infant who bounces up and down in a jumper, or that of the adult who diligently performs a hundred push-ups. Instead of repeating the same action, toddlers vary their behavior, as if they were trying to discover all the possibilities of the world they live in.

Tertiary Circular Reactions This exploration and experimentation are typical of stage-five sensorimotor intelligence. Unlike the primary and secondary circular reactions, in which babies repeat the same action again and again, in the tertiary circular reaction toddlers vary their behavior. A toddler might first hit a toy drum with a drumstick, then, in turn, hit it with a pencil, a block, and a hammer.

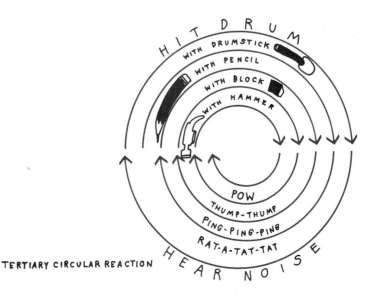

TERTIARY CIRCULAR REACTION

Figure 7.6 *The "busy scientist" in one of his many laboratories. Unfortunately, toddlers in stage five of the sensorimotor period are much better at taking things out and pulling them apart than they are at putting them back or together. This means that a family's sense of humor is more important at this stage than their sense of order.*

The Little Scientist   Piaget compares the toddler's active experimentation in stage five to a scientist who "experiments in order to see." On one occasion, Piaget's son Laurent dropped a small piece of bread again and again, watching intently as it fell. Then with equal attentiveness he crumbled it up and dropped the pieces.

Stage-five thinking is much more creative than earlier sensorimotor thought. Stage-five toddlers go one step beyond the stage-four process of deciding whether to suck, drop, or shake a given object. They seem to ask, "What *else* can I do with this? What happens if I take the nipple off the bottle, or turn over the trash basket, or pour water on the cat?"

Because of this willingness to experiment, toddlers find new ways to achieve their goals. They learn, for instance, that they can bring a toy to them by pulling on the string tied to the end of it, or that they can "reach" the plate of cookies in the middle of the dinner table by pulling on the tablecloth. No doubt, parents of toddlers could add many other examples, from the mischievous to the disastrous.

Stage Six: New Means Through Mental Combinations (18 Months to 24 Months)

At this stage, toddlers begin to anticipate and solve simple problems by using mental combinations before they act. That is, they fit one idea with another in their minds, rather than simply combining one action with another as they did at earlier stages. Consider what Jacqueline Piaget did at 20 months.

> Jacqueline arrives at a closed door with a blade of grass in each hand. She stretches out her right hand toward the knob but sees that she cannot turn it without letting go of the grass. She puts the grass on the floor, opens the door, picks up the grass again and enters. But when she wants to leave the room, things become complicated. She puts the grass on the floor and grasps the doorknob. But then she perceives that in pulling the door toward her she will simultaneously chase away the grass which she placed between the door and the threshold. She therefore picks it up in order to put it outside the door's zone of movement. [Piaget, 1952]

In this example, Jacqueline did not need to experiment; she was able to imagine the various problems involved with opening the door and to invent solutions to them without resorting to trial and error, as a younger child would.

Mental Representation Another characteristic of stage-six thought is improved memory. Children develop mental representation, the ability to remember, or represent mentally, what they have seen or experienced. For example, Jacqueline was fascinated when a neighbor's child had a temper tantrum in a playpen; he screamed, shook the playpen, and stamped his feet. She had never seen anything like it.

The very next day, Jacqueline had a tantrum of her own, complete with stamping. If she had imitated her friend's tantrum immediately, or if she had seen it dozens of times before, her behavior would not have demonstrated mental representation. However, Jacqueline's acting out of a detailed mental image she had retained for twenty-four hours is an example of deferred imitation, which is typical of stage-six thought.

Pretending Once children have reached the stage of mental combinations, they can pretend. A toddler might lie down on the floor and pretend to go to sleep, and then jump up, laughing. Or a child might sing a lullabye to a doll before tucking it into bed. This is a marked contrast to the behavior of the younger child, who treats a doll like any other toy, biting, throwing, or sitting on it.

Figure 7.7 *Pretending becomes possible when toddlers reach the stage of mental combinations, at about 18 months. At this point, imagination primarily consists of specific actions performed with a doll or toy animal, but it soon evolves into the elaborate dramas of the preschool and school-age child.*

Two Cautionary Comments

Piaget's stages of sensorimotor thought, especially the development of object permanence, have proven to be reasonably reliable indicators of mental development in children (Wachs, 1975; Uzgiris and Hunt, 1975; Kramer et al., 1975). However, like every other measure of intelligence, Piaget's stages can be too rigidly interpreted.

In the first place, each child's experience will affect when that child reaches a specific stage (Wachs, 1976). Actually, Piaget's own children reached the various stages of sensorimotor intelligence earlier than the ages given here, probably because Piaget, in constantly testing their abilities, gave his children more practice and experience than most children receive.

Then, too, just because a child has reached a certain stage does not mean that the child thinks at that level all the time. Ten-month-old children do not always search for hidden objects, and twenty-month-olds do not always remember what they have seen the day before.

The Development of Object Permanence

As we have already seen, in the first six months of life, out of sight is literally out of mind. Toward the end of stage-three, at about 8 months, the baby begins to search for disappearing objects. But these searches last only for a moment, and the object must be quickly found or the baby will forget all about it.

By stage four, the search lasts longer and is more determined, but the infant is capable of a fascinating mistake. Suppose a 10-month-old is playing with a ball which rolls under a chair. The infant will crawl after it, even if the crawling takes a good deal of effort. But if after being recovered the ball disappears again, this time at the opposite side of the room under a couch, and is not found quickly, the stage-four baby will look for the ball where it was last found—under the chair.

The stage-five toddler will not make that mistake. As long as the toddler sees the object disappear, the toddler knows where to look. However, the stage-five child cannot imagine "invisible" displacements, that is, hiding places the child has not seen. When Piaget hid a coin first in his hand, and then put his hand under a blanket, leaving the coin there,

Jacqueline looked for the coin in his hand but didn't think of looking for it under the blanket.

By stage six, Jacqueline looked first in his hand, and then, without hesitation, under the blanket. Her ability to use mental combinations enabled her to imagine where the coin might be, even if she did not actually see it go there. At this point, object permanence is fully developed.

Object permanence is more than a curious aspect of infant development. Once infants realize that objects exist even when out of sight, and that they can be found by careful searching, infants become more knowledgeable and purposive, demanding specific people and certain toys to which they have become attached. One infant cries for several minutes after his mother leaves; another bangs at the door that closed behind her departing father; a third refuses to go to sleep without a particular blanket; a fourth mourns the disappearance of a pet kitten. By age 1, toddlers try many ways to bring lost objects back, calling and crying, searching and wishing. In short, by understanding one of the simple laws of nature and acting on this understanding, infants become less malleable and more recognizably human.

Figure 7.8 *The inability to see usually retards the development of the concept of object permanence. This need not be the case, however, if the parents are able to provide sufficient auditory and tactile stimulation to compensate for the loss of vision. This little girl's parents make sure she has frequent play periods with noise-making toys and graspable objects, including one of the best playthings of all, her brother.*

Finally, it is probably not a coincidence that children reach the stage of active experimentation just when their motor skills become more mature. It is much easier for an infant to be a busy little scientist if he or she is agile enough to get to interesting "experiments" and to handle objects with some skill. Does this mean that a child who walks later or is physically handicapped and unable to reach many objects would become mentally retarded? The answer probably depends on the environment of the particular child. The child who cannot walk need not be mentally handicapped if the various objects that walking children discover are placed within reach. Even blind children develop normally if they are encouraged (with bells, furry objects, music boxes) to explore their world as a sighted child would (Fraiberg, 1977a).

"The American Question"

These cautionary comments bring us back to the disagreement between Piaget and many North American psychologists about how cognitive development occurs. As you can see from Piaget's stages, he views infants as actively organizing their experiences themselves. He speaks of children adapting their reflexes, making interesting sights last, finding new ways to achieve their goals—and makes little mention of the role of parents or specific learning experiences. He does not think development should be accelerated. In fact, he calls "What should we do to foster cognitive development?" the "American question," because it is one of the first questions Americans ask when he lectures to them. He implies that something about American society, rather than something about infant development, makes us ask that question.

Teaching and Learning in Infancy

Whatever the reason, Americans not only ask the question, they also set about to answer it, demonstrating that infants can be taught to do many things, if the learning process is correctly programmed. For instance, with proper reinforcements, such as a pleasant taste or an interesting sight, infants can be taught to turn their heads in a particular sequence, kick their legs at a target, vocalize more often, or perform almost any other behavior within their capacity (Sameroff, 1972; Fitzgerald and Brackbill, 1976). (Attempts to speed up the maturational sequences of infancy, however, have been less successful.)

For example, Siqueland and Lipsitt (1966) found that the rooting reflex in the newborn (turning the head toward an object that brushes against the cheek) is a weak response, occurring about 25 percent of the time. Setting out to strengthen this response, they brushed babies' cheeks and gave them a bottle of sugar water to suck for 2 seconds every time they displayed the reflex. Within half an hour, the rooting reflex was being exhibited 75 percent of the time. This experiment and others like it that show the role of reinforcement in infant learning contain a lesson for parents. How they respond to their baby teaches the baby how to act in the future. For instance, when newborns first try to suck to be fed, their lack of experience might make their responses weak and inefficient. But very quickly, if the parents' behaviors (how they hold the infant, how they present the nipple) are constant and the feeding process enjoyable, baby and care-giver will adjust to a mutually satisfying routine.

In addition to learning through conditioning, infants also seem to be primed for social learning. Even in the first weeks of life, babies try to imitate what they see. (Try sticking your tongue out at an infant, and notice his or her delightful response.) Later, many babies learn how to crawl down stairs (backwards and feet first), or what to do on a potty, by watching a slightly older baby perform. Babies probably also learn how to interact with other people by watching how people respond to each other.

Enrichment Because of the research proving that infants can be taught many skills, some psychologists have tried to improve infants' cognitive development by providing special enrichment. In one study, thirty premature babies from low-income families were randomly assigned to two groups (Scarr-Salapatek and Williams, 1973). The fifteen infants in the control group received normal hospital and home care. The other fifteen premature infants were given special stimulation in the hospital: bright decorations suspended above their isolettes within a few hours after birth and daily "play" periods with a nurse as soon as the infant could maintain constant body temperature. A psychologist taught the mothers of the experimental group special techniques for playing with their babies and visited them regularly in the first year to provide new games and encouragement. After one month, the babies in the experimental group began to surpass the control group in motor and perceptual abilities. By the end of one year, they were advanced in many ways, including scoring an average of 10 points higher on a test of infant intelligence.

Another researcher, Burton White (1971), studied infants' ability to reach for an object. All the babies in his research were in a hospital, awaiting adoption or foster care. White's first study traced the development of reaching in a group of babies receiving normal hospital care, which included their spending most of their time on their backs in cribs with solid white bumpers designed to keep the babies clean and to prevent them from hurting themselves. However, these bumpers also made it impossible for the infants to see anything except what was directly above them, until they discovered their hands at about 2 months and stared at them. This group of babies did not develop the ability to grasp an object with one hand until they were about 5 months old (150 days).

Figure 7.9 *Does it make a difference whether infants have toys within reach as they lie in their cribs? White and Held (1966) discovered that, at least for institutionalized infants waiting to be placed in foster homes, it does: babies in the "enriched" environment developed the ability to grasp an object almost two months earlier than babies in the sterile, dull cribs did.*

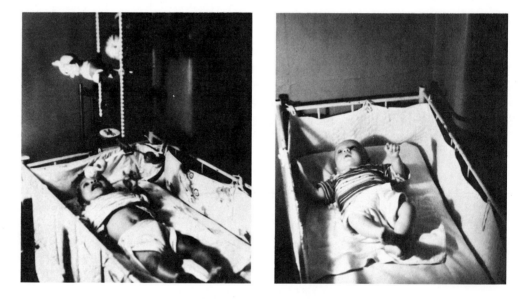

A second group had an enriched environment beginning at one month: colorful bumpers; some time each day on their stomachs, when they could look around at other people; and a stabile* that included a mirror, rattles, and several other objects that could be visually and tactilely explored. These babies were able to grasp by 98 days, significantly earlier than the first group.

A final group received more carefully controlled stimulation: first, a red-and-white bumper; a pacifier fastened on the side of the crib within easy reach; and then, at two months, the stabile. Care was taken not to overstimulate them, as may have happened with the group in the enriched environment (that group may have

---

*A stabile is a three-dimensional toy that dangles above a crib. It is similar to a mobile, but it does not move.

experienced some difficulties in coordinating vision and hand movements, because they had so many objects to choose from). These infants developed more rapidly than the infants in either the deprived or enriched group: they were able to grasp at less than 3 months (89 days).

Most other experiments in special enrichment of the infant's environment have likewise been successful, especially when the goal is to expand the perceptual skills of babies who live in institutions or in homes that lack the varied experiences and individual attention that characterize the normal middle-class American home. These findings have led some popular writers to give advice such as this suggestion from *How to Raise a Brighter Child*: "You should begin filling your infant's life with sensory stimuli and motor activity the first week you bring him home from the hospital" (Beck, 1975).

Such advice worries many psychologists, who fear that parents might overstimulate their infants. Each baby has an individual appetite for the amount of stimulation he or she receives. In addition, some forms of stimulation are more appropriate at certain times in an infant's life than others (Greenberg and O'Donnell, 1972). White (1975) feels infants benefit from activities they enjoy and toys that stimulate their natural curiosity, but he is critical of elaborate enrichment activities and expensive educational toys. Normal loving and playing with an infant usually provide adequate stimulation.

Faster Isn't Always Better Psychologists point out that the baby who focuses, reaches, or walks earlier than normal will not necessarily be a smarter, more able, adult. In fact, there is often no correlation between the IQ scores measuring sensorimotor abilities attained by normal babies and their subsequent IQ scores: the baby who learns to reach early is sometimes the child who learns to count late (Bayley, 1970). As Kagan and Klein (1973) observe: "There is no reason to assume that the caterpillar who metamorphoses a bit earlier than his kin is a better adapted more efficient butterfly."

Can any practical conclusion be drawn from this ongoing controversy? Probably that it is best to try to steer a middle course, recognizing that each baby has an inner timetable and motivation to learn about the world, while at the same time realizing that outside influences, especially the kinds of experiences and the specific nature of the stimulation available, will affect the baby's development. Neither extreme—ignoring the baby's experiences or programming every learning moment—is wise. Given a stimulating environment and patient parents, babies will probably learn as well and as quickly as they can.

Babies Are Active Learners In fact, no matter what theoretical background they come from, psychologists studying babies have been impressed by infants' delight in learning. This is what Piaget calls "a process of equilibrium," an "internal mechanism" "of self-regulation . . . a series of active compensations." The essential idea is that infants search for knowledge rather than waiting passively to receive what their biology or society gives them (Piaget and Inhelder, 1969).

Researchers from various theoretical perspectives have come to conclude that Piaget is correct in describing infants' eagerness to learn. Experiments in perception show more than infants' ability to use their senses; they also demonstrate that babies are born with considerable curiosity. Infants work very hard—sucking, pulling, poking, dropping—in order to repeat a novel experience. When the experience loses its novelty, they become bored or habituated, showing excitement again when changes occur. Other research suggests that the most interesting experiences of all for an infant are those that are somewhat different from the same old routine, but not too different (Kagan, 1978). Taken together, these two characteristics make it seem quite likely that babies, like adults, will learn best when they are neither bored nor bewildered but are presented with challenges that are within their capacities. This is not too different from a basketball team that plays best against a slightly better team rather than against a team that is either twice or half as good.

The infant's internal motivation to learn has been good news to parents and psychologists who thought it was up to them to foster mental development. Nevertheless, few people who care about infants are content to sit back and ignore the learning processes. The question is, How do we make sure each baby has sufficient stimulation and challenge without overstimulation or frustration? The answer has emerged from many areas of research in infant development, but the study of language has been particularly helpful.

Language Development

December 23, 1976, 6:50 A.M.: interchange between Elissa, age 11 months, 19 days, and her mother, age 34.

First sounds from Elissa's crib:
"Aah."
Long pause.
"Aah, aah."
Shorter pause.
"Da, da."
Pause.
"Aah, aah, aah, aah."
Pause.
"Ma, ma."

First sounds from mother's bed:
"Mama."
Immediate response from Elissa's crib:
"Aah."
Mother responds again:
"Mama. Mommy's coming."
Mother enters Elissa's room. Elissa, already standing up, sees mother and smiles. Mother smiles back.
"Hi, honey. How are you today?"
Elissa answers, "Haah," *and flexes her legs in a half jump of excitement.*
"Hi. You want to come up?"
Elissa smiles, says nothing. Mother holds out her hands.
"Come?"
Elissa holds out her hands, leaning on the crib for support. Mother picks baby up.
"Come. Let's get clean diapers for Elissa."
Elissa, in mother's arms, smiles and rests her head on mother's shoulder, nuzzling her cheek.

Does Elissa show any understanding of language in this "conversation"? It depends on our definition of language. If we view Elissa's contribution to this interchange in terms of language structure, that is, the particular rules of grammar and combinations of sounds that make up English, or Spanish, or any other language, we would have to say that Elissa has yet to demonstrate any language ability. However, if we view it in terms of language function, that is, the communication of ideas and emotions by one person to another, then it can be said that Elissa and her mother engaged in an extensive dialogue. Elissa communicated that she was awake and wanted someone to come to her, and then she expressed delight at her mother's voice and subsequent appearance. When Elissa did not respond to "You want to come up?" her mother tried again with one word and a gesture. Elissa got the message and responded, showing her willingness to be picked up and her pleasure at being held. Psycholinguists, psychologists who study language development, believe that both structure and function are important in the development of the child's ability to communicate.

Ways to Study Early Language

Months before demonstrating any knowledge of language structure, infants are remarkably skilled at communicating through cries, gestures, and facial expressions. By age 2, most children have mastered some of the structure of language: they know dozens of words and are able to use them to express many kinds of ideas. What accounts for this rapid language development? Until recently, how psycholinguists answered this question depended on how they approached the study of early language.

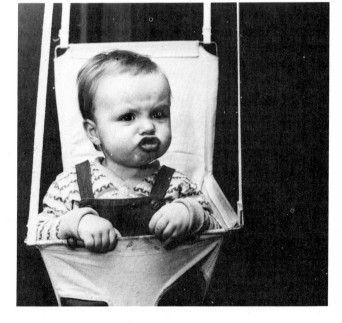

Figure 7.10 *The child achieves eloquence in the language of facial expressions and gestures long before attaining intelligibility with words.*

Skinner's Theory   Some researchers, led by B. F. Skinner (1957), have maintained that children are conditioned to talk. As Skinner explains it, when a baby babbles "ma-ma-ma" and Mommy comes running over to smile, talk, and hold the child, the baby is likely to say "ma-ma-ma" again. How rapidly and how well a child talks, according to Skinner, depends primarily on how often the child hears speech and how well the child is reinforced for talking.

As time goes on, the infant learns that "mama" brings Mother, and that other sounds bring other results. Actually, say behaviorists, the words and phrases children learn depend on the conditioning within their particular family. Some toddlers are given a cookie when they say "cookie"; others must say "cookie please." In a family that values verbal communication, a toddler who asks questions and makes requests will usually be rewarded for these behaviors and will be more likely to say them again. In other families, children are to be seen and not heard, and sometimes are even punished for talking. In fact, behaviorists believe that the main reason that later-born children are less verbal than first-born is that older siblings and tired parents are more likely to respond with annoyance than with delight at the youngest child's verbal production.

Learning by association, without specific reinforcement, is also part of the process. One infant's mother habitually labeled everything that she did for her daughter. Among this little girl's first words were "fispin" and "uddipin," which she would say as she handed the "first" pin and then the "other" pin to her mother at the appropriate time in the diapering process.

According to the principles of conditioning, if the young child hears sufficient speech and gets enough reinforcement for talking, the process of expressing ideas in words eventually becomes reinforcing in itself—so much so, in fact, that many parents find it necessary to teach their older children to be quiet when sitting in church or temple and when others are talking. In adolescence and adulthood, language has become so reinforcing that many people spend hours each day talking to others or writing down their ideas.

Chomsky's Theory   Rather than concerning themselves with parents' reactions to their baby's first words, other researchers, led by linguist Noam Chomsky (1968), psychologist David McNeill (1970), and biologist Eric Lenneberg (1967), studied the milestones in infant-language development (see chart). They discovered that children all over the world attain very similar language skills at about the same age, despite the great differences among cultures, families, and native languages.

Chomsky explains this similarity by suggesting that all human beings have an inborn ability to learn language. To emphasize the inborn, automatic nature of this ability, Chomsky decided to call it language acquisition device (LAD). (Obviously, neither he nor anyone else thinks that the predisposition to learn language is actually a device located somewhere in the brain.) According to Chomsky, the innate language-learning ability causes babies to listen attentively to speech sounds in the early weeks of life and to imitate speech sounds and patterns throughout infancy. LAD triggers babbling at about six months, the first word at about a year, and the first sentences about two years after birth, no matter whether the child is black or white, rich or poor, or growing up in Indonesia or Brazil.

Part of the human predisposition to learn language, according to Chomsky, is an inborn understanding of the basic structure of language, which Chomsky calls the deep structure. For instance, infants do not have to learn that vocalization is an important way to communicate, that small differences in the way words are said may be significant, that some sentences are questions and some are not. The particular vocabulary and grammar of each language (called surface structure), of course, takes time to learn. However, Chomsky believes that children learn the surface structure as rapidly as they do because their comprehension of the deep structure is already present, guiding their efforts to grasp the underlying rules of grammar from the flawed and incomplete sentences that most adults speak.

Language Development

3 MONTHS	Markedly less crying than at 8 weeks; when talked to and nodded at, smiles, followed by squealing-gurgling sounds, usually called cooing, which is vowel-like in character and pitch-modulated; sustains cooing for 15–20 seconds.
4 MONTHS	Responds to human sounds more definitely; turns head; eyes seem to search for speaker; occasionally some chuckling sounds.
5 MONTHS	The vowel-like cooing sounds begin to be interspersed with more consonantal sounds; . . . acoustically, all vocalizations are very different from the sounds of the mature language of the environment.
6 MONTHS	Cooing changes into babbling resembling one-syllable utterances; neither vowels nor consonants have very fixed recurrences; most common utterances sound somewhat like ma, mu, da, di.
8 MONTHS	Reduplication (or more continuous repetition) becomes frequent; intonation patterns become distinct; utterances can signal emphasis and emotions.
10 MONTHS	Vocalizations are mixed with sound-play such as gurgling or bubble-blowing; appears to wish to imitate sounds, but the imitations are never quite successful; beginning to differentiate between words heard by making differential adjustments.
12 MONTHS	Identical sound sequences are replicated with higher relative frequency of occurrence and words (mama or dadda) are emerging; definite signs of understanding some words and simple commands (show me your eyes).
18 MONTHS	Has a definite repertoire of words—more than three, but less than 50; still much babbling but now of several syllables with intricate intonation patterns; no attempt at communicating information and no frustration for not being understood; words may include items such as "thank you" or "come here," but there is little ability to join any of the lexical items into spontaneous two-item phrases; understanding is progressing rapidly.
24 MONTHS	Vocabulary of more than 50 items (some children seem to be able to name everything in the environment); begins spontaneously to join vocabulary items into two-word phrases; all phrases appear to be own creations; definite increase in communicative behavior and interest in language.
30 MONTHS	Fastest increase in vocabulary with many new additions every day; no babbling at all; utterances have communicative intent; frustrated if not understood by adults; utterances consist of at least 2 words, many have 3 or even 5 words; sentences and phrases have characteristic child grammar; that is, they are rarely verbatim repetitions of an adult utterance; intelligibility is not very good yet, though there is great variation among children; seems to understand everything that is said to him.

Source: Lenneberg, 1967

Disagreements Of course, linguists and behaviorists disagree about whether Chomsky's or Skinner's theory is the more accurate. Many linguists think Skinner's theory is too simplistic, because it does not explain the child's language learning as it really happens. If children talk because they are reinforced, why, linguists ask, do they learn new words slowly for months and then learn rapidly? The fact that the language-learning ability changes even though the rate of reinforcement does not suggests that some inborn predisposition reaches maturity at a certain age in much the same way as the readiness to walk does. Another question linguists ask is, How, if children repeat only what they hear, do we explain word combinations that adults never use, like "no sleepy" for "I don't want to go to bed" or "more page" for "Read to me some more"? It would seem apparent that, rather than simply parroting the speech they hear, children create much of the language they speak, using their own understanding of the rules of grammar.

In any case, most parents reinforce their children for the *content* of their speech rather than for its grammar. For instance, Eve, at 18 months, pointed to her mother and said, "He a girl." "That's right," her mother said, pleased that her daughter knew the difference between male and female and not troubled at all by the incorrect grammar (Brown, 1973). As Roger Brown wryly points out, we are much more likely to reinforce our children for speaking honestly than for speaking correctly, nevertheless our children usually grow up to speak grammatically, but not always truthfully. This tends to disprove the behaviorists' theory that children learn to speak correctly because they are rewarded for doing so.

On the other hand, behaviorists point out that the existence of LAD or the deep structure of language has not been proven, whereas a substantial body of research supports certain aspects of Skinner's view. Infants babble more when people babble back (Rheingold et al., 1959; Weisberg, 1963), and preschool children whose parents listen to them appreciatively become much more verbal than children whose parents ignore them. In addition, carefully applied conditioning techniques, especially in teaching speech to mentally retarded and emotionally disturbed children, have proven themselves again and again (Sloane and MacAulay, 1968; Gray and Ryan, 1973).

Motherese

Neither side had much luck in convincing the other, until psycholinguists began to study parent-child *interaction,* recording precisely what each half of the partnership said and did rather than looking first at parent behavior. This led to a discovery that proved both the behaviorists and the linguists to be partly right, specifically, the discovery of baby talk. The term "baby talk," as used here, does not refer to the way people think babies talk—the "goo-goo-ga-ga" that few infants actually say. Rather, it refers to the particular way people talk to infants, a distinct form of language that some psychologists have nicknamed Motherese. Baby talk differs from adult talk in a number of features: it is distinct in its pitch (higher),

Figure 7.11 *Exaggeration of facial expression and pronunciation, and simplification of words and sentences are among the many features of the special language adults speak to infants. As this mother and her 4-month-old baby demonstrate, the partners in the simple "conversations" of early infancy often participate simultaneously, making it difficult to decide who is imitating whom.*

intonation (especially low-to-high fluctuations), vocabulary (simpler and more concrete), and sentence length (shorter). Adults speaking baby talk use more questions, commands, and repetitions, and fewer past tenses, pronouns, and complex sentences, than they do in adult talk. It is baby talk, rather than the usual forms of language, that infants first learn to speak.

Psychologists have detected implicit rules for creating the special words of baby talk (Ferguson, 1977): Avoid consonants such as "r" and "l" that are hard for infants to pronounce ("bunny" is used for "rabbit"). Choose words that are supposed to sound like the object referred to ("train" becomes "choo-choo," "dog" becomes "bow-wow," "urination" becomes one of dozens of onomatopoeic words). Repeat syllables ("mama," "dada"). And end words in a "y" sound ("tummy," "beddy," "Tommy," "Susie").

Baby talk probably originates in the interaction between parent and child, as each tries to communicate with the other. For instance, after parents first said "stomach," and infants tried to repeat it, perhaps saying "tomma," the parents learned to simplify it to "tummy." Of course, standard words of baby talk, such as "tummy," do not need to be rediscovered by every parent and child. However, in many families, a private vocabulary develops with words that are meaningful only to that parent and infant but nevertheless follow the general rules of baby talk in their use. Nicknames for hard-to-pronounce words such as "pacifier," "blanket," and "grandmother" are examples.

These characteristics of baby talk are as true in Russian, Japanese, and Arabic as they are in French, English, and Spanish. One study of baby talk in six languages found that parents from every linguistic community copy the child's pronunciation, not only using words like "tummy" and "bow-wow" but even going to such lengths as "bootiful bunny wabbit" (Ferguson, 1964). Motherese is spoken by almost every mother throughout the world; it is also spoken by fathers, other relatives, and strangers. Children as young as 3 use it to talk to dolls, stuffed animals, and babies; lovers occasionally use many features of baby talk in intimate moments.

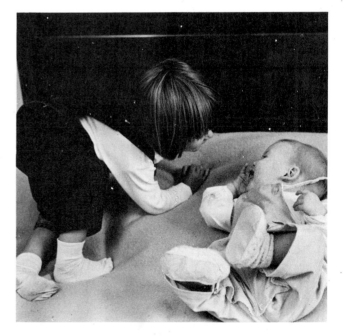

Figure 7.12 *Even pre-schoolers can speak Motherese. They do it with dolls, puppets, and, if they have a chance, babies. In turn, most infants are more responsive to the antics and conversation of a slightly older child than they are to anyone else's except their own parents'.*

Careful study of baby talk has shown that, contrary to Chomsky's contention, many adults are amazingly skilled in attuning their speech to the child's level of comprehension, so instead of hearing an ungrammatical mishmash, young children frequently hear clear, concise sentences. For instance, one sentence-by-sentence analysis of how many words twenty adult strangers used per sentence to talk to a 2-year-old boy showed that sentence length was directly related to the child's previous response. If the child indicated that he did not understand a statement, the next sentence was significantly shorter (Bohannon and Marquis, 1977).

Many conversations between parent and child show the parent interpreting the child's imperfect speech and then responding with short clear sentences the child can understand, often with special emphasis on important words. Naturalistic observation is the best way to study this interaction, for facial expression and intonation are as much a part of baby talk as the words spoken. However, recorded dialogues help give the flavor. At the end of the following conversation, for instance, the Motherese mode is made especially clear when the mother switches out of Motherese to make a comment to herself (quoted in Lindfors, in press):

Child: I say no
Mother: *No what?*
Not like.
You don't like cabbage?
No.
Well, just leave it there, OK? Just leave it there.
Eat the fish.
You can eat some fish.
Put the cabbage here.
(She puts the cabbage where child indicated.) Yeah, let's put the cabbage . . . let's put the cabbage like you do when you don't care for something. You just sorta leave it there. You taste it and you be polite and you taste it and then you just put it there and then you just eat everything else. Would you like some more fish?
I like more fish.
All right. Child, you're gonna have table manners yet!

In this conversation, as in most episodes of baby talk, the child is an active participant, responding to the mother and making his needs known. While Chomksy was wrong in underestimating the parents' role in language learning, he was right in crediting children with an inborn willingness to listen, to try to understand, and to respond.

Steps in Language Development

In the "conversation" between Elissa and her mother with which we introduced this section, Elissa, like almost every infant her age, demonstrated an inborn predisposition to learn language by babbling to herself, listening intently when her mother spoke, and responding with noises and gestures. Elissa's mother, like most mothers of 11-month-olds, was making possible the kind of interaction necessary for language learning by responding to her daughter with simple phrases, repeating and expanding the infant's babbling. We have already touched upon these beginnings of language development in the chart on page 221, but now let us look more closely at the emergence of this quintessential skill.

First Communications   Normal babies are born able to cry in several ways, as researchers have discovered by analyzing recorded cries (Wolff, 1969). The usual "hunger," or "rhythmic," cry follows this pattern: short cry (about .6 second), brief pause (about .2 second), intake of breath (.2 second), pause, and another short cry. The "mad" cry follows the same pattern, but with more force. The "pain" cry is longer and louder, with a long rest between cries; one typical 3-day-old expressed the pain of a heel prick by crying 4 seconds and then pausing 7 seconds before the next 4-second-long cry.

The difference between these cries is apparent even to inexperienced new mothers, as Peter Wolff found in a series of experiments in which he played a recording of a pain cry after a mother had left him with her baby and gone to another room. In each case, the mother ran anxiously back to the experiment room as soon as she heard the pain cry. All the mothers in this experiment were relieved to learn that their infant was not really crying. (Many of them were also angry that Wolff had tricked them in this way, an emotion most psychologists would agree was justified.) With several other mothers, Wolff played a recording of the basic rhythmical cry. That these mothers could distinguish this cry was demonstrated by the fact that they responded in a less rushed and more relaxed manner than the mothers who had heard the pain cry.

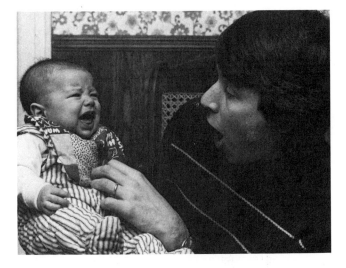

Figure 7.13 *The first reflexive cries quickly become the first form of communication, if care-givers treat them as such. If a parent responds to an infant's crying by making a relatively loud and steady comforting noise along with an exaggeratedly pleasant facial expression, the infant may become sufficiently interested to stop crying in order to listen.*

These early cries are reflexes, activated in response to pain or displeasure rather than in a deliberate attempt to communicate. But just as other reflexes are, according to Piaget, the starting point for the acquisition of differentiated responses, the newborn's first cries probably become adapted to the social world that surrounds the infant, and parent-child communication develops as the first needs of the newborn are attended to.

As we have seen, crying is not the only communication that occurs in early infancy. In the first months of life, babies have facial expressions and body movements that provide clues about their feelings. The pleasure smile (a relaxation of the facial muscles) evidencing contentment (Oster, 1978), and the arm-waving that indicates excitement, are two examples that are apparent even in the first days of life. With responsive parents, babies soon learn that these gestures are meaningful.

As early as 5 weeks of age, babies make noncrying sounds when they see faces or hear voices. The uttering of these sounds is called cooing, because the infant repeats the same vowel sounds again and again, varying the pitch slightly, the way a pigeon does when it coos (Lenneberg, 1967).

RESEARCH REPORT **Responding to the Baby's Cry**

Many parents are afraid of spoiling an infant by responding whenever the baby cries. Their fears seem to be supported by behaviorist theory, which holds that most behaviors will occur more frequently if they are reinforced. Since nothing is more rewarding to an infant than a care-giver's attention, behaviorists would predict that the more often parents pick up their infants when they cry, the more crying there will be. Indeed, research with nursery-school children (Hart et al., 1964) and babies in a hospital nursery (Etzel and Gewitz, 1967) suggests that crying occurs less often when crying is ignored, especially if noncrying forms of communication, such as smiling, are reinforced.

However, this does not seem to be the case with infants who live at home. Silvia Bell and Mary Ainsworth (1972) used naturalistic observation techniques to study twenty-six mother-infant pairs at home throughout the first year. Observers kept careful records of the frequency of infant crying, and the nature and frequency of maternal response. They found that all the infants cried less as they grew older—the average infant cried 7.7 minutes per hour in the first three months of their first year (one fretful infant cried 35 percent of the time) and 4.4 minutes per hour in the last three months. When frequency and duration of crying for each baby in the first quarter were compared to the same measures in the last quarter, there was no particular pattern. In other words, we cannot predict from data on early crying whether a fussy 3-month-old will still be relatively fussy at 12 months.

However, maternal responsiveness in the early months correlated with maternal responsiveness in the later months. (The range of responsiveness was very large: one mother responded to 96 percent of her baby's cries; another mother responded to only 3 percent.) Bell and Ainsworth discovered that the infants whose mothers responded most often in early infancy tended to cry *least* as they approached 1 year of age, communicating instead with gestures, facial expressions, and vocalizations. By contrast, the infants whose mothers had responded to their cries less frequently tended as 1-year-olds to cry more often and for longer time periods, and to use fewer alternative modes of communication.

This study has been criticized by two behaviorists, Gewirtz and Boyd (1977), who contend that because it did not distinguish one cry from another (for instance, a reflexive hunger cry from a cry for attention), it does not really prove that responding to early cries for attention will make a baby less fussy later on. Gewirtz and Boyd are concerned that parents, learning of the Bell and Ainsworth study, will feel compelled to respond to every cry instantly, thus creating 2-year-old tyrants who use temper tantrums to always get their own way.

In a reply to this criticism, Ainsworth and Bell (1977) explained that they knew "full well that the sensitive, responsive mothers would not be so foolish" as to respond immediately to every cry, and would likely respond with greater alacrity to hunger and pain cries than to mere fussing. They also insist that, just because babies cry when they want attention from their care-givers is no reason to ignore their cries; in fact, babies who learn to signal their needs for human company by crying are likely to be better able to signal the same needs in more mature ways later on than are babies whose crying is ignored.

Babbling By 20 weeks, babies have added several consonant sounds to the vowels of cooing, and by 6 months, utterances include several distinct sounds and combinations of sounds. Continual repetition of the same sound, called babbling (partly because "ba-ba-ba" is one of the first repetitions), helps babies utter their first words, which are usually made up of the sounds they babble most.

Listening and Responding At first, babies probably babble for the pure physical pleasure of making movements and noises with the mouth, tongue, lips, and throat, in much the same way they enjoy kicking their legs or moving their fingers. In fact,

A CLOSER LOOK: **Babbling and First Words**

All over the world, babies make the same first sounds, beginning with vowel sounds similar to "a," "e," and "o," and then sounds similar to the consonants "m," "d," "b," "n," "p," "w," "k," and "t." In many languages, the names for the things most important to babies are made of those same sounds, often said twice, since babies frequently repeat sounds. For example, look at the names for mother, father, and baby in the ten languages listed in the chart.

It seems as if languages all over the world are structured to encourage speech in babies. The twentieth-century American nickname for father is a fascinating example. Logically, the nickname should be a combination of the "f" and "th" sounds, perhaps "faftha" or "fathy." However, both those sounds are difficult for babies to say. Instead, the nickname has become "dada" or "daddy," as if American fathers had decided to accept one of the baby's first babblings rather than wait for "father."

	Mother	Father	Infant (Child)
English	mama, mommy	daddy	baby
Spanish	mama	papa	niño nene
French	maman, mama	papa	bébé
Italian	mamma	babbo, papa	bambina, bimba, bimbo
Syrian Arabic	mama	baba	bubbu
Bantu	ba-mama	taata	mu-ulu
Swahili	mama	baba	mtoto
Sanskrit	nana	tata	bala
Hebrew	ema	abba	teenok
Japanese*	haha	chichi	akago, akanbo, kodomo

*In present-day Japanese, "mama" and "papa" are often used to mean mother and father. "Mama" also means food.

babbling seems to decrease at about 8 months, when infants become more attentive to what other people say. Vocalization then increases again toward the end of the first year as babies begin to babble in conversation rather than simply for the delight in practicing a new motor skill (Beckwith, 1971).

There is another interesting change in babbling patterns in the second half of the first year. At first, infants are likely to vocalize while someone else is talking, as if to join in the general noise-making. But by 8 months or so, the typical infant is still while someone talks, and then responds with a babble, and then listens again. It seems as if the baby has learned the first rules of conversation: Don't talk when someone else is talking, and respond politely when it's your turn.

This can be seen as an example of stage-three cognitive development, as the infant begins to develop secondary circular reactions, while trying to "make interesting sights last." Turn-taking is part of many of the games parents and babies play in the second half of the first year, such as peek-a-boo, patty-cake, and you-give-me-the-toy-and-I-give-it-back-to-you. Bruner (1974–1975) believes this mutual game-playing is the first step in language learning. Turn-taking is also evident in early conversations between parent and child, as Catherine Snow (Snow and Ferguson, 1977) discovered when she recorded them. Between 5 and 7 months, Snow found, mothers began to treat burps, smiles, yawns, gestures, and babbling as part of a conversation. For instance, this mother asks and answers several questions, as if the baby's smile and burp are significant communications:

Child: (Smiles)
Mother: *Oh, what a nice little smile! Yes, isn't that nice? There.*
There's a nice little smile.
(Burps)
What a nice wind as well! Yes, that's better, isn't it?

Timing is another important feature of conversations between parents and pre-verbal infants. Many parents talk to their babies, wait for the baby to respond by a motion, a facial expression, or a noise, and then talk again. Even when the baby does nothing, the timing is very similar to that of a polite adult conversation. A mother says, "Aren't you my cutie?" pauses 1.43 seconds for the baby to think and respond, and then says, "You sure are," in agreement with the imagined response (Stern, 1977).

Is it foolish to talk to an infant like that? Not at all, according to most psycholinguists. Even though a newborn's crying, cooing, and babbling are all reflexive, responding to these noises as though they were statements helps the infant learn to use noises to communicate.

First Words Even before infants utter their first words, they begin to learn the intonation of language, and using a single sound can express happiness, distress, a command, and a question. A psychologist from the Soviet Union, Tonkova-Yampol'skaya (1973), recorded the rise and fall of voice tones for babies and adults expressing each of these four types of communication and found that the infant pattern closely follows the adult pattern (see Figure 7.14).

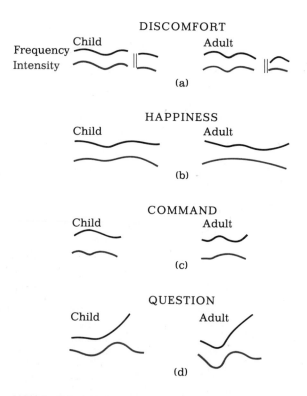

Figure 7.14 *Intonation patterns of infants younger than 12 months are surprisingly similar to those of adults, both in sound intensity and fundamental tone frequency, as shown from vocal responses recorded on magnetic tape. The pattern for distress or discomfort* (a) *is apparent in the first month of life; for happiness* (b), *by 3 months; for a command* (c), *by 10 months; and for a question* (d), *by 12 months.*

The other development that precedes the first speaking of words is the first understanding of words. As the infant begins to anticipate events (stage four of cognitive development), words such as "hot!" "no!" or "bye-bye" are connected with an experience.

Finally, at about 1 year, the average baby speaks one or two words, not pronounced very clearly or used very precisely. Many 12-month-olds have not started speaking at all, and even the most precocious usually have less than a dozen words in their vocabulary.

A CLOSER LOOK   **Deaf Babies**

Normal babies enjoy conversations with themselves, with mirrors, with toys, with animals, with insects, and especially with older people who babble back. Deaf babies babble the same sounds at 6 months as hearing babies, but since they cannot hear themselves or others' responses, there is no circular reaction. Consequently, they communicate with gestures rather than sounds, and their early babbling disappears rather than turning into speech.

Since they do not understand or develop speech, most deaf or hard-of-hearing babies are severely handicapped in language development, usually experiencing difficulties with written vocabulary and grammar all their lives (Meadow, 1975). However, recent research on deaf infants whose parents communicated with them using American sign language (Ameslan), just as other parents would have used words, found that these deaf babies developed sign language as fast as hearing babies develop spoken language. One little girl, Ann, signed her first two words at 10 months ("pretty" and "wrong") and used 142 signs and 14 letters of the manual alphabet at 19½ months (Schlesinger and Meadow, 1972).

In Ann's case, testing for deafness was done in the first days of life, because both her parents were congenitally deaf. However, most parents simply take it for granted that their baby hears normally, and many hearing problems are not suspected until there are such secondary problems as a 2-year-old's not having begun to talk, or a 5-year-old's still not being understood verbally. By this time the hearing problem may have become a lifelong handicap, because the first years of language development are crucial.

Hearing problems are often not noticed in infants, since even deaf babies babble and normal babies sometimes ignore noises that would startle an adult. However, an infant's never turning to find a noise or never responding to voices in the first months probably signals a hearing problem. Ear infections and other diseases may cause hearing problems, so an infant who seemed to hear perfectly in the early months but who does not vocalize as much in later months should be checked by a doctor. When a hearing impairment is diagnosed early enough, hearing aids, surgery, or special education can usually prevent the difficulty from becoming a major handicap (Bolton, 1976).

The first words a child speaks are not necessarily the words a child has heard most often; they are the words that are most important to the child. The majority usually involve some movement or action the child can do, as might be expected, since the child is at the sensorimotor stage of development. For instance, Katherine Nelson (1973) followed the language development of eighteen children for a year, beginning at about their first birthdays. She found that none of the eighteen toddlers had "diaper," "table," or "crib" as one of their first fifty words, but eleven had "shoe," seven had "clock" (meaning watch as well), and six had "key," all objects a 1-year-old can play with.

As children learn their first words, they usually become adept at expressing intention. Even a single word, used with the proper intonation and gestures can express a whole thought. When a toddler pushes at a closed door and says in a demanding tone, "bye-bye," the meaning is clear. If a toddler holds on to Mother's legs and says "bye-bye" as soon as the babysitter arrives, the meaning is equally clear though quite different. Single words such as these are called holophrases, so named because the whole phrase, or sentence, is expressed in one word.

A child's success in one-word communication usually depends on the willingness and ability of other people to interpret the child's efforts. In fact, the age at which a baby "talks" depends partly on when the baby's family is ready to listen. Few children master adult pronunciation until they are 7 or 8 years old, and in the first years of talking, sympathetic listening is often essential if the child's meaning is to be communicated.

This raises an important question: Should children be considered to be talking when they seem to say a word, even if the word is not intelligible? Such an attribution might be overly generous, because all 1-year-olds sometimes make noises that sound like sentences but are not intended to mean anything. Gesell aptly called these noises expressive jargon. On the other hand, children make meaningful sounds that are not in the dictionary. One linguist's daughter at 10 months said "nenene" to scold somebody and "tt" to call the squirrels (Leopold, 1949). In a case like this, when a child's private vocabulary is understood by others, "nonwords," such as the daughter's "nenene" and "tt," probably should be considered words.

For practical purposes it would certainly seem that they should be. Nelson's study of the eighteen children found that those children who had the most extensive language development by age 2 had mothers who accepted the child's early vocalizations as meaningful. Correspondingly, those children whose mothers rejected their early efforts were more likely to be relatively slow in language development. Here are two examples quoted by Nelson, first an accepting mother and then a rejecting one:

> Mother: Jane. Here's a bottle. Where's the bottle? Here's a bottle.
> Jane: *Wah wah.*
> Bottle.
> *Bah bah.*
> Bah bah.
> *Bah bah.*
> Oh, bah bah. Here's a ball.
> *Baw.*
> Ball. Yes.
> *Uh. Uh boo?*
> Ball.

> Paul: *Go.*
> Mother: What? Feel.
> *Fe.*
> What's that? A dog. What does the dog say? One page at a time. Oh, that one over there. What's that one there?
> *Boah.*
> What? You know that.
> *Bah.*
> What?
> *Ah wah.*
> What?
> *Caw.*
> Car?
> *Caw, awh.*
> Little kitty, you know that. [Nelson, 1973]

Nelson found other interesting correlations between the toddler's life and language achievement at age 2. The children who were most advanced spent proportionately more time with adults than with other young children, went on more outings, and watched less television than the children whose language developed more slowly.

Children differ in the ways in which they use their first words. Some children are referential; they are interested in cataloguing everything ("wha dat?" "wha dis?") and refer to objects more than people. Others are expressive; they are involved with people and personal desires ("bye-bye," "mama," "more," "daddy come," "pick me up") (Bloom et al., 1975). The difference between these two styles of language learning would logically seem to result from the way mothers talk to their children; that is, one might expect referential mothers to have referential children, and expressive mothers, expressive children. However, in her study of language acquisition, Nelson (1973) found as many cases of unmatched styles as she found matched. In those instances in which the child's style and the mother's were dissimilar, Nelson noted that there was a period of slowed-down language acquisition during which the child appeared to adopt the mother's style. Thereafter language learning proceeded at a normal pace.

The Slow Growth of Vocabulary You might think that once a child could say a few words, additional words would come easily. But this is not the case. Vocabulary increases gradually, perhaps a few words a month. By 18 months, the average baby knows somewhere between three and fifty words (Lenneberg, 1967).

No one is sure why vocabulary increases so slowly at first, or why some children talk at 12 months and others wait until 2 years. Shirley (1933) has suggested that children in the first half of the second year are so busy learning to walk and run that they do not have time to focus on language. Her explanation would account for the early talkers who are late walkers, and vice versa. Lenneberg (1967) sees talking as a biological development, just as dependent on physical maturation as walking is.

Piaget's research suggests that the child must reach stage six of sensorimotor development, the stage of mental representation, before language learning can become rapid. Piaget's explanation seems plausible, for in order to really grasp the connection between words and referents, a toddler must be able to think about an object or action without using sensorimotor skills. A firm sense of object permanence is also necessary to enable the child to connect the word "ball," for instance, with an actual ball, whether the child is playing with it or is about to get it out of the toy box. Many of the toddler's first sentences seem to show that mental representation ("See dis," "Wha dat?") and object permanence ("Where dis," "Allgone dat") are ideas of such significance that they are often put into words.

Once vocabulary begins to expand, toddlers seem to "experiment in order to see" with words just as they do with objects. The "little scientist" becomes the "little linguist" exploring hypotheses and reaching conclusions.

At first, infants take words to mean much more than they do. This characteristic, known as overextension, might lead one child to call anything round "moon," and another to call every four-legged creature "doggie." But once the toddler is ready to become the linguist, new words are learned almost as rapidly as the knowledge of what they refer to. It is not unusual for 2-year-olds to walk down the street pointing to every animal, asking "doggie?" "horsey?" "kitty?"—apparently in order to test their hypotheses with many real-life examples, like scientists testing a theory.

It is important to note that vocabulary size is not the most sensitive measure of early language learning. Rather, the crux of early language is function, not structure, communication, not vocabulary. If parents are concerned about their nonverbal 1-year-old son, they should look at his ability and willingness to make his needs known and to understand what others say. If those skills seem to be normal, and if the child hears enough simple language addressed to him every day (through someone's reading to him, singing to him, talking about the food he is eating and the sights he sees), he will probably be speaking in sentences by age 2½.

The Next Steps Once a child has mastered a few words, the next step is to put words together, which usually occurs about 6 months after the first words. Late speakers, who do not utter a word until age 2, frequently speed up this process. Instead of speaking a first word, they might speak a first sentence.

Combining words demands considerable linguistic understanding because, in English and in most other languages, the order of words affects the meaning of the sentence. It could make a big difference to a toddler's immediate future whether he explains the screaming of his younger sister as "Baby bite me" or "Me bite baby." However, even in their first two-word sentences, toddlers demonstrate that they have figured out this rule, commanding "More juice" or "Baby eat" rather than the reverse. (The process of learning grammar, and the rapid vocabulary expansion that follows the slow acquisition of the first words, are explored in Chapter 10, where the language development of preschool children is discussed.)

Measuring Cognitive Development

Many people want to know if a baby is learning quickly or slowly, and are curious about ways to measure cognitive development in infancy (see Table 7.1). But what factors should be looked at in deciding how well an infant is learning? We know that all babies coo, cry, and babble, so these activities cannot be used as indices of intelligence. Besides, we also know that some intelligent children do not talk until they are 2.

In addition, we know that babies who walk or reach at a younger age than average are not necessarily smarter than average, although babies who are very

TABLE 7.1   **Sample Items from Two Tests of Infant Development**

Bayley	Gesell and Amatruda
At about 6 months, an average baby	
Accepts second cube (while infant holds one cube, examiner places second cube within easy reach, and infant takes it).	Lifts head.
	Sits erect for a moment.
Reaches persistently when second cube is just out of reach.	Grasps cube with radial palmer grasp.
	Holds two cubes for longer than a moment.
Vocalizes pleasure.	Babbles "m-m-m" and polysyllabic vowel sounds.
Vocalizes displeasure.	
Picks up cube deftly.	Eats solid food well.
Babbles several syllables.	Brings feet to mouth.
When examiner shows infant his or her face in a mirror, infant approaches mirror.	Pats mirror image.
At about 12 months, an average baby	
Responds to "no, no."	Walks with one hand held.
Repeats performance when someone laughs at what he or she does.	Says two words besides "mama" and "dada."
Imitates words when examiner says "mama," "dada," "baby," etc.	Gives a toy on request.
Imitates action. When examiner rattles a spoon in a cup, as if stirring, infant imitates, producing similar noise.	Cooperates in getting dressed.
	Tries to build a tower of cubes, with some success.
Responds to request. When examiner hands a cup to child and says, "Take a drink," child holds cup in both hands as if to drink.	

Source: Adapted from Kessen et al., 1970.

slow in acquiring these skills are a cause for concern. And even though infant mastery of Piagetian tasks (such as searching for a hidden object) indicates something about mental development, we know that Piaget himself thinks attempts to measure the rate of mental growth are senseless.

Consequently, we should not be surprised that attempts to develop tests of infant intelligence have not been very successful, except in spotting infants who are doing very poorly. But for the average infant in a normal home, infant IQ tests are not good predictors of future intelligence scores or school performance (Bayley, 1965).

However, in the first months of life, there is one important clue to future cognitive development—the quality of the home environment. The progress infants make on the steps of thinking and communication outlined here depend more on their relationships with family members than on any other circumstance.

Since the key to good cognitive development, as with all other areas of human development, is suitable interaction, parents who want to help their infant's cognitive growth should play with their baby at a level appropriate to the stage of development the baby is in at the moment. Just like an active toddler, the parent should "experiment in order to see" what produces a fascinated stare or a happy grin in the baby, and what produces overexcitement, boredom, fear, or frustration. The active baby will show the sensitive parent how to teach.

Figure 7.15 *Parent-child interaction is the most powerful determinant of cognitive ability in infancy. As object permanence becomes more firmly understood, most infants enjoy games of appearance and disappearance—first the simple peek-a-boo at about 8 months, and then hide-and-seek at about 18 months, when the ability to pretend adds to the excitement.*

SUMMARY

How Cognitive Development Occurs

1. Both maturation and learning are necessary for cognitive development, although psychologists disagree about which is more important. Piaget does not think cognitive development should be "pushed," but Bruner thinks an infant's environment should be "enriched."

Sensorimotor Intelligence

2. Infant thought is called sensorimotor intelligence because babies think with actions, using their senses and motor abilities to understand their world. They learn to adapt their reflexes, respond to people and experiences, and, by the end of the first year, figure out how to accomplish simple goals.

3. In the second year, toddlers find new ways to achieve their goals, first by actively experimenting and then, toward the end of the second year, by mental representation—working problems out in their heads.

4. Babies think that objects no longer exist when they are no longer in sight, but gradually the concept of object permanence develops. By about 1½, toddlers know where to look for something that has been hidden in one hand and then put in the other hand, even though they did not see the actual transfer.

"The American Question"

5. Experiments in learning have proven that infants can be taught many things, using conditioning techniques and social modeling. Enrichment programs do improve the cognitive skills of deprived infants. For normal infants, parents should find a middle ground between too much and too little stimulation.

Language Development

6. Skinner thinks children learn language through association and reinforcement. Chomsky thinks language ability is inborn, ready to emerge as soon as the culture provides clues about what particular surface structures are to be used.

7. Baby talk has been recognized as a special language, used all over the world to communicate with babies. Mothers and infants coordinate their conversations, even before the baby can say a single word. How well a child communicates depends on how ready and willing the family is to listen.

8. Language skills begin to develop at birth, as babies communicate with noises and gestures, and practice babbling. Infants understand a few words toward the end of the first year, and say a few words at the beginning of the second year. By age 2, most toddlers can combine two words to make a simple sentence.

9. Children vary in how rapidly they learn vocabulary, as well as in what kinds of words they use. In the first two years, it is more important to attend to the child's comprehension of simple words and gestures, and willingness and ability to communicate feelings and needs than to the rate at which vocabulary increases.

Measuring Cognitive Development

10. Infant intelligence tests are not very accurate in predicting a child's later achievement, although they can be used to spot an infant whose development is extremely slow. The parents' ability to tune-in to their infant's level of cognitive growth, and to provide appropriate stimulation, is more important than whether the infant walks or talks earlier or later than other babies.

KEY QUESTIONS

What is the traditional controversy about cognitive development in infancy?

What is the modern version of that controversy?

What is the basic characteristic of infant thought according to Piaget?

Give an example of a circular reaction.

Why is the 1-year-old referred to by Piaget as "the little scientist"?

What makes it possible for the toddler to pretend?

Why should one be cautious in using Piaget's stages as a measure of cognitive development?

What kinds of behaviors can be conditioned during infancy?

What are the differences between Skinner's and Chomsky's theories of early language development?

Why is baby talk important?

How are the words of baby talk invented?

When and why should parents respond to a baby's cries?

How does a baby practice language skills before uttering the first word?

How would one measure the language development of a child under age 2?

KEY TERMS

sensorimotor	deep structure
circular reactions	surface structure
primary circular reaction	baby talk
secondary circular reaction	Motherese
object permanence	pleasure smile
tertiary circular reaction	cooing
mental combinations	babbling
mental representation	holophrases
deferred imitation	expressive jargon
enriched environment	referential
language structure	expressive
language function	overextension
psycholinguists	
language acquisition device (LAD)	

RECOMMENDED READINGS

Piaget, Jean. *The origins of intelligence in children.* New York: Norton, 1963.

Piaget is never easy to read, not even for psychologists who specialize in cognition. But his ideas provide the context for most contemporary notions of cognitive development in childhood, so the effort to understand him may be worth it. This book of 419 pages is entirely about the six stages of sensorimotor intelligence. It includes many examples taken from Piaget's experiences with his three children.

Gesell, Arnold, Ilg, Frances, and **Ames, Louise.** *Infant and child in the culture of today.* New York: Harper & Row, 1974.

Beck, Joan. *How to raise a brighter child.* New York: Pocket Books, 1975.

These two books balance each other out, for the Gesell book advises letting infants develop at their own pace, while the Beck book gives all kinds of suggestions for accelerating cognitive development, promising to increase a child's IQ 20 points or more. As you read these books, remember that some developmental psychologists think too much emphasis on letting children grow at their own pace might result in insufficient stimulation. On the other hand, keep in mind that overstimulation can be a problem as well.

White, Burton. *The first three years of life.* Englewood Cliffs, N.J.: Prentice-Hall, 1975.

White tries to apply research on infant cognitive development to the practical business of raising an infant. He gives suggestions for toys and games that babies like in the first three years of life. This book tends to be repetitive, but has many useful suggestions nonetheless.

Brown, Roger. *A first language: The early stages.* Cambridge, Mass.: Harvard University Press, 1973.

Brown looks primarily at the beginnings of grammar, at age 1½ or 2. This book is not easy, but it is well written and provides insight into the way psycholinguists explore child language.

The First Two Years: Psychosocial Development

Babies control and bring up their families as much as they are controlled by them; in fact, we may say that the family brings up a baby by being brought up by him.

Erik Erikson
Childhood and Society

I waited so long to have my baby, and when she came, she never did anything for me.

Mother of severely abused 4-year-old girl
The Battered Child

CHAPTER 8

Emotions and Personality

Attachment

Self-Concept

Friendliness

Individual Differences

Theories of Infant Emotions

Freud

Erikson

Bowlby and Spitz: Maternal Deprivation

Dennis: Stimulus Deprivation

Babies in Families

Day Care

The Quality of Home Care

HOME

The Harvard Preschool Project

Synchrony

Problems in Parent-Child Interaction

Child Abuse and Neglect

True or False?

An infant is much more likely to be frightened by a stranger who is a midget than by one who is of normal height.

The more securely attached infants are to their mothers, the less likely they are to venture forth in search of adventure.

Once toddlers have developed a sense of "me" and "mine," it is very difficult for them to share willingly.

Day-care centers are adequate alternatives to mothering only in countries like China and Russia, where the emphasis is on the group rather than on the individual.

Babies who do not respond positively to cuddling are not being cuddled properly.

Adults who were abused children are least likely to be abusing parents because of their sensitivity to the problem.

It is not easy to interpret a baby's emotions. Infants obviously cannot tell us whether they feel timid or courageous, elated or depressed. Even when we can plainly see that a baby is happy or sad or afraid, we usually know little about the origin or the importance of those emotions. Is an 11-month-old's clinging to Mother and crying pitifully when she leaves a sign of deprivation or spoiledness? of love or anger? of panic or simple frustration? And how great an effect on the child might repetitions of this scene have? Should the mother avoid incidents like this at all costs or decide that her child will simply have to "grow up"? Questions such as these plague many care-givers as they try to decide how best to satisfy the emotional needs of an infant.

The field of child development is replete with studies, facts, and theories that point to answers to these questions; and psychologists are full of suggestions, for in spite of the problems inherent in the study of infants, they have done surprisingly well in charting the development of emotions during the first two years of life. Nevertheless, most psychologists shy away from rules of child-rearing, focusing instead on the relationship between parent and child, an interaction that varies from pair to pair, day to day. This chapter begins with facts and theories relating to the psychosocial development of the infant and ends with the moment-by-moment interaction between parent and child, an interaction that can bring satisfaction and joy when it goes well and tragedy when it does not.

Emotions and Personality

Most emotions in the first months of life are simple reactions to everyday experiences (see the chart on page 239), a fact that leads some psychologists to wonder if the infant's early cries or smiles should be called emotions. They seem more like reflexes—that is, automatic responses to a particular stimulus—than the complex feelings of a thoughtful human being. For instance, the social smile (a smile at another person) is equally broad for almost everyone, and the precise age at which it appears depends more on conceptual age (the number of weeks since the baby

Development of Three Basic Emotions: Birth to Age 2

	Birth to 6 Months	6–12 Months	12 Months On
DISTRESS	Infants have many reasons for showing distress. They cry due to hunger, fatigue, pain, cold, loud noises, or sudden loss of support (if it seems that they are being dropped).	Most babies cry less during this period, for their digestion is more stable, and their interest in the world distracts them. However, before each new tooth appears, some babies are miserable for days.	The phrase "as easy as taking candy from a baby" definitely does not apply to most toddlers, who cry when virtually anything is taken from them. Almost any frustration, from being put to bed when they don't feel tired to being unable to reach the record player, can make them utter cries that sound much more like anger than the sadness or pain typical of the younger infant.
PLEASURES, SMILES, AND LAUGHTER	Contentment occurs when the neonate is securely wrapped or cuddled, rocked back and forth, or well fed. Babies also seem to enjoy looking at interesting sights and hearing soothing noises (especially rhythmic ones like heartbeats or lullabyes). For many babies, sucking is such a pleasure that it distracts them from other troubles, as the word "pacifier" testifies. Smiles begin early—with a half-smile at a pleasant noise or full stomach in the first days of life and a social smile in response to someone's face at about 6 weeks. By 4 or 5 months, smiles become broader, and babies laugh rather than grin if something is particularly exciting.	At about 8 months, babies are much more likely to laugh in *anticipation* of an enjoyable experience (Sroufe and Waters, 1976) rather than just *while* their stomachs are being kissed or they are splashing in the bath. Curiosity grows stronger, and interesting sights become even more fascinating.	Toddlers smile and laugh for most of the same reasons younger children do, although their greater fears sometimes inhibit them. However, toddlers are especially delighted by actions they perform themselves, and, as they grow older, by play with other children.
FEAR	In the first months of life, babies sometimes look scared when they are first placed in a warm bath, are held aloft like an airplane, or are otherwise subjected to new experiences. But usually infants under 6 months are intrigued rather than intimidated by such novelties. They seem as delighted with the antics of a stranger as they are with the playful noises and faces of their own parents.	Many new fears appear in the second half of the first year, grow stronger, and then decline. For instance, Sandra Scarr and Philip Salapatek (1970) presented babies with six potentially frightening things—a visual cliff, a strange adult, a jack-in-the-box, a toy dog that moved, a mask, and a loud noise. Babies younger than 7 months rarely showed any fear; babies older than 7 months often were wary; and babies between 11 and 18 months were most likely to be frightened by all six experiences. Then at about 1½ years, fear declined again.	

was conceived) than on any other factor. Premature babies smile at people later than full-term babies do—forty-six weeks past conception rather than six weeks past birth (Bower, 1977).

In the second half of the first year, infant reactions are recognizable as true emotions. The 12-month-old's fear of strangers, for example, is not a mindless reaction to all strangers. Instead, it depends on the specific situation: it tends to be weak if the infant is in a familiar place and with a familiar person, absent if the stranger is a child, and strong if the stranger behaves strangely, by making scary noises, for example, or by coming too close to the baby's face. The stranger's appearance is important too: babies are less wary of midgets than of taller adults, for instance (Brooks and Lewis, 1976). By age 1, an infant's response to any new or stressful situation also depends on the infant's relationship with his or her parents, as we will soon see.

Figure 8.1 *The "pleasure smile" of this sleeping infant is probably an inborn response to the satisfactions of a full stomach and a smoothly functioning digestive system, just as most of the early cries are automatic responses to hunger or indigestion.*

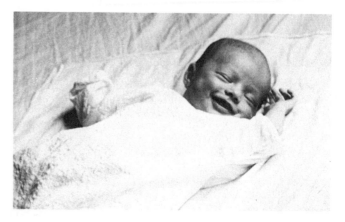

Most of the basic human emotions, including joy and sorrow, love and anger, fear and fascination, are already present at 1 year. But the toddler's new physical and cognitive development changes the way these emotions are experienced. If personality is "the characteristic way a person reacts to people and experiences" (a definition accepted by many psychologists), then the typical toddler's personality is quite different from the infant's.

Consider the adjectives used by Benjamin Spock and Arnold Gesell (probably the best-known chroniclers of early childhood) to describe American toddlers: demanding, assertive, mercurial, precooperative, contrary, obstinate, exasperating, imperious, balky, negativistic, bossy, and overfussy (Gesell et al., 1974; Spock, 1976). Most of these adjectives are well-deserved, although the toddler is not to blame. The ability to walk, run, and climb, coupled with a sense of independence and an enormous curiosity, makes it almost inevitable that toddlers explore, experiment, and get into trouble. That leads directly to frustration, for in most families, someone is bound to shout "No!" or take a plaything away or put the toddler in a crib or playpen—at least several times each day. Frustration sometimes leads to clear demonstrations of anger. Toddlers may throw their food on the floor, scream and kick their legs, or even hold their breath until someone panics and gives them what they want.

Figure 8.2 *The "terrible twos" is a popular epithet for toddlerhood when young tyrants say "No" and "Mine" much more often than "Yes" or "Let's share." Indeed, Gesell sees many similarities between the typical toddler and the typical adolescent in that the growing independence and self-assertion of each makes life more difficult for all concerned. However, just like teenagers, toddlers have another side to their personalities: they can also be cooperative, friendly, and affectionate.*

Having outlined the emotions evident in the first two years, we will now look in detail at the development of attachment, self-concept, and friendliness, three facets of personality development in toddlerhood that often vary from child to child.

Attachment

One emotion that develops during infancy has been studied in detail because it may reflect the quality of the relationship between care-giver and child. This emotion is attachment, a form of love. According to Ainsworth (1973), "an attachment may be defined as an affectional tie that one person or animal forms between himself and another specific one—a tie that binds them together in space and endures over time." When people are attached to each other, they try to be near one another, and they interact with each other often. Infants show attachment by "proximity-seeking" behaviors, such as approaching, following, and clinging, and "contact-seeking" behaviors, such as crying, smiling, and calling (Ainsworth and Bell, 1970).

As we noted in Chapter 1, Ainsworth (1967) began investigating attachment in a village in Uganda, observing the relationship between twenty-eight babies and their mothers. She used many criteria to measure attachment, among them whether the baby cried, smiled, or vocalized differently with the mother than with other people; whether the baby cried or tried to follow the mother when she left; whether the baby used the mother as a secure base for exploration (going forth to explore and then coming back to reestablish contact); and how often the baby clung to, or scrambled up on, the mother. (Kissing was also among Ainsworth's original criteria, but she discovered that mothers and babies in Uganda never kiss each other.)

Ainsworth found that no one specific maternal behavior makes a well-attached baby, and that no one measure of attachment is sufficient. Instead, an overall sensitivity to the child's needs, and an ability to satisfy those needs, were crucial. This generalization proved just as true in our own society, as Ainsworth found in later research. *Quality* of care, especially with regard to mother-infant play, is more important in establishing attachment than *quantity* of care (Ainsworth and Bell, 1974).

Ainsworth became interested in not only the formation of attachment, but also its consequences, specifically the relationship between attachment and the infant's willingness to explore the environment. To measure this relationship, she developed the standard laboratory procedure described in Chapter 1 (page 17), in which infants in seven successive episodes were left in a well-equipped playroom with their mother, a stranger, and by themselves. The comings and goings of the mother and the stranger were designed to be a mild stress on the infants, and their reaction to that stress was taken as an index of the nature of their attachment to their mothers.

For most infants, the mother's presence in the room was enough to give them courage to explore; her departure was a source of distress; and her return was a signal for the infants to reestablish contact (with a smile or by climbing into the mother's arms) and then resume playing. These are all signs of secure attachment.

Other infants, however, showed signs of insecure attachment. Some clung to their mother even before her initial departure, cried loudly each time she left, and refused to be comforted when she returned—either pushing the mother away or continuing to sob even when they were back in her arms. Others showed no signs of stress when the mother left, but on her return, they avoided reestablishing contact,

Figure 8.3 *Securely attached toddlers get comfort and courage from hearing, seeing, or touching their mothers. Reassuring responses like this mother's help children adjust to new experiences.*

sometimes even turning their backs. Ainsworth found that infants who were most securely attached were most likely to explore their environment and, therefore, most likely to learn. Those who displayed insecure attachment were least likely to do so.

Other research by Alan Sroufe and his colleagues has confirmed that secure attachment at age 1 sets the stage for more exploration and more mature personality development at ages 2 and 3. Observations in nursery school showed that, compared to insecurely attached children, 3-year-olds who had been rated securely attached at age 1 were significantly more curious, self-directed, and sympathetic to other children. They also were more likely to be sought out as a friend and to be chosen as a leader. By contrast, the insecurely attached 1-year-olds were more apt to grow up to be withdrawn and hesitant at age 3 (Sroufe, 1978).

The Developmental Sequence of Signs of Attachment Attachment probably begins in the first months of life, for even 1-month-olds become accustomed to the way they are cared for, and show some signs of distress (irregular sleeping or eating patterns) if an unfamiliar person cares for them (Sander et al., 1970). But for the most part, babies in the first six months are quite flexible, willing to let any attentive person hold or feed them. Attachment becomes much more apparent in the second half of the first year and at the beginning of the second, when babies hold onto familiar people and cry when they leave.

Evidence of attachment changes as the child grows older. One researcher studied attachment by observing 100 babies in their homes. She found that babies at the end of their first year were the most likely to cry when their mothers left and to cling to them when they returned. In the middle of the second year, they were more likely to search for their mothers than cry. At 24 months, they showed relatively little distress when their mothers left, but seemed delighted when they returned, often running to hug and kiss them (Serafica, 1978).

This sequence closely follows the development of separation distress, in which a child shows that he or she is unhappy when a familiar care-giver leaves. The first signs of separation distress appear at about 6 months; by 9 months, the reaction is much clearer and becomes even stronger by 15 months. Then it gradually weakens. Most children younger than 2 cry when their parents leave them at nursery school, but few 3-year-olds do (Jones and Gill, 1972).

The practical implications of these studies are clear. The hardest time for a baby to begin nursery school, to change care-givers, or to move to an unfamiliar house is probably between 9 and 18 months. If such a change is necessary during these months, parents should try to make the transition as easy as possible—perhaps staying with the child in school for a few days, or bringing a familiar blanket or stuffed toy to the new bed.

Attachment to Father The emphasis on attachment to mother does not mean that fathers are unimportant in the first year. The reverse is true. Several researchers have found that the father's presence is just as effective as the mother's in making babies secure enough to investigate their surroundings (Kotelchuck et al., 1975). When left alone with a stranger, those babies whose fathers spent the most time with them cried the least—an average of 8.8 seconds in one experiment, compared to an average of 40.5 seconds for babies whose fathers rarely cared for them. The babies whose fathers were active in their care also showed more interest in exploring their environment (Spelke et al., 1973).

Other research has shown that fathers may fill a special role in their infant's lives because father's play tends to be more physical and more exciting than mother's. Fathers are likely to swing their toddlers around, or "wrestle" with them on the floor, or crawl after them in a "chase," while mothers are more likely to read their children a book or help them play with their toys.

One researcher studied fourteen families in their homes and found that although 20-month-old toddlers spent the same amount of time smiling, vocalizing, and playing with their mother as with their father, they responded more to playing with their father (Clarke-Stewart, 1978). By 30 months, differences were even more apparent: the children were more cooperative, involved, and interested in their father's games, and judging by their smiles and laughter, had more fun playing.

This study also found a correlation between the child's score on the Bayley IQ test and three measures of paternal attitudes: how much the father enjoyed playing with the child, how positively he felt about the child, and how long his play sessions with the child lasted. The consensus of the researchers who have studied father-infant interaction is that the bond between a man and his child can be as strong and important as the mother-infant bond, although it may be expressed in somewhat different ways.

Figure 8.4 *For many toddlers, a perch on their father's shoulder is very exciting, especially if he is pretending to be a large animal or a fast-moving vehicle. Fathers are more likely to swing and carry their children aloft than mothers are, one reason children usually laugh more when playing with their fathers.*

Self-Concept

The sense of self emerges gradually over the first two years. In the first months, infants have no awareness of their bodies as theirs, as shown when 2-month-olds "discover" their hands when they catch sight of them, become fascinated by the way they move, then "lose" them as they slip out of their line of vision. Even 8-month-olds often don't seem to know where their bodies end and someone else's body begins, as can be seen when a child at this age grabs a toy in another child's hand and reacts with surprise when the toy "resists."

As object permanence develops, babies realize, first, that other people exist and, eventually, that they themselves exist. Michael Lewis and Jeanne Brooks (1975) found that when 1-year-olds see pictures of their families, they name the members "Daddy, Mommy, Baby." Not until between 21 and 24 months do toddlers label themselves with their own name—despite the fact that most babies respond to their own name by 10 months, about the same time they react to "No!" and "Hot!"

Figure 8.5 *In their second year, infants begin to develop a sense of themselves. Among other things, they come to realize who their mirror image is.*

Further evidence of the emerging sense of self was shown when babies looked in a mirror after a dot of rouge had surreptitiously been put on their noses. If the babies knew that they were seeing *themselves* in the mirror, according to Lewis and Brooks (1978), they would react to the unfamiliar redness on their noses. One study of ninety-six babies between 9 and 24 months showed a clear developmental shift. While even some of the youngest babies responded to their mirror image by acting coy or touching their bodies, none of those between 9 and 12 months tried to touch the mark; most of those between 12 and 24 months did.

As toddlers develop an awareness of who they are and what they can do, they acquire two new emotions, pride and shame, which of course are impossible to experience before having a sense of self. Consider these two examples. One toddler learns in nursery school how to put on his snow jacket by laying it open on the floor, putting his arms through the sleeves, and then flipping it over his head. He is so proud that he insists on donning his jacket every time he leaves the house, even when winter is long over. Another toddler enjoys picking up the phone whenever it rings but is forbidden to because, instead of speaking, she merely listens while the caller keeps repeating "Hello?" The prohibition stops her—except when she is alone in the room. Then she picks the receiver up, listens, and slams it down shamefacedly when someone enters the room! Such moments of pride and shame may become part of the child's self-concept, that is, her idea of what kind of person she is. This idea will be discussed further when Erikson's second stage, autonomy versus shame and doubt, is explained.

Friendliness

Because babies smile at everyone in the first months of life, delight in playing with attentive adults, and are fascinated by other babies, children, and animals, most people think of them as being friendly. Strictly speaking, however, we do not consider people friendly unless they have the option of not being friendly, so in this sense the automatic smile of infants cannot be regarded as a friendly gesture; infants do not even realize they are smiling.

But toddlers do know the difference between themselves and others, and between familiar people and strangers. This enables them to be both friendly and unfriendly. In fact, toddlers are infamous for being the latter: it is thought that they are afraid of strangers, often unwilling to share, and not above grabbing a toy from another child or pushing and biting to get their way. And they are, but only under certain circumstances. Parents, teachers, and psychologists are now realizing that far from being asocial by nature, toddlers can be very friendly as long as they are familiar with other people and feel reasonably secure and happy.

One series of experiments demonstrated the willingness of 18-month-olds to share when they were in a playroom with their mother and another child-mother pair (Rheingold et al., 1976). All the children shared with their mothers, and three-fourths of them shared with the other child. The same researchers conducted further experiments with other toddlers to see how extensive sharing during toddlerhood is. They found that the toddlers were willing to share almost anything, including food, dolls, and blocks, with almost anyone, including fathers and adult strangers. They even shared with inanimate objects: one child gave a toy to a doll, another showed a lemon to a toy cow. In all cases, the children shared on their own initiative, without prompting or praise.

Another study of children between 10 and 24 months also found that even the youngest children responded to each other, smiling, talking, and sharing in a play situation, although the older the child was, the more social play transpired (see Figure 8.6) (Eckerman et al., 1975). In this study, children could play with their mothers or with another child. In the middle of the second year, children were more likely to play with their mothers than younger and older children were, but by the end of the second year, children were almost four times as likely to play with another child as they were to play with their mothers. The researchers speculate that more play with their mothers at 18 months prepared children for more play with other children at 24 months.

This research confirms that children begin to develop social skills when they are toddlers. Of course, it takes a long time before children can learn more complicated social skills, such as sharing toys that they don't want to share, or accepting another child's version of the rules to a particular game. But given sufficient experience, toddlers can become quite friendly.

Figure 8.6 (a) *Watching children who were in the presence of their mothers and another child, researchers observed each child for forty 15-second observation periods, noting whether the child's behavior during each period was of social or solitary play. As shown here, the average 24-month-old spent twice as much time in social play as the average 12-month-old. (b) In addition, two types of social play were observed: play with mother and play with peers. Play with mother increases from age 1 to age 1½, and then declines, as play with peers doubles from age 1½ to age 2.*

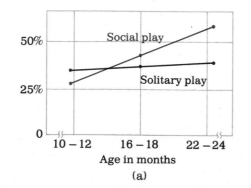

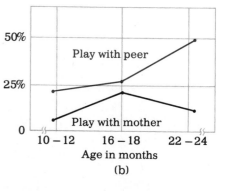

Individual Differences

An infant's early distress, happiness, and curiosity seem to be maturational rather than learned behavior, since infants all over the world cry, smile, and explore for the same reasons and at about the same ages. Even blind and deaf infants follow the same sequence, which suggests that maturation triggers smiles at 2 months and fears at 8 months. Babies meeting other babies seem interested at 10 months, fearful at 20 months, and ready to play at 30 months.

However, simple maturation is not the only cause of early emotional growth, because there are evident differences that maturation alone does not explain. For instance, most emotions, including fear of strangers, separation distress, and attachment, appear a few months later in some babies than in others. Blind infants are about two months behind their sighted peers, for example (Fraiberg, 1977a). Infants also differ in the intensity of these emotions; some seem terrified of strangers, while others simply look a bit cautious. A few babies, even some reared by their mothers at home, never show clear signs of attachment. Finally, while almost all toddlers are more willful than they were as infants, some are much more compliant than others.

RESEARCH REPORT　　　**Sex Differences in Infant Personality**

Although several studies have found that infant boys and girls differ in their emotional responses, we do not yet have enough evidence about these difference to pinpoint their causes. One study of seventeen pairs of boy-girl twins, aged 12 to 15 months, found that the girls stayed closer to their mothers and looked at them more often (Brooks and Lewis, 1974). Another study found that 13-month-old boys were more likely to try to figure out how to open the catch on a gate that separated them from some toys than were girls, who tended to just stand there and cry (Goldberg and Lewis, 1969). When Moss (1967) studied 3-month-old first-born infants, he found that girls usually slept more and cried less than boys.

Does research like this confirm the popular notion that girls are easier to care for, but more dependent, than boys? Before jumping to that conclusion, let's look more closely at the evidence. First, all the studies found much variation in the behavior of babies of either sex. As parents can testify, there are many noisy, difficult, and independent girls, and many peaceful, easy, dependent baby boys. This means that other factors besides gender must cause many temperamental differences. In addition, the sex differences that have been found between the average boy and girl *might* be inborn, but they could just as well be the result of early differences in treatment.

Let us consider the biological evidence. Although the average girl weighs a few ounces less than the average boy, she is physiologically more mature. This is shown, for instance, in bone age, that is, how much of the child's cartilage has become bone. At birth, girls' bone age is, on

According to Goldberg and Lewis, boys and girls by toddlerhood show many differences in their typical play behavior. Given a choice, boys are more likely than girls to play with toys involving gross motor skills—choosing to pound with a hammer, for instance, rather than playing less actively with a toy dog or cat. They

also respond differently to frustration. As shown here, when faced with a barrier, the typical girl cries helplessly, whereas the typical boy tries to get around it. These facts, of course, indicate nothing about whether such early sex differences are learned or innate.

average, two weeks ahead of boys', and by the end of the first year, girls are eight weeks ahead of boys (Tanner, 1974). Advanced physical maturity could explain why girls are less likely to cry, since more mature digestive systems would

Some of these differences may be inborn differences in temperament. However, cultural patterns can be crucial. Babies who grow up in a community where strangers are rare and their mothers are always nearby usually show fear of strangers and separation distress later and more intensely than do infants who regularly see strange faces and experience the mother's departure every day. For example, among !Kung babies of Namibia, who spend the first months of life in a carrier strapped to their mother's chest and know everyone in their village, *all* 15-month-olds cry when they are separated from their mothers. In many cultures, the peak of separation distress occurs earlier than 15 months; and in other cultures, some babies never cry at separation (Kagan, 1976).

These differences are apparent even among babies from the same genetic background, which further rules out inheritance as the only source of variation in emotional development. For instance, Israeli children raised in a kibbutz are shy with unfamiliar children at age 1½, just as family-raised Israeli children are. But by age 2, the kibbutz children are less inhibited and more likely to play than their family-raised contemporaries (Zaslow, 1977). As we saw in the research on attachment, the quality of family care, even within the same culture, makes some infants more confident and curious, or more clinging and distressed, than others.

---

mean fewer stomach pains and hunger pangs, the most common causes of infant crying.

Most studies of neonates find no differences between boys and girls, although there is some evidence that girls are more sensitive to taste and smell in the first hours of life (Maccoby and Jacklin, 1974). One study found sex differences in newborn responses as measured by the Brazelton scale: males were higher in reactivity (they became excited faster, cried more, and were harder to console), and females were higher in responsiveness (they attended more to a face and a voice) (Osofsky and O'Connell, 1977).

If females are indeed born more responsive, this would suggest that the infant girl's easier temperament and greater dependence are a result of gender, not culture. However, British studies find fewer differences between male and female newborns than American studies do. One explanation is that the baby boy's greater irritability and lesser responsiveness may be the result of circumcision rather than inborn temperament (Richards et al., 1976). In the United States, 83 percent of newborn boys are circumcised, while less than 1 percent of British boys are.

Now let's look at evidence that infant girls and boys are treated differently. Mothers tend to talk more to daughters than to sons, and fathers usually roughhouse more with sons than with daughters (Kagan, 1971; Parke, 1979). Parents give girls and boys different toys and decorate their rooms differently, even in the first months of life (Rheingold and Cook, 1975). According to a study of mothers and their 10-month-olds, mothers of boys were quicker to come when their babies cried than mothers of girls were, even though the cause of the tears (separation from mother) was the same for all the babies (Carter and Bow, 1976).

Finally, in one study, 204 college men and women saw a film of a 9-month-old infant playing with unfamiliar toys (Condry and Condry, 1976). Half the students were told that the infant was a boy named David; the other half were told that the infant was a girl named Dana. The students who thought they were watching David "saw" more pleasure and less fear in the infant's emotions than the students who thought they were watching Dana. In one instance, when the baby reacted negatively to a jack-in-the-box, the students were more likely to interpret David's reaction as anger and Dana's response as fear. Male students were especially likely to differentiate between David and Dana.

As the authors of this last study point out, such differences in the way adults perceive male and female infants probably affect the way they treat boy and girl babies. Adults are more likely to comfort the "scared" baby girl than the "angry" baby boy, differences in treatment that might affect personality development.

Research such as this suggests that cultural values cause some sex differences, but it does not exclude the possibility of important biological differences in the ways male and female infants respond. Final judgment on the relative strength of biological and cultural influences cannot be made without more definitive research.

Cognitive development also affects emotional development. It is likely, for instance, that the ability to recognize mother and father, realize that they still exist when they are out of sight, and remember them when they are gone may be prerequisites for the more obvious signs of attachment. Some psychologists even consider "person permanence" a special type of object permanence that emerges earlier or later than conventional object permanence, depending partly on the experience of the infant (Ainsworth, 1973).

In the same way, cognitive development affects when a child is able to experience pride and shame, since to feel either, a child must know that he or she exists. As we have pointed out, infants do not have this awareness. Toddlers do, however, which is one reason 2-year-olds say "me" and "mine" so often.

Many psychologists believe that self-knowledge, emotional development, and cognitive growth are interrelated. As is apparent from Table 8.1, the development of language and sensorimotor skills also seems linked to emotional growth. The variation among infants in emotions and personality probably depends on interaction among many biological, cognitive, and cultural influences.

TABLE 8.1 **Interrelated Aspects of Development**

Age (in months)	Self-knowledge	Emotional Experience	Cognition	Language	Sensorimotor Skills
0–3	Emergence of self-other distinction.	Unconditioned responses to stimulus events (noise, hunger, etc.).	Reflexes and circular reactions involving own body.	Cries and coos.	Lifts head; senses becoming more acute and adapted.
4–8	Emergence of self-other categories.	Specific emotional experiences (fear, happiness, love attachment).	Circular reactions involving self and others.	Babbling.	Reaches and holds on; sits up, rolls over. Perception well developed.
9–12	Consolidation of self-other permanence.	Conditioned responses (strangers, incongruity, surprise).	Object permanence, anticipation, means and ends.	Responds to words, and usually utters first word.	Crawling, standing, climbing.
12–24	Consolidation of basis of self-categories (age, gender, self-recognition).	Development of empathy, shame, embarrassment, pride.	More complex means and ends, exploration and experimentation, mental representation, imagination.	Talks. Vocabulary of three to fifty words at 18 months. Uses own name at end of second year.	Walking, running.

Source: Columns for self-knowledge, emotional experience, and cognition are adapted from Lewis and Brooks, 1978.

Theories of Infant Emotions

Many psychologists have examined the development of emotions and theorized about the possible consequences of the failure to meet the infant's basic emotional needs. As we will see, while many of their observations are remarkably similar, their theories have led them to quite different conclusions.

Freud

Freud (1960, originally published in 1935) called the first stage of his developmental sequence the oral stage, because he thought the mouth is the infant's most important source of sensual gratification. According to Freud, not only is the mouth the instrument for attaining nourishment, it is also the main source of pleasure: sucking, especially at the mother's breast, is a joyous, sensual activity for babies.

Freud believed that infants who are frustrated in their urge to suck might become frustrated adults, still trying to get oral satisfaction by excessively eating, drinking, chewing, biting, smoking, or talking. He also theorized that oral people tend to be generous, disorganized, and habitually late; that is, they act "babyish" so someone will "mother" them.

In the second year, Freud maintained, the chief pleasure zone is the anus. Accordingly, he referred to this period as the anal stage. Since this period is the usual time of toilet training, it can be fraught with parent-child conflict. Freud believed that premature toilet training (occurring before the age of 1½ or 2, when children are physiologically mature enough to hold their urine for several hours, and psychologically mature enough to participate in the toilet-training process) or overly strict toilet training produces "anal types," who chronically worry about constipation or diarrhea and overemphasize neatness, cleanliness, precision, and punctuality. People with anal personality structures have difficulty relaxing and are overcautious about meeting new people or participating in new experiences—problems which, in Freud's view, could have been avoided if only their toilet training had been less unpleasant.

Figure 8.7 *Toilet training is an important event in the life of the toddler, according to psychoanalytic theorists. If parents make the experience pleasant, toilet training can foster independence and pride, rather than obsessive concern with cleanliness or nagging feelings of shame and doubt.*

Erikson

According to Erikson (1963), the infant's task is to solve the problem of trust versus mistrust vis-à-vis the world, by deciding whether or not the world is a good, comfortable place. Babies learn trust if they are well fed, warm, and dry significantly more often than they are hungry, cold, and wet.

Like Freud, Erikson emphasizes the importance of feeding, but he believes that the overall pattern of infant care is more important than any one aspect of it. Babies begin to develop a sense of who they are when they experience "consistency, continuity, and sameness of experience." Erikson explains that "the amount of trust derived from earliest infantile experience does not seem to depend on absolute quantities of food or demonstrations of love, but rather on the quality of the maternal relationship."

Of course, Erikson realizes that infants cannot always be content and comfortable. He acknowledges that teething, for example, is painful no matter how comforting the parents are. However, Erikson thinks that if comfort is the rule, the baby is likely to become an adult who believes that life is good and people trustworthy; if comfort is the exception, the child is likely to become a pessimistic, suspicious, and unhappy adult.

Erikson sees the conflict of toddlerhood as autonomy versus shame and doubt for toddlers want to rule their own actions and bodies. Indeed, the drive for autonomy is present in every aspect of the toddler's life. Toddlers love to do everything from feeding and dressing themselves to pushing their own strollers—no matter that they often spill their milk, put their clothes on inside out, and push their strollers in directions no one else wants to go.

Figure 8.8 *The toddler's growing independence is a mixed blessing. The girl in this photo may be starting to get herself ready for bed. On the other hand, it is equally likely that her mother has just finished dressing her.*

Erikson thinks that toilet training can be a difficult experience if parents instill a sense of shame and self-doubt in the toddler who defecates at the wrong time and place. While Erikson agrees with Freud that too strict toilet training is harmful, he also disapproves of too little discipline:

> Firmness must protect him [the toddler] against the potential anarchy of his as yet untrained sense of discrimination, his inability to hold on and let go with discretion. As his environment encourages him to "stand on his own feet," it must protect him against meaningless and arbitrary experiences of shame and of early doubt. [Erikson, 1963]

Bowlby and Spitz: Maternal Deprivation

John Bowlby believes that maternal love and care are the most important influences on the infant's future development. After reviewing many studies on infants separated from their mothers, Bowlby concluded that any break in the early mother-child relationship could cause severe emotional, intellectual, and social consequences (Bowlby, 1952). Specifically, he maintained that children who lose their mothers in infancy, or who are separated from them because of hospitalization, maternal employment, or other circumstances, are likely to become depressed, physically and mentally retarded, or delinquent. Their state is the result of maternal deprivation, which literally means loss of mother but has come to mean either loss of, or separation from, the infant's main care-giver. Thus a baby who is separated from a father or grandmother who provided most of that baby's care might suffer maternal deprivation. Infants, such as orphans in hospitals, who never had a primary care-giver are also considered to be maternally deprived.

The Foundlings   In order to understand how Bowlby reached his conclusion, consider the following study, which has become a "classic," not because the research was so well done, but because the conclusions are so disturbing.

In 1945, René Spitz reported on the development of unwanted infants in a foundling home. In this institution, babies received good nutrition and medical care. For the first months of life, they were breast-fed, either by their own mothers, or by wet nurses, and they were visited regularly by a doctor, who made sure their diet was good and their surroundings clean.

After being weaned, the foundlings were cared for by several nurses, who changed shifts and days frequently, so no particular nurse was responsible for any particular baby. The ratio of infants per care-giver was about eight to one. The babies lay on their backs almost all of the time in their cribs, without toys, playmates, or individual attention, unable even to sit up, at first because their physical development had not progressed sufficiently, and later because they had worn hollows in the mattresses, making sitting-up impossible.

While the foundlings' development was more advanced than normal in the first months, by 1 year their average score on a test of development was in the mentally-retarded range. They were apathetic, rarely smiling, talking, or crying. In addition, even though the staff of the institution took many precautions against disease, and hygiene was impeccable, these babies were extremely susceptible to illness. All of them caught measles during an epidemic, and twenty-three of the eighty-eight children under 30 months died from the disease, a death rate of one child in four. At that time in the community, home-reared infants who caught measles had less than 1 chance in 200 of dying.

Spitz compared these foundlings with infants housed in another institution, called the Nursery, where they were cared for by their mothers, themselves institutionalized for delinquency. Although the quality of diet and medical care for the Nursery infants was found to be somewhat below that provided for the foundlings, the Nursery infants fared much better, developing normally throughout the first year. The reason, according to Spitz, is that they had their mothers with them, providing love and individual attention, whereas the foundlings lost such "mothering" when breast-feeding was discontinued.

Bowlby's Conclusions   On the basis of evidence such as this, as well as his own research on hospitalized children, Bowlby (1969) believes that disturbances in the mother-child relationship are the cause of many of the psychological and social problems of the Western world. The most common disturbances, Bowlby states, result from too little mothering, or mothering from a succession of different people. He also says that it is possible for a child to be "overmothered," with the mother insisting on providing too much care and not allowing the child to have time to relax or develop his or her own skills. Mothering involves emotional responsiveness as well as physical care. Bowlby (1973) believes that "a mother can be physically present but emotionally absent," with tragic results.

Spitz (1965) agrees. He also thinks babies suffer maternal deprivation if their mother is emotionally disturbed. In this case, "the mother's personality acts as a disease-provoking agent, as a psychosocial toxin," poisoning the development of the child.

Dennis: Stimulus Deprivation

There is an alternative explanation for the retardation of the babies in Spitz's and in Bowlby's studies. It comes from the American psychologist Wayne Dennis, whose early research was reported in Chapter 1.

The orphanage Dennis studied in Iran in the 1950s was similar to the foundling home reported by Spitz. Here too, the care-giver–child ratio was about eight to one, and the babies, who had been abandoned by their mothers, had almost no opportunity to see, hear, or interact with anyone or anything. Dennis reported that they were very slow in developing basic motor skills (see Table 8.2).

A CLOSER LOOK   **Applications of Theories**

Each of these theories has changed the way infants are cared for. Prior to the popularity of Freud's ideas, many European and American parents seriously discouraged babies from thumb-sucking, sometimes going so far as making them wear mittens or tying their hands by their sides. Also common was breast-feeding according to a strict schedule, allowing babies to nurse for ten or twenty minutes every four hours. The result of both these practices was a lot of frustrated and hungry babies.

The general acceptance today of demand feeding, thumb-sucking, and pacifiers is due in part to Freud's concern for infants' sucking pleasure. While many psychologists disagree with Freud's predictions of far-reaching consequences due to frustration at the oral stage (and some orthodontists bemoan the results of years of thumb- or pacifier-sucking), almost all psychologists agree that, at least in the first months of life, babies should be allowed to suck as much as they want.

Erikson's emphasis on trust and continuity has led to the realization that even infants can be affected by differences in care, especially if parents fluctuate in the way they feed, hold, or attend to their infant from day to day. The idea that consistency, love, and continuity may be more important than any particular "right" way to raise a child has gained acceptance over the past few years. So has the idea that freedom to explore must be balanced by a clear sense of limits.

Spitz's and Bowlby's ideas have revolutionized the care of institutionalized infants. Thirty years ago, orphans were

A happy, active, preschool child sucking on a pacifier is a common sight in contemporary America. Although many adults from older generations or other cultures consider pacifiers "ugly" or *"unhealthy," most parents of young children accept the popularized interpretation of Freud's theory and let their children have pacifiers even when infancy is over.*

TABLE 8.2 **Percent of Children Who Can Perform Basic Motor Skills**

	Children Studied by Dennis		Normal Children	
	Age 12–24 Mos.	*Age 24–36 Mos.*	*At 12 Mos.*	*At 24 Mos.*
Sit alone	42%	95%	100%	100%
Creep or scoot	14%	75%	100%	100%
Stand holding on	4%	45%	95%	100%
Walk holding on	2%	40%	80%	100%
Walk alone	0%	8%	50%	100%

These infants were also severely retarded in talking, and in other cognitive and social skills (Dennis, 1960; Dennis and Najarian, 1957). Dennis blames this retardation on "paucity of handling" and "restricted learning opportunities" rather than on maternal deprivation. He notes that the foundlings in Spitz's study were deprived of stimulation as well as mothering, whereas Spitz's comparison group of Nursery babies had not only mothers but also toys, better lighting, and opportunities to see, and play with, each other.

placed in large institutions, often to wait for months or years until prospective parents could see what kind of personality and intellect their child-to-be would have. Now that it is recognized that body, mind, and spirit can atrophy in an institution, adoptable children are placed with parents as soon as possible. If the biological parents cannot care for their children but are not ready to have them adopted, the children are placed with foster families. The psychologist's goal is to find a permanent home for the child as soon as possible. Unfortunately, many judges and lawyers still do not realize how important the time factor is (Goldstein et al., 1973).

Many modern hospitals have changed their policies in order to make hospitalization less frightening for a child. Parents are encouraged to visit their sick children often, or even better, to stay with them day and night. In order to reduce stranger-anxiety, two or three nurses are assigned to care for all the needs of a small group of children, a marked contrast to the experience of the sick adult, who often sees dozens of members of the hospital staff in a few days.

Dennis' research has led us to realize that institutionalized children need personal care and adequate stimulation. If they receive both, such children thrive, as Tizard and Rees (1974) found when they followed the development of sixty-four children who spent their first two years in British institutions. As infants, they were given many toys, taken on outings, and provided with other stimulating experiences; and although they were cared for by many different nurses,

the infant–care-giver ratio was low (about one to one). At age 2, their development was normal for the most part, although language development was a bit slow.

In the next two and a half years, some of these children were adopted, some were returned to their biological parents, and some remained in the institutions. Which of these three alternatives befell the child was not affected by the child's personal development; instead, external factors, such as whether the parents found employment or agreed to release their child for adoption, determined the child's fate. At age 4½, all the children were given the Wechsler IQ test. Those who had been adopted scored well above average (115), those still in the institutions scored above average (105), and those who had been returned to their original families had average scores (100). The slow language development of two years earlier turned out to be only a temporary problem, since in most cases, verbal scores were as high as nonverbal scores.

According to the researchers, the reason the children who were returned to their original parents had the lowest scores is that they had less intellectual stimulation, specifically owning fewer toys and being read fewer books, than the adopted or institutionalized children. On the basis of evidence like this, many psychologists think that the intellectual needs of young children can be met in institutions. Although emotional needs are harder to measure, it seems probable that they are harder to satisfy in an institution, unless there is a personal relationship with a caring adult.

In a follow-up study of the Iranian orphans, Dennis (1973) found that even though the average IQ of 2-year-olds had been the same for both sexes (50), by age 16 the average IQ for boys was 81, while the average IQ for girls was still about 50. The reason for the difference lay in the orphans' later schooling: boys were given much more education and more varied experiences than the girls. This finding confirmed Dennis' theory that lack of stimulation was the crucial variable that explained the poor development of the foundlings.

However, both Spitz's and Dennis' studies have been criticized on methodological grounds. One criticism is that in both cases the people who tested the infants knew not only the goals of the study but also which babies lived in which institutions, making it improbable that experimenter bias was avoided.

An additional criticism is that the babies in both Spitz's and Dennis' research were deprived of *both* mothering and stimulation. As Rutter (1974) points out in his excellent review, almost all psychologists now agree that infants growing up without personal attention *and* stimulation will be harmed. Neither maternal deprivation nor an unstimulating environment is an adequate explanation by itself for the slow development of institutionalized infants, or for the long-range effects of poor infant care.

Babies in Families

What do the theories tell us about babies growing up in families? Is Freud right in his assertion that early feeding and toilet-training experiences can determine future personality? Is the trust-and-autonomy stage as important as Erikson believes? Is Bowlby right in holding that mother, and only mother, should provide almost all the necessary care in early childhood? The answer to all three questions is, Probably not. Most psychologists respect the work of Freud, Erikson, and Bowlby, and some find their theories helpful in understanding emotionally disturbed children and adults. But few psychologists accept these theories as they were originally stated. Freud's theories especially have fared poorly.

Freud's Theories   Research has failed to tie the personality of the adult, or even of the 5-year-old, to specific experiences in the first two years. Whether a child was fed on schedule or demand, or toilet-trained at 8 months or 3 years, does not seem to matter much at age 5, or 10, or 30. The parents' overall love and attention to their child is more important than when the child gives up the bottle or wears the last diaper (Caldwell, 1964; Martin, 1975).

For example, one study of 375 children found that those who were toilet-trained before 12 months were no more likely to have emotional problems than those trained later (Sears et al., 1957). However, children whose mothers were cold and strict *were* more likely to become upset whenever they were trained, and were more apt to be still wetting their beds at age 5. Most psychologists today advise waiting until the child is old enough to cooperate in toilet training.

Erikson's Theories   Erikson's theories about the first years have fared better than Freud's because they emphasize the overall pattern of fostering trust in the first year and allowing autonomy in the second; and researchers *have* found that an overall atmosphere of warmth and acceptance in the home does correlate with happy, self-confident children (Caldwell, 1964; Martin, 1975).

The idea that trust is important in the first year and autonomy important in the second has been repeated in different words by many psychologists who are astute observers of young children. Mary Ainsworth, for example, speaks of attachment leading to exploration; John Bowlby speaks of secure attachment leading to self-reliance; Margaret Mahler speaks of the mother's acting as a "shielding membrane," allowing the child to develop individual and independent characteristics (Mahler et al., 1975). This all sounds very similar to the idea of providing "basic trust."

Another of Erikson's accepted ideas is that children naturally seek to do things on their own, a fact confirmed by teachers, parents, and psychologists, who find that toddlers spend hours trying to master new skills—from putting on their pants to using their potty.

However, Erikson's theory that too many disruptions in the first year or too little autonomy in the second will have a lifelong impact has not been substantiated. The trend of psychological research now points in the other direction; even children with an extremely deprived, unloving, or restricted infancy sometimes become normal, happy adults (Kagan and Klein, 1973; Winick et al., 1975; Clarke and Clarke, 1976). While the first two years are important, they no longer seem as critical as Erikson and many others once believed.

Bowlby and Dennis   No one disagrees with Bowlby's and Dennis' contention that infants need individual attention and cognitive stimulation in the first years of life. Babies growing up in normal households get both.

However, some psychologists have interpreted Bowlby's research to mean that infants need their mothers with them virtually all the time. Following this line of

---

A CLOSER LOOK   **People as a Source of Stimulation**

The emphasis on the importance of stimulation is sometimes interpreted to mean that babies need toys and activities more than they need social interaction with people. This interpretation is wrong, for people are usually far better sources of stimulation than any manufactured plaything.

Imagine how a face looks to a baby. It has bulges for the nose and cheekbones, indentations for the eyes and mouth, and protuberances for ears. The skin tones are varied, and the eyebrows, nostrils, eyes, and lips provide contrasting color and texture. The whole object is surrounded by hair—sometimes bushy, silky, curly, or straight; sometimes black, brown, red, blond, white, or gray. Beards, glasses, hats, freckles, wrinkles, and earrings make the object even more fascinating. The entire face, as well as the individual parts, can move in lots of different ways: the teeth and tongue, for instance, constantly appear and disappear.

As if all this were not enough, faces also make thousands of noises—everything from the sounds of speech to clicks, squeals, laughs, grunts, whines, and kisses. What's more, faces can be touched, patted, pulled, poked, smelled, licked, tasted, and bitten. Most exciting of all, faces respond to the baby's own movements and noises.

No wonder developmental psychologists stress parent-infant relationships, not only for affection but also for the stimulation that people provide.

reasoning, Selma Fraiberg concluded that good maternal care is "every child's birthright." She thinks that rather than subsidizing alternatives to mothering, such as day care, our society should help inadequate mothers improve their relationship with their infants (Fraiberg, 1977b). This argument is one reason the United States government provided less money in the last half of the 1970s for infant day care and for preschool education than it did in the first half.

However, most contemporary psychologists do not agree that mothers must be the sole care-givers for young children. They believe that it is fine for several people to share responsibility for the child, as long as there are not too many care-givers and as long as each gives the child the love and the stimulation that babies need.

Day Care

The debate over alternatives to mothering has led to a closer examination of day-care centers, the chief question being whether spending time away from both parents harms the cognitive or social development of the child. Evidence from other countries is clear. Children have been successfully raised in day-care centers in Israel, China, and the Soviet Union, even from the time they were a few weeks old (Bettelheim, 1969; Bronfenbrenner, 1973; Kessen, 1975).

But evidence from another culture does not always prove that the case would be the same in North America. Research here has shown that how much a child benefits from day care depends on the quality of care in both home and center. Children from inadequate homes are likely to learn more in a good day-care center than they would at home (Robinson and Robinson, 1971; Doyle, 1975). On the other hand, poor-quality day care slows down cognitive development, as Mary Peaslee (1976) found when she studied 2-year-olds in a center where there were sixteen children per adult. Not surprisingly, these children scored lower on the Bayley test of mental development and on language skills than home-reared children from similar backgrounds.

What about normal children in day-care centers where there are enough adults? One careful study compared babies who spent five full days a week in a day-care center from the time they were 3 months old with babies of the same economic and ethnic background who remained home with their mothers (Kagan et al., 1978). The total group of ninety-nine children included Caucasian and Chinese babies from middle-class and working-class homes.

At this particular center, each care-giver was assigned to only a few children (a ratio of one adult for every three infants and one adult for every five toddlers), thus ensuring that each child would receive consistent care from a familiar person. The curriculum was structured to provide appropriate learning experiences and stimulation for each child. Care-givers made sure to play with each infant individually several times a day, among other things, providing discrepancy experiences (saying "boo," showing a new rattle, etc.). With toddlers they sang and read and encouraged exploration of almost any sort.

This study found no important differences between day-care and home-care children in emotional, social, or cognitive development. For instance, the children in both groups were, according to Ainsworth's criteria, equally attached to their mothers. The authors concluded that professional day care, when carefully structured, has no negative psychological effects (Kagan et al., 1978).

Other research reports confirm Kagan's conclusion that infants usually fare equally well in a good home or a good day-care center. Nevertheless, there is,

A CLOSER LOOK   What to Look for in a Day-Care Center

Warmth and Sensitivity in the Adults

Do the adults lower themselves to child height to talk to the children? Do they listen to the toddler's imperfect words and try their best to understand? Do they anticipate when a fight is about to begin and find a way to avoid it? Do they initiate play with an infant? Are they comforting, encouraging, and guiding—all at the appropriate moment?

The Adult-Child Ratio

The number of children per care-giver is an important determinant of how much individual care each child will get. With children under age 2, five children is about all one adult can care for. An even lower ratio is better.

Opportunity for the Children to Explore

Is the space ample and safe? Is there a place for the babies to crawl without being stepped on by running older children? Are there interesting toys—puzzles, blocks, dolls, cars—within reach of the children?

The Curriculum

Activities such as reading books, dancing to music, painting, and playing games take extra effort on the part of the adults, but they are creative enterprises for children of almost any age. Watching television, even educational television, is a poor substitute.

Teacher-Parent Relationships

Are the teachers receptive to parents' questions and ideas? Do they welcome parental observation and help? At the same time, are they confident of their own ability and

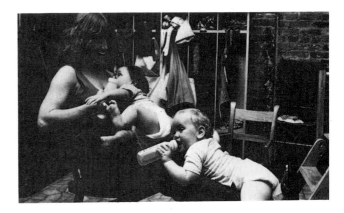

Even an enthusiastic and energetic adult cannot care for too many children at once. With toddlers, who need diapering and feeding as well as love and stimula-tion, good day-care centers have no more than five children per adult. As you can see here, even two children is sometimes a handful.

sensitivity in caring for children? In other words, do they respect the parents and respect themselves?

Provision for the Sick Child

Sudden fevers, rashes, and diarrhea are frequent in early childhood. Does the day-care center have adequate space and staff to isolate and care for a child who suddenly becomes sick? Does it have hygiene procedures to keep illnesses from spreading? Finally, are the policies about such things as required vaccinations, continued school attendance of sick children, and medical-emergency procedures acceptable to the parents?

---

apparently, at least one difference between home care and center care, and that is in the care-giver–infant interaction. Rubenstein and Howes (1979) found that mothers and day-care workers behaved differently with toddlers because their relationship to them was different. Mothers caring for their children at home talked to them more, in particular, giving them more orders, directions, and reprimands. In the day-care centers, the workers talked less with the children but touched, smiled at, and played with them more. The children were more social in the center and cried more at home. The authors concluded that although neither centers nor homes are more stimulating for infants, infant care may be "more pleasurable for both infants and care-givers in a social rather than isolated context."

What does the research on day care mean for the parent of a young child? We can probably conclude that for most children, the quality of daytime care is more important than whether it comes from the mother or father at home or a teacher at school. Good day care is certainly no worse than home care; in some cases it may be more enjoyable and more stimulating for the children than home care.

The Quality of Home Care

What distinguishes a good home from a bad home or from a home that is merely adequate? Is there any way to assess the quality of care given to a young child? And is there any way to help people become better parents? These questions were the starting point for two groups of researchers, who chose opposite strategies.

HOME

Bettye M. Caldwell and her associates set out to construct a measure by which any home environment could be graded. They began by pouring over the literature (Elardo et al., 1975; Bradley and Caldwell, 1976; Elardo et al., 1977). They read all the psychologists and educators they could find who had described criteria for a good learning environment for children under the age of 3. From this research, they developed a list of specific characteristics that could be observed by a visitor to a child's home, then tested the list by going to the homes of infants and toddlers. The original list was revised, retested, edited, and revised again. Finally, they selected forty-five questions, divided them into six categories, and called the result HOME, an acronym for Home Observation for the Measurement of the Environment.

The Six Subscales of HOME

1. *Emotional and verbal responsiveness of mother.*   Example: Mother responds to child's vocalizations with vocal or verbal response.

2. *Avoidance of restriction and punishment.*   Example: Mother does not interfere with the child's actions or restrict child's movements more than three times during the visit.

3. *Organization of the physical environment.*   Example: Child's play environment appears safe and free of hazards.

4. *Provision of appropriate play materials.*   Example: Child has one or more toys or pieces of equipment that promote muscle activity.

5. *Maternal involvement with child.*   Example: Mother tends to keep child within visual range and to look at the child often.

6. *Opportunities for variety in daily stimulation.*   Example: Mother reads stories to child at least three times weekly.

One interesting aspect of HOME is that fathers and other care-givers are not neglected. Although the word "mother" is used on the list, credit is given if someone else does the "mothering." Caldwell notes that an older sibling might be the one who reads books to the child, or a father, grandmother, or other babysitter might be the primary daytime care-giver, in which case he or she would be the person to observe with the child. Also, fathers are specifically included on two HOME items: "Father provides some caregiving every day" and "Child eats at least one meal per day with mother and father." The authors note that the "father" does not have to be the biological father, as long as he plays a fathering role and has daily contact with the baby.

HOME has been used to evaluate the environment of young children from many racial and cultural groups, with better success in predicting the children's later cognitive development than either conventional IQ tests or measures of social class. Suppose a baby from a family on welfare does not score particularly high on

Figure 8.9 *Among the routines in infancy that correlate with later intelligence, according to Bettye Caldwell's HOME, are the father's providing some daily care-giving and the child's being taken on several outings a week.*

an infant intelligence test, but has a high HOME score, showing that the mother talks and reads to the child and provides appropriate playthings and a safe play space. By contrast, suppose a middle-class baby does fairly well on an infant intelligence test but has a low HOME score because the mother is cold and unresponsive and the child has no good place to play. The chances are that by age 3 the welfare child will outperform the middle-class child in language and cognitive development.

The Harvard Preschool Project

Another research team, led by Burton L. White and Jean Carew Watts (1973), began their study, called the Harvard Preschool Project, not in the library, but in kindergarten. There they found decided differences in the following social and cognitive skills even though the children were similar in physical and perceptual abilities.

Characteristics of Competent Children

SOCIAL SKILLS
1. Getting and maintaining adult attention in socially acceptable ways.
2. Using adults as helpful resources.
3. Expressing hostility and affection to adults.
4. Leading and following peers.
5. Expressing hostility and affection to peers.
6. Competing with peers.
7. Praising oneself and showing pride in one's accomplishments.
8. Involving oneself in adult role-playing, or otherwise showing a desire to grow up.

COGNITIVE SKILLS
1. Linguistic competence—ability to understand and communicate.
2. Intellectual competence, including ability to deal with numbers, rules, and understand other points of view.
3. Executive abilities, such as planning complex activities.
4. Attentional ability, specifically, the ability to work on one's own project while being aware of other people.

Figure 8.10 *Several studies have found that toddlers who are read to every day are more likely to be verbal, intelligent schoolchildren than are toddlers who are rarely read to.*

White and Watts wondered when the differences in competence in these skills first appear. Looking at preschool children and toddlers they found that some children were already superior in these social and cognitive skills by age 3, while other 3-year-olds were lagging behind. But when they subsequently studied infants, they found no clues (except in cases involving serious abuse, neglect, or mental retardation) to indicate which infants would eventually become competent kindergarteners. On the basis of these findings, they concluded that toddlerhood is the most critical period for North American children, for during these years some children begin to surpass their peers in the skills they will need in school.

The next step was to find out what happens during those critical years to turn toddlers into "competent" or "incompetent" 3-year-olds. The Harvard team decided that the answer must be in the way mothers relate to their children. Consequently, they determined which kindergarten children from their first study had younger siblings, and then they spent hours observing these toddlers and their mothers* in their homes. They were looking for differences between the child-rearing characteristics of the mothers (called "A" mothers) who fostered competent children and those of the mothers (called "C" mothers) who raised incompetent children.

"A" mothers all showed several characteristics. They enjoyed their toddlers and talked to them at a level they could understand. The child's learning and happiness were more important to them than the appearance of the house, so they organized the environment to be safe and interesting for the toddler. They allowed their children to take minor risks and, at the same time, set reasonable limits. For instance, a 2-year-old might be allowed to climb up the stairs but not allowed to jump off the couch. Finally, they were busy and happy rather than unoccupied or depressed.

While all "A" mothers were similar to each other, there were several differences among "C" mothers. Some were depressed, disorganized, and listless. They seemed to have stopped trying to provide adequate stimulation for their children.

---

*White has been criticized for studying only mothers, not fathers and other care-givers. He says that mothers were the primary care-givers for all the toddlers he studied, so he described the social world of the toddlers as it was, not necessarily as it might be.

Figure 8.11 *Toddlerhood is the most difficult period for parents and the most crucial time for children, according to Burton White. One question is how to encourage exploration while setting reasonable limits.*

Others were overprotective, constantly interfering with their children's natural curiosity and independence. Still others were more interested in the housekeeping than in their children's activities, and consequently ignored their toddlers most of the time.

White and Watts feel that most mothers can be "A" mothers, even if they do not have much time, education, or money. In the original study, "A" mothers did *not* spend all their time with their toddlers. They were nearly always available for answering a question, setting up a new activity, adding an encouraging comment, and the like, but they spent less than 10 percent of their time with the toddlers actually caring for them. Some of the "A" mothers had part-time jobs; some had several other children. In fact, one was the mother of eight. While poverty makes it harder to be an "A" mother, neither money nor higher education is necessary. Some "A" mothers were on welfare; some had not graduated from high school.

Synchrony

One factor comes up again and again in examples of successful child-rearing in the first years of life. Ainsworth calls it sensitivity to the child's needs; White refers to it as the mother's enjoyment of the child; HOME labels it emotional and verbal responsiveness in the mother; psycholinguists speak of it as the fine-tuning of baby talk.

This common factor has led psychologists to film the interaction of parent and child, often with awe-inspiring results. Frame-by-frame analysis of the mother-infant interaction has revealed an astonishing split-second timing on the part of each partner in the relationship. This carefully coordinated interaction, called synchrony, has made psychologists who describe it turn to metaphors. They write about the intricate meshing of a finely tuned machine (Snow, 1977), a dialogue of exquisite precision in its patterning (Schaffer, 1977), and the interplay of musicians improvising a duet and of dance partners executing a piece of skilled choreography (Stern, 1977).

The specific behaviors of care-givers playing with their babies are most certainly not impressive in themselves: mothers and fathers open their eyes and mouths wide in expressions of mock surprise, make rapid clucking noises or repeated one-syllable sounds ("ba-ba-ba-ba-ba," "di-di-di-di," "bo-bo-bo-bo," etc.), raise and lower the pitch of their speech, change the pace of their movements (gradually speeding up or slowing down), tickle, pat, lift, and rock the baby, and do many other simple things. Nor is the infant's contribution very surprising: babies stare or look away, vocalize, widen their eyes, smile, and laugh, move forward or back. But the synchrony of parent and baby at play becomes more awesome the more carefully one examines it.

One Mother-Baby Interaction   Consider the following written account of a mother and her 3-month-old: actually it only begins to hint at the complexity of synchrony that can by seen in films and videotapes of mother-child interaction.

> Until this point, a normal feeding, not a social interaction, was underway. Then a change began. While talking and looking at me the mother turned her head and gazed at the infant's face. He was gazing at the ceiling, but out of the corner of his eye he saw her head turn toward him and turned to gaze back at her. This had happened before, but now he broke rhythm and stopped sucking. He let go of the nipple and the suction around it broke as he eased into the faintest suggestion of a smile. The mother abruptly stopped talking and, as she watched his face begin to transform, her eyes opened a little wider and her eyebrows raised a bit. His eyes locked on to hers, and together they held motionless for an instant. The infant did not return to sucking and his mother held frozen her slight expression of anticipation. This silent and almost motionless instant continued to hang until the mother suddenly shattered it by saying, "Hey!" and simultaneously opened her eyes wider, raising her eyebrows further, and throwing her head up and toward the infant. Almost simultaneously, the baby's eyes widened. His head tilted up and, as his smile broadened, the nipple fell out of his mouth. Now she said, "Well, hello! . . . hello! . . . Heello . . . Heeelloo!", so that her pitch rose and the "hellos" became longer and more stressed on each successive repetition. With each phrase the baby expressed more pleasure, and his body resonated almost like a balloon being pumped up, filling a little more with each breath. The mother then paused and her face relaxed. They watched each other expectantly for a moment. The shared excitement between them ebbed, but before it faded completely, the baby suddenly took an initiative and intervened to rescue it. His head lurched forward, his hands jerked up, and a fuller smile blossomed. His mother was jolted into motion. She moved forward, mouth open and eyes alight, and said, "Ooooooh . . . ya wanna play do ya . . . yeah? . . . I didn't know if you were still hungry . . . no . . . nooooo . . . no I didn't . . ." And off they went. [Stern, 1977]

Visual recordings of mother-infant play have shown that most mothers make dozens of carefully timed eye, head, and mouth movements to get their infant to smile (Stern, 1977). Fathers develop these skilled motions too, especially when they are the baby's main care-giver (Field, 1978).

Figure 8.12 *Episodes of playful interaction are an important part of parent-infant interaction. Each parent-infant pair seems to develop their own favorite games and rituals of communication.*

A seemingly more difficult task is knowing, not how to amuse a baby, but when to stop the game. Some babies need less stimulation than others, and all babies need to break off from the excitement of play after a few minutes. See how the same mother-infant pair stopped their game, with the baby first suggesting, then insisting, that the play end.

During the next four cycles of the renewed and slightly varied game, the mother did pretty much the same, except that on each successive cycle she escalated the level of suspense with her face and voice and timing. It went something like: "I'm gonna get ya . . . I'mmmmm gonna get ya . . . I'mmmmmmmmmm goooonaa getcha . . . I'mmmm goooooonaaa getcha!!" The baby became progressively more aroused, and the mounting excitement of both of them contained elements of both glee and danger . . . As the excitement mounted he seemed to run that narrow path between explosive glee and fright. As the path got narrower, he finally broke gaze with mother, appearing thereby to recompose himself for a second, to deescalate his own level of excitement. Having done so successfully, he returned his gaze to mother and exploded into a big grin. On that cue she began, with gusto, her fourth and most suspenseful cycle, but this one proved too much for him and pushed him across to the other side of the narrow path. He broke gaze immediately, turned away, face averted, and frowned. The mother picked it up immediately. She stopped the game dead in its tracks and said softly, "Oh honey, maybe you're still hungry, hun . . . let's try some milk again." He returned her gaze. His face eased and he took the nipple again. The "moment" of social interaction was over. [Stern, 1977]

In this interchange, the mother failed to read the baby's initial breaking of his gaze as a sign that he had had enough of the game. But as soon as he turned away, averted his eyes, and began to frown, she saw what he wanted and "stopped the game dead in its tracks." Infants have many ways to indicate that they have had enough: they look blank or look away; fuss or frown; yawn or close their eyes; turn their bodies away or fold their arms and legs closer to themselves; or punch or kick someone or something away (Brazelton et al., 1974). If none of this works, babies cry loudly or even let their bodies go limp.

Usually infants enjoy playing many times a day, but only for a few minutes at a time. In the mother-infant game partially described above, the entire episode lasted about four minutes.

Sensitivity in Other Care-giving Routines As we saw in Chapter 7, effective language learning depends on the parents' attuning themselves to the child's level of comprehension. Similar sensitivity occurs in many aspects of infant care. Adjusting the feeding schedule to meet the baby's demand and postponing toilet training until the toddler is ready are two examples.

Parents even learn to adjust their handling of babies, as shown by a longitudinal study of thirty-seven babies (Schaffer and Emerson, 1964). Throughout infancy, nineteen of the thirty-seven babies were "cuddlers," who enjoyed being held and comforted by their mothers for hours at a time. Nine others were "cuddlers" to a lesser degree. The remaining nine were "noncuddlers": they did not enjoy being held.

Traditional psychological theories would lead us to think it is the mother's fault if a baby does not enjoy cuddling. We would assume that these nine infants wanted cuddling but that their mothers responded improperly, turning them into noncuddlers.

But Rudolph Schaffer and Peggy Emerson found no support for this idea. Rather, the noncuddlers had never wanted to be held by anyone, even in infancy. Nor did they seek substitutes for the maternal cuddling they were supposedly lacking; in fact, as they grew older, they were less likely than other babies to enjoy cuddly toys, favorite blankets, or even their own thumbs. It would seem, then, that an infant's desire to be cuddled is determined by inborn factors rather than by maternal care.

Some of the mothers of the noncuddlers wished that their infants wanted to be held more often (one mother said wistfully, "He is just like his father—not one for a bit of love"), but they adjusted to their babies' preference. They comforted their noncuddlers by talking to them, and put them to bed without trying to rock them to sleep.

As this example shows, infants have individual patterns of sensitivity and enjoyment. The more a person comes to understand a particular baby, the better the person will become able to comfort and please that baby. Thus, when all goes well, parents feel the pride of being able to make their baby stop crying, and smile, faster than anyone else can. At the same time, each infant will learn to prefer his or her parents, not only because they are the most familiar people in the baby's world, but also because they are the most skilled.

Problems in Parent-Child Interaction

Unfortunately, the interaction between parent and infant does not always go well. One reason is that parents sometimes try to follow a general rule about how infants should be raised rather than looking to the particular baby for clues to how that baby might best be handled. As Anneliese F. Korner (1974) explains: "A mother's conviction that even very young babies require a good deal of stimulation may severely hamper an excitable baby's success in achieving any kind of homeostasis. A mother's fear of 'spoiling' an infant may make her refrain from soothing efforts which he requires to settle down."

Figure 8.13 *A mismatch be-*
tween a parent's idea of
what infants are like and the
individual infant's actual
temperament leads to prob-
lems for both: round babies
do not fit into square holes.

Sometimes parent-child interaction is restricted because the parent underesti-mates the child's potential. Tulkin and Kagan (1972) found that a group of working-class mothers talked to their infants less than a group of middle-class mothers talked to theirs, partly because the working-class women did not believe that babies listen or communicate. One working-class mother who *did* talk to her infant said her friends criticized her for "talking to the kid like she was three years old." As we saw in the discussion of baby-talk research in Chapter 7, parents who communicate with their infants help the infants to communicate in return.

Often there is a clash between the baby's temperament and the parent's person-ality: a parent who would find it easier to care for a quiet baby frequently ends up caring for an active one, and vice versa (Escalona, 1968). Sometimes, however, a baby creates problems no matter what the care-giver's personality. According to Thomas et al. (1968), about one baby in ten is downright difficult—active, irregular, intense, and unhappy—through no fault of either parent or child. These babies try the patience of even the most loving and experienced parents.

Fortunately, there is encouraging news for parents of difficult babies. A longitu-dinal study of 187 children showed that most infants who were difficult between 4 and 8 months were less difficult at ages 3 to 7 (Carey and McDevitt, 1978). On the other hand, most easy infants became less easy, although the early temperamental differences had not completely disappeared. Other studies show that most difficult babies become normal adolescents. In fact, it is almost impossible to predict the eventual adjustment of a person based on temperament in the first weeks of life (Murphy and Moriarty, 1976).

If parents recognize their children's difficult characteristics, and respond with patience and consistency, children can learn to express their temperament con-structively. On the other hand, if a difficult baby happens to be born in a family where "good" babies are considered evidence of the parents' worth, and "bad" babies are an indictment, both baby and parents suffer.

Child Abuse and Neglect "Difficult" children are more likely to be abused than other children, but it would be a mistake to see this fact in terms of cause and effect. Many abusing parents consider normal infant behavior difficult and deliberate: they punish infants for "crying too much" or toddlers for being unable to control urination or defecation. One mother of a 2-year-old said, "I don't know what happened. I felt just fine—no worries—and suddenly when she couldn't get her body shirt undone and peed on my freshly waxed floor, something snapped and I threw her across the room as if she had killed somebody or something" (Kempe and Kempe, 1978).

Especially in the first two years of life, children are abused or neglected more because of who they are than what they do. Babies who are unwanted, or who are the "wrong" sex, or who have minor physical problems, sometimes become the victims of their parents' disappointment. The baby's appearance, as in the case, say, of the little boy who looks just like the father who left the mother early in pregnancy, or the little girl who reminds her father of his mother who abused him, can trigger rejection instead of love. Among white families, babies who were premature are more often abused than babies who were full-term. (Among black families, this discrepancy does not exist, possibly because the rate of prematurity is twice as high among blacks, making it less likely that they would view prematurity as abnormal.)

Figure 8.14 *When brought to the hospital, this 3-year-old told attendants, "Mommy said she would hit me until my head broke." His mother had beaten him because he spilled a glass of milk, and had told him to say that he had fallen down a flight of stairs. Emergency-room personnel are trained to spot unlikely "accidents" and to use x-rays to prove long-term abuse. The earlier the abusing parent can be recognized, the better the chances of preventing extreme abuse.*

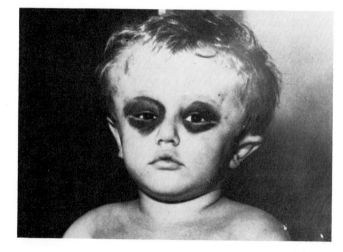

Problems with the Parents According to Ruth and Henry Kempe (1978), of every ten parents who severely abuse their children, one is so mentally ill as to be untreatable. Such persons have delusions ("God is telling me to kill this child") or they communicate only by bashing. They are cruel or fanatical, and completely closed to reason. With these parents, the only solution is removal of the child from the home.

But most abusive parents are not very different from average parents. They love their children, and want the best for them. They also get angry at their children, and do things they later regret. While child abuse cuts across nearly all social categories, it is especially likely to occur among young and uneducated parents, for their self-esteem is often low and their need for social support is usually high. In their immaturity, they expect too much from their babies. When the infant cries, they interpret the crying as deliberate misbehavior, intended to blame and anger them.

As the Kempes write:

> Many parents have told us they see persistent crying as accusatory. An average mother will regard a crying or fussy baby as hungry or wet or full of gas. She will proceed to feed, change, burp him, and then put him down in the crib and say, "Baby, you're tired," close the door, then turn on the radio or talk to a friend. The abusive parent is unable to leave the crying child, and tries harder and harder to pacify him until in a moment of utter frustration she is overwhelmed by the thought that the baby, even at two weeks of age, is saying, "If you were a good mother I wouldn't be crying like this." It is precisely because the parent tries to be extra good, to be loved and earn the love of the child, that intractable crying is seen as total rejection and leads to sudden rage. The abuse is clearly not a rational act. It is not premeditated, and it is often followed by deep grief and great guilt. Such parents are seen by doctors and nurses as being very solicitous. Third parties find it hard to believe that so loving a parent could have inflicted such serious injury. [Kempe and Kempe, 1978]

Parents who themselves were rejected as infants have a particularly difficult time responding to their babies with love, for they have neither the experience nor the patience needed. One such example was the actress Joan Crawford, who was abused, neglected, and sexually exploited as a young girl and continued this destructive pattern with her own adopted children. In her case, as in many others, alcohol made the problem worse (Crawford, 1978).

Figure 8.15 *Now that the facts of Joan Crawford's abusiveness as a parent are known, it is possible to look at this photo and read all kinds of ominous signs into the apparent unresponsiveness of her adopted daughter Christina.*

Stress and Loneliness Studies of abusive and neglectful parents show that when they are under stress, they are less able to show affection to their children. Usually, a particular crisis—an eviction notice, a fight with a spouse, dismissal from a job—provokes a particular act of abuse, but the overall pattern of economic or interpersonal stress sets the stage. Parents who have no friends, family, or neighbors to help them during periods of stress are more likely to take out their problems on their children. This social isolation triggers another problem: no one tries to help the abused child or report the parents until the pattern is well established and considerable harm has been done. (Sometimes, of course, other people actually can make the problem worse, offering such comments as "Can't you stop that baby from crying!" or "If that were my son, I know what I'd do.")

Another factor that increases the incidence of abuse is a bad marriage. The Kempes write (1978): "In our experience, single parents are rather less abusive than couples, which is surprising because one would think that a spouse would provide support in the face of crisis. In fact a spouse who is not supportive is worse than no spouse at all when it comes to childrearing."

Poverty The incidence of abuse and neglect rises as income falls; very poor parents (family income under $5000 per year) are the most likely to abuse their children (Pelton, 1978), especially if the living conditions are crowded and available friends and helpers are few. One reason may be that the hardships of poverty often make it more difficult to be patient with children, and the inability to provide for basic physical needs may produce the kinds of frustration and despair that make emotional needs harder to serve. When each trip to the grocery store puts a large dent in the budget, and a night at the movies or a trip to the zoo is a major undertaking, many family members, old and young, find their patience in short supply.

When abuse and neglect lead to death, the fault is usually not limited to the family alone. Follow-up reports almost always show that social workers and school authorities were already aware that a serious problem existed, as we saw with Cynthia Feliccea.

Incidence of Abuse and Neglect The incidence of abuse and neglect is large and growing. Nationwide, approximately 1 case is *reported* each year for every 700 children under age 14. Public awareness of the problem, and state laws that require pediatricians and hospital personnel to report injuries that might not be accidents, caused the number of reported cases to jump dramatically in many states between 1968 and 1972: for instance, from 4000 to 40,000 in California; from 10,000 to 30,000 in Florida; from 721 to 30,000 in Michigan (Kempe and Kempe, 1978). For these states, the rate in 1972 was higher than 1 case for every 100 children.

Problems of Definition. Throughout this discussion, you have probably wondered what, exactly, constitutes abuse and neglect. The problem of definition plagues professionals as well, which is one reason two authorities, both in 1973, came up with very different figures for the rate of abuse in the United States. One told a Senate hearing that there are 30,000 cases of "truly battered" children per year (U.S. Senate, 1973); another estimated that there are actually 1,500,000 cases of child abuse annually (Fontana, 1973).

In fact, abuse and neglect can be seen as a continuum. At one end are cases of abuse or neglect that lead to the death of the child. There are about 700 such cases in the United States each year (Fontana, 1973), or two a day. According to recent statistics, in infancy, death from neglect is more common than death from abuse. For instance, one of the most careful chroniclers of abuse and neglect, James Weston (1974), listed all such deaths in Philadelphia from 1961 to 1965. Of the thirty-eight infants under 1 year who died from these causes, twenty-three died from neglect and fifteen from abuse. In twelve of the latter cases, the reason given for the abuse was that the infant "cried too much." By toddlerhood, death from abuse is more common than from sheer neglect.

At the other end of the continuum are the most moderate forms of abuse and neglect. At least one investigator believes that spanking and slapping are forms of violence, even though most parents do, in fact, spank or slap their children on occasion (Gelles, 1978). Others see such things as letting a child go to school on a snowy day without boots, mittens, or a hat, or giving a child a candy bar and a soda for lunch, as forms of moderate neglect. By this definition, most of us who are parents probably do neglect our children at one time or another. Being able to admit that they are not perfect helps parents to remedy their mistakes and keeps them from expecting their children to be angelic rather than human.

Ruth and Henry Kempe (1978) see a continuum of parent care, from the highly pathological at one end to "the only possible claimant to perfection as a mother, the Madonna" at the other. "But let us not forget," they caution, "Mary also had the perfect child." The Kempes estimate that between 20 and 30 percent of all parents have considerable difficulty caring for their children adequately (see Figure 8.16).

Figure 8.16 *This chart shows the range of parenting styles delineated by the Kempes, with most parents being "good enough" and relatively few being highly pathological or, at the other end of the scale, excellent. The Kempes believe that up to 30 percent of all parents are potentially abusive or neglectful, a potential that may become realized in times of stress.*

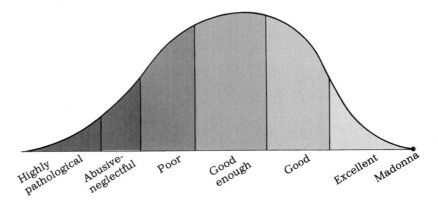

Highly pathological — Abusive-neglectful — Poor — Good enough — Good — Excellent — Madonna

Help for Parents and Children Child abuse and neglect is a depressing topic, especially when one realizes that the problem is self-perpetuating. Children learn how to love from their parents: consequently, abused and unloved children often become abusive and unloving parents.

Treatment. Nevertheless, there is some reason to hope. The Kempes (1978) found that 80 percent of abusing parents can be helped so that they no longer physically punish their children. Both short-term help (a hotline for parents to call when they find themselves losing control, an around-the-clock crisis nursery where parents in need of a few hours' peace can drop off their children), and long-term help (individual and family therapy, a home worker or lay therapist assigned to the family) are needed.*

Early detection of abuse can prevent serious problems. Colorado's new laws and programs to help abused children and their parents have had a dramatic impact on the number of abused children who die in the hospitals of Denver. The death rate dropped from twenty a year in the early 1960s to less than one a year in the mid-1970s.

_____

*An organization called Parents Anonymous, with chapters in every major city, helps abusing parents in much the same way that Alcoholics Anonymous helps alcoholics.

Prevention. Babies "at risk" can be spotted at birth and helped before abuse becomes a reality. The Kempes (1978) studied 350 families (with their consent) in the labor and delivery room, looking for worrisome signs such as an apparent lack of love between the parents, a failure on the part of parents to look their newborns in the eye or touch them, or parental disappointment over the baby's sex or appearance. They found a hundred "high-risk" families and gave them all routine services. In addition, fifty of the families were assigned a pediatrician who saw the baby for check-ups, including a postnatal examination followed by a consultation with the parents. The doctor also called the family at least once a week to provide encouragement and answer questions.

This personal intervention did not transform the parents, nor did it protect the infants from all forms of abuse and neglect. In fact, twenty of the fifty families showed signs of "abnormal parenting practices," and three of the babies were so below height and weight for their age that they were treated for "failure to thrive." But the pediatrician's attention did stop physical abuse: whereas by age 2, five of the fifty nonintervention group needed hospital treatment—for, among other injuries, a fractured femur, a fractured skull, barbiturate poisoning, a subdural hematoma (hemorrhage on the surface of the brain), and third-degree burns—none of the fifty intervention-group babies was hospitalized for abuse or neglect. Results such as this should be encouraging to everyone who cares about the quality of care young children receive.

Since poverty, youth, and ignorance correlate with poor parenting, measures that raise the lowest incomes, discourage teenage parenthood, and increase the level of education will probably lower the rate of abuse. And since social isolation and unrealistic expectations make it harder to provide good care for young children, any program that fosters friendly contact with others and an accurate understanding of the needs of children should be encouraged. With a little experienced guidance, most parents can become better at appreciating their children and learning how to relate to them with greater respect and with mutual delight.

SUMMARY

Emotions and Personality

1. The development of emotions in the infant follows an orderly pattern, from reflexive cries and smiles in the first six months, to fear and pleasure related to specific events in the next six months. By age 2, most of the cries and fears of the 1-year-old have become milder and less frequent.

2. Signs of attachment—attempts to stay close to a familiar person, and cries of protest when a familiar person leaves—grow stronger as the infant grows older. These attachment behaviors peak in the first half of the second year. Two-year-olds are usually delighted to see a familiar person return, but they cry less than they used to when that person leaves. Secure attachment aids cognitive and social development, by making the child feel safe.

3. Toddlers become increasingly aware of who they are. This makes them more assertive and independent, and capable of feeling proud or ashamed. They also become able to play and share with other children.

4. The timing and balance of emotional development are affected by maturation, culture, and family. Gender may influence the emotional development of infants, either because boys and girls are biologically different, or because parents treat them differently. Cognitive development probably affects emotional development and vice versa.

Theories of Infant Emotions

5. Freud called the first year of life the oral stage, because infants get so much pleasure from their mouths, and the second year the anal stage, in accordance with the shift in the chief zone of pleasure. Erikson emphasizes the infant's need for trust and continuity, and the toddler's need for autonomy, or independence.

6. Babies in institutions where they get impersonal care develop more slowly and are more often ill than babies in a

normal home. Bowlby and Spitz believe a lack of mothering causes this problem; Dennis thinks insufficient stimulation is the cause.

7. Each of these theories has led care-givers to be more concerned about meeting the psychological needs of infants and toddlers. However, none of these theories is accepted wholeheartedly by most psychologists today, partly because the theories tend to underemphasize the father's role, underestimate the value of a good day-care center, and ignore many of the individual differences in mother-infant interaction.

The Quality of Home Care

8. The researchers who developed HOME as well as those in the Harvard Preschool Project agree that the mother's responsiveness to her child, and the organization of the play space, are significant determinants of infant development. Other researchers have found extraordinary mutual sensitivity in mother-infant interactions. The synchrony of movement and gesture is reminiscent of a well-choreographed dance.

9. Parent-child interaction does not always go smoothly. Child abuse and neglect are increasing, partly because many parents do not know what normal child behavior is. Social isolation and poverty make the problem worse. Programs to prevent and treat child abuse have had some success.

KEY QUESTIONS

What emotions develop in the first year?

What factors influence whether a baby will be afraid of a stranger?

How does attachment affect cognitive development, and vice versa?

What are some consequences of the toddler's growing sense of self?

How do maturation and culture affect emotional development?

What are the possible causes for sex differences in infant emotional development?

How did Bowlby reach his conclusions?

How can day-care centers benefit, and harm, infants?

How might parents adjust their care-giving routines in response to their infants' particular characteristics?

What are some of the reasons parent-infant interaction does not always go well?

How common is child abuse and neglect?

What can be done to help abused children and their parents?

KEY TERMS

social smile
fear of strangers
personality
attachment
secure attachment
insecure attachment
separation distress
self-concept
bone age
oral stage
anal stage

trust versus mistrust
autonomy versus shame and doubt
maternal deprivation
HOME
The Harvard Preschool Project
synchrony
abuse
neglect

RECOMMENDED READINGS

Brazelton, T. Berry. *Infants and mothers.* New York: Dell, 1966.

Describes the actual practice of meeting the needs of three types of babies, the active baby, the quiet baby, and the average baby. Should be very helpful to parents who wonder why their baby doesn't act the same as the baby next door.

Erikson, Erik. *Childhood and society.* 2nd ed. New York: Norton, 1963.

Erikson's classic work describing each of his eight stages. Particularly relevant to this chapter is Erikson's explanation of the effect of infancy on later development. This is shown in the case history of an emotionally disturbed girl and in his discussion of childhood among the Sioux and Yurok Indians.

Rutter, Michael. *The qualities of mothering: Maternal deprivation reassessed.* New York: Aronson, 1974.

A careful evaluation of the attachment, "mothering," and stimulation needs of the young child. The book includes a discussion of Bowlby's and Dennis' research and concludes that "the concept of maternal deprivation . . . has served its purpose and now should be abandoned."

Stern, Daniel. *The first relationship.* Cambridge, Mass.: Harvard University Press, 1977.

Describes research in mother-infant interaction, as well as practical application of this research. Includes what can go wrong ("missteps in the dance") and an honest appraisal of what psychologists know and do not know about parent-child relationships.

Kempe, Ruth S., and Kempe, C. Henry. *Child abuse.* Cambridge, Mass.: Harvard University Press, 1978.

The best book to date on child abuse, written by two authors who are famous for their work on the detection and care of abuse victims in Denver, Colorado. The book includes discussion of child neglect and sexual abuse, but the focus is on the treatment and prevention of physical abuse.

The Play Years

PART III

The period from age 2 to 6 is usually called early childhood, or the preschool period. Here, however, these years are called the play years to underscore the importance of play. Play occurs at every age, of course. But the years of early childhood are the most playful of all, for children spend most of their waking hours at play, acquiring the skills, ideas, and values that are crucial for growing up. They chase each other and dare themselves to attempt new tasks, developing their bodies; they play with words and ideas, developing their minds; they play games and dramatize fantasies, learning social skills and moral rules.

The playfulness of young children can cause them to be delightful or exasperating. To them, growing up is a game, and their enthusiasm for it seems unlimited, whether they are quietly tracking a beetle through the grass or riotously turning their play area into a shambles. Their minds seem playful too, for the immaturity of their thinking enables them to explain that "a bald man has a barefoot head," or that "the sun shines so children can go outside to play."

If you expect them to sit quietly, think logically, or act realistically, you are bound to be disappointed. But if you enjoy playfulness, you might enjoy caring for, listening to, and even reading about children between 2 and 6 years old.

The Play Years: Physical Development

He who would learn to fly one day must first learn to stand and walk and run and climb and dance: one cannot fly into flying.

Nietzsche
"On the Spirit of Gravity"

True or False?

A preschooler's refusal to take part in roughhousing is usually a sign of precocious social sophistication.

If preschoolers who had hearty appetites as infants suddenly begin merely picking at their food, their diets must usually be supplemented with vitamins.

Some psychologists believe that emotional stress and lack of affection can stunt your growth.

Unless you write in Chinese or Hebrew, your penmanship is at a disadvantage if you are left-handed.

The only reason most children cannot read by age 5 is that they have not received proper instruction.

Bed-wetting after age 4 is usually either the result of laziness or an act of revenge.

Asian-American children run a lower risk of having accidents than do children of any other ethnic group in the United States.

The primary topic of this chapter is the body and brain development that makes the average 6-year-old so different from the average 2-year-old in terms of size, shape, and acquired skills. But before describing the changes involved in this development, let us look at three of the ways preschool children play. Once we can picture the differences in how children use their bodies as they grow, the significance of changes in height, weight, and motor skills will be easier to understand.

Physical Play

As you will recall from Chapter 7, children in early infancy engage in sensorimotor play, delighting in such things as watching a mobile or kicking the side of the basinette. Such pleasure in sensory experiences and motor skills continues throughout early childhood. If allowed to, for example, preschool children can spend many happy hours exploring the sensations provided by their food, experiencing various textures as they mix noodles and meat together with their hands, watching peas float after they put them in their milk, listening to the slurping sound as they suck spaghetti. Most families restrict play with food, but children find similar opportunities for sensorimotor play in the sandbox, bathtub, or mud puddles. The joys of touch, taste, and smell contribute to each child's understanding of the physical environment.

Much of the play of early childhood leads to the mastery of new skills, and is therefore called mastery play. Preschool children love to roll down a hill, thrilling to the careening of their bodies, the topsy-turvy whirl of sky, trees, and grass, and the overpowering dizziness they experience when they try to get up. They will climb to the top of a jungle gym and fearlessly hang upside down by their legs, or pump themselves high on swings and then leap off. Almost anything, from a parent's saying "I'll race you to the corner" to a tree that seems too high to climb, becomes a challenge that the young child wants to meet and master. As the child grows older, mastery play comes to include more intellectual games, such as play with words or ideas.

Rough-and-tumble play is one of the most descriptive phrases in developmental psychology. The term arises from ethologists' observations of young monkeys wrestling, chasing, and pummeling each other, behaviors the ethologists learned were playful when they were done with a play face, that is, when the monkeys' facial expressions seemed to suggest that the monkeys were having fun. The same behaviors accompanied by a frown usually meant a serious conflict. In human children, too, rough-and-tumble play is quite different from aggression, which may involve serious hitting and pushing (Jones, 1976).

This distinction is useful, for rough-and-tumble play seems an important part of the daily activities of many children in preschool, especially after they have had to sit quietly for a period of time (Jones, 1976). Adults who wonder when to break up a "fight" may be helped by knowing that facial expression is as significant in children as it is in monkeys: children almost always smile, and often laugh, in rough-and-tumble play, whereas they frown and scowl in real fighting.

Rough-and-tumble play is a social activity that usually occurs between children who know each other well. It takes a longer time for newcomers to nursery school, younger children, and only children to join in rough-and-tumble play than it does in any other form of play (Garvey, 1976), probably because they have had fewer social experiences. This implies that the next time you see two children playfully wrestling in the dirt, you could compliment them on their social development!

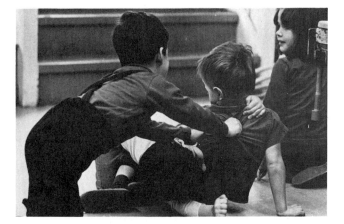

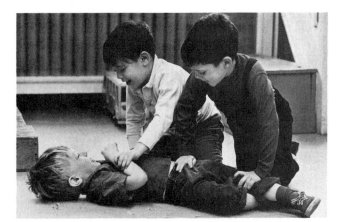

Figure 9.1 *The clue to whether these photos depict bullying or rough-and-tumble play is the boys' facial expressions. If this had been a real fight, frowns and grimaces would be evident in the last picture.*

A CLOSER LOOK   **Work and Play**

Many observers are struck by the similarity between the play of young animals and the skills needed by full-grown animals. Some of these skills are patterns of motor behavior. Consider the play of kittens (Egan, 1976). They will sniff and pat any mouse-sized object. If it moves, they crouch and pounce. If it is furry, they will also bite it, carry it around, shake it, and toss it. If the object is alive, and a kitten is hungry, the furry creature is then killed and eaten. But when the kitten is not hungry, the object is played with for a long time, especially if it continues to move. Well-fed kittens play as much as hungry kittens; they just don't eat their prey when they are done. Obviously, kittens who become skilled at kitten's play will become cats who are skilled at catching prey.

For primates, social skills are even more important for survival than motor skills. In order for a group of monkeys to live together peacefully, all the adults must know how to assert their rights without antagonizing other monkeys to the point of a serious fight.

Once again, these important survival skills are learned by playing. Baby monkeys learn complicated behaviors of dominance and submission by pretending to fight with each other. If they do not have playmates when they are young, even monkeys who receive normal mothering become socially withdrawn and unusually aggressive during adolescence, sometimes picking a fight with a much larger male monkey, or a female monkey with an infant. Such aggression leads to quick, and sometimes fatal, counterattack. If these "unsocialized" monkeys survive adolescence, they can become adults who seem normal, although too much aggression and too little affection often remain part of their personality (Suomi and Harlow, 1976).

Animal studies such as these have helped psychologists see the value of all forms of human play (Vandenberg, 1978). While most people think of play as the opposite of work, and many parents complain that their children play too much, and sometimes even punish them for "playing around," psychologists think that even the most carefree, spontaneous play is related to serious productive work (Garvey, 1977). If they never played, children might never become skillful or loving adults.

Size and Shape

Preschool children's bodies grow steadily taller and stronger, enabling them to run faster and reach higher with each passing year. To be specific, from age 2 through 6, children gain about 4½ pounds (2 kilograms) and add almost 3 inches (7 centimeters) per year. By age 5, the average North American child weighs about 40 pounds (18 kilograms) and measures 43 inches (109 centimeters). As Figure 9.2 shows, many children are taller or shorter than these averages. Weight is especially variable: about 10 percent of American 5-year-olds weigh less than 35 pounds and another 10 percent weigh almost 50 pounds (National Center for Health Statistics, 1976).

The ranges of normal height and weight are even greater when children from different parts of the world are compared. In general, children from northern Europe have the tallest average height, and children from southern Asia, the shortest. For instance, 3-year-olds from the Netherlands average 38 inches (97 centimeters), almost 6 inches (15 centimeters) taller than their contemporaries from Bangladesh. In fact, 3-year-old Dutch children are taller, on average, than 5-year-olds from several other countries.

Reasons for Variation   Howard Meredith (1978) reviewed more than 200 studies of the height of preschool children in various parts of the world and found that the two most significant causes of height differences are ethnic origin and nutrition. Partly because they receive better nourishment and health care, urban children, upper-class children,

Figure 9.2 *As these charts show, boys (black line) and girls (brown line) grow more slowly and steadily than they did in the first two years of life. Consequently, weight gain is particularly slow, with most children losing body fat during these years. The weight that is gained is usually bone and muscle.*

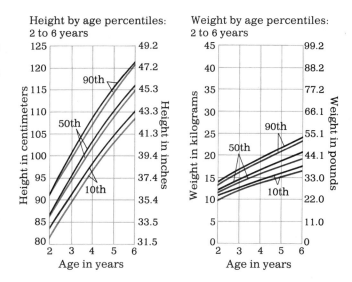

Height by age percentiles: 2 to 6 years

Weight by age percentiles: 2 to 6 years

and first-borns are all somewhat taller than rural children, lower-class children, and later-borns. (Meredith also reports that if a mother smoked during pregnancy, her child will be about half an inch shorter at age 5; and that children living high above sea level will be slightly shorter than their cousins living close to sea level.) Since most North American preschoolers obtain enough food for their bodies to grow as rapidly as their genes allow, ethnic differences in the height of Americans are primarily genetic, not nutritional. Generally, Afro-American children are tallest, followed by Caucasian Americans, and then Asian-Americans.

Whether a child is short or tall, annual height and weight gains are much smaller from age 2 to 6 than during the first two years of life. In fact, an average child gains less weight per year at ages 2 and 3 than at any other age until 17. Since preschool children need fewer calories per pound than they did from birth through toddlerhood, their appetites are smaller, causing many parents to worry about their preschooler's diet. Indeed, about a third of all mothers of 5-year-olds think their children have finicky appetites (Sears et al., 1957).

Actually, most parents shouldn't worry if their preschool children are eating less, for if a young child is offered a variety of healthy foods, he or she will usually eat enough to meet the basic nutritional requirements. (Serious malnutrition is much more likely to occur in infancy and in adolescence than in early childhood [Abra-

Figure 9.3 *Infants often guzzle, and older children sometimes seem to gobble, but preschoolers tend to be picky eaters. The reason is biological: their growth has slowed down. Consequently, "Take a taste of everything" is a more reasonable parental demand to make on them than "Finish everything on your plate."*

ham et al., 1974].) Of course, candy, soda, and sweetened cereals can spoil a small appetite faster than a large one, so they should be limited to make sure the child consumes enough vitamins, minerals, and protein.

Taller and Thinner

Preschool children lose their baby fat as their bones grow longer, thicker, and harder. Bone growth can be seen with x-rays, which reveal how much of the cartilage has hardened into bone. The rate of ossification, or hardening, determines the bone age of the child, which is measured by comparing a particular child's x-rays with x-rays showing average skeletal maturity for that child's age.

Changes in body proportions are easy to see by comparing the shape of the average 2-year-old with that of the average 5-year-old. The kindergarten child no longer has the protruding stomach, round face, short limbs, and large head that are characteristic of the toddler. On the whole, the preschooler's growth is up rather than out. The old-fashioned custom of dressing young children in short pants and short dresses, even when adults all wore long pants and long dresses, had a very practical origin: children outgrow clothes much more slowly if the clothes are not designed to cover the legs.

Figure 9.4 *This boy's short pants and long-waisted jacket are typical of children's clothes in the nineteenth century, when one wool suit had to fit for several years.*

Growth Problems

If you look at a group of nursery-school children, all more or less the same age, you will probably see one or two who are noticeably bigger or smaller than their classmates. In all likelihood, they are perfectly normal and in the best of health; they are simply genetically destined to be tall or short at this stage of development.

However, about one child in a thousand suffers an extreme growth disorder, either dwarfism, which results in abnormal shortness, or giantism, which results in abnormal tallness. Because children do not grow much from year to year in early childhood, height and weight charts for this period usually do not distinguish normal from abnormal growth. Checking to see if skeletal maturity, or bone age, corresponds to chronological age is a much better way to spot problems (Lowrey, 1978). If bone age is much different from chronological age and height, growth problems are to be suspected. A tall 4-year-old is too tall if the bone age is 3 (height in this case is outdistancing skeletal maturation); just right if the bone age is 5; and too short if the bone age is 7 (height here is progressing more slowly than skeletal maturation) (David Sinclair, 1973).

Whether or not unusual height is a medical problem, it often causes psychological stress. Adults and children tend to judge maturity by size, so the short child is apt to be treated like a baby, and the tall child may be expected to talk and behave with more sophistication than he or she possesses. If these children play with children who are the same size, or if adults do not adjust their expectations to the children's age rather than their size, the short child might indeed become more babyish than is appropriate, and the tall child might feel stupid and clumsy.

Causes of Growth Problems   There are three general causes of growth problems. The first is congenital: a genetic condition or prenatal abnormality results in unusual shortness or, less often, unusual tallness. Many people having growth deficiencies can be helped to approach average height through treatment with growth hormones in childhood (Lowrey, 1978).

The second cause is a physical problem that appears during childhood. Chronic infections (such as hookworm or dysentery), untreated diabetes, and severe malnutrition all stunt growth. If these problems are treated, a growth catch-up allows the child to reach normal height (Lowrey, 1978).

Finally, a third cause of growth problems may be emotional. According to some psychologists, too much stress and not enough affection can prevent normal production of growth hormones, even if genes, medical care, and nutrition are adequate. This problem is called deprivation dwarfism.

Lytt Gardner (1972), reports such a case involving a pair of twins, a boy and a girl, who grew normally for the first four months. Then their mother became pregnant with an unwanted baby, and their father lost his job. Each spouse blamed the other, and the husband left home. According to Gardner, the mother focused her hostility on the only male around, her infant son. While the girl grew normally, the boy twin at 13 months was no bigger than an average 7-month-old. Following hospitalization, he grew rapidly, a fact that shows his problem was not congenital. Then his father came back home, and the little boy was discharged from the hospital. By age 3½, both twins were approximately the same height, only slightly less tall than an average child.

This boy was fortunate. According to Gardner, most children suffering from deprivation dwarfism grow rapidly in the hospital, but stop growing or even lose weight when they go back home. Since the cause is neither physical abuse nor apparent malnutrition, it is hard to get counseling for the parents, and even more difficult to remove the child from the home. If the parents voluntarily give up children suffering from deprivation dwarfism, and the children then get good foster care, they grow normally (Gardner, 1972).

Motor Skills

Preschool children spend most of their waking hours in motion, using large body movements—such as running, climbing, jumping, throwing—or smaller movements, such as those involved in pushing toy cars, dressing dolls, or painting pictures. Large and small movements such as these demonstrate the underlying gross motor skills and fine motor skills that make it possible and enjoyable for the child to play.

Partly because the child's body becomes slimmer, stronger, and less top-heavy, gross motor skills improve dramatically between ages 2 and 6. Two-year-olds are quite clumsy, falling down frequently and often bumping into stationary objects. But by age 5, many children are both skilled and graceful. Most 5-year-olds can ride a tricycle, climb a ladder, pump a swing, and throw, catch, and kick a ball. Some of them can even skate, ski, and ride a two-wheeled bicycle, activities that require balance as well as coordination. In fact, almost any gross motor skill that does not require much strength or judgment can be learned by most healthy 5-year-olds, if they have a patient teacher and plenty of time and space to practice (Caroline Sinclair, 1973).

Figure 9.5 *By age three, most children can peddle and steer a tricycle. It will be about two years before this little girl's body and her sense of balance will have matured sufficiently for her to be able to ride a bicycle.*

Fine motor skills, however, are much harder for young children to master. Such things as pouring juice from a pitcher (into a glass, that is), cutting food with a knife and fork, and achieving anything other than a scribble with a pencil are usually difficult for preschoolers. They can spend hours trying to tie a bow with their shoelaces, often producing knot upon knot instead.

The chief reason for these difficulties is simply that many preschool children have not developed the muscular control or careful judgment needed for fine motor skills, a liability complicated by their still having short, fat fingers. If utensils, toys, and clothes for the preschool child are not selected with this in mind, frustration and destruction can result: preschool children will burst into tears when they cannot button their sweaters, or will mash a puzzle piece in their attempt to make it fit into the wrong position.

Figure 9.6 *Writing your name is no easy task during the preschool years. With a thick pen, a large piece of paper, and a sample to copy, Michael manages to do quite well. In another year, he will probably learn to begin his letters on a level, make the middle line of the "E" shorter, and remember the "H."*

Children's Art

As in most other areas, limited skill in "artistic" endeavors does not keep pre-schoolers from trying. When young children see a pencil, pen, crayon, or magic marker, their first impulse is to draw—on paper, walls, or themselves. These early markings look random to most adults, but psychologists who study them find an amazing sense of order and design (Goodnow, 1976).

The first drawings are not intended to be representational. The child prefers shapes and designs over pictures of real things, and many young children are mystified at the typical adult question, "What is it?" Kellogg (1970) has identified four stages of artistic development:

1. *Placement stage: until age 3.* The child experiments with placing marks on paper, using various scribbles to cover all or part of the page.

2. *Shapes stage: age 3.* The child tries to make basic shapes, a circle, an "x," a square.

3. *Design stage: age 3½.* The child uses basic shapes and scribbles to make designs—a circle within a circle, or a series of crosses.

4. *Pictorial stage: ages 4 to 5.* At this stage the child tries to form pictures of people, animals, and buildings, gradually adding more detail as he or she grows older.

Once children begin drawing people and things, they expect everyone else to understand exactly what they have created. To them, two vertical lines topped by a circle with two dots inside is obviously Mommy (Figure 9.7). Why would anyone need to ask "What is it?"

It is interesting to speculate why children's drawings at the pictorial stage include, or omit, the particular features that they do. Why, for instance, do drawings of people usually include head, eyes, legs, arms, hair, and often even hands and feet before they begin to include the trunk? That children simply do not perceive the torso would seem a very unlikely explanation, especially since children know something is missing when they see a doctored photograph that shows a person with a "missing" midsection.

Figure 9.7 *Mommy.*

(a)

(b)

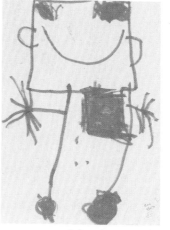

(c)

(d)

Figure 9.8 *These drawings of a person by a preschooler named Randy cover a two-year period and demonstrate not only Randy's increasing skill at manipulating a pen, but also his perceptual and cognitive development. (a) His "circle" person, drawn at 3 years, 5 months, might be called a scribble by the uninformed. (b) Six months later, his person is represented as a whole, with head, feet, and belly button, all enclosed by* one line. (c) *At 4 years, 4 months, Randy attaches the legs to the head and the arms to the legs, a typical pattern followed by preschoolers throughout the world. (d) At 5 years, 2 months, Randy's drawing of "Daddy" shows recognition of the torso, but evidences Randy's difficulty in attaching it to the legs. (e) Finally, at 5 years, 5 months, Randy draws a person complete with hat, teeth, and even the correct number of fingers.*

(e)

A cognitive explanation is more plausible: children draw body parts in order of their importance to them, and the torso is less important, perhaps because it does not do anything visible, as hands and feet do. It is also possible that children consider the trunk to be included in their circle-and-line figures. When Goodnow (1977) asked children to add a stomach or belly button to their stick figures, for instance, the children did not act as if they had omitted part of the body; they simply added a dot, a circle, or a few lines in the appropriate place.

Handedness

Most infants fluctuate between left- and right-handedness, and many 4-month-old babies who will become right-handed show a temporary preference for the left hand. By age 2, some children have a strong preference for one hand (Gesell and Ames, 1947). Other children alternate hand preferences throughout early childhood, first showing a preference for one hand (as well as one foot, one ear, and one eye) in elementary school. For most children, hand preference becomes obvious between ages 2 and 5, with about one child in ten preferring the left hand (Hardyck and Petrinovich, 1977).

Figure 9.9 *Before left- or right-handedness is firmly established, some children find that the most efficient and enjoyable way to draw or paint is with both hands. By age 6, the two-handed approach is rare.*

Left-handedness Traditionally, left-handedness was considered wrong, and right-handedness, right. The English words "sinister," meaning evil, and "dextrous," meaning skilled, come directly from the Latin words for left and right, *sinister* and *dexter*. In fact, the words for "left" in various languages almost always connote something negative:

> *Mancino* means "deceitful" in Italian; *linkisch*, "awkward" in German; *na levo*, "sneaky" in Russian. In Spanish *zurdo* also means "malicious," and *no ser zurdo*, "to be not left-handed," in addition means "to be very clever.". . . moreover, the French word for left, *gauche*, is applied to those social misfits who make a habit of putting their foot in their mouth. [Fincher, 1977]

Because of this view, many left-handed children have been forced by parents and teachers to become right-handed. If they refused, they were considered stubborn and disobedient, or even a child of the devil.

Recent evidence points toward genes and perhaps prenatal environment as the origin of most instances of hand preference (Hardyck and Petrinovich, 1977; Fincher, 1977), so certainly it is foolish for parents to blame a child for being a lefty. And if nothing more, it is obviously frustrating for a left-handed child to be forced to become right-handed. Some educators suspect that forcing a left-handed child to make the switch creates other problems, such as stuttering or reading difficulties, although research has not confirmed this (Spache, 1976).

Left-handedness and Handicaps. Left-handed people are as capable as right-handed people. Sometimes they even have an advantage, in that they show a greater tendency toward ambidexterity than right-handed people do (Fincher, 1977). However, left-handed children are handicapped in mastering one basic skill, handwriting. For one thing, it is hard to use the left hand to write languages that read from left to right, such as English, without smudging the paper as the writing hand moves along the line just written. It is true that some languages are easier for the left-handed person to write than others because they are written from top to bottom, like Chinese, or from right to left, like Hebrew. However, no matter where they are placed on the page, letters or characters in almost every language are usually formed from left to right and counterclockwise. This presents a difficulty for lefties, who naturally draw from right to left and clockwise (Linksz, 1973). They would rather write this way: **ꟼfeⅬ**, than this way: **Left**. For these reasons, left-handed children may need extra encouragement and patience when it comes to learning penmanship.

In fact, Arthur Linksz (1973) feels that left-handed children should be taught to write with their right hand, and allowed to use their left hand for everything else. However, most psychologists believe that a child who shows a clear preference for the left hand is probably obeying genetic instructions and should not be switched.

Developing Motor Skills

Most young children practice their motor skills wherever they are, whether in a well-equipped nursery school with climbing ladders, balance boards, and sandboxes, or on their own, with furniture for climbing, fences for balancing, and gardens or empty lots for digging up. As long as the child has the opportunity to play with other children in an adequate space, motor skills will develop as rapidly as maturation and body size allow. On the whole, preschool children learn basic motor skills by teaching themselves and learning from other children, rather than by specific adult instruction. (Complex skills, such as riding a bicycle or playing the piano, obviously require some tutelage.)

Figure 9.10 *In every culture and every historical period, children seem to be natural-born climbers, as suggested by this sixteenth-century German painting by Brueghel and this contemporary photo of children in Sweden.*

Games that preschool children love, such as tag, hide-and-seek, and follow-the-leader, seem designed to accommodate differences in children's abilities as well as the universal childhood urge to try new skills. In follow-the-leader, usually no one objects if a smaller child cannot copy the leader precisely. In tag, each child decides how much time to stay on base, and whether or not to run close to whoever is "it" with taunts of "Can't catch me." Informal agreements usually make sure everyone gets a turn at chasing and being chased. In many other chasing games, such as cops-and-robbers, all the children spend most of their time running. Especially during early childhood, confusion and uncertainty about who is chasing whom, and what to do when someone is caught, does not slow down the game at all.

Space   One thing adults do need to do to enhance the development of children's motor skills is to provide safe and spacious places for playing. This problem has become greater with increasing urbanization. A study by Murphy and Moriarty (1976) describes playing conditions that, given an urban setting, seem, if not ideal, at least fortunate:

> . . . little traffic and practically no danger from marauders. Ways of life of neighboring families were sufficiently similar so that most mothers permitted the preschool and school-age children to explore freely and to develop friendships with the children in the neighborhood. This meant that it was possible for the child to get outdoors much of the time through his own efforts, even before the age of two, and roam a wide area. . . . Even the homes of most of the poor . . . at that time . . . still had yards up to 50 feet wide and 100 feet deep. [Murphy and Moriarty, 1976]

But the authors were writing about Topeka, Kansas, in the 1950s, a city they regarded as unique in its accommodation of children. Many young urban children today are not so fortunate as the Topeka children were, especially lower-class children in large cities. Play space inside the apartments is scarce; halls, elevators, and sidewalks are dangerous. Ecological studies have shown that poor children younger than 9 use public parks infrequently, because the parks are usually too distant, crowded, or dangerous for the small child (Gump, 1975).

This deprivation may cause a child to become clumsy. According to Caroline Sinclair (1973), who has studied the development of motor skills in early childhood, "if . . . space is restricted, . . . clothes too tight, or if [the child] is not allowed on the floor, or on the ladder, or up a tree, his [or her] inborn motor complexes will not develop into smoothly operating movement patterns." Other studies have found that children growing up in low-income urban neighborhoods are more likely to fail physical fitness tests than are children in any other group. Lack of exercise due to a lack of good play areas is probably one of the reasons, although poorer nutrition, health care, and physical education also play a role.

The Importance of Motor Skills

Although parents and teachers are often forced to pay extra attention to the active child, developmental psychologists are more concerned with the inactive child than the active one, for two reasons.

First, they believe that children who have not mastered basic motor skills tend to lack pride in themselves, a fact that obviously could hinder development of a healthy self-concept (Caplan and Caplan, 1974). Children as young as 4 compare themselves with other children and are quick to judge themselves superior or inferior, even if the comparison is not valid (Masters, 1967). A 6-year-old city child who never had a bicycle might feel stupid and babyish if he or she were to move to a neighborhood where all the children can ride bikes. In addition, inactive children who have not mastered motor skills seem less able than active, competent children to cope with many demands, challenges, and frustrations (Murphy, 1962).

Second, some psychologists believe that children who have problems with motor skills in early childhood are more likely to have difficulty with academic skills in middle childhood. Some educators have found that gross motor skills, such as hopping, balancing, and even crawling, are precursors of the three Rs (Hallahan

Figure 9.11 *Children who have not developed the same motor skills as their peers (for example, because of a move from one type of neighborhood to another) often feel embarrassed and inadequate.*

and Cruickshank, 1973). Other studies link fine motor skills, such as drawing a straight line or copying a rectangle, with later reading, writing, and spelling abilities (de Hirsch et al., 1966).

You have probably noticed that these two reasons are given as possibilities. Psychologists are not positive that children feel less good about themselves or learn more slowly in school because they are slow to develop motor skills. Perhaps poor nutrition, perceptual problems, or a lack of motivation is the underlying cause of both Johnny's inability to read and his trouble balancing on one foot or drawing a straight line (Torgeson, 1975). However, many psychologists and teachers believe that children should be encouraged to run, dance, and draw, not only for their happiness and pleasure, but also for increased confidence and ability.

Brain, Eyes, and Inner Organs

Changes in size, shape, and skills are the most visible signs of physical development between ages 2 and 6. However, less visible changes in the nervous system and in various organs are probably even more important for the child's psychological development. They make it possible for the 6-year-old to sit in a first-grade classroom and learn for hours at a time, something even the brightest 2-year-old cannot do.

Brain Maturation

The brain develops faster than any other part of the human body. In a 2-year-old, it weighs about 75 percent of its weight at adulthood. By age 5, the brain has attained about 90 percent of its full weight, even though the average 5-year-old's body weight is less than one-third the average adult's (Tanner, 1970).

Several important changes in the functioning of the cortex occur during early childhood that *may* enable a 6-year-old to concentrate, think, and learn more like an adult than like a younger child. James Tanner (1970) suggests that the emergence of stages of mental functioning, as described by Piaget, "is very likely dependent on progressive maturation and organization of the cortex."

One of the most important aspects of the development of the brain has to do with its being organized in left and right hemispheres, each controlling one half of the body. Oddly enough, the left hemisphere of the brain controls the right side of the body, including the right ear and right hand, while the right half of the brain controls the left half of the body.

As the brain matures, it becomes more specialized; that is, particular parts of the brain tend to be used for certain abilities. The brain center for speech, for instance, is usually located in one part of the left hemisphere, as are most other parts of the brain that aid language; the center for spatial skills and visual imagery is usually located in part of the right hemisphere. Left-handed people sometimes have spoken language skills located in the left hemisphere, sometimes in the right, and occasionally in both.

Brain specialization is probably beneficial. Just as a society can accomplish more for its members if some people specialize in certain tasks and some in others, so the brain can be more efficient if each of its functions is performed by a special part. An individual probably can master more skills if each part of the brain is responsible for different types of knowledge. At the same time, however, such specialization makes it harder for the brain to compensate for loss of function of particular parts due to injury.

Brain specialization for language skills probably begins early in development, according to several recent studies. For instance, forty-two right-handed preschool children listened through stereophonic headphones to pairs of digits, hearing one with the right ear and the other with the left (Hiscock and Kinsbourne, 1977). When asked to report the numbers they heard, even the 3-year-olds were significantly more correct when reporting what they heard with their right ear. This would seem to suggest that the left hemisphere is already more attuned to the sounds of speech than the right hemisphere is.

However, brain specialization for language is not complete until adolescence, as demonstrated by right-handed accident victims who suffer damage to the language area of the brain. If full grown, the victim may be forever mute. However, a child might lose the entire speech area of the left half of the brain and readily learn to talk again by using the right hemisphere (Lenneberg, 1970). Left-handed children and adults tend to have an easier time switching from one half of the brain to another following brain damage (Hardyck and Petrinovich, 1977).

There are several intriguing relationships between brain specialization and handedness. Not only do most right-handed people use their left brain for language and their right brain for spatial skills; most of them use their right hand for tasks that require skill or strength and their left hand for tasks that require tactile sensitivity. A study of fourteen right-handed blind children, for instance, found that they read Braille more quickly and accurately with the fingers of their left hand than with the fingers of their right (Hermelin and O'Connor, 1971). (This study was prompted by a blind child who had injured his left hand and said he could not do his schoolwork because his "reading hand" was hurt.)

Given the evidence for a relationship between hand preference and brain specialization, many psychologists reasoned that a child who had definite left- or right-hand preferences would have a more specialized brain than a child who had mixed preferences. Some took this to mean that degree of hand preference would indicate when a young child was ready to learn to read, add, or perform other school skills: they considered a 4-year-old who always used the same hand to draw to be ready for kindergarten, and a 6-year-old who switched from one hand to another, not ready.

At first, evidence supported this idea. Compared with regular schools, schools for mentally retarded or brain-injured children have a greater proportion of children who are confused about which hand to use for many specific tasks. However, in normal children, degree of hand preference does not seem to be related to school achievement (Belmont and Birch, 1965; Lyle and Johnson, 1976). Many children with poorly developed hand skills are nevertheless ready for reading and math.

Eye Development

Although readiness to do elementary-school work does not seem directly related to degree of hand preference or to brain specialization, it is related to the maturation of the visual apparatus.

Until age 5 or 6, children are usually farsighted; that is, they can see better at a distance than they can up close. Their eyes are not mature enough to focus on a line of normal-sized print, nor can they scan systematically from one word or picture to another in one direction (Vurpillot, 1968). Children at this age are likely to guess at a word on the basis of the first letter rather than looking at the entire word.

By age 6, most children can focus and scan reasonably well, although they are still much less skilled at scanning than adults are (Mackworth and Bruner, 1970). By age 8, most children are able to read small print.

Vision Tests   The problems of a 6-year-old whose vision is less acute or less mature than other children's are not usually spotted by parents or teachers. Since adults more often have trouble with distance vision than near vision, they sometimes mistakenly assume that a kindergarten child who can recognize someone a hundred feet away must see perfectly well. Unfortunately, the routine vision test (reading letters or shapes from a chart several feet away) does not detect problems with near vision; nor does it spot blurriness that appears after several minutes of focusing or double vision that occurs when both eyes do not focus on the same detail. Most educators recommend a thorough visual examination before the first grade, including tests of nearsightedness, eye strain, and binocular vision (the ability of both eyes to work together).

However, the ability to see a letter clearly is only one small part of being able to read a word. The child has to scan it correctly, connecting letters with sounds, mentally forming alternative pronunciations (the phonics method) or memorizing which configurations are which words (the look-say method). Reading demands many perceptual and conceptual skills. Most children who develop reading problems perform perfectly well on a vision test, as long as the test does not use recognition of letters as the measure of acuity. The link between eye development and reading seems to fall into the same category as the link between brain specialization and reading—an intriguing but not very helpful notion.

Reading Readiness

When is a child ready to learn to read, then? Until the middle of the twentieth century, the answer to this question was straightforward: in the first grade. Reading began in the first grade because most children were sufficiently mature at age 6.

Using age as an indicator of readiness-to-read worked well for the average child, but children who matured early became bored and those who matured late became frustrated. Educators subsequently decided that some children were not ready to start reading until age 8 and that others were ready at age 5, so they developed reading-readiness tests (e.g., Ilg and Ames, 1965) that asked 5-year-olds to draw a man, or copy a rectangle, or tell a story. Depending on the results, some kindergarteners were taught to read and other children were kept at playing with blocks and dolls until age 7 or 8 (Cicourel et al., 1974).

Many parents objected to this solution, for children labeled "unready" in kindergarten were likely to be at the bottom of the academic heap throughout their school career. Some educators thought that the schools should adapt to the less mature children, rather than waiting for the reverse to occur (Beller, 1970). On the other hand, many teachers thought it was a mistake to teach reading to children who did not seem ready to learn, for they had seen too many first graders crying in despair because they could not master the printed page.

Figure 9.12 *"Reading" the paper in imitation of their parents is fun for many pre-school children. Actually, however, the eye and brain maturation that makes reading a small line of news-print possible rarely develops before age 7.*

This controversy is not yet settled. A popular book for parents is *How to Teach Your Baby to Read* (Doman, 1975), which advises beginning reading at age 2, partly because early reading at home will supposedly make a child smarter and less frustrated than children who learn to read in school. The author suggests overcoming problems of visual immaturity by using large letters to write the toddler's first words. Agreeing with Doman, Donald Emery (1975) calls the idea that children are not ready for reading until age 6 a "paralyzing prejudice."

However, *Better Late than Early* (Moore and Moore, 1975) takes the opposite viewpoint. The authors say that many children, especially boys, are not ready for any kind of formal education, particularly reading, until age 8, 9, or even 10. According to them, late starters are better achievers and less frustrated than children who were forced to begin first grade too early.

Which point of view is right? Probably most developmental psychologists would agree with David Elkind (1978), a cognitive psychologist who has tried to figure out what basic abilities make reading possible. Elkind concluded that "reading English, far from being a simple matter of discriminating letters and associating sounds, involves complex mental processes from the very start." The child has to be able to regulate the many perceptions, both visual and auditory, involved in word recognition.

Elkind thinks that formal reading instruction probably should be delayed until the child is about 6 or 7. At the same time, he thinks that those 4-year-olds (about 1 in 100) who are eager and able to learn reading should be allowed to, without pressure from parents to master the skill.

Figure 9.13 *Reading—like father, like son.*

Psychologists Eleanor Gibson and Harry Levin (1975) hold a similar view and enumerate the many experiences a preschool child should have before beginning reading instruction, including scribbling, looking at books, and playing rhyming games. They add:

> Reading, word games, printing, and so on, should not be forced on a child or formalized. They should be fun, not work. . . . "Home learning" kits of various kinds are advertised like patent medicines, and the consumer would do well to be equally wary of them. The only magic in learning to read is the magic that the child supplies himself when a rich and responsive environment gives him the chance.

Other Body Changes

In addition to those already discussed, many other parts of the child's body become noticeably more mature between ages 2 and 6, permitting children by their sixth year to be less dependent on their families and more ready for the demands of formal education.

As children grow older, their sleeping patterns begin to approximate adult patterns, and their stomachs and bladders grow larger and more stable. This means that 5-year-olds can go for longer periods without a nap, a snack, or a trip to the bathroom. Other body changes mean 5-year-olds have fewer colds and intestinal upsets than they did when they were younger (Bayer and Snyder, 1971). Stomach aches are less common as the digestive system becomes more regular; ear infections are rarer as the distance from the inner ear to the outer ear becomes greater; respiratory illnesses are less severe as the trachea (windpipe) grows longer; and fevers are not so high as the normal body temperature becomes lower and more stable (the average temperature of a 1-year-old is 99.7°F, or 37.6°C; by age 5, it is 98.6°F or 37.0°C [Lowrey, 1978]).

Many parents find that by age 6 their "sickly" child is ill less often, the allergic child is less sensitive to foods and dust, and the bed-wetting child is usually dry. As is almost always true in maturation, these changes are gradual, and individual differences are common. For example, about 21 percent of all 6-year-olds sometimes or always wet their beds, and one child in eight still has this problem at age 10 (National Center for Health Statistics, 1971).

Part of the reason some children are slow to develop nighttime bladder control is physiological; a child might have a smaller bladder or a sounder sleep pattern than other children the same age. Emotional factors are often involved as well, as shown by a rise in the incidence of bed-wetting when children sleep away from home, visiting relatives or attending camp, for example. Thus, punishing a child for wetting the bed in most cases only compounds the problem, for punishment usually produces stress. Establishing routines to make bed-wetting less likely, and reinforcing the child for staying dry, might solve the problem if the child is physiologically mature enough to respond.

Activity Level Between ages 2 and 6 the child's activity level decreases (heart rate and breathing rate slow as well). In one study, researchers measured changes in activity level from age 3 to 9 (Routh et al., 1974). During the first part of the study, each child was allowed to play wherever he or she wanted to in a playroom. During the second part, the child was asked to play in one special area. Researchers kept track of how often the child stopped playing with one toy and started playing with another, as well as how often the child moved from one part of the designated play area to another. In both conditions, and with both measurements, activity level decreased markedly from age 3 to 6, and continued to decrease at a slower rate from 6 to 9.

In the same study, parents were asked about their child's activity level at home—whether, for instance, the child wriggled when watching television, fidgeted when eating, or moved a lot during sleep. Again, scores decreased with age, with one exception. Age 6 saw a small increase, perhaps because the children were temporarily more restless at home in response to the new restrictions of school.

Accident Rate The child's gradual decrease in activity, as well as the development of motor skills and cognitive maturity, helps explain why a child's likelihood of being seriously injured in an accident decreases with each passing year after age 3. (Of the accidents that result in death, fatal poisoning occurs most often at age 1; drowning is most frequent at age 2; and death resulting from being struck by a motor vehicle is highest at age 3.) Older children are given more freedom of movement and are more likely to be exposed to danger than are younger children, but they are more able to regulate their behavior. A 3-year-old, for instance, is more likely to run in front of a moving car chasing after a ball than an 8-year-old is; indeed, 8-year-olds are sufficiently cautious as to be able to play ball in the street in relative safety.

This gradual development of caution should not give the wrong impression, however. Throughout childhood, accidents are by far the leading cause of death, killing more young people than the next five or six causes combined. About 1 child in every 3000 dies an accidental death each year, and most children need stitches or a cast sometime before they are 10 years old.

Figure 9.14 *Because many children who live in crowded cities must play either in the street or in debris-filled lots, they run a higher risk of accidents than children who can play in the yards and parks of suburbia. The rate of accidental deaths among children in the Bronx, N.Y., for instance, is twice that in Scarsdale, a wealthy suburb less than 5 miles away.*

A child's chances of having an accident depend primarily on three factors: the amount of adult supervision, the safety of the play space, and the child's activity level. Some groups of children have many more accidents than others, because these three factors differ. For instance, Asian-American children have fewer accidents than any other American ethnic group, probably because their parents traditionally keep them nearby; this makes the children safer, although more dependent (Kurokawa, 1969). Poor children have more accidents than wealthier children, probably because their play areas are more hazardous. Boys are more active than girls, and are expected to be more daring; consequently, they have more accidents than girls, about one-third more at age 1, and twice as many at age 5.

Sex Differences and Similarities

The difference in accident rates for boys and girls raises the intriguing question of sex differences. Boys and girls follow almost identical paths of physical development during early childhood. They are about the same size, and can do almost the same things at the same age. Knowing a preschool child's sex alone provides little in the way of clues concerning that child's physical development.

However, when averages based on groups of boys are compared with those of groups of girls, several interesting differences appear. Boys are slightly taller and more muscular. They lose their baby fat sooner, and have somewhat less body fat throughout childhood. Girls, on the other hand, mature more rapidly in several ways. For instance, their bone age is usually a year or more ahead of the bone age of boys the same chronological age (Lowrey, 1978). They lose their "baby" teeth earlier, and their brains show earlier signs of specialization.

Drawings by Charles Schulz; © 1972 United Feature Syndicate, Inc.

Figure 9.15 Batting a ball is one skill that boys generally perform better than girls, partly because, except for a year or two during early adolescence, the average male has stronger hands and arms than the average female of the same age. Another reason is that boys receive more encouragement for ball playing— for instance, most Little League teams are still all male. Until girls have an equal opportunity to accept or reject the rewards for athletic skill, we will not know how high their batting averages could be.

These physical differences may underlie differences in particular motor skills between girls and boys. By ages 4 and 5, boys are usually superior in most gross motor skills, especially those like throwing and hitting that involve arm strength. At the same time, girls are more coordinated in skipping and galloping (Caroline Sinclair, 1973). Some studies have found girls to be better than boys in certain fine motor skills, especially when speed is involved (Laosa and Brophy, 1972; Ilg and Ames, 1965). Six-year-olds who cannot print the letters of their names legibly are more often male than female.

Of course, with all skills, male-female differences could be caused by differences in the amount of practice children have had in certain skills, rather than basic body or brain differences. For instance, we know that preschool boys spend more time playing outside, running, climbing, and riding tricycles than girls do, while girls spend more time at arts and crafts than boys do (Harper and Sanders, 1975; Rubin, 1977). Whether the difference in play preference is biological or cultural, the fact is that boys get more experience with gross motor skills, and less with fine motor skills, than girls do.

At the same time, the advantage of one sex over the other in most skills is very slight. One researcher compared the running and jumping skills of kindergarteners, first-graders, and second-graders (Milne et al., 1976). While the average boy was ahead of the average girl at every age, there was a great deal of overlap. For instance, while half of the boys in kindergarten could jump 35 inches in the standing long jump and could run 400 feet in 50 seconds, so could about 45 percent of the girls. The range of ability in running was as great for the girls as for the boys. This means that most boys at this age know several girls in their class who can jump farther and run faster than they can.

Most of the variation in strength and skills among children is caused by individual, rather than male-female, differences. With the exception of hand and forearm strength (boys are usually stronger), girls and boys of the same size and shape are very similar in strength until puberty (Tanner, 1970). On most eye-hand–coordination tasks, sex differences are not significant (Eckert and Eichorn, 1974).

SUMMARY

Physical Play

1. Play is the work of early childhood. Through sensorimotor play, mastery play, and rough-and-tumble play, children develop their bodies and skills.

Size and Shape

2. During early childhood, children grow about 3 inches (7 centimeters) a year. Normal variation in growth is caused primarily by genes and nutrition, although physical and emotional health can also affect height.

Motor Skills

3. Gross motor skills improve dramatically during this period, making it possible for the average 6-year-old to do many things with grace and skill.

4. Fine motor skills, such as holding a pencil or tying a shoelace, also improve, but more gradually. Many 6-year-olds, especially left-handed ones, find writing difficult.

Brain, Eyes, and Inner Organs

5. The child's brain and eyes become more mature during these years. This maturation is probably necessary before the child can do typical first-grade work, although the precise relationship between brain, eyes, and learning is not clear. Reading is a complex perceptual and conceptual task, which demands much more than left-right distinctions and visual maturity.

6. Children's chances of injuring themselves depend partly on age: the accident rate decreases as age increases. Supervision, play space, activity level, and the sex of the child also correlate with the frequency of accidents.

Sex Differences and Similarities

7. The average boy plays more active games and is taller and more muscular than the average girl. He is usually better at gross motor skills, such as throwing a ball, than she is, but she is usually better at fine motor skills, such as drawing a person. During these years, however, the similarities between the sexes are much more apparent than the differences.

KEY QUESTIONS

What causes variations among children in height and weight during early childhood?

How does the shape of the child's body change during early childhood?

In what motor skills have average 5-year-olds developed competence?

What are the advantages and disadvantages of left-handedness?

How do motor skills develop?

What is the relationship between motor skills in early childhood and learning in elementary school?

What are some of the brain developments during early childhood?

What visual developments occur in early childhood?

Why is there a controversy about when children should learn to read?

What conclusions can be drawn from statistics on accident rates among children?

What are the main similarities and differences in the physical development of boys and girls in early childhood?

KEY TERMS

mastery play	gross motor skills
rough-and-tumble play	fine motor skills
play face	handedness
ossification	brain specialization
bone age	farsighted
dwarfism	binocular vision
giantism	reading-readiness tests
deprivation dwarfism	

RECOMMENDED READINGS

Sinclair, Caroline. *Movement of the young child: Ages two to six.* Columbus, Ohio: Merrill, 1973.

This book gives many practical suggestions for helping children develop their motor skills, as well as providing information about the abilities of the average boy and girl at each of the years from 2 to 6.

Goodnow, Jacqueline. *Children drawing.* Cambridge, Mass.: Harvard University Press, 1977.

Goodnow discusses the order and progression of children's drawing. She believes that "drawings can tell us something not only about children but also about the nature of thought and problem-solving among both children and adults." The book proves her point, and is illustrated with thousands of sketches from her own children and from the preschool children who have been the primary subjects of her research.

Murphy, Lois B., and Moriarty, Alice F. *Vulnerability, coping and growth: From infancy to adolescence.* New Haven, Conn.: Yale University Press, 1976.

This book describes the results from a longitudinal study of a group of children growing up in Topeka, Kansas, in the 1950s and 1960s. Much fascinating detail is included, showing how many stresses "normal" children experience, and how many coping skills children develop. As a longitudinal study, this book is relevant to almost every chapter of this text, but it is listed here because it helps one see the antecedents and consequences of preschool development.

The Play Years: Cognitive Development

"Mommy, I'm so sorry for the baby horses—they cannot pick their noses."

"I'm barefoot all over."

"Why do they put a pit in every cherry? We just have to throw the pit away."

Preschool children quoted in Chukovsky, 1968

True or False?

If preschoolers were only given full, yet simple, logical explanations of their parents' dos and don'ts, they would be able to listen to reason in most cases.

When shown a picture of, say, seven dogs, four of which are collies, the typical 5-year-old will say there are more collies than dogs.

Because preschoolers are self-centered, they are more selfish at this age than at any other.

The average 2-year-old who knows 50 words will probably know over 10,000 words by age 6.

One of the things guaranteed to give a preschooler fits is conversation with a peer who keeps changing the subject.

To study cognitive development in early childhood, most psychologists use one of two approaches. Either they try to understand what goes on within the child's mind, recording the growth of logic and language, or they attempt to determine what intellectual abilities should be evident by, say, the first grade, and then try to discover which learning experiences and which teaching methods will help children to meet these standards.

Both approaches begin with the mind of the young child, but one describes while the other prescribes. One focuses on thinking, the other, on learning; one centers on the cognitive characteristics shared by all children, the other, on the differences between one child and another. Even the methods are different: psychologists taking the first approach prefer naturalistic observation; those choosing the second are more likely to use control groups, experimental procedures, and standardized tests.

We will look at both approaches in this chapter, first describing the child's thinking and language, and then exploring the teaching that homes and schools provide. The ideas generated by one approach do not always seem relevant or even correct to the advocates of the other, but you will see that these approaches are closely related. Knowing how a child thinks is very useful to teachers and parents who want to help a child to learn.

Preoperational Thought

In the last stage of sensorimotor thought, children 1½ years old began to figure things out mentally. Toddlers occasionally stop to think before acting, instead of hurtling pell-mell into each new idea. As their second birthday approaches, they become able to pretend and can imitate behavior they saw hours, or even days, before. These budding mental abilities come to full flower between ages 2 and 6, as imagination and language open up new ways of thinking and playing. Preschool children can think symbolically, although they still lack the logical abilities of older children.

Symbolic Thinking

A symbol is something that stands for, or signifies, something else. A flag symbolizes a country, a handshake symbolizes friendship, a skull and crossbones symbolizes poison. Words are the most common symbols, whether spoken or written. For instance, the sound "dawg" symbolizes a dog, as do the three written letters "d-o-g." The word "dog" signifies a general concept of dogness, enabling a young child to see an unfamiliar canine and identify it as a dog, no matter whether it is a Great Dane, a toy poodle, or a mutt. Knowing the symbols that stand for the dog makes it easier to talk about dogs, remember them, and think about them.

Once children become capable of symbolic thought, they learn to use thousands of words, as well as many objects and gestures, to represent ideas, actions, and things. It becomes easier for them to remember the past, imagine the future, and deal with the present. A 2-year-old might stop crying upon hearing "Mommy is coming soon," or might give serious thought to "Remember when you fell down?" Most 3-year-olds are more adept at pretending than 1-year-olds are, partly because they can use props (such as high-heels or a hat) but mostly due to their use of words as symbols.

Figure 10.1 *When the stage of symbolic thought has been reached, two potholders make a doll's bed, and lace curtains and a sheet of aluminum foil make a queen.*

Consequently, *creative play* is a favorite activity during the preschool years, when children are old enough to pretend but not yet able to distinguish fantasy from reality very well. Imagination becomes more apparent with each passing year. Whereas the 1-year-old might play with a cup and saucer independently, banging them on the floor, and the 2-year-old might place the cup on the saucer and pretend to drink, the 3-year-old can transform the cup and saucer into almost

Figure 10.2 *Imaginative play becomes more elaborate as children grow older. This little girl's tea party is obviously more complex than simply pretending to drink tea from an empty cup, but had it been organized by an older child, it might have been so intricate as to have involved sending invitations, decorating the room, seating a variety of "guests," and serving an imaginary five-course meal.*

anything (Lowe, 1975). The child might begin by pretending to pour tea and eat an imaginary cookie, then use pieces of paper, or marbles, or anything handy to make an entire meal. But at a moment's notice, the cup and saucer could just as easily become a space ship, a hat, or a domed dwelling. By the end of early childhood, at age 5 or 6, the imaginary objects can be invisible, existing solely in the child's mind.

The First Symbols   Given the importance of symbols, it should come as no surprise that cognitive psychologists highlight the first use of symbols in thought. In Piaget's terms, the symbolic function distinguishes preoperational thought from earlier sensorimotor thought; in Jerome Bruner's, the symbolic mode joins the more primitive cognitive abilities of the infant. Both men describe the 2-year-old as no longer solely dependent on the senses and motor abilities that characterized early thinking. Reflection joins action as a way of understanding the world.

Piaget's Private Symbols.   Piaget sees the first signs of symbolic thinking in a toddler's pretending that a piece of cloth is a pillow, or that a piece of paper is food. The child's first words are symbols too, although often they are "private symbols" rather than "social signs" understood by the larger language community (Flavell, 1963). For many 2-year-olds, "mommy" means "I want something." If they want to be held, they raise their arms and say "mommy" to whomever happens to be nearby, including daddy, brother, or a passing stranger. Learning to talk so that others will understand what they want to say takes preschoolers a long time. Even 5-year-olds use words and phrases that are difficult to interpret.

Bruner's Iconic Thinking.   Agreeing that symbolic thinking develops gradually, Jerome Bruner (1973b) describes a mode of thinking, called iconic thought, that appears before true symbolic thought. Bruner derives his term from the religious sense of "icon," that is, an image or likeness that is worshiped, not just as a symbol of a deity, but as an object that possesses the very characteristics of the god it represents. (Followers of some faiths might believe, say, that touching a certain statue can help a sick person become well.)

   In somewhat the same way, Bruner contends, a child at the iconic stage of thinking uses words and things, not as symbols, but as the objects they represent. For example, Daddy's photograph might become Daddy when he is gone; a stuffed animal might become a best friend. A child's name can be a powerful icon, as well:

for instance, Elkind (1978) suggests that children will be much more willing to share their possessions if their name is written on the toy in question because "to a child, a written symbol is a more potent sign of entitlement than use." Similarly, a young child who is called a baby may fear that the word itself will make him or her become a baby.

One sister's way of teasing her little brother shows the power of iconic thinking. At first she called him "Baby, Baby, Baby," which made him cry, but also made their mother angry at her for upsetting her brother. So the sister sang the lyric, "Yes sir, that's my baby," producing the same result in her brother while keeping herself out of trouble. In the end, all she had to do was hum the song to make him cry and to make her mother tell him, "Stop crying, she's not doing anything to you."

The private symbols of the young child's speech can continue for years. However, once symbolic thinking is possible, many ideas become easier to understand and express. Communication, imagination, and reflection all become possible.

Prelogical Thought

The ability to perform logical operations does not appear until middle childhood. To emphasize this fact, Piaget refers to the cognitive period from age 2 to 7 as the period of prelogical thinking, or preoperational thought

The Problem of Conservation To adults, it is obvious that a given quantity of liquid remains the same no matter what the shape of its container. But as we saw in Chapter 2, conservation, the idea that amount is conserved when shape changes, is not at all obvious to young children. Rather, they are impressed solely by the height of the liquid in the container.

Preschool children usually have the same problem with regard to *conservation of matter*. Ask a 4-year-old child to make two balls of clay of equal amount, and then instruct the child to roll one of them into a long skinny rope. When this is done, ask the child whether both pieces still have the same amount of clay. Almost always, 4-year-olds will say that the long piece has more. Not until age 6, 7, or 8 does the average child realize that the amount of matter remains the same despite any change of shape.

Explanations for Inability to Conserve. Often students wonder if the child's inability to give the correct answer to Piagetian conservation problems is due to difficulties in language rather than thought. Does a 4-year-old know what "the same amount of clay" really means? Psychologists sensitive to this possibility have tried to ask the crucial question in words the child understands, such as, "Let's pretend this clay is cake, and we'll both have a piece. You have the long, thin one and I'll have the round one. Does one of us have more to eat, or do we both have the same?" No matter how the question is phrased, preoperational children think the two lumps of clay are unequal.

Many older children, and even some adults, are likewise unable to apprehend conservation *visually:* to them, a tall, thin quart bottle on the supermarket shelf seems to hold more than a short, wide one. But adults and older children understand two logical operations, identity and reversibility, that help them to deduce the consequences of conservation. In the example of the clay rope and ball, identity would involve the realization that no matter how the shape of the clay is altered, nothing is being added to it or subtracted from it. Reversibility would involve the realization that the clay can be returned to its original state by reversing the shape-changing process. In fact, when asked how they know the clay rope and ball contain the same amount of matter, many 9-year-olds simply roll the rope back into a ball. Identity and reversibility also are underlying concepts for mathematics: 5 is always 5, whether it is expressed as 1 + 4 or 2 + 3 (identity); and if 3 − 2 = 1, then 1 + 2 must be 3 (reversibility).

The fact that preschool children do not understand the concept of conservation is of little practical import: they do not need to understand it in their daily lives, and they will master it long before they become cooks or chemists. However, Piaget's research on conservation is significant for developmental psychology because it proves that ideas that seem simple to adults are beyond the cognitive capacity of even the brightest and most verbal 4-year-old. The ideas of a preschool child are organized with different principles, or *schemes*. The child interprets the taller glass of lemonade or the longer piece of clay by assimilating it into the scheme "taller and longer are bigger," without accommodating other apparent facts, such as narrower is less.

Tests of Various Types of Conservation

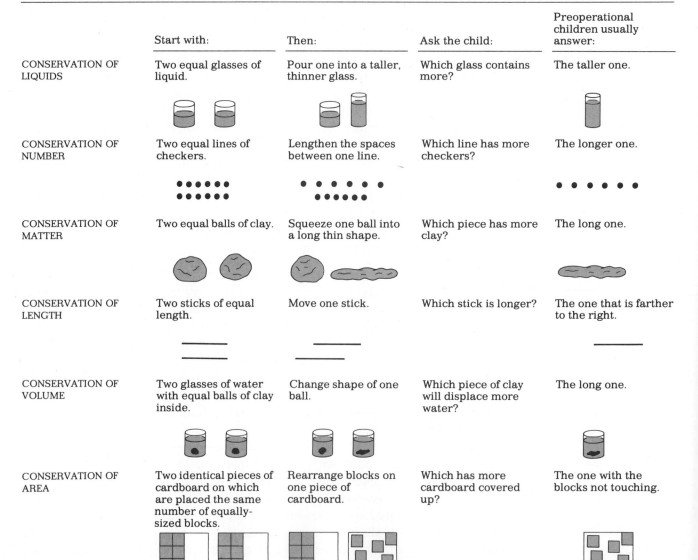

	Start with:	Then:	Ask the child:	Preoperational children usually answer:
CONSERVATION OF LIQUIDS	Two equal glasses of liquid.	Pour one into a taller, thinner glass.	Which glass contains more?	The taller one.
CONSERVATION OF NUMBER	Two equal lines of checkers.	Lengthen the spaces between one line.	Which line has more checkers?	The longer one.
CONSERVATION OF MATTER	Two equal balls of clay.	Squeeze one ball into a long thin shape.	Which piece has more clay?	The long one.
CONSERVATION OF LENGTH	Two sticks of equal length.	Move one stick.	Which stick is longer?	The one that is farther to the right.
CONSERVATION OF VOLUME	Two glasses of water with equal balls of clay inside.	Change shape of one ball.	Which piece of clay will displace more water?	The long one.
CONSERVATION OF AREA	Two identical pieces of cardboard on which are placed the same number of equally-sized blocks.	Rearrange blocks on one piece of cardboard.	Which has more cardboard covered up?	The one with the blocks not touching.

Difficulty Understanding Change Preschool children's difficulty with logical operations makes it hard for them to perceive gradual transformations. As a result, children do not understand that aging is a continual process. On the morning of her fifth birthday, one little girl got out of bed and asked, "Mommy, am I five yet?" When told that she was, she spread out her hands and looked at them in amazement. "Look at my 5-year-old fingers. How big they are!" she said.

Another puzzled preschooler asked her 16-year-old babysitter, "Where are your children?" When the babysitter replied that she didn't have any, the preschooler responded, "If you are still a child, how can you be a babysitter?" Using the same reasoning, children looking at photographs in the family album find it difficult to believe that those pictures of little children are really of Daddy, Mommy, or an older brother or sister.

Centration Many of these examples show a characteristic of preoperational thought called centration, that is, the focusing, or *centering,* of attention on one feature of a situation to the exclusion of all others. A child centers on one aspect of the appearance of the liquid in a glass—its level—and decides that one glass must contain more than another if the height of its contents is greater—in spite of having seen the same amount of liquid poured into each glass. Children also center on what family members mean to them exclusively: they do not understand that their father is also a son and possibly a brother too.

Figure 10.3 *Centration often leads preschoolers to reason that a son is a little boy, not a grown man, and that Grandma is too old to be a mommy.*

The ability to reconcile two conflicting or complementary facts spontaneously does not usually appear until age 7, although a child can be *taught* that he or she is, say, Baptist, an American, and 4. Three psychologists (Hartley et al., 1948) who asked 4-year-olds about their religious identity received some amusing responses from children who had not yet been so taught. Replied one child, "I'm not Catholic, I'm Richie"; another said she would become Jewish, but now she was 4.

Classification Another logical idea that appears gradually is classification, the sorting of objects into categories or classes (Inhelder and Piaget, 1970). For example, a child's parents and siblings are all members of the class called family. Toys, animals, people, and food are other everyday categories. Most preschool children understand these words, but many do not understand that they are categories. A preschool child might tell a sibling, "If you hit me, you can't be in my family," and at the same time consider that family to include the pet dog and a litter of gerbils.

Preschoolers' limited understanding of the general category "dogs" and of the subcategories of particular breeds of dogs can be seen in the following experiment, modeled on a series of experiments conducted by Piaget. An examiner shows children seven toy dogs. Four of them are collies, and the other three are a poodle, an Irish setter, and a German shepherd. First, the examiner questions the children to make sure they know that all the toys are dogs and can name each breed. Then comes the crucial question: "Are there more collies or more dogs?" Until the concept of classification is firmly established, usually not until age 7 or 8, most children say, "More collies." They cannot make the mental shift from the subcategory "collie" to the general category "dogs."

A CLOSER LOOK   **Doubting Piaget**

When one of my students first heard about Piaget's experiment with a category and a subcategory, she was convinced his conclusions were wrong, chiefly because she felt that he had made his classification task unnecessarily difficult by using categories such as breeds of dogs. She decided that her bright 5-year-old, Tyrone, would demonstrate an understanding of classification if she devised an experiment with material Tyrone knew well.

That evening after class, she put some yellow vitamins and a greater number of red vitamins in her hand and asked her son, "Are there more vitamins or more red vitamins?" To her amazement, Tyrone said, "More red vitamins." Reformulating her question, she asked, "Are there more red vitamins, or more vitamins?" Once again, he said, "More red vitamins," just as Piaget would have predicted.

My student's initial skepticism is typical of many Americans at first hearing Piaget's predictions about the mental abilities of young children. After all, one would think that any intelligent child who has spent hours pouring water in and out of various containers and making balls and snakes and whatnot from Play-Doh would understand such obvious concepts as conservation of liquids or matter. However, most parents, teachers, and psychologists who have duplicated Piaget's experiments have found that Piaget knew what he was talking about. Today's children sometimes show logical thinking earlier than Piaget's subjects, but the difference is not as great as one might expect. Philip Cowan reports the experience of one psychologist, the father of a 5-year-old:

The father had apparently made repeated attempts to drill the child on the conservation of water problem. One day the father proudly demonstrated the child's skill. On the first two trials, the boy said, "There's more water in this glass; it's higher." The father's face fell. Given a third try, his son said, "Oh, it's the same, it's still the same amount of water." The father beamed proudly, while the son added in a tiny whisper, "But it really isn't." [Cowan, 1978]

The child's insistence on maintaining his preoperational perception despite his father's instruction is typical of a child who has not yet developed concrete operational thought. However, special instruction may speed the progress of children in the transitional period, from 5 to 7 (Inhelder et al., 1974). According to one report, even 4-year-olds sometimes learn conservation after careful instruction, including demonstrations, descriptions of what occurred, and an opportunity for the children themselves to perform the experiments, with the experimenter telling them how well they are doing (Denney et al., 1977).

The fact that instruction can hasten the onset of concrete reasoning does not make Piaget's basic ideas invalid. He has always insisted that he was interested in the sequence of stages rather than the exact ages at which each stage appeared. Cross-cultural research verifies that the sequence is almost always the same, although the ages at which particular concepts are mastered depends somewhat on the experience of the child and the emphasis of the culture.

Another experiment involves several levels of classification, with multicolored shapes that can be subdivided by color, or by shape, or by both color and shape. Inhelder and Piaget (1970) found that most children between 2½ and 5 were unable to sort multicolored shapes into categories correctly. Typically, a 4-year-old would start by putting a circle next to a circle, but then, noticing that the second circle was blue, would put a blue square next to it. In all Piaget's experiments in classification, children younger than 7 rarely show full comprehension of categories and sub-categories.

Many psychologists think Piaget underestimates the logical abilities of preschool children. Nancy Denney (1972), for one, believes that classification appears much earlier than age 7. She gave 2-, 3-, and 4-year-old children (thirty-six at each age) cardboard figures, in four shapes, two sizes, and four colors. She asked each child to "put the things that are alike or the things that go together into groups." As shown in the chart below, half of the 2-year-olds made groupings that showed at least some similarity, as did thirty-two of the 3-year-olds. By age 4, twenty-three of the children were completely correct, dividing all the shapes into categories by color, or by form, or by both color and form. Most of these 4-year-olds achieved "true classification" on this test much earlier than predicted by Piaget's findings. Denney suggests that nursery-school experience, middle-class homes, and "Sesame Street" might be the reasons for this difference.

Nancy Denney's Experiment with Classification

NO SIMILARITY

The child made no response, or the response seemed random, or the child made a design with no apparent recognition of similar form. For example:

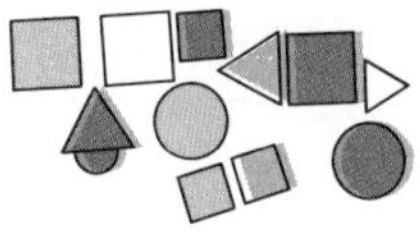

INCOMPLETE SIMILARITY

The child sorted some by shape, color, or size, but others randomly. For example:

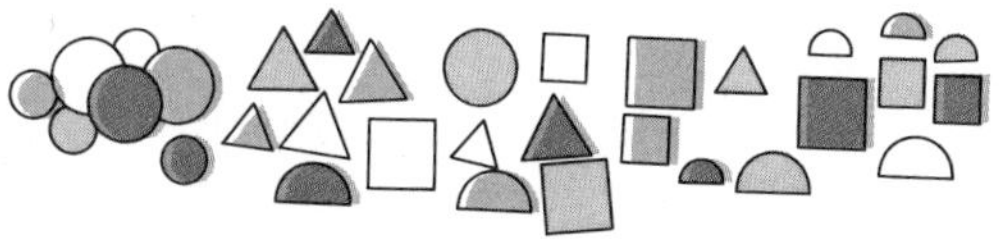

COMPLETE SIMILARITY

The child sorted all thirty-two shapes by one category, or by two categories. For example:

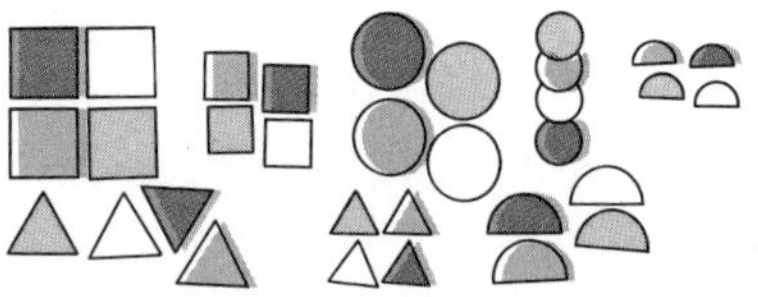

RESULTS	Age of Child	No Similarity	Incomplete Similarity	Complete Similarity
	2 years	18	16	2
	3 years	4	19	13
	4 years	4	9	23

Cause and Effect   Another consequence of prelogical thinking is that children have trouble understanding cause and effect, partly because they center on one aspect of an event rather than on the relationship between events. As a result, children who fall down might blame the sidewalk, or another child several feet away, or even God. Because they do not understand chance, preschool children sometimes interpret the phrase "it was an accident" to mean "don't blame me." Thus, a child might very well hit her brother deliberately and then protest, "It was an accident." Adults who understand the cognitive characteristics of preschool children will realize that this little girl is not lying.

Piaget's research also explains why nursery-school children tend to get worked up if everyone in class isn't given juice in identically shaped glasses and why they believe 4-year-olds are much bigger than children between 3 and 3¾. And it also confirms the all-too-obvious fact that arguing with preschool children is usually futile, for they find it hard to "listen to reason."

Egocentrism

At every stage of development, a child's thought processes reflect egocentrism (Elkind, 1978); that is, the child's ideas about the world are restricted by the child's own narrow point of view. To say that the child is egocentric means only that the child is naturally self-centered, not that the child is selfish (Piaget, 1959).

Egocentrism appears in different forms at various ages. During early childhood, it is expressed in the child's difficulty imagining what it would be like to be someone else. Children assume everyone reacts to the world as they themselves do. A 3-year-old boy hearing his father crying, for instance, might try to comfort his daddy by bringing a teddy bear, a lollipop, or a Band-Aid. Obviously, this child is not selfish: he is willing to give up something of his own. But he is egocentric: he assumes daddies are consoled by the same things that comfort little boys.

Children's descriptions of natural phenomena often show egocentric thought, as when preschool children declare that it has snowed so that they can make a snowman or that the grass grows so that they won't hurt themselves if they fall. This aspect of preschool thought is illustrated by a folk tale about a young princess who thought the moon was so pretty that she insisted on having it. When the king told her it would be impossible to get it for her, she pined away, neither eating nor playing, as all the king's doctors and philosophers tried in vain to cure her. Finally, when she was near death, a clever boy asked her, "How big is the moon?" "As big as a silver coin," she answered. "And what would happen if you were to get the moon?" he asked. "Another moon would grow," she replied. In a wink the boy fashioned a silver disk as big as a coin and gave it to her, making, needless to say, the princess happy, the king grateful, and himself wealthy and respected all his life.

Understanding the egocentric nature of preschool thought can help in real life, too. Take the case of a 3-year-old boy who asks his father how the wheels on his toy car work. The father patiently tries to explain friction and axles, but the boy keeps asking more questions. Finally the boy's aunt, who is wise in such matters, tells him that the car has wheels on it so it will move when someone pushes it. "That's right!" says the boy, as he stops asking questions and starts pushing the car. His question about how the wheels work was really "How does this affect me?"—the implied question underlying many children's inquiries at this stage.

Artificialism and Animism   Their egocentrism makes many young children think that everything in the world is alive, just as they are. Such a view is referred to as

RESEARCH REPORT   ## The Origin of Babies

The development of the child's concept of "where babies come from" is an example of the gradual maturation of thought. Most 3- and 4-year-olds believe that babies come ready-made and that parents buy them in a store or hospital. One preschool boy carefully saved all his money and gave it to his mother so that she would be able to buy him a little brother or sister. Another child knew that babies grow inside mothers, so he asked his mother to grow a baby or a puppy, whichever she wanted (Chukovsky, 1968). By the time one 3-year-old asked his mother where babies came from, she had already decided to answer all his questions honestly, so she sat him down and explained the entire process of intercourse, conception, prenatal development, and birth. When she had finished, he smiled and said, "That's the silliest story I ever heard" (Lipton, 1973).

Two psychologists (Bernstein and Cowan, 1975) tested sixty children, aged 3 to 12, who were older brothers or sisters in families where questions about conception and pregnancy were usually answered factually. The psychologists assessed each child's level of cognitive development on Piagetian tests, and then asked the child about the origin of babies.

Since they had seen their mothers pregnant, and had been told the truth, even the youngest children knew that their little brother or sister had come from their mother's body rather than from a store. Nevertheless, they displayed preoperational thought patterns. Most of the 3- and 4-year-olds believed the baby was always there, rather than created from a sperm and an ovum. When one child was pressed to explain how his younger sibling could have been inside the uterus even when he himself was in his mother's body, he clung to his basic idea but added some additional facts he had heard. He said that the younger baby was first in another woman's tummy, and then it came out of her vagina and into his mother's tummy after he himself was born.

Older preschool children more often thought that babies are manufactured: one suggested that the mother bought the bones and blood at a store and then put the baby together in her tummy, or that she bought a rabbit or a duck and then ate it, turning it into a baby. The fascinating aspect of all these childish versions is that the children combine bits of fact, such as the baby's being inside the mother, into their own scheme of the way the world functions. This is a

Preschool children delight in hearing the heartbeat and feeling the movement of their future brother or sister. They also ask many questions about the origins of babies. However, even when their questions are answered truthfully, many preschoolers still believe that babies are made in heaven or purchased in a store.

charming example of Piaget's idea that children assimilate and accommodate the information they hear.

Bernstein and Cowan also found that each child's understanding of conception and birth was closely related to his or her performance on Piagetian tests. A child who thinks babies are made by someone's painting their picture (as did one child in this study) is likely to think that night comes because Mother puts the light out, and that you can make more clay by squeezing a clay ball into a long, skinny coil. This finding confirms Piaget's idea that all aspects of cognitive development are interrelated. A child who is egocentric and illogical about conservation will probably be egocentric and illogical about other ideas as well.

This does not imply that all the interrelated logical structures of concrete operational thought appear simultaneously. In this study, children's understanding of night and day was usually more advanced than their understanding of conception and prenatal growth. Other research shows that years elapse between the first application of conservation concepts and the final mastery of the concept.

animism Animistic children might bump into a table and then punish the table for hitting them, or when they drop a stuffed animal, they might begin to cry because they think they have hurt it. The child might ask such questions as, "Why does the radio talk so loud?"

Other children might egocentrically reason that because they themselves make many things from blocks, sand, and the like, everything, living things included, is made in a similar fashion. Children whose thinking is influenced by this artificialism might try to manufacture a puppy out of sticks and mud, or might imagine God creating the world by building a fire to make the sun.

Both artificialism and animism seem amusing to older children and parents, who prefer scientific explanations of natural phenomena. However, preschool ideas probably make sense if one does not know or believe in the rules and findings of science. Indeed, the preoperational child's concepts are very similar to those of legends, myths, and early religion and philosophy.

Death, Illness, and Divorce The limitations of preoperational thought often make it hard for children to understand death, illness, or divorce. Children often blame themselves for these events. A 4-year-old boy might think he killed Grandma by disobeying her, or that God made his tonsils infected because he said a bad word, or that Mommy and Daddy are separating because he got dirt on the carpet.

Explanations to relieve the child's anxiety should be phrased in terms the preoperational child can understand. One little girl heard that her grandmother had died of old age, so she refused to eat any cake at her own birthday party, crying, "I don't want to be 5. I don't want to die." In such a situation, parents who believe in religious ideas of afterlife have a less difficult task than parents who do not, since it is much easier for a preoperational child to believe Grandma died because she was ready for heaven than to understand the gradual deterioration involved in the aging process.

Preschool children who are told that their parents are divorcing because they no longer love each other often wonder if the parents will fall out of love with them as well. It is important to explain to children in these circumstances that love between parent and child is a bond that cannot be severed by divorce or weakened by time. Uncertainty is even harder on a preoperational child with egocentric thought patterns than it is on an adult. For this reason, it is easiest for the child if the divorce process is quick, without custody fights or temporary reconciliation. (Chapter 14 discusses children's adjustment after the divorce is finalized.)

Understanding Another Point of View

By calling preoperational thought prelogical and egocentric, we might be overstating the limitations of preschool cognition. In fact, egocentrism declines and logic begins years before children master the concrete operations of the next period of cognitive development at age 7 or 8. Children gradually become able to decenter, no longer focusing only on one aspect of a situation or on their own point of view.

Piaget's Three Mountains The research on children's understanding of another person's point of view shows this development. In a classic experiment, Piaget and Inhelder (1963) showed children, aged 4 to 11, a three-dimensional exhibit of three mountains (see Figure 10.4). Each child was seated on one side of the table that held the exhibit, with a doll seated on another side. Then each child was asked to choose one of a series of photos that showed how this scene would look to the doll.

Children younger than 6 thought that the doll would view the mountains the same way they did, no matter where the doll sat. By age 6 or 7, most children realized that perspective is affected by position, but they did not choose the correct

Figure 10.4 (a) *Replications of Piaget's three-mountains experiment are used to measure the ability to imagine a different point of view. The child is first shown a display model of three mountains, and then is shown ten drawings of various views of the mountains. The child is asked to select the drawing that most accurately portrays the point of view of a doll seated at various positions around the table. For instance, if a child were sitting in position 1 looking at the three-mountain display (here shown in an overhead view) and asked how the display would look from sitting position 4, which picture— (a), (b), or (c)—should the child select? Preoperational children often wrongly select their own view (b) rather than correctly choosing (a).*

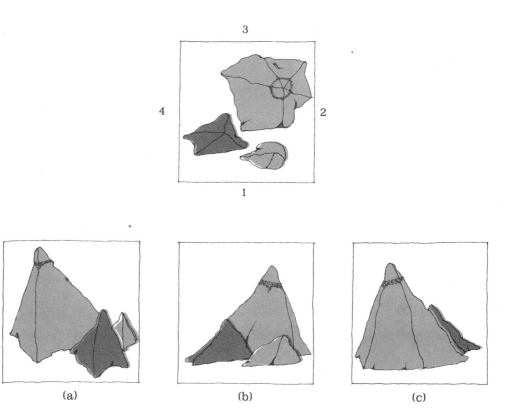

(a)   (b)   (c)

photo. Between 7 and 9, some children chose correctly, with occasional errors. Not until ages 9, 10, and 11 could most of the children perform this task perfectly. From these results, Piaget concluded that children under 7 were too egocentric to understand another point of view.

Experiments That Make It Easier for the Child.   Piaget's conclusion may have been too hasty. Simpler experiments have shown that even preschool children can begin to understand another's perspective. By age 4, children could choose how the "Sesame Street" character Grover would view a rural scene (a lake with a sailboat, farm animals, and a house) from different positions (Borke, 1975). In another experiment, preschool children could guess what color someone else saw through tinted glasses (Liben, 1978).

This early development of social understanding is shown even more clearly in an ingenious experiment reported by Flavell (1975). Forty children, ten at each age from 3 to 6, were asked to pretend that they were giving presents to themselves, their parents, their siblings, and their teacher. They could choose from five objects: a truck, a doll, a necktie, an adult book, and a pair of silk stockings.

All twenty-one girls and nineteen boys chose gifts for themselves that the experimenters considered "appropriate": nineteen girls chose the doll and fifteen boys chose the truck. Two girls and one boy chose the book, two boys chose the tie, and one 3-year-old boy chose a pair of boots he saw lying in a corner of the testing room and refused to make a second choice. None of the girls chose the truck or the necktie; none of the boys chose the doll or the stockings. (These choices would have been inappropriate, according to the experimenters.)

When the children's choices for other people were tallied, some selections were what the experimenters judged to be inappropriate for the recipient's age or sex (see Table 10.1). Six of the ten 3-year-olds made "most inappropriate" choices, but none of the older children did. Only one of the 3-year-olds made "completely appropriate" choices for everyone, but all the 6-year-olds did.

TABLE 10.1 **"It's the Thought That Counts"**

Age	Most Inappropriate*	Somewhat Inappropriate†	Completely Appropriate‡
3 years	6	3	1
4 years	0	7	1
5 years	0	5	5
6 years	0	0	10

*"Most inappropriate" choices were a truck for the mother or a doll for the father.
†"Somewhat inappropriate" choices were a truck for the father or a doll for the mother, an adult gift for a sibling, or a child's gift for a teacher.
‡"Completely appropriate" choices were gifts deemed suitable for both the age and sex of the recipient.

These results show that preschool children gradually become able to imagine what kind of present someone else would want, even if it is not what they would choose for themselves. This decentration is evidence of declining egocentrism. (The experiment also demonstrates attitudes in children and in psychologists about "appropriate" sex roles, a topic discussed in Chapter 11.)

It Depends on the Situation Piaget's three-mountains experiment has been criticized as being too difficult because it requires children to imagine various spatial perspectives in addition to adopting another point of view. On the other hand, asking children to choose an appropriate present for Daddy, and giving them credit for some social understanding as long as they don't choose a doll, might be too easy. It is apparent that how well a child understands another point of view depends on the specific situation, as well as on the child's cognitive maturity.

General Conclusions When all the research is considered, it appears that social understanding grows and egocentrism declines throughout the preschool years, although most 6-year-olds have trouble with the more complex tests of understanding another point of view (Shantz, 1975). At age 7 or 8, there is often noticeable improvement. Of course, as we know from our daily experience, just because someone *can* understand another point of view doesn't mean that he or she always *will* understand it, a truism for adults as well as for children.

In considering all the examples of cognitive development during early childhood, we must take care neither to overestimate nor to underestimate how much children understand. Before Piaget's research, few adults realized that preschool children are so illogical and egocentric. Now we need to avoid the opposite mistake of assuming that 4-year-olds can never think logically or understand someone else's viewpoint.

As we will see, language development during these years follows a pattern similar to that of the development of logic. On the one hand, it is astonishing how easily children learn words and grammar. At the same time, several aspects of language are very difficult for young children, because their cognitive immaturity makes some words and grammatical forms hard to understand.

Figure 10.5 *These recipes (from* Smashed Potatoes, *edited by Jane Martel) show many characteristics of preschool thought, among them literal interpretation of words ("Sometimes you can call it a bird, but it's not") and an uncertain idea of time ("Cook them for plenty of time") and quantity ("A giant lump of stuffin' ").*

A whole turkey

1 big bag full of a whole turkey
  (Get the kind with no feathers on
  not the kind the Pilgrims ate.)
A giant lump of stuffin'
1 squash pie
1 mint pie
1 little fancy dish of sour berries
1 big fancy dish of a vegetable mix
20 dishes of all different candies; chocolate balls,
  cherry balls, good'n plenties and peanuts

Get up when the alarm says to and get busy fast. Unfold the turkey and open up the holes. Push in the stuffin' for a couple hours. I think you get stuffin' from that Farm that makes it.

I know you have to pin the stuffin' to the turkey or I suppose it would get out. And get special pins or use big long nails.

Get the kitchen real hot, and from there on you just cook turkey. Sometimes you can call it a bird, but it's not.

Then you put the vegetables in the cooker—and first put one on top, and next put one on the bottom, and then one in the middle. That makes a vegetable mix. Put 2 red things of salt all in it and 2 red things of water also. Cook them to just ½ of warm.

Put candies all around the place and Linda will bring over the pies.

When the company comes put on your red apron.

Chops

Some chops that are enough to fill up your pan
Fresh salt and pepper
Fresh flour
1 ball of salad lettuce
1 sponge cake with ice cream

Put the chops in the bag and shake them for 5 hours—and the flour too.

Put them in a skillet pan on the biggest black circle on the roof of your stove. Cook them for plenty of time.

Fringe up the lettuce in little heaps in all the bowls.

Go on the porch and bring the high chair and have your supper everybody!

Note: But stoves really is dangerous—and you shouldn't go
    near one till you get married.

Language Development

As adults, we are sufficiently accomplished in language use that we can adapt our speech to diverse listeners (old and young, male and female) in a range of situations (school, work, home) to express many functions (to persuade, inform, entertain, and criticize).

When did we learn these complex abilities? The language-learning process, which begins in the first days of life in the interaction between infants and care-givers, continues into old age. But the most rapid language learning occurs during the language explosion of the preschool years. By middle childhood, language skills have developed so well that psycholinguists are more surprised by what children do not seem able to communicate than by what they can. The child's ability, or lack of it, to use language as a tool for communication and thought is discussed at the end of this section. For the moment, we will consider the raw material of language itself, specifically the rules, words, and sounds that facilitate communication.

Vocabulary

In the beginning, vocabulary grows slowly. The first few words at 1 year are nor-mally followed by a few new words each month: the 18-month-old knows between three and fifty words, and the 24-month-old knows fifty words or more. From then on, as the child masters symbolic thought, vocabulary increases so rapidly that Smith (1926) found vocabulary between ages 2 and 4 doubling every six months. In other words, children between 2 and 4 learn several new words each day! Accord-ing to Carey (1977), the average 6-year-old knows between 8000 and 14,000 words.

Some children seem to understand and use almost any specific term they hear: they have the ability to use correctly words and phrases that most high-school students do not even know, "bamboozle," "biodegradable," and "sibling rivalry," among them. Very few 6-year-olds actually know these words, because few adults use them when talking to young children. But if a 6-year-old hears, say, "sibling rivalry," and someone explains it as "brothers or sisters fighting about something they both want," the child can report accurately, "There's a lot of sibling rivalry at my house."

Another, less charming, kind of "advanced" language usage is seen in the child who comes home spouting profanity picked up from neighborhood children. Any words that shock adults are exciting to a child, so an angelic 3-year-old who has seen the look this new vocabulary produces in Mom may rush off to try it on Grandma too. Whispering and giggling about feces and urine seems to hold par-ticular delight for preschool children.

Limitations of Vocabulary Despite the young child's ability to learn new words more rapidly than at any other age, vocabulary is limited in several ways by the child's preoperational thought processes. Egocentric thinking enables children to create a word (for instance, anything squishy may be "fufula"; buttocks, "plumps"; a pair of stockings, "stocks") and expect others to understand. At the same time, the definition of some words expands and contracts for reasons that are not always apparent. For many 2-year-olds, "daddy" can refer to any man, or any man with a moustache, or only to their own father, depending on how they want to define the word at that moment (Thompson and Chapman, 1977) .

The world is so
you have something
to stand on

Little stones are for little children
to gather up and put in little piles

A hole is to dig

When preschool children define words, they usually think about actions a child could do, and come up with egocentric definitions such as "A hole is to dig." Because preschool children emphasize action and specific objects, their vocabulary consists mainly of verbs and concrete nouns, with very few abstract nouns such as "justice," "economy," "government."

Another vocabulary limitation results from the fact that young children, through a kind of verbal centering, tend to believe everything literally: if a word means one thing, it cannot mean another. When a mother, exasperated by her son's continual inability to find his belongings, told him that someday he would lose his head, he calmly replied: "I'll never lose my head. I'll find it and pick it up." Another child laughed when his grandmother said winter was coming soon. "Do you mean that winter has legs, and is walking here?" (Chukovsky, 1968). Before age 6, children understand that a light can be bright, or a rock, hard, or ice cream cold, but they are too literal-minded to understand why an intelligent child is called "bright," a stern grandparent, "hard," or an unfriendly neighbor, "cold" (Asch and Nerlove, 1960).

Finally, words expressing a comparison, such as "tall" and "short," "near" and "far," and "deep" and "shallow," are hard for children to use correctly (de Villiers and de Villiers, 1978). Once they know which end of the swimming pool is the deep one, they might obey instructions to stay out of deep puddles by splashing through every puddle they see, insisting that none of them are deep. Many 4-year-olds get angry at being called little, even in comparison to an adult: to them, babies are little; they themselves are big.

Grammar

Grammar includes the techniques, such as word order and word form, that languages use to communicate meaning. Dan Slobin (1974) says that "grammar lies between the speech sounds you hear or say and the meanings you connect with them."

If you think of grammar as what you studied in school about forming the subjunctive and choosing between "whoever" and "whomever," you might not believe that toddlers use grammar. However, basic, everyday grammar, such as putting the subject before the verb, is apparent in the first two-word sentences a child utters. Some psychologists see a primitive grammar even in one-word utterances.

By age 3, children demonstrate extensive grammatical knowledge. They can form the plural of nouns, the past, present, and future of verbs, and the subjective, objective, and possessive forms of pronouns. Most children speaking the same language master the grammar forms in the same sequence. When Roger Brown (1973) studied the language development of three children, Adam, Eve, and Sarah, in great detail, he found that they all could add "-ing" to verbs, use the prepositions "in" and "on," and form the plural by adding "s" before they could form the past or future tense. Jill and Peter de Villiers (1973) found the same sequence when they studied speech progression in a larger cross section of English-speaking children.

Of course, preschoolers do not know *why* the different grammatical forms are used. Neither do most adults, who cannot explain the various forms of the first-person singular pronoun, but can say, "That is *my* book. *I* bought it *myself*. It is *mine*, so give it to *me*." This impressive capacity of the young child to discover and apply the rules of grammar can create trouble when they are learning a language such as English that has many exceptions for many rules.

Overregularization   Bright preschoolers apply the rules of grammar even when they shouldn't. This tendency is called overregularization, because children make the language more regular than it actually is. For example, many 2-year-olds, who are still learning new words one by one, use irregular verbs correctly: "came" for the past tense of "come," "went" for the past tense of "go." They are simply repeating what they have heard. But when they are older and wiser about the rules of forming the past tense, they talk about people who "comed" and "goed."

Once preschool children learn a rule, they can be surprisingly stubborn in applying it. Jean Berko Gleason reports the following conversation with a 4-year-old:

> She said: "My teacher *holded* the baby rabbits and we *patted* them." I asked: "Did you say your teacher *held* the baby rabbits?" She answered: "Yes." I then asked: "What did you say she did?" She answered again: "She *holded* the baby rabbits and we *patted* them." "Did you say she *held* them tightly?" I asked. "No," she answered, "she *holded* them loosely." [Gleason, 1967]

Although technically wrong, such overregularization is actually a sign of verbal sophistication, since children are applying rules of grammar. After children hear the correct form often enough, they spontaneously correct their own speech, so parents can probably best help development of grammar by example rather than explanation or criticism.

Overregularization hinders children's comprehension, as well as production, of language. In English, the normal word order is subject-verb-object, an order children follow in their earliest sentences as they say, "Mommy give juice," or, "I want ball." But preschool children have great difficulty understanding the passive voice, in which the order is reversed. When they hear, "The truck was bumped by the car," they think the truck did the bumping.

They also think sentence order is a clue to time sequence (de Villiers and de Villiers, 1979). When they hear, "You can go outside after you pick up your toys," they think they can play first and pick up later; and they might eat without washing up if they hear, "Before you eat your cookie, you must wash your hands."

Mean Length of Utterance   Both vocabulary and grammar show the growing language ability of the child. One way to measure this ability is to calculate the average number of morphemes a child uses per sentence. (A morpheme is the smallest meaningful unit of speech.) This measure is called mean length of utterance (MLU). Brown (1973) believes that MLU is the best measure of a child's verbal sophistication, because MLU reflects both vocabulary and grammar. Most 2-year-olds average two or three morphemes per sentence; 3-year-olds average between three and four morphemes.

One reason MLU is a useful measure of grammatical sophistication is that the longer the sentence, the more likely it is to employ grammatical constructions and complex phrases which are difficult to learn. During the preschool years many conjunctions, including "because," "then," "therefore," and "although," are poorly understood (Piaget, 1959). For instance, children younger than 7 might say, "I love you because I am kissing you."

Articulation

A child's ability to articulate words clearly and correctly often lags behind the child's vocabulary and grammar (McCarthy, 1954). In order to understand what preschool children are trying to say, it is helpful to know that pronunciation during these years follows orderly patterns.

One common pattern is to simplify words beginning with a double consonant. Some children do this by dropping the first consonant. "Poon" is "spoon," "mack" is "smack." Others prefer to replace both with another sound, so "truck" and "train" become "guck" and "gain." Another pattern is to make all the consonants in a word the same, so "doggie" becomes "goggy" or "doddie."

Children also prefer to have voiced consonants such as "b," "d," and "g," which are formed without expelling much breath, at the beginning of words, and unvoiced consonants, such as "p," "t," and "k," at the end of words. Thus, they may make "toe" "doe," "pop," "bop," and "dog," "dok" (de Villiers and de Villiers, 1979). These preferences do not necessarily mean the child cannot form certain sounds. One linguist's son always replaced "th" with "f," so "thick" became "fick." At the same stage, he replaced "s" with "th," so "sick" became "thick" (Smith, 1973).

Once parents and teachers understand a child's preferences, they can figure out what the child is saying, despite the odd pronunciation. Correcting or teasing the child, or withholding something until the child uses the right pronunciation, not only is unhelpful but might make the problem worse. This is certainly the case with stuttering, a problem many preschoolers have to some extent.

The way adults *can* make it easier for children with articulation difficulties is to teach them to talk more slowly and to find alternate ways of saying something when they find they are not being understood. Most children with articulation problems outgrow them by elementary school, although some sounds (especially "l" and "th") still give many 7-year-olds difficulty. If a 4- or 5-year-old still has trouble making himself or herself understood, a speech therapist should be consulted. At this age many children are able to do exercises and practice sound combinations that will help their speech.

A Critical Period?

A male finch sings an elaborate song to attract a female finch and to tell other finches that a particular territory is his. In order to produce the song correctly, he must hear other finches sing it before he reaches puberty. If he doesn't, the song he instinctively develops in adulthood will not have the necessary characteristics to help him find a mate or stake out his territory. Similar instances occur throughout the animal world.

Is there a similar critical period for people? Eric Lenneberg (1970) believes so. He thinks that the years before puberty, especially the preschool years, are the critical time for learning language. The ear, brain, and voice are primed for learning language, ready to absorb it like a sponge if someone provides the proper input. Evidence to support this hypothesis comes from the fact that child victims of damage to the speech area of the brain can relearn language much better than adults who suffer the same damage. In addition, when children and their parents move to a community where another language is spoken, the children usually learn this second language with much less effort than their parents. Chances are, the adults will never speak the new language without a foreign accent. In this situation, the children often become their parents' interpreters.

However, there is evidence refuting the theory of a critical period. Some adult victims of brain damage do learn to speak again using the other hemisphere of their brains; and adults do learn new languages, sometimes mastering half a dozen or more distinct tongues. The fact that their accent is imperfect is a minor problem which pales next to this accomplishment. But the real test of the critical-period hypothesis is not adults' recovering from brain damage or the learning of a second language. The crucial question is whether a person can learn a first language after puberty. There is no way to answer this question experimentally, for we cannot temporarily deafen children as ethologists did with baby finches.

But a girl named Genie, who was born in California in 1957, has provided some answers. Genie's father hated children; her mother was terrified of him and virtually blind. For the first twenty months of her life, Genie was underfed and ignored most of the time. Then the real abuse began. As Susan Curtiss (1977) describes it:

> . . . Genie was confined to a small bedroom, harnessed to an infant's potty seat . . . Unclad, except for the harness, Genie was left . . . to sit, tied up, hour after hour, often into the night, day after day, month after month, year after year. At night when Genie was not forgotten, she was removed from her harness only to be placed in another restraining garment—a sleeping bag which her father fashioned to hold Genie's arms stationary . . . Therein constrained, Genie was put into an infant's crib with wire mesh sides and a wire mesh cover overhead. Caged by night, harnessed by day, Genie was left to somehow endure the hours and years of her life.

Not only did no one speak to her, but she was beaten whenever she made a sound. Her father treated her as if he were a wild dog, baring his teeth, barking and growling, and scratching her with his nails.

When she was rescued, Genie could not talk or even stand up straight. She was 13½ years old and weighed 59 pounds. Since she was long past the age when children learn to talk, move, and relate to people, most psychologists would have predicted a grim future for her, devoid of language and normal social interaction.

But Genie has surprised the psychological community. After six years, first in a hospital and then with a foster family, Genie can talk in sentences, move around her neighborhood, and take a bus to school. She expresses normal emotions, including affection for her new care-givers, and has been able to communicate some of her memories of her terrible childhood.

Genie's progress proves that language can develop after puberty. (One interesting part of her language production is that she followed many of the same sequences, and made some of the same errors, that preschool children do. She dropped the "s" before words like "spoon" and "stop," and used the word "no" at the beginning of a sentence to make positive statements negative, as in "No take me home" and "No want to eat breakfast.")

However, her speech is still far from normal. She does not use personal pronouns or the words "this" and "that"; she rarely uses auxiliary verbs (as in "I *have* eaten," or "I *was* jumping"); and she has problems with articulation. The fact that these errors persist implies that her early language deprivation, coupled with abuse and malnutrition, has permanently restricted her language-learning capacity. Although early childhood is not the only time a person can learn language, it certainly is the best time.

Now that we have described the acquisition of the sounds, words, and rules that make up language, it is time to examine how these pieces fit together to help the child communicate and think.

Conversation Skills

Inasmuch as the chief function of language is communication with others, children have a lot to learn about language, despite their impressive vocabulary and grammar. In one of his studies Piaget (1959) found that about half the statements made by preschool children were egocentric, in that the children did not even try to consider the viewpoint of anyone else. Some of this egocentric speech was a simple monologue, in which children talked to themselves or to other people without waiting for a response.

Figure 10.6 *Egocentric speech includes talking to oneself, talking to someone else without considering his or her role or interest in the conversation, or talking to a doll, as this little girl is doing. Nevertheless, egocentric speech occurs more often in a social context than in isolation. In other words, preschool children talk more to themselves or to their doll when someone else is within earshot.*

Another form of egocentric speech, the collective monologue, occurs when two children have a conversation but neither one listens or responds to what the other says. Here is a collective monologue between two 4-year-olds, enjoying their togetherness and politely taking turns at speaking:

> Jenny: They wiggle sideways when they kiss.
> Chris: *(Vaguely) What?*
> My bunny slippers. They are brown and red and sort of yellow and white. And they have eyes and ears and these noses that wiggle sideways when they kiss.
> *I have a piece of sugar in a red piece of paper. I'm gonna eat it but maybe it's for a horse.*
> We bought them. My mommy did. We couldn't find the old ones. These are like the old ones. They were not in the trunk.
> *Can't eat the piece of sugar, not unless you take the paper off.*
> And we found Mother Lamb. Oh, she was in Poughkeepsie in the trunk in the house in the woods where Mrs. Tiddywinkle lives.
> *Do you like sugar? I do, and so do horses.*
> I play with my bunnies. They are real. We play in the woods. They have eyes. We *all* go in the woods. My teddy bear and the bunnies and the duck, to visit Mrs. Tiddywinkle. We play and play.
> *I guess I'll eat my sugar at lunch time. I can get more for the horses. Besides, I don't have no horses now.*

According to the nursery-school teacher who reported this conversation, neither child seemed even aware, let alone upset, that the other child was not responding to the same topic (Stone and Church, 1973).

Piaget calls the other half of the preschool child's statements socialized speech, which he defines as conversation in which two or more people make at least three statements about the same topic. Even in socialized speech, preschool children often lack communication skills. Their dialogue is sometimes an argument, with each child insisting on his or her point of view. Here, for instance, are two 3-year-olds, Ruth and Hans, discussing railroads in heaven:

> Hans: Ruth, look, up there is the railway that goes to heaven.
> Ruth: *No, there aren't any railways up there.*
> But there are railway lines.
> *No, there aren't any railway lines up there. There are no railway lines in heaven. God doesn't need any railway lines.*
> Yes, he does.
> *No, God doesn't need any railway lines nor any trains.*
> But there must be a railway line for a train. [Piaget, 1959]

Much to the exasperation of their parents, the socialized speech of preschool children often consists of their asking a question, getting an answer, and then refusing to accept the answer. Preschool children also do not realize when they must explain something to another person (Flavell, 1975). A child might say, "Remember the dog?" to someone who never saw the dog. Or, "I want my toy," without specifying which toy is wanted. That the child does not realize the incompleteness of the request is indicated by the child's becoming angry and upset if someone fetches the wrong toy.

In fact, the distinction between egocentric speech and socialized speech is somewhat arbitrary. In their investigation of communication skills in young children, Spilton and Lee (1977) invited pairs of 4-year-olds, who were strangers to each other, to play in a well-equipped playroom. Whenever one child said something and the other child asked for clarification, the researchers noted if the response was adaptive (providing additional information) or nonadaptive (repeating the same words, or saying something irrelevant). The 4-year-olds did quite well: 66 percent of their responses were adaptive. But even the adaptive responses showed egocentric thinking as well as socialized speech. Consider this dialogue between Kathy and Morgan. (In the preceding playtime, neither has mentioned or played with a sink, bathroom, or kitchen.)

> Kathy: A sink too.
> Morgan: *What?*
> There's a sink and a bathroom.
> *What?*
> There's a sink here and a bathroom in case you want to go.
> *What?*
> There's a bathroom and two sinks so you and me can wash.

Despite the fact that all her responses were adaptive, Kathy could not get Morgan interested in sinks or bathrooms. At the end of this interchange, he wandered off.

Although Kathy and Morgan still have a lot to learn about conversation and communication, Morgan did persist in asking "What?" when he didn't understand, and Kathy finally explained herself with a complex twelve-word sentence that contained only one grammatical mistake. If Morgan had said, "Oh, that's nice," before he wandered off, and if Kathy had started her conversation with something less cryptic than "A sink too," this dialogue between 4-year-olds would have sounded almost like adult conversation. At every age, the art of conversation is difficult. Gertrude Stein said that there are no conversations, only intersecting monologues—and she had adults in mind.

Thought and Language

How are thought and language related? Does the child first get an idea and then try to find words to express it, or does the child's language ability enable the child to think new thoughts? Are 6-year-olds more likely to know what they mean than they are how to say it? Do they talk to themselves in order to figure out what they think? The answers to these questions have practical implications for anyone who wants to encourage cognitive development.

Piaget believes that cognitive development comes first, making language development possible. In one experiment (1976), he asked children to crawl, and then to describe what they did. Even the 3-year-olds could crawl without hesitation, but not until age 5 or 6 could any of the children describe what they did when they crawled. Most of them mistakenly said they moved both hands together and then both knees, or the right hand with the right foot and then the left hand with the left foot. Even adults sometimes have difficulty with this task. Piaget points out that, at least in this case, having the necessary motor skills and vocabulary does not mean a child has the necessary cognitive ability to understand and explain what he or she has done.

Jerome Bruner (1964) disagrees with Piaget. He thinks that by kindergarten, language ability affects almost every aspect of a child's thought and behavior, and that language becomes a "means, not only for representing experience, but also for transforming it." In stressing the impact of language this way, Bruner is echoing an idea expressed fifty years ago by the Russian psychologist Lev Vygotsky (English edition, 1962). Vygotsky thought that beginning with symbolic thinking, about age 2, cognitive development and language development become interrelated, the progress of one thereafter affecting the progress of the other.

Most psychologists agree with Piaget that very young children form concepts first and then find words to express them. But many psychologists also agree with Bruner and Vygotsky, believing that, at some point during early childhood, language helps form ideas. In Lois Bloom's (1975) words: "There is a developmental shift between learning to talk and talking to learn." According to some evidence, this shift occurs at about age 4 or 5.

Words and Deeds   The temporal relationship between action and language during early childhood lends support to the idea of a developmental shift. When children first learn to speak, talking is often an afterthought. A little boy might put on his pants and then say, "Put on pants." Gradually, children talk to themselves more and more while they are doing something, saying, for example, "Up and down, up and down," while they swing. Finally, children use language to describe what they are going to do.

These three stages were shown when children aged 3 to 6 were asked to draw pictures. The 3-year-olds were usually silent throughout the drawing process, apparently not using words to help them work. The 4- and 5-year-olds sometimes talked about what they were creating *while* they were drawing ("... a head, now legs, now eyes, now a hat") or announced the theme of the drawing *after* they had finished. However, by age 6, most children announced what they were going to draw *before* they began to work (Zaporozhets and Elkonin, 1971).

Inner Speech   When language becomes a way of formulating ideas to oneself, it is called inner speech, to distinguish it from normal speech that is used to communicate ideas to another person. Inner speech does not necessarily mean silent speech. Children often begin inner speech by talking to themselves out loud; next they whisper; and then they silently mouth the words they are thinking. Finally, they form the words in their heads as adults do, without giving any visible or audible clues that they are talking to themselves.

Psychologists see many important uses for inner speech. Bruner (1964) says that it helps children delay gratification. Six-year-olds are better able to wait until after dinner for dessert, or to finish three arithmetic problems before recess, because they can tell themselves what the reward will be. In addition, increased use of inner speech enhances memory as children grow older (Flavell, 1970).

According to a theory first expressed by A. R. Luria (1961), who was one of Vygotsky's students, inner speech becomes a mediator between thought and action, a "go-between" that enables children to think before doing. This idea, called the verbal mediation theory (Kendler, 1970; Kohlberg et al., 1968), is illustrated by children crossing the street at a traffic light. A 4-year-old can tell herself to wait for the green light, and then follow her own command. By age 6, she might use words to regulate her progress. If she were part way across the street when the light turns red, she could tell herself to "hurry, hurry, hurry" to the other side, or to "go back and try again." Many children's games that are popular at about age 6 seem to be based on this new ability to relate words to actions. "Simon says" and "red light, green light" are two examples.

Children can be taught to put inner speech to practical use. Practicing simple self-commands is especially helpful for impulsive children, who do not usually think before they act. Simply teaching them to say "Stop and think" helps them become more reflective (Meichenbaum and Goodman, 1971). Children who have

Figure 10.7 *Actions and words become more closely related during preschool years. Games and songs that link words and deeds, such as "Put your hands up to the sky, very high," demand concentration, as shown by the facial expressions of these children.*

trouble going to sleep can be taught to tell their toes, then feet, then legs, and so on, to relax. A child who forgets to bring the necessary books to school can be taught a simple rhyme that lists them.

Are there any other practical implications of language development? If language is the foundation of many cognitive abilities, then fostering its development should be a major emphasis during early childhood. On the other hand, if Piaget is right, and language follows rather than precedes the development of logical concepts, then teaching language skills is of secondary importance. Most American educators take the former view.

Teaching and Learning

As we have outlined, during early childhood, logic emerges, egocentricity declines, vocabulary multiplies, and sentences lengthen. These developments seem self-evident now, but thirty years ago most psychologists were unaware of the learning potential of the young child. Whatever cognitive growth people noticed was attributed to maturation rather than learning. For this reason, parents, teachers, and psychologists paid little attention to education before first grade.

However, once psychologists concentrated their attention on the cognitive accomplishments of young children, they were impressed with what they saw. They asked themselves the next logical question: Can preschool children be taught? Should they be given instruction? Or do all normal children learn as much as they can on their own, regardless of their home and community environment?

Similarities and Differences in Cognitive Development

It is clear that all young children show similarities in their cognitive development. They are all egocentric and illogical, but gradually become less so as they grow older. They all learn language rapidly, following the same sequence from nouns and verbs to adjectives and adverbs. They all have certain difficulties with conversation skills.

These similarities led some developmental psychologists to think that cognitive development during early childhood is regulated primarily by internal forces—genes, maturation, and the child's own natural curiosity. This idea was supported by the failure of most attempts to teach a child logical concepts or grammatical forms before a certain level of development. In addition, some studies show that children who are "pushed" to learn faster actually learn slower if their parents don't show enough warmth and acceptance of their children as they are. In fact, children with affectionate, encouraging parents score higher on IQ tests than children with critical parents who always want them to do better (Moss and Kagan, 1958; Radin 1971; Radin and Epstein, 1976).

However, there is another possible interpretation to all this: Perhaps psychologists trying to teach specific skills, or parents trying to speed up their children's learning, are simply going about it incorrectly. While it is true that there are many similarities in the cognitive development of all children, there are also many differences.

For instance, Piaget's studies have always found that children develop logical abilities at different ages, a finding confirmed by cross-cultural research. The sequence of stages remains the same, but one child might understand at age 4 what still puzzles another at age 6. The children between 2 and 4 years old studied by Denney (1972) in the 1970s were classifying shapes as well as the children between 5 and 7 studied by Piaget in the 1950s. Language skills also vary from child to child, with some 5-year-olds knowing twice as many words as others do. One of Roger Brown's three subjects spoke in complex sentences at age 2, an accomplishment usually not reached until age 4 (Brown, 1973).

As with any other aspect of development, whenever psychologists find marked differences like these between children the same age, they look to the interaction of heredity with many factors—early health care, family, culture, and schooling among them—for the explanation.

Home and Learning

Many psychologists feel that the young child's experiences at home are by far the most important influence on learning. Others think that the significance of the specific teaching done by parents during early childhood has been exaggerated. Especially by age 3 or 4, they contend, the characteristics of the child or of the community are much more influential than what the parents do or do not do. Let us look at one aspect of cognitive development, language, to show why home influences are controversial.

Language Differences Many researchers have discovered patterns of language differences that have appeared in many cultures over several generations: among them, girls are usually more verbal than boys; middle-class children are more verbal than lower-class children; first-borns are more verbal than later-borns; single-born children are more verbal than twins, who, in turn, are more verbal than triplets (Rebelsky et al., 1967).

Psychologists who try to explain these differences usually examine the children's parents. Some studies show that mothers talk more to daughters than to sons (Goldberg and Lewis, 1969; Cherry and Lewis, 1976); that middle-class parents provide their children with more elaborate explanations, more responsive comments, and fewer commands than lower-class parents (Hess and Shipman, 1965;

Figure 10.8 *Some research indicates that little girls talk earlier and communicate more often than little boys, who are said to spend more of their time in rough-and-tumble play than in play that involves conversation, such as talking to a friend on a toy telephone. Recently, several psychologists have questioned this conclusion, claiming that there are so many individual variations, as well as so many reasons for these variations, that the generalization "females are more verbal than males" is misleading, and perhaps mistaken.*

Zegiob and Forehand, 1975); and that parents talk more to first-borns and single-borns than to later-borns or twins (Jacobs and Moss, 1976; Lytton et al., 1977).

However, these data need to be considered in the light of other findings. Reviewing all the studies of sex differences in language, for instance, Maccoby and Jacklin (1974) found that many studies show no differences between girls and boys, either in ability or in the verbal stimulation they receive from their parents. Maccoby and Jacklin wonder if research that finds sex differences is published and quoted more often than research that finds no differences, thus creating a false impression.

Even if girls are more verbal, and even if parents do talk more to their daughters than to their sons, that fact does not prove that the parents' talking *causes* the girls' language skills. Maybe maturation of the language center of the brain occurs earlier in girls than boys, just as bone maturation does. If this is true, then girls talk more because their brains are more mature, and parents talk more to daughters because the daughters talk more to them, rather than the other way around.

Socioeconomic Differences. Class differences are even more controversial than sex differences. The evidence is quite clear, but the interpretation is not (Deutsch, 1973). Most researchers have found that lower-class children are less verbal than middle- or upper-class children. The lower language scores attained by lower-class children hold true whether class is measured by family income, residence, education, occupation, or a combination of these indexes. It is just as true within ethnic groups as among groups. For instance, middle-class black children have higher IQs and more extensive vocabularies than lower-class black children (Hess and Shipman, 1965).

Many psychologists have traced these class differences to the ways middle-class and lower-class mothers interact with their children. For example, Helen Bee and her colleagues (1969) compared lower- and middle-class mothers of 4-year-olds. (In this study, the lower-class mothers were, for the most part, below the poverty line set by the federal government; the middle-class mothers were associated with the University of Washington, either as students or staff.)

The researchers found that the lower-class children were less verbal and more impulsive, and that their mothers were less skilled in teaching them. Observation of mothers and children in the waiting room prior to the experiment revealed that the lower-class mothers made twice as many controlling and disapproving statements as the middle-class mothers did. During the experiment, when the children had to solve a problem with blocks, the middle-class mothers were more likely to praise and give suggestions ("Now where does this yellow one go?"); the lower-class mothers were more likely to disapprove and give nonverbal help (such as putting the block where it belonged).

The implication of this research is that middle-class children are more verbal and better at problem-solving because their mothers are better at interacting with them. If this implication is correct, then lower-class children would become more verbal if their mothers could talk to them more and criticize them less.

How Valid Is This Kind of Research?   Other psychologists criticize studies such as this one (Cazden, 1976; Tulkin and Konner, 1973). One of their criticisms is that the very design of most language-ability tests favors middle-class children who speak standard English and penalizes lower-class children. This is especially true when the lower-class children do not speak English as their first language, or speak the dialect known as Black English (see page 414) which has different grammatical rules than standard English (Labov, 1972).

A second criticism centers on the testing situation. As Alan Sroufe (1970) points out in a critique of Bee's research, lower-class mothers are more likely to be nervous in a testing room on a campus than are middle-class mothers who are already familiar with the university. In addition, when most of the testers are white, middle-class university students or staff, and most of the lower-class mothers are black, the lower-class mothers are likely to be nervous. This might make them more controlling and critical of their children than they ordinarily are and might even make the preschool children more likely to misbehave in the waiting room and become unusually nonverbal in the testing situation.

Psychologists have tried to respond to these two criticisms by changing the tests and the test conditions, but have had mixed results. Quay found that giving test instructions in Black English did not improve the test performance of disadvantaged black children on verbal or nonverbal test questions (Quay, 1972); and Scott found that black 2- and 3-year-olds performed as well for a white tester as for a black tester (Scott et al., 1976). Meanwhile, researchers comparing white middle-class mothers or black middle-class mothers with lower-class mothers from the same ethnic group continued to find the same differences in maternal style.

On the other hand, Zigler and his colleagues (1973) showed that economically disadvantaged children scored much better on a vocabulary test when they were familiar with the examiner and the format of the test, and when they felt relaxed. Testing children's language in a spontaneous play situation and in formal testing, Johnson (1974) found that in both conditions, lower-class children did as well as middle-class children when both groups had the same performance IQ (measured by nonverbal tests, such as putting puzzles together). And Cazden (1976) reports that the language of lower-class children becomes much more elaborate when they are personally involved with the topic.

There is a third criticism of all research such as this: that it looks for problems in the child and the home and ignores underlying problems of poverty and of prejudice and discrimination in the school, the culture, and the economy. Many social scientists and lower-class parents feel this is an interjection of middle-class bias (Sroufe, 1970; Tulkin and Konner, 1973).

Community and Learning

Children growing up in different cultures show marked differences in cognitive development as well as the similarities we have already described. One reason for these differences is that each culture emphasizes different tasks and varying rates of response (Goodnow, 1976). For instance, some cultures stress abstract skills and others stress manual skills; some cultures criticize their children for being "slow as molasses in January" and others are more likely to remind them that "haste makes waste."

One cross-cultural difference is that urban children learn to emphasize speed and language, whereas rural children emphasize carefulness and more concrete skills. Michael Maccoby and Nancy Modiano (1966) compared the cognitive styles demanded by various cultures and noted that they were "struck by how much more the Mexican city children are like children from the Boston suburbs than like children from the Mexican villages."

Community differences appear as well. In fact, children from one part of a town often do better in school and on IQ tests than children from another part of the same town. Unfortunately, it is hard to separate the effect of locale from the influence of genes, home, or income, because people with similar characteristics tend to live in the same community. It is not easy to decide if a little girl who lives in a slum does poorly in school because of her parents' education, her poverty, her mother's teaching style, or the deprivation of her neighborhood.

However, a study done in eastern Norway proved that neighborhood can have a significant impact. Marida Hollos and Philip Cowan (1973) compared three groups of children, all from low-income, two-parent families with an average of three children per family. Ethnic background, religion, and parents' education were the same for all three groups.

Neighborhood was the only difference among the three groups of children. One group lived on isolated farms and spent most of each day playing alone or watching their mother work, the parents and children rarely speaking to each other. The second group lived in a small town, playing with other children most of the time. The third group lived in a town that was not only larger than the second group's (though still small compared to the cities of southern Norway or North America) but was also an educational and cultural center. They played with other children, came into contact with strangers of various ages, and attended occasional cultural events.

Using conservation and classification tasks, the researchers tested each child's mastery of logical operations. They also measured how well each child could understand another point of view. Test performance was very similar for the children from the two towns. However, at age 7, the farm children scored much better at logical operations than their town contemporaries, but much worse at understanding another point of view. By age 9, the town children caught up to the farm children in logic, but the farm children were still low in understanding another's perspective.

Thus, it would seem that if in a particular neighborhood children are left to play by themselves and to observe their parents in a workaday environment, their thinking is likely to develop along lines of concrete logical operations. If, on the other hand, children in a particular neighborhood interact often with other children and adults outside of the family, they will be more adept at understanding points of view other than their own. They will, in other words, be more flexible and open-minded.

Preschools and Learning

Once research suggested that some young children learned less because they were "disadvantaged" by their home environment or "culturally deprived" by their community, many educators and psychologists proposed special preschool education that would compensate for these deficiencies and give such children a headstart in elementary school. In 1965, preschools across the nation hastily opened their doors to give such "impoverished" 4-year-olds cognitive stimulation as well as good care.

The first results from Project Headstart were encouraging (Horowitz and Paden, 1973). Children learned a variety of intellectual and social skills between September and June of their Headstart year, averaging a gain of 5 IQ points. By the end of the program, they had fewer behavior problems and greater motivation. Even children who attended Headstart classes for only a summer showed some gains.

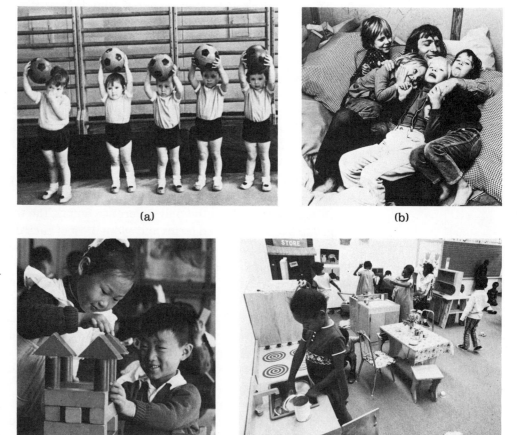

Figure 10.9 *Almost all preschools encourage the development of basic physical, cognitive, and social skills. However, each school also reflects the values of the culture, as these four photographs illustrate. (a) In the Soviet Union, physical education is stressed from an early age. Each child practices specific physical skills according to a curriculum that requires all the children to do the same activity at the same time. (b) In Sweden, equality of the sexes, physical affection, and emotional expression are among the values emphasized in day nurseries. (c) In China, structured activities that promote cooperation between one child and another are preferred. (d) Whereas in all three of these countries, preschool education is provided by the state, day care in North America is mostly private, and therefore characterized by greater variety. As in this instance, many classrooms are set up with various interest areas to allow the children to choose their own activities. The part of the room shown here is the center for playing house or store; other areas are for reading, science, and art work.*

(a)

(b)

(c)

(d)

However, the first analysis of long-term effects showed that the children who attended preschool lost their early advantage in a few years. By third grade, according to one large study, children who attended Headstart were indistinguishable from their "impoverished" peers who did not (Westinghouse Learning Corporation, 1969).

The most recent analyses are neither as encouraging as the first reports nor as discouraging as the early follow-up reports. Many of the social and cognitive gains that children receive from Headstart are imperceptible after a few years, but some programs do produce long-term differences (Horowitz and Paden, 1973). Children who participate are less likely to be kept back or placed in special classes, and they score higher on achievement tests and school report cards (Zigler, 1973).

The Headstart programs that are the most successful usually emphasize cognitive development and language skills and are staffed by teachers who try to make sure the curriculum is neither too easy nor too hard. For long-term changes, parent involvement in the program is often the determining factor (Palmer, 1977).

Interaction of Child, Home, Community, and School

In retrospect, the idea that a summer or a year of Headstart would transform the intellectual future of a child was naive, We now believe cognitive development includes many more skills and develops over a much longer time period than we once thought, so few developmental psychologists today would expect that the effects of years of deprivation could be remedied by a single preschool program.

Psychologists are still not sure precisely how much difference a year of preschool can make, or which programs are best. They suspect that some of the changes in the child may be subject to a *sleeper effect*; that is, they may not become apparent until several years later, toward the end of elementary school. At this point, children who attended preschool have lower rates of school failure and are less likely to be placed in remedial classes (Brown, 1979). As the research report on page 330 shows, the relationship among preschool education, teacher characteristics, home environment, and future schooling is so complex that the degree of influence of any single factor is difficult to determine.

Psychologists no longer think that nursery school is the keystone of future cognitive development. It is one of the building blocks, but not the most important one, for home and community influences are also important, not just at age 4, but beginning at birth. Indeed, the most successful efforts to raise intellectual achievement during early childhood tap the resources of home, community, and specific educational programs. Consider two of these attempts.

Toy Demonstrators   In one program, mothers are visited at home twice a week for two years, when their children are between 24 and 28 months old (Levenstein, 1970). The visitor is called a "toy demonstrator," because she brings a toy or book as a gift each time and shows the mother how to play cognitive games with her child, especially games that stress language.

Children regularly involved in the toy demonstrations have shown gains in cognitive skills that are still evident in the third grade. In the first years of this program, the visitors were professionals (social workers or psychologists). In later years, people from the community were trained to visit other families; some of the original mothers joined the project as toy demonstrators themselves. Follow-up studies show that many nonprofessionals taught the mothers and fostered learning in the children as well as the professionals did (Levenstein et al., 1973; Madden et al., 1976).

This project is remarkable for its simplicity and success. That a relatively small effort by professionals, community people, and parents affected the cognitive growth of the children is encouraging. It suggests that most parents could make a difference in their child's future schoolwork simply by spending some time each day reading books to, and playing with, their young children, particularly in ways that encourage them to explore, use their imagination, and communicate.

A Comparison of Preschools

Setting up their research with great care, Louise Miller and Jean Dyer (1975) attempted to compare the achievement of children who attended four types of preschools with children who attended no preschool. They randomly assigned an experimental group of 214 children to one or another of fourteen experimental classes. The control group of 34 children lived in the same neighborhoods but did not attend preschool. Most of them were on the waiting list for Headstart. The fourteen experimental classes all had about the same number of children, a teacher, and an aide, and all the programs lasted for a school day, from 9 A.M. to 3:30 P.M. The only difference among them pertained to educational philosophy and practice. Four types of preschools were represented:

1. *Bereiter-Englemann.*   Two behaviorists designed this program especially for disadvantaged children, who need to learn basic concepts and behavior patterns. The atmosphere of the school is "business-like and task oriented." The curriculum is carefully structured, with workbooks and small-group instruction and drill in language, reading, and arithmetic skills and ideas. Toys are limited (for instance, crayons are allowed but paint isn't), so the children will not be distracted by too many stimuli. The children are frequently given positive reinforcement, especially praise, for specific accomplishments such as trying, working hard, and getting the right answer. They are also always told when they make a mistake.

2. *Darcee.*   This program was developed at George Peabody College in Tennessee, where it was called the Early Training Project. It includes formal instruction with small groups of children, who learn to understand and work with various stimuli and a wide range of materials. Language skills are emphasized, especially how to listen carefully and say precisely what one means. The children are encouraged to develop good work habits and attitudes, among them, persistence, concentration, delay of gratification, and the desire to achieve. A special feature of this program that recognizes the importance of the parents' role in helping children learn is that teachers consult with parents in the home.

3. *Montessori.*   This program was developed by Maria Montessori seventy years ago for the slum children of Italy. The curriculum stresses individual work in exploring the senses and in academic skills, with materials especially

Montessori materials are designed to help the child see and correct his or her mistakes as well as to provide visual and tactile stimulation, as this letter board does. Each time this child tries to fit a letter into the board, she will immediately discover if she has placed it correctly.

designed for self-education. Since children are seen as curious and competent, teachers need provide only learning opportunities and materials, not motivation or reinforcement.

4. *Traditional Headstart.*   In traditional Headstart programs, children spend most of the day in free play in an enriched environment, with many toys—building blocks, dress-up materials, books, beads, tricycles, trucks, puzzles, paints, animals, fish—enabling them to develop creativity and skills at their own pace. The curriculum is determined by the individual desires and needs of each child, although language growth, especially in conversation, is a goal strived for with all the children. Teachers are told to be warm and affectionate, establishing a relationship that will make the children want to behave as the teacher does.

The research design called for many measures of change in the children, including tests of intelligence, language skills, and curiosity, and measures of ambition, social interaction, and aggression. The children were tested in October and

The Milwaukee Project   The second project is remarkable for its intensity. Focusing on the black ghetto of Milwaukee, Rick Heber began his program with newborns who would probably become mentally retarded unless something were done. Giving IQ tests to mothers of newborns, he found forty women with scores below 75 (the mentally retarded range). Half of the mother-infant pairs in this group were

June of the Headstart year, and again in kindergarten, first grade, and second grade. The researchers also obtained the children's scores on the standard elementary-school tests of achievement.

Results

Children at each of the four types of schools showed gains in all cognitive and noncognitive skills during the preschool year. They gained especially in the skills emphasized by each curriculum. For instance, those in the Bereiter-Englemann school were highest on language and math skills; those in the Montessori school were highest in inventiveness and curiosity.

But these gains became less apparent during kindergarten, and by second grade, the children who attended preschool scored no better, and sometimes worse, on all the tests of cognitive skills. The scores on the Stanford-Binet Intelligence Test show this decline:

	B-E	Darcee	Montessori	Traditional	Controls
Prekindergarten	98	97	97	96	91
Second grade	87	91	93	90	93

The experimental children maintained their advantage over the controls on several of the noncognitive skills, however. In second grade, they were more curious, ambitious, and social, as well as less aggressive, than the children who had not attended preschool.

Conclusions

These results make it *seem* that:

1. Cognitive gains that result from preschool education are likely to fade when the children begin elementary school, although improvement in noncognitive skills may be more lasting.

2. Those programs that emphasize academic skills most, such as the Bereiter-Englemann, are most likely to produce only temporary gains, whereas programs that emphasize curiosity and self-motivation, such as the Montessori program, will show the greatest long-term gains.

However, neither of these conclusions is definitive. Although the researchers tried to design a perfect study, they encountered two problems that cast doubt on these two conclusions. The first problem was that only two Montessori teachers could be found for the study, and they were different from the other teachers in several ways. They were younger (by twelve years, on average), better educated, and less experienced. They also were both white, while only two of the other twelve teachers were. Any or all of these differences *could* have caused the Montessori children to respond a little differently to preschool or elementary school.

The second problem was that the control children, even though they came from the same neighborhoods as the experimental children, turned out to be more advantaged than the children who attended the preschools. A significantly higher percentage of the control children lived with both parents, and one out of four of the control children was white, compared to only one out of twenty among the experimental children. In addition, the parents of the control children were more than a year older, on average, than the parents of the experimental children, and their family income was slightly higher. All of these differences would have favored the control children, so their higher achievement at second grade should come as no surprise. The crucial question, that is, how the experimental children would have done in second grade without the preschool program, is unanswerable.

These flaws do not mean this research is worthless. On the contrary, it confirms two results found in other studies: that the IQ gains during preschool do not necessarily last throughout elementary school and that programs that develop independence and self-motivation may have longer-lasting effects than teacher-directed programs. Concentrating on the development of noncognitive skills may be more fruitful during preschool than teaching specific cognitive skills.

subjected to the experimental conditions, the other half became the control group, for whom nothing was done except periodic retesting.

In the experimental group, a teacher worked with each infant five days a week beginning at 6 weeks of age. The teachers, who were members of the same ghetto community, had been trained to teach young children. They followed a structured curriculum designed to foster cognitive development and they were given professional assistance and encouragement whenever they needed it. In addition, the mothers were shown how to stimulate their babies' cognitive growth at home, and they were kept informed about their children's accomplishments at school. They were also given help in homemaking skills, as well as in qualifying for better jobs.

This project continued throughout the children's preschool years. As hoped, dramatic differences appeared between the experimental children and the control children. At age 3½, the experimental children could understand complicated sentences that the controls were not able to understand until they were 5½.

When the experimental children entered elementary school, Heber, his co-workers, and many other educators and psychologists held their breath. Would the cognitive gains fade, as they had in the case of Headstart? At first, the worst fears seemed realized. The average child lost more than 5 IQ points between kindergarten and second grade. But the most recent reports are very encouraging. IQ scores have risen again (see Figure 10.10), and these children, born to retarded mothers in a slum, are above average. Their test contemporaries who had no special education during their first five years are now averaging IQ scores of about 80, low enough to qualify them for classes for mentally retarded children.

Figure 10.10 *In the Milwaukee Project, repeated IQ testing of children born to retarded mothers shows that the children who received special early education maintain an advantage over their peers who did not receive this education. At about age 5 (60 months), when they enter kindergarten, the control group (children who received no special help) shows a temporary increase in IQ. However, their scores decline again, hovering around 80 from 86 months to 180 months (about 7 to 15 years), placing them in the bottom 15 percent of American children. The experimental group's scores fall during the first two years of elementary school, but they then rise to about 105 by age 15. That is 5 points above average, higher than half of all American children.*

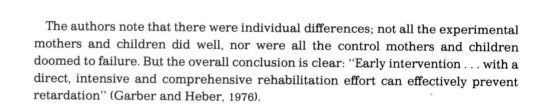

The authors note that there were individual differences; not all the experimental mothers and children did well, nor were all the control mothers and children doomed to failure. But the overall conclusion is clear: "Early intervention . . . with a direct, intensive and comprehensive rehabilitation effort can effectively prevent retardation" (Garber and Heber, 1976).

Implications What are the implications of these studies for children who are not considered deprived? It is clear that cognitive development in the early years can be affected by many things. While it is not easy to teach a child specific concepts or grammatical forms, the overall learning environment in the home, school, and community can and does influence how much a child learns and how long those cognitive accomplishments last.

SUMMARY

Preoperational Thought

1. When children become capable of symbolic thought—that is, of using words, objects, and actions as symbols—their ability to understand, imagine, and communicate increases rapidly.

2. Preoperational thought is prelogical. For instance, preoperational children cannot figure out the logical principles of conservation, classification, chance, or gradual change. They center on one feature of an experience rather than looking at the relationship among several features.

3. The preoperational child believes that other people and even objects think and act the same way he or she does. This general characteristic is called egocentrism, which is quite different from selfishness. One consequence of egocentrism is that preoperational children have difficulty understanding a point of view other than their own.

Language Development

4. Language accomplishments during early childhood include learning 10,000 or so words, and understanding almost all basic grammatical forms. However, as you might expect with prelogical children, they often misunderstand grammatical rules, metaphors, and abstractions. For many children, articulation lags behind other aspects of language development.

5. Children learn many aspects of language, including pronunciation, so rapidly during early childhood that psychologists wondered if this was a critical period for language development. However, while these are the best years for learning to talk, language skills can develop at a later age.

6. Children who are at the egocentric stage of development have difficulty with conversational skills. They are as likely to talk in monologues or collective monologues as they are to engage in socialized speech.

7. As language becomes better developed, it becomes a tool for forming ideas and regulating action. This shift occurs at about age 4 or 5, according to proponents of the verbal-mediation theory.

Teaching and Learning

8. There are many similarities in the nature and sequence of cognitive development in all children. However, there are differences as well, especially in how rapidly children pass each milestone of intellectual growth.

9. One source of these differences is the child's home, particularly with regard to how the parents interact with their children. The precise impact of home environment is controversial, however, especially when we try to explain why middle-class children develop language skills faster than lower-class children.

10. The community can have an important influence on preschool learning. Children who play with other children and meet a variety of people develop different skills than do children who live in isolated communities where they play alone.

11. Preschools that do try to improve the intellectual abilities of young children, notably Headstart, have had some success, but not as much as their founders had hoped. Preschool gains in noncognitive skills are more likely to persist during elementary school.

12. The interaction between child, home, community, and early education is probably the crucial factor in determining the cognitive growth of any particular young child. This makes it difficult for any single program to affect a child's intellectual development very much, unless all these factors are taken into account. The Milwaukee Project, a program that tried to do just that, has been astonishingly successful with children who otherwise would probably have become mentally retarded.

KEY QUESTIONS

How does symbolic thinking expand the cognitive potential of the young child?

What are several examples of the concept of conservation?

Why doesn't the young child understand conservation?

What aspects of classification are difficult for young children?

How well can young children understand another point of view?

What are the impressive language accomplishments of the young child?

What are the limitations of language ability of the young child?

How does the relationship between thought and language change during childhood?

What are at least two interpretations of the differences between the language skills of lower-class and middle-class children?

Give an example of the effect of the interaction between home, community, and school on a child's learning.

What are some of the different programs that preschools offer?

KEY TERMS

symbol	decenter
symbolic function	grammar
iconic thought	overregularization
preoperational thought	mean length of utterance (MLU)
conservation	
identity	egocentric speech
reversibility	monologue
centration	collective monologue
classification	socialized speech
egocentrism	inner speech
animism	verbal mediation
artificialism	Project Headstart

RECOMMENDED READINGS

Chukovsky, Kornei. *From two to five.* (Rev. ed.) Berkeley, Calif.: University of California Press, 1968.

Chukovsky presents hundreds of children's sayings, questions, and dialogues, which he collected over a forty-year period. His conclusion—that preschool children have a kind of genius for language that they lose at about age 6—seems valid after reading this charming collection.

Singer, Dorothy G., and **Revenson, Tracey A.** *How a child thinks: A Piaget primer.* New York: New American Library, 1978.

This is a readable summary of Piaget's ideas, including many examples from Piaget and from other sources. Thinking during early childhood is presented with particular care. The last chapter, "Beyond Piaget," includes some thoughts about the ways teachers, parents, and television influence the learning of preschool children.

Edgerton, Robert B. *Mental retardation.* Cambridge, Mass.: Harvard University Press, 1979.

This is an accurate and readable book about the forms, causes, prevention, and treatment of mental retardation. It emphasizes the crucial role of the family in helping a child learn and points out what schools can and cannot be expected to do.

de Villiers, Peter A., and **de Villiers, Jill G.** *Early language.* Cambridge, Mass.: Harvard University Press, 1979.

The de Villierses are a husband-wife team who are experts in child language. In this book, they explain the process of learning a language between birth and age 6. The book is filled with charming examples from the children of linguists, and also includes references to the early language of deaf, retarded, and autistic children, to shed light on the normal process.

The Play Years: Psychosocial Development

Lady…lady, I do not make up things, that is lies. Lies is not true. But the truth could be made up if you know how. And that's the truth.

Lily Tomlin, as Edith Ann

CHAPTER 11

Three Theories
Psychoanalytic Theory

Behaviorism

Cognitive Theory

Which is Most Valid?

Play
Social Play

Dramatic Play

Parenting
Hostility and Affection

Patterns of Parenting

Punishment

Television
Commercials

Violence

Attempts to Improve
Children's Television

Not Enough Time to Play?

Possible Problems
Aggression

Imagination

Serious Psychological
Disturbances

Sex Roles and Stereotypes
Roles and Attitudes

Androgyny

The Three Theories Reconsidered

True or False?

Most 3-year-olds think that wearing the clothes of the opposite sex will change their gender.

Children of strict parents who sternly punish misconduct become, on the whole, high-achievers.

All other factors being equal, the children most likely to develop into delinquents are those who are harshly punished by their parents.

Punishing a child for dependent behavior will most likely increase dependent behavior.

By age 3, children are fully aware that TV cartoons are pure fantasy.

Psychologists generally agree that educational TV programs like "Sesame Street" can make one of the most important contributions to preschoolers' cognitive development.

Parents usually worry much more about the physical health or intellectual growth of their preschool children than they do about the development of self-concept, social understanding, or moral codes. Yet, of the three domains of development we have been considering, the psychosocial is perhaps the most important. Can you imagine an adult who has no understanding of self and others, or who is unaware of any distinctions between male and female, or who has no sense of right and wrong? Without these crucial concepts, it would be impossible for a person to live a normal life.

The development of these concepts begins during early childhood, as children become able to define who they are ("I am . . . I can . . ."), who they were ("When I was a baby, I couldn't . . ."), and who they will be ("When I grow up, I will be able to . . ."). They become aware of sexual differences and moral distinctions, often with a prejudice (girls can't be doctors) and severity (if children tell lies, their tongues will fall out) that astonish their parents. This chapter describes how these ideas begin to develop.

Three Theories

Almost all psychologists agree that children begin to learn morals and sex roles during early childhood. They also agree that the interactions experienced at home and during play with other children are the main sources for most of this learning. But how they describe the actual dynamics of the process of learning about self and society depends on whether they favor a psychoanalytic, behaviorist, or cognitive perspective.

Psychoanalytic Theory

According to both Freud and Erikson, young children develop powerful fantasies that result in overwhelming guilt, which, in turn, produces fear of terrible punishment. But Freud and Erikson differ in their hypotheses about the content of those fantasies. In keeping with his theory of infantile sexuality, Freud held that the child's fantasies are primarily sexual; Erikson does not.

The Phallic Stage Freud (1938) called the period from about age 3 to 7 the phallic stage because he believed its center of focus is the penis. In other words, at about age 3 or 4 a boy becomes aware of his penis, begins to masturbate, and develops sexual feelings about his mother, who has always been an important love object for him. These feelings make him jealous of his father—so jealous, in fact, that, according to Freud, each son secretly wants to kill his father. Freud called this phenomenon the Oedipus complex, after Oedipus, son of the king of Thebes in ancient Greek mythology. Abandoned as an infant and raised in a distant kingdom, Oedipus later returned to his birthplace, unwittingly killed his father, and married his mother. When he discovered what he had done, he blinded himself in a paroxysm of guilt.

According to Freud, little boys feel horribly guilty for having the lustful and murderous thoughts of the Oedipus complex and imagine receiving terrible punishments, among them blindness and castration, should their fathers ever find out. They cope with this guilt by using identification, a defense mechanism through which people imagine themselves to be like a person more powerful than themselves. (Many adults use this defense mechanism when they identify with sports heroes, movie stars, or political leaders, and get vicarious pleasure from the accomplishments of these public figures.)

According to Freud, little boys come to identify with their fathers, copying their masculine behavior and adopting their moral standards. In this process, they develop their *superego*, or conscience, to control the forbidden impulses of the *id*. (Freud believed that if a boy does not experience the Oedipus complex—because, say, there is no father in the household to make the boy jealous—he is likely to identify with his mother too much, thereby increasing his chances of eventually becoming homosexual.)

Freud offered two overlapping descriptions of the phallic stage as it occurs in little girls. One form, the Electra complex, follows the same pattern as the Oedipus complex: the little girl wants to get rid of her mother and become intimate with her

Figure 11.1 *According to psychoanalytic theory, the relationship between father and daughter becomes particularly important at about age 5, when, on the basis of their father's attitudes and behaviors, girls form their images of the kind of woman they want to be and the kind of man they want to marry.*

father. In the other version, the little girl becomes jealous of boys because they have a penis and she does not, an emotion called penis envy. Somehow the girl decides that her mother is to blame for this state of affairs, so she becomes angry at her and decides the next best thing to having a penis of her own is to become sexually attractive so that someone with a penis, preferably her father, will love her (Freud, 1965; originally published in 1933).

A CLOSER LOOK **Berger and Freud**

As a woman, and as a mother of daughters, I have always regarded Freud's theory of female sexual development as ridiculous, not to mention antifemale. I am not alone in this opinion. Psychologists generally agree that Freud's explanation of female sexual and moral development is one of the weaker parts of his theory, reflecting the values of middle-class Viennese society at the turn of the century more than any universal pattern. Karen Horney (1967), a psychoanalyst who is one of Freud's disciples, criticizes him particularly on the idea of penis envy. She believes that girls envy the male's higher status more than his sexual organs, and she suggests that boys experience a corresponding emotion in the form of *womb envy,* the wish that they could have babies and suckle them.

However, my view of Freud's theory as complete nonsense has been somewhat modified by the following conversations my two oldest daughters had with me as each reached 4 years of age.

Rachel: When I get married, I'm going to marry Daddy.
  Me: Daddy's already married to me.
Rachel: (With the joy of having discovered a wonderful solution to this problem) Then we can have a double wedding!

Bethany: When I grow up, I'm going to marry Daddy.
  Me: But Daddy's married to me.
Bethany: That's all right. When I grow up you'll probably be dead.
  Me: (Determined to stick up for myself) Daddy's older than me, so when I'm dead, he'll probably be dead too.
Bethany: That's all right. I'll marry him when he gets born again.
  (Our family's religious beliefs, incidentally, do not include reincarnation.)

At this point, I couldn't think of a good reply. Bethany must have seen my face fall and taken pity on me.

Bethany: Don't worry, Mommy. After you get born again, you can be our baby.

Obviously, these two conversations do not prove that Freud was correct; but they have made me decide that Freud's description of the phallic stage is not as outlandish as it first appears to be.

Theodore Lidz (1976), a respected developmental psychiatrist, offers a plausible explanation of the process evident in my daughters and in many other children. Lidz believes that all children must go through an Oedipal "transition," overcoming "the intense bonds to their mothers that were essential to their satisfactory pre-Oedipal development." As part of this process, children imagine becoming an adult and, quite logically, replacing the adult of their own sex who they know best, their father or mother. This idea must be dispelled before the sexual awakening of early adolescence, otherwise an "incestuous bond" will threaten the nuclear family, prevent the child's extrafamilial socialization, and block his or her emergence as an adult. According to Lidz, the details of the Oedipal transition vary from family to family, but successful desexualization of parent-child love is essential for healthy maturity.

In both versions, the consequences of this stage are the same for girls as for boys: guilt and fear, and then adoption of sex-appropriate behavior and the father's moral code. By the time this stage is over, children of both sexes have acquired their superego (although, according to Freud, a girl's is not as well developed as a boy's). This strict conscience makes it difficult for people of any age to break the moral codes or transcend the sex roles they learned in childhood.

Initiative versus Guilt Erikson agrees with Freud that the child's relationship with the parents is very important, and that some of the young child's guilt arises from wanting to surpass or destroy the father or mother. But Erikson emphasizes the positive side of this stage: the child's becoming a more independent person.

According to Erikson (1963), the psychosocial crisis that characterizes this stage of development involves initiative versus guilt. In Erikson's words, the child comes into "free possession of a surplus of energy which permits him to forget failures quickly and to approach what seems desirable . . . with undiminished and more accurate direction . . . the child appears 'more himself,' more loving, relaxed and brighter in his judgment, more activated and activating." The child initiates new activities with boldness and exuberance. "The danger of this stage is a sense of guilt over the goals contemplated and the acts initiated in one's exuberant enjoyment of new locomotor and mental power." A little boy might think about stealing a candy bar, or might even actually steal one, and then have nightmares of being locked in jail forever.

Behaviorism

Some behaviorists (e.g., Miller and Dollard, 1941) believe that children learn sex roles and moral behavior because they have been rewarded for appropriate behavior and punished for inappropriate behavior. These reinforcements become internalized, so by middle childhood, children connect good feelings with "good" behavior—no longer needing external praise or criticism to maintain their socially appropriate behavior. According to this theory, then, the typical 8-year-old boy may not want to play with dolls because, when he was younger, people called him a sissy if he tucked a doll into bed.

Social learning theorists (Sears et al., 1965; Mischel, 1970; Bandura, 1969) combine the psychoanalytic emphasis on parents and the behavioristic emphasis on learning. They say that children learn much of their sexual and moral behavior by observing other people, especially people whom they perceive as nurturing, powerful, or similar to themselves. For all these reasons, parents are important models during childhood. Whether children see their parents act with compassion or indifference, with honesty or deception, they try to follow their example. Children also imitate attractive or powerful people they see in the neighborhood, or on television, especially if they see them reinforced for what they do.

Cognitive Theory

Cognitive theorists (Piaget, 1965) focus on the child's ability to understand. As we have seen, preschool children are too egocentric to reason about moral questions or to understand other points of view. But once the child has sufficient understanding, consistent moral behavior can occur.

Sex roles develop the same way. Children need to be at least 4 or 5 before they realize that they are permanently male or female. Once they understand this, they try to adopt appropriate sex-role behavior, at first with the rigidity typical of the initial stages of comprehension of an idea, and then with more flexibility.

For example, Lawrence Kohlberg and Dorothy Ullian (1974) interviewed boys and girls of many ages and discovered an orderly progression of attitudes toward sex roles.

Age 3. Children know what sex they are, but do not realize that maleness and femaleness are permanent characteristics, based on genital differences rather than external characteristics. Boys think they could become mommies; girls think they could become daddies; and both sexes think boys would be girls if they wore dresses and girls would be boys if they had their hair cut very short.

Age 6.   Children realize that sex is a permanent characteristic. Usually they are pleased to be whatever sex they are, for they believe that their own sex is the "better" one. For example, 6-year-old boys think males are stronger, smarter, and more powerful than females. In addition, children of both sexes believe sex identity is defined by observable physical signs, such as strength, depth of voice, clothes. One boy, asked why he thought men were smarter than women, said they had bigger brains. This emphasis on physical differences is true for 6-year-olds in many cultures and in many types of families, including fatherless ones.

Figure 11.2 *At the age when maleness or femaleness is thought to depend on external trappings, children enjoy dressing to conform to traditional sex stereotypes. After admiring her hair ribbons and four necklaces, this girl will probably head straight for the powder puff and perfume bottle.*

Age 10.   Children emphasize social roles more than physical characteristics, believing that "men should act like men and women like ladies." In today's world, with social roles changing as they are, a 10-year-old's ideas of what proper behavior is for men and women depend a great deal on the community and culture in which he or she lives.

Age 14.   Adolescents emphasize psychological differences rather than physical or social differences. For instance, they think that women cry more easily than men and that men are more aggressive than women. These emotional differences shouldn't predetermine a person's life, according to 14-year-olds, who think everyone has "a right to live their life the way they want to."

Age 18.   At this age, many young people think stereotypes should be abolished, but realize that their own behavior is sometimes stereotypic. One college student said, "I can't help what has been put into me over the years," and called himself "moronic," "biased," and a "male chauvinist" for his ideas.

Attitudes about sex roles, according to cognitive theory, parallel the child's stage of cognitive development: 3-year-olds confuse appearance with reality in sex roles just as they do in the conservation experiments.

Which Is Most Valid?   Which of these theories is most accurate? Our approach to answering this question in the rest of this chapter will be to examine the behavior of preschool children and explore how play, parents, and television seem to affect that behavior. Evidence that seems to support one theory or another will be noted, not to prove the superiority of an entire point of view, but to present an interesting explanation for one part of the preschool child's psychosocial development. At the end of the chapter, we will look at three problems of early childhood—aggression, withdrawal, and sex stereotypes—and ask again which theory seems to be the most convincing.

Play

In addition to the kinds of play discussed in earlier chapters, children develop social skills and roles through social play and dramatic play.

Social Play   Introduce two adults to each other, and they will probably begin to converse. Show two infants to each other, and they will most likely stare. But put two preschool children together and, chances are, they will soon begin to play.

In all forms of play, children become more social as egocentrism declines, as Mildred Parten (1932) discovered half a century ago when she studied preschool children and observed five ways children play when other children are around:

1. *Solitary play*   A child plays alone, seemingly unaware of the other children.

2. *Onlooker play*   A child watches other children play.

3. *Parallel play*   Children play in similar ways with similar toys, but they don't interact.

4. *Associative play*   Children interact, including sharing materials, but they don't seem to be playing the same game.

5. *Cooperative play*   Children play together, helping each other or taking turns.

Figure 11.3 *Children must be able to play cooperatively in order to play team games such as tug-of-war. In the game pictured here, the two sides are not as unequal as they appear, for most of the children on the right seem to be at the stage of associative play.*

RESEARCH REPORT   ## The Harlows' Monkeys

For the past twenty years, thousands of rhesus monkeys at the Wisconsin Primate Laboratories have provided developmental psychologists with insights about the needs and behavior of human children. In early research, monkeys were raised in social isolation, with no contact with their mothers or their peers (Harlow and Harlow, 1962). Some of the monkeys were raised in cages with two surrogate mothers, a wire one with a bottle of milk, and a warm, cloth one with no milk. These monkeys much preferred the cloth mother, clinging to it for hours on end and leaving it to suck on the bottle only when they were very hungry. (The implication of this facet of the research—that physical contact might be even more important to the mother-child relationship than feeding—is one reason psychologists today advise picking up and cuddling an unhappy baby.)

Normally, monkeys are curious, social creatures, like the animal on the right. The monkey on the left, *reared in social isolation, initially cringes from other monkeys, but will attack if approached too closely.*

No matter which kind of artificial mother the socially isolated monkeys had had, when they joined a normal monkey troop in adulthood, they were unable to adjust. Sometimes they hid in a corner, burying their head in their arms; if they tried to mate, they were unable to position themselves correctly; sometimes they attacked older and larger monkeys, or mothers with infants, and were seriously injured. These aberrant behaviors were irreversible if the monkeys had been in isolation six months or more. If they became mothers (through artificial insemination), these monkeys often attacked and destroyed their own babies.

The Harlows next set out to learn which aspect of social isolation was the crucial one, isolation from mother or isolation from peers. Some monkeys were raised with their biological mothers, but without peers. Others had only cloth mothers, but were given daily play periods

Onlooker play is most common at age 2; associative and cooperative play become common at 5. Parten's classification is still useful today, although various studies show different percentages of the types of play, depending on the background of the children (Rubin et al., 1976). For instance, preschoolers who have had experience with other children are likely to chase each other (rough-and-tumble play), chatter together (language play), and simply enjoy each other's company, all signs of associative and cooperative play. Today, some children pass the stage when onlooker and parallel play predominate by the time they are 3 years old.

Lawrence Sherman (1975) found in a study of preschool classes that all children will sometimes begin laughing, or even screaming, jumping up and down and clapping their hands in joy, a phenomenon of social play he called group glee. Group glee is not usually triggered by a funny story or by good news, since such a reaction to events of this kind requires a level of cognition beyond that of most 3-year-olds. Instead, group glee usually begins with an unexpected event (a child's spilling milk down his front) or a physical activity (dancing, running, jumping). The larger the group, and the older the children, the more frequent the delight.

The Importance of Social Play   That social play is enjoyable and interesting proves nothing about its importance. Would there, in fact, be any harm done if a preschool child never played with other children? Perhaps an isolated farm family has only one child, or perhaps a city mother wants to keep her child at home, away from the

Monkeys raised together without their mothers often cling to each other for security. If placed with normal monkeys, they will gradually develop normal monkey behavior.

Could the socially isolated monkeys be rehabilitated? Harlow and Suomi (1971) tried reinforcing normal social contact and punishing inappropriate behavior, but this did not work. They then tried social play, putting monkeys raised in isolation for six months together with normal monkeys the same age, but the maladjusted newcomers were attacked and rejected. Finally the psychologists tried putting an isolated monkey with a younger monkey. Success! The smaller monkey did not intimidate the maladjusted older monkey. The two learned to play together, and by age 1, the disturbed monkey had totally recovered from the early deprivation. In other such efforts, even monkeys who had been isolated for over a year have been rehabilitated by playing with younger "therapist" monkeys (Novak and Harlow, 1975).

with normal age-mates. Both groups fared better in adulthood than did the monkeys who had been completely isolated, but the monkeys raised by their mothers did not behave normally, either in sexual or social relations with the monkey troop. The monkeys who had played with peers were essentially normal.

Monkeys and humans are different in many ways, so conclusions from such primate research cannot be applied wholesale to people. For instance, we know that children, unlike monkeys, can grow up without obvious signs of maladjustment even if they did not play with other children. Perhaps greater intellectual skills help humans adjust to other people if they did not learn these skills from direct early childhood experiences. However, in underscoring the importance of social play in nonhuman primates, this research suggests that social play helps teach human primates the skills of interaction they need to learn, just as other forms of play teach other skills.

dangers of the street. Couldn't the child in either case learn social skills from adults, or from other children at elementary-school age?

To some extent the answer is yes. Children are adaptable, and they can learn most essential skills in many ways and at many ages. But there is evidence that suggests social play in early childhood provides crucial experiences that would be hard for adults to provide or for children to acquire at a later stage of life. We saw some of this evidence in the previous chapter: Norwegian children on isolated farms were still less skilled at understanding others' viewpoints, even after two years of elementary school, than were their peers who played with other children during the preschool years; children who attended Headstart usually had better social skills in elementary school, even if their intellectual advantage over non-Headstart children had faded. Suggestive evidence also comes from research on social deprivation in monkeys.

Dramatic Play

The beginnings of dramatic play coincide with the achievement of symbolic thinking and can be clearly seen in a child's "feeding," cuddling, and punishing a doll or stuffed animal. As children get older, they can create elaborate scenarios for these inanimate creatures. However, the aspect of dramatic play that is of interest to us here is the social development that occurs when two or more children cooperate in creating their own drama.

Catherine Garvey (1977) found many examples of dramatic play when she studied forty-eight preschool children ranging in age from 2 years and 10 months to 5 years and 7 months. Each child was paired with a playmate the same age; then both children were taken to a well-equipped playroom and left to do whatever they wanted.

Many of these pairs, even some of the youngest, chose to engage in dramatic play. The 2- and 3-year-olds often played a mother-and-baby game; the older children sometimes played a parent-child game or, if they were of the opposite sex, a husband-wife game. Older children created many other roles, including Hänsel and Gretel, Dr. Jeckel and Dr. Hines (sic), and St. George and the dragon. The children's creativity was shown not only in their choice of roles also but in their willingness to change their dramatic play to suit each other's whims.

Garvey found that most dramatic play employs certain standard plots. Many center around simple domestic scenes. Others involve such things as one player announcing that a child or pet is sick or dead and the other player automatically becoming the healer, administering food or medicine, or performing surgery, to restore life and health. In a third standard type of drama, one child announces a "sudden threat" (the appearance of a monster, for instance), then both children take the role of victim or defender, attacking or fleeing. The episode can end happily ("I got him!") or unhappily ("He ate me. I'm dead."), unfolding naturally yet without prearrangement.

Figure 11.4 *In dramatic play, preschoolers are usually quite willing to accept each other's fantasies, as long as the imaginary creatures keep things lively.*

Interesting age and sex differences appeared in Garvey's research on sudden-threat dramas. For instance, 2- and 3-year-olds were usually victims; 4- and 5-year-olds were usually defenders. When an older pair of children were of the opposite sex, the boy was more likely to be a defender, and the girl, an observer or victim.

One episode between two 5-year-olds illustrates this pattern. A boy and girl were playing that they were a husband and wife at home. Suddenly the girl announced a fire. The boy immediately quenched it with a toy snake (transformed to a fire hose), making water noises as he did so. The girl then declared that the fire had started up again, so the boy put it out once more. When fire appeared yet again, this time in heaven and threatening to burn God, the boy declared the snake-hose magical and destroyed the fire once and for all!

Dramatic play such as this is not only fun; it also helps children try out social roles, work out their fears and fantasies, and learn to cooperate. It is the most sophisticated form of social play, so it probably teaches social skills that simpler forms of social play do not.

The Three Theories   In watching children's dramatic play, one can find support for each of the three theories of psychosocial development. Psychoanalytic psychologists would notice that the standard plots (involving family interaction or conflict between good and evil) seem designed to help children work out parent-child, male-female, and id-superego conflicts. In the preceding example, for instance, the transformation of the rubber snake into a hose putting out the fires can be seen as the boy's fantasizing that his penis is so powerful that it can conquer all threats, rescuing himself, his girlfriend, and even God. The girl, having put herself in a dependent role, but nevertheless finding new threats for the boy to master, can be seen as expressing envy and hostility, as well as admiration.

Behaviorists, on the other hand, say there is no need to connect dramatic play with unconscious conflicts. As they tend to view it, dramatic play is a form of social learning, in which children model the behaviors they have seen in daily life or on television. Even when the episodes of dramatic play are imaginary, behaviorists would point out that the basic plots are similar to events the child has witnessed.

Emphasizing other aspects of dramatic play, cognitive theorists point out that children must be able to think symbolically before they can begin dramatic play and that the complexity of dramatic play is related to the age of the children engaging in it. At the same time, dramatic play seems most spontaneous and creative when children are still too young to be restricted by concern for reality and logic. Preoperational thinking is well suited to pretending.

Thus all three theories have a different view of one of the most important parts of the young child's life, play with other children. Now let us look at the other crucial influence on young children, parents.

Figure 11.5 *Being a bride with a long white gown and attendants is a popular role in the dramatic play of young girls. Psychologists from various theoretical perspectives might see this role as, among other things, an acting out of the daughter's wish to take her mother's place, an imitation of the ideal roles of the culture, or an exaggeration of visible sexual stereotypes.*

Parenting

How does the parents' behavior affect the child? What kinds of families foster happy, confident, friendly children or unhappy, insecure, hostile children? In large measure, answers depend on the age, sex, and temperament of the child, as well as on the culture in which the family lives. Each child is an individual, as is each parent, so the best parent-child relationship is hard to detail. There is no simple formula for child-rearing.

Hostility and Affection

However, part of the answer is clear (Martin, 1975). Parents who are hostile and rejecting toward their children are likely to have hostile and antisocial children. Thus, if parents are critical, derogatory, and dissatisfied with their children, their children are likely to become dissatisfied with themselves. If parents are insensitive to the child's point of view, the child will be less able to understand the viewpoints of others. The opposite is also true. Warm parents who are understanding and accepting of their children generally raise children who are happy and friendly.

Although parents' attitudes toward their children are important throughout childhood, they are especially so during the preschool years, partly because the child's self-concept is in the early stages of formation at this time, and partly because most preschool children think of their parents as all-powerful and all-knowing and take their judgments as definitive. Nevertheless, the generality that a parent's hostility or warmth forms a child who is antisocial or loving should not blind us to the fact that, in some cases, the antisocial behavior in a child may be the cause of parental hostility rather than the result of it (Bell and Harper, 1977). Be that as it may, parents are the adults, and presumably more capable of patience and understanding than children, so they have a greater responsibility for the nature of the parent-child interaction.

Patterns of Parenting

That parents should be loving and understanding with their children is, of course, not news. Nor does it address the question of *how*.

In fact, what general styles of child-rearing are there, and what are their effects? To answer this question, Diana Baumrind (1967) observed 110 3- and 4-year-old children in nursery school, grouping them by personality types. She then interviewed both parents, and watched parent-child interaction in two settings, at home and in the laboratory. On the basis of her findings, she described three basic patterns of parenting.

The first is authoritarian: the parents' word is law, not to be questioned, and misconduct is punished. Authoritarian parents seem aloof from their children, afraid to show affection or give praise.

The second pattern is permissive: the parents make few demands on their children, hiding any impatience they feel. Discipline is lax, and anarchy frequently reigns.

The third pattern is authoritative: the parents in this category are similar in some ways to authoritarian parents, in that they set limits and enforce rules, but they are also willing to listen receptively to the child's requests and questions. Family rule is more democratic than dictatorial.

To see the differences among these three patterns more clearly, imagine that it is five minutes before bedtime for a 4-year-old boy. In the authoritarian family, the child would probably already be getting ready, brushing his teeth and putting on his pajamas. If he were to ask, "Can I please stay up another half hour?" the parents would probably say, "You know the rule. Get to bed now, right this minute."

In the permissive family, the parents would say, "Don't you think it's time for you to go to bed?" to which the child would likely respond, "I want to watch one more TV program." The parents might then suggest that the show is not worth watching, but the boy would probably stay up anyway, finally falling asleep in front of the television.

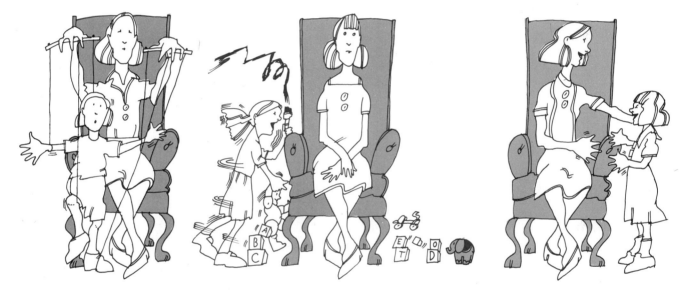

Figure 11.6 *While authoritative parenting requires the most time and patience, it is also most likely to produce a happy child rather than a distrustful puppet or an uncontrolled little devil.*

In the authoritative family, the child might ask to stay up later, explaining that he wanted to watch one more show. The parents would probably listen to the request, ask what show it is, and, if there were school the next day, refuse with an explanation. Occasionally, if the show is particularly worthy, they might let the child see it—*after* he has brushed his teeth, put on his pajamas, and promised to wake up without complaining in the morning.

According to Baumrind (1967, 1971), the following generalizations tend to be true. The sons of authoritarian parents tend to be distrustful, unhappy, and hostile; and neither the sons nor daughters of such parents are high-achievers. The children of permissive parents are the least self-reliant, the least self-controlled, and the most unhappy. (The boys are low-achievers, although the girls do quite well in school.) The children of authoritative parents are the most self-reliant, self-controlled, and content and are friendly, cooperative, high-achievers.

The basic conclusions of this study have been confirmed by other research. Children who grow up in families that give them both love and limits are most likely to become successful, happy with themselves, and generous with others. Children whose parents are overly strict are likely to be obedient but unhappy; those whose parents are overly lenient are likely to be aggressive and lack self-control.

Once again, however, generalizations such as these must be cautiously interpreted (Martin, 1975). Hostile, unfriendly children may produce authoritarian parents rather than the reverse being the case. Likewise, children who have some measure of self-reliance and self-control may produce relaxed, flexible parents.

A CLOSER LOOK   **It Sounds Easy But . . .**

When I teach my students about these three styles of parenting, most of them readily accept the conclusions arrived at by Baumrind. Some of them even see the authoritarian parents' methods as coming close to child abuse, or the permissive parents' as approaching child neglect. Most of them readily accept the authoritative style as the best, although a few students think the permissive approach is not as bad as the research suggests it is, and that the 4-year-old boy who doesn't have to go to bed will soon learn for himself that late bedtimes make difficult mornings. Students who champion the permissive approach may have a point, for one longitudinal study found that although loving, permissive families tend to produce difficult children, these children eventually become cooperative, caring adults (McClelland et al., 1978).

However, the most vocal complaints about Baumrind's description of three parenting styles come from students who are parents themselves. They say that she makes maintaining a consistently authoritative pattern sound much simpler than it actually is. Suppose you tell the 4-year-old that he should go to bed because the particular program he wants to stay up for is not worth watching, and suppose he insists it is. As one student said, "You know you shouldn't hit him, and you know you shouldn't let him watch, but what else can you do?" "Simple. Pull the plug," a nonparent student

answered. The parent replied: "I tried that. My children put the plug back in, and we almost played tug-of-war with the cord. I ended up yelling at them to get in bed before I counted to ten or else . . . ." The problem is that without the child's cooperation, push often comes to shove, and the authoritative parent feels obliged to become authoritarian.

Punishment

The task of setting and enforcing limits without resorting to the hostile tactics of the authoritarian parent is not easy. One problem is that physical punishment seems, at first, to be effective. It stops the child from misbehaving at that moment, and it provides an immediate outlet for parental anger. Unfortunately, parents who are quick to use physical force in punishing their children rarely realize the long-term effects that almost every research study has found.

Effects of Physical Punishment When Martin (1975) reviewed the literature on punishment, he cited twenty-seven different studies on the effects of harsh punishment. The precise definition of "harsh" varied from study to study, but, generally, it referred to punishment that is more severe than that used by other parents in the same community.

Because harshly punished children might be temporarily obedient, their parents appear to think that harsh punishment is good. However, it seems that children store up frustration at this punishment, and when they finally vent it, at school, or against their parents in later years, they are likely to use the mode of expression they have become accustomed to—violence. In twenty-five of the studies reviewed by Martin, harsh punishment at home correlated with aggression against other children, against teachers, and against society. Children who were harshly punished in childhood were more likely to become antisocial delinquents in adolescence. This relationship is especially clear for boys, who, significantly more often than girls, are harshly punished in childhood, are considered "problem children" in elementary school, and are arrested for violent crimes in adolescence. (Apparently the connection between harsh punishment and misbehavior is not so clear during the preschool years, since the only two studies in Martin's review that did not show such a link were those based on interviews with mothers of preschool children.)

Figure 11.7 *When children misbehave, parents have many options, from providing a patient explanation of why the child's actions were wrong, to using physical punishment. Many factors affect the parents' choice, among them the culture (physical punishment is much rarer among Asian-Americans and Native Americans than among other groups) and the child's sex (boys are more often physically punished than girls). A fact that might help parents who are trying to decide on methods of discipline is that children model their behavior on that of their parents. Children whose parents usually discuss problems with them become more verbal, rational, and compassionate than children who are frequently punished harshly.*

The Effects of Criticism   Parents who do not use physical punishment can be very hostile in other ways, especially by being critical and derogatory. Such treatment is more likely to make children become withdrawn and anxious than violent—especially if the child is a boy and the hostile parent is the father (Martin, 1975). Since, again, these consequences are not clear until middle childhood, the man who tells his shy 4-year-old son that he is acting like a sissy does not realize that he is making the boy more frightened and withdrawn rather than less.

In much the same way, parents trying to make preschool children less dependent sometimes merely worsen the problem. Many mothers report that their children are even more likely to whine, cling, and make demands following a scolding for being too dependent (Yarrow et al., 1968). Punishing dependence probably leads to increased dependent behavior because the child, feeling rejected, tries to get reassurance, and one way young children get reassurance is by acting babyish. Usually the parent of a crying, clinging child gets tired of pushing the child away before the child gets tired of crying.

Children sometimes ask for more attention precisely when their parents are least able or willing to give it. This was briskly demonstrated in an experiment that compared the reactions of nursery-school children when their mothers were busy filling out a questionnaire and then when their mothers were ready to help them. As any experienced mother might have guessed, the children asked the most questions when the mothers were the most busy (Sears et al., 1965).

Suggestions   Obviously, how to reprimand a child effectively without doing physical or emotional harm is a complicated problem. Nevertheless, developmental psychologists, no matter what their theoretical orientation, almost all agree with the following suggestions (Parke, 1977):

1. Positive reinforcement for good behavior is more effective, in the long run, than punishment for bad behavior. Parents who want their children to be more independent, for instance, should encourage them to do things on their own, rather than yelling at them when they cling.

2. Expected behavior should be within the physical, cognitive, and psychological capacity of the child. For instance, preschoolers particularly have trouble understanding complex situations involving cause and effect or accident and intention.

3. Rules should be explained in advance, including the reasons for the rules and the consequences for breaking them. While preschool children will not always understand the reasons, explaining them emphasizes the necessity of the rule and prepares children for the next step of cognitive development.

4. Punishment should be consistent and immediate whenever the child breaks a rule he or she understands. Putting a little girl in her room for three minutes the moment she begins to bite her sister is more effective than yelling, "Stop fighting—and just wait until your father hears how you've been acting!"

5. Children follow the example set by others. If parents find their children misbehaving, they should make sure they themselves are not providing the wrong behavior model.

6. If the child breaks rules frequently, parents should consider the possibility that the problem lies in some aspect of the home situation rather than in the child. For instance, the rules may be too vague or difficult, or the child may not get enough attention for good behavior and therefore may misbehave to attract notice. Or the child may be tired or hungry or sick, or the parents may be under a great deal of

Figure 11.8 *The old saying "An ounce of prevention is worth a pound of cure" applies to parent-child relationships. Children whose parents spend time teaching them and playing with them are usually less likely to get into mischief and more likely to try to please their parents than children who feel ignored or unwanted.*

stress. A "difficult child" who has trouble sitting still or sharing toys may need to spend more time playing outside, where sitting still is not necessary and there is less need to share toys.

With punishment, as with every other aspect of child development, it is important to look at the total picture. The child's needs and abilities, the parents' personalities, the home atmosphere, and the community environment all affect each isolated incident.

The Three Theories   Although most psychologists agree on the six suggestions just listed, as well as on the overall type of parenting that is best, there is some difference in their emphasis. Psychoanalytic thinkers, mindful of the child's difficult fantasy life (the Oedipal complex), suggest that parents not be overly strict if the child errs. (Freud's followers usually feel that more harm is caused by excessive strictness than by excessive permissiveness.) Behaviorists tend to emphasize the idea that much correct behavior can be learned if parents are clear and consistent. Cognitive theorists, by contrast, would remind parents that the preschool child lives only in the present, understands only his or her own point of view, and confuses cause and effect, so parents should not expect too much. Nevertheless, advocates of all three theories agree that children grow best when limits are clearly set and love is abundantly given.

Television

Interaction with parents and play with other children have been the main forces shaping social skills since the beginning of human history. In the last 30 years, however, a third influence has emerged—television.

Virtually every child in the United States watches television (it is estimated that 95 percent of all households have one or more TV sets). According to a study of preschoolers' TV viewing in California, the average 3- or 4-year-old watches two or more hours of television a day, starting a habit that will occupy more time than attending school, playing with friends, or talking to family members (Stein et al., 1975). There is a great deal of variation, however; some mothers of preschoolers report that their children watch 5 hours a week; others report 100 hours of viewing!

Almost all parents have discovered that television is a convenient babysitter, a way to keep children quiet and inactive. However, many critics feel that these hours of daily peace may be purchased at too high a price, and they cite three major problems: the effect of commercials; the content of programs; and the time that could be better spent.

Figure 11.9 *The one-eyed monster can be addictive, not only for children who never seem to get their fill of cartoons, but also for the parents who find they can spend Saturday morning in bed if the television is on.*

Commercials

Preschool children usually accept commercial messages uncritically, because, being preoperational, they are unable to understand that advertisements are intended to sell products, rather than entertain or report the whole truth. Because young children thus have virtually no sales resistance, the burden of restraint is on the parents, who must either resist the demands of their children, or succumb, buying everything from expensive toys that soon become boring or broken to sugared cereals and drinks that promote tooth decay. At times the gullibility of preschool children can be dangerous. One 4-year-old spent two days in intensive care in the hospital after swallowing forty children's vitamins: he had gotten the idea from TV commercials that the vitamins would make him "big and strong real fast" (Liebert, 1973).

Violence

The second major criticism of children's television has to do with the amount of violence it portrays. Many psychologists maintain that television violence promotes violence in children, primarily through example. Albert Bandura, a social learning theorist who has studied the influence of models (see pages 50–51), has found that a child who sees an example of violence is not only likely to copy that example immediately but is also likely to refer to that example for future behavior (Bandura, 1969). The effect is interactive and cumulative: children who watch a lot of television are more likely to be aggressive than children who do not, and children who are aggressive are likely to watch a lot of violence on television.

Preschool children are even more likely to be influenced by violence on television than older children are, because they have an especially hard time differentiating reality from fantasy. In television cartoons, which are beamed primarily at young children, physical violence occurs an average of seventeen times per hour. The good guys (Popeye, Underdog, Road Runner) do as much hitting, shooting, and kicking as the bad guys, and the consequences of their violence are never portrayed as bloody or evil. Parents assume, or hope, that young children know that the cartoons are "just pretend." But after a careful review of the literature, Stein and Friedrich (1975) concluded that, if anything, the mayhem in cartoons has a stronger impact on preschoolers than similar violent drama with real people would have, perhaps because cartoons are simpler and can exaggerate events more than actual human beings can.

Attempts to Improve Children's Television

Many educators and parents have tried to reform children's television, their most successful efforts being through Action for Children's Television (ACT), begun in Boston in 1968. By 1972 they had helped to ban children's vitamin commercials and advertisements with a TV hero directly promoting a product, as Buffalo Bob had done on the Howdy Doody shows that the first generation of television children watched in the 1950s. They have also reduced the total advertisement time allowed on children's programs from sixteen minutes per hour to twelve. Thanks to ACT, violence on television is less now than it was: in 1969, for instance, violence in cartoons averaged thirty incidents per hour, almost double the current rate (Stein and Friedrich, 1975).

At the same time, public television has developed special educational programs, such as "Sesame Street," which teaches numbers and letters, and "Mister Rogers," which encourages creativity. Although these two programs differ in method and content, research has shown that both succeed in their teaching efforts, especially when parents watch with their children (Cook et al., 1975; Tower et al., 1979).

Not Enough Time to Play?

Nevertheless, a growing group of critics is concerned that even the best television does more harm than good because it robs children of play time, making them less creative, less verbal, less social, less independent (Singer and Singer, 1977; Winn, 1977).

Some support for this idea comes from an experiment with certain families in Denver, Colorado, who voluntarily gave up television for a month. The parents of these families reported that their children played and read more, that siblings fought less, that family activities became more common, that mealtimes were longer, and that bedtimes were earlier (Winn, 1977). Unfortunately, this experiment lasted only a month, and the families were volunteers who answered an article in the *Denver Post* titled, "Would You Free Your Children from the Monster?" Thus, this study, though provocative, was certainly not a carefully controlled, scientific experiment. The families knew what the premise of the experiment was, and were hoping it would be borne out.

In fact, a controlled scientific experiment on the effects of television is almost impossible, because families that do not have television are so rare. It is virtually impossible to find two groups of children who are similar in every way except that some watch television and some do not. However, studies have shown that children who watch a lot of television tend to be lower achievers than children who watch a little television (Stein and Friedrich, 1975).

One reason for this correlation may be that language skills cannot be mastered in the early years without individualized communication between adult and child. Among the evidence for this statement is the case of Jim, a normal child born to deaf parents who hoped their son would learn to talk by watching television, which he did, in fact, watch for hours each day. However, Jim did not begin to talk at all until age 2½; and by 3 years, 9 months, his language was immature and abnormal. He was using sentences with grammatical structures that would be usual for normal 2-year-olds, such as "Be down go" and "Big two crayon." At that point, with intensive, personal, language therapy, Jim learned in five months what he hadn't learned in forty-five months of television viewing. At 4 years, 2 months, his language was normal for his age (Bard and Sachs, 1977).

What can a parent do? Some professionals recommend no television at all, especially for preschoolers. Others suggest that parents watch with their children, so that they can personalize the learning on educational programs and criticize or censor the content of noneducational television. Many parents have found it easier to impose a simple rule—only an hour a day, or only before dinner, or only on Saturday—than to try to prohibit television completely or censor each program. Virtually no psychologist who has studied the effects of children's television thinks parents should let their preschoolers watch whatever and whenever they want.

Possible Problems

No matter how loving, attentive, understanding, patient, and judicious parents are, there are some problems in early childhood that cannot be avoided. As part of the process of developing social skills, children do and say things that worry their parents. They seem too ready to strike out at others, or they insist that imaginary creatures are real, or they refuse to play with anyone. Are these serious problems? If so, what can be done about them?

Aggression

When children first start playing with other children, in toddlerhood, they are rarely deliberately aggressive. They might pull a toy away from another child or even push someone over, but they do so to get an object, or remove an obstacle, rather than to hurt. As children grow older, the frequency of deliberate physical aggression increases, normally reaching a peak sometime during the preschool years, and then declining.

In one study, 102 children between the ages of 4 and 7 were observed in six classes (Hartup, 1974). Each time a child was physically or verbally abusive to another child, the observer recorded what happened before and after the incident,

Figure 11.10 *Having just smeared his neighbor's arm with paint, the boy on the right, according to Hartup's findings, stands a 50–50 chance of being similarly decorated.*

as well as the age and sex of the aggressor. According to this study, aggression decreased markedly as the children grew older, especially instrumental aggression, which involves quarreling over an object, territory, or privilege. That is to say, younger children were much more likely than older children to fight over who was to be at the front of the line, or who had a particular toy first. Hostile aggression, aggression that is an attack against a specific someone rather than a fight about some thing, did not decline as rapidly.

Another interesting age difference appeared. With regard to being the recipient of a derogatory comment from a peer ("dumb-dumb," "fatso," or the like), younger children were almost as likely to respond physically as verbally (48 percent to 52 percent, respectively). Older children were much more likely to react with a threat or another insult (78 percent) than with a push or punch (22 percent). The developmental trend toward less aggression is equally apparent in both sexes, although boys were involved in more aggressive instances than girls at every age. This boy-girl difference has been found in many cultures, and in nonhuman primates, even those in the Harlows' studies who had no experience with older monkeys. This suggests a biological component, although culture is an influence as well.

Family and neighborhood influences, as well as age and sex, affect how aggressive a particular child will be. As Berkowitz concluded in his summary of the research on aggression "violence ultimately produces more violence." Children whose parents use physical punishment, who watch violent television, and who play with aggressive children are likely to be more aggressive than children without such examples (Berkowitz, 1973).

The importance of the parents' example is stressed by psychologists from all three theoretical camps. They also all agree that some physical aggression is normal in young children, although each has a somewhat different explanation of this fact: the psychoanalytic theorist stresses the poorly developed superego; the behaviorist says that the child has not yet learned more appropriate ways to satisfy basic needs; the cognitive theorist emphasizes the egocentrism of the young child.

Psychologists also agree that although the physical aggression of the young child should be accepted as normal, it should not be encouraged, for children need to develop their superegos, or appropriate behaviors, or awareness of the needs of others. In other words, theory confirms common sense: adults should stop a child from hitting another on the head, even while they realize that such a show of force is a normal 3-year-old's response to provocation.

Some psychoanalytic thinkers, including Freud, believe in *catharsis;* that is, they believe that expressing emotions like anger or sadness will make the person feel less hostility or sorrow. Again, this is not to suggest that an angry child should be encouraged to hit. Instead, the child should be helped to find another way to express anger, perhaps sticking to words rather than blows, or punching a pillow rather than a person.

Preventing and controlling acts of aggression and punishing children when such acts occur are only part of the answer. In the long run, children need to learn to share and cooperate, and to understand the needs of others. These *prosocial skills* begin to develop during early childhood. Even in nursery school, the most popular children are those who are friendly and cooperative (Moore, 1967). (The development of prosocial behavior is explained in Chapter 14, because it is even more important in middle childhood than in early childhood.)

Figure 11.11 *When the importance of cooperation is emphasized, even young children can be very helpful to each other.*

Imagination

Another characteristic of preschool children is that they sometimes have vivid nightmares, elaborate daydreams, and imaginary friends and enemies. This can worry their parents, but in fact this active fantasy life is normal and healthy. Children at the preoperational stage of thinking have difficulty distinguishing reality from fantasy; for them, dreams are believable. A child waking up from a nightmare might insist that there is a rhinoceros under the bed, and refuse to be comforted by assurances that rhinoceroses are confined to zoos and, in any case, cannot fit under beds. Instead of trying logic, parents should use actions—perhaps turning on the light, looking under the bed, and announcing that the animal must have gone away.

Figure 11.12 *For many pre-school children, nightmares don't stop when they wake up. After all, when you have trouble distinguishing fantasy from reality and you are not sure how much room there is under your bed at night, almost anything could be hiding there.*

Other things are frightening too. Young children often are genuinely frightened at the sight of a friend wearing a Halloween costume, or of a parent pretending to be a lion. They worry about the wholeness of their bodies, and can be troubled when they see a legless person, probably because they connect physical appearance with identity. The same logic that defines a girl as someone with long hair defines a person as someone with a complete body. Even a minor cut can cause concern. In addition, everyday objects that make things disappear—the toilet bowl, vacuum cleaner, or bathtub drain—seem ominous to many small children, because they wonder if these devices might make them disappear too.

When an irrational fear, or phobia, becomes so strong that it interferes with the child's normal functioning, psychologists recommend two techniques to help solve the problem. The first is gradual desensitization, in which the child slowly becomes accustomed to the feared object or experience. A child who is afraid of dogs might begin by sitting near a friendly small dog who is docile, quiet, and passive; then pet the dog; then gradually become accustomed to larger and more active dogs. The second technique is modeling, through which the phobic child observes another child happily experiencing the feared object (for instance, a child who is afraid of the ocean may gain courage seeing another child playing in the water). These two techniques, used together, are much more effective than criticism or forced exposure to what is feared. A child who is terrified of dogs should never be told that only babies are afraid of dogs, nor should a child who is afraid of the water be thrown into it so that he or she will "get over" the fear.

Because their thinking is so centered, young children can imagine something and then act as though they believe it is real. For instance, many children, especially those with few real playmates, create imaginary playmates, who serve as companions for games, and sometimes as scapegoats for mischief or accidents. Children usually take these imaginary playmates quite seriously, and anyone who denies their existence (say, by sitting down on a chair said to be occupied by one) is likely to be confronted by an angry child. Selma Fraiberg (1968) was well aware of this when she encountered her niece's imaginary playmate Laughing Tiger (so named because he always laughed and never bit):

> At dinner that evening my niece did not take notice of me until I was about to sit down. "Watch out," she cried. I rose quickly, suspecting a tack. "You were sitting on Laughing Tiger!" she said sternly. "I'm sorry. Now will you please ask him to get out of my chair." "You can go now, Laughing Tiger," said Jan. And this docile and obedient beast got up from the table and left the company without a murmur.

In this incident, by taking Laughing Tiger seriously, Fraiberg was able to show her respect for her niece as well as reclaim her chair.

Preschool children with such creative imaginations are neither lying nor disturbed; they are simply showing a normal characteristic of preoperational thought. In fact, they may be smarter, more creative, and better adjusted than children who do not have such vivid fantasies (Pines, 1978).

Serious Psychological Disturbances

Although vivid fantasies and irrational fears are usually nothing to be concerned about in early childhood, severe psychological problems can occur, and are generally signalled by abnormal human relationships.

The most severe disturbance of early childhood is called autism, from the word element "auto-," meaning self. Autistic children are so self-involved that they hardly recognize that other people exist, and prefer self-stimulation to stimulation from others. They are given to performing the same behavior again and again, and can spend hours on end turning a toy around and around in their hands or even banging their heads against the wall. The least change in their world can produce pathological terror.

The first signs of autism appear in infancy. Autistic babies do not cuddle when held but become rigid or limp, and they cry and avert their eyes, rather than smile, when familiar people greet them. The diagnosis is confirmed if at age 2 or 3 the child still does not play with others or try to converse (Ornitz and Ritvo, 1976).

Autistic children are usually mute, but sometimes they engage in a type of speech called echolalia, echoing, word for word, such things as singing advertisements or the questions put to them. Ask an autistic child, "Are you hungry?" and, if there is any response, it will most likely be, "Are you hungry?"

Other children seem normal in infancy, but become withdrawn during childhood. Instead of maturing, their thought processes and social skills gradually deteriorate, as their speech becomes disorganized, their nightmares more terrifying, and their emotions less predictable. The usual diagnosis in these cases is childhood schizophrenia

Causes At first, psychiatrists and psychologists were convinced that early parent-infant relationships were the probable causes of most of the emotional problems that children exhibit, so they blamed the parents in cases of autistic or schizophrenic children. Apparent confirmation for this theory came from observation of the typical personality structure of these parents: the parents of an autistic child often seemed cold, aloof, and unusually intellectual; the parents of schizophrenic children often seemed to have a love-hate relationship with their child, showering affection one moment and rejecting the child the next (Achenbach, 1974).

But more recent evidence suggests that both autism and childhood schizophrenia are strongly influenced by congenital factors. Autistic children often have a history of prenatal rubella, postnatal seizures, or other early signs of possible brain damage; and the first symptoms of autism itself appear so early that it is highly unlikely that the parents' behavior could be the cause of the condition. A 4-week-old baby with seemingly normal parents who prefers to look away from faces, for instance, is so abnormal at such a tender age that the cause must be inborn. In addition, it is exceedingly rare for parents to have more than one autistic child, which suggests that something in the child, not in the parents' behavior, causes the disorder.

The evidence that parent-child relationships do not contribute to childhood schizophrenia is less clear. We know schizophrenia in adults is partly genetic, but we do not know if recessive, dominant, or polygenic inheritance patterns predominate, nor are we sure that childhood schizophrenia follows the same genetic patterns as adult schizophrenia. Most important, we do not know what role environment plays. However, we are convinced that some children are born with a greater vulnerability to schizophrenia than others, so that abnormal parenting is not the sole cause (Achenbach, 1974). It is probably safe to conclude that if parents of autistic children seem aloof and cold, or if parents of schizophrenic children seem inconsistent, this parental response is more a reaction to, rather than the cause of, the children's condition (Bender, 1973).

Cures Fortunately, both these problems are rare; only 6 children in 10,000 are diagnosed as autistic or schizophrenic (Werry, 1972). Unfortunately, most children with either problem never recover completely. For autistic children, the chances of recovery improve if the child develops useful speech before age 5; for schizophrenic children, the chances of recovery improve if the first symptoms appear relatively late in childhood. For both disorders, "love is not enough" (Bettelheim, 1950). The most successful treatment methods usually combine behavior therapy with individual attention and concern: autistic children can sometimes learn to talk, and schizophrenic children, to control their anxiety, if a step-by-step conditioning process is set up and reinforcement is carefully delivered. For the severe self-destructive acts some seriously disturbed children engage in, such as banging their heads against a wall, sudden punishment, such as an electric shock, usually eliminates the behavior (Lovaas and Simmons, 1969; Simmons and Lovaas, 1969).

Figure 11.13 *The first step in trying to teach autistic children to communicate is to get them to pay attention to someone else. In this case, the teacher sits right in front of her pupil, rewarding him with a sip of juice if he looks her in the eye.*

Parental participation in the child's treatment is often the most important factor affecting the future of the child, with improvement being more common if the parents are stable and well-adjusted than if they are guilt-ridden and unstable. But it is much easier to state that parents of disturbed children need to be stable and consistent than it is to suggest just how they might manage to be so, given the stresses of their situation, especially since psychologists and psychiatrists themselves do not always agree on what factors make a particular child emotionally disturbed or what measures will foster long-term improvement. Consider Noah, the son of Josh and Fuomi Greenfeld, who was diagnosed as autistic. His parents spent years finding special therapy and providing patient education for him, but by the time Noah was 10, they became depressed and discouraged. Noah's father says he feels guilty

for all the things I no longer do for Noah. Such as run after doctors or seek out miracle cures. I just try to take him for granted.

Which means: I take for granted that I have to live in a house with blankets chewed, pillows strewn about, chairs upturned. I take for granted that I have to be constantly wary of his bowel movements . . . I take for granted that I have to sit with him as he eats and that I have to brush his teeth twice a day and that he has to be coached in the acts of dressing and undressing . . . I take for granted that I must walk with him in the evenings, that I must drive him to school each day, that I must pick him up in the late afternoons. I take for granted that I constantly have a baby to care for.

I also take for granted that what I do is so little, that what Fuomi does is so much more. [Greenfeld, 1978]

Sex Roles and Stereotypes

Parental attitudes and behavior may very well be the determining factor in the development of the young child's conception of masculinity or femininity. Children learn about gender very early. Most 2-year-olds know whether they are boys or girls, identify strangers as mommies or daddies, and know that Daddy has a penis and that Mommy has breasts. By age 3, children can consistently apply gender labels (Thompson, 1975).

These accomplishments do not mean that children understand that gender is biological. Until age 4 or 5, they are likely to think sexual differences depend on clothes, hair, or maturation, rather than on biology, believing that a girl would be a boy if she cut her hair short or that a boy might become a girl if he wore a dress. One preschool girl visited the neighbor's new baby, who was having a bath. Later, her parents asked if the baby was a boy or a girl. "I don't know," she replied, "it's so hard to tell at that age, especially when it's not wearing clothes" (Stone and Church, 1973).

Figure 11.14 *This girl's pleasure at her newly acquired figure is typical of children aged 4 to 6, who usually believe the appearance of femininity or masculinity equals the fact, and that more is better. At this age, boys are given to sticking objects in their pants to exaggerate the size of their penis, and children of both sexes (not yet sure of the internal anatomical differences between male and female) like to stuff the front of their shirts with a pillow "baby."*

Children at 4 and 5 often exaggerate sex stereotypes of behavior, as is apparent in their play. Garvey (1977) found that preschoolers are usually quite willing to let the other child change the plot in dramatic play but they are not willing to let the daddy cook while the mother goes off to work. Many children even adopt the role of Super Mommy or Super Daddy. One little girl busily cared for all of her twenty-six children, one for each letter of the alphabet. One boy, playing a husband-wife game with a girl, walked through the door and announced, "Okay, I'm all through with work, honey. I brought home a thousand dollars."

Figure 11.15 *Children simplify and amplify the roles they play—doctors always heal, cops always catch robbers, and mommies and daddies are powerful, rich, and loving.*

In this day of greater equality for women, many parents are astonished to hear their 5-year-old daughters ask for hair ribbons and organdy dresses or express hopes of becoming stewardesses and nurses, despite the parents' suggestions that they become pilots or doctors. Five-year-old boys have stereotyped ideas of the male role as well. One told his father, a professor who lived a sedentary, academic life, "Oh, Daddy, how old will I be when I can go hunting with you? We'll go in the woods, you with your gun, me with my bow and arrow. Daddy, wouldn't it be neat if we could lasso a wild horse? Do you think I could ride a horse backward if someone's leading me like you?" (Kohlberg, 1966).

RESEARCH REPORT **Sexual Stereotypes in 3-Year-Olds**

We all are aware of the changes in traditional sex roles over the last decade. More women are serving in public office, or working as lawyers, or training as engineers than ever before. More men are sharing in the care of their children and in the housework. These trends are particularly apparent among younger, better-educated people, although changes in sex roles have occurred in every community.

We would expect these changes to reach little children, especially children of college students and faculty, like those at the Stanford University nursery school. However, this turns out to be only partially the case, according to Deanna Kuhn and her colleagues (1978), who found that 2- and 3-year-olds at that school already believed many traditional sex-role concepts.

The research design was simple. Each child was shown two paper dolls, one named Lisa and one named Michael, and then asked which doll would do or say certain things. For some of the statements, the children were equally likely to pick Lisa or Michael. But for other statements, Lisa was more likely to be picked to do traditional female things, and Michael to do traditional male things.

Both boys and girls held the following stereotypes:

Girls Are More Likely To

play with dolls
help mother
talk a lot
never hit
say "I need some help"
clean the house
become a nurse

Boys Are More Likely To

help father
say "I can hit you"
become a boss
mow the grass

The following stereotypes were held by boys but not girls:

Girls Are More Likely To

cry
be slow
cook the dinner

Boys Are More Likely To

be loud
be naughty
grow up to be a doctor or a governor

These stereotypes were held by girls but not boys:

Girls Are More Likely To

look nice
give kisses
say "I can do it best"
take care of babies

Boys Like To

fight
be mean

This study found evidence that some sexual stereotypes are declining. The children held no sex stereotypes for

playing ball
playing house
running fast
being smart
being messy
being dirty
being the leader
being kind
being neat
saying "I can do it"
washing the car
washing the dishes

Best of all, no sex stereotype was shown when the children had to choose whether Lisa or Michael was more likely to say "I love you."

Roles and Attitudes

Obviously, some sex differences are biological facts of life: boys can't become mothers and girls can't become fathers. It is equally clear that some sex differences are cultural: 4-year-old boys wear one-piece bathing suits; 4-year-old girls, with nothing more to conceal, wear two-piece suits. However, trying to distinguish biological from cultural differences is not always easy. Moreover, some cultural differences are harmful and others not; some biological tendencies should be encouraged and others controlled. Whether one believes the sexism of small children is a problem to be counteracted or a fact of life to be celebrated depends on one's own perspective and experience. Psychologists from the three major theoretical camps are themselves divided on this matter.

Psychoanalytic Theory Freud believed that the foundation for our adult sexuality is laid during the years from 3 to 6, with our love, jealousy, and fear of our parents determining how successfully we learn sex-appropriate behavior. Consequently, Freudians are neither surprised nor worried when a 4-year-old exaggerates sex roles considered appropriate to his or her gender.

They are concerned, however, when a child seems indifferent to sex roles or, worse yet, seems to prefer roles of the opposite sex. One cause of such problems, according to this theory, is single-parent families, which do not provide the child with the opportunity to go through the normal love, hate, and identification phases of the Oedipus complex. This lack of normal sex-role development may produce an adult with sexual problems, such as frigidity or homosexuality.

This theory is not generally accepted today, for children from single-parent families usually become well-adjusted, heterosexual adults. In addition, psychologists no longer consider homosexuality per se a sign of emotional disturbance. To the best of our knowledge, a person's sexual preferences are influenced by a host of biological and psychosocial factors at many stages of life, not just by the experiences of early childhood. But Freudian theory has led to two ideas held by many psychologists:

1. Parents should not be very worried if their child exaggerates sex roles. This may be the child's way of working out a complex identity.

2. Young children should know and love adults of both sexes. Especially when the father is not part of the child's life, a relationship with another man (perhaps a grandfather, an uncle, or a teacher) is important.

Behavior Theory Behaviorists take another view about sexual attitudes during early childhood. They believe that virtually all sexual patterns are learned, rather than inborn, and that parents, teachers, and society are responsible for any ideas or patterns the child demonstrates. Behaviorists are not surprised when preschool children seem precociously and dogmatically conscious of sex roles, for most parents of preschool children follow traditional male and female roles, even if the parents don't necessarily hold traditional sex-role views. For instance, imagine a couple who, prior to their first child, try to avoid traditional sex roles, both of them being employed and both sharing the housework. Then the wife becomes pregnant. The most likely sequel is that she will take a maternity leave, quit her job, or work part-time. This traditional pattern is reinforced by the biological fact that only the woman can breast-feed, the sociological fact that relatives and friends generally expect the woman to provide most infant care, and the economic fact that the husband's salary is usually higher than the woman's. Once the wife is home, it seems likely that she will do more than half the housework.

In addition to being influenced by the role adoption they see in the house, preschool children, according to behaviorists, are reinforced for behaving in the ways deemed appropriate for their sex and punished for behaving inappropriately. Research does not always substantiate this hypothesis. In the first place, most parents of preschool children expect their children of both sexes to behave in similar ways: they punish both for being aggressive and encourage both to be independent. If anything, sex stereotypes are reversed, boys getting more punishment for aggression and girls getting more reinforcement for independence (Maccoby and Jacklin, 1974).

However, several interesting sex differences do appear from the research. First, boys are criticized more often for wanting to play with the traditional girls' toys than girls are for wanting to play with boys' toys. Even in toddlerhood, boys are criticized for playing with dolls (Fagot, 1978). Second, fathers are more likely to expect their girls to be "feminine" and their boys to be "masculine" than mothers are. Fathers are more gentle with their daughters than they are with their sons, and are more likely to engage in rough-and-tumble play with their sons than they are with their daughters (Maccoby and Jacklin, 1974).

Studies of children's play show that children expect to be punished if they stray too far from traditional sex roles. In one study, a 5-year-old girl decided to be the father and told a 5-year-old boy to be the mother (Grief, 1976). The boy was clearly upset, saying he *had* to be the father. The girl ignored his complaints until he appealed to authority, threatening to "tell" on her if she didn't let him be the father. At this threat, she gave in. She must have thought that adults would not have let her get away with her game of role reversal.

The behaviorist idea that sex roles are learned has caused many parents, teachers, and psychologists to rethink their interaction with young children. If we want little girls to become active, independent women, we should encourage them to participate in rough-and-tumble play, and try to expose them to books and real-life situations in which women occupy positions of responsibility and power. If we want little boys to become fathers actively involved with their children, we should encourage them when they act out such a role: a 3-year-old boy who tenderly sings a lullabye to a doll should be praised, not teased.

Cognitive Theory Most cognitive psychologists would probably take a position halfway between the psychoanalytic and the behaviorist. While they realize that role models and education help children develop sex roles, they also believe that a child's mental immaturity makes some misunderstanding inevitable. A 4-year-old boy may want to be a mommy when he grows up because he is not yet old enough to realize that gender is a biological fact, virtually impossible to change. Despite her mother's explanation that she can play much more easily in pants, a 5-year-old girl may insist on wearing dresses and hair ribbons to kindergarten because she believes that her femininity depends on frilly clothes.

According to cognitive theory, the child's own mental processes lead first to the idea that sexual differences are a matter of external appearance (compare this with the two glasses in the conservation experiments) and then to a more flexible and mature interpretation of masculinity and femininity. Parents can explain and suggest, but the sex roles children eventually adopt are influenced more by their own understanding and preferences than by their mother's or father's.

Androgyny

Each theoretical position has merit. Obviously, sex differences are both inborn and learned, and cognitive maturity is needed before one can grasp the complexity of modern sex differences and similarities. But this generality is of little help to a parent or teacher trying to decide which qualities to encourage or discourage in a child. Although almost everyone recognizes that traditional sex roles are too restrictive, many parents hesitate to treat their daughters and sons in the same way, because they worry that their girls might become too masculine or their boys too feminine.

A new concept, androgyny, has been developed to counter the misconception that masculinity and femininity are exact opposites—an assumption that leads a great many people to believe that the less one follows the feminine role, the more masculine one becomes, and vice versa. Androgyny—strictly speaking, the state of having both male and female sexual characteristics—has come to be used in connection with a person's defining himself or herself primarily as a human being, rather than as a male or female (Bem, 1974).

In this sense, androgynous men and women share many of the same personality characteristics, instead of following the traditional sex-role patterns. For instance, traditional males rate significantly higher than traditional females on a personality trait labeled "dominant-ambitious," but androgynous males and females score about the same, because the men see themselves as less dominant than the traditional male does, while the females see themselves as more dominant than the traditional female does (Wiggins and Holzmuller, 1978). Androgynous people of both sexes are nurturing and independent, and neither sex tries to be unemotional or passive.

People who are flexible in their sex roles, and able to display the best qualities of both traditional stereotypes, are more competent and have a higher sense of self-esteem than people who follow traditional sex-role behavior (Spence and Helmreich, 1978). This suggests that it is good to encourage children to develop all their potential characteristics, letting them engage in rough-and-tumble play outside as well as quiet play in the doll corner. Instead of saying, "Boys don't cry," or "Girls don't fight," we should apply the same standards to both sexes, either advising, "Children should settle their own arguments," or "Nobody fights," as the situation demands.

Figure 11.16 *Nearly all of the games of early childhood, from the physical release of running and chasing games to the emotional pleasure of caring for a family of dolls, can be fun for children of both sexes. Allowing and encouraging preschoolers to play with a variety of materials helps them develop their own abilities and preferences, whether "masculine," "feminine," or androgynous.*

The Three Theories Reconsidered

At the beginning of this chapter, the three theoretical explanations of the young child's psychosocial development seemed to have little in common. But now that we have looked at the thoughts and actions of young children, the three theoretical explanations seem to agree on several points: that the spontaneous social play of the young child helps to develop the understanding of social rules; that the parents' interaction with the child is crucial to the formation of the early self-concept; that television is a potentially harmful influence; and that physical aggression, powerful fantasies, and sexual stereotypes are normal during early childhood.

Although the theoretical underpinnings of the three approaches are quite different, their practical applications are similar. As long as young children have parents who love them and friends to play with them, they could be raised according to psychoanalytic, behaviorist, or cognitive principles and would, in all three situations, develop a healthy sense of who they are and how to live with others.

SUMMARY

Three Theories

1. While all psychologists agree that children begin to learn sex roles and moral values during early childhood, they disagree about how this occurs.

2. Freud believed that the guilt and fear that children feel because of the fantasies of the Oedipal complex result in the development of their superegos. Erikson stresses the child's initiative and exuberance, noting that the child sometimes feels guilty when this energy gets out of bounds.

3. Behaviorists think children learn their values from the reinforcement they receive for acting appropriately, and from the punishment they get for behaving inappropriately. The example set by their parents, as well as the role models they see in their community or on television, is also important.

4. Cognitive theorists remind us that young children are illogical and egocentric. We should not expect them to understand moral values, or the nature of sex roles. For example, the typical preschool child thinks maleness and femaleness are the result of clothes and hair style rather than biology.

Play

5. Playing with other children prepares preschoolers for the demands of school and the social relationships they will later develop. As children grow older, they spend more time in associative and cooperative play than in the more simple onlooker or parallel play of the younger child.

Parenting

6. Parent-child interaction is complex, with no simple answers about the best way to raise a child. However, in general, authoritative parents, who are warm and loving but willing to set and enforce reasonable limits, have children who are happy, self-confident, and successful. Authoritarian families, in which punishment is strict, tend to produce aggressive children. Children from permissive families often lack self-control.

7. Preschool children need to know clear and consistent rules, and what the consequences are for breaking them. The most effective punishments are temporary removal of something the child enjoys (television, a tricycle) rather than harsh punishment.

Television

8. Television can be educational for young children. But television is also a harmful influence, because young children tend to believe advertisements, follow the example of televised violence, and spend time watching television which could be better spent playing.

Possible Problems

9. Normal preschool children sometimes use physical force to get what they want and sometimes have vivid fantasies that they think are real. These behaviors are to be expected in a child who is trying to cope with the many ideas and problems of social interaction but is without the thought processes available to older children and adults.

10. Some children show signs of serious psychological problems, for example the autistic or the schizophrenic child. The causes of these disturbances are multifactorial. The best chances for improvement lie in a structured treatment program in which parents participate.

Sex Roles and Stereotypes

11. For many reasons, children become more conscious of sex roles toward the end of early childhood. The response of parents and teachers to this development depends on their own ideas of appropriate masculine, feminine, or androgynous behavior.

KEY QUESTIONS

According to Freud, how and why does the superego develop?

According to behaviorists, how do children learn sex roles and moral values?

According to cognitive theorists, why do 5-year-olds have particularly stereotyped ideas of sex roles?

Why is social play important?

As children grow older, how does their dramatic play change?

What kinds of punishment are worst for young children and why?

What kinds of punishment are best for young children and why?

What three things are critics of children's television particularly concerned about?

What are the essential disagreements between Freud and the behaviorists about the origin of sex roles during early childhood?

What are the essential agreements among theorists of all three camps about psychosocial development during early childhood?

KEY TERMS

phallic stage	authoritarian parenting
Oedipus complex	permissive parenting
identification	authoritative parenting
Electra complex	harsh punishment
penis envy	instrumental aggression
initiative versus guilt	hostile aggression
social play	phobia
dramatic play	gradual desensitization
solitary play	modeling
onlooker play	imaginary playmates
parallel play	autism
associative play	echolalia
cooperative play	childhood schizophrenia
group glee	androgyny

RECOMMENDED READINGS

Garvey, Catherine. *Play.* Cambridge, Mass.: Harvard University Press, 1977.

This is a scholarly and lively presentation of the many forms of play and the many things children learn while playing. Garvey includes many quotations from children engaged in dramatic play, showing how children develop their social ideas and skills.

Greenfeld, Josh. *A child called Noah.* New York: Pocket Books, 1972. *A place for Noah.* New York: Pocket Books, 1978.

These two books tell about Noah Greenfeld, a child diagnosed as autistic and later considered brain-damaged, and about his parents and older brother as they try to live with Noah. By reading both books, you will understand some of the hope, despair, and anger of the parents of severely disturbed children. You will also get an idea of the kinds of help psychologists and educators can provide, and of the many ways the entire community—professionals and lay people alike—fail to offer the support that the Greenfelds, and thousands of other families like them, need.

Bettelheim, Bruno. *The uses of enchantment: The meaning and importance of fairy tales.* New York: Vintage Books, 1977.

Bruno Bettelheim is famous as a child psychologist from the Freudian tradition who has worked with emotionally disturbed children. In this book he analyzes children's fairy tales and shows how they express and explain the child's fantasies, especially those of the phallic stage.

The School Years

PART IV

If someone asked you to pick the best years of the entire life span, you might choose the years from 7 to 11 and defend your choice persuasively. To begin with, physical development is usually almost problem-free, making it easy to master dozens of new skills.

With regard to cognitive development, most children are able to learn quickly and think logically, providing the topic is not too abstract. Moral reasoning has reached that state where right seems clearly distinguished from wrong, with none of the ambiguities that complicate moral issues for adolescents and adults.

Finally, the social world of middle childhood seems perfect, for most school-age children think their parents are helpful, their teachers fair, and their friends loyal. Their future seems filled with promise—at least most of the time it does.

However, school and friendships are so important at this age that two common events can seem crushing: failure in school and rejection by peers. Some lucky children escape these problems; others have sufficient self-confidence or family support to weather them when they arise; and some leave middle childhood with painful memories, feeling inadequate, incompetent, and inferior for the rest of their lives.

The next three chapters celebrate the joys, and commemorate the occasional tragedies, of middle childhood.

The School Years: Physical Development

Once riding in old Baltimore
Heart-filled, head-filled with glee
I saw the whole of Baltimore
Keep looking straight at me.

Now I was eight and very small
And he was no whit bigger
And so I smiled, but he poked out
His tongue, and called me "Nigger."

I saw the whole of Baltimore
From May until December
Of all the things that happened there
That's all that I remember.

Countee Cullen, 1925
"Incident"

CHAPTER 12

Size and Shape

Variations

Childhood Obesity

Motor Skills

Children with Handicaps

Separate Education

Mainstreaming

Learning Disabilities

Hyperactive Children

True or False?

Obesity is a serious problem for adults, but it is not significant in childhood because it is so easily outgrown.

During middle childhood, at least, boys have the advantage over girls in nearly all physical activities.

The old saw "All work and no play makes Jack a dull boy" has academic as well as social validity.

According to teachers, about one-fourth of all school-age children in the United States have a handicap that warrants special educational help.

Learning disabilities such as extreme difficulty in reading and writing can usually be traced to prenatal brain damage.

Children who are troublemakers because they are hyperactive are generally unaware of, or indifferent to, the difficulties their behavior creates.

In general, physical development in middle childhood seems smooth and relatively uneventful for a number of reasons. For one thing, disease and death are rarer during these years than during any other period. For another, most children master new physical skills quickly, provided they have an opportunity to practice them. In addition, sex differences are minimal, and sexual urges seem to be submerged, so the task of understanding sexual identity remains simplified for the time being.

However, for many school-age children, the way their bodies look and move becomes a source of embarrassment and concern—not because new physical problems appear but because old problems suddenly become much more important. This shift occurs largely because of increased cognitive development. As we will see in detail in the next chapter, egocentrism, a hallmark of preoperational thought, declines during middle childhood. As a result, children become much more aware of the opinions of others and are much more likely to note, and react to, differences among peers. Thus children with physical problems—whether minor ones such as needing glasses or major ones such as needing crutches—are likely to be teased or stared at. In similar fashion, children who are physically less skilled than their siblings or classmates are likely to be made to feel clumsy and inferior.

At the same time, the social world of the school-age child becomes much broader, as elementary school usually brings together children who have differing backgrounds and abilities. Preschool children who can't tie their shoes, or speak clearly, or read the letters of the alphabet are usually unaware that many of their peers can. However, in elementary school, children compare themselves to one another, and those who are "behind" their classmates in areas related to physical maturation may feel themselves to be deficient. Physical development during this period even affects friendships, for they become based, in part, on physical appearance and competence. Consequently, children who look "different," or who are noticeably lacking in physical skills, often become lonely and unhappy.

Thus, the change in children's thought processes and the expansion of their social world during middle childhood can transform physical differences into psychological problems during these years. With this in mind, we are ready to examine normal and abnormal physical development.

Size and Shape

Children grow more slowly during middle childhood than they did earlier or than they will in adolescence. Gaining about 5 pounds (2¼ kilograms) and 2½ inches (6 centimeters) per year, the average child by age 10 weighs about 70 pounds (32 kilograms) and measures 54 inches (137 centimeters).

During these years the average child becomes proportionally thinner as he or she grows taller. Muscles become stronger each year, enabling the average 10-year-old, for instance, to throw a ball twice as far as the average 6-year-old. The capacity of the lungs increases, and the heart grows stronger, so each year of middle childhood enables the child to run faster and exercise longer than before.

These changes can be affected by experience as well as maturation, as shown by studies of girls who trained for serious competitive swimming, often beginning at age 8 or earlier to swim three or four hours a day. By adolescence, the lung and heart capacity of these girls was significantly greater than that of their peers who were comparable in body type and strength before the training (Eriksson, 1976).

Variations

Many healthy children are much larger or smaller than average. The range is so great that, for example, if 8-year-olds who are among the tallest and heaviest 10 percent of their age group were to stop growing for one year while their classmates grew normally, they would still be taller than half their contemporaries and heavier than three-quarters of them (National Center for Health Statistics, 1976).

In some regions of the world, most of the variation in height is caused by malnutrition, with wealthier children being several inches taller than their contemporaries from the other side of town—whether the town is Hong Kong, Rio de Janeiro, or New Delhi. But as we saw in Chapter 6, most children in North America get enough food during middle childhood to grow as tall as their genes allow. So heredity, rather than diet, causes most of the variation we see (Eveleth and Tanner, 1976).

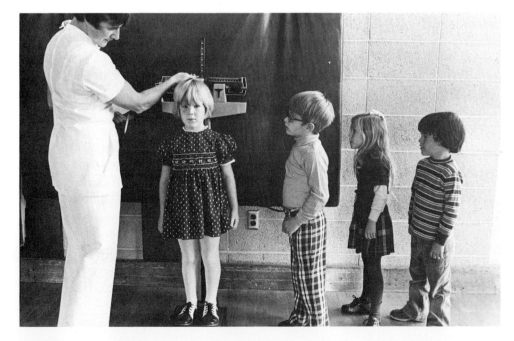

Figure 12.1 *Genes rather than diet cause most of the variations in body build and height among elementary school classmates in North America. Of course, in countries where severe malnutrition is prevalent, the effects of diet are much more apparent.*

Children grow less during middle childhood than at any other time, a fact especially apparent when one realizes that a 3-inch increase for a toddler who is 2½ feet tall is proportionately much greater than for a 10-year-old who is almost 5 feet tall. As you can see, girls begin their adolescent growth spurt a year or two earlier than boys—so growth tables can be unisex until age 10 but must separate the sexes at that point.

TABLE 12.1   **Expected Increase in Height Per Year**

Age	Both Sexes	
	Inches	*Centimeters*
Birth to 1 year	9.8	24.9
1–2	4.8	12.2
2–3	3.6	9.1
3–4	2.9	7.4
4–5	2.7	6.9
5–6	2.7	6.9
6–7	2.4	6.1
7–8	2.2	5.6
8–9	2.2	5.6
9–10	2.0	5.1

Age	Boys		Girls	
	Inches	*Centimeters*	*Inches*	*Centimeters*
10–11	1.9	4.8	2.3	5.8
11–12	1.9	4.8	2.5	6.4
12–13	2.2	5.6	2.6	6.6
13–14	2.8	7.1	1.9	4.8

Source: Lowrey, 1978.

Rates of maturation also vary. For instance, a relatively tall 7-year-old might still have the muscle maturity and coordination more typical of a 5-year-old. At the other end of middle childhood, some 10- and 11-year-olds begin to undergo the changes of puberty, and may find that they are superior to their peers, not only in height but in strength and endurance as well. These variations also follow genetic, and perhaps cultural, patterns. French-speaking Canadian children, for example, tend to be smaller, stronger, and to have greater heart and lung capacity than their English-speaking Canadian peers (Shephard, 1976).

While it may be comforting for parents and teachers to know that healthy children come in all shapes and sizes, it is not always comforting to the children

Figure 12.2 *The second boy is not only slower, he is a bit confused about the research on Canadian children. What might have helped him do better in this race would have been French ancestors, not French lessons.*

themselves. As we saw in Chapter 10, toward the end of the preschool period children become less egocentric as their awareness of the opinions of others increases. This trend continues in middle childhood. However, school-age children are not very adept at anticipating how their own comments might affect someone else, so they are very likely to tell each other "You're so short, you look like a first-grader" or "Your long legs make me think of a spider"—without realizing that such comments can make a child feel abnormal and ashamed. Deliberate insults, like the one in the Cullen poem at the beginning of this chapter, are even worse.

Childhood Obesity

The hardest size difference to bear in middle childhood is obesity. Although the point at which an overweight child qualifies as "obese" depends partly on the child's body type, partly on the proportion of fat to muscle, and partly on the culture, there is no doubt that at least 5 percent of all North American elementary-school children can be classified as obese. Compared to the average child who weighs about 66 pounds at 53 inches, children in this group weigh more than 85 pounds at the same height (National Center for Health Statistics, 1976). These children are overweight by almost everyone's standards.

Obesity is a physical and medical problem at any stage of life, for the overweight person usually exercises less and runs a greater risk of serious illness; and except in the early years, it is often a psychological problem as well. Preschool children are not usually troubled much by the fact that they are fatter than their friends, but in middle childhood, fat children are teased, picked on, and rejected. They know they are overweight, and they often hate themselves for it.

For example, Robert Staffieri (1967) showed children between 6 and 10 years old silhouettes of three people—one fat, one thin, and one muscular—and asked which adjectives on a checklist described each one. The children labeled the fat silhouette "forgetful," "cheating," "argumentative," "lying," "sloppy," "mean," "ugly," "dirty," and "stupid" at least twice as often as they did the thin silhouette and three times as often as they did the muscular silhouette. Even children who thought they themselves were overweight chose negative adjectives to describe the fat silhouette.

Obese children have fewer friends than other children (Staffieri, 1967); and when they are accepted in a peer group, it is often at a high price: they are usually forced to answer to nicknames like "Tubby," "Blubber," or "Fat Albert," and must suffer jokes about their shape. To make matters worse, obesity occurs more often among low-income children than among middle-income children, so many overweight children must cope with both liabilities (Eveleth and Tanner, 1976).

Help for Overweight Children   Clearly, an overweight child needs emotional support for a bruised self-concept, as well as help in losing weight. But reducing is difficult and psychological encouragement is often scarce, partly because obesity is usually fostered by family attitudes and habits that are hard to break. Obese children sometimes try crash diets, which make them irritable, listless, and even sick—adding to their psychological problems without accomplishing much long-term weight loss. To make matters even more difficult, nutritionists caution against strenuous dieting during childhood, since cutting down on protein or calcium could hinder important bone and brain growth (Winick, 1975). Generally, they recommend stabilizing the weight of obese children to allow them to "grow out" of their fat.

Causes of Childhood Obesity

Nutritionists believe that a combination of many factors causes obesity (Weil, 1975). These influences begin in infancy, continue through childhood, and are still important in adulthood. Five are particularly important.

1. *Heredity.*   Body type, including the distribution of fat, as well as height and bone structure, is inherited.

2. *Activity level.*   Inactive people burn fewer calories and are more likely to be overweight than active people. This is just as true in infancy and childhood as in the rest of life.

3. *Types of food eaten.*   Besides the obvious culprits, many common foods, from cornflakes to ketchup, have sugar as a major ingredient. Children who eat too much of these foods become overweight. On other diets—such as breast milk for infants or vegetarian diets for adults—it is hard to become fat.

4. *Attitude toward food.*   Some people consider food a symbol of love and comfort, and eat whenever they are upset. This pattern may begin in infancy, if parents feed their babies whenever they cry rather than first figuring out if the baby is lonely or uncomfortable rather than hungry (Heald, 1975). It continues through childhood, when parents, teachers, and even pediatricians use sweets as a reward or consolation.

5. *Quantity of food eaten.*   In some families, parents take satisfaction in watching their children eat, always urging them to have another helping. The implication is that a father's love is measured by how much food he can provide, a mother's love, by how well she can cook, and a child's love, by how much he or she can eat. This is especially true when the parents or grandparents grew up where starvation was possible. In those places, overweight was a sign of health and wealth. An extra layer of fat was a valuable resource the child's body could use when food became scarce.

Childhood obesity correlates with adult obesity. In fact, fat babies are more likely than average-weight babies to become fat children, who are more likely than average-weight children to become fat adolescents, who are more

likely than average-weight adolescents to become fat adults. One theory to explain this correlation is that overfeeding in the first years may produce an excess of fat cells in the infant's body (Knittle, 1972).

How can too much food create too many *cells*? For most of life, the number of fat cells in a person's body remains the same no matter what that person eats. Adults become fatter because each fat cell becomes fuller, or thinner because each cell gets emptier; but new cells are not formed.

However, before birth, in the first two years of life, and during early adolescence, the size *and* the number of the cells can increase. This number is related to nourishment, for malnutrition slows down the rate of cell multiplication. If this process works in the other direction, overfeeding an infant might produce a superabundance of fat cells (Winick, 1975). Fat babies and adolescents would become adults who want more food and gain weight more easily than people who were not overfed as children. Even when these adults dieted and lost weight, their bodies would still contain those extra cells, just waiting to soak up calories like a sponge.

This theory would explain why chubby babies are more likely than average-weight babies to become overweight children and obese adults. However, scientists do not believe that there is a direct path from infant overfeeding to extra fat cells to adult obesity, for fat babies do not always become fat children or adults, and even those who follow this path may be directed by genes rather than childhood diet. Whatever the precise cause of obesity, it is a major health problem, with one in five adults being 30 percent or more over their "ideal" weight. There is no doubt that overweight children need help in changing their eating and exercise habits in order to make childhood more enjoyable and adult obesity less likely.

When Father's role is to "bring home the bacon," and Mother's role is to prepare home-baked goodies, Junior is often expected to do his part by eating and enjoying everything he is offered.

Figure 12.3 *Because many obese children have come to associate food with love and comfort, they seek solace from criticism by stuffing themselves with food—even when what they have been criticized for is their fatness.*

The best solution is increased physical activity, especially since overweight children tend to be less active than their peers, burning fewer calories and adding pounds even when they eat less than other children (Mayer, 1968). More exercise would mean stronger muscles and less fat. However, exercise is hard for overweight children, for they are not often chosen to play on the team, and they are likely to be teased when they try to join in group activities.

Parents and teachers can help overweight children to do the kinds of exercise in which their size is not much of a disadvantage—walking to school rather than taking the bus, or doing sit-ups at home—or even an advantage, as it might be in swimming or football. Parents can also exercise with their children, not only making activity easier and providing a good model, but bolstering the child's self-confidence as well.

Figure 12.4 *Overweight children seem to resist exercise for a number of reasons. For one thing, physical activity is more difficult for them than for normal-weight children. Then, too, there is the question of self-consciousness, especially in a class setting: most gym outfits seem designed to reveal extra weight rather than hide it.*

Motor Skills

The fact that children grow more slowly during middle childhood may be part of the reason they become so much more skilled at controlling their bodies during these years. (Compare this control, for instance, with the clumsiness that typically accompanies sudden changes in body shape and size during puberty.) School-age children can perform almost any motor skill, as long as it doesn't require very much power or judgment. The skills of average North American 8- and 9-year-olds include swinging a hammer well, sawing, using garden tools, sewing, knitting, drawing in good proportion, writing or printing accurately and neatly, cutting fingernails (Gesell et al., 1977), riding bicycles, scaling fences, swimming, diving, roller skating, ice skating, jumping rope, and playing baseball, football, and jacks (Stone and Church, 1973).

A CLOSER LOOK   **Benefits from Physical Activity**

Physical activity in middle childhood has many benefits. Besides the obvious fact that it can help regulate weight and strengthen muscles, it also appears that exercise in childhood may slow down or even prevent the development of serious health problems (Bailey, 1977). For example, heart disease and high blood pressure are less common in adults who exercised regularly when they were children, even if they have become more sedentary in adulthood.

In addition, children who master a physical skill, whether it be turning a cartwheel or catching a football, think better of themselves (McGowan et al., 1974) and enjoy greater acceptance by other children (Clarke and Greene, 1963; Nelson, 1966). This is especially important for children who are having trouble in other spheres of competence, such as understanding schoolwork or making friends.

Finally, physical activity may help a child think and learn better. This was shown in France, where elementary-school children usually attend school six days a week, leaving little time for active play. Over a decade ago, some French schools began an experimental program: children spent two-thirds of their schoolday in academic work and one-third in physical exercise, including swimming, gymnastics, games, and free play. Educators hoped that the advantages of this physical activity would outweigh the disadvantages of less classroom time—and they did. Children in the experimental schools actually improved in academic skills, surpassing children who spent most of their time studying. School officials also reported that health improved and that discipline problems became fewer. In 1969, the play program was adopted throughout France (Bailey, 1977).

Unfortunately, many physical-education programs in North America emphasize competitive team sports rather than physical activity per se. Especially for children who are not very good at hitting a baseball or catching a football, and so are the last to be chosen for the team, or the least likely to get into the game, such programs may be worse than nothing at all.

Boys and girls are just about equal in physical abilities during these years, except that boys have greater forearm strength (Tanner, 1970) and girls have greater flexibility. Boys thus have an advantage in sports like baseball, whereas girls have the edge in sports like gymnastics. But for most physical activities during middle childhood, neither body size nor sex is as important as age and experience. Short children can become fast runners, boys can do cartwheels, and girls can hit home runs, if they spend enough time practicing.

Figure 12.5 *Increased body control during middle childhood makes climbing, swinging, and jumping among the favorite activities of school-age children.*

However, the maxim "Practice makes perfect" does not necessarily hold (Åstrand, 1976). Every motor skill is related to several other abilities, some depending on body size, others on brain maturation, others on practice. Take softball, for example. It is much easier for an elementary-school child to throw a ball than to catch one, for catching involves more judgment and eye-hand coordination. Reaction time, that is, how much time it takes to respond to a particular stimulus, is longer the younger a child is: younger children are therefore apt to drop a ball after it lands in their mitt because they are slow to enclose it, or to strike out by swinging too late. In fact, many of our national sports are very difficult for elementary-school children because they demand precisely those skills that are hardest to master. Ideally, the physical activities of elementary-school children should center around skills that most children can perform reasonably well.

Children with Handicaps

Can a blind 6-year-old be expected to learn in a classroom with children of normal vision? Can a child in a wheelchair play with other third-graders? What about the child who is mentally retarded, or has a learning disability, or is hyperactive?

Teachers estimate that about 25 percent of all school-age children in the United States need special educational help because they have some kind of handicap (Roberts and Baird, 1972). This includes children with vision, hearing, and speech problems, children who cannot use their limbs normally, and children who have specific learning disabilities. The United States Congress gives a more conservative estimate: it allows the states to designate 12 percent of all children between the ages of 5 and 15 as educationally handicapped.

Separate Education

Because teachers did not feel prepared to handle them, and parents wanted to protect them from loneliness and mockery, many handicapped children used to stay at home, educated by their parents or a tutor or not taught at all. Others spent their school years in classes for special children.

Such segregation to some degree seems warranted, since school is the place where a child is most intensely compared with other children. Often all children the same age are expected to be able to accomplish the same things at the same time. Consequently, the first-grader who can't sit still when the teacher asks for quiet, the third-grader who can't read out loud, and the fifth-grader who can't do multiplication are all made aware of their inadequacies. So is the rest of the class, often making it even harder for the disabled child to learn.

Figure 12.6 *These photos of a class at the Lexington School for the Deaf show several of the advantages of special education. The curriculum is designed to accommodate the students' disability (note the many visual aids), the class size is small, and because the students all have the same problem and all are wearing a hearing aid, no one feels "different."*

However, educators and parents have realized that separate education is not always best for children with special problems—either obvious problems like blindness or less apparent difficulties such as moderate mental retardation. For one thing, handicapped children need to learn many cognitive skills that are best learned in a regular classroom. Studies have shown, for instance, that most retarded children learn more in a regular class than in a class for slow learners (Blackman and Heintz, 1966). In addition (and probably even more important than the question of cognitive achievement), children, in preparation for adulthood, should learn to cope in a world of many kinds of people. Most children, handicapped or not, learn social and survival skills best by playing and learning with other children; so normal children and special children should benefit from sharing a classroom.

Another argument against separate education is that once children become labeled as handicapped and are segregated, their adjustment to special treatment within a self-contained classroom where they never play with normal children may make it difficult for them to outgrow the stereotype or the special educational milieu. The deaf child who has to learn with other hearing-impaired children might not learn to lip-read; the child who was mentally retarded at age 7 because of a temporary family problem (such as a death, or a bitter divorce) might, if placed in a special classroom, remain classified as retarded at age 11. Once a child is labeled as needing special education, the label tends to stick, even when the child's needs change.

We may be "digging the educational graves of many racially and/or economically disadvantaged children by using an I.Q. score to justify the label 'mentally retarded'! This term then becomes a destructive, self-fulfilling prophecy." These forceful words were part of a journal article written in 1968 by Lloyd Dunn, a leading researcher in the area of special education. His words and the ideas behind them heralded mainstreaming, a new approach to educating handicapped children.

Mainstreaming

Many educators now believe that handicapped children should be integrated with normal children as much as possible and as early as possible (Nix, 1976; Dunn, 1973; Gardner, 1977; Deno, 1973). This practice is called mainstreaming, because the handicapped children join the main group of children. Federal laws currently guarantee the rights of all children, no matter what their handicaps, to public education, within regular classrooms if possible.

Figure 12.7 *Friendship between children may be the greatest advantage of mainstreaming.*

However, children should not be left to "sink or swim" when they join the mainstream. Many need supportive services to help them learn in the regular classroom, and some children still need special classrooms and schools, at least for part of their education. One technique adopted by many schools is the creation of a resource room, with special learning materials and specially trained teachers, where children with learning difficulties can receive help. One advantage of this solution is that a child can be assigned to the resource room for several hours a day, even in midyear, without disrupting friendship patterns or identification with a regular class. In the same way, a child who no longer needs special help can rejoin the regular group easily. In addition, communication between regular and special teachers, which is essential to the child's optimal learning, is facilitated when both types of teachers have classrooms within the same school.

Sometimes educators and psychologists who plan for the handicapped child ignore the special needs of the child's parents, who experience many stresses that other parents do not (as suggested by the fact that parents who have a congenitally handicapped child are twice as likely to become divorced as the parents of normal children are [Tew and Lawrence, 1975]). Simple tasks that schools expect of normal students, such as getting to school on time or completing a homework report that requires library research, often mean additional stress for the parents of a disabled child. Consequently, the decision to mainstream a child should be made by teachers, parents, and, if possible, the child as well, so that each person concerned understands what the mainstreaming will mean personally.

A CLOSER LOOK   **The Educational History of David**

David's mother had a sore throat in March 1967 when she was four weeks pregnant. Her experience as a pediatric nurse led her to think that she might have rubella, and she was prepared to consider an abortion. But her illness was misdiagnosed as scarlet fever, and she and her husband decided to accept the diagnosis rather than persist in their unconfirmed suspicions.

In November, her son David was born with rubella syndrome, including a serious heart defect and cataracts covering his eyes. Survival was in doubt during the first weeks, but heart surgery repaired some of the heart deficiency at one month. An operation to allow some light to pass around the cataract in one eye failed, destroying that eye completely.

Given such tragic conditions, many parents are too numbed to think about what they can do to foster normal development in their handicapped infants. Luckily, David's parents invited a worker from the Kentucky School for the Blind to visit their home and give them advice. One of the suggestions they followed was to provide David with a large rug for a play area, rather than confining him to a playpen. When he crawled onto the floor, his parents would say "No" and place him back on the rug, thus enabling him to learn where he could explore safely without bumping into walls or furniture.

David's parents were equally fortunate with regard to preschool education, which is hard to find for infants such as David, who, at age 2, did not walk, talk, or feed himself. A new job took the family to Boston, where the Perkins School for the Blind had just begun a program for 2-year-olds and their mothers. Observing a teacher work with David, David's mother learned specific methods used to develop motor and language skills in multihandicapped children, and she in turn taught them to David's father and older brothers. The family spent hours rolling balls, doing puzzles, and singing with David.

Mainstreaming can be very successful, even when it places special demands on teachers and children. This blind boy (not David) is able to use a typewriter in class, lift weights in gym, and play with friends during recess.

At age 3, tests showed David to be mentally retarded, which was not surprising since he did not talk and could not coordinate his hands or fingers very well. However, David's hearing was found to be normal, making him one of the lucky ones, for 72 percent of rubella syndrome 3-year-olds have hearing defects (Chess et al., 1971).

At age 4, David was walking and saying his first word, "Dada." Open-heart surgery corrected the remaining heart damage, and an operation removed the cataract on his other eye. His parents moved back to Kentucky and found four schools that would accept David. He attended two schools for victims of cerebral palsy, one in the morning, in Lexington, and another in the afternoon, forty miles away. (He ate lunch in the car with his mother.) On Fridays these two schools were closed, so he attended a school for the mentally retarded, and on Sunday he spent two hours in Sunday school, his first experience with mainstreaming.

Learning Disabilities

Many children (estimates range from 2 to 40 percent) have specific learning disabilities, perhaps in reading (dyslexia), writing (dysgraphia), or arithmetic (dyscalcula). Children with a learning disability seem normal—at least there is *no apparent problem in vision, hearing, intelligence, or motivation*—but they have great difficulty learning some particular skill that other children the same age learn easily.

What Causes a Learning Disability?   The precise cause or causes of learning disabilities are hard to pinpoint, but to many professionals it looks as if some parts

At age 7, David entered first grade in a public school. He was legally blind (his vision with heavy glasses was still far from perfect); his motor skills were poor (among other things, he had difficulty controlling a pencil); and his social skills were immature (he pinched people he didn't like and cried and laughed at inappropriate times). But his intellectual development was adequate for regular school. In some skills, he was advanced; he could multiply and divide in his head.

By age 11, David, having skipped a grade, was a fifth-grader. He read with a large magnifying glass—at the eleventh-grade level—and was labeled "intellectually gifted" according to a test of verbal and math skills. For about an hour each day, he was tutored by a teacher for special children, but the rest of the time he was in a regular class. He began to learn a second language and to play the violin. In both areas, he proved to have an extraordinary auditory memory and acuity. Even his social skills had improved, although the other children teased him because he still looked and acted "different." His teacher found him "difficult," and wondered if he should see a psychiatrist (this

same teacher failed David in a math test because he had refused to do long division, yet admitted that he was the best math student in the class).

As this book goes to press, David is approaching his twelfth birthday. He still is difficult, but his parents remember how much harder he used to be. More than that, they rejoice that their legally blind child can see well enough to read; and that their "severely retarded" child is now "intellectually gifted."

They hope David has found enough understanding from regular teachers and normal children that, by adulthood, he will interact with people as well as he now plays with words and numbers.

David's progress is exceptional. Few children who do not begin to speak until age 4 are so advanced by age 11. We do not know how much his family's devotion, his early special education, and his later mainstreaming each contributed to David's remarkable development. But David does show that predictions are difficult. Children who seem hopelessly handicapped or retarded may eventually learn in a regular classroom and live a normal life.

of the child's brain do not function as well as they might. In other words, there seems to be a minimal brain dysfunction that impairs learning ability.

The symptoms of minimal brain dysfunctions are *sometimes* similar to those of adults who have sustained brain damage, that is, damage to the structure of the brain. For instance, a woman with a brain tumor was presented with the following problem: "A boy is eight years old. His father is thirty years older, and his mother is ten years younger than the father. How old is she?" The woman tried three times—first adding 8, 30, and 10 to get 48 and then dividing by 3; then subtracting 10 from

Figure 12.8 *Dyslexia takes many forms. One of the simplest is "mirror" reading, in which letters, sentences, or, as in this case, words, are read backward.*

30; then subtracting 10 from 30 again—finally she added 8 and 30, subtracted 10, and got the correct answer, 28 (Luria, 1966). Her difficulty sounds familiar to anyone who has taught children or adults with dyscalcula. The interesting fact, however, is that this woman's disability disappeared when the tumor was removed (Farnham-Diggory, 1978).

(a)

(b)

(c)

Figure 12.9 *The classroom behavior of children with learning disabilities is usually normal until they are faced with a situation beyond their capacities. (a) This boy listens to his teacher's question, (b) thinks, (c) gets part of the answer, (d) then temporarily despairs at getting the rest.*

(d)

Other victims of brain damage sometimes lose their ability to read, write, spell, or speak normally, even though other aspects of their functioning are normal. This fact led early researchers to think that brain damage (perhaps sustained during prenatal development or in the birth process) was the cause of childhood learning problems too. However, many professionals now believe that although brain dysfunction is sometimes attributable to an injury to the brain, a more common cause is probably an inherited difficulty in brain functioning—perhaps involving connections between the left and right brains or the sensory areas, such as those having to do with vision and hearing (Farnham-Diggory, 1978). This theory seems plausible because siblings and other relatives of children with learning disabilities often have some learning difficulties themselves.

For at least two reasons, however, we must be cautious in hypothesizing organic causes for learning disabilities. First, it is difficult to prove that a particular form of brain damage or pattern of inheritance, or, for that matter, a particular drug taken by the mother during pregnancy or a disease contracted by the child in infancy, causes a particular learning problem. More important, the assumption that the cause of a learning disability is organic sometimes leads to the belief that it is almost impossible to remedy the disability through education. In fact, no matter what the cause of learning disabilities, the way teachers and parents respond can make an enormous difference to the child's chances of overcoming the problem. If teachers and parents realize that a given child is neither lazy nor stupid, but has a learning disability, they can help the child become a competent adult.

That might seem to be an overly optimistic statement about a 9-year-old who is "word blind," unable to read even the simplest words, or a 13-year-old who spells brother "brith" and helicopter "throccatei" (Farnham-Diggory, 1978). But many such children learn basic skills eventually, especially if they are given patient, individual tutoring. And in adulthood, we all find ways to compensate for our specific disabilities.

Take going to the supermarket to pick up some groceries, for instance. It's a simple task; almost every adult can do it. But many adults have difficulty with some aspect of the task, and have learned to compensate. Those with poor memories may bring a shopping list; those with a poor sense of location may memorize landmarks; those who have trouble reading look for pictures on labels; those with a weakness in math may just assume that larger sizes are more economical rather than trying to calculate the price per ounce.

Each of us has some skills that we are less proficient in than most other people are, and each of us has found ways to keep these deficiencies from becoming serious handicaps. Some do quite a good job of it: Hans Christian Anderson, Woodrow Wilson, and Nelson Rockefeller were all dyslexic.

Hyperactive Children

The same note of optimism, and awareness of individual differences, will help us attempt to understand one of the most puzzling problems that sometimes occurs in middle childhood—hyperactivity. A hyperactive child is one who is considered too active, impulsive, distractible, and excitable, especially at the wrong times and places. Although these characteristics are present in preschool years, children are not usually labeled "hyperactive" until elementary school, when it becomes apparent that they cannot sit quietly in one spot and concentrate on schoolwork. Many hyperactive children have a learning disability, which compounds the problem. In fact, according to some professionals, hyperactivity is itself a form of learning disability, whether or not it is accompanied by specific difficulties in learning particular skills. Most hyperactive children (at least 80 percent) are boys, and the majority come from families of low socioeconomic status (Cantwell, 1975). Whether this is so because school life is more difficult for boys and lower-class children or because these children are more vulnerable to the problem is not certain. Both factors are probably involved.

A CLOSER LOOK · **Reactions to the Hyperactive Child**

Some handicaps evoke more sympathy than others. Everyone feels compassion for blind children, and it is nearly everyone's impulse to help them. (For one thing, schools for the blind are the most generously funded special schools in the nation.)

Hyperactive children, on the other hand, are in the opposite position. Their underlying problem is invisible, and their behavior makes almost everyone reject them. We are so used to thinking that all it takes to concentrate is a little will power and that a quiet manner in the classroom, a doctor's office, or a restaurant is natural, that we don't sympathize with the child who finds concentration or stillness a monumental task and frequently gets into trouble as a result. Nobody wants a troublemaker for a student, a friend, a son, or a daughter.

But troublemakers suffer too, as is clear from the following remarks of three hyperactive children.

Boy, 6 years, 11 months: . . . I would like it a lot if Mrs. Miller (teacher) would just once in a while, even once in the whole of second grade, say, 'Here's a boy who's really moving up fast' to me like she did to Stu and Jackie . . . And I also would like to do some things good like Elliot (older brother) does right from the start. Elliot hit a baseball right off, and he just catches good, and my dad says, 'That boy is a natural,' and I would like it if I was natural at something.

Boy, 8 years, 4 months: I just wish I could be just an *ordinary boy*, like I mean OK in school but not all A's and have the other kids ask me to play ball, and most of all I wish I would not cry when I get mad. It's really terrible when you can't stop crying and everyone's looking.

Boy, 6 years, 11 months: I am very tired of everything always being wrong and having to go for tests and my mom and dad look awful worried and soon I might have to go to another school. And what I would like a lot would be if I could just sit still and be the way the other kids are and not have all these things happen. And most of all I wish I did not break that mirror at Teddy Work's birthday party. [Ross and Ross, 1976; quoted in Farnham-Diggory, 1978]

Causes of Hyperactivity   When confronted with a child who is considerably more active than other children and can't concentrate very well, it is not easy to explain that child's behavior. However, we do know at least five reasons why some children are much more active than the normal child.

1. *Brain injury,* perhaps as a result of a complication during the birth process, can make it hard for a child to concentrate or sit still.

2. *Brain dysfunction* can make it hard to relax. For example, one child's brain may need an unusual amount of stimulation to arouse the central nervous system, so the child must keep moving in order to think clearly.

3. *Temperamental* differences make some children more active than others. As Thomas, Chess, and Birch (1968) found, some children kick a lot in the uterus, run around as soon as they can walk, and want to keep active every minute of the day.

4. The *environment* may cause hyperactivity. Children with no place to play may get restless. Watching television day after day makes some children irritable and aggressive.

5. *Eating* certain substances affects activity level. As an extreme example, ingestion of a few flakes of lead-based paint makes it impossible for a child to think clearly. (Such paint is now illegal for toys or interior walls, but many old, poorly maintained buildings have layers of lead paint on the walls.) Severe vitamin de-

ficiencies, especially of the B vitamins, impair concentration. Finally, certain foods, such as milk, chocolate, sugar, and cola, and certain chemical additives, seem to make some children restless.

In any given case, of course, the explanation for a child's excessively active behavior is likely to involve a combination of some of these factors.

A CLOSER LOOK   Science and Testimony on the Feingold Diet

Benjamin Feingold, a physician working at the Kaiser-Permanente Health Care facilities, began to wonder if the hyperactivity of certain of the children he saw could be the result of some of the chemicals added to processed foods, a suspicion that arose from his experience as an allergist. As a result of his research into this possibility, he suggested that hyperactive children be put on a diet completely free of artificial colors and flavoring, the preservatives BHT and BHA, and aspirin—no easy task since virtually all commercially available baked goods, cereals, luncheon meats, frozen dinners, ketchups, mustards, and toothpastes, and almost all medicines prescribed for children, contain one or more of the forbidden additives. For some children, Feingold also recommended that certain foods containing natural salicylates, such as apples, oranges, cucumbers, strawberries, tomatoes, and tea, also be avoided.

Feingold's book outlining his diet, *Why Your Child Is Hyperactive* (1974), has been read by thousands of parents who subsequently tried the diet on their children. According to their testimony, the diet brings marked improvement in a third or more cases (Buckley, 1977). Consequently, grateful mothers have formed hundreds of Feingold associations to promote the diet as well as to compel the government to require more accurate food labeling (Cott, 1977).

Despite all this testimony and advocacy, however, there are no reliable data showing that the Feingold diet works (Spring and Sandoval, 1976). As we saw in Chapter 1, good research techniques to reduce subjectivity include having

experimental and control groups and keeping all the participants "blind" concerning which individuals are given which treatments. The typical "proof" given for the Feingold diet comes from parents who so desperately want their child to quiet down that they change the child's entire diet. Given this, it is easy to suggest other reasons for the success of Feingold's plan:

1. Some children benefit from extra attention, and become less difficult.

2. Some children improve with time, and this improvement is misinterpreted as proof that the diet works.

3. Some parents and teachers simply imagine improvements.

Robert Sieben (1977) puts the case against the Feingold diet, and other controversial, unproven treatments for hyperactivity, most forcefully:

Anecdotal case reports . . . are, by their very nature, biased, subjective, and impressionistic . . . . It is unfortunate that the understandable desire of both teachers and parents to find a quick and easy cure has encouraged widespread acceptance of very dubious medical treatments. There is no such ready cure. The treatment of these problems is largely a laborious educational and social one.

Feingold (1977) admits that years of investigation are necessary before his diet can be proven effective, but he points out that there is no harm in trying to follow his recommendations. Whether one agrees with his critics probably depends on other attitudes, such as one's opinion about processed foods and about scientific evidence.

Help for Hyperactive Children   What should be done to help hyperactive children? Some people believe that nothing should be done, since many hyperactive children settle down during adolescence. Others suggest changes in the environment, such as less television and more play (Winn, 1977), or eliminating certain foods from the child's diet (Feingold, 1974), but evidence that these changes work is hard to find. (However, there is some evidence that the caffeine in coffee quiets hyperactive children rather than exciting them [Firestone et al., 1978; Harvey and March, 1978].) Another, more difficult change is to set up the child's home and school with as few distractions as possible and with a simple routine that eliminates confusion. Some hyperactive children quiet down and learn to do much better in such an environment (Cruickshank, 1977).

Yet another approach has been the use of psychoactive drugs that calm down the hyperactive child. At least 150,000 children take such medication each day (Sroufe, 1975), especially amphetamines, which enable some hyperactive children to concentrate for the first time in their lives (Wendler, 1971; Levy, 1973). However, critics have maintained that these drugs dull the child's mind, stunt growth, cause addiction, and distract parents and teachers from their responsibility to meet the child's needs (Schrag and Divoky, 1975; Whalen and Henker, 1976).

Just who is right is hard to say, because good evidence on the long-term effects of these drugs is scarce (Sroufe, 1975). Nevertheless, it now appears that neither the highest expectations nor the worst fears about psychoactive drugs can be substantiated. Psychoactive drugs do make many hyperactive children quieter, but they do not, as hoped, improve learning ability. At the same time, they appear not to stunt growth, cause drug addiction, or dull the mind (Paluszny, 1977). However, both proponents and opponents agree that psychoactive medication is sometimes prescribed for children without proper diagnoses or without follow-up examinations—an abuse that can harm the child. For instance, children are sometimes prescribed an overly large dosage and become lethargic, or they sometimes continue to be given the psychoactive drug even when the basic hyperactivity has abated.

Given the many causes of hyperactivity, the wide range of individual differences in normal children, and the frequency of drug abuse, most professionals agree that children should be labeled "hyperactive" with extreme care. Children need to be examined individually, by educators and psychologists, as well as by physicians, and the home and the school need to be evaluated before children are given medication that might affect their future development (Baxley and LeBlanc, 1976).

The same careful approach should characterize all attempts to understand and meet the needs of school-age children. And when there does appear to be a special problem, we must remember that each child is an individual, with some of the strengths and liabilities typical of children in middle childhood, but also with capabilities and problems that few others share, and all of these in unique combination. This is, of course, true whether the origin of the problem seems to be in the body and brain, as discussed in this chapter, or in the cognitive, cultural, and social aspects of development, which we shall investigate in the next two chapters.

SUMMARY

Size and Shape

1. Children grow more slowly during middle childhood than at any time until the end of adolescence. There is much variation in the size and rate of maturation of healthy North American children, primarily as a result of genetic, rather than nutritional, differences.

2. Overweight children suffer from peer rejection and poor self-concept. More exercise, rather than severe dieting, is the best solution.

Motor Skills

3. School-age children can perform almost any motor skill, as long as adult strength or judgment is not a prerequisite. Physical exercise during these years aids psychological development as well as biological growth. Unfortunately, most competitive games that adults enjoy demand skills that are hard for children to master.

Children with Handicaps

4. Children with obvious physical handicaps often were excluded from regular schools, assigned to special classes, limited to home tutoring, or given no education at all. Now

the law requires that these children must be provided public education, in the regular classroom if possible.

5. Children with learning disabilities such as dyslexia (severe reading problems) or hyperactivity (high activity levels with low concentration ability) have generally been part of the regular classroom, but they need special attention and help to learn to cope with their problems.

6. Learning disabilities may originate in a brain dysfunction of some sort, but whether the cause is organic or not, many educational and psychological measures can help children with these disabilities. Psychoactive drugs also help some children, but these should be used carefully and cautiously.

KEY QUESTIONS

What causes the variation in physical growth and skill in middle childhood?

How does obesity affect a child's development?

What are the advantages of mainstreaming?

What are the disadvantages of mainstreaming?

What are the symptoms of learning disability?

What are the possible causes of hyperactivity?

What are the arguments for and against use of psychoactive drugs to control hyperactivity?

KEY TERMS

obesity
mainstreaming
resource room
specific learning disabilities
dyslexia

dysgraphia
dyscalcula
minimal brain dysfunction
brain damage
hyperactivity

RECOMMENDED READINGS

Farnham-Diggory, Sylvia. *Learning disabilities.* Cambridge, Mass.: Harvard University Press, 1978.

A readable and scholarly discussion of learning disabilities, including hyperactivity as well as the disabilities that affect specific academic skills. The author's discussion of the definitions, causes, and treatments of learning disabilities makes one realize how much we have yet to learn on this subject.

Mayer, Jean. *Overweight: Causes, costs, and control.* Englewood Cliffs, N.J.: Prentice-Hall, 1968.

This book was written for the educated public by a leading nutritionist at Harvard University. It provides a sensible and straightforward discussion of obesity and health, including interesting material on young people and exercise.

The School Years: Cognitive Development

I hear, and I forget.
I see, and I remember.
I do, and I understand.

Ancient Chinese proverb

Ten years from now I will be 19, and probably in
college, and live away from home . . .
But if I don't go to college, I will romp and roam.

Ten years from now I will be quite pretty,
and have lots of dough . . .
and if I don't, Oh No!

Ten years from now everything will be fine,
and I WILL BE MINE.

Rachel, age 9
"Ten Years from Now"

CHAPTER 13

Cognitive Changes During Middle Childhood

Humor

The Stage View

Concrete Operational Thought

Implications of Piaget's Theory for Educators

The Information-Processing View

Matching Skills to Be Taught with the Child's Learning Style

Language

Vocabulary

Grammar

Communicative Competence

Measuring Cognitive Development

Teacher Opinions

Achievement Tests

Aptitude Tests

True or False?

It is quite possible for a child to be able to recite numbers from 1 to 30, yet not be able to count five people in a room correctly.

No matter what their age, children's notions about the meaning of death seem to have little to do with the religious teachings they may have been exposed to.

The fact that most cultures begin the formal education of children at around age 7 proves that a maturational increase in the complexity of thought takes place at this age.

Until 7 or 8, most children would probably think that "The boy was bitten by the dog" means that the boy did the biting.

Black English sentences like "He be goin' to school" actually adhere to grammatical rules.

IQ scores are generally good predictors of occupational level and accomplishment.

The expectations that children have of themselves change rapidly during middle childhood. Remember the difference between the first day of first grade and the beginning of fifth grade? Six-year-olds enter school filled with excitement and fear, often dressed in their Sunday best and clinging tightly to their mother's or father's hand. By age 10, children arrive at school with new notebooks and sharpened pencils, ready for the serious business of learning. They appear casual and confident, even when they aren't, and they would angrily balk if their parents offered to walk them to the classroom. While first-graders worry about getting lost or wetting their pants, fifth-graders worry about finishing a report on time, or failing a test.

There is a vast difference in what teachers expect of them, too. If first-graders can learn to stay quiet when they are supposed to, read simple words, and add simple numbers, that's considered accomplishment enough. Fifth-graders are expected to memorize multiplication tables and spelling rules; they are supposed to understand the morals of the books they read and the general principles underlying the mathematical formulas they use; and they are urged to plan their work ahead and hand it in neatly and correctly.

School report cards reflect these different expectations. Most first-graders, if they are marked at all, are given a "good" in academic skills. In most schools, the important part of the report is the teacher's assessment of whether the child listens to rules, knows when to sit still, and seems to be trying. By fifth grade, some children are earning an A or an "excellent" in various subjects; others are failing. Fifth-graders' accomplishments are compared with their classmates', with the teacher's standard of what fifth-graders should be learning, and with the achievements of 10-year-olds throughout the country.

These changes in the behavior and attitudes of children, teachers, and parents reflect, in part, the growth of children's cognitive abilities between ages 6 and 11, abilities that can be seen in the reasoning strategies children use, the school-related skills they master, and even in the jokes they tell. This chapter describes the cognitive development that underlies these skills, as well as the rating systems, such as IQ and achievement tests, used to measure them.

Cognitive Changes During Middle Childhood

Between ages 7 and 11, children become much more accomplished at thinking, learning, remembering, and communicating, because their cognitive processes become less egocentric and more logical. Evidence of this growth includes the simple facts that most fifth-graders can figure out which brand and size of popcorn is the best buy, can be taught to multiply fractions, can memorize a list of twenty spelling words, and can use irony appropriately—accomplishments beyond virtually every first-grader. The disciplines of psychology and education have much to tell us about the nature, the causes, and the consequences of this cognitive growth, although some of the information from various researchers and theorists is conflicting. As Roger Landrum (1978) explains, "the complexities of classroom settings defy the elegance of psychological theory . . . the relationship between education and psychology is a labyrinth." Before trying to make our way through this maze, let's look at one spontaneous behavior of school-age children that shows evidence of the logic, memory, and language development that are typical during these years, specifically joke-telling.

Humor

The joke-telling of school-age children demands several skills not usually apparent in younger children: the ability to listen carefully; to know what someone else will think is funny; and, hardest of all, to remember the right way to tell the joke. Telling a joke is beyond most preschool children. If asked to do so, they usually just say a word (such as "pooh-pooh") or describe an action ("shooting someone with a water gun") that they think is funny. Even if they actually use a joke form, they usually miss the point. As one child said after listening to her older sisters tell jokes on a long car trip, "What happens when a car goes into a tunnel?" "What?" her sisters asked. "It gets dark." By contrast, almost every 7-year-old can tell a favorite joke upon request (Yalisove, 1978).

Daniel Yalisove (1975, 1978) analyzed children's jokes in considerable detail. He has found three types of humor that flourish during middle childhood, each one reflecting different aspects of cognitive development.

Reality Riddles Consider these two favorite riddles of first- and second-grade children.

> How many balls of string does it take to reach around the world?
> (One, but it had better be a big one.)

> What is even worse than biting into an apple and finding a worm?
> (Finding half a worm.)

Yalisove calls riddles like these reality riddles, because the child must have a notion of the way things really are in order to perceive the humor in the riddles. To appreciate the first riddle, the child must have a sense of relative size and distance, and in the second, a sense of cause and effect. These ideas are beyond most preschool children, who are in the period of preoperational thought. But school-age children are able to reason about specific events and observable objects, and take

Figure 13.1 *During middle childhood, children come into their own as joke-tellers, punsters, and comic raconteurs. No matter what kind of funny business children share, their relating it in secret adds to the hilarity.*

delight in using their growing mental powers. Their new way of thinking (which characterizes concrete operational thought, as we will soon see) enables them to realize how big a ball of string would have to be to reach around the world and to know where the other half of the worm must be (McGhee, 1971).

Language-Ambiguity Jokes   Yalisove calls many of the favorite jokes during middle childhood language-ambiguity jokes, for they center on a play on words. Here are four examples:

> Why didn't the woman leave the house even when a bear was chasing her?
> (Because she didn't want to be seen with a bare behind.)
>
> What is the difference between a jeweler and a jailer?
> (One sells watches and the other watches cells.)
>
> Order, order in the court!
> (Ham and cheese on rye, your honor.)
>
> If April showers bring May flowers, what do May flowers bring?
> (Pilgrims.)

In order to understand jokes like these, the child must not only know that words can have two meanings, and that certain words that sound the same have different meanings, but must also be flexible enough to switch quickly from one meaning to the other. Jokes involving language play become increasingly popular as the child progresses through elementary school and becomes more comfortable with double meanings. Yalisove (1978) found that two out of every three riddles asked by fourth- and fifth-graders involved puns or some other form of language ambiguity. Older and younger children did not rely on these devices as often.

The process of asking a riddle shows another characteristic that develops during middle childhood—the excitement of teasing or tricking someone, especially an adult. Whereas a 7-year-old is likely to deliver the punch line as soon as the listener says "I don't know," or even before, a 10-year-old is more likely to demand several guesses before giving the correct answer with a self-satisfied grin. If the adult guesses the answer correctly, the child is crestfallen.

Some jokes are designed to catch the listener off guard by supplying new answers to old questions. For instance, everyone knows the traditional answer to "What is black and white and red all over?" But there are also new answers, including "An embarrassed zebra," or "A sunburned skunk," or "A flag Betsy Ross made by mistake"—none of them as clever as the original, but all serving to let the joke-teller arrogantly say "Wrong!" when an adult confidently says "A newspaper."

Many of the jokes popular in middle childhood illustrate another facet of these years: an awareness of social conventions. Jokes such as those about the woman with the bare behind, the criminal ordering a sandwich from the judge, and Betsy Ross making a mistake poke fun at these standards and are funny to school-age children partly because they are familiar with these standards and take them seriously.

Absurdity Riddles A third type of joke becomes more common toward the end of middle childhood. Yalisove calls these absurdity riddles. For example:

> How do you fit six elephants into a VW?
> (Three in the front and three in the back.)

> What did the wild-game hunter do when a herd of elephants wearing sunglasses stampeded toward him?
> (Nothing. He didn't recognize them.)

> What's the easiest way to sink a submarine?
> (Knock on the door.)

In order to find these riddles funny, a person has to be able to understand that once the absurd premise of the riddle is accepted, the absurd answers are actually logical. Assuming that elephants can be fitted into a VW, that sunglasses thoroughly disguise appearance, or that sailors in submarines open the door when someone knocks, the answer in each case is sensible. A grasp of the logic within the absurdity is what makes these jokes funny rather than stupid, and requires an understanding of hypothetical ideas and logical consequences which begins to emerge at about age 11 and is characteristic of adolescent thought (more about that in Chapter 16).

The Stage View

Joke-telling is only one of the new cognitive abilities to appear between ages 5 and 7. According to several psychologists who have studied cognition during this period, there is a change not only in the complexity of thought but also in the *way* children think during these years. In summarizing this research, Sheldon White (1965) calls these two years a time of "unusually significant change" in the "character of children's learning."

White cites twenty-one aspects of mental development that display a 5-to-7 shift. For instance, 7-year-olds are likely to use complex reasoning, to make long-term plans, and to seek intellectual rewards such as the satisfaction of getting the right answer. In contrast, 5-year-olds use simple reasoning, little or no planning, and

Figure 13.2 *In order to learn to read, children must be able to recognize small differences in the position and direction of letters, such as those that distinguish "mom" from "wow," or "was" from "saw," or "dad" from "bad." According to some researchers, the ability to make these distinctions improves noticeably between ages 5 and 7.*

work for praise and attention rather than for the right answer. Between ages 5 and 7, children usually become able to tell their left from their right, to focus on the shape of an object rather than on its color, and to distinguish positioning differences of like figures, as in the case of "p," "q," "b," and "d" (White, 1965). Selective attention often improves noticeably at about age 6, enabling the 6-year-old to concentrate and screen out distractions better than the 4-year-old can (Wright and Vlietstra, 1975). As we saw in Chapter 10, the ability to use language, especially "inner speech," to facilitate thinking also improves during this period.

In addition, several memory skills seem to improve during these years. One example is the memory for a group of numbers. On both the Wechsler Intelligence Scale for Children (WISC) and the Stanford-Binet intelligence tests, children listen to a series of digits, such as 3-5-4-8-7, and then are asked to repeat them, either forward or backward. Children's performance on this task, which gauges short-term memory, improves dramatically between ages 5½ and 7½, and then develops more slowly from 7½ to 15 (Wechsler, 1974). (Other intellectual skills grow more slowly in childhood, and reach a peak in adulthood.)

Finally, in Piaget's theory of the sequence of cognitive development, the years from about 5 to 7 are a transitional period, in which the child has not quite abandoned preoperational thought nor reached concrete operational thought. Piaget notes that although children sometimes intuitively grasp the right answer to tests of concrete operational logic, they frequently are unable to explain how they arrived at it or to understand the underlying principles that led them to their conclusion (Cowan, 1978). For instance, many 6-year-olds seem to apply the concepts of conservation or classification, but, when asked to explain their mental processes, might act as if reasons are unnecessary because the problem is so obvious. (The adult's "Why?" is typically answered with "Because.") They also might fail to arrive at the correct answer to another problem that depends on the same underlying principle. For instance, a child might correctly answer that both glasses contain the same amount in the conservation-of-liquids experiment (see page 58), but then, if the liquid from one of the glasses is poured into six smaller glasses, insist that the amount of liquid has increased.

Concrete Operational Thought

By contrast, in Piaget's theory, the years from 8 to 10 are usually a time when children can reason about almost anything they perceive. They have passed through the confusions of the 5-to-7 shift and they have not yet reached the complications caused by the adolescent's ability to imagine dozens of solutions to every real or imagined problem.

Between ages 8 and 10, children usually understand logical principles, as long as the principles can be applied to specific, or concrete, examples. They can watch water being poured from a thin glass into a wide one and explain why the quantity of liquid remains the same (conservation). They can sort dogs into breeds or flowers into species without confusion (classification). They are quick to say that 8 is greater than 5, and just as quick to confirm that 11,108 is greater than 11,105 (seriation). Since the first two of these concepts are discussed in detail on pages 303–307 in Chapter 10, we will concentrate here on the third.

Seriation and Number   Seriation refers to the arrangement of objects in a series, as in the laying out of sticks from shortest to longest, or of crayons from lightest to darkest. Like other logical operations, seriation begins to be understood toward the end of the preoperational period, but the concept is usually not firmly established until age 7 or 8. A typical 6-year-old, asked to arrange a series of ten sticks

Figure 13.3 *During middle childhood, many children become ardent collectors, not only categorizing and labeling their possessions, but also arranging them in a series. A grasp of seriation would, for instance, enable this budding geologist to arrange his specimens in order of their hardness, or their smoothness, or their value.*

according to length, might first put together three sticks—a short, medium, and long—and then insert the others, rearranging several of the sticks before getting the correct order. A typical 8-year-old, in contrast, would look at the whole jumble of sticks, pick out the shortest, then the next shortest, and so on, systematically and quickly arranging the series.

One practical example of seriation is number sequence. Many North American children, having watched "Sesame Street" since toddlerhood, can count from 1 to 10, or even to 20, before age 4. This is quite an achievement, for in pretelevision decades, many kindergarteners entered school counting "1, 2, 3, 5, 8, 10, 7, 17, 19, 20-teen," without realizing that anything was amiss.

However, just because a child has memorized the number sequence does not mean that he or she understands that numbers are a series and that they correspond to specific quantities. When asked to count the number of people in a room, a child might count and point to each person but say the numbers faster than he or she points, consequently counting six people as ten. In such a case, the child clearly does not understand the one-to-one correspondence between object and number.

Even children who can count objects correctly often do not grasp other aspects of the number system. Five-year-olds, who are in the transitional period between preoperational and concrete operational thought, are often puzzled by simple questions such as "Which is greater, 6 or 8?" or "What number is one less than 5?" (Piaget and Szeminska, 1965). These concepts take a long time to develop: many first-graders need to do much finger-counting and hard thinking in order to add simple sums such as 2 plus 3 and 4 plus 1. Other math difficulties occur because classification concepts are a prerequisite for a firm understanding of place value. Thus many elementary-school children have trouble understanding the difference between, say, 501, 51, and 15, a difference that seems simple and obvious to adults.

Figure 13.4 *Counting blocks and keeping track with their fingers helps children make the connection between spoken numbers and written symbols. According to Piaget, this is a much better way to understand math than rote learning is.*

Once children understand the number system, at about age 7 or 8, and logical ideas such as identity, reversibility, and reciprocity, they learn to add and subtract, and, later, divide and multiply, by applying these basic concepts to each new problem. (Identity, you will remember, is the idea that something remains the same, no matter what form it takes; reversibility, the idea that a process can be reversed to restore the original form. *Reciprocity* is the idea that two dimensions are reciprocal; that is, that "it's taller but it's thinner" or "it's shorter but it's wider" explains why different-sized glasses can hold the same amount of water.) Applied to math, identity reveals, for example, that whether it is formed by 2+4 or 3+3, 6 is still 6; reversibility reveals that if 2 plus 1 equals 3, then 3 minus 1 must be 2; and reciprocity reveals that the area of a rectangle that is 6 inches wide and 4 inches high is that same as that of a rectangle that is 3 inches wide and 8 inches high.

Time Told the date of the first automobile, or of Emancipation, a 6-year-old might ask his or her parents if they were alive before cars were invented, or if they saw the slaves being given their freedom. At least one 6-year-old boy made the opposite mistake, deciding that he was born before his father. This boy also believed that he would grow older with time but that his father would remain the same age and that his mother wouldn't grow older "because she is old already" (Piaget, 1970a).

Such mistakes are rare by age 8, when the basic thought processes of concrete operational thought enable children to understand the passage of time much better. This is probably one reason why television programs that show life in earlier times ("Little House on the Prairie," "The Waltons," "Happy Days") and future times ("Star Trek," "Battlestar Gallactica") become popular with this age group.

Distance Distance concepts are so poorly understood before middle childhood that after looking at a map, a 6-year-old might talk about taking a walk from California to New York or, even more telling, from Toronto to Canada. This lack of a sense of distance, plus a lack of classification skills, makes trying to teach first-grade children the geographical distinctions between cities, states, and countries very frustrating.

Figure 13.5 *When they were a few years younger, at the preoperational stage, these children might have thought that a walk around the actual continental United States would not take much longer than this one.*

A CLOSER LOOK   Concepts of Death

Children younger than 6 rarely think that death is universal, inevitable, and final. Instead, they often think that only people who want to die, or who are cowardly, evil, or careless, actually succumb, and that dead things can be revived, perhaps by giving them hot food, or keeping them warm. Between the ages of 5 and 7, these ideas fade, and children become more aware of the reality of death.

That attitudes toward death are closely tied to age was first reported in 1948, when Maria Nagy studied attitudes toward death among Hungarian children. She found that most children between ages 3 and 5 denied the reality of death. Those between 6 and 9 believed that death exists but tended to cope with this idea by thinking of death as a person who carries away only certain people. Children older than 9 recognized death as an inevitable, biological phenomenon.

Similar shifts are reported by Gerald Koocher (1973), who first tested seventy-five children, aged 6 to 15, to determine the cognitive stage they were in, and then queried them about death. When asked "What makes things die?" preoperational children gave egocentric or illogical answers, such as "When God reads your name in a book" or "Going swimming alone." By contrast, concrete operational children were likely to think of specific violent causes for death, such as "Guns," "Bows and arrows," "Eating rat poison," "Getting beat up." Finally, children at the formal operational stage of thinking realized that old age, illness, and a "worn-out body" are the most likely causes of death.

Koocher also discovered that cognitive maturity was a deciding factor in children's answers to the question "When do you think you will die?" The answers of preoperational children showed the most variety: one said, "Three hundred," and another, who was 6 years old, said, "Seven." By contrast, virtually all of the concrete or formal operational children gave answers between 60 and 100.

Koocher did not find any evidence of the personification of death, as Nagy had. Instead, he found that children in middle childhood became interested in the specific details about death as a way of mastering their fears. For instance, if Grandpa dies, a school-age child might want to know the words of the doctor's report on the cause of death, and might ask about each detail of the funeral arrangements.

In most Western cultures, families sometimes find it hard to respond honestly to the child's inquisitiveness about death. However, Geoffrey Gorer (1973), a British physician who has studied attitudes toward death, believes that a society that treats death as "unmentionable" engenders the furtive excitement produced by the "pornography of death"—the horror comic, the sick joke, and so forth—rather than fostering realistic understanding. By contrast, Gorer says, parents who provide a good model for the child are those who are honest in discussing death with the child—avoiding

The process of bereavement, which this girl is experiencing because of her father's death, should include concrete gestures of mourning, a chance to discuss emotions, and the opportunity to take comfort from daily life.

However, once children attain concrete operational thought, they understand that some places are at a distance much farther than they can see or walk to, and that one geographical area can contain smaller areas. Sometimes they delight in their new understanding so much that in giving their addresses, they include not only their names, streets, cities, and states, but also "United States, North America, the Western Hemisphere, the World, the Solar System, the Milky Way Galaxy."

Combining the concepts of time, speed, and distance is much harder than understanding any one of these ideas separately. When shown two toy trains that move along a track, one of them stopping farther along than the other, preoperational children always say that the one in front is the faster—regardless of when or where the trains started or how fast they actually went (Piaget, 1970b). The ability to judge euphemisms ("Grandpa passed away"), or worse, falsities ("He went to heaven" spoken by a parent who does not believe in God or heaven)—and who are willing to express their own emotions and fears. With death, as with other topics, discussion aids cognitive development.

We might expect that religious beliefs or parental education, as well as cognitive maturity, would determine what a child believes about death. However, among contemporary North American children, at least, this does not seem to be the case. Helen Swain (1979) interviewed 120 Canadian children between the ages of 2 and 16 and found that the only variable that affected attitudes toward death was the age of the child. No matter what their religious or educational background, for instance, few children between 2 and 4 thought they would die; half the children between 5 and 7 thought they would; and almost all of the children older than 7 thought they would. Several of the teenagers had religious or

philosophical ideas about death, but, again, these ideas did not seem related to specific religious teachings in childhood. Koocher also found religion relatively unimportant in children's attitudes toward death. When asked "What will happen when you die?" most of the children talked about funeral arrangements. Only 10 percent said they didn't know, and a mere 5 percent mentioned God.

One final aspect of children's ideas about death should be mentioned. Some children, when they first realize that they themselves will die, develop irrational fears, or *phobias,* refusing, for example, to eat a certain food or to sit in the front seat of the car. Based on the research, we can conclude that such phobias will disappear as the child becomes more mature and that, given a supportive family, children will develop their own way of coping with fears about death, just as they develop more rational ideas about conservation and classification.

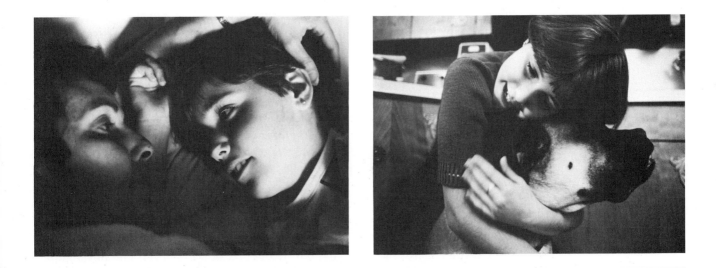

the relationship of time, speed, and distance develops gradually throughout middle childhood, and by age 12, most children have grasped the general principles. Even in adulthood, however, applying these principles in specific situations is not simple, as researchers found when they tested college undergraduates, as well as children, on more difficult versions of the two-trains problem (Siegler and Richards, 1979).

Children in middle childhood also have difficulty considering several logical operations at once. Not until adolescence (and often not even then) do young people develop a systematic use of several logical ideas, which is a characteristic of formal operational thought.

Cause and Effect   Finally, concrete operational children have a much firmer grasp of cause and effect, especially when compared to preoperational children who may think it is sunny because they wished it to be, or rainy because God is angry at them. The development of causality may be shown in the explanations given by children of various ages for the origin of a fight. For instance, children under age 5 often do not understand that a fight has a specific cause. One preschooler's response to her mother's criticism for picking a fight was, "But Mommy, what can I do when the fight just crawls out of me?" (Chukovsky, 1968). By kindergarten, children realize that someone starts a fight, but they are usually convinced they are innocent.

In middle childhood, children are more likely to present an elaborate sequence. A pair of quarreling 9-year-old girls might explain that one of them refused to share her gum, which made the other call her a pig, which lead to an exchange of insults, causing one to push and the other to shove, until finally both were punching and kicking. Although they might have different opinions about which insults or blows exceeded the appropriate response and escalated the quarrel, both girls would probably agree on what the causal sequence of events was.

Fighting 9-year-olds also usually realize that either one of them could have stopped the argument before the first blow, and that they both share the blame for the fight. The school-age child's increased ability to understand another's point of view, combined with a greater appreciation of cause and effect, makes settling a quarrel between 9-year-olds a lot easier than trying to convince two 6-year-olds to shake hands and say they are sorry.

Implications of Piaget's Theory for Educators

The educational significance of what we know about cognition during middle childhood depends partly on which theoretical perspective one considers most valid in explaining the reasons for cognitive growth, and partly on which particular skills or abilities one wants to teach. Naturally, Piagetians and behaviorists have different opinions on this matter.

From Piaget's Followers   Piagetians generally believe that middle childhood is characterized by the acquisition of certain logical concepts that develop in a period of disequilibrium and transition at about age 6 or 7 and are brought into equilibrium at the concrete level of thought by the end of this period. The development and application of these ideas depend primarily on the individual child's rate of mental maturation and organization. While Piagetians acknowledge that children can be nudged a bit when they are at the brink of a new idea, they maintain that, in general, the school's role is to provide materials and the opportunity for children to do their own thinking and discovering rather than to inculcate specific ideas or facts.

These Piagetian ideas have a number of implications for educators. First, since Piaget believes that children learn by actively exploring their environment, it follows that the emphasis in the classroom should be on learning by doing: counting blocks, or adding nickels and dimes, or measuring the length and width of the classroom is more instructive than watching the teacher solve arithmetic problems on the board. Likewise, building a grass house, molding a clay pot, baking bread, and then writing about the process is more enlightening and memorable than reading about these activities in a social studies book. This approach is especially important in early elementary school when most children are in a

Figure 13.6 *A rabbit in the classroom can provide a real close-up on biology, and also help students develop a sense of responsibility.*

transitional stage. Then the classroom must be a place where they can experiment, explore, and discuss, rather than learn specific bits of knowledge at particular times.

The second crucial idea from Piagetian theory and research is that the rate of development is different for each child. One child might begin the 5-to-7 shift at age four; another child, not until age 8. Whatever the timing, each stage of development evolves gradually and depends on inner adaptations to the child's experiences. Consequently, children should not be "pushed" through this process. As Elkind (1969) writes, "from the Piagetian perspective, there are 'optimal periods' for the growth of particular mental structures which cannot be rushed." Once a child grasps the logical ideas that characterize concrete operational thought, it takes time and experience before each general principle is applied in all situations. For instance, an understanding of conservation of liquids precedes that of conservation of volume by several months or years.

For these reasons, a teacher, ideally, should allow each child to set the pace for the assimilation of new ideas and concepts. The classroom should have specific materials that will aid discovery of things such as number facts and classification concepts, but there should be no preordained plan as to which particular ideas should be understood when. This viewpoint is well stated by Eleanor Duckworth (1972):

> It is almost impossible for an adult to know exactly the right time for a given question for a given child—especially for a teacher who is concerned with thirty or more children. Children can raise the right question for themselves when the setting is right.
>
> [Schools] can help to uncover parts of the world which children would not otherwise know how to tackle . . . Schools and teachers can provide materials and questions in ways that suggest things being done with them; and children, in the doing, cannot help being inventive. [This means] providing a setting which suggests wonderful ideas to children—different ideas to different children—as they get caught up in intellectual problems that are real to them.

Figure 13.7 *There are many ways for a child to "discover" the essential workings of the number system: one is with a schoolroom version of an abacus, which has ten beads on each row.*

Piagetians sometimes put the case even more strongly, maintaining that a system that uses rewards, such as grades or gold stars, or compares one child's accomplishment with another's, as do standardized tests, is actually destructive to the child's active, self-regulating search for cognitive equilibrium.

This does not mean that Piagetian theory would have teachers sit idly by, waiting for children to learn. Rather, it suggests which kinds of activities might be most educational. For instance, once children understand the basic concepts of classification, usually by age 8 (Inhelder and Piaget, 1964), they happily apply it in dozens of situations, often collecting anything and everything—stamps, baseball cards, string, pebbles, bubble-gum wrappers, bottle caps—in order to count, organize, and categorize. Their learning environment, therefore, ought to include many opportunities for them to exercise their new abilities, from alphabetizing words and differentiating parts of speech to, say, categorizing species of fish in an aquarium.

In addition, since another important cognitive achievement of middle childhood is increased ability to understand another point of view, children should be encouraged to discuss ideas. For instance, having small groups of children plan such things as a class trip, or ways to earn money, or the games to be played in gym time encourages them to listen to each other and helps them become less egocentric.

The Information-Processing View

Because Piaget's primary interest is in the mental structures, or schemes, of cognitive development, much of his research has been concerned with the concepts, such as conservation and seriation, that school-age children usually possess and preschool children usually do not.

An alternative way to look at cognitive development comes from psychologists who see similarities between the workings of the human mind and the information processing done by computers. The output of a computer depends primarily on three factors: the input, or material fed into it; the capacity of the computer; and the program the computer has for organizing the input. Following this model in order to understand school-age children's cognitive output, psychologists look at their ability to receive, store, and organize information.

Figure 13.8 *According to information-processing theory, the output of the human mind depends not only on the input but also on the capacity of the brain to store, organize, and retrieve what it has received.*

Receiving Information The first step in cognition is attention. Unless a child is able to attend to a sensation or experience, that child will not understand it or learn anything from it. Selective attention, as we saw in the chapters on infancy, begins at birth, when neonates are more likely to attend to some stimuli and ignore others. During middle childhood, children become much better at concentrating on the task at hand and are less easily distracted by irrelevant stimuli.

In one study, children aged 6 to 12 were asked to remember the background colors of a series of pictures—an elephant, a scooter, a water bucket, and so forth (Maccoby and Hagen, 1965). They were not asked to remember the subjects of the pictures. As expected, memory for background colors improved steadily with age; 12-year-olds remembered almost twice as accurately as 6-year-olds. Then the children were asked to name the subjects of the pictures. Ability to remember in this case improved only slightly with age, and then declined. In fact, 12-year-olds apparently had learned to focus their attention and ignore unnecessary information so well that they were actually worse than 6-year-olds at remembering which subjects were on which backgrounds!

A review of the research on selective attention (Pick et al., 1975) found that the ability to screen out distractions and concentrate improves steadily during middle childhood, although, of course, it is affected by the specific context in which it functions. In general, selective attention improves when children are told to attend ("Listen carefully . . ." "Pay attention to . . ."); when they tell themselves to concentrate ("Think hard, you can do it"); and when they are motivated to attend. Other research has shown that if children are asked to pay attention to someone else, they are more likely to attend closely if the model is like them in age, sex, or other identifiable characteristics.

Selective attention may also be enhanced by specific reinforcement. For instance, in one study, seventy-two fourth-, sixth-, and eighth-graders were asked to remember forty-eight words, each of which was worth 1¢, 3¢, or 5¢ for its being remembered (Wilson et al., 1978). Not surprisingly, the children remembered more nickel words than penny words.

The Development of Memory Several psychologists studying memory have suggested that there are two aspects of memory that should be considered separately. The first is pure memory capacity—how much information the brain can hold and how quickly it can be processed and stored. The second, metamemory, involves the ability to use various techniques to keep things in mind.

Memory capacity is quite well developed by age 6. In fact, preschool children sometimes surprise their parents by remembering the details of a trip they took or a picture they saw, or by repeating the words of a nursery rhyme or television commercial with perfect accuracy. A more subtle type of memory capacity seems just as well developed in 5-year-olds as in adults. This is the sensory register, which *temporarily* stores sensory information (as in the afterimage that occurs like an instant photo upon closing your eyes). In both children and adults, the sensory register functions for less than a second; then the sensory memory fades, and in order for the information to be remembered longer, it must be stored. At this point, a person's capacity to remember correlates directly with age; adults are better than children; 10-year-olds are better than 5-year-olds (Morrison et al., 1974).

The main difference in memory ability between 6-year-olds and 12-year-olds is in metamemory (Ross and Kerst, 1978; Brown and DeLoache, 1978). Older children are much more likely to use both logical and illogical mnemonic, or memory-aiding, devices. One such technique is rehearsal, the repetition of the items to be remembered; another is chunking, the grouping of items into categories; a third technique is memorizing general rules rather than specific examples. For instance, poor spellers often rely on such devices as " 'i' before 'e' except after 'c,' " " 'Separate' has a 'rat' in it," "The only time 'full' is spelled with a double 'l' is when it stands alone, so be careful," and dozens more. These techniques come spontaneously to some children, but they also can be taught. Even a short practice session with instruction in rehearsal or chunking usually results in improved memory performance in school-age children (Hagen et al., 1975).

Older children are also more likely to understand what the instruction "Try to remember" means and to devise strategies to help them remember. For example, in one experiment, preschool, first-grade, and fifth-grade children were shown a series of pictures (Appel et al., 1972). Half of them were told to *look at the pictures,* and the other half were told to *try to remember the names of the pictures.*

The preschool children usually just stared at the pictures under either instruction, and when told to remember, remembered almost exactly the same percentage of the nine pictures they were shown (46 percent, an average of about four pictures) as when told to look (48 percent). By first grade, children remembered 66 percent of twelve pictures when told to remember, and 63 percent when told to look—an insignificant difference.

But the fifth-graders responded differently in the two conditions. When told to remember, they were much more likely to repeat the names of the pictures to themselves, and to organize the pictures into clusters to make remembering easier. Even though they had fifteen pictures to study, they remembered 81 percent when told to remember and 62 percent when told to look. The conclusions one can draw from this experiment are similar to those from other research: By age 10, most children have learned how to use mnemonic devices, and are ready to apply them when faced with a memory task.

When all the research on memory development during childhood is considered, it becomes clear that the development of memory depends on several factors, including maturation, experience with the material to be memorized, experience with memorizing, ability to develop and use strategies for memorizing, and motivation. All these develop during the ordinary course of elementary school, where experience, motivation, and specific instruction are frequent.

The Behaviorist View Psychologists who consider cognitive growth from a behaviorist perspective believe that Piaget underestimates the role of specific teaching and external reinforcement. Each skill and each acquisition of a concept, they say, can be seen as the result of a chain of learned responses. Consequently, rather than waiting until a child's internal self-regulation produces an understanding of subtraction, a teacher can give the child math lessons, beginning with simple counting exercises, then adding, then subtracting. If the process is carefully planned, and the child is reinforced at each step, the child will learn math concepts and facts earlier and better than children who are left to discover these ideas on their own.

In addition, whereas Piagetians are chiefly interested in the *process* of learning, behaviorists look more at the *product,* giving the children guidance so that they will arrive at the right answers with increasing frequency. Behaviorists therefore emphasize the importance of correcting children's mistakes as well as rewarding their accomplishments. Behaviorists also believe that facts are best learned if they are *overlearned,* and that repeated practice in penmanship, spelling, and math skills is the best way to ensure that they will be remembered years later. This approach obviously seems sensible for rote learning, such as memorizing multiplication tables or developing better penmanship. Other types of learning, such as mastering scientific concepts or developing reading comprehension, seem to depend more on the child's cognitive readiness, and therefore one might think the Piagetian tactics are best. However, many behaviorists think the idea of "readiness" has been overemphasized, and that by middle childhood, most children are ready to learn almost any skill or concept if the curriculum is well programmed and the teacher sufficiently adept.

Their emphasis being on the importance of external reinforcement and curriculum sequences set by the teacher, behaviorists naturally contend that Piaget's stages are actually a result of influences in the environment, rather than the result of the child's own search for equilibrium. For instance, Piagetians take as evidence of a universal 5-to-7 shift the fact that many cultures begin formal education at about age 7. Behaviorists regard this view as looking at the facts in reverse. They contend, rather, that the 5-to-7 shift can be explained as the *result* of school rather than the reason for school. Once children spend a year or two in formal education, of course, they will develop better skills in memory, language, and logic—that's what school is all about.

In a typical classroom, the teacher rewards learning with gold stars, smiles, words of praise, and the like. Such procedures work very well, the behaviorists contend, for most children, most teachers, and most learning situations. Reading, writing, and arithmetic have been learned by generations of children because the tasks are specific (memorizing the ×3 table, for instance) and the reinforcement valued ("excellent" written next to the "100%"). When students do not learn, say the behaviorists, it is because the teacher rewards poor performance with attention, or because the goals are set too high—not because certain concepts have not yet been attained.

Figure 13.9 *Among many effective rewards for learning, a gold star is something young scholars will eagerly hitch their intellectual wagons to. However, some educators believe that using such rewards as a motivation for good schoolwork detracts from the intrinsic joys of learning.*

Matching Skills to Be Taught with the Child's Learning Style

Taking into account all the research, there is evidence that supports both the Piagetian and the behaviorist approach to elementary-school education. Rather than choosing one perspective and rejecting the other, we should probably look closely at the particular skill we want to teach and at the particular child to whom we want to teach it. For example, the rules of spelling can be learned much more efficiently through instruction than by being figured out. On the other hand, the ability to think logically, and not be swayed by perceptual "evidence" (as in the conservation problems), probably demands a level of brain maturity that few children reach before age 6.

In addition, the most helpful approach takes into account the cognitive pattern and style of the particular child. For instance, Jerome Kagan (1965) has made a distinction between reflectivity and impulsivity in conceptual tempo. Some children tend to be impulsive, blurting out the first answer that comes to mind without examining other possibilities. These children might benefit from specific educational measures designed to help them organize their thoughts and test their conclusions. On the other hand, some children seem more reflective, tackling problems thoughtfully, and enjoying figuring out the answers on their own. A schoolroom where children have a chance to find their own problems and work out their own solutions might be best for these children.

Finally, the efforts of parents and teachers should complement rather than contradict each other. A child raised to be respectful, obedient, and controlled might have a difficult time in a classroom where children are expected to be independent and questioning. The child's parents might be upset that the child cannot read, spell, or multiply at age 8, and might not understand the teacher's insistence that certain cognitive concepts must be mastered first. The opposite conflict might appear when a child who is used to challenging every statement at home is placed in a classroom where children are expected to be quiet and disciplined. The parents may not understand, for example, why their child has to stay after school for demanding of the teacher, "How do you know?"

Traditional versus Open Education In the 1970s there was a debate between advocates of two forms of elementary-school instruction, with different methods, assumptions, and goals proposed by each side. One form was traditional education: the teacher set the curriculum, which emphasized reading and math skills, and had all the children doing the same work at the same time. The other form was called open education, partly because many learning areas were open to the child at once. What each child did depended largely on what the child wanted to do, for it was assumed that children know best what they want to learn and how they want to learn it. Children of various abilities, and often of various ages, learned together in the same open classroom.

Critics of traditional education said that it fostered prejudice, passive learning, and competition, while discouraging creativity, social skills, and emotional development (Silberman, 1970; Featherstone, 1971; Howe, 1974). Critics of open education said that it produced children who not only had not mastered basic skills but, at the same time, overestimated their own intelligence and wisdom. It was also said to be inefficient, with children taking an hour to figure out for themselves something that a teacher could have explained to them in a minute.

Professionals as well as parents still disagree about which form of education is better, but both forms have been modified to allow greater flexibility and individual instruction. We now recognize that a method that works for a particular child learning a particular skill may not work as well for another child or for another skill. According to one study that compared children in several British schools, traditional education is better for teaching traditional academic subjects, especially with anxious children who need to know precisely what they are supposed to do (Bennett, 1976). Open education, on the other hand, may provide the best milieu for developing certain abilities, such as creativity and social interaction, and for some children, especially those who do not need a structured environment.

The important thing, then, is to match the children's needs and personalities to the type of education they receive. No matter which skills or which child one is teaching, it is also important for teachers and parents to look for the "teachable moment"—the best time to introduce a new idea—and to pay attention to "headfitting," making sure the curriculum fits the intellectual ability of the particular child. As long as the child finds school an enjoyable place to learn new skills and ideas, the question of which pedagogical method should be used becomes secondary.

Figure 13.10 (a) *In a traditional school, the children all work individually on the same task. This structure seems especially helpful for children who tend to be anxious, worrying about what they should do next.* (b) *Many open classrooms have "mixed age-groupings," which allow older, wiser children to help teach their younger peers. Research shows that this benefits the "teacher" as much as the "learner," especially with children who become shy or angry when adults try to correct them.*

(a)

(b)

Language

As discussed in Chapter 7, the rate of language production in the first months of life is limited by brain capacity and organization. The immature brain of most infants does not enable them to connect word with object and pronounce the result any more than their immature legs can support their standing weight. Nor can most children put two words together to form primitive sentences until they are at least 18 months old. By early childhood, however, the brain seems to be capable of learning vocabulary and grammar rapidly. As a matter of fact, children growing up in countries where almost everyone is bilingual or trilingual seem to master two languages as easily as most North Americans master one. In addition, prekindergarten children develop their language skills without any special tutelage. Indeed, language instruction for preschoolers seems pointless, as was shown in Chapter 10 by Gleason's unsuccessful efforts to get a 4-year-old to say that the baby rabbits were "held" rather than "holded."

During the school years, however, children enter a new phase of language learning, when they are able to benefit from explicit instruction. Consequently, most schools emphasize language skills during middle childhood. This includes imparting knowledge about roots, prefixes, and suffixes to build vocabulary, teaching and applying the rules of grammar, and developing the ability to use language abstractly, independent of contextual clues. Probably as a result, the growth of these aspects of language in the average schoolchild is impressive.

Vocabulary

The average child acquires about 5000 new words between ages 9 and 11. Which new words are added is noteworthy. For instance, looking at the first page of the "S" section of the dictionary, the average 9-year-old would probably know that "Sabbath" means a day of rest, that "sack" refers to a bag, and that "sad" means unhappy. In the next two years, the average child learns that "sacred" means holy, that "sacrifice" refers to an offering to a god, and that "saddler" indicates a person who makes saddles (Dale and O'Rourke, 1976). These additional words are easy for the child to learn because "sacred" and "sacrifice" have the same root, and "saddler" is related to the more common "saddle." If school-age children are helped to see the way words are related, they will develop an extensive vocabulary. As demonstrated by Kenneth Koch's (1970) and Richard Lewis' (1977, 1978) collections of poems written by children, as well as by the jokes children tell and the secret languages they create, children can truly *enjoy* words. In this regard, it should be remembered that as important as school experiences are, family experiences may be even more important, for children from families in which conversations and discussions are part of daily life score much higher on tests of language than those from families in which emotions are expressed with gestures and dinner-table conversation is preempted by television.

Grammar

The same kind of progress occurs in grammar. Although most of the everyday grammatical constructions are mastered before age 6, knowledge of syntax continues to develop throughout elementary school, perhaps because children are increasingly able to use grammar to understand the connections between words. They are not fooled by word order, or apparent meaning. For instance, Carol

Chomsky (1969) found that upon hearing "John promised Mary to shovel the driveway," only children younger than 8 would be likely to be misled by their understanding that the subject of a sentence is usually the noun preceding the verb and conclude that Mary is going to do the shoveling. Likewise, children younger than age 6 often have trouble understanding the passive voice, but by middle childhood most children realize that "The truck was bumped by the car" does not state that the truck did the bumping (de Villiers and de Villiers, 1978).

Children over age 7 are also less likely to get confused by irrelevant information, once they understand syntactic structure. In an experiment analogous to Piagetian tests of conservation, Chomsky presented children with a large doll and asked, "Is this doll easy to see or hard to see?" Even preschool children answered correctly. But when Chomsky put a blindfold on the doll, most of the sixteen 5- and 6-year-olds answered the same question by saying the doll was hard to see. Only three of the fifteen children aged 7 or 8 made this mistake, and none of the nine children aged 9 or 10 were misled by the blindfold.

Age of Child	Wrong (Percentage Answering "Hard to see")	Correct (Percentage Answering "Easy to see")
5	78%	22%
6	57%	43%
7	14%	86%
8	25%	75%
9	0%	100%
10	0%	100%

Other language abilities also seem closely related to concrete operational thought. For instance, an understanding of comparatives ("longer," "deeper," "wider"), of the subjunctive ("If you were a millionaire . . ."), and of metaphors (that is, of how someone could be a dirty dog or a rotten egg) is dependent upon the achievement of a certain level of cognitive development. This is true even with languages in which the actual structure of the grammar is relatively simple. For instance, the subjunctive is much less complicated in Russian than in English, but Russian-speaking children do not master the subjunctive earlier than English-speaking children, because the concept must be understood before the form can be (de Villiers and de Villiers, 1978).

Communicative Competence

Finally, the school-age child becomes much better at using words and grammar as a communication tool, to be adapted to the particular topic, audience, and intent. An 8-year-old child might use one type of vocabulary and grammar with a teacher, another with an adult relative, and a third with neighborhood friends. Preschool children can do some of this spontaneously, as shown when they talk baby talk to a doll, but they lack the ability to analyze what they are doing, and thus, to refine their skill in using different forms of speech.

One example of the developing child's consciousness of language as a tool comes from studies that probe the child's understanding of the word "word" (Papandrapoulou and Sinclair, 1974). Most children younger than 7 confuse a word with

Figure 13.11 *Singing helps children learn language. The children singing "Winter Wonderland," in this photo, for instance, are learning rhymes, alliteration, and perhaps new vocabulary ("glistening," "parson," etc.). In some songs, children learn regional dialects and sometimes words from other languages.*

the object it refers to. Thus, they say that "car" is a "real word" because "you can drive it"; however "is," "very," and "but" are not because "you can't see them." In the same way, preschool children trying to decide if a sentence is grammatically correct judge solely on the basis of whether the sentence makes sense ("The mouse chased the cat" would be wrong). Later they judge on the basis of how they themselves would say the sentence ("Me and Suzy quarreled" is considered more correct than "Suzy and I quarreled"). Finally, by the end of middle childhood, they are able to apply the rules of grammar correctly when asked to, even if they don't apply them in their own everyday speech. Of course, understanding textbook grammar usually depends on specific instruction, especially if no one in the child's immediate world speaks it.

Black English   When trying to teach "correct" English, instructors have come to realize that some forms of nonstandard English are a source of group identification and pride. This is most apparent in Black English, a form of English spoken by many black Americans. Black English used to be considered simply poor English until linguists realized that the so-called errors were actually consistent alternative grammatical forms, some of which originated in African linguistic patterns. For example, the word "be" in standard English is primarily used as part of the infinitive "to be." But in Black English, "be" can also be used to indicate a repeated action or existential state (Labov, 1972). Thus, in Black English, one cay say, "I am sick" or "I be sick." The first means "I am sick at this present moment"; the second includes the recent past as well as the present. To express the second concept in standard English, one might say, "I have been sick for a while and I still am sick."

Another difference occurs in the expression of negation. Almost all children spontaneously use the double or even triple negative, saying "I don't want to see no doctor" or "Nobody never gives me nothing." But since these forms are wrong in standard English, middle-class children are usually corrected by their parents and older peers, and use only one negative per sentence by middle childhood. However, speakers of Black English tend to resist, consciously or unconsciously, such correction, because in Black English the double negative for emphasis is correct.

Such seeming exceptions to standard English sound like gross errors to someone who has not heard much Black English, just as a heavy regional accent may seem like wholesale mispronunciation to someone unfamiliar with it. Actually, however, the differences between Black English and standard English are relatively easy to understand, especially when one realizes that Black English has consistent grammatical rules. Many black Americans can switch easily from Black to standard English, depending on the context, just as many Americans modify their accents to fit their audience. However, many others, especially children, speak only Black English because that is the form of English spoken almost exclusively by their peers and family members. This fact can lead to both academic and emotional problems in school. Writing a composition becomes very difficult when one's grammar and pronunciation, constantly reinforced in daily nonschool life, make it hard to formulate a sentence in correct standard English or even to learn correct spelling or punctuation. In addition, if the teacher takes the attitude that all nonstandard English is wrong, the effect on children who speak nonstandard English can be quite destructive. As Dorothy Seymour (1971) writes:

> A child is quick to grasp the feeling that while school speech is "good," his own speech is "bad," and that by extension he himself is somehow inadequate and without value. Some children react to this feeling by withdrawing; they stop talking entirely. Others develop the attitude of "F'get you, honky." In either case, the psychological results are devastating and lead straight to the dropout route.

On the other hand, if the teacher recognizes Black English as a legitimate dialect, with its own grammar, pronunciation, and vocabulary, and consequently not only accepts but also echoes the dialect the students speak, the children will be penalized when they enter the larger world where proficiency in standard English is expected. Therefore, the best solution seems to be to help children achieve competence in standard English, at the same time accepting their communications in nonstandard English as valid. The same basic tactic can be used for children who speak with marked regional accents and phrases, or whose first language is not the one spoken in the school. Unlike preschool children, who learn language best through exposure, speaking as many languages as the people around them, school-age children are able to analyze and apply language rules, so they can be systematically taught a new language or dialect, even if it is not the one they usually hear.

Figure 13.12 *The function of language is to serve the human need to communicate. However, people often focus on form rather than function, forgetting that what is proper speech to one person may be dialect to someone else. In such cases, they may try to instruct another in "respectable" speech with all the sensitivity Brer Rabbit showed the Tar Baby.*

" 'I'm gwine ter larn you howter talk ter 'spectubble fokes ef hit's de las' ack,' sez Brer Rabbit, sezee."

Measuring Cognitive Development

Especially in our society, where the skills taught in school are considered crucial for success in later life, parents and teachers want to know how well the process of education is going. Is the child learning as quickly and as much as possible? Would another class, another teacher, another curriculum be better? Is a slow-learning second-grader going to be slow throughout the elementary school years? These questions are sufficiently important in our culture that educators and psychologists have found several ways to answer them.

Teacher Opinions

Teachers base their evaluation of a schoolchild's performance on many factors—test scores, homework, schoolwork, classroom attitude, neatness, and work habits among them. If, in addition, experienced teachers confer with concerned parents, they can often arrive at an even more accurate estimate of how well a child is doing, and of what can be done to facilitate the child's learning. School systems that encourage parent-teacher cooperation have found that pupil achievement rises as a result.

Of course, teachers' and parents' judgments are not infallible. A problem may arise if a particular teacher has specific ideas about which skills are important to learn at what age. When these views conflict with those of the parents or of teachers in other grades, the child may suffer.

For instance, some teachers focus on behavior and devalue intellectual accomplishments. Assigning her students to sections of the first grade, one kindergarten teacher decided to place a particular child in the "Junior First"—the lowest of four first-grade sections—because, although he was "extremely verbal" with a "fantastic vocabulary" and "knew all his sounds and letters," he was also "very silly and immature" (Cicourel et al., 1974). A decision of this nature may not be wrong if subsequent teachers keep such children sufficiently intellectually challenged so that they can be advanced when their social skills mature. Otherwise, they may not be taught the things they are intellectually ready to learn.

Achievement Tests

Teacher reports on students are helpful, but an objective assessment of how well each child is learning, and how well each teacher is teaching, is also needed. Achievement tests, which measure how much a child has accomplished, are used for both purposes.

At least 200 million achievement tests are given each year in the United States (Holman and Docter, 1972). Ideally, these tests help teachers know which students need special attention and which children need more challenging work, and they help parents and administrators know which teachers are teaching well. Achievement tests can be used to determine if a student will graduate, or have to repeat a grade. Within each grade they are sometimes used to group students in classes, so the poorest achievers are in one class and the better achievers in another.

Creating an accurate achievement test is a complex process. First of all, the test must be valid; that is, it must measure what it is supposed to measure. It must also be reliable, so that the same findings are arrived at over several testings. To take an example from physical measurement, if you wanted to measure weight gain, the most valid way would be to use a scale—not a tape measure. And you would want the scale to be reliable, not susceptible to changes in humidity.

Now let's take the example of developing a math-achievement test for grades two to six. For the test to be *valid,* the questions must reflect the actual math curriculum in American schools as well as measure proficiency in standard math skills. For the test to be *reliable,* the questions must be clearly written, and must not require any special knowledge of nonmathematical factors. For instance, if all the problems had to do with shopping in a supermarket, children who had not shopped in a supermarket might be unfairly penalized. More basic, the directions must be clear and simply written, so that the test does not inadvertently test ability to read and follow directions. In addition, there must be enough questions at every level so that the test will not only spot children achieving at kindergarten level and at ninth-grade level, but will also draw the fine distinction between children in the first and the second month of fourth grade.

Once the questions are written, they must be field-tested—tried out with hundreds of children of different ages, grades, races, and family incomes. Some of the children are tested and retested to make sure the test is reliable; that is, not subject to much unexpected variation from one test date to the next. On the basis of this field-testing, some questions are eliminated and others are rewritten, until the test seems sufficiently valid, reliable, and sensitive.

Then the test is standardized by giving it to a large group of children typical of the overall population who will take the test. From the performance of this sample, the testers determine what score should be considered average for each month of school. Thus, twenty correct answers to fifty questions might be the average score in the second month of the third grade (3.2); twenty-one correct might be the score of the fourth month of the third grade (3.4); and so forth. Even after all these steps are taken, no test is completely valid and reliable. To compensate for this, the examiners' manual reports how the test was constructed, validated, and standardized, so that testers will exercise caution in interpreting the test results.

Even the most carefully designed achievement tests can be invalid or unreliable for a particular child or group of children, for three reasons:

1. Some children are much better at taking tests than others. They enjoy the challenge, work quickly but carefully, and guess well. Other children are poor test-takers, perhaps because they are so anxious that they cannot think, or because the test format is confusing to them.

2. Achievement scores depend partly on the child's preparation for the test, and teachers can boost their students' scores by giving them practice at test-taking and by making sure they are familiar with the kind of material that is going to be on the test. When teachers and principals feel their jobs depend on achievement scores, both innovation in the curriculum and honesty may be sacrificed.

3. Even when achievement scores are fairly accurate, they may lead to inaccurate conclusions. It is easy to conclude that students who score poorly on achievement tests are slow learners, when, in fact, some of them need glasses, others are dyslexic, still others are bilinguals who have not yet mastered English, and so forth.

Aware teachers and parents know that an achievement test provides only a clue to any child's accomplishment. It does not tell the whole story, no matter how carefully it is constructed. Unless the various problems inherent in this kind of test are kept in mind, perhaps thousands of children will be misjudged each year.

Aptitude Tests

Whereas achievement tests are intended to measure how much a child has accomplished, aptitude tests, theoretically, measure how much a child could accomplish, if given the opportunity. However, it is impossible to measure potential without measuring a sample of present ability in order to predict future ability. As Jencks writes: "In principle, achievement tests tell whether students have mastered some body of material that the tester deems important. Aptitude tests (such as IQ tests) theoretically tell whether students are *capable* of mastering a body of material that the tester deems important. In practice, however, all tests measure both aptitude and achievement" (Jencks et al., 1972). This is a point we will return to later, when we discuss how much faith can be placed in aptitude tests.

Intelligence Tests   In elementary school, the most commonly used aptitude tests are intelligence tests. The first one was developed by Alfred Binet in 1905 to find which boys in the Paris schools could not benefit from normal instruction because their mental development was retarded. He felt that if a test could spot these students early, years of effort on the part of teachers and pupils would be saved. Since boys who failed to complete their work were shamed and even whipped in those days, the IQ test was a blessing to the pupils, who were no longer faced with an impossible task, as well as to the teachers and parents who knew the retarded boys were not "just lazy."

Figure 13.13 *In most nineteenth-century schools, children who did not complete their work for any reason were beaten with birch rods and scorned by their classmates. The assumption that slow learners are simply not trying hard enough was proven false by Alfred Binet in 1905. His first intelligence tests showed that some children are much faster at mastering memory or reasoning tasks than others are.*

Following Binet's lead, American psychologists have developed several IQ tests, the most widely used individual ones being the Stanford-Binet and the Wechsler tests (one for preschoolers, one for schoolchildren, and one for adults—WPPSI, WISC, and WAIS, respectively), all of which test general knowledge, reasoning ability, mathematical skill, memory, and vocabulary.

The following pairs of questions are indicative of the easiest and hardest of the many questions in five of the WISC subtests (the range of difficulty covers kindergarten through high school; as long as a child continues to answer most items correctly, the examiner asks questions of increasing difficulty).

General knowledge: How many thumbs do you have?/Who wrote *The Divine Comedy*?

Reasoning ability: How are a child and an adult alike?/How are an elephant and a whale alike? (Two points credit for the category both belong to: humans for the first question, mammals for the second; one point for less sophisticated, albeit correct, answers.)

Mathematical skill: What is 4+1?/If a train traveling at 32 miles per hour takes three days to get from one place to another, how fast must a train go to travel the same distance in half a day?

Memory: Repeat these numbers: 963./Repeat these numbers backward: 7832916.

Vocabulary: What is a spoon?/What is a mortgage?

Such items as these make up half of the Wechsler test. The other half measures nonverbal skills, such as putting a puzzle together, arranging a series of pictures in a sequence that tells a story, and creating designs with colored blocks to match those shown in sample pictures. (The Stanford-Binet test differs from the Wechsler test in that it has fewer nonverbal tests and tallies speed of completion less frequently.)

For many reasons, these tests measure ability much better than achievement tests do. They are given to children one at a time by a psychologist or counselor trained to establish rapport. Thus, the examiner can make sure that the child is not anxious, sick, or upset, and that the child understands each question. The tester reads the test to the child, so poor readers are not handicapped. (Some tests of intelligence are given to a group of children together, and are usually less valid than the individual tests.)

What IQ Scores Are Supposed to Mean.   Originally, the intelligence quotient was truly a quotient, arrived at by dividing mental age by chronological age and multiplying by 100. Thus, a 10-year-old who scored at the 12-year-old level would have an IQ of 120; and a 15-year-old who scored like a 12-year-old would have an IQ of 80. Today, the system for determining actual score is more refined, but the scores are still roughly equivalent to the old system. Specific labels are used to designate children who score several years above or below the expected score at that age.

Above 130	Gifted
115–130	Superior
85–115	Average
70–85	Slow learner
Below 70	Mentally retarded
50–69	Educable (can learn to read and write)
25–49	Trainable (can learn to care for self)
0–24	Custodial (will need to be cared for)

As you can see from this listing, the range of average scores goes from 85 to 115 (100 is considered exactly average). About two-thirds of all people score within this range, and only about 2 percent score above 130. (The labels applying to the three lowest score ranges must be considered rough predictions: many people labeled "retarded" learn more than their IQs would predict.)

The Purpose of Intelligence Tests.   Today IQ tests serve two purposes. They predict school achievement and diagnose learning problems. For example, they help teachers know how able a child is, allowing them to give more challenging work to the faster student and easier work to the slower student. They also help spot the

---

A CLOSER LOOK   **The Gifted Child**

When asked "What can you do with a brick?" most elementary-school children think of less than ten uses, almost always incorporating the brick as building material or as a weapon. But a few children think of many more uses, and some of their suggestions are highly imaginative: for instance, tying the brick to a raft and using it for an anchor; or grinding it up to make paint; or putting it next to a water fountain so small children can stand on it to drink. Children who give these kinds of responses are considered highly creative. Their thinking processes can be described as *divergent,* for they lead to many solutions to every problem, in contrast to those of the *convergent* thinker, whose mind searches for *the* one, correct answer for any question.

High creativity is only one form of giftedness that becomes apparent in elementary school; other types include very high intellectual ability or unusual talent, such as that of the mathematical or musical prodigy. Each of these gifts can create problems for the elementary-school child, who may have trouble finding friends who accept someone with such special ability.

But of all the gifted children, creative children are the ones most likely to get into trouble at school, for their ideas may seem out of place when the emphasis is on conforming and knowing the "right" answers—both valued in the usual elementary-school classroom. Creative children are often exasperating to teachers, especially when they come up with a new way to do long division which they consider better, or refuse to eat the school lunch because it contains certain ingredients, or when they daydream when they are supposed to memorize their spelling words, or when they ask bothersome questions about the history lesson. Creative children develop a reputation for having "wild and silly ideas," and they tend to be excluded from group activities (Torrence, 1972).

One study found that school is particularly hard for children who score relatively high on tests of creativity but low on tests of intelligence, for they often lose confidence in themselves and retreat from classroom interaction (Wallach and Kogan, 1965). Children high in both creativity and intelligence may be bored, but usually are able to do well on conventional school assignments and tests. The child who is at the lower end of the scale in both creativity and intelligence often learns to value social activities more than academic ones. And finally, the child high in intelligence and low in creativity is likely to become addicted to school achievement.

Most educators and psychologists who study gifted children believe that they need special encouragement and enrichment at school, beginning in the early grades, in order to develop their self-esteem and social skills, as well as their talents. Otherwise, they might drop out or fail in their grades, as did Thomas Edison, Albert Einstein, Winston Churchill, Gamul Abdul Nasser, Émile Zola (who got a zero in literature), and Pablo Picasso (who refused to do anything but paint).

In fact, in a study of famous people from all over the world, Victor and Mildred Goertzel (1962) found that 60 percent hated their years in school. Many of them misbehaved, played hooky, or dropped out, responses to education that were likely to occur in all types of schools (public, private, and parochial) and in every culture. It is reassuring to realize that these extraordinary people overcame their early educational experiences, and perhaps we should sympathize with their teachers as well as with them. However, the biographies of such people lead us to wonder how many future inventors, artists, and world leaders are now suffering through boring classes with unsympathetic teachers and peers. Another question is even more disturbing: How many other gifted young people, who may have had a little less persistence, talent, or luck, never learned to appreciate their talents or develop their skills?

very bright child, who might need a special class for the gifted or an opportunity to skip a grade, and to spot the mentally retarded child who might need a special class for slow learners.

Probably more important is the help they provide counselors in discovering why a child is having a learning problem. If a hard-working, healthy child is failing and scores 70 on an IQ test, it would seem clear that the regular work is probably too hard for that child. On the other hand, a failing child with an IQ of 110 must have another problem—perhaps a poor teacher, a discouraging home environment, or a reading difficulty. As one part of a battery of tests, IQ tests also help diagnose minimal brain damage and emotional disturbances.

Problems with IQ Tests. It is impossible to construct a completely fair test of aptitude in a society where educational opportunities are not equal and cultural differences are apparent. For instance, some questions on IQ tests—say, "Why is it better to give to an organized charity rather than to a street beggar?" or "Where does the sun set?"—would be more difficult for children who are poor and live in the inner city. Even attempts to develop culture-free tests, such as asking a child to draw a person and then noting how detailed the drawing is, are hindered by cultural variations. For one thing, some children do much more drawing at home or school, and this affects how they draw people.

In addition, test-taking is easier for some children than for others. Many children, for example, have been told not to talk to strangers, especially strange men of a different race. Thus, a black 8-year-old girl might say to a white male psychologist, "I don't know," rather than guess at an answer.

Another problem is that most IQ tests are standardized on American-born, English-speaking children, even though they are sometimes used to decide the educational future of immigrant, non-English-speaking children. Precisely for this reason, a California court recently ruled that the standard intelligence tests could

Figure 13.14 *Many psychologists are looking for alternatives to the standard IQ tests, which give the child points for each correct answer. In these photos, Gilbert Voyat, a psychologist who studied with Piaget, gives classification problems to two preschool girls and a conservation task to a school-age boy. Rather than trying to compare one child with another, as is done in most standard intelligence tests, Voyat is more interested in each child's approach to the problem. He looks at the* process *of thinking more than the* product.

Correlation Between School Grades, Test Scores, and Adult Success

There is a positive correlation between school grades, achievement test scores, and intelligence test scores; in other words, someone who scores high on one of these measures is likely to score high on the others. This is not surprising, for all three are designed to measure similar skills and abilities.

At first glance, the relationship between childhood achievement and adult success seems clear-cut as well. In his long-term study of children with IQs above 130, Terman found that they had greater success and less failure as adults than the general population in their respective communities (Terman and Oden, 1959). For example, they were happier with their marriages, their occupations, and their incomes. Children who have high marks in the sixth grade tend to do well in high school, college, and adulthood, and people who occupy high-status occupations tend to have high IQs (Jencks, 1979).

However, this general tendency does not always predict individual accomplishments, as was evidenced by the large cross section of adults given the Army General Classification Test during World War II, when almost every able-bodied man of fighting age was tested before joining the armed forces.

While average scores follow the expected trends, the range for each occupation is so great that trying to predict occupation based on IQ is risky (G.C.T. scores correspond roughly to scores on other intelligence tests). Thus one teacher had a score of 76 (slow learner), and a radio repairman a score of 56 (mentally retarded). There are men with very high scores in every occupation, and men with very low scores (theoretically not able to learn to read, write, or add) gainfully employed as sales clerks, truck drivers, and machinists.

Mean G.C.T. Scores and Range of Scores for Army Air Force White Enlisted Men By Civilian Occupation

Occupation	Mean G.C.T. Score	Range
Accountant	128.1	94 – 157
Lawyer	127.6	96 – 157
Engineer	126.6	100 – 151
Teacher	122.8	76 – 155
Bookkeeper	120.0	70 – 157
Clerk-general	117.5	68 – 155
Clerk-typist	116.8	80 – 147
Radio repairman	115.3	56 – 151
Salesman	115.1	60 – 153
Artist	114.9	82 – 139
Musician	110.9	56 – 147
Machinist	110.1	38 – 153
Sales clerk	109.2	42 – 149
Mechanic	106.3	60 – 155
Butcher	102.9	42 – 147
Cook and baker	97.2	20 – 147
Truck driver	96.2	16 – 149
Farmer	92.7	24 – 147
Miner	90.6	42 – 139

Source: Harrell and Harrell, 1945.

Jencks and his colleagues (1972) found that Americans who earned salaries in the top 20 percent were paid six times as much as those in the bottom 20 percent. They found that this enormous income differential could be explained much more by differences in years of schooling, family background, motivation, and an unexplained factor called "luck" than by differences in achievement or aptitude test scores. Many people with high IQs are far from wealthy, and many college graduates who avoided flunking out by a hair's breadth become quite successful. Thus IQ tests or school grades are not always accurate indications of future status or income.

no longer be used as the major criterion of "special class" placement, a practice that had resulted in a disproportionate number of children born in other countries being put in classes for the mentally retarded.

Professionals who are trained in writing and using IQ tests are often among the most cautious in interpreting them, for they are aware of their shortcomings as well as their strengths (Holman and Docter, 1972). They know that social class, racial prejudice, and even family size affect IQ scores (Brody and Brody, 1976), that IQ tests measure achievement as well as ability, that individual scores sometimes change 20 points or more from year to year, and that IQ tests in childhood are not a very accurate way to measure success in adulthood.

Consequently, many psychologists believe that IQ tests should be used only to diagnose problems, not to predict future accomplishment. Kenneth Clark writes:

> The I.Q. cannot be considered sacred or even relevant in decisions about the future of the child. It should not be used to shackle children. An I.Q. so misused contributes to the wastage of human potential. The I.Q. can be a valuable educational tool within the limits of its utility, namely, as an index of what needs to be done for a particular child. The I.Q. used to determine where one must start, to determine what a particular child needs to bring him up to maximum effectiveness, is a valuable educational aid. But the I.Q. as an end product or an end decision for children is criminally neglectful. The I.Q. should not be used as a basis for segregating children and for predicting—and therefore determining—the child's educational future. [Clark, 1965]

Differing views of the value of IQ tests often amount to pitched battle. Some psychologists reject them totally, maintaining that intelligence tests are biased and misleading and have no valid place in the educational system (Jackson, 1975). Others think that the tests themselves are accurate, and that blaming them for the larger social ills that they measure is equivalent to the ancient Greek custom of killing the messenger who brought bad news.

As will become apparent in the next chapter, influences of the family, peer group, and society can aid or impede every aspect of achievement in middle childhood, from standard test scores to personal self-esteem. Just as it is shortsighted to use only one measurement to evaluate a child's cognitive development, it is probably also a mistake to blame low achievement on any one factor—whether it be a poor teacher, an inept child, or a misused test.

SUMMARY

Cognitive Changes During Middle Childhood

1. School-age children enjoy telling jokes, evidence of their developing memory, logic, and social skills. Jokes involving language ambiguity are the most popular.

2. According to some developmental psychologists, the years from ages 5 to 7 are a time of transition, when new memory skills, reasoning abilities, and willingness to learn appear. During this period, children sometimes intuit the right answers to logical questions without knowing how they got them.

3. According to Piaget, beginning at about age 7 or 8, children are able to think using the logical structures of concrete operational thought. They can apply their logic to problems involving conservation, classification, and seriation and can distinguish cause and effect. The relationship between time, space, and distance is also better understood, as are others' points of view.

4. According to information-processing research, cognitive growth during middle childhood is a result of how much information children are given, how efficiently they learn to process it, and how motivated they are to understand and reproduce it. During middle childhood, children learn new strategies for concentrating and remembering, which makes them much more able to master academic skills.

5. Piaget's theory implies that teachers should provide the materials and time children need to develop their ideas, rather than try to force all the children to learn specific skills at particular times. Each child's own search for cognitive equilibrium, rather than external reinforcement, will help that child master whatever body of knowledge he or she is ready to understand.

6. Behaviorists believe that giving each child specific learning tasks, correcting mistakes, and reinforcing right answers is the more effective way to teach. They point out that cross-cultural evidence shows that environmental factors exert a sizable influence on what skills and concepts are mastered.

7. No matter which theory one holds, educators and psychologists agree that education should be suited to the needs and abilities of each child. Teachers and parents usually do this well, when they can cooperate and agree.

Language

8. Language abilities continue to improve during middle childhood, partly because schools and families encourage this learning, and partly because increased cognitive development makes it easier to grasp difficult grammatical distinctions.

9. The ability to understand that language is a tool for communication makes the school-age child more able to use different forms of language in different contexts, as does, for example, the child who uses Black English on the playground and standard English in the classroom.

Measuring Cognitive Development

10. Achievement tests and aptitude tests can help spot children who are not learning as well as they should, and can diagnose the problem. However, they must be carefully written and cautiously interpreted.

11. Intelligence tests were originally developed to identify children who could not learn in normal classes, and they are still used to diagnose which children should have special education. However, IQ scores fluctuate much more than was formerly realized, so they are not as good predictive instruments as they were once thought to be.

KEY QUESTIONS

What skills are necessary to enjoy telling jokes?

What are some of the characteristics that appear during the 5-to-7 shift?

What must children understand before they can use the number system?

What are the educational implications of Piaget's theory of cognitive development?

What does cross-cultural research on Piaget's stages find?

What language abilities develop in middle childhood?

What is the difference between an achievement test and an aptitude test?

What are the uses of intelligence tests?

What are the problems with intelligence tests?

KEY TERMS

reality riddles	impulsive
language-ambiguity jokes	reflective
absurdity riddles	traditional education
5-to-7 shift	open education
seriation	Black English
information processing	achievement tests
selective attention	valid
metamemory	reliable
sensory register	field-tested
mnemonic	standardized
rehearsal	aptitude tests
chunking	

RECOMMENDED READINGS

Jencks, Christopher, et al. *Inequality.* New York: Basic Books, 1972.

This is a provocative discussion of the reasons for inequality in America. The influence of intelligence, school, family background, and socioeconomic class are all considered. The book makes one think about the relationship between democracy, income, and achievement, although many people will not agree with Jencks' conclusions.

Dillard, J. L. *Black English.* New York: Vintage, 1972.

The definitive history of Black English, showing its roots in Africa and its use as a dialect today.

Ginsburg, Herbert. *The myth of the deprived child.* Englewood Cliffs, N.J.: Prentice-Hall, 1972.

Ginsburg argues that "deprived" or "disadvantaged" children are as competent as more privileged children. The apparent differences in IQ scores of children from various social classes are more an artifact of the test and of the standard school curriculum than an accurate measure of true differences.

The School Years: Psychosocial Development

The child does not know that men are not only bad from good motives, but also often good from bad motives. Therefore the child has a hearty, healthy, unspoiled, and insatiable appetite for mere morality, for the mere difference between a good little girl and a bad little girl.

G. K. Chesterton

True or False?   The quest for independence from parents during middle childhood is typical only of modern industrial societies.

Although American children generally are aware of differences in skin color at age 3, it is not until middle childhood that they become aware that social significance has been attached to those differences.

One of the chief roles of parents during middle childhood should be that of mediator, interceding in conflicts between children before they escalate into fights.

All that is required for a child to learn social skills is other children to play with.

Psychologists have determined that five basic cultural characteristics foster cooperative behavior: the United States is lacking in all but one of them.

Divorced women are better able to care for their children than divorced men are, as is reflected in the fact that 90 percent of single-parent households are headed by women.

At first glance, it might seem that the social world of children during middle childhood is quite similar to that of early childhood, since, for the most part, no new elements are added in this later period; family, friends, and even school are already part of the life of most 5-year-olds. But each element does change during middle childhood. Children become less dependent on their parents for moment-to-moment care, and more responsible for choosing and donning their own clothes, preparing and eating their own breakfasts, organizing and cleaning their own rooms. As the parents' role seems to diminish, the influence of other children grows. Playing with friends and fighting with enemies, and deciding who is which, are a central part of middle childhood. Finally, school becomes serious business: it is a place for learning about oneself as well as learning the three Rs.

All these changes occur because children themselves change, becoming much more competent and self-aware than they were. They also begin to develop their own moral codes and values with which to judge everyone, including parents, teachers, peers, and themselves. This chapter begins by discussing the characteristics of school-age children, and then shows how these children interact with their widening social world.

Theories about Middle Childhood

In the chapter on psychosocial development during early childhood (Chapter 11), we saw that the major theories could be viewed as alternative ways of explaining the same phenomena. For instance, the exaggeration of male-female differences that is evident in most 5-year-olds could be seen as a symptom of the Oedipal complex, a result of watching stereotyped situation comedies on television, or a sign of increased cognitive maturity. However, with regard to middle childhood, each theory focuses on a different characteristic of development.

Psychoanalytic Theory

According to Freud, most instinctual impulses during middle childhood are hidden and quiet; this is the period of latency. Compared to the jealousy, passion, and guilt of children at the phallic stage, children's lives during middle childhood are much steadier, freeing them from the emotional bonds that tied them to their parents during the preschool years. Freud hypothesized that the reason for latency is that the superego has become strong enough to keep the forces of the id—particularly the sexual and aggressive urges that appeared during the phallic stage—under control, thus allowing the ego to grow. (When the sexual pressures of adolescence emerge at puberty, this temporary harmony will be broken—but that's another age and another chapter.)

Erikson agrees that the Oedipal wish to establish a sexual future with the mother or father is over by age 7 and that "violent drives are normally dormant" in middle childhood, giving children new independence from their parents. But Erikson goes one step further. Once the child realizes that "there is no workable future within the womb of his family, . . . [the child] becomes ready to apply himself to given skills and tasks."

According to Erikson, the goal of this period is industry, as children busily master the skills needed in their culture. During the industry versus inferiority stage, children develop a view of themselves as good workers or failures, or, in Erikson's words, as industrious and productive or inferior and inadequate.

Although many psychologists disagree with the psychoanalytic explanation of the reasons for the relative calm of middle childhood, this theory does point to two basic characteristics of middle childhood: growing independence from parents and increased readiness to work at whatever skills the culture values. In fact, independence from parents is sought by almost all children this age. Boys in Kenya, for example, prefer to herd the cattle without adult supervision (Whiting, 1963), just as children in the United States are happy to play without their parents being nearby. The working parents' "latchkey kids," who let themselves into their empty homes or apartments with the housekeys they wear around their necks, may be pitied by the neighbors, but they are often envied by other children.

Erikson's emphasis on industry is in accord with anthropologists' observations. In many cultures, school-age children master many skills, from weaving to penmanship. Indeed, adults often rely on children between ages 7 and 10 to perform important work. According to a detailed account of children in six cultures (Whiting, 1963), Nysango children in Kenya weed, harvest, shuck, grind, and cook corn, and herd cattle. Rajput girls in India pick water chestnuts, vegetables, and cotton, while the boys pasture the cattle and work in the fields. The children in Okinawa, Japan, use sharp cutting tools (sickles, knives, and saws), twist straw into rope, and harvest rice. Mixtecan Indian children in Mexico care for the animals, including turkeys, chickens, goats, and burros, and help in the fields, as do children in the Philippines. In all these cultures, caring for younger children, washing, and sweeping are also part of the daily responsibilities of offspring in middle childhood.

The same study found that, at least in middle-class towns, American children between ages 6 and 8 have virtually no household responsibilities, and those between 9 and 12 have only a few. They are generally "expected to keep their rooms orderly when reminded . . . and . . . to help wash dishes." Consequently, these children learn few domestic skills and remain dependent on their parents' ability to maintain the household. (The recent increase in employed mothers has altered this picture somewhat, adding more household responsibilities to the lives of many school-age children, a welcome change according to Lois Hoffman [1977].)

(a)

(b)

(c)

Figure 14.1 *The work done by school-age children is essential to many families in developing countries, as is the labor of these industrious children from* (a) *Ghana,* (b) *Guatemala,* (c) *Brazil,* (d) *Nigeria, and* (e) *El Salvador.*

(d)

(e)

On the whole, it seems, North American children are expected to develop their competencies outside the home: their testing ground is the school or the playing field. Schoolchildren develop reading, writing, and computational skills, and by middle childhood, they are often eager to build science models, write stories, or trace and color maps with only minimal assistance from parents or teachers. They also develop nonacademic skills through sports and lessons—baseball and karate,

Figure 14.2 *North American children often use sports as a way to develop their competence. Despite recent efforts to make athletic activities equally available to both sexes, many girls are less practiced at dozens of sports skills—including holding a bat.*

Hebrew and Chinese, pottery and ballet, being a few among the hundreds of possibilities. While some children develop competence with a great deal of adult assistance, learning how to steal a base in Little League or how to play the scales on the violin, others develop skills on their own, from scaling fences, to building treehouses, to stealing a candy bar.

Unfortunately, there is the other side of this stage—in Erikson's terms, inferiority. In a society such as ours, where competition and comparison are an integral part of most classrooms and sports, many school-age children decide that they are stupid, clumsy, and worthless, a problem we will discuss in more detail later in this chapter.

Behaviorism

The development of skills during middle childhood is a theme also recognized by behaviorists. They are interested in the particular situations that promote learning, whether they are those of the classroom or of the general socialization processes that occur in family and community. Three characteristics of school-age children make them good candidates for the application of behaviorist techniques.

1. They are much more aware of the actions and attitudes of others than previously. Of course, modeling is possible even with infants, who can stick out their tongue or say "ba-ba-ba" in imitation of someone else. But during middle childhood, children become much more astute at observing other people. School-age children model themselves after not only their parents but also their teachers and friends, choosing people they see as successful (Bandura, 1977).

2. School-age children also become more receptive to many types of reinforcements. While younger children respond better to tangible rewards—a cookie, a new toy, a hug—school-age children are more open to social reinforcement, such as praise or attention, as well as intrinsic rewards, such as pride in work well done (Bandura, 1977). Robert White (1959) stresses the drive for competence, which he considers as reinforcing as the traditional sexual drives recognized by Freudians or the basic needs (hunger, thirst, etc.) emphasized by early behaviorists. White thinks competence and mastery are motives at every period of life, but he believes that when children become better able to evaluate their own performance, at about age 7, they become much more willing to work to master a skill. The pride of the child who gets a 100 on a spelling test or hits a home run is almost palpable.

Figure 14.3 *Young gymnasts in Moscow hold aloft trophies previously won by students from their school. During middle childhood, symbolic reinforcers, such as trophies and medals, and social rewards, such as public recognition of one's accomplishments, become sufficiently powerful that many aspiring athletes and musicians practice long hours to attain them.*

Figure 14.4 *Being better able to understand logical sequences—"If this, then that"—children in middle childhood can often make great efforts in the name of future rewards, like getting to school on time every day in order to get a brand new bike.*

3. They are more able to understand cause and effect. This works both in the short-term ("Be home by 6 o'clock or you can't watch television") and in the long-term ("If you are on time for school all fall, you can have a bike for Christmas"). Of course, some children are better at understanding consequences and the postponing of rewards than others, but almost all 9-year-olds have a firmer grasp of these concepts than they did at age 6.

All three of these developments make school-age children good subjects for operant conditioning. Interestingly, at about age 6, children become less susceptible to classical conditioning (White, 1965). If Watson had tried to condition a 7-year-old to be afraid of white furry objects, he would have had a much harder time than he had with little Albert (see page 26).

Learning Self-Control Children of this age are also better able to exercise self-control, as was demonstrated by a series of experiments on a process called resistance to temptation (Mischel, 1978). For instance, children were allowed to pick between two treats (say, between a small notebook and a large one, or between one cookie and two), one of which they could have immediately; the other—the better—they would have to wait for. School-age children were much more able to wait for the better treat than younger children were, partly because they knew how to make the wait easier—by not looking at the treat and by distracting themselves from the temptation.

In another version of this experiment, children at three levels (preschool, third grade, and sixth grade) were shown two marshmallows and told they could have both if they waited until the experimenter came back to the room but only one if they pushed a buzzer that signaled the experimenter to return immediately. Then they were given the choice of waiting with the marshmallows in plain view or covered by a cake tin. Picking the alternative that would make waiting harder, 58 percent of the preschoolers asked to have the marshmallows left in view, whereas only 30 percent of the third-graders and 23 percent of the sixth-graders did. When asked "What can you say to yourself that will help you wait?" most of the preschoolers replied that they did not know. However, all the older children came up

Figure 14.5 *Not having acquired techniques for self-control, preschoolers are usually at the mercy of their immediate appetites, whereas older children are often able to distract themselves from temptation. In this resistance-to-temptation experiment, there seems to be little doubt about which child will be able to hold out.*

with strategies, such as lecturing themselves ("Boy, Jenna, if you ring that bell you only get one"), distracting themselves ("Think of Christmas"), or making the treat seem temporarily undesirable ("I'd say that the marshmallows are filled with an evil spell, and if you eat or touch it, you will be under a spell for five years").

Awareness of self-control techniques, as shown by this example, is also apparent in dozens of examples from the daily life of school-age children. They resist temptation (deciding not to sit next to their best friend in school in order to concentrate harder), postpone pleasure (saving their money for a big treat), and show sophistication about their own behavior in other forms as well. A child trying to become a better athlete, for instance, might decide to practice a particular skill (such as running for stamina, shooting baskets, or swimming laps in the pool) for an hour as soon as school is over, before watching TV, playing with friends, or getting a snack. Another child might decide that it's time to get organized, and draw up a schedule of all the things to get done during the course of each day. A religious child, on the other hand, might devise a personal schedule of penances for behavior deemed sinful.

Of course, many children have difficulty sticking to their plan for more than a few days, but the very fact that such self-control techniques appear spontaneously demonstrates the maturation of the school-age child.

Cognitive Theory

The way concrete operational children think about their world affects how they learn and what they are capable of learning, as we saw in the previous chapter. In addition, it affects their understanding of themselves and others. This change is most noticeable in their growing ability to decenter and understand another point of view. John Flavell (1975) has traced this development in a number of experiments, such as asking children to describe an object to someone who can't see it, to tell a story to someone who has never heard it, or to persuade someone to do something that person would rather not do. Skill at tasks such as these develops gradually, as shown by the differences in approach between two third-graders (about age 8) and two seventh-graders (about age 12) when asked to pretend they were asking their fathers to buy them a television.

First, the third graders:

> Come on, I want a television for my own room. Come on. Please. Daddy, come on. Buy me a television. I want one for my room. Come on. Come on, Daddy. I want you to. There!

> Daddy, would you buy me a TV set? . . . If you don't I'm gonna make the money, and go around selling things. And I . . . I know it looks nice in my room, and I think I should have it . . . And if you don't get it for me, I won't bring you any birthday or Christmas present . . . And if you don't I won't—I won't like you and . . . if you don't get me a TV set . . . I'll get . . . . If you don't get me a TV set I'll just say you just better.

Now, the seventh graders:

> Oh Father—er, wait a minute—oh, Dad. I just was down shopping and I saw this most lovely, most beautiful TV I ever saw and it's a portable too. And I was wondering—it didn't cost very much, and you could put it on your charge account down there, and I was just wondering if you could kinda buy it for me, for my birthday or Christmas present to have in my own room. Ah—I'm sure that you'd like it, and well, if you want it, you buy one for your room too. They're kinda cheap, I mean, well, what you can get out of a TV, they're pretty nice, and oh, it'd just match all the furniture in my room. And I promise I wouldn't let any of my friends come in and watch it, or any of my sisters and brothers to wreck it.

> Oh, hello, Dad. How are you today? Do you want your slippers changed or something? Here, have a cigarette? Oh, you don't want one? Oh, okay. Do you want me to do anything for you? Ah—let's see—hey, Christmas is coming. I'll review my list for you. Now there's only one thing I want and that is a television set. Ah—if you get me that you don't have to get me anything else, unless you want to, of course. But you know I need one real much, and ah—and if I don't feel good I have to come into the living room and watch the TV. I can stay right in my room and be very rested. And ah—you know I can use it a lot. And ah—and when my friends come over they don't have to pack in front of the television. They could stay right in my room and be very quiet. Um, yeah, yeah. And they're real pretty and they make a room look real nice, and they're real small ones too, that you can use if you want—wanted. They wouldn't take up any room and—well, you could get a pretty cheap one. Maybe a used one, a secondhand one. They'd only be used a few times. Anything you want to get me, as long as it's a television set. Okay?

The seventh-graders not only talked longer and gave more reasons, they also used more persuasion and fewer threats. Apparently they had learned that threats do not work when negotiating with someone who has greater power, an important lesson for school-age children who must interact with authorities (such as school principals and police officers) and threatening figures (such as the class bully or the neighborhood tough).

A CLOSER LOOK   **Pride and Prejudice**

In North America, racial attitudes usually begin very early in childhood. Mary Ellen Goodman (1964), after reviewing research on the development of racial prejudices, describes three overlapping phases:

Phase I. Awareness of racial differences, beginning at about age 2½ to 3.
Phase II. Orientation toward specific race-related words and concepts beginning at about age 4.
Phase III. True *attitude* toward various races, beginning at about age 7.

Goodman's delineation has been corroborated by recent research in many parts of the United States and Canada. In one study, black and white 3-year-olds in South Carolina were already aware of racial differences (Ballard and Keller, 1976). Another study found that 3-year-old black children and 4-year-old white children in New England were already aware that white is the racial identity favored by that society (Porter, 1971). By age 5, the white children could rationalize their prejudices. At the same age, black children felt ambivalent about being black and had feelings of hostility and envy toward whites. In Porter's study, social class was an important variable, with lower-class white children having more antiblack attitudes than middle-class whites, and middle-class black children revealing more antiblack attitudes than lower-class blacks.

Other studies of young children show that the most prejudiced children are those with the most prejudiced and authoritarian parents, who use strict disciplinary techniques and are inflexible in their attitudes toward right and wrong (Katz, 1975; Boswell and Williams, 1975). By contrast, children whose parents are more tolerant usually are more able to respect themselves and are better able to appreciate someone else.

One solution to the problems of prejudice is to teach racial pride and interracial understanding. Taking this approach, one California school district where most of the children are white and middle class has set up a special curriculum that is intended to reduce prejudice. Among the instructional objectives for kindergarten children are to instill the ideas that "all people have similar feelings even though they have different colors of skin, hair, etc." and that "differences between people are good and make people interesting." A comparison of the racial attitudes of 7-year-olds in that district with those of their contemporaries of similar racial and economic background from a neighboring district revealed that the children who experienced the special curriculum were significantly less prejudiced toward nonwhite children (Westphal, 1977).

Another solution is to teach children, especially minority children, to be proud of themselves, including their appearance and culture. This has been one of the educational goals of black parents, churches, schools, and the media over the last twenty years.

Evidence that such education has improved the self-image of black children may be seen in doll-preference tests, which have been used by psychologists for decades as a measure of racial attitudes. (In the standard test, a child is shown two dolls, identical in every way except that one has brown skin, brown eyes, and black hair, while the other is a blue-eyed blond. Then the child is asked questions to determine which doll he or she prefers.) In his studies conducted in the 1930s in Washington, D.C., Kenneth Clark found that only 32 percent of the black children tested preferred to play with the black doll (Clark and Clark, 1939). Similar tests have been conducted many times over the years, the more recent ones showing considerable improvement in self-image. For instance, thirty years after Clark's study, Fox and Jordon (1973) tested 360 black children in New York City, and found that 59 percent preferred the black doll.

A more obvious indication of a shift in self-image among blacks is the very use of the word "black." Prior to the 1950s, blacks were "Negroes" to each other as well as to whites, and "black" was considered an insulting epithet, even when used by a black. By contrast, Afro-American children today identify themselves as black with pride.

On the basis of the findings of doll-preference tests, this photo might be seen as de- *picting both tolerance and self-respect.*

Ethnic Awareness Growing awareness of others' opinions makes the school-age child much more vulnerable to social criticism, and at the same time, better able to empathize with others. Consider the development of racial, religious, and national attitudes. By middle childhood, almost all children know their own racial and religious background, and their group's relative social position. They have also become more aware of the circumstances of other groups, and according to several studies of contemporary children, are more likely to sympathize with children of minority groups (e.g., Zinser et al., 1976) and more likely to see other nations in a favorable light (Allen, 1976). Obviously, positive changes such as these depend on the culture surrounding the child, as well as on the specific information the child is given. But at least it is cognitively possible for children between 7 and 11 years old to appreciate differences among people, something that is much harder to do at a younger age.

Now that we have glimpsed a few of the contributions of the major theories, what picture of the school-age child appears? The typical child is seen as gaining independence from parents, becoming industrious, more ready to learn, and better able to master skills with each passing year. Most school-age children are aware of themselves in the larger society and, given the right environment, are learning to appreciate their own qualities and understand the characteristics of others.

However, the picture is not complete until we describe one important influence that shapes the life of many school-age children, making them far less independent than they at first seem to be. This influence comes from their peers.

The Society of Children

For many children, independence from parents is linked to dependence on peers. Compared to preschool children, who are willing to play with anyone or by themselves, school-age children are more particular about playmates and more unhappy without friends. According to a nationwide survey of parents, school-age children spend several hours each day playing with friends, more time than they spend watching television—and more time than reading, playing alone, and working combined (Roberts and Baird, 1972).

While playing together, children in middle childhood transmit and develop their own subculture—referred to by social scientists as the society of children—complete with language, dress codes, and rules of behavior that adults often do not notice. Pig Latin, Ubby Dubby, abbreviations, and secret codes flourish during these years, as do standards of dress that include everything from the necessity of wearing a particular style and brand of sneakers to avoiding certain color combinations, especially on certain days of the week.

Vocabulary

School-age children develop their own vocabulary for all manner of situations. For the adult nonplayer, the rules for a game as simple as jacks, for example, can become a mystery of specialized lingo, including "kissies," "haystacks," "flipsies," "interference," "fancies," "garbage," "poison fives," and "raindrops." In their study of schoolchildren's language in England, Opie and Opie (1959) found dozens of variations for any number of words: to give but a few instances of one example, "time out" could be indicated by "kings," "cruses," "creams," "cree," "vain," "fain," "schinch," "barley," "pax," "locks," and "nix."

In addition, there is a traditional vocabulary that children have drawn on for generations for many of their activities. Many American readers of this book will remember "one potato, two potato," "pepper," "one, two, three, O'Leary," and "starlight, star bright," as only a few of the many special words and rhymes associated with such things as choosing players on a team, jumping rope, bouncing a ball, and getting one's wish (Knapp and Knapp, 1976). Some of this vocabulary even goes back to games played centuries ago in England—"London Bridge is falling down," "eeny, meeny, miney, moe," "buck-buck" (also known as "Johnny on a pony"), and "ring-around-the-rosey," among them. The fact that many of these terms have been passed from generation to generation of children, without the assistance of adults or books, attests to the power of the culture of children.

At this age, children have a touching faith in the potency of words. Many schoolyard fights are justified with the assertion "He called me a name." The fighting potential of particular insults depends more on local custom than literal meaning. For instance, one normally well behaved boy suddenly attacked another boy in the classroom. When the teacher told him he should know better, he explained, "He said my mother wears combat boots, and you know I couldn't let him get away with that." Another example of the power of words is the response of children when someone doubts their word. "Honest to God" or "I swear" is usually thought sufficient proof of truth-telling. If more powerful evidence is needed, "Cross my heart and hope to die, drop down dead if I tell a lie" or "Crisscross the Bible, never tell a lie, if I do my mother will die" can be used (Opie and Opie, 1959).

As children grow older, they realize that they can combat words with words, and they become more likely to answer an insult with an insult than with a blow. The dialogue can become so skilled that a pair of verbal 10-year-olds "playing the dozens" attract as large a playground audience as a pair of wrestling 7-year-olds. If a younger or less articulate child begins to get the worst of a verbal duel, he or she often resorts to physical fighting, or responds with "Sticks and stones can break my bones, but words can never hurt me"—a defense that makes the victim feel better and exasperates the attacker, proving again the power of words..

Although adults who care about children may welcome the switch from physical to verbal fighting, the school-age child who is sensitive to criticism and rejection might much rather come home with a bloody nose than with the wounded pride caused by a classmate's criticism.

Codes of Behavior

In the society of children, the most important codes are those that govern behavior. Many of these rules involve independence from adults: children whose parents walk them to school or kiss them in public are pitied; "cry babies" and "teachers' pets" are criticized; children who tattle or "rat" to adults are despised. Adults may be amused, or bored, when one child says to another something like "Cry baby, cry baby, stick your head in gravy; wash it out with bubble gum, and send it to the navy"; but the impact of such taunts on children can be considerable. In fact, adult help may occasionally be needed in such situations to maintain a child's dignity and independence. The teacher who uses shame as a disciplinary technique, or the parent who calls an elementary-school child "baby," is probably not aware of the psychological harm that such strategies may be causing.

Figure 14.6 *Adults who think it is constructive to call a child "baby" for immature behavior have apparently forgotten what it was like to be a child and the focus of everyone's scorn.*

The importance of social codes to school-age children is perhaps most obvious in their organization of clubs or gangs, in which much attention is given to details concerned with rules, officers, dress, and establishing a clubhouse. Typical of children's industry at this stage, creating the club is usually more important than maintaining it. Often the club has no announced purpose, its only apparent function the exclusion of adults and children of the opposite sex. From a developmental psychologist's perspective, however, such clubs serve many functions, including building self-esteem, sharpening persuasive abilities, and teaching social cooperation.

Rejection   The ebb and flow of children's fashion and favor causes almost every school-age child to feel rejected at some point by other children. The child not chosen to play on the team, excluded from the club, or not invited to the party feels that a crucial part of his or her world has been shattered. Such rejection is made harder when it occurs for reasons the child does not understand or cannot change—perhaps an accent, a way of dressing, or physical appearance (Kleck et al., 1974), or even the child's name (McDavid and Harari, 1966). Sometimes children are shunned because their parents are thought to be too rich or too poor or of the wrong religion or race. Sometimes newcomers are automatically rejected until they prove themselves worthy. Social skills are also important in determining

Figure 14.7 *The huskier, older children in a neighborhood play group often tell the other children what to do—even to the point of getting them to voluntarily accept punishment. In general, there are limits to the authority of these leaders, and if the leader oversteps them, the other members of the group are likely to rebel.*

A CLOSER LOOK   **The Development of Social Competence**

Strongly influenced by Piaget's account of children actively seeking to assimilate and accommodate, Robert White (1959) offered the theory that among the most powerful motives for human behavior is the urge to be competent. According to White, people of all ages strive to develop various motor, cognitive, and social skills that will help them understand and control their environment, whether or not external reinforcement for these skills is forthcoming. This basic idea has been accepted by almost all developmental psychologists, who see evidence of *competence motivation* in virtually every skill children master. Indeed, some psychologists, on discovering the intricacies of the society of children, have interpreted the internal drive for social competence to mean that all a child requires in order to develop social skills is other children to play with.

Recently, however, White has cautioned against this simplistic interpretation (White, 1979). Simply putting a child with other children and expecting social competence to develop is naive at best and destructive at worst. In support of this contention, White describes three types of social incompetence that can occur despite frequent play periods with other children.

1. *Social anesthesia.* Some children can spend most of their time with other children without recognizing the consequences of their behavior or becoming sensitive to the feelings of others. The impulsive child, the poor sport, and the bully often need help to understand the consequences of their antisocial behavior.

2. *Social isolation.* In today's world, White says, "the experience of most children is that parents, peers, teachers, counselors and group workers are united in pushing for social participation; it is something of a miracle to get off by oneself." As a result, some children become adept at withdrawing when they are with others, averting their eyes, remaining expressionless, and reluctantly answering question with monosyllables. Such social isolation serves the short-term purpose of allowing privacy, but it does not permit the child to develop healthy patterns of social interaction.

3. *Social enslavement.* Some children are so afraid of rejection by others that they become slaves to their peers, constantly helping and placating them and agreeing with everyone. They do not risk expressing their own ideas, for fear of ridicule or rejection. This attitude often backlashes, for the person who is overly anxious to please becomes one of the least interesting, and therefore most expendable, members of the group.

White concludes that

Historically we have clamored too loud for social adjustment. We have not been sensitive to the dangers of throwing children together regardless of their anxieties and their own social needs. We have been enchanted with peer groups, as if the highest form of social behavior were getting along with age-equals . . .

It is clear, then, that although children learn many social skills from playing with their peers, such play is not the only, nor necessarily the best, way to develop social competence. Time spent alone, or with people who are older or younger, can be very useful in learning to function in the social world.

Poor sports who chronically quit if they can't have their way seem to suffer from a kind of social anesthesia, making them unaware of the real effects of their behavior.

acceptance: children who rarely praise their peers, who have difficulty communicating, and who do not know how to initiate a new friendship are unlikely candidates as friends (Gottman et al., 1975). A child who cheats, whines, or is a poor loser is unwelcome in most children's groups.

If a child is very unpopular, or the group of children particularly rough, the child may be subjected to jeers or special torments, perhaps being routinely pushed, poked, pinched, or beaten up, or being forced to hand over lunch money, or lunch itself. When bullying goes too far, it may provoke some of the other children to turn against the bully.

For the most part, however, adults are the ones who must deal with the question of bullying. When a child tearfully says "Everyone teases me," or comes home with a bloody nose and a torn shirt, many adults are confused about whether, and how, to intervene. Obviously, conflicts that are physically dangerous or likely to produce long-lasting emotional scars should be halted. But psychologists generally believe that children learn important social skills from each other when they are in conflict, so parents who are overprotective, or who try to "even the score" after the fight is over, probably do their children a disservice. What adults might best do is help chronically bullied children figure out why they are picked on and what methods of defense to use. At the same time, an effort might be made to make the children who do the bullying understand the impact of their mischief.

Cognitive Conceit

The society of children is maintained partly because many school-age children think they know more than adults. One reason for this is that by age 10 or 11, most children in some ways *are* more skilled and knowledgeable than their parents. They often can beat them at board games, surpass them in memory quizzes, teach them new math, or lecture them about science. This sometimes fosters a know-it-all attitude, called cognitive conceit (Elkind, 1974), a familiar phenomenon to the parent who has been told "You don't know anything," or the teacher who has been called stupid.

Figure 14.8 *As a result of their cognitive conceit, children in middle childhood sometimes take a single victory over a parent as a sign that they themselves are brilliant and the parent stupid.*

Further evidence of cognitive conceit comes from the literature popular with school-age children. The overall theme of clever and curious children helping each other outwit foolish or insensitive adults is apparent in classics like *Peter Pan* (the children don't need parents, and the adult villain, Captain Hook, is fooled by a ticking clock) and *Huckleberry Finn* (Huck helps Jim escape from slavery), in standards like *Nancy Drew* and *The Hardy Boys*, and current best sellers like *The Chronicles of Narnia*, in which adults are absent from the action entirely, or the Judy Blume books, in which adults are peripheral and foolish.

In one example from Blume's *Blubber* (1974), the fifth-grade teacher, Mrs. Minish, misses every clue that a confrontation between Wendy, the class bully, and Blubber, the class scapegoat, is brewing. On the showdown day, the teacher leaves the class during lunch, cautioning them, as usual, to be good. When she is out of earshot, the class, en masse, locks Blubber in the closet to await the outcome of her trial "for being a stool pigeon, a rat, a fink and a tattletale." Jill, the class lawyer, will give evidence against Blubber to the jury (the class) and the judge, Wendy. Wendy has already charged the jury: "Ladies and gentlemen of the jury, it is your job to decide if Blubber is lying. Frankly, as the judge, I'm sure she is."

A hitch appears when another member of the class says Blubber needs a lawyer. Jill, the narrator, comments:

> Right that minute it didn't matter to me whether or not she had told on us. It was the trial that was important and it wasn't fair to have a trial without two lawyers. So I faced Wendy and I said, "I'm sick of you bossing everyone around. If Blubber doesn't get a lawyer then Blubber doesn't get a trial."
>
> "No lawyer!" Wendy folded her arms across her chest.
>
> "Then no trial!" I shouted, running to the supply closet. Before Wendy knew what I was doing I unlocked the door and flung it open. "Come out! I just cancelled your trial."
>
> "You'll pay for this," Wendy told me. "You'll be sorry you were ever born, Jill Brenner!"
>
> For the first time I looked right into Wendy's eyes and I didn't like what I saw.
>
> That afternoon Mrs. Minish said, "You've been such a nice, quiet class since lunch. I wish you'd act this way more often."

The teacher's ignorance of what has actually been going on in her classroom conforms to the view of many children that adults are foolish or ineffectual in the social world of childhood.

Moral Development

This passage from *Blubber* shows another dimension of middle childhood, the development of morals. There are at least two aspects to moral development: thinking about right and wrong, and behaving in a moral or immoral way. These two aspects are somewhat correlated in middle childhood—children who think in more advanced ways are more likely to behave in a more ethical manner—but the correspondence is far from perfect. Let's consider them separately.

Thinking about Right and Wrong

As cognitive theorists have discovered, before age 7, children tend to think that rules are sacred and unchangeable and, at the same time, tend to apply them in an egocentric manner. Consequently, trying to play a serious game of checkers with a 4-year-old can be frustrating, because the child may apply different rules as the game progresses—unaware that the changes are a result of individual whim rather than mutual consent. Piaget (1965) found that although preoperational children thought the rules for playing marbles came from the town elders, their grandfathers, or even God, they actually played marbles with little regard for rules.

During the years of middle childhood, rules are still important as codes that must be respected (Blubber is on trial for tattling on her classmates); but rules can be changed (Jill is trying to change the rules of the trial). According to Piaget, by age 11 most children have rejected the idea held by the typical 6-year-old that rules are absolutes that must always be obeyed.

During these years, the concept of fairness changes too. When Piaget asked children to give instances of unfair behavior, they responded with examples that fit one of four categories.

1. Everything that is forbidden ("Telling lies," "Children who make a noise with their feet during prayers").

2. Going against the rules of a game.

3. Inequality ("Giving a big cake to one and a little one to another," "When both do the same work and don't get the same reward").

4. Social injustice ("A mother who won't allow her children to play with children who are less well dressed").

There were clear age trends, with older children being likely to give more sophisticated answers. However, as shown by the chart below, even older children tend to equate unfairness with inequality rather than with social injustice. This becomes apparent in everyday life, when children fight over who got to wash the blackboards yesterday or who has the biggest piece of pie, or when they complain that a certain teacher is more likely to yell at one child than at another. The idea that various children might need various punishments for the same misbehavior is hard for most school-age children to accept.

Unfairness Is . . .

	Doing What's Forbidden	Breaking Rules of a Game	Inequality	Social Injustice
6 TO 8 YEARS OLD	64%	9%	27%	0%
9 TO 12 YEARS OLD	7%	9%	73%	11%

Stages of Moral Thinking Following in Piaget's footsteps, Lawrence Kohlberg (1963) studied moral reasoning by telling children and adults stories that posed ethical dilemmas. One of them was the following:

A woman was near death from cancer. One drug might save her, a form of radium that a druggist in the same town had recently discovered. The druggist was charging $2000, ten times what the drug cost him to make. The sick woman's husband, Heinz, went to everyone he knew to borrow the money, but he could only get together about half of what it cost. He told the druggist that his wife was dying and asked him to sell it cheaper or let him pay later. But the druggist said "no." The husband got desperate and broke into the man's store to steal the drug for his wife. Should the husband have done that? Why?

Kohlberg examined the responses to such dilemmas and found three levels of moral reasoning—preconventional, conventional, and autonomous—with two stages at each level.

1. *Preconventional (emphasis on avoiding punishments and getting rewards).*

> *Stage 1 Might makes right (punishment and obedience orientation).*   At this stage the most important value is obedience to authority in order to avoid punishment.

> *Stage 2 Look out for number one (instrumental and relativist orientation).*   Each person tries to take care of his or her own needs. The reason to be nice to other people is so they will be nice to you. In other words, you scratch my back and I'll scratch yours.

2. *Conventional (emphasis on social rules).*

> *Stage 3 "Good girl" and "nice boy."*   Good behavior is considered behavior that pleases other people and wins their praise. Approval is more important than any specific reward.

> *Stage 4 "Law and order."*   Right behavior means obeying the laws set down by those in power, being a dutiful citizen.

3. *Autonomous (emphasis on moral principles).*

> *Stage 5 Social contract.*   The rules of society exist for the benefit of all, and are established by mutual agreement. If the rules become destructive, or if one party doesn't live up to the agreement, the contract is no longer binding.

> *Stage 6 Universal ethical principles.*   General universal principles determine right and wrong. These values (such as "Do unto others as you would have others do unto you," or "Life is sacred") are established by individual reflection and meditation, and may contradict the egocentric or legal principles of earlier reasoning.

At every age, according to Kohlberg, *how* people think, rather than *what* conclusions they reach or what actions they take, determines what stage they are in. For example, someone whose moral reasoning is at stage 3 could argue either that the husband should steal the drug (because people will blame him for not saving his wife) or that he shouldn't steal the drug (because he had already done everything he could legally and people would call him a thief if he stole).

While Piaget found that most of his marble players had reached the social-contract idea by age 11, Kohlberg found that many 10-year-olds were still at stage 1 or 2, and that many adults never reach stage 5 or 6 (Kohlberg and Elfenbein, 1975). Researchers have found that giving children a chance to discuss moral issues and to hear arguments at the stage of moral development above the one they are in helps them develop more complex ethical thinking. This explains why children reach higher moral levels when thinking about such issues as the rules of marbles or the fairness of adults than when thinking about ethical dilemmas such as the relative merits of life and property, or individual freedom and social order. It also suggests that adults who want to transmit moral values to schoolchildren should have discussions about moral issues rather than dictating moral rules.

One aspect of moral discussions at this age is that children often endorse more rigid moral standards than they actually care to follow. It is not uncommon, say, for a fourth-grade class to propose inflexible rules ("No one should ever be late") and strict punishments ("Latecomers should stand in the corner all day"). However, when these same children are themselves late, they tend to look to extenuating circumstances ("I couldn't find my shoes") to get them off the hook. The translation of the intellectual understanding of rules into moral behavior is far from automatic.

Moral Behavior

When a person decides how to behave in any given situation, he or she is influenced not only by moral reasoning but also by the behavior of others, by personal wishes, and by the standards of the society. Most children have been told that cheating is wrong, and they can usually explain why it is. But many (almost all?) children cheat when their friends put pressure on them to do so, or when the chance of being caught is slim. This was discovered in a classic series of studies published in 1929 (Hartshorne et al.), which underscored for social scientists the fact that virtues such as honesty and goodness are abstract ideals. Actually, most people are both honest and dishonest, good and bad, depending on the circumstances.

This same variability is also found in prosocial behaviors, which are actions performed to benefit someone else without expectation of reward for oneself. Whether or not a child will be helpful or cooperative is affected by the specific situation and cultural context (Mussen and Eisenberg-Berg, 1977).

Cooperation   By age 6 or 7, children are much more able to cooperate and share, because they have become less egocentric. How willing children are to use this ability can vary from culture to culture, however. In some cultures, cooperation increases throughout childhood; in others, it decreases because competition is the preferred mode of interaction.

Cooperative behavior is most likely to occur in societies with the following five characteristics (Mussen and Eisenberg-Berg, 1977):

1. stress on consideration of others, sharing, and orientation toward group;

2. simple social organization;

3. assignment of women to important economic functions;

4. members of the extended family (grandparents, aunts and uncles, cousins) living together;

5. early assignment of tasks and responsibilities to children.

Not surprisingly, in contemporary American society, with complex social organization and small nuclear families where children have few responsibilities, children become less likely to cooperate as they grow older (Mussen and Eisenberg-Berg, 1977; Bryan, 1975).

Cooperation, as well as other forms of prosocial behavior, is also affected by the specific situation, as shown by dozens of experiments reviewed by Paul Mussen and Nancy Eisenberg-Berg (1977). Children are more likely to cooperate if they have been rewarded for cooperating, or if they have seen someone else cooperating. Children are also more likely to cooperate and share with someone they like or admire, or with someone who needs their help.

Also of particular importance is family example: children who see their parents cooperating and following ethical values are likely to do so as well. Sociologists

RESEARCH REPORT   **Cooperation**

Millard Madsen and his colleagues at UCLA developed a game to measure cooperation and competition (Madsen, 1971). Each player has partial control of a pen that moves over a piece of paper on which there are four circles, one at each side.

In the "cooperative condition" of this experiment, all the players are rewarded each time the pen crosses all four circles. In other words, the more the children work together, the more they all win. In the "competitive condition," each child is rewarded only when the pen crosses his or her circle. Obviously, even in this situation, cooperation is the best policy, for if the children take turns helping each other, each child can win as often as every other child. However, during middle childhood, this fact does not seem to occur to most American children. They pull the pen in their own direction, and no one wins. In fact, even in the cooperative condition, some children prefer to compete rather than earn rewards that would be shared.

Madsen compared the performance of rural Mexican children with that of American children on this game and found the Mexicans much more cooperative. He also discovered that Mexican-Americans are part way between these two groups—not as competitive as Americans, nor as cooperative as the rural Mexicans (Madsen and Shapira, 1970). In fact, children who were second- or third-generation Mexican-Americans were more competitive than first-generation Mexican-Americans.

Similar trends are found in other countries. For instance, Israeli children living in cities are much more competitive in this game than Israeli children living on rural kibbutzim (Shapira and Madsen, 1969).

We may or may not agree that competitiveness is an inevitable consequence of living in an urbanized, industrialized society; however, it does seem clear that children in such societies learn to value competition more than cooperation.

Figure 14.9 *The coopera-tion required to build this hut for the Holi festival is part of the daily lives of these children in Imphal, India.*

have found that growing up in a large family is one factor that makes children more generous, although other factors, such as the age and sex of the siblings, are also important (Ribal, 1963; Sawyer, 1966). Finally, mood affects prosocial behavior. Children who feel happy and successful are more generous than children who feel like failures.

To summarize, cognitive, cultural, situational, and family factors all make some children more ethical, cooperative, generous, and helpful than others. While these factors affect children throughout their lives, it is during middle childhood that patterns begin to emerge. A child develops a characteristic way of responding to others by about age 7.

Consequently, adults who are concerned about the values of the next generation should provide a model for young children to follow, and should encourage school-age children to discuss and determine the ethics they will try to adopt.

The Child's Social Milieu

There is much variation in how children express their needs to become more independent, competent, and social, and in how successful they are in meeting them. As with moral development, much depends on culture, community, and home—in other words, on the social milieu. Particularly important are the two institutions that affect every aspect of development during middle childhood— family and school. In Erikson's words, "Many a child's development is disrupted when family life has failed to prepare for school life, or when school fails to sustain the promise of earlier stages" (Erikson, 1963).

The Critical Years

Before detailing the impact of these two social institutions, it is important to stress how crucial the experiences of middle childhood can be. Sometimes parents and psychologists become so concerned with the "critical period" of the first five years of life that they underestimate the significance of middle childhood.

It is true that, for most children, personality characteristics and general intelligence at age 6 are closely related to the same attributes at age 10 or age 20. One could interpret this to mean that the first years are the determining ones. But as Kagan (1978) points out, most children are subject to the same environmental influences in the second five years as in the first five, so there is every reason to expect a continuity of behavior. Logically, one could argue that the second five years are actually the determining ones. Studies of adopted children who change families after age 5 find that children can change in personality, behavior, and intelligence during middle childhood (Kadushin, 1970), as is dramatically shown in the Research Report on the next page.

Family

Although many aspects of child care become easier by middle childhood, there are new needs in this period that parents must meet. Nevertheless, the same qualities of parenting that are important at earlier stages are important now—warmth, encouragement, and authoritative guidelines without authoritarian control (Martin, 1975). Explaining rules and reasons for punishment, and listening to the child's opinions and ideas, are especially important when the child has attained concrete operational thought and can think logically about specific events. In general, instead of doing things for their children, parents must provide guidance and support while allowing the children to think for themselves.

Deciding Values It seems especially necessary that parents decide what moral values to encourage, and then provide both information and example. Sex education, for instance, is important during these years, for children need to know about the physical changes they will be experiencing in a few years and to think about the cultural conflicts surrounding sex before they reach adolescence. Talking with a child about the physical, ethical, and emotional aspects of sex helps clarify misconceptions and establish a channel of communication that might be crucial in a few years. In addition, it should be kept in mind that children deduce a good deal on this subject from the attitudes parents reveal in their relationship with each other and in their dealings with other adults. This is equally true with regard to many other areas in which children must make value decisions, from education, economics, or religion to drugs.

Adoption During Middle Childhood

In one extreme case, reported by Koluchová (1976), after a year in a children's home following their mother's death, a pair of twin boys spent five and a half years, from ages 1½ to 7, in extreme deprivation. They lived with their father and stepmother

. . . in almost total isolation, separated from the outside world; they were never allowed out of the house or into the main living rooms in the flat, which was tidy and well furnished. They lived in a small, unheated closet, and were often locked up for long periods in the cellar. They slept on the floor on a polythene sheet and were cruelly chastised . . . . The twins also suffered physically from lack of adequate food, fresh air, sunshine, and exercise.

During the trial, the people next door testified that they had often heard queer, inhuman shrieks which resembled howling, and which came from a cellar leading to the back court. The father was once seen beating the children with a rubber hose until they lay flat on the ground unable to move. The neighbors, however, did not interfere in any way because they did not want to risk conflict with the children's stepmother, who was known to be a selfish, aggressive woman.

At age 7, the twins were taken away from their parents. They were fearful and unable to talk. Professional predictions about their chances of ever becoming normal were pessimistic. Each boy's mental age was "about three years."

However, they were given excellent special education in a well-staffed institution. By age 9, it was clear that they were learning well, and psychologists thought they would do better if they were with a loving foster family and in a normal

school rather than in the school for the mentally retarded they had been attending. One way to measure their development is with the WISC IQ test (see the chart below). Note the rapid progress, especially in the year between ages 9 and 10, which was their first year in a normal family and school. From age 12 on, their scores hover within a few points of 100, precisely average.

Their emotional development is harder to assess, of course, but the indications are that it is normal. The boys show strong love for their foster mother, and are deeply attached to each other. Relationships with classmates as well as with other members of their new family are good. The psychologist who has worked with them reports that "in the development and personalities of the boys, no psychopathological symptoms or eccentricities appear at present. It is possible to say that there are no consequences of deprivation remaining which would cause retardation or damage to their development."

Probably one crucial reason that these boys did so well is that, even in their five years of misery, they had each other's support. In addition, the emotional and educational care they received after they were rescued was outstanding. Of course, we do not know what their achievements might have been without the deprivation of their early years: perhaps they could have been geniuses, rather than simply average. Nevertheless, their experiences do show that home and school can reverse, at least in part, severe deprivation in early childhood.

When the twins were first removed from their home, they were impossible to test because they did not understand how to follow even the most simple instructions. Psychologists estimated that their IQ was in the 40s. By age 8, they were testable, and scored in the moderately retarded range. As this graph shows, their scores increased each year until adolescence, when they leveled off at about 100.

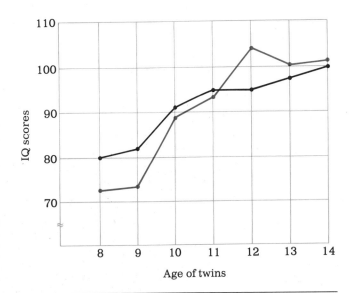

Help with School   Parental involvement in the child's school life can be another important undertaking for parents during middle childhood. Parents who attend parent-teacher conferences, and who help their child with homework—either by seeing to it that the child has a time and place to do it, or by sitting with the child to provide encouragement—have children who enjoy school more and who score higher on achievement tests. This is more than a simple correlation between parental attitude and child performance, as shown by one carefully designed British study that compared children's achievement before and after a special program that encouraged parental participation in school activities (Young and McGeeney, 1968). In general, the children's achievement improved as their parents became more aware of the school's methods and curricula, and as they discussed homework with teachers and other parents. While most parents decided that they would give their children more help with their schoolwork, some parents realized that they had been erring in the opposite direction by implicitly putting too much pressure on their children through overinvolvement. In both cases, the parents' adjustment improved their children's performance.

Father's Involvement   The father's involvement with children during middle childhood is as important as the mother's. While it is hard to measure the quality of fathering, one crucial variable seems to be how much time the father devotes to his children. For instance, there is a correlation between how often and how long fathers are in the presence of their children and how well the children perform on achievement tests (Blanchard and Biller, 1971; Landy et al., 1969). Unfortunately, most fathers today spend relatively little time in child-centered activities. One study of fathers in several Western countries, including the United States, found that the average employed father spent twenty hours a week in the presence of his children but only two hours per week actively involved with them (Szalai et al.,

Figure 14.10 *Fathers provide a male role model and much needed encouragement for school-age children. However, more than 25 percent of all elementary-school children do not live with their biological father, and most of these children do not see their father regularly.*

1972). In other words, many fathers ate dinner and watched television with their children daily, but few spent much time reading, playing, or even conversing with them.

Another important variable is the father's expression of affection and encouragement, according to a careful review of the literature (Pilling and Pringle, 1978). Boys who have warm relationships with their fathers in middle childhood are more likely to be good students and less likely to become delinquents than are boys who have cool or hostile relationships with their fathers. In addition, they are more pleased with themselves, more secure in their masculinity, and better liked by their peers. Several studies show that girls are also positively affected by warm relationships with their fathers, although the impact does not seem to be as great.

Possible Problems

The impact of home life in middle childhood makes it important to evaluate family patterns and problems that *might* affect children, such as divorce, single-parent families, maternal employment, and poverty.

Divorce Since 1970, the divorce rate in the United States has been about 50 percent. In other words, each year the number of divorces is about half the number of marriages. Fortunately, many of these divorces do not involve children. Nevertheless, an estimated one-third of all children in the United States have already experienced their parents' divorce, or will do so before they reach 18 years of age.

Analyzing the impact of divorce on those children is a complex research task. For one thing, the degree of feuding between parents, of disruption in the children's routine, and of financial strain following divorce varies from household to household. For another, vulnerability to these factors varies from child to child. It also varies from one period of development to another: a divorce during transitional periods such as the beginning of first grade or the onset of adolescence is harder for a child than one during relatively smooth periods of development.

One conclusion seems fairly well substantiated: divorce is almost always difficult for a child, and the first year after the divorce is usually the hardest. According to one study, in the typical divorce in which the mother has custody of the children and the father has visitation privileges, mothers usually become stricter and fathers more indulgent in the first few months after divorce. Changes in daily life, such as where the children live or go to school, what rules they are expected to follow, and what responsibilities they are supposed to assume, also are common soon after divorce. As a result of all these changes, children frequently experience a decline in their school achievement and often become more demanding and less obedient in the first year after their parents' divorce (Hetherington et al., 1977).

The long-term effects of divorce are harder to measure. For one thing, obviously, it is impossible to know how well the children would have fared if the parents had stayed together. However, John Santrock (1972) did find that achievement dipped more in the year *before* a bitter divorce than after, which suggests that some children, at least, are better off with one divorced parent than with two feuding ones. When the mother remarried within five years, achievement scores of the children tended to rise.

Probably the fairest conclusion is that variables such as the parents' continued concern for their children, family economic stability, and the willingness of the school to understand temporary declines in school performance are more important than the precise legal status of the parents' relationship.

Single-Parent Families   One in every six children in the United States, and one in every ten Canadian children, lives in a single-parent family, about 90 percent of which are headed by the mother (Schlesinger, 1975).

How does it affect children to live in a fatherless home? In the review of the research on this topic, Marybeth Shinn (1978) found most studies to show that children without fathers in the home tend to do less well academically, especially in quantitative (mathematical) skills, than children with fathers in the home. However, it seems that *if* children have another man (perhaps a grandfather, uncle, or stepfather) who cares for them, and *if* the father's absence does not mean lower income, and *if* the mother or someone else gives the child extra attention to compensate for time not spent with the father, there are few, if any, negative consequences (Wilson et al., 1975; Shinn, 1978). (It should be noted that much of the research on fatherless households has been flawed by the assumption that divorced fathers are necessarily absent fathers. Although, in fact, some divorced fathers never do see their offspring, many others take major responsibility for their day-to-day care.)

A divorced father's taking an active father role may be as important for him as for the child. In one study of separated or divorced upper-middle-class fathers, the men who were the most active in caring for their children were also the most stable and self-satisfied after the divorce (Keshet and Rosenthal, 1978). This study does not prove cause and effect. It could be that men with the most stable personality structures are those who choose to stay in the fathering role after separation. However, it is also possible that a father's organizing his life to spend time with his children is, itself, a restorative experience after divorce.

Although fathers as single parents have not been studied as extensively as mothers, in general they have been found to be as capable as mothers. However, families headed by a single father do have some problems that families headed by a single mother do not. An extensive study of 588 such families found that many men are less prepared than women to handle the simultaneous demands of children and career (George and Wilding, 1972). Single fathers also were less willing to ask for help, financial as well as psychological, when problems become too difficult to handle alone.

Employed Mothers   Slightly more than half the women who have school-age children, but no children younger than 6, are employed,* as are a third of the women who have children under 6. The most common reason mothers work is to earn needed money, but another important motivation is a psychological one. The personal satisfaction and social status of the employed woman are usually greater than those of the woman who stays at home—especially if routine housework is the only activity to fill the empty hours while the children are at school. A large survey of working mothers found that they are physically healthier (only 7 percent reported any symptoms of ill health compared to 25 percent of the housewives), they have a more positive self-image (80 percent reported positive personal characteristics compared to 65 percent of the housewives), but a larger proportion felt inadequate as a parent (Feld, 1963). More recent research shows that this sense of

---

*All homemakers are, of course, employed, in the sense that taking care of a household is indeed work. Here, however, "employed" refers to work in a paying job.

inadequacy as a parent is still present in today's working woman, especially among those women whose primary reason for working is personal satisfaction rather than financial necessity (Beckman, 1978). Traditionally, of course, the accepted view was that a woman who held a full-time job was automatically doing her children an injustice. Today the tendency is to reserve judgment for individual cases. In some ways, children of wage-earning mothers fare better than children of mothers who stay home. For instance, although employed women still do more housework than the other members of their families, their husbands and children help out more than do the husbands and children of women who are housewives. Consequently, the children learn responsibility as well as household skills, and experience the positive example of a father who helps with child care and other tasks (Hoffman, 1977).

Figure 14.11 *Boys and girls whose mothers are employed are more likely to learn to do household tasks than children whose mothers are not. The opportunity to take on responsibilities can be especially important for children in middle childhood, who take pride in performing useful work.*

In middle childhood, daughters of working women are likely to have positive conceptions of being female. According to a review of the literature, they think of females as competent, effective, and active, and they look forward to becoming a woman themselves. By contrast, daughters of housewives are more likely to associate femininity with restrictions on physical, social, and economic possibilities (Hoffman and Nye, 1974).

At the same time, there is some evidence that *sons* of employed mothers are less likely to say their father is the man they most admire than are sons of housewives. This finding is most frequent in lower-class families, where women are more likely to work because the husband has a low-paying job or no job at all (Hoffman and Nye, 1974). Thus, it could be that the father is less important to the son because he earns little, not because the wife is employed.

A Canadian study of 223 10-year-olds also found that while maternal employment did not affect daughters, the sons of employed mothers were more likely to have problems than the sons of nonemployed mothers. Specifically, within working-class families, sons of employed mothers were described more negatively by their fathers, were more shy and nervous, disliked school more, and had lower grades.

Within middle-class families, the sons of working mothers had lower math and language-achievement test scores. Two factors moderated these potential problems: if the father was actively involved with his children, and if the mother was satisfied with her roles, the children tended to have fewer problems, no matter what sex they were or what their mother's employment history was (Gold and Andres, 1978).

In practice, how maternal employment affects a child depends on many factors that vary from family to family. We know that, on average, employed mothers spend only five and a half hours a week in child-centered activities, compared to eleven hours a week for housewives (Szalai et al., 1972). If a child particularly needs attention, and if the family has several children but only one adult, an employed mother, the child might suffer. (The same is true for households headed by a single employed father [George and Wilding, 1972].) On the other hand, if children get enough attention from their parents or other adults, the children might benefit from their increased independence, the additional income, and the expanded role models that result from maternal employment.

Since adults who are happy with their lives appear more able to love other people, including their children, it would seem that the mother who enjoys her job and the mother who enjoys staying home will probably be better mothers than women who are unhappy with their roles, whatever they are. In fact, another review of the research concludes that "satisfied mothers—working or not—have the best adjusted children" (Etaugh, 1974).

Finally, the availability of adequate child supervision is one important factor in how satisfied the employed mother is, as well as how the child fares. In a review of the research, Doria Pilling and Mia Kellmer Pringle (1978) found that mothers were less happy and children more likely to show some signs of strain when the child was unsupervised while the mother was away at work. However, they conclude, as long as "there is adequate out-of-school supervision, it seems that the primary school child should not, in general, suffer adverse effects from maternal employment."

Socioeconomic Status   One of the most powerful influences on children's lives in middle childhood is their family's socioeconomic status. About a third of America's children suffer basic deprivation because their families do not have sufficient income to provide for them (Keniston, 1977). This is especially crippling in middle childhood, since, as the last two chapters have shown, children during these years tend to think in concrete terms and base their self-concept partly on how they compare to other children in terms of possessions, skills, and achievements. Low-income children not only have fewer things, they also have less opportunity to develop their abilities. As Erikson (1963) describes it, they often settle for inferiority rather than industry, which may hinder them all their lives.

Simply finding an environment where independence and competence can develop is hard in some low-income neighborhoods. In the words of Kenneth Keniston (1977):

> Poor children live in a particularly dangerous world—an
> urban world of broken stair railings, of busy streets serving
> as playgrounds, of lead paint, rats and rat poisons, or a rural
> world where families do not enjoy the minimal levels of
> public health . . . It is a world where even a small child learns
> to be ashamed of the way he or she lives. And it is frequently
> a world of intense social dangers, where many adults, driven

by poverty and desperation, seem untrustworthy and unpredictable. Children who learn the skills for survival in that world, suppressing curiosity and cultivating a defensive guardedness toward novelty or a constant readiness to attack, may not be able to acquire the basic skills and values that are needed, for better or worse, to thrive in mainstream society.

In some ways, we might even say that such children are systematically trained to fail . . . Such children are smart enough to sense from an early age that the world of mainstream America defines them as no good, inadequate, dirty, incompetent, and stupid.

Keniston's statement is corroborated by psychological research. Lower-class school-age children are more likely than their better-off peers to be poor achievers, and to get worse each year. In addition, they are less likely to set realistic goals for themselves, either in schoolwork or future lives (Jencks et al., 1972). This situation sets up a vicious cycle, with low achievement making it hard to set realistic goals, and vice versa.

Figure 14.12 *While the material deprivations of poverty are difficult to live with, the psychological costs are probably even greater. For instance, if this boy is ashamed of his home and refuses to invite other children over to play, he is less likely to develop the social skills he needs. If he sees himself as inferior because he is poor, he is likely to retain this self-concept all his life.*

Partly because their present status seems more dependent on factors over which they have no control, such as their parents' employment and their landlord's decency, lower-class children are more likely to believe they have little control over their future (Bartel, 1971), and therefore, they try less hard and accomplish less (Maehr, 1974). Children who do not feel they are in command of their school performance are more likely to suffer a decrease in self-esteem and think their teacher expects too much of them and blames them too much (Bryant, 1974). Especially in cases such as this, teachers need to make sure the children know specifically what they can do to help themselves to learn, so they can gain experience in controlling their own destiny (Gilmor, 1978).

Coping with Stress

Given all the disruptions that often occur in middle childhood, one might well wonder how it is that a great many children manage to survive with any confidence and competence. In fact, most children not only survive, they thrive, later remembering middle childhood as one of the happiest times of their life.

Children's methods of coping with stress are as diverse as the situations they must respond to. In their longitudinal study, Murphy and Moriarty (1976) found that all the children in their sample had encountered unexpected stress, and almost all had coped quite well. Among many instances, the authors describe one girl's compensating for her chronically ill mother's unavailability by spending most of her time with a "second mother," a next-door neighbor. In another case, a boy overcame his mother's wish to keep him a baby by devoting all his energy to sports. The coping strategies typical of middle childhood described in this study were sometimes thoughtful, conscious responses: a tomboy, for example, "decided to be a girl when I was seven"; another girl "decided to stop being shy" at age 10; and a boy whose parents had separated during his preschool years decided to begin another life, forgetting the first one. Sometimes, of course, the coping strategies were unconscious, as in the cases of two seriously ill children who used the defense mechanisms of fantasy and regression to help them endure pain.

The overall conclusion drawn by the authors is that most children are much more resilient than previous clinical studies of emotionally disturbed children would indicate. Those children who had difficulty coping tended to be the ones who had repeated problems or very serious stresses, and who did not have steady support and encouragement from any adults.

Similar conclusions about the resilience of school-age children were reached by researchers studying children who had to cope with extraordinary pressures. Norman Garmezy (1976) studied inner-city black children and children born to schizophrenic parents, both groups being considered "at risk" of having serious developmental problems. The former are vulnerable because poverty, racism, and a crowded urban milieu correlate with academic and emotional problems. The latter are "at high risk" of emotional illness partly because schizophrenia has a genetic component and partly because the disorganized, disoriented behavior of a schizophrenic parent makes a normal parent-child relationship difficult. Nevertheless, Garmezy found that many children in both these groups do surprisingly well, sometimes showing more competence in terms of school achievement and social relationships than their more advantaged peers.

Garmezy refers to these children as *invulnerables* because they seem to be stress-resistant. In probing for the reasons for their ability to cope, he notes that the influence of a caring adult (perhaps a parent, teacher, neighbor, or doctor) can have a protective effect. So can the child's ability to use imagination and, in cases involving a schizophrenic parent, to understand that some of the parent's ideas are delusions. Indeed, every kind of competence, whether it be cognitive, emotional, or social, helps these children overcome the risk factors that characterize their lives (Garmezy et al., 1979).

Michael Rutter (1979) is another psychologist who has studied the effects of extraordinary stress on the emotional stability of children. He identified six family variables that were strongly and significantly associated with child psychiatric disorders:

1. severe marital discord

2. low social status

3. overcrowding or large family size

4. paternal criminality

5. maternal psychiatric disorder

6. admission into the care of the local authority

Then he studied a large sample of 10-year-old children, noting the presence or absence of these six characteristics, as well as the incidence of psychiatric problems. An intriguing result is that children with one risk factor were no more likely to have psychiatric problems than children with no risk factors (see Figure 14.13).

However, when two of the risk factors occurred together, the incidence of problems more than doubled. When four or more of the risk factors were present, psychiatric problems were four times as likely as when there were two. It seems that there is an interactive relationship between risks. As Rutter writes, "The stresses *potentiated* each other so that the combination of chronic stresses provided very much more than a summation of the effects of the separate stresses considered singly."

Both Rutter and Garmezy have tried to determine what helps a high-risk child succeed rather than fail. Schools that are supportive, families that function smoothly, and close relationships with an adult (who need not be a parent) all seem to be factors that help children growing up in very stressful circumstances. According to these researchers, it also helps if the child is a high achiever in school, has an adaptable temperament, and is a girl.

Few children face the problems that Garmezy's invulnerables faced, and thus few children need the inner strength and environmental support that help a child at risk of serious psychological breakdown. Instead, most children enter middle childhood eager to learn and to make friends; and with relatively little effort on the part of parents, teachers, and the community, most of them succeed. The needs for independence and encouragement, new skills and loyal friends, are usually satisfied in middle childhood, so that most people remember these years as a happy time. By age 11, the average child has a right to feel competent and self-satisfied, and even to display some cognitive conceit. Most 11-year-olds are ready and eager for the next stage of development—adolescence.

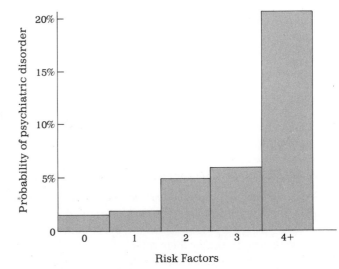

Figure 14.13 *Rutter found that children who had to cope with one serious problem ran virtually as low a risk of suffering a psychiatric disorder as did children who faced no serious problems. However, when the child had two problems, the chances more than doubled. Four or more problems produced about ten times the likelihood of psychiatric disorders as one. About one child in five who experienced four or more serious stresses actually became emotionally disturbed.*

SUMMARY

Theories about Middle Childhood

1. Freud believed that most of the child's emotions are latent during middle childhood, especially sexual and aggressive urges. This enables the child to become less dependent on parents, and more interested in friends of the same sex.

2. Erikson calls middle childhood the industry-versus-inferiority stage, because children like to be busy learning new skills. If they don't develop the competencies their society values, they don't develop their self-esteem and thus feel inferior.

3. Behaviorists stress the school-age child's increasing ability to learn, as intrinsic reinforcements, social influences, and ability to control oneself all develop.

4. Cognitive theory notes that children become less egocentric during these years. They become more vulnerable to others' opinions, and more able to understand another point of view.

The Society of Children

5. School-age children develop their own subculture, with language, values, and codes of behavior. The child who is not included in this society often feels deeply hurt, for social dependence on peers is strong at this age, even as independence from adults is valued.

Moral Development

6. Children become able to reason about moral dilemmas during middle childhood. According to Piaget and Kohlberg, they move through stages of moral reasoning, from the self-centeredness of the younger child to an emphasis on moral principles.

7. Moral behavior is affected by reasoning ability, and also by culture, situation, and family influences. Prosocial behavior, such as cooperation, can be encouraged or discouraged depending on the child's social world.

The Child's Social Milieu

8. Family, school, and neighborhood can profoundly affect a child's personality and achievement during middle childhood. One important factor is how much adult attention the child receives. This may or may not be a problem for children whose fathers are absent, whose parents are divorced, or whose mothers are employed.

9. Socioeconomic status can determine a child's ability to develop the independence, competence, and friendships that school-age children need. However, even children who have several strikes against them sometimes appear to be invulnerable, emerging from middle childhod unscathed.

KEY QUESTIONS

How is latency expressed in the activities of school-age children?

What are some of the cultural differences in the development of skills?

What makes school-age children easier to teach, according to behaviorists?

As children learn to decenter, how does their social world change?

What evidence is there that the society of children is a powerful force in middle childhood?

What are the differences between Piaget's and Kohlberg's views on the development of moral judgment?

What affects whether children will follow their moral beliefs?

How can one argue that the second five years of life are as important as the first?

How does the parent's role in middle childhood differ from that of early childhood?

How does parental divorce affect a child?

How does the absence of the father affect a child?

What factors tend to make maternal employment beneficial or harmful to a child's development?

Why is it important for a child to feel in control of his or her life?

How does socioeconomic class affect the development of skills in middle childhood?

What can help a child cope with stress?

KEY TERMS

latency
industry versus inferiority
resistance to temptation
the society of children
cognitive conceit
preconventional moral reasoning

conventional moral reasoning
autonomous moral reasoning
prosocial behaviors
invulnerables

RECOMMENDED READINGS

Piaget, Jean. *The moral judgment of the child.* New York: The Free Press, 1965.

Piaget's careful research on the rules of marbles and ideas of justice is illustrated with many quotations from the children themselves. It also includes discussion of adult morality and ethical theory, which is provocative but heavy reading.

Mussen, Paul, and **Eisenberg-Berg, Nancy.** *Roots of caring, sharing, and helping.* San Francisco: Freeman, 1977.

A fine review of the research on prosocial behavior, this book should be useful to anyone wanting to know how to impart standards of what to do, rather than perpetuating our usual emphasis on what not to do.

Jewett, Claudia L. *Adopting the older child.* Harvard, Mass.: The Harvard Common Press, 1978.

In a practical, sympathetic book, Jewett describes the problems and the joys of adopting children aged 6 and older. For example, the book gives useful advice about handling many of the problems that older adoptees display when they first arrive in a new home, such as sleeping problems, overdressing, lying, temper tantrums, and withdrawal. The book concludes with a hopeful follow-up on some children who were adopted, noting that the parents of older adoptees "talk about a sense of enormous personal growth, of satisfaction at having sought a meaningful challenge and met it, and the privilege of having shared something of lasting value with another human being."

Coles, Robert. *Children of crisis: A study of courage and fear.* New York: Delta, 1964.

In this sensitive study of the first black children to attend the newly integrated schools of the South, the psychiatrist Robert Coles reveals the strength and resilience of many of those children. The book illustrates the concept of "invulnerables," while describing some of the family and community resources that allowed the children to survive psychologically in a stressful environment.

Adolescence

PART V

Adolescence is probably the most challenging and complicated period of life to describe, study, or experience. Between the ages of 10 and 20, more changes occur, and greater individual variation is evident, than during any other period. Children's bodies suddenly show the signs of sexual maturing and childish faces become less round and more angular. These biological changes of puberty are universal, but in their particular expression, timing, and extent, the variety shown is enormous and depends, of course, on sex, genes, and nutrition. There is great diversity in cognitive development as well: many adolescents are as egocentric in some respects as preschool children, while others reach the stage of abstract thinking that characterizes adult cognition at its best. Psychosocial development shows even greater diversity, as adolescents develop their own identity, choosing from a vast number of sexual, moral, political, and vocational paths.

Yet such differences should not mask the commonality of the adolescent experience, for all adolescents are confronted with the same developmental tasks: they must adjust to their new body size and shape and to their awakening sexuality, think in new ways, and strive for the emotional maturity and economic independence that characterize adulthood. As we will see in the next three chapters, the adolescent's efforts to come to grips with these tasks are often touched with confusion and poignancy.

Adolescence: Physical Development

Lots of kids I know, they feel all of a sudden they can't be kids anymore. They call themselves kids but they don't feel the same way about it . . . Their parents may tell them how they act irresponsibly, like kids, but in their minds they aren't thinking irresponsible thoughts . . . you can tell by looking at them too; their bodies aren't kids' bodies either. It's hard to guess people's age nowadays because everybody looks older; even if they don't, they act older . . . You think, Hey, I know I'm not old, but it's fun to try, because if I want, I can fail miserably at it. You can pull off this big mask of yours and say "Hi, everybody, it's really me and I'm really a kid . . . " You hate to admit it, but there are lots of times you wish you still were a little kid, nodding at all the questions people ask."

Jeannie Melchione, age 16
quoted in Cottle, 1979

True or False?

Because of the radical hormonal changes that occur during adolescence, this period of growth is on the whole a time of stress and agitation.

No matter how sexually active they are, adolescent girls are much less likely to become pregnant during the first year of menstruation than they are during young adult years.

Unlike the growth of early childhood, physical development that is prevented by poor nutrition during puberty cannot be made up for later.

Sexual attitudes have changed to such an extent in the past twenty years that girls are now as likely to engage in casual sexual relations as boys are.

Masturbation is as commonly practiced among girls as among boys, but girls tend to feel much more guilty about it.

Because of the particular kinds of hormonal changes that teenage girls go through, adolescence is more difficult for them than for boys.

The Stormy Decade?

What should we expect from young people during their adolescent decade—from about age 10 to 20? Until recently, most psychologists believed that this period is inevitably characterized by storm and stress—that is, emotional turbulence and psychological strain—as young people try to cope with their rapid physical development, their emerging sexuality, and the problems of identity and independence that must be faced as adulthood approaches.

In an influential two-volume treatise titled *Adolescence*, G. Stanley Hall (1904) persuasively set forth the view that erratic physical growth coincides with erratic emotional and moral development. According to Hall, adolescence is a time of

Figure 15.1 *Seated front and center is G. Stanley Hall, the leading American proponent of the storm-and-stress view of adolescence. Surrounding him, and lending support to his theory, particularly with regard to adolescent sexuality, are the prime movers of the psychoanalytic movement: Sigmund Freud, A. A. Brill, Ernest Jones, S. Ferenzi, and Carl Jung. (This photo was taken in 1909 in Worcester, Mass.)*

rebirth: physiological maturation not only changes the adolescent's size; it also changes the young person's way of seeing the world. Consequently, stated Hall, each new generation is capable of surpassing previous generations in moral and intellectual leadership, because the young are idealistic, altruistic, and self-sacrificing. At the same time, however, the worst of human potential can, and does, appear. In Hall's words:

> The momentum of heredity often seems insufficient to enable the child to achieve this great revolution and come to complete maturity . . . every step of the upward way is strewn with wreckage of body, mind, and morals, . . . Modern life is hard, and in many respects increasingly so, on youth. . . . Normal children often pass through stages of passionate cruelty, laziness, lying and thievery. [Hall, 1904]

Psychoanalytic Theory

Psychoanalytic theorists generally agreed with Hall. They particularly thought that there was little parents could do to protect their children from the stresses of adolescence, since the adolescent's rapid sexual maturation and powerful sexual drives would inevitably conflict with the culture's prohibitions against their free expression. As Peter Blos (1962) put it, "No one is exempt—no matter how warm and understanding the family background. The comfort and security of having been loved may help sustain the adolescent in this moment of terror, but no parent, however devoted and well intentioned, can spare the child this frenzied conflict."

One reason psychoanalytic theorists believed parents cannot prevent the "frenzied conflict" of adolescence is that, in part, they themselves cause it. According to Freud (1960, originally published in 1935), the impulses and fantasies of the Oedipal complex, which are repressed during latency, reemerge at puberty because repression is no longer sufficiently powerful to defend the ego against the strong sexual urges of adolescence. Before the young can reach the genital stage, when sexuality is expressed with contemporaries, they must free themselves of their sexual feelings toward their mother or father. Often this is done by temporarily replacing their respect and love for their opposite-sex parent with contempt and hate, a defense mechanism called reaction formation

Figure 15.2 *According to psychoanalytic theory, the psychological hallmark of the onset of puberty—and the reason for the supposed turbulence of adolescence—is the reawakening of sexual impulses that have been repressed during latency.*

Indeed, psychoanalytic theory was so accepting of the inevitable conflict of adolescence that Freud's daughter Anna believed we should be more worried about the psychological health of the adolescent who does *not* seem to be emotionally upset than about the one who does. As she explained it:

> We all know individual children who as late as the ages of 14, 15, or 16 show no such outer evidence of inner unrest. They remain, as they have been during the latency period, "good" children, wrapped up in their family relationships, considerate of their mothers, submissive to their fathers, in accord with the atmosphere, ideas, and ideals of their childhood background. Convenient as this may be, it signifies a delay of normal development, and is, as such, a sign to be taken seriously . . . These are children who have built up excessive defenses against their drive activities and are now crippled by the results, which act as barriers against a normal maturational process . . . They are, perhaps, more than any others, in need of therapeutic help to remove the inner restrictions and clear the path for normal development, however upsetting the latter may prove to be. [Freud, 1968]

Since both Hall's scientific research and psychoanalysts' clinical experience seemed to confirm the idea that adolescence is destined to be difficult, it is not surprising that this view has dominated development psychology for most of this century. There was some conflicting evidence from anthropology: for example, Margaret Mead reported that adolescence for girls in Samoa is peaceful and happy (1961; originally published in 1928). But such exceptions from distant societies did not disprove the general belief that, at least in the Western world, adolescence would typically be a time of moodiness, depression, and disobedience.

Recent Research

Within the last twenty years, however, more careful research has been done on wider samples of young people. We have learned that *most adolescents, most of the time, are calm and predictable rather than turbulent and erratic* (Bandura and Walters, 1959; Douvan and Adelson, 1966; Offer, 1969). Joseph Adelson (1979) explains one reason that psychologists had overestimated adolescent turmoil:

> . . . our concentration on atypical factions of the total body of the young—on addicted, delinquent, and disturbed youngsters, or on the ideologically volatile, or on male (far more impulsive and rebellious than females)—has led us to generalize from qualities found among a minority of the young to adolescents as a whole . . . If we examine the studies that have looked fairly closely at ordinary adolescents, we get an entirely different picture. Taken as a whole, adolescents are *not* in turmoil, *not* deeply disturbed, *not* at the mercy of their impulses, *not* resistant to parental values, *not* politically active, and *not* rebellious. [Adelson, 1979]

Some psychologists, parents, and journalists probably still make the mistake of generalizing about all adolescents on the basis of the behavior of the adolescents we are most likely to notice—the disrespectful, the disturbed, and the delinquent.

Although we now know that adolescence need not be a turbulent period, we should not lose sight of the fact that it is not always smooth. For instance, Daniel and Judith Offer (1969; Offer and Offer, 1975) studied a group of boys from early adolescence through young adulthood. They found that 80 percent of their study population could be categorized in one of three ways. Of the whole group, 22 percent experienced tumultuous growth—the turbulent, crisis-filled maturation that Hall and Freud would have predicted. Nearly the same number, 23 percent, experienced continuous growth. For this group, adolescence was characterized by a "smoothness of purpose and self-assurance" and a "mutual respect, trust, and affection" between them and their parents. Finally, 35 percent of the boys experienced surgent growth. They were reasonably well adjusted and coped with the tasks of adolescence quite well, but they also went through periods of anger, regression, and repression before they moved toward a more mature way of coping with the increased demands their bodies and their cultures placed on them.

Figure 15.3 *Psychologists have become increasingly aware that teenagers cannot be pigeonholed according to the statistically atypical extremes of adolescent behavior. The current tendency in psychology is to view adolescent growth in terms of general patterns—i.e., tumultuous, continuous, or surgent.*

Thus, as we read about the details of physical development during adolescence, we should assume neither that these biological changes occur routinely nor that they create emotional havoc. Instead the question is, Which changes will create what problems for whom?—a question answered, in part, at the end of this chapter.

Puberty

The period of physical growth that ends childhood and brings the young person to adult size, shape, and sexual potential is called puberty. Generally, the many changes of puberty are grouped into two categories, those that are primarily related to the overall growth of the young person's body, and those that are specifically related to the development of male or female sexual characteristics.

This distinction is somewhat misleading, for sexual dimorphism, or differences in the appearance of males and females, is present in every aspect of pubescent growth. For instance, while both sexes grow rapidly during adolescence, boys typically begin this accelerated growth about two years later, and end it with relatively more height, less fat, and stronger muscles, than girls do. It is also true that some of the changes that we consider exclusively male, such as lowered voices, or exclusively female, such as breast development, actually occur to young people of both sexes—although, obviously, by the end of puberty, male voices are markedly lower than female voices, and female breasts are markedly larger than male breasts. Nevertheless, as long as we keep in mind that the distinction between sexual growth and other physical growth is not precise, it will be useful to discuss them separately.

Figure 15.4 *Because boys experience the accelerated growth of puberty approximately two years later than girls do, difference in height is sometimes one of the most noticeable distinguishing features between the sexes in early adolescence.*

The Growth Spurt

The first biochemical indication of puberty is increased concentrations of certain hormones in the bloodstream; and the first signs of puberty perceptible as such to the young person usually involve sexual characteristics—the initial enlargement of the girl's breasts and the boy's testes (Katchadourian, 1977). However, the first readily observable sign of the onset of puberty is the beginning of a period of rapid physical growth, generally referred to as the growth spurt.

The growth spurt begins with a rapid weight gain. Toward the end of middle childhood, both boys and girls become heavier, primarily through the accumulation of fat, especially on their legs, arms, buttocks, and abdomen. Soon after the weight spurt occurs, a height spurt begins, redistributing some of the fat and burning up the rest.

A CLOSER LOOK   **Body Image**

In a culture such as ours, which places a premium on physical attractiveness and uses beautiful bodies to sell everything from clothes and cosmetics to stereos and auto parts, it is no wonder that with the onset of the growth spurt most adolescents begin spending hours of every day in front of a mirror, tirelessly checking and rechecking their clothes, their physiques, their complexions, the part in their hair. As Tanner (1971) explains:

For the majority of young persons, the years from twelve to sixteen are the most eventful ones of their lives so far as their growth and development are concerned. Admittedly, during fetal life and the first year or two after birth, developments occurred still faster, and a sympathetic environment was probably even more crucial, but the subject himself was not the fascinated, charmed, or horrified spectator that watches the developments, or lack of developments, of adolescence.

Anna Freud believes that narcissism, a seemingly excessive self-absorption, is actually a normal aspect of adolescent behavior. Psychologists generally agree that one of the tasks of adolescence is developing one's body image, or the concept of one's physical appearance.

However, in the process of acquiring their body image, most adolescents refer to the cultural *body ideal*—the slim, shapely woman and the tall, muscular man promoted by movies, television, and advertising. Obviously, few people measure up to the model standards set by the likes of Farrah Fawcett, Bo Derek, Robert Redford, and O. J. Simpson. But whereas most adults have learned to accept the discrepancy between the cultural ideal and their own appearance, few adolescents are satisfied with their looks. One nationwide study of young people between 12 and 17 years old found that 49.8 percent of the boys surveyed wanted to be taller, and

48.4 percent of the girls wanted to be thinner. A scant majority of the boys (55 percent) were reasonably satisfied with their build, while most of the girls (60 percent) were not satisfied (Scanlan, 1975).

Other studies show that girls are dissatisfied with more parts of their bodies than boys are. Both sexes, for example, are likely to be concerned about facial features, complexion, and weight, and boys worry about the size of their penis in much the same way girls worry about the size of their breasts. But girls are much more likely to worry about the size and shape of their buttocks, legs, knees, and feet as well (Clifford, 1971).

The adolescent's concern over appearance is more than vanity—it is a recognition of the role physical attractiveness plays in gaining the admiration of the opposite sex. Hass (1979) found that the characteristics that boys sought in girls were, in order, good looks, good body, friendliness, and intelligence; girls wanted boys to be intelligent, good looking, have a good body, and be good conversationalists.

The fact that physique is valued by both sexes, and that adolescents can spend hours in front of the mirror, and many dollars on clothes and cosmetics to make themselves appear more attractive, is understandable, for there is a strong relationship between how adolescents feel about their bodies and how they feel about themselves (McCandless, 1960). To the adolescent, looking "terrible," or feeling regarded as looking "terrible," is often the same as *being terrible*. Consequently, adolescents' concern for their appearance should be an occasion for adults' sympathy, rather than their derision.

Given the standards of the body beautiful against which adolescents, especially girls, feel compelled to measure themselves, it is little wonder that they seem obsessively concerned with physical looks.

Records of individual growth during this period make it obvious why the word "spurt" is used to describe these increases (Tanner, 1971). During the twelve-month period of their greatest growth, many girls gain as much as 20 pounds (9 kilograms) and 3½ inches (9 centimeters), and many boys gain up to 26 pounds (12 kilograms) and 4 inches (10 centimeters). Some grow even faster, adding as much as 6 inches in six months. About a year after the greatest height increase, the period of greatest muscle increase occurs: consequently, the pudginess of the typical child in early puberty generally has disappeared by late pubescence, two years later.

The growth process does not occur in every part of the body simultaneously (Katchadourian, 1977). In most cases, adolescents' hands and feet lengthen before their arms and legs do, and the torso is the last part to grow. Thus, growth in puberty, unlike that of earlier periods, is distal-proximo (far to near). In addition, the nose, lips, and ears usually grow before the head itself reaches adult size and shape. Thus, a 12-year-old girl might wear a woman's shoe size while still wearing children's sizes in all her other clothes; and a 14-year-old boy might fear that his nose is the only part of him that is getting any bigger. Even more disturbing to the growing person can be the fact that the two halves of the body do not always grow at the same rate: one foot, breast, or ear can be temporarily larger than the other. None of these anomalies lasts very long, however: once the growth process starts, every part of the body reaches close to adult size and shape in about three years.

Figure 15.5 *The fact that growth during puberty is distal-proximo leads to the bane of many young adolescents' lives: disproportionately big feet.*

Internal organs also grow during this period. The lungs increase in size and capacity, allowing the adolescent to breathe more deeply and slowly, and the heart doubles in size. In addition, the total volume of blood increases. These organic changes give the person greater endurance in physical exercise; many teenagers can run for miles, or dance for hours, without stopping to rest. The digestive system increases in capacity also, although not so rapidly that the typical adolescent can be satisfied with only three meals a day.

Finally, many relatively minor physical changes during puberty can have substantial impact. For instance, oil, sweat, and odor glands become much more active during puberty. One result is acne, a problem for about two-thirds of all boys and half of all girls between the ages of 14 and 19 (Schacter et al., 1971). Another

Figure 15.6 *The dramatic increase in heart and lung capacity and overall body strength during adolescence makes many teenagers seem capable of going full tilt without ever needing a break. One of the socially creative expressions of this new endurance popular with high schoolers is marathon dancing for a charitable cause.*

example is a change in the shape of the eyes, which makes many adolescents sufficiently nearsighted to require glasses. On the positive side, the lymphoid system, including the tonsils and adenoids, *decreases* in size at adolescence, which makes the teenager less susceptible to certain respiratory ailments than the child. For this reason, about half the victims of childhood asthma improve markedly in adolescence (Katchadourian, 1977).

Nutrition

The rapid height and weight gain of puberty obviously requires that the adolescent consume additional calories, more than during any other period of life. In addition, the adolescent body needs more of several specific minerals and vitamins, including calcium, iron, and vitamins A, B_2, C, and D. There is also a greater need for protein than there is during childhood, but the usual North American diet is sufficient in this case (Heald, 1969). The nutrient most commonly deficient in the adolescent's diet is iron—a special problem for adolescent girls once their period begins. Iron-deficiency anemia is more common among adolescent females than among any other part of the population.

Figure 15.7 *The American craving for so-called junk foods seems particularly suited to providing pubescent children with the extra calories required by the growth spurt. Whether it provides the required nutrients may be an entirely different question.*

Adolescents are particularly susceptible to the latest crash diets or food fads, in part because cognitive and psychological development leads them to experiment with new ideas and life styles. Such diets can have serious consequences. For instance, the Zen macrobiotic diet, which, at the final and most "purified" stage, involves eating solely cereals, can result in anemia, scurvy, and kidney disease (Katchadourian, 1977). Exotic diets are potentially harmful at any age, but are particularly so during the critical years of adolescence, when, unless the body has sufficient nourishment to sustain rapid growth, full growth potential will not be realized. The problem is compounded, of course, for pregnant teenagers, who need an extraordinarily nutritious diet to provide for the full growth of their fetus as well as themselves. Malnutrition is one major reason mothers under age 16 are more than twice as likely to have premature or stillborn babies as are mothers in their twenties.

While the growth spurt is taking place, another set of changes occurs that transforms boys and girls into young men and women. Before puberty, the physical differences between boys and girls are relatively minor—boys are an inch or so taller and have greater arm strength; girls are somewhat shorter and have greater body flexibility. At puberty, however, many significant body differences develop as sex organs mature and secondary sexual characteristics appear.

Changes in Sex Organs   During adolescence, all the sex organs become much larger. In girls, the uterus begins to grow and the vaginal lining to thicken, even before there are visible signs of puberty. In boys, the testes begin to grow, and about a year later, the penis begins to lengthen and the scrotal sac enlarges and becomes pendulous.

Toward the end of puberty, the young person's sex organs reach sufficient size and maturity to make reproduction possible. For girls, the specific event that is taken to indicate fertility is the first menstrual period, called menarche. For boys, the comparable indicator of reproductive potential is ejaculation, that is, the discharge of seminal fluid containing sperm. Ejaculation can occur in a nocturnal emission (a wet dream), through masturbation, or through sexual intercourse, with masturbation being the most common cause for the first ejaculation (Kinsey et al., 1948).

Actually, both menarche and ejaculation are simply one more step toward full reproductive maturity, which occurs several years later. In fact, a girl's first menstrual cycles are usually anovulatory; that is, ovulation does not occur. Even a year after menarche, most young women are still relatively infertile: ovulation is irregular, and if fertilization does occur, the probability of spontaneous abortion is much higher than it will be later, because the uterus is still relatively small. In the case of boys, the concentration of sperm necessary to fertilize an ovum is not reached until months or even years after the first ejaculation of seminal fluid. (As many teenagers discover too late, unfortunately, this relative infertility does not mean that pregnancy is impossible at puberty; it is simply less likely.)

Secondary Sex Characteristics   Changes in many other parts of the young person's body also indicate that sexual maturation is occurring. In addition to increased height and a lower percentage of total body fat, the most obvious change to have occurred in the general body shape of the typical boy by the end of puberty is the widening of his shoulders. In the typical girl, noticeable changes include her wide hips and relatively narrow shoulders.

RESEARCH REPORT **Menarche and Self-Concept**

Do young girls feel differently about themselves after they have their first period? If so, are they proud or ashamed of their burgeoning femininity? Elissa Koff and her colleagues (1978) set out to find some answers to these questions. They administered a group of tests and asked eighty-seven seventh-grade girls dozens of questions on two occasions, first when their average age was 12 and then again half a year later.

Twenty-three of the girls had already reached menarche on the first test date, thirty reached menarche between the two test occasions, and thirty-four still had not menstruated by the second test session. By looking for differences in the test results among these three groups, the researchers hoped to discover if having had their first period made a difference in the way the girls thought about themselves and their femininity.

The results show that it did, as demonstrated by the draw-a-person test, for example. First the girls were asked to "draw a whole person . . . not a stick figure." Then they were asked to indicate the sex of the figure and to draw a second person of the opposite sex. The drawings were rated on two characteristics: which sex was drawn first, and how different the male and female portrayals were in body shape, body parts, hair, and clothes. (The scorers were "blind," not knowing who made which drawing, so the scoring was not influenced by knowledge of the girls' menarcheal status.) The girls were also asked how satisfied they were with various parts of their bodies—seventeen parts in all, including "feminine" parts such as breasts and buttocks, as well as "nonfeminine" parts, such as hands and feet.

After menarche, girls were more likely to draw a female person first in the draw-a-person test (see Table 15.1), and they differentiated male and female persons more clearly in their sketches. They also expressed more satisfaction with the feminine parts of their bodies, even though the actual change in breast size over a six-month period is small, and even though some premenarche girls were more shapely than some postmenarche girls. The authors of this study concluded that "menarche is a pivotal event for reorganization of the adolescent girl's body image and sexual identification . . . it is menarche, in particular, rather than puberty, in general, that is critical in precipitating a change in the adolescent girl's image of the body and acceptance of herself as female."

The fact that, in these girls, menarche led to a more favorable attitude toward womanhood is encouraging. As shown by Paula Weideger's (1976) study, historical and cultural attitudes toward menstruation have been predominantly negative, including such ideas as that menstruation is an unclean time, a curse, and that a

TABLE 15.1 **Percent of Seventh-Grade Girls Who Drew a Female Figure First, When Asked to Draw a Person**

	First Test Occasion	Second Test Occasion
Group 1: Girls who had not reached menarche	68%	68%
Group 2: Girls who had reached menarche between first and second test	77%	97%
Group 3: Girls who had already reached menarche before the first test	100%	100%

menstruating woman is potentially dangerous to men and to growing plants. As archaic as these notions are, their effects have continued to be felt. Indeed, according to a study of young girls from several American subcultures (Henton, 1961), positive attitudes toward menstruation were rare as recently as a generation or two ago. The results from the Koff study suggest not only that negative attitudes toward menstruation are now less common but that the experience of menarche itself may promote positive attitudes about womanhood.

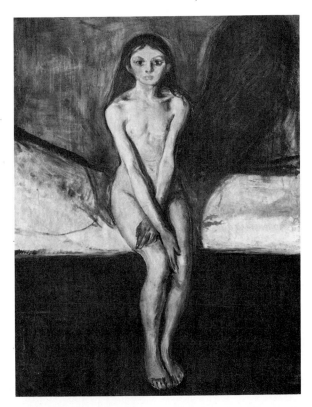

Edvard Munch's haunting image of female adolescence seems to reflect perfectly the shame and uncertainty *that have characterized many young girls' entry into womanhood.*

Breast Development.   Another obvious difference in the shape of the female body, and the one most focused on in Western cultures, is the development of breasts. For most girls, the first sign that puberty is beginning is the "bud" stage of breast development, when a small accumulation of fat causes a slight rise around the nipples. From then on, breasts develop gradually for several years, with full breast growth not being attained until almost all the other changes of puberty are over. Since our culture takes breast development to be symbolic of womanhood, girls whose breasts are very small or very large often feel worry and embarrassment, despite the fact that breast size does not reflect ability to respond to erotic stimulation or to nurse an infant.

For boys, the diameter of the areola (the dark area around the nipple) increases during puberty. Much to their consternation, many find that they are developing some breast tissue as well. However, their worry is needless; about 40 percent of all adolescent boys experience some breast enlargement, usually at about age 14 (Roche et al., 1971), but this enlargement almost always disappears by age 16.

Hair.   In both sexes, head and body hair usually becomes coarser and darker during puberty, and axillary (underarm), pubic, and facial hair appears, usually beginning with a few light-colored straight strands of pubic hair. As puberty continues, pubic hair becomes darker, thicker, and curlier, and covers a wider area. Girls reach the adult pubic-hair pattern in about three years; for boys, the process takes six years or more.

Facial and body hair are mistakenly considered signs of manliness in our society. Actually, the tendency to grow facial hair is inherited; how often a man needs to shave is determined by his genes rather than his virility. In addition, facial hair is usually the last secondary sex characteristic to appear, sometimes long after a young man has become sexually active. Finally, girls typically develop some facial hair during puberty—a sign, not of masculinity, but of sexual maturation.

Voice.   The adolescent's voice becomes lower as the larynx grows, a change most noticeable in boys. (Even more noticeable, much to the chagrin of the young male, is his occasional loss of voice control, throwing his newly acquired baritone into a high squeak.) Girls also develop lower voices, a fact reflected in the recognition of a low, throaty female voice as "sexy."

Gender Differences in Sex Drive

One of the most difficult questions to answer is how the sex drive, that is, the need or desire to experience sexual stimulation and achieve sexual satisfaction, differs in male and female adolescents. Until recently, most people, including psychologists, believed that the sex drive is much stronger in males than in females. This view has been given particular support by Helene Deutsch (1944), a psychoanalyst Freud acknowledged as an expert on women. In her view, females were destined to be passive and receptive, and males, to be active and aggressive, by the very nature of their genitals, a fact that would, naturally, make these sexual traits universal.

The Double Standard   One consequence of this idea was the double standard, a separate code of sexual behavior for males and females. Since her sex drive was considered less strong, the female was expected to stop the sexually aggressive man rather than become carried away with passion herself. The male, on the other hand, was expected to try to get as much sexual gratification as possible. According to a study of high-school students conducted by Gary Schwartz and Don Merten

Figure 15.8 *Until recently, the traditional psychoanalytic view of sexual determinism has reinforced the stereotype of the male as a caveman conqueror and the female as passive, though oft-protesting, prey.*

(1967), the double standard was still strong among many adolescents in the mid-1960s. The students felt that a boy attained status by "providing some concrete evidence for frequent and exaggerated boasts about sexual prowess," whereas a girl "must allow herself to reach a relatively high level of sexual excitement and intimacy without giving in to what are described as persistent demands for greater sexual favors."

Consider one girl's answers to the following questions:

> Question: Whose responsibility is it [regarding how far things go sexually on a date]?
>
> Answer: The girl's. I mean because guys can't help it. I mean they are born that way. . . .
>
> Question: Are all guys like this or just particular guys?
>
> Answer: Some guys would get as far as they could get, just for kicks, but there are other boys who are just as nice as they can be, but any boy who likes a girl enough . . . I don't think he would do it intentionally to hurt her, but he just can't help trying to get as far as he can get. I don't think even the nicest guy can help being that way.

As the authors of this study summarize their findings:

> Though girls admit that they also have strong sexual feelings, they agree that they and not the boys are capable of rational control, of setting limits. Thus, girls claim that nature has burdened them with the responsibility of keeping petting relationships within prescribed moral limits. In a basic sense, girls see boys as morally defective—or, if not as morally defective, at least as morally immature. Boys are said to be simply incapable of realistically assessing the negative consequences of giving free rein to sexual impulses in a dating situation. And, from what we have been able to observe, boys often fulfill these cultural expectations which have been phrased in such biological terms. [Schwartz and Merten, 1967]

Another extensive study of adolescents in the 1960s, conducted by Elizabeth Douvan and Joseph Adelson, described the differences between the male and female sex drives. For boys, the sex drive is "imperious and biologically specific . . . [the boy] must . . . find within himself the means of obtaining sexual discharge without excessive guilt, and means of control without crippling inhibitions." For girls, on the other hand,

> sexuality is not experienced as such; it very easily becomes spiritualized, idealized, etherealized. . . . erotic gratification as such is likely to remain secondary to—or at least closely related to—fulfillment of other needs such as self-esteem, reassurance, affection, and love. For most girls, the overall relationship with the individual boy whom she loves—the extent to which the relationship is characterized by trust, concern, and a mutual sharing of life experiences—takes precedence over specific sexual release. Consequently, control of impulses is likely to constitute a considerably less urgent problem for girls. [Douvan and Adelson, 1966]

Although no firm conclusion can yet be drawn with regard to the relative strength of the sex drive in boys and girls, all available evidence does indicate that the double standard has declined considerably over the last two decades. One indicator of this is that the number of girls at any given age who have experienced sexual intercourse is almost as high as the number of boys (Hass, 1979; Sorensen, 1973; Hopkins, 1977). Indeed, one study of college youth found that males and females reported identical rates of nonvirginity (Vener and Stewart, 1974). According to another survey, most teenage girls believe that women enjoy sex as much as men (Hunt, 1970).

However, there is also evidence that adolescent male and female sex drives and attitudes are not identical. The best information we have on adolescent sexual attitudes and behavior comes from Robert Sorenson's (1973) extensive, careful survey of a cross section of Americans between the ages of 13 and 19 that covered 200

Figure 15.9 *Although the double standard per se seems to have declined sharply among teenagers, there still appear to be some distinct attitudinal differences between the genders: Sorenson (1973) found that whereas nearly one out of four males engaged in casual sexual relations, less than one in sixteen girls did.*

communities. Although a majority of the young people surveyed believed that sexual activity between males and females should reflect their total relationship, more boys than girls accepted the idea that recreational sex, with no commitment to the opposite partner, is permissible. The boys also tended to have had more sexual partners and more varied sexual experiences, with 24 percent of the boys, but only 6 percent of the girls, falling into the category Sorenson termed sexual adventurers, that is, "nonvirgins freely moving from one sexual intercourse partner to another."

Sorensen also found that boys, especially in early adolescence, are more worried about their sexuality: for instance, 57 percent of those between 13 and 15 years old answered yes to the statement "Sometimes I think I am addicted to sex, the way some people are addicted to drugs." Older boys, and girls of all ages, answered yes to this question only about 25 percent of the time.

Masturbation   Another difference in the sexual attitudes and behaviors of adolescent boys and girls is apparent with regard to masturbation. Few adolescents today believe what almost everyone thought a century ago—that masturbation causes a variety of mental and physical illnesses, from schizophrenia and tuberculosis to acne and nearsightedness (Miller and Lief, 1976). However, adolescent boys are more likely than girls to masturbate (80 percent compared to 59 percent, according to Hass [1979]; 83 percent to 45 percent, according to Miller and Lief [1976]), *and* are more likely to feel guilty about it. Hass found that whereas only one-fifth of the girls who masturbated felt guilty, about half of the boys did, and those who did not feel guilty often had other negative reactions, such as feeling ashamed, stupid, or abnormal. These negative feelings may disappear as the young person becomes more mature, as was suggested by a study of West German youth between the ages of 11 and 16. This particular study found that only one boy in four under age 14 thought masturbation was "OK as often as you want," compared to 55 percent of the 15- and 16-year-olds (Schoof-Tams et al., 1976).

The Timing of Puberty   The changes of puberty occur in predictable sequence and tempo. The entire process begins when hormones from the hypothalamus (a part of the brain) trigger hormones in the *pituitary* gland (often called the master gland and located in the base of the skull), which in turn trigger increased hormonal production by the *gonads,* or sex glands (the testes in the male and the ovaries in the female).

For girls, the most important hormones produced by the sex glands are estrogen and progesterone, which cause, usually in this sequence, the beginning of breast development, first pubic hair, widening of hips, the growth spurt, menarche, and completion of breast and pubic-hair growth. For boys, the most important hormone is testosterone, which produces, usually in this sequence, growth of the testes, growth of the penis, first pubic hair, capacity for ejaculation, growth spurt, voice changes, beard development, and completion of pubic hair growth. Once the hormonal concentrations start the biological changes of puberty, the process is rapid, with most major changes occurring within three years.

However, while the sequence of pubertal events is very similar for all young people, there is great variation in the age at which it starts. Healthy children begin puberty any time between ages 8 and 16. The child's sex, genes, body type, and nourishment all play a role in this variation.

A CLOSER LOOK **Factors Affecting When Puberty Occurs**

Male-female differences are one factor affecting when a particular person will experience puberty. The average time differential between female and male development depends on which particular event in puberty is being compared. The first signs of reproductive capability appear only a few months later in boys than in girls: the average girl reaches menarche at age 12 years, 8 months while the average boy first ejaculates at age 13 (Zacharias et al., 1976; Schoof-Tams et al., 1976). However, since the growth spurt appears later in the sequence of pubertal changes in boys, the average boy is two years behind the average girl in this respect. Consequently, between ages 12 and 14 most girls are taller than their male classmates.

Genes are also an important factor in the age at which puberty begins. This is most clearly seen in the case of menarche, the pubertal event that is easiest to date. Although most girls reach this milestone between 11 and 14, the age of onset varies from 9 to 18. However, the difference in the age at which sisters reach menarche is, on the average, only 13 months; and the difference for monozygotic twins averages a mere 2.8 months.

Body weight and the proportion of fat are also important in determining the onset of puberty. Short, stocky children tend to experience puberty earlier than those with taller, thinner builds. Menarche in particular seems related to the accumulation of a certain amount of body fat. It is less likely to occur in spring and summer, when most children gain more height than weight, and more likely in winter. Females who have little body fat, such as runners and other athletes, menstruate later and more irregularly than the average girl, while those who are generally inactive menstruate earlier. (This is one explanation for the fact that blind girls, who are usually less active than sighted girls, normally have their first period earlier than sighted girls.)

Some researchers (Frisch and Revelle, 1970) believe that there is a critical weight (about 100 pounds) that young women must attain before they can reach menarche. This may or may not be the case today, for while it is true that thin girls enter puberty later, it is not clear whether weight gain promotes menarche or is merely a sign that the hormonal processes have begun. However, in earlier times, lower body weight as a result of inadequate nutrition was probably the main reason puberty occurred later than it does now. In the nineteenth century, for instance, most women had their first menstrual period between ages 15 and 17 instead of today's average of 12 to 14.

Poor nutrition also diminishes the growth spurt at puberty and thereby limits the total height attained. Consequently, a century ago, the average man was 5 feet 6 inches tall instead of today's average of 5 feet 11 inches (Tanner, 1971). With each new generation over the past hundred years or so, young people have been experiencing puberty earlier and growing taller than their parents, a phenomenon called the secular trend. In contemporary North America and Europe, nutrition and medical care for most children are now sufficient to allow genes and gender, rather than health and nutrition, to determine the age at which puberty begins. As a result, the average maximum height and the age of puberty are the same today as they were ten years ago. Although most American adults reached puberty at an earlier age than their parents and grandparents, most of today's children will experience their growth spurt and develop their sexual characteristics at the same age that their parents did.

As a result of the secular trend, a boy soprano's voice today usually begins to crack around age 12. In the eighteenth century, however, it usually didn't break until the middle or late teens. J. S. Bach, for example, was a mainstay of the soprano section of St. Michael's choir in Lunëburg until he was sixteen. Franz Josef Haydn was nearly seventeen before his voice broke and forced him to retire from the royal choir in Vienna. (The year before, the choir master had unsuccessfully sought permission to have Haydn castrated to preserve his voice.)

Storm and Stress: Who, When, and Why?

Now that we have examined the nature of physical growth and related developments during puberty, we are better able to anticipate potential problems during adolescence. And we can predict that people with certain characteristics are particularly likely to experience a stormy adolescence.

Early and Late Puberty

First let us consider the probable impact of the extreme variation in the age at which puberty begins. It is not uncommon for a differential as great as seven years to exist between the age early-maturing girls enter puberty and the time late-maturing boys do. Young people in these circumstances must spend years of their lives in contradiction to the norm that males are taller than females. In addition, it is virtually impossible for these adolescents to find contemporaries of the opposite sex who are at the same stage of sexual development. Girls who are taller and more developed than their classmates find that they have no peers who share their interests or problems. Prepubescent girls call them "boy crazy," and boys tease them about their big feet or emerging breasts. Almost every sixth-grade class has an 11-year-old pubescent girl who slouches so she won't look so tall, wears loose shirts so no one will notice her breasts, and buys her shoes a size too small.

In a case such as this, the problem is generally temporary; studies show that by seventh or eighth grade, the early-maturing girl is more likely to be respected and liked (Faust, 1960). For one thing, she is attractive to older boys, making her the target of envy more than scorn. After a year or two of awkwardness and embarrassment, she is able to advise her less mature girl friends about topics that they find increasingly important, such as bra sizes, dating behavior, menstrual cramps, and variations in kissing.

For average late-maturing boys, the problems may be more general and long-lasting. They must watch themselves be outdistanced, first by the girls and then by most of the boys in their class, and they are forced to endure the patronizing scorn of those who only recently were themselves immature. Extensive longitudinal data from the Berkeley Growth Study found late-maturing boys to be less

Figure 15.10 *The late-maturing male is apt to go through a double phase of feeling immature and socially inferior: first he is physically overshadowed by many of his female classmates, who are about two years ahead of him in growth; then he is out-stripped by his male peers, who may enhance their newly acquired sense of manliness by treating him like a kid.*

poised, less relaxed, more restless, and more talkative than early-maturing boys, who were more often chosen as leaders (Jones and Bayley, 1950). The late-maturing boys were more playful, more creative, and more flexible, qualities that are not usually admired by other adolescents, although they may be more appreciated in adulthood.

Follow-up studies of the same late-maturing individuals when they were 33 years old, and again when they were 38, found that most of them had reached average or above-average height but that some of the personality patterns and social inferiority of their adolescence persisted nevertheless (Jones, 1957; Jones, 1965; Mussen and Jones, 1957). Compared to early- or average-maturing boys, those who had matured late were less likely to hold positions of leadership in their jobs or in their social organizations; they tended to be less controlled, responsible, or dominant; and some of them still had feelings of inferiority and rejection. However, in several positive characteristics they scored better. They were likely to have a better sense of humor and to be more egalitarian and more perceptive than their early-maturing peers, who tended to be more moralistic and self-satisfied.

Of course, not all late-maturing boys feel inferior during adolescence or later life. Some find other ways to excel, using their minds and talents to become the class genius, or musician, or comedian. In addition, late maturation today may be less difficult than it was decades ago; for example, because of the greater freedom allowed young girls, the late-maturing boy can now gain social and sexual experience dating girls several years younger than he is. If he attends a school influenced by Piaget's ideas, where most classes are composed of students who share interests and abilities rather than age, he will be less likely to feel inferior and more likely to develop his creative talents. Nevertheless, the research suggests that parents and teachers need to be particularly conscious of the special emotional needs of early- and late-maturing adolescents.

Boys' Problems

As we have seen, girls have their share of problems during puberty. In general, however, boys have the more difficult time. Their physical growth occurs later, which means that the average boy is not only shorter but also weaker than the average girl for a two-year period from about age 12 to 14. And because their growth is more rapid than girls', they and their families must adjust to increased appetites, new clothes sizes, and changing self-image even more rapidly than girls and their families. In addition, many of the physical changes of puberty seem to fall more harshly on boys than girls. For instance, boys are more likely to develop acne, and their voices are more likely to squeak before they mature.

Sexual developments create even more problems for boys than physical growth. Many are worried that they will have a visible erection at an embarrassing moment, such as when reciting in class or dancing with a girl. As we have seen, guilt about masturbation is greater in boys than girls, and many of them worry about being oversexed (Sorensen, 1973).

Since boys experience more problems as a result of the biological changes of puberty than girls do, we would expect boys, more than girls, to show signs of emotional distress during adolescence, and there is evidence for this speculation. For one thing, boys are three times as likely as girls to be arrested (ten years ago they were four times as likely to be), and they are more likely to report having difficulty with their parents and teachers. For instance, 25 percent of the boys in Sorensen's study agreed with the statement "I have pretty much given up on ever being able to get along with my parents," compared to only 6 percent of the girls.

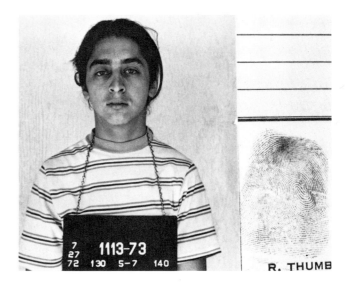

Figure 15.11 *The fact that teenage boys are arrested three times as often as teen-age girls is one of several in-dicators suggesting that the pressures of adolescence are felt more acutely by males.*

What's more, the rate of accidental death, homicide, and suicide (the three leading causes of adolescent death) is about three times higher for boys than for girls.

Of course, none of these statistics applies to every boy. Indeed, as the Offers (1975) found, about a fourth of their sample of boys had a smooth adolescence, and about a third had only transitory problems. Nevertheless, taken as a whole, boys are more likely to have a difficult time during adolescence than are girls.

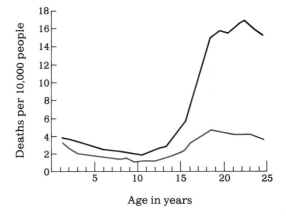

Figure 15.12 *According to 1976 statistics, males (black line) 16 to 17 years old are three times more likely to die from accidents, violence, or poisoning than are females (color line) the same age. Males from 18 to 24 are four times more likely than their female count-erparts to meet such un-timely ends.*

Early and Late Adolescence

Because the years between 11 and 14 typically include the greatest hormonal changes and physical growth, and the first experience with menarche and ejacula-tion, this period is ripe with adjustments, for the parents as well as for the adoles-cent. And as we saw in Chapter 4, adjusting to any change, even a positive one, puts stress on the people involved.

Early adolescence is very stressful for families. For example, the Offers found that minor parent-child bickering about details of eating, dressing, or cleanliness were common in many families. Another study provides interesting confirmation that early adolescence is especially difficult. Roberta Simmons and her colleagues (1973) asked 1917 subjects between 8 and 18 years old questions designed to mea-sure four dimensions of self-concept:

1. *Self-consciousness.*   Example: "If a teacher asked you to get up in front of the class and talk a little bit about your summer, would you be very nervous, a little nervous, or not at all nervous?"

2. *Stability of self.*   Example: "A kid told me, 'Some days I like the way I am. Some days I do not like the way I am.' Do your feelings change like this?"

3. *General self-esteem.*   Example: "Are most things about you good, bad, or . . . about the same?"

4. *Specific self-esteem.*   Example: "Do you consider yourself smart, good looking, truthful . . . ?"

All four measures of poor self-concept showed a steep increase between ages 11 and 13 or 14, and then most dimensions of self-concept improved, with adolescents between 16 and 18 years old thinking even better of themselves, in general, than 8-year-olds did.

However, even though most 15-year-olds have fewer quarrels with their parents, like themselves better than they did a few years earlier, and have adjusted to the physical developments of adolescence, they face new problems. As we will see in Chapter 17, while biological changes begin adolescence, culture, rather than biology, ends it. In order to reach adulthood, the young person must forge his or her own identity, which is no easy task. Those young people who do not have parental and peer support may find the psychosocial tasks of late adolescence much more difficult than the biological upheaval of early adolescence. Before discussing these problems, we should learn about adolescent cognitive development, development that makes it easier for adolescents to solve many social problems, including their own.

SUMMARY

The Stormy Decade?

1. Until recently, most psychologists believed that adolescence is inevitably a time of storm and stress, or emotional turbulence. Freudians thought that the sexual needs of the adolescent have to conflict with parental authority in order for the young person to develop normally.

2. However, recent research has shown that most adolescents, most of the time, are calm and predictable rather than turbulent and erratic. While only a minority experience a completely smooth adolescence, few are distressed most of the time.

Puberty

3. The growth spurt—first in weight, then height, then strength—is the first obvious evidence of puberty, although some hormonal changes precede it. During the year of fastest growth, an average girl grows about 3½ inches (9 centimeters) and an average boy about 4 inches (10 centimeters).

4. Growth usually begins with the extremities and proceeds toward the torso. The head, lungs, heart, and digestive system also change in size and shape during this period.

5. During adolescence, more calories and vitamins are needed than at any other time of life. Undernourishment, exotic diets, and pregnancy can all prevent normal growth during this period.

6. During puberty, all the sex organs grow larger and the young person becomes sexually mature. Menarche in girls and ejaculation in boys are the events usually taken to indicate reproductive potential, although full fertility is reached years after these initial signs of maturation.

7. Most secondary sexual characteristics—including changes in the breasts and voice and the development of pubic, facial, and body hair—appear in both sexes, although there are obvious differences in the typical development of males and females.

8. The sexual attitudes and experiences of adolescent males and females are much more similar today than they once were. However, females still emphasize the importance of

the love relationship more than males do, while boys are more often concerned and worried about the expression of their sexual needs, in masturbation or intercourse.

9. While the sequence of pubertal events is similar for most young people, the timing of the onset of puberty shows considerable variation. Normal young people experience their first bodily changes any time from 8 to 16. The individual's sex, genes, body type, and nutrition all affect age of puberty, with boys, thin children, and malnourished children typically reaching puberty later than their opposites.

Storm and Stress: Who, When, and Why?

10. While not all teenagers have a difficult adolescence, early-maturing girls and late-maturing boys are more likely to be distressed by their physical development or lack of it. This problem is temporary for most girls, but the lack of confidence of the typical late-maturing boy may continue into manhood.

11. Neither sex necessarily has a troubled puberty, but, in general, boys find adolescence more difficult than girls do.

12. The years of early adolescence, when the greatest biological changes occur, are often characterized by parent-child bickering, and by a lack of self-confidence in the young person. These problems usually disappear after the main biological milestones of puberty are passed, although other problems may be more severe during late adolescence.

KEY QUESTIONS

What was Hall's view of adolescence?

What was the psychoanalytic view of adolescence?

How "stormy" is adolescence in North America today, according to recent research?

What are the main nonsexual biological changes that occur during puberty?

What are the main sexual changes that occur during puberty?

What are the similarities between male and female sexual attitudes and experiences during adolescence?

What are the differences in male and female sexual attitudes and behavior during adolescence?

What is the usual sequence of changes that occurs in puberty?

How can we predict when puberty will occur for a given individual?

How can the age at which puberty occurs affect psychological development?

Which changes of puberty are more difficult for boys than girls, and which are more difficult for girls than boys?

What problems are more common in early adolescence than in late adolescence?

KEY TERMS

storm and stress
genital stage
reaction formation
tumultuous growth
continuous growth
surgent growth
puberty
sexual dimorphism
growth spurt
menarche
ejaculation

anovulatory
secondary sexual characteristics
sex drive
double standard
sexual adventurers
hypothalamus
estrogen
progesterone
testosterone

RECOMMENDED READINGS

Frank, Anne. *The diary of a young girl.* New York: Washington Square Press, 1972.

Making this Dutch girl's unique account of months of hiding from the Nazis all the more poignant are the experiences that she has in common with young girls everywhere. Anne reaches menarche, falls in love, and bickers with her parents in much the same way millions of other adolescents do.

de Beauvoir, Simone. *Memoirs of a dutiful daughter.* New York: Harper & Row, 1974.

Simone de Beauvoir remembers her girlhood, including her shame and embarrassment at the changes in her body as puberty began. Her parents' insensitivity to her development helps remind us of the importance of adult understanding and sympathy during this period. The book also raises the question of the degree to which sex differences are biological or cultural. For instance, Simone was told that she thought "like a boy," but she was not permitted the same education her male cousins received.

Group for the Advancement of Psychiatry. *Normal adolescence; Its dynamics and impact.* New York: Scribner, 1968.

This book clearly states the view—held by many psychiatrists and psychologists until recently—that the biological changes of puberty bring a measure of disequilibrium and emotional disturbance to most young people. At the same time, the authors recognize that parents, culture, and individual personality differences play a role in the actual course of adolescence, and that even the most disturbed adolescent shows periods of "relative quiescence."

Adolescence: Cognitive Development

I see no hope for the future of our people if they are dependent on the frivolous youth of today, for certainly all youth are reckless beyond words. . . . When I was a boy, we were taught to be discreet and respectful of elders, but the present youth are exceedingly wise and impatient of restraint.

Hesiod (Eighth century B.C.)

True or False?

The following statement is false: "Either a football is round or it is not two-dimensional."

Someone who protests in support of civil liberties can safely be assumed to have reached the highest level of moral reasoning, which recognizes that universal principles must be obeyed.

The recent increase in the number of teenage pregnancies is explained by two factors: an increase in sexual activity among teenagers and a lack of sex education.

Most teenagers would prefer to receive information about sex from their parents rather than from sources outside the family.

The percentage of adolescents at each age who use any of the three most widely used drugs (alcohol, tobacco, marijuana) is fairly constant for each drug in different communities throughout the United States.

The biological changes of puberty are universal and, for the most part, visible, transforming children by giving them adult size, shape, and sexuality. However, another change that typically occurs between ages 13 and 15 is just as important: the intellectual maturation that enables adolescents to reason and analyze much better than children.

Formal Operational Thought

Piaget was the first to recognize what many psychologists now consider the distinguishing feature of adolescent thought: an emphasis on possibility rather than reality (Inhelder and Piaget, 1958). Before adolescence, the child has "an earthbound, concrete, practical-minded sort of problem solving approach . . . [the child] hugs the ground of detected empirical reality rather closely, and speculations about other possibilities . . . occur only with difficulty and as a last resort. An adolescent or adult is likelier to approach problems the other way around . . . reality is subordinated to possibility" (Flavell, 1977).

On the whole, adolescents are able to speculate, hypothesize, and fantasize much more readily and on a much grander scale than children who are still tied to concrete operational thinking. By the end of adolescence, many young people can understand and create general principles or formal rules to explain many aspects of human experience. Consequently, Piaget calls the last stage of cognitive development, attained at about age 15, formal operational thought, the stage at which the adolescent "begins to build systems or theories in the largest sense of the term" about literature, philosophy, morality, love, and the world of work (Inhelder and Piaget, 1958).

Development of Logic   Inhelder and Piaget (1958) undertook a classic series of experiments that traced the development of logic by finding out if children between the ages of 5 and 15 could deduce certain laws of physics by manipulating specific materials. Children were asked to put objects in a pail of water and explain why some sank and others floated; they were given different weights to hang on a string pendulum and asked to figure out which factors might affect the speed of the pendulum's swing (length of string, size of weight, height of release, force of the release); they were asked to roll marbles down an incline onto a flat surface and estimate how far they would go. In all these experiments, Piaget and Inhelder found that logical abilities developed gradually in the years before adolescence, culminating at about age 14 with an understanding of the general principles.

For instance, the children in one experiment were asked to balance a balance scale using weights that could be hooked onto the arms of the scale at several places.

This task was completely beyond the ability of most preoperational children (one 4-year-old put two weights on the same side of the scale and none on the other).

By age 7 (the usual age for the beginning of concrete operational thought), children realized that the scale could be balanced by putting the same amount of weight on both sides, but they didn't realize that distance from the center is also important.

By age 10 (near the end of the concrete operational stage), they were often able, through trial and error, to see that the farther from the fulcrum a given weight is, the more force it has (in one child's words, "At the end, it makes more weight"), and to find several correct combinations that would balance the scale.

Finally, at about age 13 or 14, some children had a firm grasp of the general law that there is an inverse relationship between a weight's proximity to the fulcrum and its force, and correctly concluded that if the weight on one arm of the balance is three times as heavy as the weight on the other, it has to be a third as far from the center as the other weight in order for equilibrium to be achieved.

Because they are able to consider theoretical possibilities, many adolescents can analyze a statement logically without becoming sidetracked by the concrete. This ability was demonstrated by a series of experiments in which adolescents and preadolescents were asked whether certain statements were true, false, or impossible to judge (Osherson and Markman, 1974–1975). For instance, the investigator hid a poker chip and said, "Either this chip is green or it is not green." Almost every preadolescent replied that the statement was impossible to judge rather than saying that it was true. They also thought that the statement "The chip in my hand is green and it is not green" was impossible to judge rather than false.

Figure 16.1 *Is this demonstrator's assertion true, false, or impossible to judge? Be prepared to blush if your answer isn't "True."*

When the examiner held a green chip so it could be seen and said, "Either the chip in my hand is red or it is not yellow," only 15 percent of the preadolescent children correctly answered "true." Beginning at age 11, however, the number of children answering correctly increased, and at age 15, about half the answers given to these logical questions were correct.

A final type of logical thinking is evident in people's reasoning about social problems. In his examination of the development of this ability, Peel (1971) told the following story:

> Only brave pilots are allowed to fly over high mountains. This summer a fighter pilot flying over the Alps collided with an aerial cable railway, and cut a main cable causing some cars to fall to the glacier below. Several people were killed and many others had to spend the night suspended above the glacier. Was the pilot a careful airman? Why do you think so?

In one group of seventy-eight children of above-average intelligence, many of those between 9 and 11 years old gave irrelevant and inconsistent responses. Some said, "Yes, he was brave," or "No, he was a showoff." Most of the 12- and 13-year-olds made their judgments solely on the basis of the content of the passage—specifically, the collision with the cable—saying such things as, "No, because if he were careful he would not have cut the cable."

Among the older subjects, however, some of the 13-year-olds and almost all of the 14- and 15-year-olds gave imaginative answers, evoking the possibility of extenuating circumstances—bad weather, sudden loss of vision, a malfunction in the plane. They usually realized that they could not decide if the pilot had been careful until they knew more about the circumstances of the accident.

Using the same technique to study logical reasoning in other areas, Peel found similar results with regard to questions demanding historical reasoning ("Why were the stones of Stonehenge placed as they were?"); ecological judgment ("What causes and prevents soil erosion?"); or sociopolitical explanations ("Were the people of Italy to blame for the water damage to art masterpieces caused by the floods in Florence?"). In addressing such questions, the adolescent was likely to see events as dynamic and consisting of many interrelated factors, and was constantly thinking of alternative possibilities.

Not a Universal Stage

It takes time for these abilities to mature. In fact, not all adolescents or adults can follow a logical argument or reach the stage of formal operational thought as measured by Piaget's criteria. In her summary of the research, Edith Neimark (1975) found many studies showing that a sizable percentage of American adults are not able to reason abstractly, and there are many cultures where no one correctly answers Piaget's tests of formal operational thought.

Piaget (1972) himself acknowledges that society and education are crucial factors in enabling an individual to attain formal operational thought. He believes that the maturation of brain and body that occurs at puberty makes these intellectual achievements possible, but certainly not inevitable. Without experiences such as an education, or social interactions that stress science, math, or logic, adults still think like concrete operational children.

The fact that not all adults attain formal operational thought has led John Flavell (1977) to state that the difference between mature and childish thought is not that adults are always logical and children never are. Rather, it is that even when adults are not being logical, they recognize the concept of logic, whereas children do not, even when, in fact, they are being logical. According to Flavell, sometime during adolescence, people begin to understand that some statements are logical and some are not, and they can usually recognize a logical flaw or acknowledge the truth of a law of physics if someone demonstrates it. As at earlier stages of cognitive development, however, there is a difference between potential and performance. While many adolescents and adults have the cognitive competence to think logically, they do not always do so, especially when thinking about themselves.

Adolescent Egocentrism

In addition to having the ability to be logical and imaginative, and to see the hypothetical and the possible, most teenagers demonstrate another cognitive characteristic—adolescent egocentrism. Adolescents are long past the egocentrism of the preoperational thought typical of preschool children, who assume that everyone thinks the same way they themselves do, and that natural wonders such as snow and flowers are put on earth for children to enjoy. By adolescence, young people know quite well that others can have different opinions; and they also know that their personal existence is largely irrelevant to the forces of nature: they are fully aware, for instance, that it doesn't rain because you forgot your umbrella—even though they may curse the heavens instead of themselves.

Nevertheless, the particular limits of adolescent judgment and logic make young people susceptible to egocentrism of another type. Instead of believing that the physical world centers on them, adolescents believe that the psychological universe revolves around them; that is, that their unique thoughts are universally held and, at the same time, that they alone understand human experiences.

As David Elkind (1978) explains, adolescents fail

> to differentiate between the unique and the universal. A young woman who falls in love for the first time is enraptured with the experience, which is entirely new and thrilling. But she fails to differentiate between what is new and thrilling to herself and what is new and thrilling to

humankind. It is not surprising, therefore, that this young lady says to her mother, "But Mother, you don't know how it feels to be in love."

Elkind also explains that adolescents often create for themselves an imaginary audience, as they fantasize how others will react to their appearance and behavior. Although pubescent boys or girls know that other people are not usually thinking the same things about them as they themselves are thinking, they sometimes have trouble realizing that others are not thinking *something* about them.

For instance, adolescents are so preoccupied with their physical appearance, sometimes spending hours in front of a mirror, that they assume that everyone else judges the final result. Anticipation of a favorable judgment can cause teenagers to enter a crowded room with the air of regarding themselves as the most attractive and admired human beings alive. On the other hand, something as trivial as a pimple on the chin can make them wish that they could enter the room invisibly. It often takes several years before this egocentrism declines and the individual can walk into a crowded room without the look of one who thinks he or she owns the world or the fearfulness of one who imagines contempt in every gaze. Elkind adds, "Whenever the young adolescent is in public, he or she is—in his or her own mind—on stage playing before an interested critical audience. Some of the boorish behavior of young adolescents in public places has to be understood in [these] terms."

Figure 16.2 *Nearly all teenagers suffer chronic anxiety about their complexions, even if they don't actually suffer acne itself. At times their thinking is so egocentric that a single blemish is enough to make them want to go into hiding, as though the whole world were waiting to condemn them for a pimple.*

Fantasies and Fables

Egocentrism sometimes leads past the possible into the impossible (Elkind, 1974). One example is the foundling fantasy, in which young people imagine that they are the offspring, not of their actual parents, but of much wiser and more beautiful people who were forced to give them up in infancy. Many fix on any of their physical characteristics that their parents don't have and decide that adoption is the most plausible explanation for the discrepancy.

Another example is the personal fable, through which adolescents imagine their own lives as heroic, or even mythical. They see themselves destined for great fame and fortune—discovering the cure for cancer or authoring a masterpiece. Piaget describes the ambitions of one graduating class (a dozen pupils) in a small Swiss town.

> One of them, who has since become a shopkeeper, astonished his friends with his literary doctrines and wrote a novel in secret. Another, who has since become the director of an insurance company, was interested, among other things, in the future of the theater and showed some close friends the first scene of the first act of a tragedy—and then got no further. A third, taken up with philosophy, dedicated himself to no less a task than the reconciliation of science and religion. We do not even have to enumerate the social and political reformers found on both right and left. There were only two members of the class who did not reveal any astounding life plans. Both were more or less crushed under strong "superegos" of parental origin, and we do not know what their secret daydreams might have been. [Inhelder and Piaget, 1958]

Thus, adolescent thought processes are usually a mixture of the abilities to imagine many logical possibilities and to deny reality when it interferes with hopes and fantasies.

Moral Development

The development of formal operational thought is related to another important aspect of cognitive maturity: the development of moral reasoning. Once young people can imagine alternative solutions to various problems in science, or logic, or social studies, they should be able to apply the same types of mental processes to thinking about right and wrong.

Stages of Moral Development

In terms of Kohlberg's delineation of the stages of moral reasoning (see pages 442–443), adolescents who are capable of formal operational thought are also usually capable of thinking ethically at the level of stage 4 (recognizing that laws should be obeyed to maintain social order), stage 5 (recognizing that laws should reflect the needs of society), or stage 6 (recognizing that universal ethical principles must be obeyed). Virtually no one under age 10 attains these loftier heights of moral reasoning, but some adolescents between 13 and 16 years old do, as do a greater percentage of those older than 16 (Kohlberg, 1975; Kuhn et al., 1977).

At the postconventional, or autonomous, level of moral reasoning (stages 5 and 6), laws are no longer to be obeyed simply because they are laws, nor are social standards to be upheld simply because others expect them to be. Nor does the preconventional idea that individuals should look out for their own best interests hold. Thus, adolescents are much more likely than younger children to be capable of self-sacrificing, idealistic reasoning, and to refuse on moral grounds to uphold rules and procedures that many authority figures, such as parents, clergy, high-school principals, college deans, and public officials, readily accept.

A CLOSER LOOK   **Implications for Education**

As the adolescent mind matures, the education that schools, teachers, and parents provide changes as well. During elementary school, the science curriculum centers on practical, visible experiences, suited to the thought patterns of the concrete operational child. An important part of elementary-school science is caring for an animal, taking nature walks, or tracing the changes in trees from fall to spring. In junior high, simple experiments such as dissecting a frog, connecting an electric circuit, or turning water into steam become possible. Because of the young person's growing ability to think abstractly in high school and college, biology at these levels can include, among other things, explanation and discussion of the cell theory; physics, calculations about the possible movements of the atom; and chemistry, formulas as well as visible transformations.

A similar shift occurs in other areas of study. High-school English no longer need center on the rules of grammar and spelling and the mechanics of reading and writing. Instead, as imagination expands, creative writing, including the use of metaphor, irony, and sarcasm, becomes easier to understand, appreciate, and produce. In fact, sarcasm, which is beyond most elementary-school children, sometimes seems to be the adolescent's favorite mode of communication.

In the social sciences, history becomes the study not only of what was but also of what might have been, and current events becomes a matter of opinion as well as of fact. Anthropology is no longer merely an account of the strange customs of strange people, but is a study of the similarities and differences of all human societies, including our own. Psychology also becomes fascinating during adolescence, although many young people apply their new-found psychological wisdom to themselves and their families under the influence of adolescent egocentrism, sometimes deciding that they are abnormal and that their parents are to blame.

All these implications are relative, their application depending on the particular teacher, curriculum, and student. As Cowan (1978) points out, since a majority of high-school students have not fully reached formal operational thought, it would be a mistake to assume that hypothetical, logical instruction should entirely replace the use of concrete examples and personal experiences. Indeed, the interplay of the specific and the general, the individual and the universal, and the inductive and the deductive modes of thought is the heart of most academic, as well as personal, knowledge.

However, since adolescents are potentially, if not actually, formal operational thinkers, instruction that takes advantage of this fact is more challenging and motivating than instruction that does not.

Although psychology can be an exciting topic for adolescents, they sometimes get carried away with their insights, reading into themselves and their parents every psychological symptom they learn about.

Certainly, in some historical periods, adolescents who have reached this stage of moral reasoning are most likely to disobey social and legal conventions. In our lifetime, we have seen that the majority of freedom marchers, civil rights activists, and Vietnam war protesters were in late adolescence, and many of them argued that they were upholding principles that were more important than social customs or government decrees.

When Norma Haan and her colleagues (1968) studied students from the University of California, they found that, in support of the principle of civil liberty, 80 percent of those who had reached stage 6 of Kohlberg's moral reasoning had participated in the free-speech demonstrations that had become the focus of campus life. Of the students at stage 5, 50 percent had participated; and of the students

Figure 16.3 *At the postconventional level of moral reasoning, right is right by virtue neither of might nor of social convention. Young people who have reached this stage of moral awareness are often likely to question, and to try to change, what they consider to be the immoral or unjust values and practices of their elders.*

at the conventional level (stages 3 and 4), only 10 percent were active protesters. These researchers also found that a majority of those in the preconventional stage were activists in this protest, but their reasons were quite different from the principled arguments advanced by the stage-6 students: rather than fighting for universal principles, they were fighting for their personal freedom to do what they wanted.

Since all the students in this study had reached late adolescence and were attending one of the best universities in the country, it should be clear that one cannot predict from a person's age, education, or behavior what stage of moral reasoning that person has reached. In fact, in the view of another cognitive theorist, Elliot Turiel (1974), Kohlberg's hierarchy is too rigid to begin with, for it assumes that people move up the ladder of moral thinking as they become more experienced and more mature. In fact, according to Turiel, adolescent moral thinking moves from a state of equilibrium to disequilibrium, variously advancing and regressing, until finally it is able to take into account the relative merits of all approaches to moral decision-making. Turiel believes that at about age 12 or 13, adolescents reject conventional rules and laws made by authorities such as teachers and parents, only to replace them, at age 14 or 15, with acceptance of social conventions set by other people. At this stage, the young person tends to think one should go along with the group, although not necessarily along with the "authorities." Then, at about age 17 or 18, the rule of the group is questioned, and rejected. Finally, at age 18 and older, the young person is able to coordinate the demands of authority, the social group, and the individual.

An Alternative View

The merit of Kohlberg's stages has been questioned by several other psychologists, who argue, among other things, that they reflect Kohlberg's personal and cultural values more than a universal hierarchy (e.g., Sullivan, 1977; Trainer, 1977). Turiel's concepts have not been sufficiently tested to see how valid they are. However, almost all developmental psychologists agree that adolescence, especially late adolescence, is often marked by changing values and standards. Classroom moral debates and late-night bull sessions become lively and compelling, and ethical stands passionately taken one year might be reversed by new reasoning the next. Kohlberg, Turiel, and most other researchers in this field believe that the solutions that young people find to moral dilemmas, whether actual or hypothetical, depend not only on their cognitive maturity but also on the moral dialogues they are able to establish with others. This suggests that when parents and teachers are confronted with moral questions by adolescents, their best long-range strategy is to listen and debate, rather than slamming the door on open discussion or laying down the law.

Figure 16.4 *Parents who refuse to discuss morals and social values with their children are not only putting off a valuable form of communication with them, but are also depriving them, and possibly themselves, of the chance to gain a broader perspective on issues of social and personal importance.*

Two Moral Issues

Of the many areas in which adults in our society must make moral decisions, at least two of them, drug use and sexual behavior, encompass a wide range of options and opinions about right and wrong. Some adults use no drugs at all. Others frequently use "social" drugs, such as cigarettes, alcohol, marijuana, and sometimes use prescription drugs, to lose weight, elevate mood, or fight insomnia. Still others use such drugs as cocaine, heroin, and LSD, which are frowned on by the larger society but wholly accepted within some subcultures.

Great diversity is apparent in sexual behavior as well: autoeroticism, homosexuality, and bisexuality are paths chosen by some individuals, and accepted by many more, as are premarital and extramarital sexual relationships. With regard to most questions in these two areas, our society, on the whole, takes the stand that adults should make their own decisions, without specific prohibition or penalty from the government. (Even when it comes to illegal drugs, the pusher is punished much more severely than the user.)

However, this freedom of choice is not offered to our adolescents. Many parents and other adults believe that adolescents are too immature to handle moral decision-making, so even alcohol and cigarettes, and in most states, sexual intercourse, are illegal for young people under 16. Although, as we will see in the next chapter, the size of the "generation gap" has been exaggerated, on the questions of sex and drugs, adults and adolescents are likely to have divergent opinions (Sorensen, 1973).

Sexual Behavior

Most psychologists believe that the attitudes of today's adolescent toward sexuality are much healthier than those of previous generations. The decline of the double standard and the increase in sexual knowledge and understanding should make it probable that most of today's young people will not be faced with the mixed feelings about sexuality that pervaded our culture only two generations ago, when

> the man or woman who learned during childhood and adolescence that it was "wrong" to examine or stimulate his or her own genitals, that it was "even worse" to have any contact with those of another person, and, particularly, that attempts at heterosexual relations were immoral, is expected to reverse completely at least some of these attitudes on the wedding night or shortly thereafter. This expectation is difficult to fulfill. If the initial lessons have been well learned, the unlearning is bound to take a long time and may never be completed. [Ford and Beach, 1951]

However, the behavior of today's adolescents leads to two social problems that make many psychologists wonder if we are allowing and even encouraging our young people to have too much sexual experience before they are sufficiently mature to handle it.

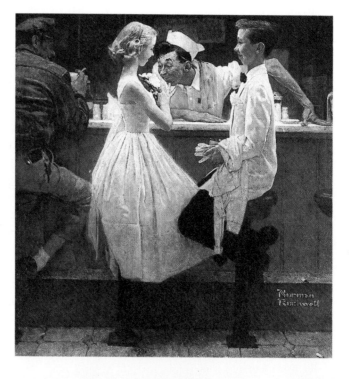

Figure 16.5 *Norman Rockwell's* Saturday Evening Post *cover "After the Prom," which appeared in 1957, reflects a still-popular image of the wholesome innocence of young love.*

Venereal Disease The first of these problems is venereal disease (VD), a name that actually covers several diseases, including syphilis and gonorrhea, that are spread by sexual contact. With the discovery of antibiotics, many physicians thought that the problem of VD could be cured once and for all. In fact, the frequency of venereal disease did decline during the 1950s, as infected people were cured with penicillin before they could spread the disease. However, in the past twenty years, the incidence of venereal disease has taken a marked upswing, especially among people under age 25, who now account for about half of all reported cases (Katchadourian, 1977).

Adolescent Pregnancy The second serious consequence of adolescent sexuality is pregnancy. As we saw in Chapter 3, the overall birth rate in the United States is declining. However, this decline is less rapid among teenagers. Indeed, girls under age 15 are the only age group today who are having more births than in any previous generation. Their birth rate in 1975—1 birth per 700 girls aged 10 to 14, or 13,000 babies in all—was double the 1966 rate for girls under 15 (Ventura, 1977). Girls under age 15 also comprise the only segment of the population in which the abortion rate exceeds the birth rate (U.S. Department of Health, Education, and Welfare, 1978). In addition, an increasing number of babies born to teenage mothers are essentially fatherless—the rate of illegitimate births increased 64 percent between 1966 and 1975, especially among mothers age 17 and younger (Ventura, 1977). In the case of babies born to married teenagers, chances are that pregnancy was the reason for the marriage.

Possible Explanations What is the reason for the high rate of these sexual problems during adolescence? At first, it might seem that the epidemics of venereal disease and teenage pregnancy are the simple result of increased sexual activity among teenagers. As we saw in Chapter 15, young people reach sexual maturity

Figure 16.6 *When Victor and Jeanette were, respectively, 12 and 13 years old, they became a couple. A year later they became parents-to-be. Every year in the United States, approximately 30,000 girls between the ages of 10 and 14 become pregnant, nearly half of them carrying the baby to term.*

sooner today than was true of earlier generations, so we might expect a rise in problems associated with increased sexual activity. But this is only part of the explanation, since the rate of venereal disease and unwanted pregnancy for sexually active adults is much lower than for adolescents.

Another explanation commonly offered is that teenagers are poorly informed about sexuality. However, this does not seem to be the case. As Schinke and his colleagues (1979) explain:

> Lack of accurate knowledge about human sexuality and lack of easy access to contraceptives also have been described as major causes of adolescent pregnancy. Accordingly, a number of programs in the late 1960s and early 1970s offered contraceptives and sex education to adolescents at little or no cost. Obtaining contraceptives without parental permission was legalized in several parts of the United States during this time, and some school systems began giving sex education classes. All these efforts reflect a straightforward assumption: given easy, low cost access to sex education and contraceptive services, young men and women will become responsible and self-regulating in their reproductive behavior, and the number of unanticipated adolescent pregnancies will drop.
>
> Programs based on this assumption have not had the intended effect. . . . access to free contraceptives has not prevented pregnancy.

Indeed, one of the most puzzling aspects surrounding teenage pregnancy is the degree to which adolescents fail to apply the facts of contraception that almost all of them have been exposed to. Zelnick and Kantner (1977) found that only one sexually active girl in four used contraceptives regularly, and Sorensen (1973) reports that only half of his nonvirgin adolescents regularly used birth control. Those who did try to prevent pregnancy most often used coitus interruptus, in which the boy withdraws his penis before ejaculation (not a very reliable method) or the pill (very effective, but not the safest for long-term use). For the most part, they did not seem to understand the pros and cons of various methods. More significant, however, is the fact that teenagers in general, and especially those who use no form of contraception, do not seem to take the possibility of pregnancy seriously. To understand this phenomenon, as well as part of the reason for the increase in venereal disease, we must apply what we know about adolescent cognition.

As Flavell (1977) explained, since many young adolescents have difficulty understanding logical hypothetical arguments, the questions "What if your partner has VD?" or "What if you become pregnant?" are not answered in rational, personal ways that would lead the young man to use a condom, or the young woman to take effective precautions, or both of them to avoid sexual intercourse until they were ready to deal with the consequences.

Adolescent egocentrism also may play a role, for many young people believe the personal fable that they cannot be touched by ills that beset others. Many sexually active young people do not really believe that pregnancy could result from *their* love-making. For instance, about a third of all the teenagers Sorensen (1973) interviewed thought that even if a girl did not take precautions, she would not get pregnant unless she really wanted to. (Interestingly enough, more nonvirgins than virgins believed this myth.) Another study found similar results, with one teenager

Figure 16.7 *Finding that many boys believe birth control is the exclusive concern of women and that an unintended pregnancy is a girl's responsibility, Planned Parenthood of Central Ohio began a campaign to change young males' attitudes. Prior to the campaign, the Planned Parenthood Hotline was averaging between 200 and 300 calls a month, only about 10 or so of them from boys. After a year of public service promotions that included TV spots like the one shown here, the number of calls had risen to about 800 a month, approximately 100 of them from boys.*

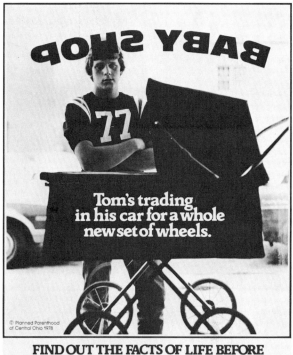

FIND OUT THE FACTS OF LIFE BEFORE
EXPERIENCE BECOMES THE WORST TEACHER

naively saying, "I don't think it [pregnancy] could happen to me. I've been having sex for two years. So far it hasn't" (Lindemann, 1974).

Another sign of cognitive immaturity, noted by Furstenberg (1976), is that because many young people like to think of sex as emotional and spontaneous, they feel it is not something that should be prepared for. Furstenberg also found the idea that "good girls don't" was still alive to the extent that "good" girls were not supposed to be sexually active unless the passion of the moment carried them away. Forethought, such as carrying a diaphragm, or even worse, taking a pill daily, meant that a girl had sex on her mind even when she was not involved in lovemaking, and therefore was "bad."

Once pregnancy is a fact, cognitive immaturity can cause additional problems. For one thing, many teenagers who have reason to think that they might be pregnant refuse to believe that they are, and put off having a pregnancy test. Consequently, many adolescents who ultimately decide to abort the pregnancy do not reach this decision until after the eighth week of pregnancy, thereby necessitating the use of abortion methods that have a higher incidence of physical complications.

For those teenagers who decide to carry the pregnancy to term, the rate of complications is about twice as high as for women between the ages of 25 and 29. Among these complications are preeclampsia (see page 124), long labor, prematurity, and still-birth. Many of these complications can be prevented if the young person obtains good prenatal care. Once again, however, adolescent girls, due partly to their cognitive immaturity, are less likely than older women to seek prenatal care. For instance, only 40 percent of pregnant 15-year-olds see a physician during the critical first three months of pregnancy, compared to 81 percent of the pregnant women between 25 and 29 years old. In fact, out of every 100 pregnant 15-year-olds, 5 give birth without ever having seen a doctor or nurse during the entire nine months of pregnancy (Ventura, 1977).

Complicating the frequent cognitive immaturity of adolescents is the fact that, as we have seen, adults themselves do not always reason at the formal operational level. Their failure to do so during discussions about sex can certainly be of no aid to their children's understanding. Furstenberg, for example, found that most mothers gave their daughters general rules about sexual behavior, such as "Keep your pants on," or "Don't do anything foolish," and most were surprised and shocked when their daughters later announced that they were pregnant. Sorensen found that 58 percent of the nonvirgin girls did not use birth-control pills because they were afraid their parents might find out. Many studies have found that while adolescents would prefer to obtain information about sex from their parents, most of them actually get it from peers (Thornburg, 1975; Dickinson, 1978).

"Damn it, Constance, I am not holding anything back! That happens to be all I know about sex."
Drawing by William Hamilton; © 1975 The New Yorker, Inc.

In their efforts to help adolescents find solutions to at least some of the sexual problems they face, parents and other adults should keep in mind a simple fact from research such as Piaget's and Kohlberg's: people who have the opportunity to discuss logical ideas and moral values are better able to understand complicated ideas and make mature decisions. If adults want adolescents to make responsible, mature judgments about sexuality, they must do much more than provide facts. They must encourage an atmosphere of open, honest discussion that will help teenagers to think carefully about their personal values, their responsibilities, and their long-term plans.

Adolescent Drug Use

What are the implications of adolescent cognitive development for the issue of adolescent drug use? Is a person who thinks in the egocentric way typical of adolescence sufficiently mature to decide whether to use drugs, or which drugs to use? These are not hypothetical questions, for adolescents are, in general, using more drugs at younger ages than in previous generations (National Commission on Marijuana and Drug Use, 1973; Johnston and Bachman, 1975). As in previous decades, the drug most commonly used is alcohol, with about half of all junior-high-school students and three-fourths of all high-school students reporting that they have used it. Tobacco is a close second, and marijuana is third, with about 40

Figure 16.8 *Among teen-agers, the most frequently used drug is alcohol, with current estimates holding that three out of four high-school seniors drink alcohol at least occasionally, and that one out of four of these has a drinking problem. Making decisions about the use of marijuana is compli-cated by vastly inconsistent research findings. Many studies have found nothing harmful about marijuana; others claim that marijuana causes, among other things, chromosome damage and lower resistance to infec-tion, and that a single joint causes as much lung dam-age as a pack of cigarettes.*

percent of high-school students reporting that they have tried it. The next most commonly used drugs are the pills—amphetamines, barbiturates, and tranquiliz-ers. Finally, less than 10 percent of high-school students have used cocaine, LSD, or other narcotics.

As one would expect, the older the adolescent, the more likely he or she is to have used one or more of these drugs. For instance, a survey of marijuana use by people of all ages found that 6 percent of those between the ages of 12 and 13, 22 percent of those between 14 and 15, 39 percent of those between 16 and 17, and 53 percent of those between 18 and 24 had used marijuana (Abelson and Atkinson, 1975). After age 25, use became less common, with only 29 percent of those between 26 and 34, 7 percent of those between 35 and 49, and 2 percent of those aged 50 and older reporting that they had ever smoked marijuana. This survey was done in 1974. Obviously, a survey today would report a larger percentage of adults as having tried marijuana, because the young people who were in late adolescence and early adulthood in 1974 are adults now. However, these results also suggest that while most young people today have tried marijuana by their early twenties, most of their parents have not, a fact that leads some young people to believe that adults overes-timate the harm, and underestimate the benefits, of the drug.

Of course, each community has different rates of drug use among adolescents. In a comparison of alcohol consumption among teenagers, Margaret Bacon and Mary Brush Jones (1968) found great variety from place to place in the number of people who had ever used alcohol, from a low of 44 percent of the young people of rural Kansas to a high of 86 percent of the young people in a wealthy New York suburb. According to a more recent survey in a Midwestern farming community, 47 percent of the students from junior and senior high schools had never tried alcohol, and 80 percent had never tried marijuana (Seffrin and Seehafer, 1976a).

Pros and Cons   However, while these facts about the incidence of drug use among teenagers are clear, the interpretation of them is not. Psychologists, like the public, differ in their attitudes toward drug use: some believe moderate drug use is a useful way to cope with the stresses of modern life; others wish our society were drug-free.

On the one hand, psychologists are aware of the many reasons adolescents use drugs: they use them to relax and cope with tension, especially on social occasions; they use them to appear more adult, especially when they are with their peers; and they use them to rebel against a society that prohibits their use among adolescents while condoning their use among adults. All of these uses are understandable, and to some psychologists, permissible, as long as the drugs are not overused (Segal, 1977; Rinder, 1978).

On the other hand, many psychologists agree that most adolescents are not yet wise enough to assess the possible long-range consequences of drug use. As Turiel (1974) points out, at some periods of adolescence, moral reasoning focuses more on rejection of the standards set by authority than on the development of one's own positive values. Certainly in this respect, then, teenagers would not seem mature enough to experiment with drugs, much less to become daily users.

The picture is further complicated by conflicting research. Several studies have shown no negative long-term effects from moderate use of marijuana (Hochman and Brill, 1973), and according to some research, moderate marijuana use among college students correlates with higher grades (Herrman et al., 1976). At the same time, many studies show a correlation between adolescent use of marijuana and/or alcohol and a lack of ambition, poor attitudes toward school, and social problems with parents and friends (e.g., Tec, 1972; Albas et al., 1978; Brunswick, 1977). Indeed, one investigator, Mark Hochhauser (1978), suggests that there may be a link between the declining scores over the last decade on the Scholastic Aptitude Test (the SAT, taken by high-school students who want to enter college) and the steady increase in legal and illegal drug use among high-school students. Hochhauser believes that these drugs may not only impede the development of cognitive processes and of study habits but that they may also impair the physiological maturation of the young person's brain.

We also know that the adolescent's use of one drug makes it more likely that he or she will use another drug, a chain that begins with beer or cigarettes and may end with narcotics. This is not to say that the scare tactics used by some in the 1960s were correct—few marijuana users become heroin addicts. However, there is a correlation between the number of drugs an adolescent uses, the frequency of use, and the probable future use. For instance, one study of high-school students found that those who do not drink alcohol rarely use any other drugs, and that those who smoke marijuana usually also drink alcohol, and many use amphetamines and barbiturates as well (Seffrin and Seehafer, 1976b). These findings imply that it is a mistake for adults to assume that the use of certain drugs is harmless exploration and experimentation during adolescence, while the use of others is taboo.

Whichever side one takes about the long-term consequences of adolescent experimentation with drugs, there is an undeniable short-term hazard with regard to alcohol and marijuana: the combination of either with driving, especially if the young person in question is blindly given to two teenage credos born of cognitive immaturity—"I can deal with it" and "It can't happen to me." In spite of whatever feelings of increased competence a teenager has when under the influence, there is no question that alcohol and marijuana impair concentration and slow down reaction time. Consider for a moment the following statistics: While only 8 percent of the nation's licensed drivers are under age 20, they are responsible for 18 percent of the fatal accidents, causing an estimated 9000 deaths each year. Authorities believe that drug use is implicated in at least half of these accidents.

The Parents' Role   For parents who are convinced that adolescents are too immature to use any drugs and who wonder what effect their feelings on this matter will
have on their teenage children, there is some comfort. Research studies indicate
that although peer use of drugs is a significant influence on the adolescent (Kandel,
1974), young people who reported close, warm relationships with their parents
were more likely to abstain from drug use (Babst, 1978; Mercer et al., 1978). There
are also some research findings that may or may not be comforting: according to a
number of studies, the adolescent's behavior with regard to drugs is significantly
influenced by the practices of the parents, with a strong correlation between
parents' use of drugs (tobacco, alcohol, and prescription psychoactive drugs) and
the young person's (primarily tobacco, alcohol, and marijuana) (Kandel, 1974;
Feldman and Rosenkrantz, 1977).

**The Adolescent
Philosopher**

If asked what the major preoccupation of adolescents is, most people would probably say "Sex!" But this answer would be, at best, only a partial truth, for the thing
that actually preoccupies teenagers most is thinking—often about sex, of course,
but also about their appearance and personality, their strengths and weaknesses,
their relationships with parents and peers, and, in later adolescence, about politics, social issues, personal morals, and, ultimately, about their own place in the
world. The transition from the reality-bound person of middle childhood, who lives
primarily in the present and still proceeds largely by trial and error, to the adolescent who can mentally project himself or herself into various situations, imagining
and testing alternative modes of behavior, is the result of the increasing maturation of the cognitive processes. This development, as impressive as it is, is
nevertheless inevitably marked by fluctuations, inconsistencies, and reversals. As
we will see in the next chapter, the outcome of the adolescent's thought processes,
as well as the impact of physical development and the resolution of the identity
crisis, depends a great deal on the influence of the adolescent's particular society,
parents, and friends.

Figure 16.9 *One of the arguments for giving 18-year-
olds the vote is that they are
cognitively mature enough
to make intelligent decisions
at the polls. As we have seen
earlier with regard to cognitive development, readiness
does not necessarily mean
accomplishment.*

SUMMARY

Formal Operational Thought

1. During adolescence, young people become better able to speculate, hypothesize, and fantasize, emphasizing possibility more than reality. Unlike the younger child whose thought is tied to concrete operations, adolescents can build formal systems and general theories that transcend, and sometimes ignore, practical experience. Their reasoning is formal and abstract, rather than empirical and concrete.

2. The ability to think logically is the hallmark of formal operational thought. Between the ages of 12 and 15, many young people become able to articulate the laws of physics when they are given Piagetian tests of formal operational thought. They are also much more able to follow logical arguments and reason about social problems.

3. Many adolescents and adults never attain formal operational thinking, as measured by Piaget's tests. However, according to Flavell, unlike children, they are able to understand general laws and logical arguments when presented with them.

Adolescent Egocentrism

4. Another characteristic of adolescent thought is a particular form of egocentrism that leads young people to overestimate their significance to others. This characteristic is sometimes expressed in a personal fable about the grand and glorious deeds they will perform in adulthood.

Moral Development

5. Moral reasoning also develops during adolescence, for the young person who can grasp general laws of physics or principles of logic is more likely to articulate moral laws and ethical principles. There is a correlation between stage of cognitive development as defined by Piaget and stage of moral development as defined by Kohlberg.

6. Most adolescents question traditional customs and laws, although only a minority develop a set of universal moral principles, reaching the last of Kohlberg's six stages.

Two Moral Issues

7. However, cognitive immaturity makes it difficult for adolescents to arrive at rational decisions about sexuality and drug use. Adolescents who believe that they are above many of the normal problems that humans experience may also believe that they will never be confronted with pregnancy, even when they don't take precautions against it, or that they cannot become addicts even though they use addictive drugs.

8. About a million teenagers in the United States become pregnant each year, and the birth rate among girls younger than 15 doubled between 1965 and 1975. Compared to older women, pregnant teenagers have a higher rate of physical complications, in part because their cognitive immaturity makes it hard for them to face reality and seek prenatal care.

9. Neither traditional sex education nor freely available contraception has been successful in curbing adolescent pregnancy. The best solution seems to be to help the adolescent reason more maturely about sexual behavior.

10. An increasing number of adolescents are using drugs, at younger ages, than ever before. This is understandable, because drugs are widely available and they alleviate some of the stresses of adolescence. On the other hand, drug use is correlated with many problems.

KEY QUESTIONS

What are some of the tests that determine whether or not a person has attained formal operational thought?

According to Flavell, what are the differences between mature and childish thought?

What stages of moral development are reached during adolescence?

How does Turiel describe the adolescent's moral reasoning?

What special problems of pregnancy are more likely to occur during adolescence than during adulthood?

What explanation might there be for the epidemics of veneral disease and teenage pregnancy?

What is the incidence of drug use among adolescents?

What arguments are there for and against drug use by teenagers?

KEY TERMS

formal operational thought	foundling fantasy
adolescent egocentrism	personal fable
imaginary audience	venereal disease (VD)

RECOMMENDED READINGS

Guest, Judith. *Ordinary people.* New York: Viking Press, 1976.

This novel tells of a young man's reaction to his older brother's accidental death. The hero attempts suicide, tries to talk to his parents, begins to develop relationships with girls, consults a psychiatrist. The power of the book is that there is no sudden event that makes everything better, just the gradual maturation of the hero as he tries to understand and cope with ordinary day-to-day living.

Thomas, Piri. *Down these mean streets.* New York: Knopf, 1967.

Another adolescent's story of the search for the purpose of life, this time that of a young man growing up in the inner-city ghetto. Thomas writes of his attempt to understand what it means to be a dark-skinned Puerto Rican in a white Anglo culture. Drugs, despair, crime, and prison all impede his positive identity formation.

Adolescence: Psychosocial Development

Now watch what you say or they'll be calling you a
radical, liberal, fanatical, criminal.
Won't you sign up your name, we'd like to feel you're
acceptable, respectable, presentable, a vegetable!

At night, when all the world's asleep,
the questions run too deep
for such a simple man.
Won't you please, please tell me what we've learned
I know it sounds absurd
but please tell me who I am.

Supertramp
"The Logical Song"

True or False?   Adolescents tend to identify more with members of their own generation than with members of their own race, sex, or religion.

The conviction of many adolescents that they understand life better than adults do seems to remain constant from one generation to the next.

The main function of the adolescent's peer group is to provide support in the struggle to gain independence from one's parents.

Nearly half of all those arrested for serious crimes in the United States are eighteen years old or younger.

The fact that the rate of adolescent suicide is half that of all adult age groups lends support for the idea that the pressures of adolescence are much less keenly felt than those of adulthood.

The physical changes of puberty begin the process of adolescence by transforming the child's body into an adult's, and the cognitive developments described in the preceding chapter enable the young person to think logically and imaginatively in planning for the future. However, it is psychosocial development, particularly the resolution of the identity crisis, that allows the young person to attain adult status and maturity.

Identity

In the 1940s, Erikson became absorbed with the question of identity as a basic human need. As he put it, "Especially in times of change in the structure of society, identity becomes as important as food, security, and sexual satisfaction" (quoted in Coles, 1970). In the last three decades, Erikson has written extensively about the search for identity as the primary task, and crisis, of adolescence, when the young person tries to integrate a quest for "a conscious sense of individual uniqueness," with "an unconscious striving for a continuity of experience, . . . and a solidarity with a group's ideals" (Erikson, 1968).

In other words, the young person wants to establish and know himself or herself as a specific individual, to maintain some connection with the meaningful elements of the past, and to accept the values of a group. In the process of "finding themselves," adolescents must establish a sexual, moral, political, and vocational identity that is relatively stable, consistent, and mature. This identity ushers in adulthood, as it bridges the gap between the experiences of childhood and the personal goals, values, and decisions that permit each young person to take his or her place in society (Erikson, 1975).

Many other psychologists, following Erikson's lead, have found the concept of identity a useful and insightful way to understand adolescent psychosocial development. Through a combination of theory, clinical case studies, and scientific research, they have determined that the precise course of the identity crisis depends partly on the young person's society, peer groups, and family. Ideally, adolescents achieve their new identity through "selective repudiation and mutual assimilation of childhood identifications" (Erikson, 1968). Thus, in optimal circumstances, the adolescent abandons some of the values and goals set by parents and society, while accepting others.

However, for some young people, this process is too difficult, with the result that foreclosure, or premature identity formation, occurs. In this case, the adolescent accepts earlier roles and parental values wholesale, never exploring alternatives or truly forging a unique personal identity. A typical example might be the young man who from childhood has thought he wanted to, or perhaps was pressured into wanting to, follow in his father's footsteps as a doctor—only to discover in his third year of medical school that what he really wants to be is a poet.

Figure 17.1 *Psychological inertia is the chief characteristic of what Erikson called identity confusion. In this state, adolescents may think that they ought to make some move forward in their lives, but are without the concrete motivation to actually do so.*

Other young people experience identity confusion (also called *identity diffusion*) when they have few commitments to goals or values—whether those of parents, peers, or the larger society—and are apathetic about finding an identity. These young people have difficulty meeting the usual demands of adolescence, such as completing school assignments, making friends, and thinking about the future. As one young man said:

> I should be getting out but I don't have the drive. Not motivated I guess. I want to move [slang for being more involved and active] too, you know. It kinda motivates me a little bit to see them [peers] going . . . I want to go too. It might motivate me for a little while. I do care but I just haven't got on it. [Quoted in Gottlieb, 1975]

Some adolescents find that the roles their parents and society expect them to fill are impossible or unappealing. However, they are unable to find alternative roles that are truly their own. Instead they take on a negative identity, that is, the opposite of the one they are expected to adopt. Erikson (1968) cites two cases that illustrate this:

In both cases the parents' weaknesses and unexpressed wishes are recognized by the child with catastrophic clarity. The [Caucasian] daughter of a man of brilliant showmanship ran away from college and was arrested as a prostitute in the Negro quarter of a southern city, while the daughter of an influential southern Negro preacher was found among narcotic addicts in Chicago. In such cases it is of utmost importance to recognize the mockery and vindictive pretense in such role playing, for the white girl had not really prostituted herself, and the colored girl had not really become an addict—yet.

Finally, instead of finding a mature identity, some young people seem to declare a moratorium, a kind of time-out during which they experiment with alternative identities without trying to settle on any one. In a society such as ours, where the number of possible roles seems infinite, Erikson believes that prolonging the final resolution of the identity crisis is often constructive. However, a moratorium becomes destructive when it lasts so long that the person reaches the chronological period of young adulthood, or even middle age, without having made adult commitments, such as choosing an ideology, a life style, a vocation, or a spouse.

Which of the many paths an individual takes toward resolving the identity crisis depends, in large part, on society, family, and friends, and so we will first examine the impact of each of these forces.

The Wider Society

Societies provide an avenue to finding an identity primarily in two ways: by providing values that have stood the test of time and that continue to serve their function, and by providing social structures or customs that ease the transition from childhood to adulthood. Whether these factors make the search for identity easy or difficult depends primarily on how much agreement there is on basic values among members of the society, and on how much social change a given individual is witness to.

In a culture where virtually everyone holds the same religious, moral, political, and sexual values, and social change is slight, identity is easy to achieve. The young person simply accepts the only values and roles that he or she has ever known.

Few contemporary societies meet these conditions, for modern communication and transportation make it likely that each young person will be exposed to dozens of conflicting values, and under the impact of modern technology and science, each generation will see social changes occur at an increasing rate (Toffler, 1970).

However, some simpler cultures, especially in earlier times, met these conditions. In Samoa, as Margaret Mead (1961; originally published in 1928) described it, the transition from childhood to adulthood was peaceful and gradual: the adolescent girl differed from her prepubescent sister only physically, and from older girls, not at all. Among all three groups, there were virtually no role differences to be noted.

Mead believed this easy adolescence was made possible partly because family ties were not strong, so there were no real bonds to be broken between adolescents and their parents. In addition, the entire community agreed on basic values, among them, that sex, both in and out of marriage, is "a natural, pleasurable thing."

In many other non-Western societies, family ties were stronger, and the tasks demanded of adults were quite different from those demanded of children, so these cultures developed rites of passage, or special initiation ceremonies to ease the transition from dependence on parents to adult independence.

Often these initiation ceremonies were both dramatic and painful, involving tests of bravery and strength, as well as separation from family and from members of the opposite sex. The young people learned religious rituals and social codes that only adults knew, and emerged from the process with a new status, new responsibilities, and, often, a new name.

Male and Female Initiation Rites

Anthropologists have found that dramatic male initiation rites are more common than female ones, and that cultures which emphasize female rites usually accord women more status and respect than cultures that do not (Brown, 1963). Other interesting male-female differences appear in rites of passage generally: boys are more often initiated together, when there are enough pubescent males to comprise an initiation group, while girls are usually initiated individually, at menarche. In addition, male initiation rites are usually more painful, often involving circumcision (cutting away the foreskin of the penis) and facial scarring. Although some female initiation rites include clitorectomy (excision of the clitoris) and scarring, they are much rarer than comparable male rites.

The goal of the male initiation rite is to make the boy a member of the larger adult male community. Female initiation rites are usually intended to prepare the young woman for the more personal experiences of courtship, marriage, and running a household. These differences are shown in the following two examples.

Painful initiation rites such as this circumcision ritual among Australian aborigines seem repugnant to most Westerners. Yet they serve a very useful function in the cultures where they are practiced, facilitating a sudden transition from childhood to adulthood.

Traditionally, at about age 15, Kikuyu boys in Kenya were circumcised, adopted by ritual parents, and anointed with a special earth. Separated from the other members of their tribe for eight days, they sang, danced, ate special foods, and learned to be strong warriors. At the end of this period, they rejoined the tribe as warriors, a role that was theirs for several years, until they married (Kenyatta, 1965; Herzog, 1970, cited in Brown, 1975).

An example of an initiation rite for girls comes from Surinam, in South America (Kloos, 1969). When a Maroni river Carib girl first menstruates, she is confined to a house for eight days so that the spirits of the river and the forest will not be offended by her bleeding and kill her. She is dressed in old clothes and must avoid eating most foods. At the end of her seclusion, she is bathed by an elderly couple known to be hard-working and industrious. After her bath, a tuft of burning cotten is placed in her hands. To avoid being burned, she must move it quickly back and forth from one hand to the other, signifying to herself that she must always keep her hands busy. Then she must put her hands into a bowl of large, biting ants, again to remind herself to work hard, as the ants do. Finally, she is given jewelry and special clothes, and the village arrives to dance, sing, and celebrate her new status.

Undoubtedly, neither of these examples strikes the modern reader as pleasant. However, anthropologists and psychologists generally agree that such vivid and memorable puberty rites allowed young people to attain adult status without the identity confusion that many young people now experience. Modern cultural changes in most societies practicing these intense rites have resulted in their modification. For instance, the contemporary Kikuyu boy is circumcised in a clinic under local anesthesia and no longer emerges from the initiation rite with all the responsibilities of a man. He is likely to feel more self-confident and to be allowed to stay out later, but he is still a student living with his parents as he did before the ceremony. Such changes in initiation rites are in keeping with the fact that in few societies today do young men become warriors or do young women go directly from menarche to marriage.

Our own society offers dozens of rites of passages (usually much milder than the foregoing) that signal a new status and help young people to establish an identity (Brown, 1975). Some are religious, such as the Catholic confirmation, the Jewish Bar Mitzvah and Bat Mitzvah, the Baptist baptism; some are social, such as debutante or sweet-sixteen parties; some confer legal sanction, such as voting, or getting a driver's license; and some are frowned upon, such as the initiation rites practiced by some street gangs, or, at the other end of the socioeconomic spectrum, the hazing that still goes on in some college fraternities. For many people, high-school graduation, with the formal diploma and ceremony, as well as the dancing, driving, and drinking until dawn, is also a rite of passage.

One form of noninstitutionalized initiation that sometimes performs certain of the functions of the puberty rites in simple societies is the first experience with sexual intercourse, according to a study of 625 teenagers, aged 16 to 19 (Hass, 1979). Of the 44 percent who had had intercourse, many felt that losing their virginity had made them more mature. As one boy put it, "I felt I'd never be the same. I had taken a step on my way to manhood." Said one girl, "I felt older, more mature too, and able to understand more about guys and their attitudes and behavior."

Figure 17.2 *College is one of the major institutions for providing a moratorium on career and marriage choices. In some cases, it also provides a moratorium on growing up.*

Another way our society eases the quest for identity is by discouraging identity foreclosure through institutionalized moratoriums on identity formation. The most obvious example is college, which usually requires young people to sample a variety of academic areas before concentrating in any one and forestalls pressure from parents and peers to choose a career and mate. A less obvious institution that performs a similar function for many young people is the military. A volunteer army that recruits women as well as men provides a way for many young people to travel, train, and test themselves while delaying lifetime commitments. Finally, a culture such as ours, which discourages early marriages, makes identity foreclosure less likely, especially for girls. The average age of marriage for young people in the United States is 21.1 for women and 23.5 for men, a year older than it was twenty years ago, despite the fact that the average age at puberty and the age of first sexual experience have declined.

Figure 17.3 *The question posed by this billboard often produces a good deal of anxiety in those young people who feel unprepared to make career decisions at the age of 18. For them, the moratorium of military service may, during peacetime at least, be a happy solution, providing travel, training, and pay while committing them to nothing more than a temporary career.*

Identity and Social Crisis   At various times, entire nations have seemed to undergo an identity crisis when their values came to appear useless or even destructive. Erikson (1968) believes that Germany experienced such a crisis after World War I, when ignominious defeat and severe economic depression made many Germans question what it meant to be German. For a generation, various groups arrived at divergent answers, with both right-wing and left-wing radicals gaining increased support. For many Germans, the national identity crisis was resolved when Hitler promulgated a series of myths that told the German people who they were: in short, the master race, destined to rule the world once they had rid themselves of their enemies. Young people were especially likely to join the Nazi party, because finding an identity was particularly important for them. As Nazi

Figure 17.4 *These photos offer an unsettling illustration of what Erikson meant by national identity. Hitler's Youth, for boys from 10 to 18, combined a fanatic emphasis on the collective over the individual with the ego-inflating devices of paramilitary uniform, drills, and codes of behavior to create the largest organization for youth the Western world has ever known. In 1932 the membership was 100,000, two years later, it was 3.5 million, and by the beginning of World War II it included nearly every adolescent German male. The equivalent organization for girls was the German Girls League of Faith and Beauty, which promoted physical culture, health instruction, and domestic sciences.*

youth, they knew who they were, what they believed, and how to behave. Meetings, parades, demonstrations, and finally war helped clarify and solidify their identity.

As Erikson (1968) points out, young people are usually the most vulnerable to the totalitarian message, especially when it claims to build on traditional values while repudiating current social considerations. From the revolution of 1917 in Russia to the revolution of 1979 in Iran, this insight seems borne out.

Contemporary North America

Between the extremes of peaceful Samoa and the turbulent Germany of the 1920s, where should we place North America in the last half of the twentieth century? Does our society make identity easy or difficult to attain? To some extent, the answer to these questions depends on the young person's subculture. For instance, Native American and French-Canadian young people today must find their political and personal identity in a period of conflicting beliefs among their elders and marked social change in their communities. Another important fact to keep in mind in analyzing our society is that social circumstances change from year to year and place to place, which means that the actual path of identity formation depends partly on when and where the young person reaches maturity. In general, finding an identity was particularly difficult for North Americans who reached puberty in the 1960s, much harder than it was for earlier and later generations. Sometimes this historical accident had long-lasting consequences for the individuals involved.

Looking back over the past three decades of American history, John Conger (1976) remarks:

> An adolescent growing up in the 1950s or probably even in 1975, as compared to an adolescent facing all the conflicting pressure and polarizations of the turbulent decade of the 1960s, inevitably faced a simpler, less confusing, and less conflict ridden task of personal and social identity formation. Many of the adolescents of the 1960s, who now as young adults find themselves struggling outside the social order as drug users, defeated dropouts, or armed revolutionaries on the run, would have found other alternatives had they not grown up in the middle and late 1960s in explosive, unstable, polarized communities.

Surveys show that young people in the 1970s were more willing to accept the values of society than were their counterparts in the 1960s (Yankelovich, 1974). For instance, 60 percent of college-age young people anticipate "no difficulty in accepting the kind of life society has to offer." A large majority value democracy, education, and family life, and most expect to have a job they enjoy, a spouse they love, and children they bear and raise with pride. All available research shows that younger adolescents are even more traditional in their values and expectations than college-age youth.

There are many possible explanations for the relative satisfaction of young people in the 1970s with their present and prospective lives. For one thing, the political climate was more stable. In the 1960s, President Kennedy, Martin Luther King, Jr., and Senator Robert Kennedy were assassinated, and the war in Vietnam escalated; in the 1970s, Nixon was forced out of office and the war ended. Another reason that the number of political, social, and sexual rebels was smaller in the 1970s was that many of the causes and values that were revolutionary in earlier years had been adopted by a majority.

This is most clear in sexual values (Conger, 1976). The sexual revolution of the 1960s precipitated several changes in attitudes and behavior, including a decline of the double standard, the legalization of abortion, and an increase in premarital intercourse. Surveys show that young people in the 1970s generally accepted the sexual revolution in principle, and many of them accepted it in practice as well. For instance, Sorensen (1973), in his national sampling of Americans between ages 13 and 19, found that only 25 percent believed that sex is immoral except between married couples. He also found that 37 percent of the youths between 13 and 15 years old, and 64 percent of those between 16 and 19 years old, had experienced sexual intercourse.

Figure 17.5 *After a decade of adolescents' questioning many of the values of the "American way of life," the 1970s showed a trend back toward more traditional views—except with regard to sexuality. At mid-decade, three-fourths of the nation's youth felt that there was nothing immoral about premarital intercourse.*

In a review of the literature, Roy Hopkins (1977) found that the number of teenagers experiencing sexual intercourse has risen with each generation since the 1930s, with the largest increase, especially among girls, occurring between 1965 and 1970. This means that, compared with the adolescents of earlier generations, young people reaching puberty during the 1980s are much more likely to find that the sexual attitudes and experiences of their older siblings, their younger teachers, and, for many, their parents, are not too different from their own. This makes the development of sexual identity much easier for them than it was for young people whose sexual values were radically different from those of their elders.

Support for the young person who does not want to become sexually active is also available. Studies have shown that young people whose families uphold traditional sexual values, and who are active members of their churches, are much more likely to uphold traditional sexual values themselves.

The fact that the search for identity has in certain ways been easier for adolescents in the 1970s than in other recent times is not to be taken as a sign that achieving identity in our society is a simple thing. Indeed, vocational identity, one of the most complex adult identities, is becoming increasingly difficult to establish, as we will see at the end of this chapter. In addition, such problems as drugs, delinquency, and teenage pregnancy often lead to identity confusion, negative identity, or foreclosure. Even sexual identity is not necessarily easy, because the young person must choose between such opposites as heterosexuality and homosexuality, virginity and promiscuity, with many stages in between. The variety of choices is shown by Sorensen, who found that 22 percent of his sample were sexually inexperienced, 17 percent were sexual beginners, 21 percent were sexual monogamists (that is, they had a steady sexual relationship with one person), 15 percent were sexual adventurers, 12 percent were sexually inactive nonvirgins (nonvirgins who had not engaged in sexual intercourse for more than one year), and 13 percent could not be categorized. About 17 percent of the boys between the ages of 16 and 19, and 6 percent of the girls of the same age, had had homosexual experiences. Indeed, other research suggests that some homosexual experience, especially mutual masturbation, is common in early adolescence. As society permits a greater range of sexual choices, sexual experimentation becomes easier, but arriving at final sexual identity may be correspondingly more complex.

Friends and Family

Given the diversity of paths toward identity available in our society, whether a particular young person will be able to delay identity formation until he or she is ready to make mature decisions, or whether identity will be premature or confused, depends a great deal on family and friends.

Peer Groups

Certainly there is no doubt that other young people are an important influence on adolescents today, for they are the main source of information about sex (Dickinson, 1978) and the chief encouragers of drug use (Kandel, 1974). They also serve as a

Figure 17.6 *"Best friends" are probably more important during adolescence than at any other time. Having a trusted contemporary to confide in and reveal one's "true" self to can be very important to the process of gaining a sense of identity.*

support group for the young person who is trying to abandon childish modes of behavior, including dependence on parents, but who is not yet ready for the independence that is expected of adults (Ausubel et al., 1977). Having a best friend is sometimes crucial in helping the young person find an identity. As Osterrieth (1969) explains:

> By means of common experiences and adventures, interminable conversations that are more or less intimate, the two partners, who are inseparable, do each other the mutual favor of helping each one to know himself: they examine themselves, placing in common their experiences, their plans, their ambitions, and their most intimate secrets. In the true sense, they explain themselves to each other, and in so doing, each explains himself to himself.

Larger groups of friends also ease the transition from the lack of interest in the opposite sex felt by many school-age children to the intimacy with one member of the opposite sex that many psychologists believe is a sign of healthy adulthood. For instance, Dunphy (1963) analyzed the social structure of adolescent peer groups in Australia twenty years ago and found several stages of development between the sexually segregated groups typical of middle childhood and the pairing-off of adulthood. First a particular group of girls begins to associate with a particular group of boys, then a larger heterosexual group forms from these two groups. At this point, young people "hang out" together, but dating, when and if it occurs, is more often done with several couples together. In either case, peers provide security and role models as well as people to talk to—avoiding the embarrassment of finding oneself alone with a member of the opposite sex without knowing what to do or say. Once couples have formed from the heterosexual group, they move away from it, seeking a private relationship. They share friendship as well as love with their mate, and the best friend of the same sex and the heterosexual peer group become less important. At this point, according to Erikson (1963), the individual has reached the next stage of development: intimacy versus isolation.

Figure 17.7 *The favorite pastime of most young adolescents seems to be "hanging out"—that is, gathering together in regular but informally arranged groups for the general purposes of just sitting around. Although such activity may strike adults as aimless, it helps young people to become acquainted with members of the opposite sex while avoiding the pressures of strictly one-on-one relationships.*

Of course, many young people find their way from indifference toward the opposite sex to general attraction and final intimacy without the peer-group stages described by Dunphy, and even without a peer group. However, for most adolescents, friends who are at the same stage of development act as a buffer between the world of children and that of adults.

This function of the peer group may be especially important for minority-group adolescents. As Ausubel explains:

> The peer group reduces the total load of frustration and stabilizes the entire transitional period. It can offer compensations not only for the deprivations associated with adolescence per se, but also for the special deprivations that confront certain adolescents by virtue of their class, ethnic, racial, or religious affiliations. [Ausubel et al., 1977]

Many young people prefer to be with a peer group of the same ethnic background. However, if they must choose between association with contemporaries of different backgrounds and adults of the same background, age, rather than race or religion, usually governs their choice. For instance, Sorensen asked a large representative sample of adolescents: "Most people identify (feel that they have a lot in common with) a lot of different groups. But they identify with some groups more strongly than others. Which *one* of the groups listed below do you identify with most strongly?" The responses were as follows:

	Boys	Girls
PEOPLE OF MY OWN GENERATION	59%	57%
PEOPLE WHO LIVE IN MY COMMUNITY	16%	21%
PEOPLE OF MY OWN RELIGION	12%	10%
PEOPLE OF MY OWN RACE	11%	9%
PEOPLE OF MY OWN SEX	2%	3%

As you can see, more young people identified with their generation than with all the other groups combined. Nonwhites were more likely to identify with their racial group than whites were, but even here, only 18 percent chose race over the other possible variables. Most of them identified with their generation, just as most of the whites did.

In each generation, many young people believe that no other previous generation understands the problems of the world, or of adolescence, as well as they themselves do. Psychologists call this attitude generational chauvinism. In the 1960s, generational chauvinism seemed rampant, its rallying cry being "Don't trust any one over 30." Today, however, it may be less strong. Most of the young people in Sorensen's study, for example, believed that there is a generation gap but that its size has been exaggerated. However, Sorensen also found that 72 percent of his sample between the ages of 16 and 19 and 62 percent of those between 13 and 15 agreed that "young people these days understand more about sex than most people in their forties and fifties." A majority also believed that young people are more idealistic and less materialistic, and that they understand friendship and "what is really important in life" better than their elders.

Figure 17.8 *According to Sorensen's national survey of American teenagers, reports of a generation gap have been greatly exaggerated.*

One explanation for generational chauvinism is offered by Elkind (1978). He says that adolescent egocentrism makes it hard for adolescents to appreciate the depth of adult experience. Consequently, teenagers, in all honesty, can believe that their parents really don't understand how love feels or what life is all about.

Parents

As important as peers are to the adolescent, there is evidence that, in most cases, they serve to supplement, rather than undermine, parental influence. In fact, at the beginning of adolescence, both parents and peers are important sources for psychological support, and as adolescence continues, the young person develops autonomy in relation to both.

Sorensen found that 88 percent of the young people he surveyed had considerable respect for their parents as individuals, although 48 percent wished they and their parents agreed more about political and social issues. These disagreements, however, tend to be on the finer points of policy rather than on the overall issue. In

Figure 17.9 *In virtually all areas, parents' views are a powerful influence on their children, even with regard to attitudes about school. Adolescents whose parents show interest in their education tend to give their best efforts in the classroom.*

fact, numerous studies have shown that parents' political, religious, educational, and vocational opinions and values have a powerful impact on adolescents. Most young people, for instance, vote for the same candidate for president and attend the same church as their parents do. Adolescents who do well in high school and college tend to be the offspring of parents who value education and did well in high school and college themselves. By contrast, most high-school dropouts report that their parents do not understand, accept, or care about them or their education (Cervantes, 1965). Vocational interests also follow in family lines. These patterns hold true for adopted children almost as much as for children born into a family, suggesting that parental ideas and values, rather than genes, account for this similarity (Grotevant et al., 1979).

Parenting Styles Investigators have found that parenting style influences how well a young person copes with the identity crisis. Glen Elder (1962), in a classic study of 7400 adolescents from unbroken homes, saw parents' orientation to their children during adolescence as falling into seven possible categories, ranging from control over every aspect of the adolescent's life to no control at all:

1. *Autocratic.* Adolescents are not allowed to express opinions or make decisions about any aspect of their own lives.

2. *Authoritarian.* Although young people can contribute opinions, parents always make the final decision according to their own judgment.

3. *Democratic.* Adolescents contribute freely to the discussion of issues relevant to their behavior and make some of their own decisions, but final decisions are often formulated by the parents and always are subject to their approval.

4. *Equalitarian.* Parents and adolescents play essentially similar roles, participating equally in making decisions.

5. *Permissive.* The adolescent assumes a more active and influential position in formulating decisions, considering, but not always abiding by, parental opinions.

6. *Laissez-faire.* Young people can decide to consider or ignore parental wishes in making their own decisions.

7. *Ignoring.* The parents take no role, nor evidence any interest, in directing the adolescent's behavior.

Elder found that the young people in his sample rated their parents in the following way:

	Mother	Father
AUTOCRATIC	9%	18%
AUTHORITARIAN	13%	17%
DEMOCRATIC	35%	31.33%
EQUALITARIAN	18%	14.33%
PERMISSIVE	24%	17.33%
LAISSEZ-FAIRE	0.6%	1%
IGNORING	0.4%	1%

In other words, 9 percent of the adolescents judged their mothers to be autocratic, 18 percent of them thought their fathers were, and so on. Elder also found that autocratic and authoritarian patterns were more common among large families, lower-income families, and families with younger adolescents. These generalities have been confirmed by other research. The fact that control is less strict for older adolescents makes sense, for ideally, as young people develop cognitive capacity and accumulate experience, they should be allowed to control more of their lives. As two parents in one study replied when asked if they restricted their son's activities:

> Mother: I don't have to do anything like that any more.
>
> Father: We trust the boy. We never question him.
>
> Interviewer: Are there things you forbid him from doing when he is with his friends?
>
> Father: At his age I would hate to keep telling him that he mustn't do this, or mustn't do that. I have very little trouble with him in that regard. Forbidding I don't think creeps into it because he ought to know at 17, right from wrong. [Bandura and Walters, 1959]

Another study found that young people begin to become more assertive in family interactions when the physical changes of puberty occur (Steinberg, 1977). In many families, the parents' first reaction is to increase their own assertiveness, but gradually they yield more often, recognizing that their child is becoming an adult. Other research suggests that as parents recognize the adolescent's authority, the adolescent reciprocates. Between the ages of 14 and 19, most young people consult with their parents about their problems more often as they grow older (Kandel and Lesser, 1969).

Elder believes that families at both extremes of his parenting-style continuum make identity formation more difficult, for a healthy interaction among family members helps adolescents find out who they are. Research comparing families with delinquent and nondelinquent sons provides confirmation of this idea.

> The parents of nondelinquents appear more willing to listen to their son and to argue vigorously and disagree openly in reaching their final joint decisions. . . . there seems to be little conflict and disagreement between nondelinquent parents, but considerable activity and assertiveness between sons and parents. . . . It is important to note that although the nondelinquent son actively intervenes in family interactions with his parents, they are able to reach agreement on a final compromise solution. Apparently members of nondelinquent families can disagree initially but are flexible enough to change their positions in a mutually acceptable fashion. [Hetherington et al., 1971]

Indeed, delinquents assert *less* power in their families than nondelinquents. Other studies also report that parents of delinquents are often at the extremes of Elder's continuum: either they are rigid and autocratic or they appear neither to know nor to care what their child does.

Salvador Minuchin and his colleagues (1978) reached conclusions similar to Elder's when they compared the families of young people who had psychosomatic illnesses with families where the adolescents' illnesses were organically caused. They found that the families in which psychosomatic illnesses were engendered had five characteristics:

1. *Enmeshment.*   Each family member is tangled in the others' lives and problems, allowing no individuality.

2. *Overprotectiveness.*   The family members elicit nurturing responses (by crying, getting sick, not eating) and the other members respond with extreme protection.

3. *Rigidity.*   Change is very difficult for these families. In adolescence, the parents and the children have trouble adjusting to the development of the child.

A CLOSER LOOK   ## Delinquency

Studies that ask teenagers to report, confidentially, if they have broken any laws in the last year show that most of them fall short of innocence. In one representative group of 522 boys and girls, aged 13 to 16, in a large Midwestern city, 83 percent confessed to one or more chargeable offenses, mostly minor crimes such as smoking marijuana, drinking alcohol, or sexual intercourse with an underage girl (Gold, 1970). Thus, only a minority of teenagers would seem to be completely law-abiding. In fact, a person is more likely to be arrested at age 16 than at any other age. Yet given the characteristics of adolescence (changing body shape and rising hormonal levels, imagination and idealism not yet accompanied by much practical experience, the need for identity and independence), a temporary rise in law-breaking at adolescence is not surprising.

By no means are all adolescent crimes minor, however. Nationwide, 45 percent of the arrests for serious crimes (murder, assault, robbery) and 30 percent of arrests in general involve youths aged 13 to 18 (U.S. Department of Justice, 1978). On the whole, young people who become arrest statistics (less than one in twenty) have lower self-esteem, poorer relationships with their family, and more difficulty in school than their peers who have not had trouble with the law. Since delinquency is both a cause and a consequence of such problems, the first offender usually needs help in order to prevent these factors from compounding each other. Almost always, when a young person is involved in a serious crime, he or she has a long history of school problems and minor offenses.

Unfortunately parents, and others, are all too likely to deny the troubled situation until it is too late. (Typifying this kind of response is the father described by Elkind [1979] as yelling "Why don't you catch some real criminals!" at a policeman who had caught his son stealing a car.) Other parents punish their child's first delinquency, but often make no attempt to strengthen family relationships and build up the young person's self-esteem, steps that would make future delinquent behavior less likely.

An additional factor influencing delinquency appears to be a socioeconomic one, since lower-class young people

Almost half of those arrested for serious crimes each year are 18 years old or younger. Three-fourths of this group *have a history of family and school problems and run-ins with the law.*

have somewhat higher rates of delinquency and much higher rates of arrest and incarceration than middle-class adolescents do. This difference can be explained in part by the fact that lower-class and racial-minority offenders often get arrested for acts that middle-class whites would merely get lectured for. At the same time, the incentive to commit crime, especially robbery, seems to be linked to chronic joblessness. The unemployment rate among black youth in the inner cities is running at about 50 percent: at the same time, the crime rate for this group is higher than that for any other group in the country. As one black 17-year-old said:

How they let this happen in a country like this, having all these kids walking around the streets, got their hands jammed down in their pockets, head down, like their necks was bent in half? What do folks think these kids gonna do, when they go month after month, year after year, without nothing that even *smells* like a job? [Quoted in Cottle, 1979]

4. *Conflict avoidance.*   These families avoid conflicts, either by insisting that all is harmony, or by diffusing problems so that none are solved.

5. *Child involvement in parental conflict.*   Children become ill in order to distract their parents from problems in their marital relationship, or are called on to take sides with one parent or another.

Minuchin has developed family-therapy techniques to help these family members gain greater individuality and more flexibility. This approach has been remarkably successful with victims of anorexia nervosa, a potentially fatal psychological illness in which a person chronically refuses to eat.

A CLOSER LOOK   ## Anorexia Nervosa

The first sign of anorexia nervosa appears in an activity almost all adolescent girls* engage in—weight watching. Typically, an anorexic begins to diet, loses weight, and then, instead of stopping her diet, eats less and less until she is little more than skin and bones. Without treatment, her life is in danger.

Anorexics might lose more than 30 percent of their body weight within a few months, weighing as little as 60 pounds, yet insist that they are neither hungry nor thin. Typically, they exercise daily, "to keep up muscle tone" as one patient put it as she jogged beside her hospital bed (Minuchin et al., 1978).

There is no physical explanation for anorexia nervosa. Nor is there a medical cure for the loss of appetite and weight, although, if blood pressure is very low and body fat completely gone, emergency medical treatment includes forced feeding, through the nose or veins, to prevent sudden death.

Without psychological help, about a third of all anorexic patients get better, and about 10 to 20 percent die. The rest remain abnormally thin (or sometimes change to become abnormally fat) and overly dependent on others for a sense of identity throughout their lives.

The kind of psychological help anorexics receive depends on which theoretical perspective the therapist holds. Psychoanalytic therapists believe that anorexics have a severe disturbance of body image. According to this theory, the anorexic is afraid of becoming a woman, so she maintains a hipless, breastless, childlike form by extreme dieting. One result is that her menstrual periods cease; another consequence is that she becomes the center of family concern and nurturing. In these ways, the anorexic is more like a young child than a young woman. Through psychotherapy, psychiatrists try to help the patient accept her burgeoning femininity, and therefore accept food (Bruch, 1973).

Behaviorists see anorexia nervosa as the result of maladaptive behavior (intended as a means of getting the parents' attention, for example), so they treat it by reinforcing weight gain and punishing weight loss. For example, each day that a hospitalized anorexic gains weight, she is given privileges: freedom to watch television, to make phone calls, to see visitors, to walk around the grounds, to comb her hair. Each day that she loses weight, she must stay in bed, without even the right to go to the bathroom. Her only permitted activity is eating.

Minuchin accepts the validity of both the psychoanalytic and behaviorist approaches, but he considers anorexia a family disease rather than an individual one and recommends that it be treated accordingly.

Indeed, family therapy does seem to be the best treatment for anorexics. Programs involving individual therapy or behavior modification usually report cure rates of between 50 and 70 percent, but programs that concentrate on helping all the family members recognize themselves as individuals, who can fight their own battles and care for their own needs, are even more successful. For example, 86 percent of the fifty-three anorexic patients treated at the Philadelphia Child Guidance Clinic recovered, having learned how to develop personal identity and independence through normal relationships with their families and peers rather than through self-starvation (Minuchin et al., 1978).

This approach is instructive for all families that include adolescents. Parents who recognize their adolescents as individuals, and who realize that family disagreements may be helpful as long as the conflict is discussed and settled, will be able to help their teenagers develop a healthy identity.

---

*Most victims of anorexia are in early adolescence, although some are as young as 8 or as old as 25 when the symptoms begin. The illness can affect young people of both sexes, and every economic bracket. However, 90 percent of those afflicted are female, and are usually from families of above average income.

Adolescent Suicide   Communication between parent and child is a crucial factor in another tragic problem faced by some adolescents—whether or not to go on living. Before discussing the family roots of suicidal impulses in adolescence, however, let us consider the statistical significance of adolescent suicide.

As can be seen in Figure 17.10, the suicide rate between ages 15 and 19 is around half that for any subsequent age group. As an index of despair, however, this differential is misleading, because it actually results from the higher failure rate of teenagers' suicide attempts. In fact, adolescents attempt suicide at about the same rate as the rest of the adult population.*

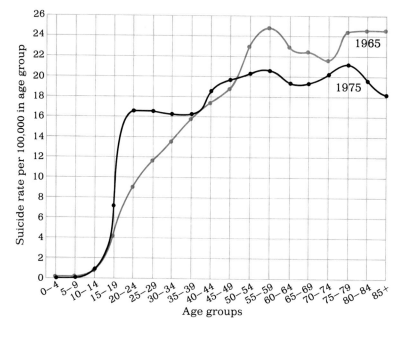

Figure 17.10 *The suicide rate for adolescents is half the rate for adults only because adolescents' attempts to kill themselves fail twice as often as those of adults. Unfortunately, the "success" rate for adolescents in the 1970s was double that of the 1960s.*

What factors cause some adolescents to reach such a state of hopelessness that they want to end their lives? Researchers have found that the precipitating event that is often taken as the "reason" for a suicide is actually the last incident in a long chain of difficulties that have beset the victim. They have also found that suicidal adolescents often come from broken or disrupted families, and feel unwanted by one or both parents (Rosenkrantz, 1978; Jacobs, 1971). In fact, Joseph Sabbath (1968) believes that many suicidal adolescents have felt for a long time that they are "expendable," not needed by anyone. In a careful study of fifty adolescents who attempted suicide, Jerry Jacobs (1971) found that most of them had a long-standing history of family problems that became worse after puberty. Another study found that most suicidal young people had little or no communication with their father, either because he was absent altogether, or because he always played the role of the disciplinarian, never the friend (Canter, 1977).

---

*Accurate statistics on attempted suicide in adolescence are hard to come by, because many attempts are hidden by embarrassed parents and many apparent accidents may actually have been suicides. However, it is generally believed that adolescents attempt suicide at least as often as adults do (Stengel, 1964). As with adults, females account for about 80 percent of all suicide attempts, while males perform about 75 percent of all "successful" suicides.

For the troubled young person, a suicide attempt is the most desperate of a series of attempts to cope with life. Jacobs (1973) found that virtually all suicidal adolescents first rebel, then withdraw, and then, in many cases, run away. When none of these actions solves their problems, they attempt suicide as a last, and most dramatic, "cry for help."

Experts have also found a number of warning signs that should alert family and friends that a young person may be becoming dangerously overwhelmed with emotional difficulties:

1. *A decline in school attendance and achievement, especially in students of better than average ability.* Jacobs (1973) found that while about a third of the young people who attempted suicide had recently dropped out of school, only 11 percent were in serious academic difficulty.

2. *A break in a sexual relationship.* This is the precipitating event for many adolescent suicides. The fact that such events are relatively common in adolescence sometimes blinds parents and teachers to the pain and depression they cause. A sympathetic shoulder to cry on is much more helpful than a statement such as "There are other fish in the sea."

3. *Withdrawal from social relationships.* The adolescent who decides that suicide is the solution sometimes seems less depressed than previously and may cheerfully say something to the effect of "It's been nice knowing you." A joking or serious "goodbye" accompanied by a sudden desire to be alone is a serious sign.

4. *An attempted suicide.* An attempted suicide, however weak it might seem, is the final effort to communicate, and must be taken seriously. If nothing changes in the adolescent's social world, an attempted suicide will probably turn out to have been a trial run for the real thing. Almost all adolescent suicides follow failed attempts.

In addition to the defeats that lead the adolescent to contemplate suicide, an important factor in converting this consideration into action is precisely the sense that nothing can change, a sense of hopelessness poignantly conveyed in the following suicide note:

> To my family and friends:
>
> I'm sorry it has to be this way. For some reason, I have set unattainable goals for myself. It hurts to live and life is full of so many disappointments and problems. . . . Please don't cry or feel badly. I know what I am doing and why I am doing it. I guess I never really found out what love or responsibility was.
>
> Bill
>
> I might also add that I had had in recent years no great desire to continue living. Saying goodbye to all of you who I was close to would only make things harder for me. Believe me, I tried to cope with my problems but I couldn't. [Jacobs, 1971]

In fact, many problems of adolescence that seem insurmountable to young people like Bill have been experienced and weathered by other people many times. Without communication with parents and friends, however, the adolescent's egocentricism prevents realization of this fact, and keeps the young person imprisoned in a sense that the future will always be like the present, a dilemma to which there seems to be only one solution. Therefore, when the warning signs have been detected, they must be taken seriously, and acted upon. As Edwin Shneidman (1978) has written:

> the act of suicide is an individual's effort to stop unbearable anguish or intolerable pain by doing "something."
> Therefore, the way to save a person's life is also to do "something," to put your knowledge of the person's plan to commit suicide into a social network—to let others know about it, to break the secret, to talk to the person, to talk to others, to offer help, to put action around the person, to show response and concern, and, if possible, to offer love.

Jobs and Careers

In terms of the development of the adolescent's cognitive abilities, career choices should become easier to make. One study found that before age 11, children's thoughts about vocations are unrealistic, based on stereotypes rather than on their own abilities or interests (Jordaan and Heyde, 1978). During early adolescence, young people are able to consider more possibilities, and, by the senior year of high school, most are able to consider their own abilities, interests, and economic circumstances in planning their future careers.

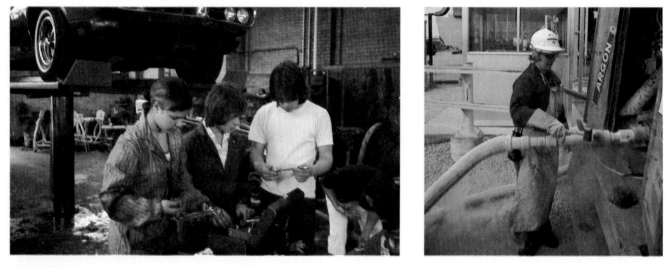

Figure 17.11 *Vocational identity in our society is more difficult to achieve than any other. This may be especially the case for women today, because of the opportunities now open to them that were formerly thought to be the exclusive province of men.*

Nevertheless, Erikson believes that, in our society, finding an occupational identity is the most difficult identity task of all for our young people. Even at age 25, one young adult in four is still uncertain what vocation he or she should choose (Super and Hall, 1978). In earlier generations, young people often simply did what their parents did, and they learned how to do it by working beside them. Today, however, the number of possible jobs and the length of time it takes to prepare for them make choosing a job field difficult for a young person. Vocational identity is usually the last aspect of identity to solidify.

Part of the problem is that the number of jobs available to young people is not as great as it was for earlier generations. One reason for this is the combined effect of the seniority system and nonmandatory retirement, especially in times of relatively high unemployment. Another reason is that the part of the job market that is

Figure 17.12 *As these figures from the Bureau of Labor Statistics show, the segments of the job market that are likely to expand significantly during the 1980s are generally those that require prior training and experience. For example, clerical workers, the largest and fastest-growing segment, must increasingly work with computers and other sophisticated office machinery.*

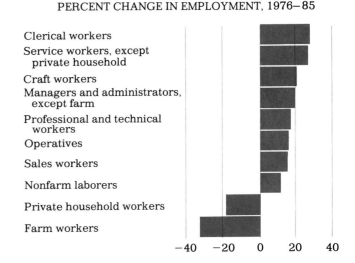

PERCENT CHANGE IN EMPLOYMENT, 1976–85

Clerical workers
Service workers, except private household
Craft workers
Managers and administrators, except farm
Professional and technical workers
Operatives
Sales workers
Nonfarm laborers
Private household workers
Farm workers

−40 −20 0 20 40

expanding (see Figure 17.12) is the part that needs trained workers, so young people must decide on a vocation years before they actually are hired. A third reason is that today's adolescents have the misfortune to follow the generation born in the baby boom of the 1950s and early 1960s. In 1974, for instance, there were 41 million people in the United States aged 10 to 19, and only 34 million aged 9 or less. Thus, by 1984, young people will have to find their way to adulthood in a society that is overloaded with people in their twenties and, ironically, prepared for more adolescents than there are. College admissions officers, for instance, will be eager to see candidates for entrance, but many employers will already have hired enough slightly older, more experienced people to fill the available slots. As a result, adolescents will be choosing and preparing for careers that may not become available to them.

However, the advice and preparation adolescents receive from their schools are usually not as appropriate as they should be. In a critique of vocational and career education, David Rogers (1973) writes, "There is still a tendency to train a surplus of students for declining occupations and too few for expanding ones. Obsolescent curricula as well as machinery remain quite common."

Figure 17.13 *The teaching profession is one area where the oversupply of trained personnel has become most apparent. Increasingly, school systems that grew prolifically to accommodate the children of the baby boom are having to close schools for lack of student population.*

Given this situation, some young people suspect that their elders' emphasis on education and preparation may be a sham to prevent them from entering the labor market or the unemployment statistics. As one young man explained:

> All school is, you know, is the great time passer. It's all a big invention to keep kids from becoming *anything*. What can you become in this society, until you're 30? . . . All it is, is a big age thing. From zero to 25, you get the big run around, the big zilch. From 25 on, or 30—maybe it's getting later and later, for all I know—they let you in. You still don't have any great skills, but you got a few wrinkles. [Cottle, 1979]

These problems relating to career choices are experienced by young people of both sexes. However, girls experience an additional problem. As Judith Bardwick and Elizabeth Douvan (1971) explained, throughout childhood girls have learned to depend on others for their self-esteem, so they try to do well in elementary school to please their teachers and parents. Then, sometime during high school, a shift occurs, when

> the establishment of successful interpersonal relationships becomes the self-defining, most rewarding, achievement task. When that change in priorities occurs—and it tends to be greatest in the later years of high school, and again in the later years of college—personal qualities, such as independence, aggression and competitive achievement, that might threaten success in heterosexual relationships, are largely given up.

Bardwick and Douvan point out that this feminine socialization devalues the very qualities that lead to most successful careers, especially where professional commitment, drive, and ambition are needed. This is one reason women tend to be employed in jobs where aggression and competition are dysfunctional—and where, not just coincidentally, pay and status are low.

We might expect that today's young women are preparing, with specific training as well as more aggressive personality patterns, for more responsible and prestigious careers. Although to some extent this may be true, research shows that quite traditional patterns are prevalent in most young women. In a survey of women in their first year of college, Harmon (1971) found that most of them planned to be housewives; many others hoped for careers in education and social work.

This persistence of traditional patterns is anticipated by recent research that confirms that the sexual differences in personality seen by earlier researchers still exist. One study shows that adolescent girls scored much higher on several measures of empathy (Eisenberg-Berg and Mussen, 1978); another, that they were less likely than boys to blame others when things went wrong (Cramer, 1979). A third study compared sex differences in attitudes toward cooperation and competition in students from the second through the twelfth grades (Ahlgren and Johnson, 1979). The students were asked to agree or disagree with statements designed to assess their feelings about cooperation (for example, "I like to learn by working together with other students") and about competition (for example, "I like to do better work than my friends"). At every age, girls preferred cooperation and boys competition, a preference most obvious in grades 8, 9, and 10.

A final factor in vocational decision making is parental encouragement and example. Daughters as well as sons tend to be ambitious, planning careers and higher education, if their parents urge them to do so. Daughters usually try to follow the example of their mothers, and boys, that of their fathers (Hoffman and Nye, 1974; Simpson, 1962). Indeed, with regard to the young person's aspiration for vocational identity, family influences seem as instrumental as they do for almost every other aspect of adolescent psychosocial development.

Conclusion

In closing our discussion of adolescence, it would seem appropriate to reiterate a point made by Erikson. Essentially, adolescence may be viewed as the dawning of commitment, to others, to ideologies, to work. And it is through these various commitments that young people begin to accomplish the task of achieving adult identity. However, as Erikson points out, identity formation goes beyond merely identifying oneself with ideal others. In part, it is a "process based on a heightened cognitive and emotional capacity to *let oneself be identified* by others as a cir-cumscribed individual in relation to a predictable universe which transcends the family." A problem that can arise in this two-way process is that adolescents may be "bewildered by some assumed role, a role forced on them by the inexorable standardization of American adolescence" (Erikson, 1964).

Within the context of the social forces that foreclose some options and encourage others, each individual attempts to chart his or her own course. Just as each infant actively searches for cognitive equilibrium, each adolescent tries to find the iden-tity that expresses his or her own individuality. In the process, adolescents make decisions about how to reach adulthood that may affect their entire lives. As Robert Frost wrote (1963):

> Two roads diverged in a wood, and I—
> I took the one less traveled by,
> And that has made all the difference.

Figure 17.14 *The pathways to identity are many, and the means of arriving there, marvelously varied. How smooth the journey is de-pends in part on how well the route and means suit the individual's personality.*

SUMMARY

Identity

1. According to Erikson, the psychosocial crisis of adolescence is identity versus role confusion. Ideally, adolescents resolve this crisis by developing a sense of their own uniqueness and a concept of their relationship to the larger society, establishing a sexual, political, moral, and vocational identity in the process.

2. Sometimes the pressure to resolve the identity crisis is too great and instead of exploring alternative roles, young people foreclose their options, establishing a premature identity. Other young people simply choose values and roles opposite to those expected by parents and society, thus forming a negative identity.

3. The process of identity formation depends partly on the society: if its basic values are consistent and widely accepted, and if social change is small, the adolescent's task is fairly easy.

4. Many societies help adolescents achieve identity by providing rites of passage, or initiation ceremonies. In some cultures, these rites are painful and dramatic, helping the young person make the transition from childhood to adolescence in a matter of days or weeks.

5. No single rite of passage can perform this function in our complex society. However, we do have institutions, such as college or the military, that help the young person declare a moratorium on final identity formation.

6. At times, an entire society undergoes an identity crisis, as Germany did in the 1920s. In such periods, the totalitarian solution—one identity that everyone must accept—is particularly attractive to many young people.

7. For young people in North America, the difficulty of identity formation depends partly on the particular community and subculture to which the person belongs. However, in general, identity seems to have been easier to achieve in the 1970s than it was in the 1960s.

Friends and Family

8. The peer group is an important source of information and encouragement for adolescents. The adolescent subculture provides a buffer between the world of children and that of adults, allowing, for example, a social context for the beginning of heterosexual relationships.

9. Many adolescents identify strongly with their generation, believing that some ideas and experiences cannot be properly understood or appreciated by adults.

10. However, parents are the most important influence on adolescents, especially when there is discussion and respect among family members. Adolescents whose parents are indifferent or overly strict tend to depend on peers for social support.

11. Minor law-breaking is common among young people of every socioeconomic class. However, serious delinquency most often occurs among teenagers who feel little reason to care about the values of their parents or their society.

12. Researchers have found that most adolescent suicides are preceded by a long sequence of negative events, including family problems and breakdowns in communication among family members. If the preliminary warning signs of suicidal behavior are heeded, many adolescent suicides can be prevented.

13. Particularly for today's young people, vocational identity may be the most difficult identity to achieve, in part because jobs are scarce and most careers demand long preparation. Girls are still especially likely to lack the necessary planning and ambition to prepare for competitive, high-status careers.

KEY QUESTIONS

What characterizes societies in which identity formation is easy?

What are some of the forms of moratorium offered by our society?

Why was identity formation in America easier in the 1970s than the 1960s?

What is the function of the peer group during adolescence?

What kinds of parenting style seem least helpful to adolescents?

What are some of the causes of delinquency?

Why is vocational identity considered particularly hard to achieve in the 1980s?

Why is unemployment particularly high among today's youth?

KEY TERMS

identity	rites of passage
foreclosure	monogamists
identity confusion	generational chauvinism
negative identity	anorexia nervosa
moratorium	

RECOMMENDED READINGS

Erikson, Erik. *Identity: Youth and crisis.* New York: Norton, 1968.

Erikson's detailed description of the many paths identity formation can take includes his analysis of literary figures, historical circumstances, and the contemporary American scene. His discussion of identity formation in women and blacks is one that most readers will probably find themselves alternately agreeing and disagreeing with.

Mead, Margaret. *Culture and commitment* (Rev. ed.). Garden City, New York: Anchor Books, 1978.

Mead reflects on the nature of the generation gap that seemed to widen during the 1960s. She concludes that our society changed for the better during the 1970s because parents and adolescents began to trust each other again.

Vonnegut, Mark. *The Eden express.* New York: Bantam, 1976.

One way to understand some of the possible problems of adolescence is to read this autobiographical account written by Kurt Vonnegut's son, Mark. He describes his schizophrenic breakdown and recovery as a young adult. Schizophrenia, of course, has many causes, but as you read this book, ask yourself if Mark would have become a mental patient if he had not spent his adolescence in the drug-filled, protesting subculture of the youth of the 1960s.

Levenkron, Steven. *The best little girl in the world.* New York: Warner Books, 1978.

This novel tells about a young woman who becomes anorexic in order to let her parents know she is not "the best little girl in the world." Quick and interesting reading.

Lasch, Christopher. *The culture of narcissism.* New York: Norton, 1979.

Lasch discusses history, literature, and psychology to analyze the values of our society. Three sections touch directly on the issue most reflected by the youth of the 1960s—the declining significance of education, family, and work. This is not an easy book, nor is Lasch's argument that we have become selfish and undisciplined a flattering one. However, it is a challenging and provocative book that forces readers to come to their own conclusions about contemporary social institutions and cultural values.

Epilogue: Adulthood and Aging

No wise man ever wished to be younger.

Jonathan Swift

*The spiritual eyesight improves
as the physical eyesight declines.*

Plato

A young man and woman have just entered adulthood. They know, and like, who they are: they have a sense of identity, not just a sexual and moral identity, but also a vocational one, for they have just landed the jobs they wanted. Given this promising beginning, what can they hope for in the sixty-odd years that, statistically speaking, lie ahead of them?

Until the last decade, psychologists could not answer this question very well. Because developmental psychology traditionally focused on childhood, the story of the individual's life, as research results seemed to show it, had "a brave beginning, an empty middle, and a sad end" (Bronfenbrenner, 1977). Now, however, we know so much more about adult development that psychologists teaching a course devoted entirely to this area of study have a hard time deciding what to exclude. Obviously, a short epilogue can offer only a glance at this burgeoning field. However, it seems fitting to include a brief report on adulthood and aging in this text, to give an indication to young people of what lies ahead, and to confirm what most older adults have already surmised: development is a lifelong process.

Work and Love

What is essential to a successful adulthood? Freud's (1960, originally published in 1935) answer to this question was *"Lieben und arbeiten"*—"To love and to work." Three decades later, Erikson (1963) described the stages after adolescence in a similar vein. The first, he said, is intimacy versus isolation, by which he meant that young adults feel the need to find someone with whom to be intimate—to experience not just sexual intimacy but also the intimacy that comes from sharing economic resources, daily routines and responsibilities, and future goals.

Figure 1 *Freud's prescription of love and work as the essential factors of successful adulthood has been seconded by many psychologists. It has also been supported by longitudinal studies, which have found significant correlations between happiness and fulfillment in these realms.*

After resolving this crisis of young adulthood through commitment to others (whether to a marriage partner, friends, or a community), adults, says Erikson, face the crisis of generativity versus stagnation. An adult becomes generative, or productive, in many ways. One is through a career. Work, which in young adulthood is often simply a means of earning money and filling time, may become much more meaningful and significant. At this stage, some adults find their current employment unsatisfactory and may change jobs or go back to college to prepare for the career they really wanted. Generativity may also be expressed in parenthood, with childbearing and child-raising becoming one of the most important concerns of life. Finally, avocations, such as hobbies or sports, and interest groups, such as churches or political clubs, can become a way to express generativity. Without some such outlet for generativity, according to Erikson, an adult stagnates.

Are loving and working as important to adults in today's world as Freud and Erikson believed them to be? Probably so. Longitudinal research such as George Vaillant's (1977) masterful study, which followed men from late adolescence to their fifties, as well as research on men and women from early adolescence to their forties (Haan and Day, 1974), shows many correlations between happiness and emotional maturity on the one hand, and satisfying marriage and successful work on the other. For instance, an ability to enjoy play, a sense of self-satisfaction, and general good health all seem to be characteristics of adults who find their occupations and emotional lives stimulating and rewarding.

Of course, not everyone need follow the usual course of career, marriage, and parenthood in order to attain emotional satisfaction. The paths to self-fulfillment are numerous and greatly varied. Indeed, many conventional views about what does and does not constitute a fulfilling way of life probably need to be revised. Vaillant's study, for example, included a 55-year-old homosexual living alone in the poorest area of San Francisco. This man had been divorced three times and was a controlled alcoholic (controlled in that he rarely drank before 5 P.M., alcoholic in that he drank himself into oblivion almost every night). Yet he impressed Vaillant with his vitality, optimism, insight, and his daily hard work as a creative writer, whose stories appeared in several excellent literary magazines. Vaillant concluded that this man "burns his candle at both ends, but not from mania or emotional illness. Ebullient energy is his way of dealing with old wounds still rubbed raw by an oppressive culture. As Edna St. Vincent Millay suggested, if such prodigal combustion is short lived, 'it gives a lovely light.' "

The Older, the Better   Developmental psychologists have discovered another fact that should be encouraging to young people who are entering adulthood: For most people, it seems, life improves with age, rather than worsens. Vaillant (1977), for instance, found that people older than 35 tended to use mature defense mechanisms more often than they did when they were younger. They were, for example, likely to cope with a problem by joking about it or deciding to ignore it for the time being, rather than by employing fantasy or repression, imagining an impossible solution or denying the existence of the problem. Those of his subjects who were still happily married after several years of marriage were likely to be even more happily married as time went on; those who were unhappily married either relieved their pain through divorce or found ways to mitigate the unhappiness.

Figure 2 *According to the longitudinal findings of Vaillant, couples who were still happy with each other after several years of marriage were likely to become even more so as time passed.*

Norma Haan and her colleagues (Block and Haan, 1971; Haan and Day, 1974) also found that maturity brought an increase in dependability and productivity, according to the self-ratings of men and women in their forties. These adults also believed that others were more likely to turn to them for advice, and that they themselves were more willing to give—not only advice, but time and material things as well. Women, but not men, were less conventional and had higher levels of aspiration in their forties than in their teens.

Another plus is that sexual satisfaction, in many cases, is easier to achieve as one grows older, partly because the uncertainty and worry that accompany the sexual expression of many teenagers and young adults decreases as adults become more experienced and less narcissistic. For one thing, the premature ejaculation that many teenage boys experience occurs less often, and the ambivalence that many teenage girls feel tends to decline. In addition, the male and female sex drives seem to become more similar in the thirties and forties. We are not sure if this change is physiological or cultural, but many people are less worried about their sexuality in middle adulthood than they were earlier. They are also more willing to seek help for their sexual problems (Masters and Johnson, 1970).

Finally, for many people, parenthood becomes more enjoyable as children grow older (Burr, 1970). Indeed, many people report that grandparenthood has most of the joys and few of the worries of parenthood.

Figure 3 *One of the benefits of grandparenthood is being able to share the joys of growing children without being burdened with all the responsibilities of raising them.*

The generality that life improves with age should not blind us to the many problems that adulthood often brings as a result of vocational and marital choices. Changing jobs, for instance, and moving from one place to another, are stresses that most adults go through many times (Toffler, 1970). Then too, almost all adults enter into marriage—itself, a stress, although usually a worthwhile one. (Especially in middle and late adulthood, married people tend to be happier than single people, who, in turn, are happier than divorced individuals [Campbell et al., 1976]). Nevertheless, almost half of all marriages end in divorce. And although, in the long term, people are generally happier out of a bad marriage than they were in it, the first year or two after divorce is almost always difficult (Hetherington et al., 1977).

Finally, child-rearing, as we have seen throughout this book, is not easy, especially during the first years of parenthood. In fact, research shows a correlation between low self-esteem, especially in women, and responsibility for one or more children under age three (Bradburn and Caplovitz, 1965; Campbell et al., 1976).

Thus adulthood brings many new problems, as well as experience and, at times, wisdom. As in other periods, how successfully people cope with these problems depends partly on the social supports they have. Friends, family, and community can make a divorce or a job change much easier or much harder. Psychologists who have studied adulthood have found that specific organizations, such as single-parent groups, and more general organizations, such as churches, often play an important role in helping adults make the transition from one set of circumstances to another.

Stages of Development

Adults do not experience stages of development in the same way that children do: such events as the first spoken words or the first signs of puberty have no exact parallel in adulthood. However, many developmental psychologists believe that there are stages of adult development set by *social* rather than biological clocks.

In her famous research on the "social clock," Bernice Neugarten found that the settings of the clock depend partly on economic status. Asking a cross section of adults such things as what they considered to be the best time to marry and what age they regarded as the prime of life, she discovered surprising agreement in the answers according to class. For instance, upper-middle-class people generally believed that the best age for a man to marry is between twenty-five and thirty-five and that the prime of life is reached at about age 40; they also agree on the stages of life: in general, men are considered young at 22, middle-aged at around 50, and old starting around 75 (Neugarten, 1968). Lower-class people, on the other hand, tended to expect marriage, parenthood, "prime of life," middle age, and grand-parenthood to occur earlier. In the lower-class view, for example, middle age begins at 40, not 50.

Historical circumstances also play a role. Women have always been "supposed to" marry at younger ages than men. However, a hundred years ago the ideal age for a woman to marry was in her early twenties, then it became her late teens (Neugarten and Datan, 1973). Now, the "ideal" age for marriage is rising, a trend directly related to the increasing numbers of women seeking higher education and better-paying jobs.

Parenthood itself affects most people's perspective on life (Flavell, 1970). For instance, having adolescent children might make an adult more concerned with upholding traditional values, in effect, advancing the social clock and pushing the adult toward middle-aged conservatism. On the other hand, watching one's teen-agers replace traditional values and life styles with new ones might serve as the impetus for liberation: a mid-life career change, for instance, might have its beginnings in a son's or daughter's questioning of values and roles.

Although social clocks are culturally set, rather than biologically predetermined, their impact is nonetheless real. Many single adults approaching age 30 decide it's time to find a mate; many married adults approaching 35 decide to have their last (perhaps only) child; many working people in their forties decide that it's time to take on maximum responsibility, or to earn maximum salary, or, in their late fifties, to prepare for retirement.

Because the ticking of the social clock is heard by most members of one's society, several psychologists who study adult development have described stages of growth that usually occur at certain times. As Daniel Levinson (1978) writes, there is

> a specific age at which each era begins, and another at which it ends. This is not to say, however, that a bell rings at precisely the same point for everyone, demarcating the eras as though they were rounds in a boxing match or classes in a highly regulated school . . . There is a range of variation . . . The variation is contained, however, within fairly narrow limits—probably not more than five or six years . . . This finding goes against the conventional assumption that development does not occur in adulthood, or, if it does, that its pace varies tremendously and has almost no connection with age. On the contrary, it seems to be closely age-linked.

Levinson came to these conclusions after an intensive study of men from a range of socioeconomic backgrounds. His work was popularized, as well as extended to women, by Gail Sheehy (1976) in the national best seller *Passages: Predictable Crises of Adult Life* (see Figure 4). The validity of the Levinson or Sheehy scheme still is a matter of research and debate. However, many psychologists agree that if the term "stage" includes social as well as biological transitions, and if the diversity of adult growth and developmental timing is recognized, then adult development can be described in stages, just as child development can.

Figure 4 *Levinson's scheme of the seasons of a man's life, as depicted here, is closely paralleled in Sheehy's study of the life cycles of men and women, a report considerably enlivened by its terminology. Sheehy describes the life stages and their subdivisions in such terms as "Pulling Up Roots" (including "Breast to Breakaway," "The Urge to Merge"); "The Trying Twenties" (including "The One True Couple," "Why Can't a Woman Be More Like a Man and a Man Less Like a Racehorse?"); "Passage to the Thirties" (including "Catch-30," "The Couple Knot, the Single Spot, the Rebound"); "Deadline Decade" (including "The Age 40 Crucible," "Switch-40s and the Couple," "The Sexual Diamond").*

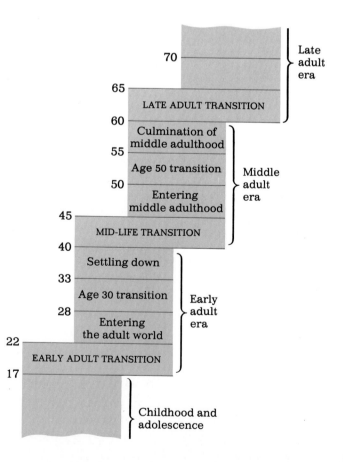

Old Age

The final era of life begins sometime after age 55, the exact year depending on whose social clock is telling the time. Younger and poorer people tend to see old age starting as early as 55; older and wealthier people tend to set 65 or 70 as the beginning of old age. Younger people also see old age more negatively, associating it with senility and dependence—a "second childhood." As Samuel Johnson once wrote:

> There is a wicked inclination in most people to suppose an old man decayed in his intellect. If a young or middle-aged man, when leaving a company, does not recollect where he laid his hat, it is nothing; but if the same inattention is discovered in an old man, people will shrug their shoulders and say, "His memory is going."

Older people are much more likely to see age positively, as a time when years of work and decades of experience finally lead to days of leisure and wisdom. In fact, their view might be summed up by the remark of the French moralist Joseph Joubert: "Old age deprives the intelligent man only of qualities useless to wisdom."

Developmental psychologists have found, on this issue at least, that the view held by older people is the more accurate. For instance, while some intellectual abilities decline with age, especially those demanding speed and memory, others hold steady, especially those involving reflection, judgment, and general knowledge. The former abilities, of course, are the ones heavily represented on conventional tests of intelligence. But it may be the latter abilities that are of greater value. This is shown by studies of productivity: historians and philosophers tend to be more productive in their sixties than in earlier years (Dennis, 1966); political leaders aged 70 or 80—such as Winston Churchill, Charles de Gaulle, Golda Meir and Mao Tse-tung—often rule powerful nations; and many artists and writers, including Robert Frost, Pablo Picasso, Giuseppe Verdi, and Marc Chagall, continue to be productive in their eighties. Three masters of developmental psychology, Freud, Piaget, and Erikson, all published books after the age of 75, and Piaget, born in 1896, and Erikson, born in 1902, continue to write and lecture.

Erikson describes the last stage of life as integrity versus despair. In Erikson's (1963) words, integrity refers to the "acceptance of one's one and only life cycle as something that had to be and that, by necessity, permitted of no substitutions," an acceptance that makes the individual "ready to defend the dignity of his own life style against all physical and economic threats." The opposite emotion, despair, is "signified by fear of death . . . Despair expresses the feeling that the time is now short, too short for the attempt to start another life and to try out alternate roads to integrity." For many older adults, grandchildren are evidence that their lives were worthwhile—the years they spent raising their children are affirmed when their children decide to follow the same path. (Again, of course, the desire for grandchildren depends on one's social clock: many adults in their fifties and even sixties consider themselves too young to be grandparents; on the other hand, other adults may want their grown children to marry and reproduce years before the children themselves consider it time to do so.)

Good health and sufficient income are important at every stage of life, but these two factors become particularly important during old age. Obviously, the percentage of people who are chronically ill increases with age, and, especially in periods of inflation, the number of elderly people on fixed incomes who find themselves below the poverty line is large. These two factors help explain why the suicide rate is so high after the age of 65.

Figure 5 *For some, old age means illness, loneliness, dependence, and despair.*

However, most older people look forward to living, even as they begin to think of age in terms of the number of years left until death, rather than the number since birth. Especially as they approach, and pass, the average American lifespan (69 years for men, 77 for women) most take heart from the knowledge that adults older than themselves continue to remain happily active. Encouragement also comes from statistical tables that show how many more years the average person who has already reached old age will live: the average 75-year-old woman, for instance, will live 11.5 more years. With each additional year of life after 75, the average age at death becomes greater, so if an adult of either sex survives to 85, chances are he or she will live to be 90.

Some psychologists, Neugarten (1975) among them, have suggested that a distinction should be made between the "young-old," who are still active, and the "old-old," who are more reflective. Levinson (1978) suggests that another stage may begin at 80. How should this last period of life be described? Perhaps the best description comes from the writer Malcolm Cowley, who, on reaching 80, wrote:

> I believe in rites and ceremonies. I believe in big parties for special occasions such as an 80th birthday. It is a sort of belated bar mitzvah, since the 80-year-old, like a Jewish adolescent, is entering a new stage of life; let him (or her) undergo a *rite de passage*, with toasts and a cantor. . . .
>
> Being admired and praised is one compensation of age, for the lucky ones, but there are other pleasures as well, including some that younger persons find hard to appreciate. One of them is simply sitting still, like a snake on a sun-warmed stone, with a delicious feeling of indolence that was seldom enjoyed in earlier years. At such times the older person is completely relaxed; he has become a part of nature—and a living part, with blood softly coursing through his veins. . . .

Figure 6 *Another writer who shared Malcolm Cowley's view of old age was Somerset Maugham, who observed in* The Summing Up: *"Old age has its pleasures, which though different, are not less than the pleasures of youth."*

Man or woman, artist or not, every old person needs a work project to keep himself more alive. The project can be one of long standing that asks to be rounded off, or it can be something completely new; perhaps a new one is better, since, as I said, persons of 80 are entering a new stage in life. It should be big enough to demand their best efforts, yet not so big as to dishearten them and lead them to subside into apathy. . . .

[And finally] Like many old people, or so it would seem, I think less about death than might be expected. The question that obsesses me is what to do with those 6.7 years, more or less, that the Census Bureau has grudgingly allowed me. [Cowley, 1978]

Glossary

This glossary provides brief definitions of the most important terms used in this book. To understand the terms more fully in context, consult the Index and read about the terms in the pages on which they first appear.

abuse   Severe harm inflicted on a child by parental use of physical force or psychological pressure.

accommodation   The process of shifting or enlarging usual modes of thinking, or schemes, in order to encompass new information. For example, many Americans would have to expand their concept of food in order to be able to consider eating octopus, even though it is a delicacy in some cultures.

achievement tests   Tests designed to measure how much mastery a person has in specific academic skills.

Action for Children's Television (ACT)   A group organized to make television more responsive to the needs of children. ACT is one of the advocates for less violence and fewer commercials during the hours children usually watch television.

adaptation   Piaget's term for the cognitive processes through which a person adjusts to new ideas or experience. Adaptation takes two forms, assimilation and accommodation.

adolescence   The period between childhood and adulthood. Adolescence usually begins at puberty and ends at the age at which the given culture first assigns a person adult responsibilities.

adolescent egocentrism   A characteristic of adolescent thought that leads the young person to think that he or she is special—unlike other people in many ways. (See *personal fable, imaginary audience,* and *foundling fantasy.*)

age of viability   The age at which a fetus can survive outside the mother's uterus if optimal care is available

(usually between twenty-four and twenty-six weeks after conception).

American Psychological Association (APA)   A professional organization made up of psychologists with various specialties (for example, developmental, clinical, and physiological psychologists). The APA publishes psychological journals, holds annual conventions, and sets standards and ethics for testing, research, training, and psychotherapy.

amniocentesis   A prenatal medical procedure in which a sample of amniotic fluid is withdrawn by syringe and tested to determine if the fetus is suffering from any problems such as Down's syndrome, Tay-Sachs disease, or Rh disease.

amniotic fluid   The liquid, contained within the amnion, which cushions the growing fetus.

analgesics   Drugs that reduce awareness of pain.

anal stage   Sigmund Freud's term for the second stage of psychosexual development (occurring during toddlerhood), in which the anus becomes the main source of bodily pleasure.

anesthetics   Medications that inhibit sensation.

animism   The belief that inanimate objects are alive, and therefore have emotions or intentions.

anorexia nervosa   A rare illness in which a person refuses to eat and consequently starves. Most victims are adolescent girls.

anovulatory   Not releasing an ovum during the menstrual cycle. Most teenage girls have anovulatory cycles during their first year of menstruation.

anoxia   A temporary lack of fetal oxygen during the birth process; if prolonged, it can cause brain damage.

anthropology   The study of the evolution of diverse human physical characteristics and cultures throughout the world.

anytime malformation   A birth defect that may have occurred at any point during pregnancy.

Apgar scale   A quick assessment of a newborn's heart and respiratory rate, muscle tone, color, and reflexes. This simple method is used to determine whether a newborn needs immediate medical care following birth.

aptitude tests   Tests that are designed to measure potential, rather than actual, accomplishment. Intelligence tests are the aptitude tests most commonly used in childhood.

artificial insemination   The injection of sperm into the uterus by means of a medical procedure rather than through sexual intercourse.

artificialism   The belief that natural phenomena, such as the growth of a flower or the rising of the moon, are manipulated rather than natural events. The idea that "Mother Nature" makes the flowers grow, or that God turns on the moon, is an example of this idea.

assimilation   Piaget's term for the inclusion of new information into already existing categories, or schemes. For example, a person may eat a new food and be unable to name it, but may nevertheless be able to guess by its taste, smell, or texture that it is, say, a fruit. In this way, a new object is placed in the preexisting category "fruit."

associative play   A form of social play in which two or more children play together, but are involved in their own separate activities. They do not cooperate with each other.

attachment   An affectional bond between a person and other people, animals, or objects that endures over time and produces a desire for consistent contact and feelings of distress during separation.

authoritarian parenting   A style of child-rearing in which the parents' word is law, and misconduct is punished—no excuses accepted.

authoritative parenting   A style of child-rearing in which the parents set limits and provide guidance, and at the same time are willing to listen to the child's ideas and make compromises.

autism   A serious psychological disturbance that first becomes apparent during early childhood, when a child does not initiate normal social contact. Most autistic children prefer to play with objects or by themselves, unlike the normal child who enjoys company.

antonomous   Independent of external control; self-regulating or unaffected by learning.

autonomous moral reasoning   Kohlberg's term for the highest stages of moral reasoning, in which the person follows universal principles, realizing that the rules of society can be broken. (Also called postconventional, or principled, moral reasoning.)

autonomy versus shame and doubt   The toddler's struggle, theorized by Erik Erikson, between the drive for self-control, and feelings of shame and doubt about oneself and one's abilities. This is the second of Erikson's eight stages of development.

babbling   Extended repetition of a combination of sounds such as "ba, ba, ba." Babbling begins at about 20 weeks of age.

Babinski reflex   A normal, neonatal reflex that causes the child's toes to fan upward when the sole of the foot is stroked.

baby talk   (See *Motherese*.)

behaviorism   A theory of psychology that holds that psychologists should study observable behavior rather than hypothesize about inner motives or unconscious needs. Behaviorism is also called learning theory, because it maintains that most human behavior is learned, or conditioned, rather than inborn.

binocular vision   The coordination of both eyes that enables a person to see one, rather than two, images.

birth catch-up   An above-average increase in weight within the first few months of life. This phenomenon is most common among underweight newborns.

birth trauma   Otto Rank's term for the infant's experience of leaving the security of the womb and entering the harsh world, a shock that Rank believed causes lifelong fear and anxiety.

Black English   A form of English with its own rules of grammar, at variance with some rules of standard English. It is called Black English because it is a dialect spoken by many black Americans. However, many black Americans do not speak Black English, and some white Americans do.

blastocyst   The mass of cells that makes up the inner portion of the blastula. The embryo develops from the blastocyst.

blastula   The human organism about one week after conception (in this form, it is a hollow sphere consisting of more than a hundred cells).

blind experimenters   Researchers who collect data without knowing what results to expect or without knowing which individuals have been subjected to special experimental conditions.

bone age   A measurement of a particular child's rate of ossification (hardening of cartilage into bone) as seen in terms of the average degree of ossification at any given age.

brain damage   Injury to the brain either through physical trauma, such as a blow on the head, or through complications of pregnancy or birth.

brain specialization The performance of certain functions by particular parts of the brain. For example, the brain center for speech is usually located in one part (called "Broca's area") of the left hemisphere.

Brazelton Neonatal Behavior Assessment Scale A rating of a newborn's responsiveness to people and strength of reflexes.

breathing reflex A normal reflex that ensures that newborns (as well as older children and adults) maintain an adequate supply of oxygen by inhaling and exhaling air.

breech birth A birth in which the child emerges from the uterus buttocks first, instead of headfirst. About one in every twenty births is a breech birth.

carriers Individuals who possess recessive genes as part of their genotype (total genetic make-up) rather than their phenotype (outward appearance). A carrier can pass on a recessive gene to his or her children, but unless the child inherits the same gene from both parents, the child will usually not develop the characteristic.

case study The research method in which the scientist reports and analyzes the life history, attitudes, behavior, and emotions of a single individual in much more depth than is usually done with a large group of people.

centration The focusing of attention on one aspect of a situation or object to the exclusion of other aspects. Young children, for example, have difficulty realizing that a mother is also a daughter, because they concentrate, or center, on one role to the exclusion of others.

cephalo-caudal development Growth proceeding from the head downward (literally, from head to tail). Human growth, from the embryonic period throughout childhood, follows this pattern.

Cesarean section A surgical procedure in which an obstetrician cuts open the abdomen and uterus to deliver the baby. This technique is used if the fetus is unable to travel safely through the birth canal.

childhood schizophrenia An emotional disturbance that can develop during early or middle childhood. Its symptoms include an unusual difficulty with social play, conversation, and emotional expression.

chromosome The microscopic particles found in every human cell that carry the genetic material transmitted from parents to children, determining their inherited characteristics.

chunking A memory technique that consists of grouping items to be memorized into categories.

circular reactions Jean Piaget's term for an action that is repeated because it triggers a pleasing response. An example of a circular reaction would be a baby's shaking a rattle, hearing the noise, and shaking the rattle again.

classical, or respondent, conditioning The process by which an animal or person learns to associate a neutral stimulus (for example, a bell) with a meaningful one (for example, food). After training, the subject will respond in the same way to the neutral stimulus as to the meaningful one.

classification The sorting of objects into categories or classes, as in sorting foods according to whether they are fruits, vegetables, or dairy products.

cognitive conceit The know-it-all attitude that many children develop in middle childhood as a result of sometimes being superior to adults in certain areas.

cognitive development That domain of human development involved with thought processes vital to perception, communication, memory, and reasoning.

cognitive theory The theory that the way people understand and think about their experiences is an important determinant of their behavior and personality.

collective monologue A "conversation" between two or more children in which the participants are talking in turn, as though in conversation, but are not actually responding to the content of each other's speech.

conception The moment of fertilization, when a sperm and ovum join to form a zygote.

concrete operational thought In Piaget's theory, that stage of cognitive development in which a person understands specific logical ideas and can apply them to concrete problems but has difficulty with abstract, hypothetical thought and logic. This period usually begins at about age 7 and tends to end in adolescence (though it sometimes ends later, or may not at all).

conditioning The process of learning that occurs either through the association of two stimuli or through the use of positive or negative reinforcement.

congenital Present at birth, either as a result of genetic or prenatal influences or specific complications of the birth process. Congenital characteristics are not necessarily apparent at birth. For example, diabetes is inherited and therefore congenital, but it does not appear until later in life.

congenital syphillis Syphillis that is transmitted from the maternal bloodstream to the fetus. This disease can cause the child to suffer serious bone, liver, or brain damage.

conservation In Piagetian theory, the principle that certain properties of a given quantity of matter (volume, weight, etc.) remain constant despite changes in shape, length, or position.

continuous development Development characterized by changes that occur steadily and gradually.

continuous growth The Offers' term for the type of adolescent growth that is characterized by smooth, problem-free development.

control group   In research, a group of subjects who are similar to the experimental group on all relevant dimensions (e.g., sex, age, educational background) but who do not experience special experimental conditions or procedures.

conventional moral reasoning   Kohlberg's term for the middle stages of moral reasoning, in which social standards are the primary moral values.

cooing   Infants' first noncrying vocalizations, usually uttered when they see a face or hear a voice. Cooing begins as early as 5 weeks of age.

cooperative play   Play in which two or more children cooperate while playing. This form of play is difficult for many preschoolers.

correlation   The degree of association or relationship between two variables.

couvade   The simulation of pregnancy and labor pains performed by fathers-to-be in "primitive" cultures. Studies of Western countries have found that fathers-to-be sometimes experience morning sickness and other pregnancy symptoms.

crawling   A skill, acquired during infancy, that involves lying on the stomach and pulling oneself ahead with the arms.

creeping   A way in which babies move by getting onto their hands and knees and coordinating movement of their arms and legs to achieve locomotion.

crib death   (See *sudden infant death syndrome.*)

critical period   Any period during which a person is especially susceptible to certain harmful or, in some instances, beneficial influences. During prenatal development, for example, the critical period is usually said to occur during the first eight weeks, when the basic organs and body structures are forming and are therefore particularly vulnerable.

cross-sectional research   Research involving the comparison of groups of people who are different in age but similar in other important ways (e.g., sex, socioeconomic status, level of education). Differences among the groups— as, for instance, between a group of 12-year-olds and group of 15-year-olds—are presumably the result of development, rather than some other factor.

decenter   To simultaneously focus on more than one aspect of a situation or consider more than one point of view. If given only a side view of an object, for example, older children are usually able to imagine how the object might look if observed from above.

deep structure   Noam Chomsky's term for the underlying rules of grammar and inherent meaning in each language.

According to Chomsky, a child's ability to understand this structure is innate (understanding, for example, that different sentence structures indicate either a statement or a question).

defense mechanisms   Behavioral or thought patterns that distort one's feelings or perceptions in order to avoid unbearable inner conflicts. In psychoanalytic theory, the ego is thought to institute these defenses when a real or imagined threat is perceived.

deferred imitation   The ability to re-create an action, or mimic a person, one has witnessed some time in the past. Infants are usually first able to do this between 18 and 24 months of age.

demand feeding   A type of infant feeding in which the timing of the feedings and the amount of food are determined by the baby's apparent desires.

deprivation   The state of being without something that is considered necessary for normal development.

deprivation dwarfism   Retardation in a child's physical growth due to emotional factors, such as parental rejection or too much stress.

depth perception   The awareness of the distance between oneself and an object. Before depth perception develops, infants reach for objects that are far too distant to grasp.

developmental psychology   The branch of psychology that scientifically studies the changes in behavior, personality, social relationships, thought processes, and body and motor skills that occur as the individual grows older.

discontinuous development   Development characterized by changes that occur rapidly during some periods and slowly or not at all during others. Most aspects of biological growth, such as changes in height and strength, are discontinuous. Many psychologists believe that cognitive and psychological development is often discontinuous as well.

disequilibrium   Piaget's term for the state of conflict that results from the inability to integrate new information into existing schemes.

displacement   A defense mechanism in which a feeling toward one object is shifted to another, less threatening, one (as when a person becomes angry at a friend rather than at the boss, who is the original object of the anger).

dizygotic twins   Simultaneously born offspring who develop from two separate zygotes, each the product of a different sperm and ovum. These twins are therefore no more similar genetically than any other two children born to the same parents.

dominant gene   A gene that exerts its full phenotypic effect in the offspring regardless of whether it is paired with another dominant gene or with a recessive gene.

double standard   The idea that males should follow one set of rules in sexual conduct, and females, another. Traditionally, females were supposed to resist the sexual advances that males were supposed to make.

Down's syndrome   A genetic abnormality caused by the presence of an extra (i.e., a forty-seventh) chromosome. Individuals with this syndrome have round faces, short limbs, and are underdeveloped physically and intellectually. (Formerly called mongolism.)

dwarfism   Extremely short stature, due either to genetic factors or psychological influences. (In the latter case, the condition is called deprivation dwarfism.)

dyscalcula   A specific learning disability involving unusual difficulty in arithmetic.

dysgraphia   A specific learning disability involving unusual difficulty in handwriting.

dyslexia   A specific learning disability involving unusual difficulty in reading.

early childhood   That period of life, usually between ages 2 and 6, when a child has some mastery of language but is not yet ready for the formal learning of elementary school. (Also called the preschool period.)

eclampsia   A serious disease that can occur during the last weeks of pregnancy. If not promptly treated, it can cause fetal brain damage and even death to the child and mother.

eclectic   Incorporating what seems to be the best, or most useful, from various theories, rather than working from a single perspective.

ecolalia   The word-for-word repetition of what another person has just said—a characteristic of the speech of many autistic children.

ecological approach   A perspective of developmental psychology that emphasizes the impact of society, culture, physical setting, and other people on the development of each individual.

ego   As conceptualized by Freud, the rational, reality-oriented part of the personality.

egocentric speech   Speech that does not take into account the point of view of the listener or fails to acknowledge the content of the speech of others.

egocentrism   Thought processes that are governed solely by one's own point of view. In the egocentrism of early childhood, many children believe that other people think exactly as they themselves do.

ejaculation   The release of seminal fluid from the penis.

Electra complex   The female version of the Oedipal complex. According to psychoanalytic theory, at about age 4, girls have sexual feelings for their father and accompanying hostility toward their mother.

embryo   The human organism from about two to eight weeks after concepton, when basic body structures and organs are forming.

engrossment   Parents' fascination with their newborn, characterized chiefly by their continued gazing at the baby.

enriched environment   A play area in which special toys are provided to stimulate the child and promote learning.

environment   The external forces, including physical surroundings, social institutions, or other individuals, that impinge on human development.

equilibrium   Piaget's term for the state of mental balance achieved through the assimilation and accommodation of conflicting experiences and perceptions.

erythroblastosis   (See *Rh disease.*)

estrogen   Hormones that are produced primarily by the ovaries and regulate sexual development in puberty. Although boys' adrenal glands produce some estrogen, it is chiefly a female hormone.

ethics   In psychology, standards of conduct intended to protect subjects of research or patients in therapy from psychological or physical harm.

experimental group   In research, a group of subjects who experience special experimental conditions or procedures.

expressive   The use of words primarily to communicate personal desires and to interact with people.

expressive jargon   Gesell's term for those apparently meaningless sounds toddlers make which are not recognizable words.

"failure to thrive"   A condition in which, for no apparent medical reason, an infant vomits rather than digests food.

farsightedness   A vision problem involving the clear perception of distant objects but difficulty in focusing on objects at close range.

fear of strangers   An infant's distress when confronted with a new person, especially an adult who acts in unusual or threatening ways.

fetal alcohol syndrome   A congenital condition characterized by a small head, abnormal eyes, malproportioned face, and retardation in physical and mental growth, that sometimes appears in children whose mothers overused alcohol during pregnancy.

fetal monitoring   Methods for assessing the growth and health of the fetus before and during birth. Fetal monitoring is used to determine whether medical intervention, such as a Cesarean section, is necessary to protect the health of the mother and/or the infant.

field-tested A term used in test construction to indicate that a particular test has been tried out on sample groups in order to refine it and determine its validity and reliability.

fine motor skills Skills involving small body movements, especially with the hands and fingers. Drawing, writing, and tying a shoelace demand fine motor skills.

first stage of labor In the birth process, the period extending from the first regular uterine contraction to the full opening of the cervix to allow passage of the child's head through the vaginal canal. The first stage of labor usually lasts between four and six hours.

5-to-7 shift The change in cognitive development between ages 5 and 7 that allows the elementary-school child to think, learn, and remember in a more mature way than was previously possible.

forceps delivery The use of large spoonlike forceps to hold the fetal head and pull the baby down the vaginal canal. This procedure is sometimes necessary if the fetus is getting too little oxygen or is having difficulty progressing through the vaginal canal.

foreclosure Erikson's term for premature identity formation, in which the young person does not explore all the identities that are available.

formal operational thought Piaget's term for the last period of cognitive development, characterized by hypothetical, logical, and abstract thought. This stage is not reached until adolescence, if at all.

foundling fantasy The idea held by some children and adolescents that they are adopted, and that their "true" parents are much better than their present "adoptive" parents.

fraternal twins (See *dizygotic twins.*)

gamete A human reproductive cell. Female gametes are called ova, or eggs; males gametes are called spermatozoa, or sperm.

gender A person's biological sex, either male or female, determined by chromosomes.

gene The basic unit of heredity, carried by the chromosomes. Genes direct the growth and development of every organism.

generational chauvinism Sorensen's term for the idea, held by many adolescents, that one's own generation is wiser, smarter, or more ethical than other generations.

generativity versus stagnation Erikson's seventh stage of development, in which adults seek to be productive through vocation, avocation, or child-rearing. Without such productive work, adults stop developing and growing.

genital stage Freud's term for the last stage of psychosexual development, in which the primary source of sexual satisfaction occurs in an erotic relationship with another adult.

genotype A person's entire genetic heritage, including those characteristics carried on the recessive genes but not expressed in the phenotype.

gentle birth Frederick Leboyer's method of childbirth in which the newborn's exposure to shocking sensory stimuli is reduced through soft lighting in the delivery room, immediate contact with the parents, and a warm bath shortly after birth.

giantism Extremely tall stature resulting from a malfunctioning of the pituitary gland.

gradual desensitization A technique, often used by behavior therapists, to reduce a person's fear of something by gradually exposing that person to the feared object.

grammar The rules of a language governing such things as word order, tense, and voice.

grasping reflex A normal, neonatal reflex that causes newborns to grip tightly when something touches their palms.

gross motor skills Those physical skills that use large body movements. Running, jumping, and climbing involve gross motor skills.

group glee A sudden outburst of joy and laughter among a group of children, usually precipitated by unexpected events or the excitement of physical activity.

growth spurt The relatively rapid physical growth that occurs during puberty.

habitat A person's usual surroundings (e.g., the home, school, or work setting).

habituation A process whereby a particular stimulus becomes so familiar that physiological responses initially associated with it are no longer present. For instance, a newborn might initially stare wide-eyed at a mobile, but gradually look at it less often as habituation occurs.

handedness Preferential use of either the right or left hand for throwing, grasping, writing, and so on. Handedness is thought to be primarily genetic.

harsh punishment The definition of harsh punishment depends on the community. Even a loud-voiced criticism may be considered harsh in some cultures, whereas spanking with a hairbrush might be the norm in others. In general, any punishment that exceeds the norm of the culture is considered harsh.

Harvard Preschool Project A research project, led by Burton White and Jean Watts, the aim of which was to discover the underlying reasons why some preschool children are more competent than others.

Headstart A special preschool educational program designed to provide culturally deprived or disadvantaged 4-year-olds with a variety of intellectual and social experiences that might better prepare them for school.

holistic A unified, or whole, view of human development, which emphasizes the interaction among the various physical, cognitive, and psychosocial aspects of growth.

holophrases A single word that is intended to express a complete thought. Young children (usually about 1 year of age) use this early form of communication.

HOME A method which measures how well the home environment of a child fosters learning. HOME looks at maternal responsiveness and involvement with the child, the child's freedom of movement, the play environment, the play materials, and the variety of activities in the child's day.

hostile aggression An attack against someone for the purpose of defending one's own self-esteem while debasing the other person's.

hyaline membrane disease (See *respiratory distress syndrome*.)

hyperactivity A state of excessive activity, usually accompanied by an inability to concentrate.

hypothalamus A part of the brain that produces hormones that regulate many aspects of physiological development.

iconic thought Jerome Bruner's term for the mode of thought in which images or words are believed to possess the same qualities as the people or objects they represent.

id As conceptualized by Freud, that part of the personality containing primitive, unconscious sexual and aggressive impulses.

identical twins (See *monozygotic twins*.)

identification A defense mechanism through which a person feels like, or adopts the perspective of, someone else. Children identify with their parents for many reasons, one of them, according to psychoanalytic theory, to cope with the powerful emotions of the Oedipal (or Electra) complex.

identity As a Piagetian term, the principle of logic which states that a given quantity of matter remains the same if nothing is added to or subtracted from it, no matter what changes occur in its shape or appearance.

identity Erikson's term for a person's sense of who he or she is as a unique individual. The main task of adolescence,

according to Erikson, is the establishment of the young person's identity, including sexual, moral, political, and vocational identity.

identity confusion Erikson's term for the experience of a young person who is uncertain what path to take toward identity formation, and therefore becomes apathetic and disoriented. (Also called identity diffusion.)

imaginary audience A term referring to the constant scrutiny that many adolescents typically imagine themselves to be under—from nearly everyone.

imaginary playmate A friend who is alive only in the imagination of a child, especially a child who has few real playmates.

implantation The burrowing of the blastula into the lining of the uterus where it can be nourished and protected during growth.

impulsive This term describes a learning style in which a person quickly selects the answer to a question. (See *reflective*.)

induced labor The artificial initiation of uterine contractions by adding a hormone (oxytocin) to the bloodstream or by breaking the membranes of the placenta.

industry versus inferiority The fourth of Erikson's eight "crises," in which the school-age child busily masters many skills or develops a sense of incompetence.

infancy That period of life before a child is able to communicate through speech, usually from birth until 18 months or 2 years. (Also called babyhood.)

infantile sexuality The idea, held by psychoanalytic theorists, that sexual pleasures and fantasies occur in childhood. Freud based his theory of psychosexual stages on changes in the sexual aims, objects, and goals of infants and children as they matured.

initiative versus guilt The third of Erikson's eight "crises" of psychosocial development. During this stage, the preschool child begins, or initiates, new activities—and sometimes feels guilty as a consequence.

inner speech The mental formulation of ideas into words. Inner speech enhances memory and the ability to delay gratification.

insecure attachment A parent-child bond marked by the child's overdependence on, or lack of interest in, the parents. Insecurely attached children are not able to be comforted by their parents and are less likely to explore their environment than are children who are securely attached.

instrumental aggression Fighting over an object, a territory, or a privilege. Examples include quarreling over a toy, a seat at the front of the classroom, or a chance to wash the blackboard. (See *hostile aggression*.)

integrity versus despair Erikson's eighth stage of development, in which elderly people evaluate their lives to decide if they have fulfilled their potential and made a lasting contribution to their family or community.

interview method The research method in which the scientist asks people specific questions designed to discover their opinions or experiences pertaining to a particular topic. Attitudes about sex, religion, or politics are usually assessed with the interview method.

intimacy versus isolation Erikson's sixth stage of development, in which young adults seek other people to share their lives with, or become isolated.

invulnerables Garmezey's term for children who appear to be stress-resistant, that is, who cope with unusual problems and still appear normal and happy.

IQ A number, or score, on an intelligence test that is designed to indicate the aptitude of a particular person for learning, especially learning in school. The average IQ is 100.

Klinefelter's syndrome (See *XXY*.)

kwashiorkor A disease resulting from protein-calorie deficiency in children. The symptoms include thinning hair, paleness, and bloating of the stomach, face, and legs.

laboratory experiment The research method in which the scientist brings people into a controlled setting, and then does something to see how the people react. For instance, children might be brought into a well-equipped playroom, and then told they can play with one, and only one, of the many toys available.

Lamaze method A technique of childbirth that involves breathing and relaxation exercises during labor.

language acquisition device (LAD) Noam Chomsky's term for an infant's inborn ability to acquire language according to a relatively stable sequence and timetable.

language function The communication of ideas and emotions through words.

language structure Particular sound combinations and rules of grammar that are at the root of any given language.

latency Freud's term for the period between the phallic stage and the genital stage. During latency, which lasts from about age 7 to age 11, the child's sexual drives are relatively quiet.

learned behavior Behavior that occurs because of specific experiences and instruction rather than because of the maturation of inborn abilities. Driving a car, solving an algebra problem, and avoiding hot stoves are all learned through some combination of personal experience, observation of others, and direct instruction.

learning by association A linking of two stimuli that causes a person or animal to respond to one stimulus as though it were the other. Having had a frightening experience during a thunder storm might make one feel apprehensive whenever storm clouds gather, for instance.

learning theory (See *behaviorism.*)

linguistics The study of the structure and development of language.

longitudinal research A long-term study of the same people that is designed to measure both changes and continuity in behavior and personality over time.

mainstreaming The practice of assigning handicapped children to regular classrooms, rather than segregating them in special classes.

malnutrition Nutrition that is so poor or insufficient that growth and health are impaired. Protein-calorie deficiency and specific vitamin or mineral deficiency are two forms of malnutrition.

marasmus A disease that afflicts infants suffering from severe malnutrition. Growth stops, body tissues waste away, and eventually death occurs.

mastery play Any form of play involving a repetition of an action or game that leads to a mastering of new skills.

maternal deprivation Inadequate mothering, or an interruption in mothering, believed to have severely negative emotional, intellectual, and social consequences. (Such deprivation can involve the biological mother or some other care-giver.)

maturation Changes in the body or in behavior that result from the aging process, rather than from learning. The child's ability to babble certain sounds at age 6 months and the loss of the front baby teeth at about 6 years are examples of changes that result from maturation.

mean length of utterance (MLU) The average number of morphemes, or meaningful linguistic units, a particular person uses in sentences. In figuring MLU, the statement "I am jumping" would count as four morphemes, "-ing" being the fourth.

meconium Fecal matter which, if expelled into the amniotic fluid, is a sign that the fetus is in distress.

meiosis The special process of chromosome duplication and cell division that occurs only in the gametes (the reproductive cells). Meiosis produces new cells, sperm or ova, each containing (in humans) only twenty-three chromosomes.

menarche A female's first menstrual period. This is taken as a sign, or even as *the* sign, of puberty.

mental combinations The mental playing-out of various courses of action before actually exercising one of them. According to Piaget, this ability usually becomes apparent between 18 and 24 months of age.

mental representation The ability, usually first evident between 18 and 24 months of age, to remember (through the creation of a mental image) an object, event, or person that has been seen or experienced.

metamemory The ability to use and explain techniques that aid memory.

middle childhood That period of life, usually from age 6 to 10 or 11, when a child is ready for the more systematic learning that occurs in elementary school.

mitosis The process of chromosome duplication and cell division that creates new cells, each containing (in humans) forty-six chromosomes with genetic information identical to that of the "original" cell.

modeling The patterning of one's behavior after that of someone else. New responses can be learned, and old ones modified, through modeling.

mongolism (See *Down's syndrome.)*

monogamists Literally, husbands who have one wife, as opposed to polygamists, who have many wives. This is Sorensen's term for adolescents who have only one sexual partner.

monologue Speech delivered out loud but with no intent to communicate to others. This is one of the types of egocentric speech typical of preschool children.

monozygotic twins Two offspring who began development as a single zygote (formed from one sperm and one ovum) that subsequently divided into two zygotes. They have the same genetic make-up, are of the same sex, and look alike.

moratorium Erikson's term for the informal pause in identity formation that allows young people to explore alternatives without making final choices. For many young people, college or military service provides such a moratorium.

Moro reflex A normal neonatal reflex in response to a sudden, intense noise or movement. In this reflex, newborns fling their arms outward, then bring them together; they may also cry with eyes wide open.

morpheme The smallest meaningful unit of speech. Most words count as one morpheme, but sometimes two words, such as "all gone" or "clackety clack," count as one, because they serve a single function; and sometimes one word, such as "cookies," counts as two morphemes, because both "cookie" and "s" are meaningful.

Motherese A term for the special language form typically used by adults to speak with infants—otherwise known as baby talk. Adults' baby talk is high-pitched, rich with intonations, and different in grammar than adult speech. Words are made simpler and modified to reflect the child's capabilities to imitate and understand them.

motor skills Those abilities which involve body movement and physical coordination, such as walking and reaching.

multifactorial characteristics Those abilities or qualities that are determined by the interaction among several genetic and environmental influences. Characteristics such as intelligence, personality, and talent, are multifactorial.

natural childbirth Childbirth in which medical assistance is minimized and psychological and physical support during delivery is stressed.

naturalistic observation The research method in which the scientist observes people in their usual surroundings (home, school, work place) performing their usual tasks. Specific methods of data collection and special training for the observers are generally used to make this method more objective than our usual daily observations of each other.

nature-nurture controversy The debate within developmental psychology over the relative importance of innate capacities ("nature") and acquired abilities ("nurture") in determining an individual's eventual achievement and personality.

negative identity Erikson's term for a chosen identity that is the opposite of the identity preferred by one's parents or society.

negative reinforcement The removal of an unpleasant stimulus in response to a particular behavior, such removal serving to increase the likelihood that the behavior will occur again.

neglect Nutritional, supervisional, or physical care of a child that is improper or inadequate.

neonate A newborn baby. Infants are neonates from the moment of birth to the end of the first month of life.

neural tube The fold of cells that appears in the embryo about two weeks after conception and later develops into the head and spine.

norms Statistical averages based on the results of research derived from a large, representative sample of a given population. Norms are not to be taken as implying "the best." For instance, the norm for an infant's first step is 12 months of age, but the infant who doesn't walk until 14 months is not necessarily less smart or less healthy than the infant who walks at 12 months.

obesity Overweight to the degree that the layer of fat on the body is significantly greater than that of the average person of the same height and age.

objective Free of biases and personal attitudes. Objectivity is a goal in carrying out scientific research.

object permanence The concept that objects and people continue to exist even when they cannot be seen. This concept develops gradually between 6 and 18 months of age.

Oedipus complex In psychoanalytic theory, both the sexual desire that boys in the phallic stage have for their mother and the associated feelings of hostility they have toward their father. This complex is named after Oedipus, a character in ancient Greek legend who unwittingly killed his father and married his mother.

onlooker play "Play" that consists of one child's watching another's active play.

open education A form of education in which both classroom space and choice of activity are more open than they are in traditional education. The classroom has separate "areas" for each activity, and children move from one activity to another in small groups or individually.

operant conditioning A learning process, conceptualized by B. F. Skinner, through which a person or animal is more likely to perform or refrain from performing a certain behavior because of past reinforcement or punishment.

oral stage Sigmund Freud's term for the first stage of life, when the infant gains both nourishment and pleasure through sucking and biting.

organization Jean Piaget's term for the process of synthesizing and analyzing perceptions and thoughts. At every stage of cognitive development, according to Piaget, people actively organize their existing ideas and adapt to new experiences.

ossification The hardening of cartilage into bones—a natural process as a child grows.

ova (singular ovum) The reproductive cells of the human female, which are present, from birth, in the ovaries.

overextension The overuse of a given word to describe several objects that share a particular characteristic. For example, toddlers often use "doggie" to label all four-legged animals.

overregularization A rigid application of grammatical rules and forms that fails to recognize exceptions and irregularities. Overregularization might, for example, lead a child to use the suffix "ed" to form the past tense of all verbs and say "bringed" instead of "brought."

ovulation The process (usually occurring two weeks after the beginning of each menstrual period) in which an ovum (egg) matures, is released by the ovary, and enters one of the Fallopian tubes.

oxytocin A hormone that is sometimes administered to a pregnant woman to induce labor, or to strengthen uterine contractions.

parallel play Play in which two or more children simultaneously use similar toys in similar ways but do not interact.

parent-infant bond The strong feelings of attachment between parents and infants.

penis envy The psychoanalytic idea that, beginning at about age 4, girls realize that boys have a penis and become jealous because they themselves do not.

perception The processing or interpretation of sensations in order to make them comprehensible.

period of the embryo From approximately the second to the eighth week after conception, during which time the rudimentary forms of all anatomical structures develop.

period of the fetus From two months after conception until birth. In a full-term pregnancy, this period lasts seven months.

period of the ovum The first two weeks after conception, during which rapid cell division occurs.

permissive parenting A style of child-rearing in which parents allow their children to do virtually anything they want to do. Permissive parents rarely punish, guide, or control their children.

personal fable The idea, held by many adolescents, that one is special—destined for great accomplishments and immune to normal troubles.

personality An individual's usual way of reacting to people and experiences.

phallic stage The third stage of psychosexual development, according to Freud, in which the penis, or phallus, is the focus of psychological concern as well as of physiological pleasure.

phenotype An individual's observable characteristics, which are caused by the interaction of the genes and the environment. (See *genotype.*)

phenylketonuria (PKU) A genetic disease, now easily detected, in which the individual is unable to properly metabolize protein. If left untreated, mental retardation and hyperactivity result.

phobia An irrational fear. Many phobias have specific names, such as claustrophobia (fear of enclosed places) aquaphobia (fear of water), and agoraphobia (fear of open spaces).

physical development That domain of development that includes changes which are primarily biological. For instance, increases in height and weight, improvements in motor skills, and development of sense organs are usually considered aspects of physical development.

physiological Pertaining to the biological and biochemical processes that occur in the body.

pituitary gland A gland in the base of the skull that produces hormones that regulate growth and trigger the biological changes of puberty.

placenta An organ made up of blood vessels leading to both the mother's and the fetus' bloodstream and having membranes to prevent mixture of the two bloodstreams. These membranes serve as screens through which oxygen and nourishment pass to the fetus and wastes pass from the fetus to the mother to be excreted through her system.

play face   A facial expression, such as a smile or laugh, that accompanies playful activity.

pleasure principle   In Freud's theory, the wish for immediate gratification of one's needs. This is the principle by which the id operates.

pleasure smile   A relaxation of the facial muscles indicating a neonate's contentment (say, after feeding or during sleep).

polygenic inheritance   The interaction of many genes to produce a particular characteristic. For example, skin color, body shape, and memory are all polygenic.

positive reinforcer   A response to a particular behavior that increases the likelihood that that behavior will occur again.

postconventional moral reasoning   (See *autonomous moral reasoning*.)

postmature babies   Neonates born two or more weeks after the due date. These infants are usually completely normal. However, babies born three or more weeks "late" sometimes suffer brain damage due to the inefficiency of the placenta after nine months.

post-partum depression   A mother's feelings of loss and sadness following the birth of her baby. Physical, psychological, and social factors all contribute to this common phenomenon.

preeclampsia   A disease of pregnancy most common during the last trimester. Early signs are high blood pressure, sudden weight gain due to water retention, and protein in the urine. If left untreated, it can develop into the sometimes fatal disease, eclampsia. (Also called toxemia.)

preconventional moral reasoning   Kohlberg's term for the first stages of moral reasoning, in which the person's own welfare is paramount and the customs or mores of society are relatively unimportant.

premature babies   Babies born more than three weeks before the due date or, according to the World Health Organization, who weigh less than 5½ pounds (2500 grams) at birth.

prenatal development   That period of development between the moment of conception and the beginning of the birth process.

preoperational thought   Jean Piaget's term for the second period of cognitive development. Children in this stage of thought, which usually occurs between the ages of 2 and 7, are unable to grasp logical concepts such as conservation, reversibility, or classification.

primary circular reaction   Jean Piaget's term for infants' repeated actions that involve their bodies (e.g., sucking the thumb or kicking the legs).

primary motor areas of the cortex   Those parts of the brain which control simple motor abilities such as waving of the arms.

primary sensory areas of the cortex   Those areas of the brain which control the five senses.

principled moral reasoning   (See *autonomous moral reasoning*.)

progesterone   A hormone that is produced primarily by the ovaries and regulates sexual development in puberty, as well as normal pregnancy.

prosocial behavior   Any behavior that benefits other people. Cooperation, helping, sharing, and generosity are all prosocial behaviors.

proximo-distal development   Growth proceeding from the center (spine) toward the extremities (literally, from near to far). Human growth, from the embryonic period through childhood, follows this pattern.

psychoanalytic theory   A theory of psychology, originated by Sigmund Freud, that stresses the influence of unconscious motivation and drives on all human behavior.

psycholinguistics   The psychological study of the acquisition and use of language.

psychosexual development   The idea, held by psychoanalytic theorists, that development occurs in a series of stages (oral, anal, phallic, and genital), each of which is characterized by the focusing of sexual interest and gratification on one part of the body.

psychosocial development   The domain of human development involving emotions, personality characteristics, and relationships with other people.

puberty   The period of early adolescence characterized by rapid physical growth and the attainment of the physiological capability of sexual reproduction. Puberty usually begins at about age 10 or 11 for girls, and 11 or 12 for boys, although there is much variation caused by genes and nutrition.

reaction formation   A defense mechanism through which a person overreacts in one direction to deny his or her feelings in the opposite direction. For instance, a couple getting a divorce, in order to deny the feelings of love they still have for each other, might convince themselves that their spouse is hateful, deceitful, and cruel.

reading-readiness tests   Tests for preschoolers designed to determine whether a child is ready to learn to read.

reality principle   According to Freud, the ego's guiding principle, which tries to mediate the demands of the id and the rules of society in order to find the most rational and productive course of action.

recessive gene   A gene that affects the expression of a particular phenotypic characteristic only when it is not paired with a dominant gene.

referential   The use of words primarily to identify objects and actions rather than to communicate with others.

reflective   This term describes a learning style that involves pausing to think and weighing all alternatives before choosing an answer to a question.

reflex   An automatic response, such as an eye blink, involving one part of the body.

regression   A defense mechanism in which an individual, under stress, will temporarily revert to a more immature form of behavior (such as bed-wetting by a 12-year-old).

rehearsal   A memory technique involving repetition of the material to be memorized.

reinforcer   Anything (for example, food, money, a smile) that increases the likelihood that a given response will occur again. For example, giving a child a warm hug for being polite will increase the chances that that behavior will be repeated.

reliable   A term used in test construction to characterize a test that will yield the same results in a variety of conditions.

representative sample   A group of subjects in a research project who have the relevant characteristics (e.g., sex, race, socioeconomic level) of the general population or of a particular segment of the population to which the experimental results are most applicable.

repression   A defense mechanism in which anxiety-provoking thoughts and fantasies are excluded from consciousness.

resource room   A classroom equipped with special learning materials designed to teach children who have learning difficulties.

respiratory distress syndrome   In neonates, irregular breathing due to insufficient surfactin. Premature babies are the primary sufferers of this problem, which is the most common cause of death in otherwise normal neonates. (Also called hyaline membrane disease.)

response   A behavior (either instinctual or learned) following a specific cue. (See *stimulus*.)

reversibility   The Piagetian principle that something that has been changed can be returned to its original state simply by reversing the process of change. For example, a ball of clay that has been rolled out into a long, thin rope can be rerolled into a ball.

Rh disease   A condition (also called erythroblastosis) that occurs when antibodies produced by the mother's blood cause damage to the fetal blood supply. This disease can now be prevented.

rites of passage   An anthropological term for any ritual that marks the transition from one stage of life to another. The initiation ceremonies at puberty are one example of a rite of passage; weddings and funerals are others.

rooting reflex   A normal neonatal reflex that helps babies find a nipple by causing them to turn their heads toward the stimulus and start to suck whenever something brushes against their cheek.

rough-and-tumble play   Wrestling, chasing, and hitting that occurs purely in fun, with no intent to harm.

rubella (German measles)   A virus which, if contracted during pregnancy, can cause the fetus to develop serious handicaps, among them blindness, deafness, and autism.

scheduled feeding   The feeding of an infant according to preset time intervals (such as every four hours) rather than in response to cries for food.

scheme   Piaget's term for a general way of thinking about, or interacting with, ideas and objects in the environment.

scientific method   An orderly procedure used to formulate questions, collect data, test hypotheses, and draw conclusions.

secondary circular reaction   Jean Piaget's term for infants' repetition of actions to produce responses from objects or people (e.g., squeezing a rubber duck or laughing while playing with an adult).

secondary sexual characteristics   Sexual features other than the actual sex organs, such as a man's beard or a woman's breasts, that are used to distinguish male from female.

second stage of labor   The period during which the baby's head moves through the vaginal opening.

secure attachment   A healthy parent-child bond in which the child feels comfort when the parent is present, experiences moderate distress at the parent's absence, and quickly reestablishes contact when the parent returns.

sedatives   A group of drugs that induce relaxation.

selective attention   The ability to focus attention on particular stimuli and ignore distractions.

self-concept   A person's sense of himself or herself as a separate person, with particular characteristics. The development of this sense of self begins at birth, but only between 1 and 2 years of age can children truly differentiate themselves from others.

sensation   The process by which the senses detect stimuli within the environment.

sensorimotor intelligence   Jean Piaget's term for the first stage of cognitive development (from birth to about 2 years old). Children in this stage primarily use the senses and motor skills (i.e., grasping, sucking, etc.) to explore and manipulate the environment.

sensory register   A memory system that functions for only a fraction of a second during sensory processing, retaining a fleeting impression of the stimulus that has just impinged on a particular sense organ (e.g., the eyes). If a person looks at an object, for example, and then closes his or her eyes, the visual image of the object is briefly maintained.

separation distress   A child's verbal or nonverbal expression of unhappiness when a familiar care-giver leaves.

seriation   The concept that items can be arranged in a logical series, as by sorting a group of sticks from longest to shortest, or arranging a group of crayons from lightest to darkest. This concept is mastered during concrete operational thought, according to Piaget.

sex drive   The need for sexual expression. Some consider this a basic human need, like the hunger drive; others do not.

sex-linked genes   Genes that are carried either on the X or Y chromosome exclusively. Sex-linked genes account for the fact that certain genetic diseases or characteristics are more likely to occur in one gender than in the other.

sexual dimorphism   The idea that the form of male and female bodies is different, not only in obvious ways, such as the difference in sex organs, but also in less apparent ways, such as the pattern of the hairline or the shape of the hands.

sickle-cell anemia   A genetic blood disease, common among Afro-Americans, that can cause fatigue, swelling of the joints, and sometimes death.

significant   A term used in statistics to indicate that specific research findings are unlikely to have occurred merely by chance. Usually, if the likelihood that a particular result occurred by chance is less than 5 in 100, the result is termed significant.

small-for-dates babies   Babies who are born weighing less than the average baby born after the same number of weeks of gestation.

social clock   Neugarten's term for the idea that the stages of life in adulthood are set by social standards rather than by biological maturation. For instance, "middle age" begins when the culture believes it does, rather than at a particular age in all societies.

socialized speech   According to Piaget, conversation in which two or more people make at least three consecutive statements about the same topic.

social learning theory   The theory that learning occurs through imitation of, and identification with, other people.

social play   Play involving two or more children who seem to be aware of each other.

social reinforcers   Rewards that come from other people in response to particular behavior and increase the likelihood that that behavior will occur again. For instance, if people smile and babble in response to the infant's first babbling, the infant is likely to babble again.

social smile   An infant's smile in response to seeing another person. In full-term infants, this kind of smile first occurs somewhere between 5 and 8 weeks after birth.

society of children   The culture of games, sayings, and traditions passed down from one generation of children to the next.

sociology   The study of the organization, structure, and function of social relationships, social institutions, and societies.

sonograph   A method of determining the size and position of the fetus by means of sound waves.

specific learning disabilities   Any of a number of particular difficulties in mastering basic academic skills, without apparent deficit in intelligence or impairment of sensory functions.

spermatozoa (singular, spermatozoon)   The male reproductive cells, which begin to be produced by the testicles at puberty.

standardized   A term that is used in test construction to indicate that norms have been established for the test answers on the basis of the actual scores of a large sample of the population for whom the test is intended.

statistics   The mathematics of the collection, organization, and interpretation of numerical data used to evaluate data and test hypotheses.

stepping reflex   A normal neonatal reflex that causes newborns to move their legs as if to walk when their feet touch a flat surface.

stimulus   An external condition or event that elicits a bodily response or prompts a particular action. For example, the sight or aroma of an appetizing meal is a stimulus to which the response is usually salivation.

storm and stress   The idea, first enunciated by nineteenth-century German philosophers and artists (*Sturm und Drang*), that adolescence is inevitably a period of emotional turbulence and social difficulty.

subjective   Influenced by biases and personal attitudes.

sucking reflex   A normal neonatal reflex that causes newborns to suck anything that touches their lips.

sudden infant death syndrome (SIDS)   The sudden death of an apparently healthy infant (usually between the ages of 2 and 4 months). The immediate cause is that the infant stops breathing; the underlying cause is not known.

superego   Freud's term for that part of the personality that contains the conscience, including the internalization of moral standards set by one's parents.

surface structure   Noam Chomsky's term for the particular vocabulary and rules of grammar that differ from one language to another. The surface structure is distinct from the deep structure of language, which includes the general rules that are shared by most languages.

surfactin   A natural substance that coats the lungs during the last weeks of fetal development and aids normal reflexive breathing during the first weeks after birth.

surgent growth   The Offers' term for the type of adolescent development that is characterized by some emotional and social problems but on the whole is a fairly smooth progression toward adulthood.

surrogate mother   In animal research, an artificial "mother" that may fulfill some of the functions of a real mother. In Harlow's research with monkeys, surrogate mothers were made of cloth or wire.

swimming reflex   A normal neonatal reflex that causes the newborn to make swimming motions when held aloft horizontally.

symbol   Sounds, written words, drawings, actions, or objects that stand for or signify something else. For example, a flag symbolizes a country, and the combination of the letters "d-o-g" symbolizes the spoken word "dog," which, in turn, symbolizes a particular kind of animal.

symbolic function   The ability to use words and images to represent objects and actions. This ability, which children usually acquire around age 2, makes it possible to remember the past, to imagine the future, and to deal with the present with more reflection and imagination.

synchrony   Carefully coordinated interaction between infant and parent (or any other two people) in which each is exquisitely, often unknowingly, attuned to the other's verbal and nonverbal cues.

teratogens   External agents, such as viruses, drugs, chemicals, and radiation, which can cross the barrier of the placenta and harm the embryo or fetus.

teratology   The scientific study of birth defects caused by genetic or prenatal problems, or by birth complications.

tertiary circular reactions   Jean Piaget's term for the repetition of certain actions with slight variations each time (e.g., hitting a drum with a stick, then with a pencil or a hammer). Tertiary circular reactions occur during the fifth stage of sensorimotor intelligence (usually between 12 and 18 months of age).

testosterone   Hormones that are produced primarily by the testes and regulate sexual development in puberty. Although girls' adrenal glands produce some testosterone, it is chiefly a male hormone.

thalidomide   A mild tranquilizer—now banned—which, when taken early in pregnancy, prevented normal formation of the fetus' arms, legs, and ears.

theory   A systematic statement of hypotheses and general principles that provides a framework for future research and interpretation.

third stage of labor   The expulsion of the placenta after a child is born.

toddler   A child, usually between the ages of 1 and 2, who has just begun to master the art of walking.

toxemia   (See *preeclampsia*.)

toxoplasmosis   A mild disease caused by a parasite often found in uncooked meat and in cat feces. If a pregnant woman contracts this disease, her fetus may suffer eye or brain damage.

transition   The period of the birth process in which the baby's head moves through the birth canal to the vaginal opening.

transverse presentation   A sideways positioning of the fetus in the uterus, requiring the fetus either to be turned around before delivery, or delivered by Cesarean section.

trophoblast   The outer cells of the blastula. These cells later form the four membranes (the yolk sac, amnion, allantosis, and chorion) that protect and nurture the embryo and fetus.

trust versus mistrust   Erik Erikson's term for the infant's basic experience of the world as either good and comfortable or as threatening and uncomfortable. Early care-giving experiences usually mold the child's viewpoint. This is the first of Erikson's eight stages of development.

tumultuous growth   The Offers' term for the type of adolescent development that is characterized by emotional and social problems.

Turner's syndrome   (See *XO*.)

umbilical cord   A tube connecting the developing fetus to the placenta. The cord contains a vein which carries nourishment to the fetus and two arteries which remove waste products.

unconscious   That part of our thoughts and memories of which we are unaware. In psychoanalytic theory, the workings of the unconscious determine much of our conscious actions and thoughts.

unemployment rate   A government statistic, calculated as the percentage of adults who are looking for work but who cannot find it, compared to the percentage who are employed. The unemployment rate does not count people who are not looking for work, such as those who are in school or those who have quit trying to find a job.

valid   A term used in test construction to indicate that a particular test will accurately measure what it is supposed to measure.

venereal disease (VD)   Any of a number of diseases, including gonorrhea and syphilis, transmitted by sexual contact.

verbal mediation   The use of inner speech to negotiate between thoughts or feelings and action in order to control one's own behavior. For instance, a 16-year-old nervously awaiting her driving test might say to herself, "Just relax. You can handle a car as well as anybody."

visual cliff   A laboratory device that consists of a ledge with an apparent drop of several feet that actually is covered by a sheet of transparent glass. Very young children will not venture beyond the end of the ledge even when coaxed by parents, a refusal that demonstrates early development of depth perception.

XO (Turner's syndrome)   A genetic abnormality occurring in females who inherit one rather than two X chromosomes. It results in incomplete sexual maturation and usually mental retardation as well.

XX   The chromosomal pair that determines that a zygote will develop into a normal female. This combination results when an ovum (which always carries an X chromosome) is fertilized by a sperm carrying an X chromosome.

XXY (Klinefelter's syndrome)   A group of genetic disorders present in males who inherit an extra X chromosome. This syndrome prevents the development of secondary sex characteristics.

XY   The chromosomal pair that determines that a zygote will develop into a normal male. This combination results when an ovum (which always carries an X chromosome) is fertilized by a sperm carrying a Y chromosome.

XYY   A genetic abnormality present in males who possess an extra Y chromosome. Men who have this disorder are generally taller and may be more prone to antisocial behavior than the norm.

zygote   The one-celled organism formed from the union of a sperm and an ovum.

Bibliography

Abelson, Herbert I., and **Atkinson, Ronald B.** *Public experience with psychoactive substances: A nationwide survey among adults and youth.* Princeton, N.J.: Response Corporation, August 1975.

Abraham, Sidney, Lowenstein, Frank W., and **Johnson, Clifford L.** *First Health and Nutrition Examination Survey, United States, 1971–1972: Dietary Intake and Biochemical Findings.* National Center for Health Statistics, DHEW publication (HRA) 76-12 19-1, Washington, D.C., 1974.

Achenbach, Thomas M. *Developmental psychopathology.* New York: Ronald Press, 1974.

Adelson, Joseph. Adolescence and the generalization gap. *Psychology Today,* 1979, **12**(9), 33–37.

Ahlgren, Andrew, and **Johnson, David W.** Sex differences in cooperative and competitive attitudes from the 2nd through the 12th grades. *Developmental Psychology,* 1979, **15**, 45–49.

Ainsworth, Mary D. Salter. *Infancy in Uganda: Infant care and the growth of love.* Baltimore: Johns Hopkins Press, 1967.

Ainsworth, Mary D. Salter. The development of infant-mother attachment. In Bettye M. Caldwell and Henry N. Ricciuti (Eds.), *Review of child development research* (Vol. 3), *Child development and social policy.* Chicago: University of Chicago Press, 1973. Pp. 1–94.

Ainsworth, Mary D. Salter, and **Bell, Silvia M.** Attachment, exploration, and separation: Illustrated by the behavior of one-year-olds in a strange situation. *Child Development,* 1970, **41**, 49–67.

Ainsworth, Mary D. Salter, and **Bell, Silvia M.** Mother-infant interaction and the development of competence. In Kevin Connolly and Jerome Bruner (Eds.), *The growth of competence.* New York: Academic Press, 1974.

Ainsworth, Mary D. Salter, and **Bell, Silvia M.** Infant crying and maternal responsiveness: A rejoinder to Gewirtz and Boyd. *Child Development,* 1977, **48**, 1208–1216.

Ainsworth, Mary D. Salter, and **Wittig, Barbara A.** Attachment and exploratory behavior of one-year-olds in a strange situation. In B. M. Foss (Ed.), *Determinants of infant behavior* (Vol. IV). New York: Wiley, 1969.

Albas, Daniel, Albas, Cheryl, and **McClusky, Ken.** Anomie, social class and drinking behavior of high-school students. *Journal of Studies on Alcohol,* 1978, **39**, 910–913.

Aleksandrowicz, Malca K. The effect of pain relieving drugs administered during labor and delivery on the behavior of the newborn: A review. *Merrill-Palmer Quarterly,* 1974, **20**, 121–141.

Aleksandrowicz, Malca K., and **Aleksandrowicz, Dov. R.** Obstetrical pain-relieving drugs as predictors of infant behavior variability. *Child Development,* 1974, **45**, 935–945.

Allen, D. J. Children's associations with their own and other countries. *Theory and Research in Social Education,* 1976, **4**, 80–92.

Als, Heidelise, and **Brazelton, T. Berry.** Comprehensive neonatal assessment (Brazelton Neonatal Behavior Assessment). *Birth and the Family Journal,* 1975, **2**, 3–9.

Ames, Bruce N. Identifying environmental chemicals causing mutations and cancer. *Science,* 1979, **204**, 587–593.

Apgar, Virginia. A proposal for a new method of evaluation in the newborn infant. *Current Research in Anesthesia and Analgesia,* 1953, **32,** 260.

Apgar, Virginia, and Beck, Joan. *Is my baby all right?* New York: Trident Press, 1973.

Appel, Lynne F., Cooper, Robert G., McCarrell, Nancy, Sims-Knight, Judith, Yussen, Steven R., and Flavell, John H. The development of the distinction between perceiving and memorizing. *Child Development,* 1972, **43,** 1365–1381.

Ariès, Philippe. *Centuries of childhood: A social history of family life.* Robert Baldick (Trans.). New York: Knopf, 1962.

Asch, S. E., and Nerlove, H. The development of double function terms in children: An exploratory investigation. In Bernard Kaplan and Seymour Wapner (Eds.), *Perspectives in psychological theory: Essays in honor of Heinz Werner.* New York: International Universities Press, 1960.

Asch, Stuart S., and Rubin, Lowell J. Postpartum reactions: Some unrecognized variations. *American Journal of Psychiatry,* 1974, **131,** 870–874.

Astrand, Per-Olof. The child in sport and physical activity: Physiology. In J. G. Albinson and G. M. Andrew (Eds.), *Child in sport and physical activity.* Baltimore: University Park Press, 1976. Pp. 19–33.

Ausubel, David P., Montemayor, Raymond R., and Svajian, Pergrouhi (Najarian).*Theory and problems of adolescent development* (2nd Ed.). New York: Grune and Stratton, 1977.

Babst, Dean V. A study of family affinity and substance use. *Journal of Drug Education,* 1978, **8,** 29–40.

Bacon, Margaret, and Jones, Mary Brush. *Adolescent drinking.* New York: Crowell, 1968.

Bailey, D. A. The growing child and the need for physical activity. In Russell C. Smart and Mollie S. Smart (Eds.), *Readings in child development and relationships* (2nd Ed.). New York: Macmillan, 1977.

Bakwin, H. Current feeding practices for infants. *Nutrition News,* 1965, **28**(3).

Ballard, Barbara, and Keller, Harold R. Development of racial awareness: Task consistency, reliability, and validity.

Balow, Bruce, Rubin, Rosalyn, and Rosen, Martha J. Perinatal events as precursors of reading disabilities. *Reading Research Quarterly,* 1975–1976, **11,** 36–71.

Baltes, Paul B. Longitudinal and cross-sectional sequences in the study of age and generation effects. *Human Development,* 1968, **11,** 145–171.

Bandura, Albert. *Principles of behavior modification.* New York: Holt, 1969.

Bandura, Albert. *Social learning theory.* Englewood Cliffs, N.J.: Prentice-Hall, 1977.

Bandura, Albert, Ross, Dorothea M., and Ross, Sheila A. Imitation of film-mediated aggressive models. *Journal of Abnormal and Social Psychology,* 1963, **66,** 3–11.

Bandura, Albert, and Walters, Richard H. *Adolescent aggression.* New York: Ronald Press Co., 1959.

Bard, B., and Sachs, J. *Language acquisition patterns in two normal children of deaf parents.* Paper presented at the meeting of the Boston University Conference on Language Acquisition, 1977.

Bardwick, Judith M., and Douvan, Elizabeth. Ambivalence: The socialization of women. In Vivian Gornick and Barbara K. Moran (Eds.), *Woman in sexist society.* New York: Basic Books, 1971.

Barker, Roger G. *Ecological psychology: Concepts and methods for studying the environment of human behavior.* Stanford: Stanford University Press, 1968.

Bartel, Nettie R. Locus of control and achievement in middle- and lower-class children. *Child Development,* 1971, **42,** 1099–1107.

Baumrind, Diana. Child-care practices anteceding three patterns of preschool behavior. *Genetic Psychology Monographs,* 1967, **75,** 43–88.

Baumrind, Diana. Current patterns of parental authority. *Developmental Psychology,* 971, **4** (Monograph I), 1–103.

Baxley, Gladys B., and LeBlanc, Judith M. The hyperactive child: Characteristics, treatment, and evaluation of research design. In Hayne W. Reese (Ed.), *Advances in child development and behavior* (Vol. XI). New York: Academic Press, 1976. Pp. 1–34.

Bayer, Leona M., and Snyder, Margaret M. Illness experience of a group of normal children. In Mary Cover Jones, Nancy Bayley, Jean Walker Macfarlane, and Marjorie Pyles Honzik (Eds.), *The course of human development.* Waltham, Mass.: Xerox College Publishing, 1971. Pp. 91–103.

Bayley, Nancy. Research in child development: A longitudinal perspective. *Merrill Palmer Quarterly,* 1965, **11,** 183–208.

Bayley, Nancy. Behavioral correlates of mental growth: Birth to thirty-six years. *American Psychologist,* 1968, **23,** 1–17.

Bayley, Nancy. Development of mental abilities. In Paul H. Mussen (Ed.), *Carmichael's Manual of Child Psychology* (Vol. I, 3rd Ed.). New York: Wiley, 1970.

Bean, Frank D., Curtis, Russell, L., Jr., and Marcum, John P. Familism and marital satisfaction among Mexican Americans: The effects of family size, wife's labor force participation, and conjugal power. *Journal of Marriage and the Family,* 1977, **39,** 759–767.

Beck, Joan. *How to raise a brighter child: The case for early learning* (Rev. Ed.). New York: Pocket Books, 1975 (originally published by Trident Press, 1967).

Beckman, Linda J. The relative rewards and costs of parenthood and employment for employed women. *Psychology of Women Quarterly,* 1978, **2**, 215–234.

Beckwith, Leila. Relationships between infants' vocalizations and their mothers' behaviors. *Merrill-Palmer Quarterly,* 1971, **17**, 211–226.

Bee, Helen L., Van Egeren, Lawrence F., Streissguth, Ann P., Nyman, Barry A., and **Leckie, Maxine S.** Social class differences in maternal teaching strategies and speech patterns. *Developmental Psychology,* 1969, **1**, 726–734.

Bell, Richard Q., and **Harper, Lawrence V.** *Child effects on adults.* Hillsdale, N.J.: Erlbaum, 1977.

Bell, Silvia M., and **Ainsworth, Mary D. Salter.** Infant crying and maternal responsiveness. *Child Development,* 1972, **43**, 1171–1190.

Beller, E. Kuno. The concept of readiness and several applications. *The Reading Teacher,* 1970, **23**, 727–737.

Belmont, Lillian, and **Birch, Herbert G.** Lateral dominance, lateral awareness, and reading disability. *Child Development,* 1965, **36**, 57–71.

Bem, Sandra L. The measurement of psychological androgyny. *Journal of Consulting and Clinical Psychology,* 1974, **42**, 155–162.

Bender, Lauretta. The life course of children with schizophrenia. *American Journal of Psychiatry,* 1973, **130**, 783–786.

Bennett, Neville. *Teaching styles and pupil progress.* Cambridge, Mass.: Harvard University Press, 1976.

Berelson, Bernard. The value of children: A taxonomical essay. In Nathan B. Talbot (Ed.), *Raising children in modern America: Problems and prospective solutions.* Boston: Little, Brown, 1974.

Berg, Alan. *The nutrition factor: Its role in national development.* Washington, D.C. The Brookings Institute, 1973 (portions with Robert S. Muscat).

Berko, Jean. The child's learning of English morphology. *Word,* 1958, **14**, 150–177.

Berkowitz, Leonard. Control of aggression. In Bettye M. Caldwell and Henry N. Ricciuti (Eds.), *Review of child development research* (Vol. III), *Child Development and Social Policy.* Chicago: University of Chicago Press, 1973. Pp. 95–140.

Bernstein, Anne C., and **Cowan, Philip A.** Children's concepts of how people get babies. *Child Development,* 1975, **46**, 77–91.

Berscheid, Ellen, Walster, Elaine, and **Bohrnstedt, George.** Body image: The happy American body: A survey report. *Psychology Today,* 1973, **7**, 119–131.

Bettleheim, Bruno. *Love is not enough: The treatment of emotionally disturbed children.* Glencoe, Ill.: Free Press, 1950.

Bettleheim, Bruno. *The children of the dream.* New York: Macmillan, 1969.

Bieliauskas, Linas A., and **Strugar, Debra A.** Sample size characteristics and scores on the Social Readjustment Rating Scale. *Journal of Psychosomatic Research,* 1976, **20**, 201–205.

Bing, Elizabeth D. *Adventure of birth.* New York: Simon and Schuster, 1970.

Blackman, Leonard S., and **Heintz Paul.** The mentally retarded. *Review of Educational Research,* 1966, **36**, 5–36.

Blanchard, Robert W., and **Biller, Henry B.** Father availability and academic performance among third-grade boys. *Developmental Psychology,* 1971, **4**, 301–305.

Block, Jack, and **Haan, Norma.** *Lives through time.* Berkeley: Bancroft Books, 1971.

Bloom, Lois. Language development. In Frances Degan Horowitz (Ed.), *Review of child development research* (Vol. IV). Chicago: University of Chicago Press, 1975. Pp. 245–303.

Blos, Peter. *On adolescence: A psychoanalytic interpretation.* New York: Free Press, 1962.

Blume, Judy. *Blubber.* New York: Dell, 1974.

Bohannon, John Neil III, and **Marquis, Angela Lynn.** Children's control of adult speech. *Child Development,* 1977, **48**, 1002–1008.

Bolton, Brian E. *Psychology of deafness for rehabilitation counselors.* Baltimore: University Park Press, 1976.

Boneau, C. Alan, and **Cuca, Janet M.** An overview of psychology's human resources: Characteristics and salaries from the 1972 APA survey. *American Psychologist,* 1974, **29**, 821–840.

Borgaonkar, Digamber B., and **Shah, Saleem A.** The XYY chromosome male–or syndrome. In Arthur C. Steinberg and Alexander G. Bearn (Eds.), *Progress in medical genetics* (Vol. X). New York: Grune and Stratton, 1974.

Borke, Helene. Piaget's mountains revisited: Changes in the egocentric landscape. *Developmental Psychology,* 1975, **11**, 240–243.

Bornstein, Marc H. Qualities of color vision in infancy. *Journal of Experimental Child Psychology,* 1975, **19**, 401–419.

Boston Women's Health Book Collective. *Ourselves and our children: A book by and for parents.* New York: Random House, 1978.

Boswell, Donna A., and **Williams, John E.** Correlates of race and color bias among preschool children. *Psychological Reports,* 1975, **36**, 147–154.

Bower, T. G. R. *A primer of infant development.* San Francisco: Freeman, 1977.

Bower, T. G. R., and **Wishart, J. G.** The effects of motor skill on object permanence. *Cognition,* 1972, **1**(2), 28–35.

Bowes, Watson A., Jr. Obstetrical medication and infant outcome: A review of the literature. Monograph of the *Society for Research in Child Development*, 1970, **35**(137), 3–23.

Bowlby, John. *Maternal care and mental health* (2nd Ed.). New York: Schocken, 1966 (originally published by World Health Organization of the United Nations, Geneva, 1952).

Bowlby, John. *Attachment* (Vol. I) *and Loss* (Vol. II). New York: Basic Books, 1969 and 1973.

Brackbill, Yvonne. Long term effects of obstetrical anesthesia on infant autonomic functioning. *Developmental Psychobiology*, 1977, **10**, 529–535.

Brackbill, Yvonne, and **Broman, Sarah H.** *Obstetrical medication and development in the first year of life.* January 15, 1979 (unpublished, but available from DHEW, American Statistics index #4478-102).

Bradburn, Norman M., and **Caplovitz, David.** *Reports on happiness: A pilot study of behavior related to mental health.* Chicago: Aldine Publishing Co., 1965.

Bradley, Robert H., and **Caldwell, Bettye M.** The relation of infants' home environments to mental test performance at fifty-four months: A follow-up study. *Child Development*, 1976, **47**, 1172–1174.

Bradley, Robert H., Caldwell, Bettye M., and **Elardo, Richard.** Home environment and cognitive development in the first 2 years: A cross-lagged panel analysis. *Developmental Psychology*, 1979, **15**, 246–250.

Brazelton, T. Berry. *Neonatal behavioral assessment scale.* Philadelphia, Pa.: International Ideas, 1974.

Brazelton, T. Berry, Koslowski, Barbara, and **Main, Mary.** The origins of reciprocity: The early mother-infant interaction. In Michael Lewis and Leonard A. Rosenblum (Eds.), *The effect of the infant on its caregiver.* New York: Wiley, 1974. Pp. 49–76.

Brennan, Barbara, and **Heilman, Joan R.** *The complete book of midwifery.* New York: Dutton, 1977.

Brody, Erness Bright, and **Brody, Nathan.** *Intelligence: Nature, determinants, and consequences.* New York: Academic Press, 1976.

Bronfenbrenner, Urie. *Two worlds of childhood: U.S. and U.S.S.R.* New York: Pocket Books, 1973 (originally published by Russell Sage Foundation, 1970).

Bronfenbrenner, Urie. Toward an experimental ecology of human development. *American Psychologist*, 1977, **32**, 513–531.

Brooks, Jeanne, and **Lewis, Michael.** Attachment behavior in thirteen-month-old opposite-sex twins. *Child Development*, 1974, **45**, 243–247.

Brooks, Jeanne, and **Lewis, Michael.** Infants' responses to strangers: Midget, adult and child. *Child Development*, 1976, **47**, 323–332.

Brown, Ann L., and **De Loache, Judy S.** Skills, plans, and self-regulation. In Robert S. Siegler (Ed.), *Children's thinking: What develops.* Hillsdale, N. J.: Erlbaum, 1978.

Brown, Bernard. (Ed.) *Found: Long term gains from early intervention.* Boulder, Colorado: Westview Press, 1978.

Brown, G. W., Sklair, F., Harris, T. O., and **Birley, J. L. T.** Life events and psychiatric disorders. Part I: Some methodological issues. *Psychological Medicine*, 1973a, **3**, 74–87.

Brown, G. W., Harris, T. O., and **Peto, J.** Life events and psychiatric disorders. Part II: Nature of the causal link. *Psychological Medicine*, 1973b, **3**, 159–176.

Brown, Judith K. A cross-cultural study of female initiation rites. *American Anthropologist*, 1963, **65**, 837–853.

Brown, Judith K. Adolescent initiation rites: Recent interpretations. In Robert E. Grinder (Ed.), *Studies in adolescence: A book of readings in adolescent development* (3rd Ed.). New York: Macmillan, 1975.

Brown, Roger. *A first language: The early stages.* Cambridge, Mass.: Harvard University Press, 1973.

Bruch, Hilda. *Eating disorders: Obesity, anorexia nervosa, and the person within.* New York: Basic Books, 1973.

Bruner, Jerome Seymour. The course of cognitive growth. *American Psychologist*, 1964, **19**, 1–15.

Bruner, Jerome Seymour. *Processes of cognitive growth: Infancy.* Worcester, Mass.: Clark University Press, 1968.

Bruner, Jerome Seymour. *Beyond the information given: Studies in the psychology of knowing.* Jeremy M. Anglin (Ed.). New York: Norton, 1973.

Bruner, Jerome Seymour. From communication to language: A psychological perspective. *Cognition*, 1974–1975, **3**, 255–287.

Brunswick, Ann F. Health and drug behavior: A study of urban Black adolescents. *Addictive Diseases: An International Journal*, 1977. **3**, 197–214.

Bryan, James H. Children's cooperation and helping behaviors. In E. Mavis Hetherington (Ed.), *Review of child development research* (Vol. V). Chicago: University of Chicago Press, 1975. Pp. 127–181.

Bryant, Brenda K. Locus of control related to teacher-child interperceptual experiences. *Child Development*, 1974, **45**, 157–164.

Buckley, Robert. Hyperkinetic aggravation of learning disturbance. *Academic Therapy*, 1977, **13**, 153–160.

Butler, Neville. Late postnatal consequences of fetal malnutrition. In Myron Winick (Ed.), *Nutrition and fetal development.* New York: Wiley, 1974.

Caldwell, Bettye M. The effects of infant care. In Martin L. Hoffman and Lois Wladis Hoffman (Eds.), *Review of child development research* (Vol. I). New York: Russell Sage Foundation, 1964. Pp. 9–87.

Caldwell, John. The placental transfer of drugs during childbirth: A possible influence on the newborn. *Journal of Psychosomatic Research,* 1976, **20,** 267–271.

Campbell, Angus, Converse, Philip E., and **Rogers, Willard L.** *The quality of American life: Perceptions, evaluations, and satisfactions.* New York: Russell Sage Foundation, 1976.

Campos, Joseph J., Hiatt, Susan, Ramsay, Douglas, Henderson, Charlotte, and **Svejda, Marilyn.** The emergence of fear on the visual cliff. In Michael Lewis and Leonard A. Rosenblum (Eds.), *The development of affect.* New York: Plenum Press, 1978. Pp. 149–182.

Campos, Joseph J., Langer, Alan, and **Krowitz, Alice.** Cardiac responses on the visual cliff in prelocomotor human infants. *Science,* 1970, **170,** 195–196.

Cantor, Pamela. Suicide and attempted suicide among students: Problem, prediction, and prevention. In Pamela Cantor (Ed.), *Understanding a child's world.* New York: McGraw-Hill, 1977.

Cantwell, Dennis P. *The hyperactive child: Diagnosis, management, current research.* New York: Spectrum, 1975.

Caplan, Frank, and **Caplan, Theresa.** *The power of play.* Garden City, N. Y.: Anchor Press/Doubleday, 1974.

Carey, Susan. The child as word learner. In Morris Halle, J. Bresman, and G. A. Miller (Eds.), *Linguistic theory and psychological reality.* Cambridge, Mass.: MIT Press, 1977.

Carey, William B., and **McDevitt, Sean C.** Stability and change in individual temperament diagnoses from infancy to early childhood. *Journal of the American Academy of Child Psychiatry,* 1978, **17,** 331–337.

Caron, Albert J., Caron, Rose F., Caldwell, Roberta C., and **Weiss, Sandra J.** Infant perception of the structural properties of the face. *Developmental Psychology,* 1973, **9,** 385–399.

Carpenter, R. G. Identification and follow-up of infants at risk of sudden death in infancy. *Nature,* 1974, **250,** 729.

Cazden, Courtney B. The neglected situation in child language research and education. In Arlene Skolnik (Ed.), *Rethinking childhood.* Boston: Little, Brown, 1976 (originally published in *Language and poverty,* Frederick Williams (Ed.). University of Wisconsin Press, 1970).

Cervantes, Lucius F. *The dropout: Causes and cures.* Ann Arbor: University of Michigan Press, 1965.

Cetron, Marvin J., and **Sugarek, Sharon E.** Zero population growth and economic growth. In *U.S. economic growth from 1976–1986* (Vol. II), *Human capital.* United States Congress, Joint Economic Committee, 1977.

Cherry, Louise, and **Lewis, Michael.** Mothers and two-year-olds: A study of sex-differentiated aspects of verbal interaction. *Developmental Psychology,* 1976, **12,** 278–282.

Chess, Stella, Korn, Sam J., and **Fernandez, Paulina B.** *Psychiatric disorders of children with congenital rubella.* New York: Brunner/Mazel, 1971.

Chomsky, Carol. *The acquisition of syntax in children from five to ten.* Cambridge, Mass.: MIT Press, 1969.

Chomsky, Noam. *Language and mind.* New York: Harcourt, Brace, World, 1968.

Chukovsky, Kornei Ivanovich. *From two to five.* Berkeley: University of California Press, 1968.

Cicourel, Aaron V., Jennings, Kenneth H., Jennings, Sybillyn H. M., Leiter, Kenneth C. W., MacKay, Robert, Mehan, Hugh, and **Roth, David R.** *Language use and school performance.* New York: Academic Press, 1974.

Clark, Kenneth B. *Dark ghetto: Dilemmas of social power.* New York: Harper and Row, 1965.

Clark, Kenneth B., and **Clark, Mamie K.** The development of consciousness of self and the emergence of racial identification in Negro preschool children. *Journal of Social Psychology,* 1939, **10,** 591–599.

Clarke, Ann M., and **Clarke, A. D. B.** (Eds.). *Early experience: Myth and evidence.* New York: Free Press, 1976.

Clarke, H. Harrison, and **Greene, Walter H.** Relationships between personal-social measures applied to 10-year-old boys. *Research Quarterly,* 1963, **34,** 288–298.

Clarke-Stewart, K. Alison. And daddy makes three: The father's impact on mother and young child. *Child Development,* 1978, **49,** 466–478.

Clifford, Edward. Body satisfaction in adolescence. *Perceptual and Motor Skills,* 1971, **33,** 119–125.

Cobb, Sidney. Social support as a moderator of life stress. *Psychosomatic Medicine,* 1976, **38,** 300–314.

Cohen, Stephen M., Allen, Martin G., Pollin, William, and **Hrubec, Zdenek.** Relationship of schizo-affective psychosis to manic depressive psychosis and schizophrenia. *Archives of General Psychiatry,* 1972, **26**(6), 539–545.

Coles, Robert. *Erik H. Erikson: The growth of his work.* Boston: Little, Brown, 1970.

Colman, Arthur, and **Colman, Libby.** *Pregnancy: The psychological experience.* New York: Bantam, 1977 (originally published by Seabury, 1971).

Condon, William S., and **Sander, Louis W.** Synchrony demonstrated between movements of the neonate and adult speech. *Child Development,* 1974, **45,** 456–462.

Condry, John, and **Condry, Sandra.** Sex differences: A study of the eye of the beholder. *Child Development,* 1976, **47,** 812–819.

Cone, Brenda. Puerpural depression. In Norman Morris (Ed.), *Psychosomatic medicine in obstetrics and gynecology.* Basel: Karger, 1972.

Conger, John J. Current issues in adolescent development. Abstracted in Journal Supplement Abstract Service, *Catalog of Selected Documents in Psychology,* 1976, **6**, 94.

Conway, Esther, and **Brackbill, Yvonne.** Delivery medication and infant outcome: An empirical study. Monograph of the *Society for Research in Child Development,* 1970, **35**(137), 24–34.

Cook, Thomas D., Appleton, Hilary, Conner, Ross F., Shaffer, Ann, Tamkin, Gary, and **Weber, Stephen J.** *"Sesame Street" revisited.* New York: Russell Sage Foundation, 1975.

Corah, Norman L., Anthony, E. James, Painter, Paul, Stern, John A., and **Thurston, Donald L.** Effects of perinatal anoxia after seven years. *Psychological Monographs,* 1965, **79**, 3 (Whole No. 596).

Corter, Carl, and **Bow, Jane.** The mother's response to separation as a function of her infant's sex and vocal distress. *Child Development,* 1976, **47**, 872–876.

Cosgrove, Benton B., and **Henderson, B. E.** Male genitourinary abnormalities and maternal diethylstilbestrol. *Journal of Urology,* 1977, **117**, 220–222.

Cott, Allan. A reply. *Academic Therapy,* 1977, **13**, 161–171.

Cottle, Thomas J. Adolescent voices. *Psychology Today,* 1979, **12**(9), 40, 43–44.

Cowan, Philip A. *Piaget: With feeling: Cognitive, social, and emotional dimensions.* New York: Holt, Rinehart and Winston, 1978.

Cowley, Malcolm. *Life.* December, 1978.

Cramer, Phebe. Defence mechanisms in adolescence. *Developmental Psychology,* 1979, **15**, 476–477.

Cravioto, Joaquin, and **DeLicardie, Elsa.** Longitudinal study of language development in severely malnourished children. In George Serban (Ed.), *Nutrition and mental functions.* New York: Plenum Press, 1975. Pp. 143–191.

Cravioto, Joaquin, DeLicardie, Elsa R., and **Birch, Herbert G.** Nutrition, growth, and neurointegrative development: An experimental and ecologic study. *Pediatrics* (Supp.), 1966, **38**, 319–372.

Crawford, Christina. *Mommy dearest.* New York: Morrow, 1978.

Cruickshank, William M. *Learning disabilities in home, school, and community.* Syracuse, N.Y.: Syracuse University Press, 1977.

Curtiss, Susan R. *Genie: A linguistic study of a modern day "wild child."* New York: Academic Press, 1977.

Dale, Edgar, and **O'Rourke, Joseph.** *The living word vocabulary.* Elgin, Ill.: Field Enterprises (Dome), 1976.

Danforth, David N. (Ed.). *Obstetrics and gynecology* (3rd Ed.). New York: Harper and Row, 1977.

Darwin, Charles. One: A biographical sketch of an infant. *Mind,* 1877, **7**, 285–294.

Davenport-Slack, Barbara, and **Boylan, Claire Hamblin.** Psychological correlates of childbirth pain. *Psychosomatic Medicine,* 1974, **36**, 215–223.

Davis, Clara M. Self selection of diet by newly-weaned infants: An experimental study. *American Journal of Diseases of Children,* 1928, **36**, 651–679.

Degenhardt, Karl-Heinz, Kerken, Hans, Knörr, Karl, Koller, Siegfried, and **Weidemann, Hans-Rudolf.** Drug usage and fetal development: Preliminary evaluations of a prospective investigation. In Marcus A. Klingberg, Armand Abramovici, and Juan Chemke (Eds.), *Drugs and fetal development* (Vol. 27). New York: Plenum Press, 1972.

de Hirsch, Katrina, Jansky, Jeannette Jefferson, and **Langford, William S.** *Predicting reading failure: A preliminary study of reading, writing, and spelling disabilities in preschool children.* New York: Harper and Row, 1966.

Denney, Nancy Wadsworth. A developmental study of free classification in children. *Child Development,* 1972, **43**, 1161–1170.

Denney, Nancy Wadsworth, Zeytinoglu, Sezen, and **Selzer, S. Claire.** Conservation training in four-year-old children. *Journal of Experimental Child Psychology,* 1977, **24**, 129–146.

Dennis, Wayne. The effect of restricted practice upon the reaching, sitting, and standing of two infants. *Journal of Genetic Psychology,* 1935, **47**, 17–32.

Dennis, Wayne. Causes of retardation among institutional children: Iran. *Journal of Genetic Psychology,* 1960, **96**, 47–59.

Dennis, Wayne. Creative productivity between the ages of 20 and 80 years. *Journal of Gerontology,* 1966, **21**, 1–8.

Dennis, Wayne. *Children of the crèche.* New York: Appleton-Century-Crofts, 1973.

Dennis, Wayne, and **Dennis, Marsena G.** The effect of cradling practices upon the onset of walking in Hopi children. *Journal of Genetic Psychology,* 1940, **56**, 77–86.

Dennis, Wayne, and **Najarian, Pergrouhi.** Infant development under environmental handicap. *Psychological Monographs,* 1957, **71**, 1–13 (Whole No. 434).

Deno, E. N. (Ed.). *Instructional alternatives for exceptional children.* Arlington, Va.: Council for Exceptional Children, 1973.

Deutsch, Cynthia P. Social class and child development. In Bettye M. Caldwell and Henry N. Ricciuti (Eds.), *Review of child development research* (Vol. III). Chicago: University of Chicago Press, 1973.

Deutsch, Helene. *The psychology of women: A psychoanalytic interpretation* (Vol. 2). New York: Grune and Stratton, 1944–1945.

de Villiers, Jill G., and de Villiers, Peter A. A cross-sectional study of the acquisition of grammatical morphemes in child speech. *Journal of Psycholinguistic Research,* 1973, **2,** 267–278.

de Villiers, Jill G., and de Villiers, Peter A. *Language acquisition.* Cambridge, Mass.: Harvard University Press, 1978.

de Villiers, Peter A., and de Villiers, Jill G. *Early Language.* Cambridge, Mass.: Harvard University Press, 1979.

Dickinson, George E. Adolescent sex information sources: 1964–1974. *Adolescence,* 1978, **13,** 653–658.

Dick-Read, Grantly. *Childbirth without fear: The original approach to natural childbirth* (Rev. Ed.). Helen Wessel and Harlan F. Ellis (Eds.). New York: Harper and Row, 1972 (originally published in Britain, 1933, first U.S. edition, 1942).

Doman, Glenn. *How to teach your baby how to read.* Garden City, N.Y.: Doubleday, 1975.

Donovan, Bonnie. *The Cesarean birth experience: A practical, comprehensive, and reassuring guide for parents and professionals.* Boston: Beacon Press, 1977.

Douvan, Elizabeth, and Adelson, Joseph. *The adolescent experience.* New York: Wiley, 1966.

Doyle, Anna Beth. Infant development in day care. *Developmental Psychology,* 1975, **11,** 655–656.

Drillien, Cecil M. *The growth and development of the prematurely born infant.* Baltimore: Williams and Wilkins, 1964.

Dronamraju, Krishna R. Multigenic inheritance. In Daniel Bergsma (Ed.), *Medical genetics today.* Baltimore: Johns Hopkins Press, 1974. Pp. 250–254.

Duckworth, Eleanor. The having of wonderful ideas. *Harvard Educational Review,* 1972, **42,** 217–231.

Dunn, Lloyd M. Special education for the mildly retarded—Is much of it justifiable? *Exceptional Children,* 1968, **35,** 5–22.

Dunn, Lloyd M. (Ed.). *Exceptional children in the schools: Special education in transition* (2nd Ed.). New York: Holt, Rinehart and Winston, 1973.

Dunphy, Dexter C. The social structure of urban adolescent peer groups. *Sociometry,* 1963, **26,** 230–246.

Eckerman, Carol O., Whatley, Judith L., and Kutz, Stuart L. Growth of social play with peers during the second year of life. *Developmental Psychology,* 1975, **11,** 42–49.

Eckert, Helen M., and Eichorn, Dorothy H. Construct standards in skilled action. *Child Development,* 1974, **45,** 439–445.

Edgerton, Robert B. *Mental Retardation.* Cambridge, Mass.: Harvard University Press, 1979.

Egan, Jane. Object-play in cats. In Jerome S. Bruner, Alison Jolly, and Kathy Sylva (Eds.), *Play.* New York: Basic Books, 1976. Pp. 161–165.

Eimas, Peter D. Speech perception in early infancy. In Leslie B. Cohen and Philip Salapatek (Eds.), *Infant perception: From sensation to cognition* (Vol. II). New York: Academic Press, 1975. Pp. 193–231.

Eimas, Peter D., Siqueland, Einar R., Jusczyk, Peter, and Vigorito, James. Speech perception in infants. *Science,* 1971, **171,** 303–306.

Eisenberg-Berg, Nancy, and Mussen, Paul H. Empathy and moral development in adolescence. *Developmental Psychology,* 1978, **14**(2), 185–186.

Elardo, Richard, Bradley, Robert, and Caldwell, Bettye M. The relation of infants' home environments to mental test performance from six to thirty-six months: A longitudinal analysis. *Child Development,* 1975, **46,** 71–76.

Elardo, Richard, Bradley, Robert, and Caldwell, Bettye M. A longitudinal study of the relation of infants' home environments to language development at age three. *Child Development,* 1977, **48,** 595–603.

Elder, Glen H. Structural variations in the childrearing relationship. *Sociometry,* 1962, **25,** 241–262.

Elkind, David. Egocentrism in adolescence. *Child Development.* 1967, **38,** 1025–1034.

Elkind, David. Piagetian and psychometric conceptions of intelligence. *Harvard Educational Review,* 1969, **39,** 319–337.

Elkind, David. *Children and adolescents: Interpretive essays on Jean Piaget.* New York: Oxford University Press, 1974.

Elkind, David. *The child's reality: Three developmental themes.* Hillsdale, N.J.: Erlbaum, 1978.

Elkind, David. *The child and society.* New York: Oxford University Press, 1979.

Emery, Alan E. H. Antenatal diagnosis: Limitations and future prospects. In Daniel Bergsma (Ed.), *Medical genetics today.* Baltimore: Johns Hopkins Press, 1974, Pp. 289–296.

Emery, Donald G. *Teach your preschooler to read.* New York: Simon and Schuster, 1975.

Enkin, M. W., Smith, S. L., Dermer, S. W., and Emmett, J. O. An adequately controlled study of the effectiveness of PPM training. In Norman Morris (Ed.), *Psychosomatic medicine in obstetrics and gynecology.* Basel: Karger, 1972.

Erikson, Erik H. *Childhood and society* (Rev. Ed.). New York: Norton, 1963.

Erikson, Erik H. A memorandum on identity and Negro youth. Journal of social issues, 1964, 20, 29–42.

Erikson, Erik H. Identity, youth, and crisis. New York: Norton, 1968.

Erikson, Erik H. Life history and the historical moment. New York: Norton, 1975.

Eriksson, Bengt O. The child in sport and physical activity: Medical aspects. In J. G. Albinson and G. M. Andrew (Eds.), Child in sport and physical activity. Baltimore: University Park Press, 1976. Pp. 43–66.

Erlenmeyer-Kimling, L., and Jarvik, Lissy F. Genetics and intelligence: A review. Science, 1963, 142, 1477–1479.

Escalona, Sibylle K. The roots of individuality: Normal patterns of development in infancy. Chicago: Aldine, 1968.

Etaugh, Claire. Effects of maternal employment on children: A review of recent research. Merrill-Palmer Quarterly, 1974, 20, 71–98.

Etzel, Barbara C., and Gewitz, Jacob L. Experimental modification of caregiver maintained high-rate operant crying in a 6- and a 20-week-old infant (Infans Tyrannotearus): Extinction of crying with reinforcement of eye contact and smiling. Journal of Experimental Child Psychology, 1967, 5, 303–317.

Evans, Hugh E., and Glass, Leonard. Perinatal medicine. Hagerstown, Md.: Harper and Row, Medical Dept., 1976.

Eveleth, Phillis B., and Tanner, James M. Worldwide variation in human growth. Cambridge, England: Cambridge University Press, 1976.

Fagot, Beverly L. The influence of sex of child on parental reactions to toddler children. Child Development, 1978, 49, 459–465.

Fanshel, David, and Shinn, Eugene B. Children in foster care: A longitudinal investigation. New York: Columbia University Press, 1978.

Fantz, Robert. The origin of form perception. Scientific American, 1961, 204(5), 66–72.

Farnham-Diggory, Sylvia. Learning disabilities. Cambridge, Mass.: Harvard University Press, 1978.

Faust, Margaret Siler. Developmental maturity as a determinant in prestige of adolescent girls. Child Development, 1960, 31, 173–184.

Featherstone, Joseph. Schools where children learn. New York: Liveright, 1971.

Federman, Edward J., and Yang, Raymond K. A critique of "Obstetrical pain-relieving drugs as predictors of infant behavior variability." Child Development, 1976, 47, 294–296.

Fein, Robert A. Men's entrance to parenthood. The Family Coordinator, 1976, 25, 341–348.

Feingold, Benjamin, F. Why your child is hyperactive. New York: Random House, 1974.

Feingold, Benjamin F. A critique of "controversial medical treatment of learning disabilities." Academic Therapy, 1977, 13, 173–181.

Feld, Sheila. Feelings of adjustment. In F. Ivan Nye and Lois Wladis Hoffman (Eds.), The employed mother in America. Chicago: Rand McNally, 1963. Pp. 331–352.

Feldman, Ben H., and Rosenkrantz, Arthur L. Drug use by college students and their parents. Addictive Diseases: An International Journal, 1977, 3, 235–241.

Ferguson, Charles A. Baby talk as a simplified register. In Catherine E. Snow and Charles A. Ferguson (Eds.), Talking to children: Language input and requisition. Cambridge, England: Cambridge University Press, 1977.

Ferreira, Antonio J. Emotional factors in prenatal environment: A review. Journal of Nervous and Mental Disease, 1965, 141, 108–118.

Ferster, Charles B., and Skinner, B. F. Schedules of reinforcement. New York: Appleton-Century-Crofts, 1957.

Field, Tiffany. Interaction behaviors of primary versus secondary caregiver fathers. Developmental Psychology, 1978, 14, 183–184.

Fincher, Jack. Sinister people: The looking-glass world of the left-hander: A scientifc shaggy-dog story. New York: Putnam, 1977.

Firestone, Philip, Poitras-Wright, Helene, and Douglas, Virginia. The effects of caffeine on hyperactive children. Journal of Learning Disabilities, 1978, 11, 133–141.

Fisher, W. M., Huttel, F. A., Mitchell, I., and Meyer, A. E. The efficacy of the psychoprophylactic method of prepared childbirth. In Norman Morris (Ed.), Psychosomatic medicine in obstetrics and gynecology. Basel: Karger, 1972.

Fitzgerald, Hiram E., and Brackbill, Yvonne. Classical conditioning in infancy: Development and constraints. Psychological Bulletin, 1976, 83, 353–376.

Flavell, John H. The developmental psychology of Jean Piaget. Princeton, N. J.: Van Nostrand, 1963.

Flavell, John H. Developmental studies of mediated memory. In Hayne W. Reese and Lewis P. Lipsitt (Eds.), Advances in child development and behavior (Vol. 5). New York: Academic Press, 1970. Pp. 182–211.

Flavell, John H. Cognitive changes in adulthood. In L. R. Goulet and Paul B. Baltes (Eds.), Life-span developmental psychology: Research and theory. New York: Academic Press, 1970. Pp. 247–253.

Flavell, John H. The development of role-taking and communication skills in children. Huntington, N.Y.: Krieger, 1975 (originally published by Wiley, 1968).

Flavell, John H. *Cognitive development.* Englewood Cliffs, N.J.: Prentice-Hall, 1977.

Fomon, Samuel J. *Infant nutrition* (2nd Ed.). Philadelphia: Saunders, 1974.

Fontana, Vincent J. *Somewhere a child is crying: Maltreatment—causes and prevention.* New York: Macmillan, 1973.

Ford, Clellan S., and **Beach, Frank A.** *Patterns of sexual behavior.* New York: Harper, 1951.

Fox, David Joseph, and **Jordan, Valerie Barnes.** Racial preference and identification of black, American Chinese, and white children. *Genetic Psychology Monographs,* 1973, **88**, 229–286.

Fraiberg, Selma. *The magic years.* New York: Scribner, 1968.

Fraiberg, Selma. Blind infants and their mothers: An examination of the sign system. In Michael Lewis and Leonard A. Rosenblum (Eds.), *The effect of the infant on its caregiver.* New York: Wiley, 1974. Pp. 215–232.

Fraiberg, Selma. *Insights from the blind: Comparative studies of blind and sighted infants.* New York: Basic Books, 1977a.

Fraiberg, Selma. *Every child's birthright: In defense of mothering.* New York: Basic Books, 1977b.

Frankenberg, William K., and **Dodds, Josiah B.** The Denver Developmental Screening Test. *Journal of Pediatrics,* 1967, **71**(3), 181–191.

Freedman, Daniel G. Ethnic differences in babies. *Human Nature* (No. 1), 1979, **2**, 36–43.

Freud, Anna. Adolescence. In A. E. Winder and D. L. Angus (Eds.), *Adolescence: Contemporary studies.* New York: American Books, 1968.

Freud, Sigmund. *The basic writings of Sigmund Freud,* A. A. Brill (Ed. and Trans.). New York: Modern Library, 1938.

Freud, Sigmund. A phobia in a five year old boy (1909). In *Collected papers* (Vol. 3), Alix and James Strachey (Trans.). New York: Basic Books: 1959. Pp. 149–289.

Freud, Sigmund. *A general introduction to psychoanalysis,* Joan Riviare (Trans.). New York: Washington Square Press, 1960 (originally published, 1935).

Freud, Sigmund. *New introductory lectures on psychoanalysis,* James Strachey (Ed. and Trans.). New York: Norton, 1965 (originally published, 1933).

Frisch, Rose E. Population, food intake, and fertility. *Science,* 1978, **199**, 22–30.

Frisch, Rose E., and **Revelle, Roger.** Height and weight at menarche and a hypothesis of critical body weights and adolescent events. *Science,* 1970, **169**, 397–399.

Frost, Robert. *Selected poems of Robert Frost.* New York: Holt, Rinehart, and Winston, 1963.

Furstenberg, Frank F., Jr. *Unplanned parenthood: The social consequences of teenage childbearing.* New York: Free Press, 1976.

Garber, H. L., and **Heber, I. R.** The Milwaukee Project: Indications of the effectiveness of early intervention to prevent mental retardation. Paper presented at the meeting of the International Association for the Scientific Study of Mental Deficiency. Washington, D.C., 1976.

Gardner, Lytt I. Deprivation dwarfism. *Scientific American,* 1972, **227**(1), 76–82.

Gardner, William I. *Learning and behavior characteristics of exceptional children and youth: A humanistic behavioral approach.* Boston: Allyn & Bacon, 1977.

Garmezy, Norman. Vulnerable and invulnerable children: Theory, research, and intervention. Abstracted in the Journal Supplement Abstract Service, *Catalog of Selected Documents in Psychology,* 1976, **6**(4), 96.

Garmezy, Norman, Masten, Ann, Nordstrom, Lynn, and **Ferrarese, Michael.** The nature of competence in normal and deviant children. In Martha Whalen Kent and Jon E. Rolf (Eds.), *Primary prevention of psychopathology* (Vol. III), *Social competence in children.* Hanover, N. H.: University Press of New England, 1979. P. 22.

Garvey, Catherine. Some properties of social play. In Jerome S. Bruner, Alison Jolly, and Kathy Sylva (Eds.), *Play.* New York: Basic Books, 1976. Pp. 570–583.

Garvey, Catherine. *Play.* Cambridge, Mass.: Harvard University Press, 1977.

Gelles, Richard J. Violence and pregnancy: A note on the extent of the problem and needed services. *Family Coordinator,* 1975, **24**, 81–86.

Gelles, Richard J. Violence toward children in the United States. *American Journal of Orthopsychiatry,* 1978, **48**, 580–592.

George, Victor, and **Wilding, Paul.** *Motherless families.* London: Routledge and Kegan Paul, 1972.

Gesell, Arnold, and **Amatruda, Catherine S.** *Developmental diagnosis: Normal and abnormal child development, clinical methods and pediatric applications* (2nd Ed.). New York: Hoeber, 1947.

Gesell, Arnold, and **Ames, Louise Bates.** The development of handedness. *Journal of Genetic Psychology,* 1947, **70**, 155–175.

Gesell, Arnold, Ames, Louise Bates, and **Ilg, Frances L.,** *Infant and child in the culture of today: The guidance of development in home, and nursery school.* (Rev. Ed.). New York: Harper and Row, 1974.

Gesell, Arnold, Ames, Louise Bates, and Ilg, Frances L. *The child from five to ten* (Rev. Ed.). New York: Harper & Row, 1977.

Gewirtz, Jacob L., and Boyd, Elizabeth F. Does maternal responding imply reduced infant crying? A critique of the 1972 Bell and Ainsworth report. *Child Development*, 1977, **48**, 1200–1207.

Gibson, Eleanor J., and Levin, Harry. *The psychology of reading*. Cambridge, Mass.: MIT Press, 1975.

Gibson, Eleanor J., and Walk, Richard D. The "visual cliff." *Scientific American*, 1960, **202**(4), 64–72.

Gilmor, Timothy M. Locus of control as a mediator of adaptive behavior in children and adolescents. *Canadian Psychological Review*, 1978, **19**, 1–26.

Gleason, Jean Berko. Do children imitate? *Proceedings of the International Conference on Oral Education of the Deaf*, 1967, **2**, 1441–1448.

Globus, Albert, Brain morphology as a function of presynaptic morphology and activity. In Austin Riesen (Ed.), *The developmental neuropsychology of sensory deprivation*. New York: Academic Press, 1975.

Goad, Walter B., Robinson, Arthur, and Puck, Theodore T. Incidence of aneuploidy in a human population. *American Journal of Human Genetics*, 1976, **28**, 62–68.

Goertzel, Victor, and Goertzel, Mildred George. *Cradles of eminence*. Boston: Little, Brown, 1962.

Gold, Delores, and Andres, David. Developmental comparisons between ten-year-old children with employed and nonemployed mothers. *Child Development*, 1978, **49**, 75–84.

Gold, Martin. *Delinquent behavior in an American city*. Belmont, Calif.: Brooks/Cole, 1970.

Goldberg, Susan, and Lewis, Michael. Play behavior in the year-old infant: Early sex differences. *Child Development*, 1969, **40**, 21–31.

Goldman, Carole Baker. *Children as a factor in marital satisfaction: A selected bibliography*. Washington, D.C.: National Alliance for Optional Parenthood, 1979.

Goldstein, Joseph, Freud, Anna, and Solnit, Albert J. *Beyond the best interests of the child*. New York: The Free Press, 1973.

Goldstein, Kenneth M., Caputo, Daniel V., and Taub, Harvey B. The effects of prenatal and perinatal complications on development at one year of age. *Child Development*, 1976, **47**, 613–621.

Goodman, Mary Ellen. *Race awareness in young children* (Rev. Ed.). New York: Collier Books, 1964.

Goodman, Richard M. Various genetic traits and diseases among the Jewish ethnic groups. In Daniel Bergsma (Ed.), *Medical genetics today*. Baltimore: Johns Hopkins Press, 1974. Pp. 205–219.

Goodnow, Jacqueline J. The nature of intelligent behavior: Questions raised by cross-cultural studies. In Lauren B. Resnick (Ed.), *The nature of intelligence*. New York: Wiley, 1976. Pp. 169–188.

Gottesman, Irving I., and Shields, James. *Schizophrenia and genetics*. New York: Academic Press, 1972.

Gottlieb, Benjaman H. The contribution of natural support systems to primary prevention among four social subgroups of adolescent males. *Adolescence*, 1975, **10**, 207–220.

Gottman, John, Gonso, Jonni, and Rasmussen, Brian. Social interaction, social competence, and friendship in children. *Child Development*, 1975, **46**, 709–718.

Gray, Burl B., and Ryan, Bruce P. *A language program for the nonlanguage child*. Champaign, Ill.: Research Press, 1973.

Greenberg, David J., and O'Donnell, William J. Infancy and the optimal level of stimulation. *Child Development*, 1972, **43**, 639–645.

Greenberg, Martin, and Morris, Norman. Engrossment: The newborn's impact upon the father. *American Journal of Orthopsychiatry*, 1974, **44**, 520–531.

Greenfeld, Josh. *A place for Noah*. New York: Holt, Rinehart, and Winston, 1978.

Greif, Esther Blank. Sex role playing in pre-school children. In Jerome S. Bruner, Alison Jolly, and Kathy Sylva (Eds.), *Play*. New York: Basic Books, 1976. Pp. 385–391.

Grimm, Elaine R. Psychological and social factors in pregnancy, delivery and outcome. In Stephen A. Richardson and Alan F. Guttmacher (Eds.), *Childbearing—Its social and psychological aspects*. Baltimore: Williams and Wilkins Co., 1967. Pp. 1–52.

Grotevant, Harold D., Scarr, Sandra, and Weinberg, Richard A. Patterns of interest similarity in adoptive and biological families. *Journal of Personality and Social Psychology*, 1977, **35**, 667–676.

Gump, Paul V. Ecological psychology and children. In E. Mavis Hetherington (Ed.), *Review of child development research* (Vol. V). Chicago: University of Chicago Press, 1975.

Guttmacher, Alan F. *Pregnancy, birth, and family planning: A guide for expectant parents in the 1970's*. New York: Viking Press, 1973.

Haan, Norma, and Day, D. A longitudinal study of change and sameness in personality-development: Adolescence to later adulthood. *International Journal of Aging and Human Development*, 1974, **5**, 11–39.

Haan, Norma, Smith, M. Brewster, and Block, Jeanne. Moral reasoning of young adults: Political-social behavior, family background, and personality correlates. *Journal of Personality and Social Psychology*, 1968, **10**, 183–201.

Habicht, Jean-Pierre, Yarbrough, Charles, Lectig, Aaron, and **Klein, Robert.** Relation of maternal supplementary feeding during pregnancy to birth weight and other sociobiological factors. In Myron Winick (Ed.), *Nutrition and fetal development.* New York: John Wiley and Sons, 1974. Pp. 127–145.

Hagen, John W., Jongeward, Robert H., Jr., and **Kail, Robert V., Jr.** Cognitive perspectives on the development of memory. In Hayne W. Reese (Ed.), *Advances in child development and behavior* (Vol. 10). New York: Academic Press, 1975. Pp. 57–101.

Haith, Marshall M., Bergman, Terry, and **Moore, Michael J.** Eye contact and face scanning in early infancy. *Science,* 1977, **198,** 853–854.

Haley, Alex. *Roots.* Garden City, N.Y.: Doubleday, 1976.

Hall, Calvin S. All the world's a stage. *Contemporary Psychology,* 1977, **22,** 690–691.

Hall, G. Stanley. *Adolescence.* New York: Appleton, 1904.

Hallahan, Daniel P., and **Cruickshank, William M.** *Psycho-educational foundations of learning disabilities.* Englewood Cliffs, N. J.: Prentice-Hall, 1973.

Hansen, Eva, and **Bjerre, Ingrid.** Mother-child relationships in low birthweight groups. *Child Development,* 1973, **3,** 93–103.

Hanson, James W., Streissguth, Ann P., and **Smith, David W.** The effects of moderate alcohol consumption during pregnancy on fetal growth and morphogenesis. *The Journal of Pediatrics,* 1978, **92,** 457–460.

Harbison, Raymond D. (Ed.). *Perinatal addiction.* New York: Halsted Press, 1975.

Hardy, Janet B. Clinical and developmental aspects of congenital rubella. *Archives of Otolaryngology,* 1973, **98,** 230–236.

Hardy, Janet B., McCracken, George H., Jr., Gilkeson, Mary Ruth, and **Sever, John L.** Adverse fetal outcome following maternal rubella *after* the first trimester of pregnancy. *Journal of the American Medical Association,* 1969, **207,** 2414–2420.

Hardyck, Curtis, and **Petrinovich, Lewis F.** Left-handedness. *Psychological Bulletin,* 1977, **84,** 385–404.

Harlow, Harry F., and **Harlow, Margaret.** Social deprivation in monkeys. *Scientific American,* 1962, **207**(5), 136–146.

Harlow, Harry F., and **Suomi, Stephen J.** Social recovery by isolation reared monkeys. *Proceedings of the National Academy of Science,* 1971, **68**(7), 1534–1538.

Harmon, Lenore W. The childhood and adolescent career plans of college women. *Journal of Vocational Behavior.* 1971, **1,** 45–56.

Harper, Lawrence V., and **Sanders, Karen M.** Preschool children's use of space: Sex differences in outdoor play. *Developmental Psychology,* 1975, **11,** 119.

Harrell, Thomas W., and **Harrell, Margaret S.** Army General Classification Test scores for civilian occupations. *Educational and Psychological Measurement,* 1945, **5,** 229–239.

Harris, Ben. Whatever happened to little Albert? *American Psychologist,* 1979, **34,** 151–160.

Harris, Florence R., Wolf, Montrose M., and **Baer, Donald M.** Effects of adult social reinforcement on child behavior. *Young Children* (Formerly *The Journal of Nursery Education*), 1964, **20**(1), 8–17.

Hart, Betty M., Allen, K. Eileen, Buell, Jean S., Harris, Florence R., and **Wolf, Montrose M.** Effects of social reinforcement on operant crying. *Journal of Experimental Child Psychology,* 1964, **1,** 145–153.

Hartley, Eugene L., Rosenbaum, Max, and **Schwartz, Shepard.** Children's perceptions of ethnic group membership. *Journal of Psychology,* 1948, **26,** 387–398.

Hartshorne, Hugh, May, Mark A., and **Maller, J. B.** *Studies in service and self-control.* New York: Macmillan, 1929.

Hartup, Willard W. Aggression in childhood: Developmental perspectives. *American Psychologist,* 1974, **29,** 336–341.

Harvey, D. H., and **March, R. W.** The effects of decaffeinated coffee versus whole coffee on hyperactive children. *Developmental Medicine and Child Neurology,* 1978, **20,** 81–86.

Haskell, Samuel D. Desired family-size correlates for single undergraduates. *Psychology of Women Quarterly,* 1977, **2,** 5–15.

Hass, Aaron. *Teenage sexuality: A survey of teenage sexual behavior.* New York: Macmillan, 1979.

Hausknecht, Richard, and **Heilman, Joan R.** *Having a Cesarean baby.* New York: Dutton, 1978.

Heald, Felix P. (Ed.). *Adolescent nutrition and growth.* New York: Appleton Century Crofts, 1969.

Heald, Felix P. Juvenile obesity. In Myron Winick (Ed.), *Childhood obesity.* New York: Wiley, 1975, Pp. 81–88.

Heinonen, Olli P., Slone, Dennis, and **Shapiro, Samuel.** *Birth defects and drugs in pregnancy.* Littleton, Mass.: Publishing Sciences Group, 1976.

Held, Richard, and **Hein, Alan.** Movement-produced stimulation in the development of visually guided behavior. *Journal of Comparative and Physiological Psychology,* 1963, **56,** 872–876.

Henneborn, William James, and **Cogan, Rosemary.** The effect of husband participation on reported pain and probability of medication during labor and birth. *Journal of Psychosomatic Research,* 1975, **19,** 215–222.

Henton, Comradge L. The effect of socio-economic and emotional factors on the onset of menarche among Negro and White girls. *Journal of Genetic Psychology,* 1961, **98,** 255–264.

Hermelin, Beate, and O'Connor, N. Functional asymmetry in the reading of Braille. *Neuropsychologia,* 1971, **9,** 431–435.

Herrman, Gerald, Schuckit, Marc A., Hineman, Sherry, and Pugh, William. The association of stress with drug use and academic performance among university students. *Journal of the American College Health Association,* 1976, **25,** 97–101.

Hess, Eckhard H. Ethology and developmental psychology. In P. H. Mussen (Ed.), *Carmichael's manual of child psychology* (3rd Ed.). New York: Wiley, 1970, 1–38.

Hess, Robert D., and Shipman, Virginia C. Early experience and the socialization of cognitive modes in children. *Child Development,* 1965, **36,** 869–886.

Hetherington, E. Mavis, Cox, M., and Cox, R. Beyond father absence: Conceptualization of the effects of divorce. In E. Mavis Hetherington and Ross D. Parke (Eds.), *Contemporary readings in child psychology.* New York: McGraw-Hill, 1977.

Hetherington, E. Mavis, Stouwie, Roger J., and Ridberg, Eugene H. Patterns of family interaction and child-rearing attitudes related to three dimensions of juvenile delinquency. *Journal of Abnormal Psychology,* 1971, **78,** 160–176.

Hill, John P., and Steinberg, L. D. The development of autonomy during adolescence. Paper presented at the Symposium on Research on Youth Problems Today. Madrid, 1976.

Hill, Reba. Drugs ingested by pregnant women. *Clinical Pharmacology Therapeutics,* 1973, **14,** 654–659.

Hillenbrand, E. D. *The relationship of psychological, medical, and feeding variables to breast feeding.* Unpublished master's thesis, George Washington University, 1965 (cited in Bell and Harper, 1977).

Hinde, R. A. *Biological bases of human social behavior.* New York: McGraw-Hill, 1974.

Hindley, C. B., Filliozat, A. M., Klackenberg, G., Nicolet-Meister, D., and Sand, E. A. Differences in age of walking in five European longitudinal samples. *Human Biology,* 1966, **38,** 364–379.

Hiscock, Merrill, and Kinsbourne, Marcel. Selective listening asymmetry in preschool children. *Developmental Psychology,* 1977, **13,** 217–224.

Hochhauser, Mark. Educational implications of drug abuse. *Journal of Drug Education,* 1978, **8,** 69–76.

Hochman, Joel Simon, and Brill, Norman Q. Chronic marijuana use and psychological adaptation. *American Journal of Psychiatry,* 1973, **130,** 132–140.

Hoffman, Lois Wladis. Changes in family roles, socialization, and sex differences. *American Psychologist,* 1977, **32,** 644–657.

Hoffman, Lois Wladis, and Nye, F. Ivan. *Working mothers.* San Francisco: Jossey-Bass, 1974.

Hollos, Marida, and Cowan, Philip A. Social isolation and cognitive development: Logical operations and role-taking abilities in three Norwegian social settings. *Child Development,* 1973, **44,** 630–641.

Holman, Milton G., and Docter, Richard. *Educational and psychological testing.* New York: Russell Sage, 1972.

Holmes, T. Stephenson and Holmes, Thomas H. Short-term intrusions into the life style routine. *Journal of Psychosomatic Research,* 1970, **14,** 121–132.

Holmes, Thomas H., and Masuda, Minoru. Life change and illness susceptibility. In Barbara Snell Dohrenwend and Bruce Dohrenwend (Eds.), *Stressful life events: Their nature and effects.* New York: Wiley, 1974. Pp. 45–72.

Hopkins, J. Roy. Sexual behavior in adolescence. *Journal of Social Issues,* 1977, **33**(2), 67–85.

Horney, Karen. *Feminine Psychology.* Harold Kelman (Ed.), New York: Norton, 1967.

Horowitz, Frances Degen, Ashton, Jennifer, Culp, Rex, and Gaddis (Eds.). The effects of obstetrical medication on the behavior of Israeli newborn infants and some comparisons with Uruguayan and American infants. *Child Development,* 1977, **48,** 1607–1623.

Horowitz, Frances Degen, and Paden, Lucile York. The effectiveness of environmental intervention programs. In Bettye M. Caldwell and Henry N. Ricciuti (Eds.), *Review of child development research* (Vol. III), *Child Development and Social Policy.* Chicago: University of Chicago Press, 1973. Pp. 331–402.

Howes, Virgil M. *Informal teaching in the open classroom.* New York: Macmillan, 1974.

Hubert, Jane. Belief and reality: Social factors in pregnancy and childbirth. In Martin P. M. Richards (Ed.), *The integration of a child into a social world.* London: Cambridge University Press, 1974. Pp. 37–51.

Humphrey, Michael. The effect of children upon the marriage relationship. *British Journal of Medical Psychology,* 1975, **48,** 273–279.

Hunt, Jane V., and Rhodes, Leanne. Mental development of preterm infants during the first year. *Child Development,* 1977, **48,** 204–210.

Hunt, J. McVicker. Wayne Dennis, 1905–1976. *Child Development,* 1977, **48,** 330–332.

Hunt, M. Special sex education survey. *Seventeen,* (Jul.) 1970, 94ff.

Ilg, Frances L., and **Ames, Louise Bates.** *School readiness: Behavior tests used at the Gesell Institute.* New York: Harper & Row, 1965.

Illsley, Raymond. The sociological study of reproduction and its outcome. In Stephen A. Richardson, and Alan F. Guttmacher (Eds.), *Childbearing: Its social and psychological aspects.* Baltimore: Williams and Wilkins Co., 1967. Pp. 75–141.

Inhelder, Bärbel, and **Piaget, Jean.** *The growth of logical thinking from childhood to adolescence.* New York: Basic Books, 1958.

Inhelder, Bärbel, and **Piaget, Jean.** *The early growth of logic in the child: Classification and seriation.* New York: Humanities Press, 1970 (originally published by Norton, 1964).

Inhelder, Bärbel, Sinclair, Hermine, and **Bovet, Magal.** *Learning and the development of cognition.* Susan Wedgwood (Trans.). Cambridge, Mass.: Harvard University Press, 1974.

Jackson, George D. On the report of the ad hoc committee on educational uses of tests with disadvantaged students: Another psychological view from the Association of Black Psychologists. *American Psychologist,* 1975, **30,** 88–93.

Jacobs, Blanche S., and **Moss, Howard A.** Birth order and sex of sibling as determinents of mother-infant interaction. *Child Development,* 1976, **47,** 315–322.

Jacobs, Jerry. *Adolescent suicide.* New York: Wiley, 1971.

Jaffe, Frederick S. Public policy on fertility control. *Scientific American,* 1973, **229**(1), 17–23.

James, William. *The principles of psychology* (Vol. I). New York: Dover, 1950 (originally published by Holt, 1890).

Jelliffe, Derrick B., and **Jelliffe, E. F. Patrice.** Current concepts in nutrition: "Breast is best": Modern meanings. *New England Journal of Medicine,* 1977, **297,** 912–915.

Jelliffe, Derrick B., and **Jelliffe, E. F. Patrice.** *Human milk in the modern world: Psychological, nutritional, and economic significance.* New York: Oxford University Press, 1978.

Jencks, Christopher. *Who gets ahead? The determinants of economic success in America.* New York: Basic Books, 1979.

Jencks, Christopher, Smith, Marshall, Acland, Henry, Bane, Mary Jo, Cohen, David, Gintis, Herbert, Heyns, Barbara, and **Michelson, Stephan.** *Inequality: A reassessment of the effect of family and schooling in America.* New York: Basic Books, 1972.

Jensen, Arthur R. How much can we boost I.Q. and scholastic achievement? *Harvard Educational Review,* 1969, **39,** 1–123.

Jirásek, Jan E. Principles of reproductive embryology. In J. L. Simpson (Ed.), *Disorders of sexual differentiation: Etiology and clinical delineation.* New York: Academic Press, 1976. Pp. 52–109.

Johnson, Dale L. The influences of social class and race on language test performance and spontaneous speech of preschool children. *Child Development,* 1974, **45,** 517–521.

Johnston, L., and **Bachman, J.** *Monitoring the future: A continuing study of the life styles and values of youth.* Ann Arbor, Mich. Institute for Social Research, 1975.

Johnston, Robert B. Motor function: Normal development and cerebral palsy. In Robert B. Johnston and Phyllis R. Magrab (Eds.), *Developmental disorders: Assessment, treatment, education.* Baltimore: University Park Press, 1976.

Jones, Kenneth Lyons. The fetal alcohol syndrome. In Raymond D. Harbison (Ed.), *Perinatal addiction.* New York: Halsted Press, 1975.

Jones, Mary Cover. The later careers of boys who were early- or late-maturing. *Child Development,* 1957, **28,** 113–128.

Jones, Mary Cover. Psychological correlates of somatic development. *Child Development,* 1965, **36,** 899–911.

Jones, Mary Cover, and **Bayley, Nancy.** Physical maturing among boys as related to behavior. *Journal of Educational Psychology,* 1950, **41,** 129–248.

Jones, N. Blurton. Rough-and-tumble play among nursery school children. In Jerome S. Bruner, Alison Jolly, and Kathy Sylva (Eds.), *Play.* New York: Basic Books, 1976, 352–363.

Jones, N. Blurton, and **Leach, Gill M.** Behavior of children and their mothers at separation and greeting. In Jones, N. Blurton (Ed.), *Ethnological studies of child behavior.* Cambridge, Mass.: Cambridge University Press, 1972. Pp. 217–247.

Jordaan, Jean Pierre, and **Heyde, Martha Bennett.** *Vocational maturity during the high school years.* New York: Teachers College Press, 1978.

Kaback, Michael M., Zeiger, Robert S., Reynolds, Linda W., and **Sonnebonn, Marquerite.** Approaches to the control and prevention of Tay-Sachs disease. In Arthur G. Steinberg and Alexander G. Bearn (Eds.), *Progress in medical genetics* (Vol. 10). New York: Grune and Stratton, 1974. Pp. 103–134.

Kadushin, Alfred. *Adopting older children.* New York: Columbia University Press, 1970.

Kagan, Jerome. Impulsive and reflective children: The significance of conceptual tempo. In John D. Krumboltz (Ed.), *Learning and the educational process.* Chicago: Rand McNally, 1965. Pp. 133–161.

Kagan, Jerome. *Change and continuity in infancy.* New York: Wiley, 1971.

Kagan, Jerome. Emergent themes in human development. *American Scientist,* 1976, **64**, 186–196.

Kagan, Jerome. The baby's elastic mind. *Human Nature,* 1978, **1**, 66–73.

Kagan, Jerome, and Klein, Robert E. Cross-cultural perspectives on early development. *American Psychologist,* 1973, **28**, 947–961.

Kagan, Jerome, Kearsley, Richard B., and Zelazo, Philip R. *Infancy: Its place in human development.* Cambrige, Mass.: Harvard University Press, 1978.

Kandel, Denise. Inter- and intragenerational influences on adolescent marijuana use. *Journal of Social Issues,* 1974, **30**(2), 107–135.

Kandel, Denise, and Lesser, Gerald S. Parent-adolescent relationships and adolescent independence in the United States and Denmark. *Journal of Marriage and the Family,* 1969, **31**, 348–358.

Karmel, Marjorie. *Painless childbirth: Thank you Dr. Lamaze.* Philadelphia: Lippincott, 1959.

Katchadourian, Herant A. *The biology of adolescence.* San Francisco: Freeman, 1977.

Katchadourian, Herant A., and Lunde, Donald T. *Biological aspects of human sexuality.* New York: Holt, Rinehart and Winston, 1975.

Katz, Phillis A. (Ed.). *Toward the elimination of racism.* New York: Pergamon Press, 1975.

Kellogg, Rhoda. *Analyzing children's art.* Palo Alto, Calif.: Mayfield, 1970.

Kempe, Ruth S., and Kempe, C. Henry. *Child abuse.* Cambridge, Mass.: Harvard University Press, 1978.

Kendler, Tracy S. Development of mediating responses in children. In *Cognitive development in children: Five monographs of the Society for Research in Child Development.* Chicago: University of Chicago Press, 1970, (originally published 1963).

Keniston, Kenneth, and The Carnegie Council on Children. *All our children: The American family under pressure.* New York: Harcourt, Brace, Jovanovich, 1977.

Kennel, John H., Jerauld, Richard, Wolfe, Harriet, Chesler, David, Kreger, Nancy C., McAlpine, Willie, Steffa, Meredith, and Klaus, Marshall H. Maternal behavior one year after early and extended post-partum contact. *Developmental Medicine and Child Neurology,* 1974, **16**, 172–179.

Kenyatta, Jomo. *Facing Mount Kenya: The tribal life of the Gikuyu.* New York: Vintage Books, 1965.

Keshet, Harry F., and Rosenthal, Kristine, M. Fathering after marital separation. *Social Work,* 1978, **23**, 11–18.

Kessen, William (Ed.). *Childhood in China.* New Haven: Yale University Press, 1975.

Kessen, William, Haith, Marshall, M., and Salapatek, Philip H. Human Infancy: A bibliography and guide. In Paul Mussen (Ed.), *Carmichael's manual of child psychology* (3rd Ed.). New York: Wiley, 1970. Pp. 287–445.

King, Maurice H. *Nutrition for developing nations.* Nairobi: Oxford University Press, 1973.

Kinsey, Alfred C., Pomeroy, Wardell B., and Martin, Clyde E. *Sexual behavior in the human male.* Philadelphia: Saunders, 1948.

Kitzinger, Sheila. *Giving birth: The parents' emotions in childbirth.* New York: Taplinger, 1971.

Klaus, Marshall H., and Kennel, John H. *Maternal-infant bonding: The impact of early separation or loss on family development.* St. Louis: Mosby, 1976.

Kleck, Robert E., Richardson, Stephen A., and Ronald, Linda. Physical appearance cues and interpersonal attraction in children. *Child Development,* 1974, **45**, 305–310.

Kloos, Peter. Female initiation rites among the Maroni River Caribe. *American Anthropologist,* 1969, **71**, 898–905.

Knapp, Mary, and Knapp, Herbert. *One potato, two potato: The secret education of American children.* New York: Morton, 1976.

Knittle, Jerome L. Obesity in childhood: A problem in adipose tissue cellular development. *Journal of Pediatrics,* 1972, **81**, 1048–1059.

Knodel, John. Breast-feeding and population growth. *Science,* 1977, **198**, 1111–1115.

Knox, David, and Wilson, Kenneth L. The difference between having one and two children. *Family Coordinator,* 1978, **27**, 23–25.

Koch, Kenneth. *Wishes, lies, and dreams: Teaching children to write poetry.* New York: Chelssea House Publishers, 1970.

Koff, Elissa, Rierdan, Jill, and Silverstone, Esther. Changes in representation of body image as a function of menarcheal status. *Developmental Psychology,* 1978, **14**(6), 635–642.

Kohlberg, Lawrence. Development of children's orientation towards a moral order (Part I). Sequence in the development of moral thought. *Vita Humana,* 1963, **6**, 11–36.

Kohlberg, Lawrence. A cognitive developmental analysis of children's sex-role concepts and attitudes. In Eleanor Maccoby (Ed.), *The development of sex differences.* Stanford, Calif.: Stanford University Press, 1966. Pp. 82–172.

Kohlberg, Lawrence, and Elfenbein, Donald. The development of moral judgments concerning capital punishment. *American Journal of Orthopsychiatry,* 1975, **45**, 614–640.

Kohlberg, Lawrence, and Ullian, Dorothy Z. Stages in the development of psychosexual concepts and attitudes. In

Richard C. Friedman, Ralph M. Richart, and Raymond L. VandeWiele (Eds.), *Sex differences in behavior: A conference.* New York: Wiley, 1974. Pp. 209–231.

Kohlberg, Lawrence, Yaeger, Judy, and Hjertholm, Else. Private speech: Four studies and a review of theories. *Child Development,* 1968, **39**, 691–736.

Kolata, Gina Bari. Infertility: Promising new treatments. *Science,* 1978a, **202**, 200–203.

Kolata, Gina Bari. In vitro fertilization: Is it safe and repeatable? *Science,* 1978b, **201**, 698–699.

Kolata, Gina Bari. Scientists attack report that obstetrical medications endanger children. *Science,* 1979, **204**, 391–392.

Koluchová, Jarmila. Severe deprivation in twins: A case study (and) A report on the further development of twins after severe and prolonged deprivation. In Ann M. Clarke and A. D. B. Clarke (Eds.), *Early experience: Myth and evidence.* New York: The Free Press, 1976. Pp. 45–66.

Konner, M. J. Aspects of the developmental ethology of a foraging people. In N. Blurton Jones (Ed.), *Ethological studies of child behavior.* London: Cambridge University Press, 1972. Pp. 285–304.

Kontos, Donna. A study of the effects of extended mother infant contact on maternal behavior at one and three months. *Birth and Family Journal,* 1978, **5**, 133–140.

Koocher, Gerald P. Childhood, death, and cognitive development. *Developmental Psychology,* 1973, **9**, 369–375.

Korner, Anneliese F. The effect of the infant's state, level of arousal, sex, and ontogenetic stage on the caregiver. In Michael Lewis and Leonard A. Rosenblum (Eds.), *The effect of the infant on its caregiver.* New York: Wiley, 1974. Pp. 105–121.

Kotelchuck, Milton, Zelazo, Philip R., Kagan, Jerome, and Spelke, Elizabeth. Infant reaction to parental separations when left with familiar and unfamiliar adults. *Journal of Genetic Psychology,* 1975, **126**, 255–262.

Kramer, Judith A., Hill, Kennedy T., and Cohen, Leslie B. Infants' development of object permanence: A refined methodology and new evidence for Piaget's hypothesized ordinality. *Child Development,* 1975, **46**, 149–155.

Kuhn, Deanna, Langer, Jonas, Kohlberg, Lawrence, and Haan, Norma S. The development of formal operations in logical and moral judgment. *Genetic Psychology Monographs,* 1977, **95**, 97–188.

Kuhn, Deanna, Nash, Sharon Churnin, and Brucken, Laura. Sex role concepts of two- and three-year-olds. *Child Development,* 1978, **49**, 445–451.

Kurokawa, Minako. Acculturation and childhood accidents among Chinese and Japanese Americans. *Genetic Psychology Monographs,* 1969, **79**, 89–159.

Labov, William. *Language in the inner city: Studies in the black English vernacular.* Philadelphia: University of Pennsylvania Press, 1972.

Landrum, Roger. Preface. *Stage theories of cognitive and moral development: Criticisms and applications.* Reprint (No. 13), *Harvard Educational Review,* 1978.

Landy, Frank, Rosenberg, Benjamin G., and Sutton-Smith, Brian. The effect of limited father absence on cognitive development. *Child Development,* 1969, **40**, 941–944.

Lang, Raven, *Birth book.* Ben Lomond, Calif: Genesis Press, 1972.

Langer, William L. Checks on population growth: 1750–1850. *Scientific American,* 1972, **226**(2), 92–99.

Laosa, Luis M., and Brophy, Jere E. Effects of sex and birth order on sex-role development and intelligence among kindergarten children. *Developmental Psychology,* 1972, **6**, 409–415.

Larsen, Spencer A., and Homer, Daryl R. Relation of breast versus bottle feeding to hospitalization for gastroenteritis in a middle-class U.S. population. *The Journal of Pediatrics,* 1978, **92**(3), 417–418.

Lebel, Robert Roger. Ethical issues arising in the genetic counseling relationship. In Daniel Bergsma (Ed.), The National Foundation, March of Dimes, *Birth Defects,* original article series, 1978, **14**.

Leboyer, Frederick. *Birth without violence.* New York: Knopf, 1975.

Lee, Lee C. *Personality development in childhood.* Monterey, Calif.: Brooks/Cole, 1976.

Leifer, A. D., Leiderman, P. H., Barnett, C. R., and Williams, J. A. Effects of mother-infant separation on maternal attachment behavior. *Child Development,* 1972, **43**, 1203–1218.

Lenneberg, Eric H. *Biological foundations of language.* New York: Wiley, 1967.

Leopold, Werner F. *Grammar and general problems in the first two years. Speech development of a bilingual child: A linguist's record* (Vol. 3) Evanston, Illinois: Northwestern University Press, 1949. (Quoted in David McNeill, *The acquisition of language: The study of developmental psycholinguistics.* New York: Harper and Row, 1970.)

Levenstein, Phyllis. Cognitive growth in preschoolers through verbal interaction with mothers. *American Journal of Orthopsychiatry,* 1970, **40**, 426–432.

Levinson, Daniel J. *The seasons of a man's life.* New York: Knopf, 1978.

Levy, Harold B. *Square pegs in round holes: The learning-disabled child in the classroom and at home.* Boston: Little, Brown, 1973.

Lewis, Michael, and **Brooks, Jeanne.** Self, others, and fear: Infant's reactions to people. In Michael Lewis and Leonard A. Rosenblum (Eds.), *The origins of fear.* New York: Wiley, 1975.

Lewis, Michael, and **Brooks, Jeanne.** Self-knowledge and emotional development. In Michael Lewis and Leonard A. Rosenblum (Eds.), *The Development of affect.* New York: Plenum, 1978. Pp. 205–226.

Lewis, Richard. *Miracles: Poems by children of the English-speaking world.* New York: Bantam, 1977.

Lewis, Richard. *Journeys.* New York: Bantam Books, 1978.

Liben, Lynn S. Perspective-taking skills in young children: Seeing the world through rose-colored glasses. *Developmental Psychology,* 1978, **14,** 87–92.

Lidz, Theodore. *The person: His and her development throughout the life cycle* (Rev. Ed.). New York: Basic Books, 1976.

Liebert, Robert M., Neale, John M., and **Davidson, Emily S.** *The early window: Effects of television on children and youth.* New York: Pergamon Press, 1973.

Linde, Shirley M. *Sickle cell: A complete guide to prevention and treatment.* New York: Pavilion, 1972.

Lindemann, Constance. *Birth control and unmarried young women.* New York: Springer, 1974.

Lindfors, Judith. *Children's language and learning.* Englewood Cliffs, N. J.: Prentice Hall, in press.

Linksz, Arthur. *On writing, reading, and dyslexia.* New York: Grune and Stratton, 1973.

Lipsitt, Lewis P. Perinatal indicators, and psychophysiological precursors of crib death. In Frances Degen Horowitz (Ed.), *Early developmental hazards: Predictors and precautions.* Boulder, Colorado: Westview Press, 1978.

Lipton, Isabel. Head teacher of the Bedford Street School. Personal communication, 1973.

Lloyd-Still, John D. Clinical studies on the effects of malnutrition during infancy on the subsequent physical and intellectual development. In John D. Lloyd-Still (Ed.), *Malnutrition and intellectual development.* Littleton, Mass.: Publishing Sciences Group, 1976. Pp. 103–159.

Lovaas, O. Ivar, and **Simmons, James Q.** Manipulation of self-destruction in three retarded children. *Journal of Applied Behavioral Analysis,* 1969, **2,** 143–157.

Lowe, Marianne. Trends in the development of representational play in infants from one to three years—An observational study. *Journal of Child Psychology,* 1975, **16,** 33–48.

Lowrey, George H. *Growth and development of children* (7th Ed.). Chicago: Year Book Medical Publishers, 1978.

Luria, Aleksandr R. *The role of speech in the regulation of normal and abnormal behavior.* New York: Boni and Liveright, 1961.

Luria, Aleksandr R. *Human brain and psychological processes.* Basil Haigh (Trans.). New York: Harper and Row, 1966.

Lyle, J. G., and **Johnson, E. G.** Development of lateral consistency and its relation to reading and reversals. *Perceptual and Motor Skills,* 1976, **43,** 695–698.

Lytton, Hugh, Conway, Dorice, and **Sauvé, Reginald.** The impact of twinship on parent-child interaction. *Journal of Personality and Social Psychology,* 1977, **35,** 97–107.

McCall, Robert B. Challenges to a science of developmental psychology. *Child Development,* 1977, **48,** 333–344.

McCarthy, Dorthea. Language development in children. In Leonard Carmichael (Ed.), *Manual of child psychology* (2nd Ed.). New York: Wiley, 1954.

McCleary, Elliott H. *New miracles of childbirth.* New York: McKay, 1974.

McClelland, David C., Constantian, Carol A., Regalado, David, and **Stone, Carolyn.** Making it to maturity. *Psychology Today,* 1978, **12**(1), 42–53, 114.

Maccoby, Eleanor Emmons, and **Hagen, John W.** Effect of distraction upon central versus incidental recall: Developmental trends. *Journal of Experimental Child Psychology,* 1965, **2,** 280–289.

Maccoby, Eleanor Emmons, and **Jacklin, Carol Nagy.** *The psychology of sex differences.* Stanford: Stanford University Press, 1974.

Maccoby, Michael, and **Modiano, Nancy.** On culture and equivalence. In Jerome Bruner, Rose Olver, and Patricia Greenfield (Eds.), *Studies in cognitive growth.* New York: Wiley, 1966. Pp. 257–259.

McConnell, James V. *Understanding human behavior* (2nd Ed.). New York: Holt, Rinehart, and Winston, 1977.

McDavid, John W., and **Harari, Herbert.** Stereotyping of names and popularity in grade-school children. *Child Development,* 1966, **37,** 453–459.

Macfarlane, Aidan. *The psychology of childbirth.* Cambridge, Mass.: Harvard University Press, 1977.

McGhee, Paul H. Cognitive development and children's comprehension of humor. *Child Development,* 1971, **42,** 123–138.

McGowan, Robert W., Jarman, Boyd O., and **Pedersen, Darhl M.** Effects of a competitive endurance training program on self-concept and peer approval. *The Journal of Psychology,* 1974, **86,** 57–60.

McGurk, Harry, and **Lewis, Michael.** Space perception in early infancy: Perception within a common auditory-visual space? *Science,* 1974, **186,** 649–650.

McIntire, Roger W. Parenthood training or mandatory birth control: Take your choice. *Psychology Today,* 1973, **7**(5), 34–39, 132–133, 143.

Mackworth, N. H. and **Bruner, Jerome S.** How adults and children search and recognize pictures. *Human Development,* 1970, **13**, 149–177.

McMillen, Marilyn M. Differential mortality by sex in fetal and neonatal deaths. *Science,* 1979, **204**, 89–91.

McNeill, David. Language development in children. In Paul Mussen (Ed.), *Handbook of child psychology* (3rd Ed.). New York: Wiley, 1970.

Madden, John, Levenstein, Phyllis, and **Levenstein, Sidney.** Longitudinal I.Q. outcomes of the mother-child home program. *Child Development,* 1976, **47**, 1015–1025.

Madsen, Millard C. Developmental and cross-cultural differences in the cooperative and competitive behavior of young children. *Journal of Cross-Cultural Psychology,* 1971, **2**, 365–371.

Madsen, Millard C., and **Shapira, Ariella.** Cooperative and competitive behavior of urban Afro-American, Anglo-American, and Mexico-American and Mexican village children. *Developmental Psychology,* 1970, **3**, 16–20.

Maehr, Martin L. Culture and achievement motivation. *American Psychologist,* 1974, **29**, 887–896.

Magenis, R. E., Overton, K. M., Chamberlin, J., Brady, T., and **Lovrien, E.** Parental origin of the extra chromosome in Down's Syndrome. *Human Genetics,* 1977, **37**, 7–16.

Mahler, Margaret S., Pine, Fred, and **Bergman, Anni.** *The psychological birth of the human infant: Symbiosis and individuation.* New York: Basic Books, 1975.

Martin, Barclay. Parent-child relations. In Frances Degan Horowitz (Ed.), *Review of child development research* (Vol. IV). Chicago: University of Chicago Press, 1975. Pp. 463–540.

Marx, Jean L. Botulism in infants: A cause of sudden death? *Science,* 1978, **201**, 799–801.

Maslow, Abraham H. *Toward a psychology of being* (2nd Ed.). Princeton, N. J.: Van Nostrand, 1968.

Masters, John C. Social comparison by young children. In Willard W. Hartup and Nancy L. Smothergill (Eds.), *The young child.* Washington, D. C.: The National Association for the Education of Young Children, 1972. Pp. 320–339.

Masters, William H., and **Johnson, Virginia E.** *Human sexual response.* Boston: Little, Brown, 1966.

Mayer, Jean. *Overweight: Causes, costs, and control.* Englewood Cliffs, N. J.: Prentice Hall, 1968.

Mead, Margaret. *Coming of age in Samoa.* New York: Morrow, 1961 (originally published in 1928).

Mead, Margaret, and **Newton, Niles.** Cultural patterning of perinatal behavior. In Stephen A. Richardson and Alan F. Guttmacher (Eds.), *Childbearing—Its social and psychological aspects.* Baltimore: Williams and Wilkins Co., 1967. Pp. 142–244.

Meadow, Kathryn P. The development of deaf children. In E. Mavis Hetherington (Ed.), *Review of child development research* (Vol. 5). Chicago: University of Chicago Press, 1975.

Meares, Russell, Grimwade, James, and **Wood, Carl.** A possible relationship between anxiety in pregnancy and puerperal depression. *Journal of Psychosomatic Research,* 1976, **20**, 605–610.

Meichenbaum, Donald H., and **Goodman, Joseph.** Training impulsive children to talk to themselves: A means of developing self-control. *Journal of Abnormal Psychology,* 1971, **77**, 115–126.

Mercer, G. William, Handleby, John D., and **Carpenter, Richard A.** Adolescent drug use and attitudes toward the family. *Canadian Journal of Behavioural Science,* 1978, **10**, 79–90.

Meredith, Howard V. Research between 1960 and 1970 on the standing height of young children in different parts of the world. In Hayne W. Reese and Lewis P. Lipsitt (Eds.), *Advances in child development and behavior* (Vol. 12). New York: Academic Press, 1978. Pp. 2–59.

Milewski, Allen E., and **Siqueland, Einar R.** Discrimination of color and pattern novelty in one-month human infants. *Journal of Experimental Child Psychology,* 1975, **19**, 122–136.

Miller, Louise B., and **Dyer, Jean L.** Four preschool programs: Their dimensions and effects. *Monographs of the Society for Research in Child Development,* 1975, **40**(5 & 6).

Miller, Neil E., and **Dollard, John.** *Social learning and imitation.* New Haven: Yale University Press, 1941.

Miller, P. M., Ingham, J. G., and **Davison, S.** Life events, symptoms, and social support. *Journal of Psychosomatic Research,* 1976, **20**, 515–522.

Miller, William R., and **Lief, Harold I.** Masturbatory attitudes, knowledge, and experience: Data from the sex knowledge, and attitude test (SKAT). *Archives of Sexual Behavior,* 1976, **5**, 447–467.

Mills, M., and **Melhuish, E.** Recognition of mother's voice in early infancy. *Nature,* 1974, **252**(5479). Pp. 123–124.

Milne, Conrad, Seefeldt, Vern, and **Reuschlein, Philip.** Relationship between grade, sex, race, and motor performance in young children. *Research Quarterly,* 1976, **47**, 726–730.

Milunsky, Aubrey. *The prenatal diagnosis of hereditary disorders.* Springfield, Ill.: Thomas, 1973.

Milunsky, Aubrey. *Know your genes.* Boston: Houghton Mifflin, 1977.

Minuchin, Salvador, Rosman, Bernice L., and **Baker, Lester.** *Psychosomatic families: Anorexia nervosa in context.* Cambridge, Mass.: Harvard University Press, 1978.

Mischel, Walter. Sex typing and socialization. In Paul H. Mussen (Ed.), *Carmichael's manual of child development* (Vol. II). New York: Wiley, 1970. Pp. 3–72.

Mischel, Walter. Toward a cognitive social learning reconceptualization of personality. *Psychological Review,* 1973, **80,** 252–283.

Mischel, Walter. How children postpone pleasure. *Human Nature,* 1978, **1,** 51–55.

Money, John, Ehrhard, Anke A., and **Masica, Daniel.** Fetal feminization induced by androgen insensitivity in the testicular feminizing syndrome: Effect on marriage and maternalism. *Johns Hopkins Medical Journal,* 1968, **123,** 105–114.

Montagu, Ashley. *Touching: The human significance of the skin.* New York: Columbia University Press, 1971.

Moore, Raymond S., and **Moore, Dorothy N.** *Better late than early.* New York: Reader's Digest Press, 1975.

Moore, Shirley, G. Correlates of peer acceptance in nursery school children. In Willard W. Hartup and Nancy L. Smothergill (Eds.), *The young child: Reviews of research.* Washington, D. C.: National Association for the Education of Young Children, 1967.

Morrison, Frederick J., Holmes, Deborah Lott, and **Haith, Marshall M.** A developmental study of the effect of familiarity on short-term visual memory. *Journal of Experimental Child Psychology,* 1974, **18,** 412–425.

Moss, Howard, A. Sex, age, and state as determinents of mother-infant interaction. *Merrill Palmer Quarterly,* 1967, **13,** 19–36.

Moss, Howard A., and **Kagan, Jerome.** Maternal influences on early I.Q. score. *Psychological Reports,* 1958, **4,** 655–661.

Moss, Melvin. Director of Medical Research for Muscular Dystrophy Foundation. *Personal Communication,* February 19, 1979.

Motulsky, Arno G., Carter, C. O., and **Emery, A. E. H.** *Genetic counseling.* New York: MSS Information Corporation, 1974.

Murphy, Lois Barclay. *The widening world of childhood: Paths toward mastery.* New York: Basic Books, 1962.

Murphy, Lois Barclay, and **Moriarty, Alice E.** *Vulnerability, coping, and growth: From infancy to adolescence.* New Haven: Yale University Press, 1976.

Mussen, Paul Henry, and **Eisenberg-Berg, Nancy.** *Roots of caring, sharing, and helping: The development of prosocial behavior in children.* San Francisco: Freeman, 1977.

Mussen, Paul Henry, and **Jones, Mary Cover.** Self-conceptions, motivations, and interpersonal attitudes of late- and early-maturing boys. *Child Development,* 1957, **28,** 243–256.

Naeye, Richard L. Coitus, and associated amniotic-fluid infections. *New England Journal of Medicine,* 1979, **301,** 1198–1200.

Nagle, James J. *Heredity and human affairs* (2nd Ed.). St. Louis: C. V. Mosby, 1979.

Nagy, Maria. The child's theories concerning death. *Journal of Genetic Psychology,* 1948, **73,** 3–27.

National Center for Health Statistics. *Anthropometric and clinical findings: Preliminary findings of the first health and nutrition examination survey, United States, 1971–1972.* Washington, D.C.: DHEW Publication No. (HRA), 1975. Pp. 75–1229.

National Center for Health Statistics. NCHS Growth charts, 1976. *Vital Statistics,* 1976, **253,** (Supp.), U.S. Department of Health, Education, and Welfare.

National Commission on Marijuana and Drug Abuse. *Drug use in America: Problem in perspective.* Second report to the President and the United States Congress, United States Department of Health, Education, and Welfare. Washington, D. C.: United States Government Printing Office, March, 1973 (No. S266–00003).

Neimark, Edith D. Intellectual development during adolescence. In Frances Degan Horowitz (Ed.), *Review of research in child development* (Vol. 4). Chicago: University of Chicago Press, 1975.

Nelson, Dale O. Leadership in sports. *Research Quarterly,* 1966, **37,** 268–275.

Nelson, Katherine. Structure and strategy in learning to talk. *Monographs of the society for research in child development,* 1973, **38,** (1 & 2, Serial No. 149).

Nettleblady, Per, Fagerström, Carl-Fredrik, and **Uddenberg, Nils.** The significance of reported childbirth pain. *Journal of Psychosomatic Research,* 1976, **20,** 215–221.

Neugarten, Bernice L. Adult personality: Toward a psychology of the life cycle. In Bernice L. Neugarten (Ed.), *Middle age and aging: A reader in social psychology.* Chicago: University of Chicago Press, 1968.

Neugarten, Bernice L., and **Datan, Nancy.** Sociological perspectives on the life cycle. In Paul B. Baltes and K. Warner Schaie (Eds.), *Life-span developmental psychology: Personality and socialization.* New York: Academic Press, 1973.

Neugarten, Bernice L. The future and the young-old. *Gerontologist,* 1975, **15,** 4–9.

Newberger, Carolyn Moore, Newberger, Eli H., and **Harper, Gordon P.** The social ecology of malnutrition in childhood. In John D. Lloyd-Still (Ed.), *Malnutrition and intellectual development.* Littleton, Mass.: Publishing Sciences Group, 1976. Pp. 160–186.

Newsday. Human milk needed to help keep baby alive. January 11, 1979, p. 23.

Newsday. 1,000 offer breast milk to baby. January 12, 1979, p. 3.

Newton, Niles. Battle between breast and bottle. *Psychology Today*, 1972, **6**(2), 68–70, 88–89.

Newton, Niles, and **Newton, Michael.** Lactation—Its psychological components. In John G. Howells (Ed.), *Modern perspectives in psycho-obstetrics*. New York: Brunner/Mazel, 1972. Pp. 385–409.

The New York Times. Taller and huskier young Japanese are attributed to increase of protein in diet since World War II. May 17, 1970, p. 12.

The New York Times. Child rearing cost is put near $85,000. September 20, 1976, p. 35.

The New York Times. F. D. A. seeks alcoholic drink warning for pregnant women. November 23, 1977, p. B-9.

The New York Times. U. N. sees population rise slowing. June 28, 1978, (City Edition).

The New York Times. Study says smoking perils baby even if halted before pregnancy. January 17, 1979, p. A-11.

The New York Times. Baby is frozen to death at heatless home in Queens. February 7, 1979, p. B-3.

The New York Times. Queens baby frozen to death also found maltreated. February 8, 1979, p. B-85.

Nix, Gary W. (Ed.). *Mainstream education for hearing impaired children and youth*. New York: Grune & Stratton, 1976.

Nobbe, Charles E., and **Okraku, Ishmael O.** Male-female differences in family size preferences among college students. *Social Biology*, 1974, **21**, 279–289.

Nott, P. N., Franklin, M., Armitage, C., and **Gelder, M. C.** Hormonal changes and mood in the puerperium. *British Journal of Psychiatry*, 1976, **128**, 379–383.

Novak, M. A., and **Harlow, Harry F.** Social recovery of monkeys isolated for the first year of life: 1. Rehabilitation and therapy. *Developmental Psychology*, 1975, **11**, 453–465.

Nyhan, William L. *The heredity factor: Genes, chromosomes and you*. New York: Grosset and Dunlop, 1976.

O'Brien, Thomas E., and **McManus, Carol E.** Drugs and the Fetus: A consumer's guide by generic and brand name. *Birth and the Family Journal*, 1978, **5**, 58–86.

Offer, Daniel. *The psychological world of the teenager: A study of normal adolescent boys*. New York: Basic Books, 1969.

Offer, Daniel, and **Offer, Judith.** *From teenage to young manhood*. New York: Basic Books, 1975.

Omenn, Gilbert S. Prenatal diagnosis of genetic disorders. *Science*, 1978, **200**, 952–958.

Opie, Iona, and **Opie, Peter.** *The lore and language of schoolchildren*. Oxford: The Clarendon Press, 1959.

Ornitz, Edward M., and **Ritvo, Edward R.** The syndrome of autism: A critical review. *American Journal of Psychiatry*, 1976, **133**, 609–621.

Osherson, Daniel N., and **Markman, Ellen.** Language and the ability to evaluate contradictions and tautologies. *Cognition*, 1974–1975, **3**, 213–226.

Osofsky, Howard J., and **Kendall, Norman.** Poverty as a criterion of risk. *Clinical Obstetrics and Gynecology*, 1973, **16**, 106–109.

Osofsky, Joy D., and **O'Connell, Edward J.** Patterning of newborn behavior in an urban population. *Child Development*, 1977, **48**, 532–536.

Oster, Harriet. Facial expression and affect development. In Michael Lewis and Leonard A. Rosenblum (Eds.), *The development of affect*. New York: Plenum Press, 1978. Pp. 43–75.

Osterrieth, Paul A. Adolescense: Some psychological aspects. In Gerald Caplan and Serge Lebovici (Eds.), *Adolescence: Psychosocial perspectives*. New York: Basic Books, 1969. Pp. 11–21.

Ostrea, Enrique M., Jr., and **Chavez, Cleofe J.** Perinatal problems (excluding neonatal withdrawal) in maternal drug addiction : A study of 830 cases. *The Journal of Pediatrics*, 1979, **94**(2), 292–295.

Palmer, Francis H. The effects of early childhood intervention. Paper presented at the Annual meeting of the American Association for the Advancement of Science, Denver, Colorado, 1977, (ERIC Document 143 427, 1978).

Paluszny, Maria J. Psychoactive drugs in the treatment of learning disabilities. In William M. Cruickshank (Ed.), *Learning disabilities in home, school, and community*. Syracuse, N. Y.: Syracuse University Press, 1977. Pp. 292–319.

Papandropoulou, Ioanna, and **Sinclair, Hermine.** What is a word? Experimental study of children's ideas on grammar. *Human Development*, 1974, **17**, 241–258.

Parke, Ross D. Punishment in children: Effects, side effects, and alternative strategies. In Harry L. Hom, Jr. and Paul A. Robinson (Eds.), *Psychological processes in early education*. New York: Academic Press, 1977, 71–97.

Parke, Ross D. The father of the child. *The Sciences*, 1979, **19**(4), 12–15.

Parten, Mildred B. Social participation among pre-school children. *Journal of Abnormal and Social Psychology*, 1932, **27**, 243–269.

Patterson, Gerald R. The aggressive child: Victim and architect of a coercive system. In Eric J. Mash, Leo A. Hamerlynck, and Lee C. Handy (Eds.), *Behavior modification and families*. New York: Brunner/Mazel, 1976, 267–316.

Pawson, M., and **Morris, Norman.** The role of the father in pregnancy and labor. In Norman Morris (Ed.), *Psychosomatic medicine in obstetrics and gynecology*. Basel: Karger, 1972.

Peaslee, Mary. The development of competency in 2-year-old infants in day care and home reared environments. Ph. D. dissertation, Florida State University, 1976.

Peel, E. A. *The nature of adolescent judgment*. New York: Wiley, 1971.

Pelton, Leroy H. Child abuse and neglect: The myth of classlessness. *American Journal of Orthopsychiatry*, 1978, **48**, 608–617.

Persaud, T. V. N. *Problems of birth defects: From Hippocrates to Thalidomide and after: Original papers*. Baltimore: University Park Press, 1977.

Piaget, Jean. *Play, dreams, and imitation in childhood*. Caleb Gattagno and F. M. Hodgson (Trans.). New York: Norton, 1951.

Piaget, Jean. *The origins of intelligence in children*. Margaret Cook, (Trans.). New York: International Universities Press, 1952.

Piaget, Jean. *The language and thought of the child* (3rd Ed.). Marjorie and Ruth Gabain (Trans.). London: Routledge and Kegan, Paul, 1959.

Piaget, Jean. *Judgment and reasoning in the child*. Marjorie Warden (Trans.). London: Routledge and Paul, 1962 (originally published in 1928).

Piaget, Jean. *The moral judgment of the child*. Marjorie Gabain (Trans.). New York: The Free Press, 1965.

Piaget, Jean. *The child's conception of time*, A. J. Pomerans (Trans.). New York: Basic Books, 1970a.

Piaget, Jean. *The child's conception of movement and speed*, G. E. T. Holloway and M. J. Mackenzie (Trans.). New York: Basic Books, 1970b.

Piaget, Jean. Intellectual evolution from adolescence to adulthood. *Human Development*, 1972, **15**, 1–12.

Piaget, Jean. *The grasp of consciousness: Action and concept in the young child*, Susan Wedgwood (Trans.). Cambridge, Mass.: Harvard University Press, 1976.

Piaget, Jean, and **Inhelder. Bärbel.** *The child's conception of space*, F. J. Langdon and J. L. Lunzer (Trans.). London: Routledge and Paul, 1963.

Piaget, Jean, and **Inhelder, Bärbel.** *The psychology of the child*, Helen Weaver (Trans.). New York: Basic Books, 1969.

Piaget, Jean, and **Szeminska, Aline.** *The child's conception of number*, Caleb Gattegno and F. Hodgson (Trans.). New York: Norton, 1965.

Pick, Anne D., **Frankel, Daniel G.**, and **Hess, Valerie.** Children's attention: The development of selectivity. In E. Mavis Hetherington (Ed.), *Review of child development research* (Vol. V). Chicago: University of Chicago Press, 1975. Pp. 325–383.

Pilling, Doria, and **Pringle, Mia Kellmer.** *Controversial issues in child development*. New York: Schocken Books, 1978.

Pines, Maya. Invisible playmates. *Psychology Today*, 1978, **12**(4), 38–42, 106.

Porter, Judith D. R. *Black child, white child: The development of racial attitudes*. Cambridge, Mass.: Harvard University Press, 1971.

Pringle, Mia Kellmer. Reducing the costs of raising children in inadequate environments. In Nathan B. Talbot (Ed.), *Raising children in modern America: Problems and prospective*. Boston: Little, Brown, 1974. Pp. 189–215.

Pritchard, Jack, and **MacDonald, Paul C.** *Williams obstetrics* (15th Ed.). New York: Appleton-Century-Crofts, 1976.

Quay, Lorene C. Negro dialect and Binet performance in severely disadvantaged black four-year-olds. *Child Development*, 1972, **43**, 245–250.

Radin, Norma. Maternal warmth, achievement motivation, and cognitive functioning in lower-class preschool children. *Child Development*, 1971, **42**, 1560–1565.

Radin, Norma, and **Epstein, Ann S.** Motivational components related to farther behavior and cognitive functioning in preschoolers. *Child Development*, 1976, **46**, 831–839.

Rank, Otto. *The trauma of birth*. New York: Harcourt Brace, 1929.

Raring, Richard H. *Crib death*. Hicksville, N. Y.: Exposition Press, 1975.

Rebelsky, Freda G., **Starr, Raymond H., Jr.**, and **Luria, Zella.** Language development: The first four years. In Yvonne Brackbill (Ed.), *Infancy and early childhood*. New York: The Free Press, 1967.

Recommended Dietary Allowances. National Research Council, Food and Nutrition Board, National Academy of Sciences, Washington, D. C., 1974.

Reed, James. *From private vice to public virtue: The birth control movement and American society since 1830*. New York: Basic Books, 1978.

Rheingold, Harriet L., and **Cook, Kaye V.** The contents of boys' and girls' rooms as an index of parents' behavior. *Child Development*, 1975, **46**, 459–463.

Rheingold, Harriet L., **Gewirtz, Jacob, L.**, and **Ross, Helen W.** Social conditioning of vocalizations in the infant. *Journal of Comparative and Physiological Psychology*, 1959, **52**, 68–73.

Rheingold, Harriet L., Hay, Dale F., and **West, Meredith J.** Sharing in the second year of life. *Child Development,* 1976, **47,** 1148–1158.

Ribal, Joseph E. Social character and meanings of selfishness and altruism. *Sociology and Social Research,* 1963, **47,** 311–321.

Richards, M. P. M., Bernal, J. F., and **Brackbill, Yvonne.** Early behavior differences: Gender or circumcision? *Developmental Psychobiology,* 1976, **9,** 89–95.

Richmond, Julius. *The Surgeon General's Report on Smoking.* Department of Health, Education, and Welfare, United States Government, 1979.

Riesen, Austin H. (Ed.). *The developmental neuropsychology of sensory deprivation.* New York: Academic Press, 1975.

Rinder, Irwin D. The effects of marijuana: A social psychological interpretation. *Psychiatry,* 1978, **41,** 202–206.

Roberts, C. J., and **Lowe, C. R.** Where have all the conceptions gone? *Lancet,* 1975, i, 498–499.

Roberts, J. Fraser. *An introduction to medical genetics* (6th Ed.). London: Oxford University Press, 1973.

Roberts, Jean, and **Baird, James T., Jr.** National Center for Health Statistics. *Parental ratings of behavioral patterns of children.* Series 11–#108, DHEW Publication, No. 72–1010, 1971.

Roberts, Jean, and **Baird, James T., Jr.** National Center for Health Statistics. *Behavior patterns of children in school.* Series 11–#113, DHEW Publication, No. 72–1042, 1972.

Robinson, Halbert B., and **Robinson, Nancy M.** Longitudinal development of very young children in a comprehensive day care program: The first two years. *Child Development,* 1971, **42,** 1673–1683.

Roche, A. F., French, N. Y., and **Davilla, G. H.** Areolar size during pubescence. *Human Biology,* 1971, **43,** 210–223.

Rogers, David. Vocational and career education: A critique and some new directions. *Teachers College Record,* 1973, **74,** 471–511.

Rose, Susan Ann. Infants' transfer of response between two-dimensional and three-dimensional stimuli. *Child Development,* 1977, **48,** 1086–1091.

Rosengren, William R. Some social psychological aspects of delivery room difficulties. *The Journal of Nervous and Mental Disease,* 1961, **132,** 515–521.

Rosenkrantz, Arthur L. A note on adolescent suicide: Incidence, dynamics, and some suggestions for treatment. *Adolescence,* 1978, **13,** 209–214.

Rosenthal, David. *Genetic theory and abnormal behavior.* New York: McGraw Hill, 1970.

Rosenthal, Robert, and **Jacobson, Lenore.** *Pygmalion in the classroom: Teacher expectation and pupils' intellectual development.* New York: Holt, Rinehart and Winston, 1968.

Ross, Bruce M., and **Kerst, Stephen M.** Developmental Memory theories: Baldwin and Piaget. In Hayne W. Reese and Lewis P. Lipsitt (Eds.), *Advances in child development and behavior* (Vol. 12). New York: Academic Press, 1978. Pp. 183–229.

Ross, Dorothea M., and **Ross, Sheila A.** *Hyperactivity: Research, theory, and action.* New York: Wiley, 1976.

Routh, Donald K., Schroeder, Carolyn S., and **O'Tuama, Lorcan A.** Development of activity level in children. *Developmental Psychology,* 1974, **10,** 163–168.

Rubenstein, Judith L., and **Howes, Carollee.** Caregiving and infant behavior in day care and in homes. *Developmental Psychology,* 1979, **15,** 1–24.

Rubin, Kenneth H. The social and cognitive value of preschool toys and activities. *Canadian Journal of Behavioral Science,* 1977, **9,** 382–385.

Rubin, Kenneth H., Maioni, Terrence L., and **Hornung, Margaret.** Free play behaviors in middle- and lower-class preschoolers: Parten and Piaget revisited. *Child Development,* 1976, **47,** 414–419.

Rudel, Harry W., Kinel, Fred A., and **Henzl, Milan R.** *Birth control: Contraception and abortion.* New York: Macmillan, 1973.

Russell, Michael J. Human olfactory communication. *Nature,* 1976, **260,** 520–522.

Rutter, Michael. *The qualities of mothering: Maternal deprivation reassessed* (originally published by Penguin in England, 1972). New York: Aronson, 1974.

Rutter, Michael. Protective factors in children's responses to stress and disadvantage. In Martha Whalen Kent and Jon E. Rolf (Eds.), *Primary prevention of psychopathology* (Vol. III), *Social competence in children.* Hanover, N. H.: University Press of New England, 1979. Pp. 49–74.

Ryder, Norman B., and **Westoff, Charles F.** *Reproduction in the United States: 1965.* Princeton, N. J.: Princeton University, 1971.

Sabbath, Joseph C. The suicidal adolescent—The expendable child. *Journal of American Academy of Child Psychiatry,* 1969, **8,** 272–289.

Salapatek, Philip. Stimulus determinants of attention in infants. In Benjamin B. Wolman (Ed.), *International encyclopedia of psychiatry, psychology, psychoanalysis, and neurology* (Vol. 10). New York: Aesculepius Publishers, 1977. Pp. 451–456.

Salter, Alice. Birth without violence: A medical controversy. *Nursing Research,* 1978, **27,** 84–88.

Sameroff, Arnold J. Learning and adaptation in infancy. In Hayne W. Reese (Ed.), *Advances in child development and behavior* (Vol. I). New York: Academic Press, 1972. Pp. 170–214.

Sameroff, Arnold J. Transactional models in early social relations. *Human Development*, 1975, **18**, 65–79.

Sameroff, Arnold J. Caregiving or reproductive casualty? Determinants in developmental deviancy. In Frances Degen Horowitz (Ed.), *Early developmental hazards: Predictors and precautions*. Boulder, Col.: Westview Press, 1978. Pp. 79–101.

Sameroff, Arnold J., and **Chandler, Michael J.** Reproductive risk and the continuum of caretaking casualty. In Frances D. Horowitz, M. Hetherington, S. Scarr-Salapatek, and G. Siegel (Eds.)., *Review of child development research* (Vol. IV). Chicago: University of Chicago Press, 1975. Pp. 187–244.

Sander, Louis W., Stechler, Gerald, Burns, Padraic, and **Julia, Harry.** Early mother-infant interaction and 24-hour patterns of activity and sleep. *Journal of Child Psychiatry*, 1970, **9**, 103–123.

Santrock, John W. Relation of type and onset of father absence to cognitive development. *Child Development*, 1972, **43**, 455–469.

Sawyer, Jack. The altruism scale: A measure of cooperative, individualistic, and competitive interpersonal orientation. *American Journal of Sociology*, 1966, **71**, 407–416.

Saxon, L., and **Rapola, J.** *Congenital defects*. New York: Holt, 1969.

Scarr, Sandra, and **Salapatek, Philip.** Patterns of fear development during infancy. *Merrill-Palmer Quarterly*, 1970, **16**, 53–90.

Scarr, Sandra, and **Weinberg, Richard A.** Intellectual similarities within families of both adopted and biological children. *Intelligence*, 1977, **1**, 170–191.

Scarr-Salapatek, Sandra, and **Williams, Margaret L.** The effects of early stimulation on low-birth-weight infants. *Child Development*, 1973, **44**, 94–101.

Schachter, Rubin J., Pantel, Ernestine S., Glassman, George M., and **Zweibelson, Irving.** Acne Vulgaris and psychological impact on high school students. *New York State Journal of Medicine*, 1971, **71**, 2886–2890.

Schaffer, H. Rudolph. *Mothering*. Cambridge, Mass.: Harvard University Press, 1977.

Schaffer, H. Rudolph, and **Emerson, Peggy E.** Patterns of response to physical contact in early human development. *Journal of Child Psychology and Psychiatry*, 1964, **5**, 1–13.

Schardein, James L. *Drugs as teratogens*. Cleveland: CRC Press, 1976.

Scheinfeld, Amram. *Twins, and supertwins*. Philadelphia: Lippincott, 1967.

Scheinfeld, Amram. *Heredity in humans* (Rev. Ed.). Philadelphia: Lippincott, 1972.

Schinke, Steven P., Gilchrist, Lewayne D., and **Small, Richard W.** Preventing unwanted adolescent pregnancy: A cognitive-behavioral approach. *American Journal of Orthopsychiatry*, 1979, **49**, 81–88.

Schlesinger, Benjamin. *The one-parent family: Perspectives and annotated bibliography* (3rd Ed.). Toronto: University of Toronto Press, 1975.

Schlesinger, Hilde S., and **Meadow, Kathryn P.** *Sound and sign: Childhood deafness and mental health*. Berkeley: University of California Press, 1972.

Schoof-Tams, Karin, Schlaegel, Jürgen, and **Walezak, Leonhard.** Differentiation of sexual morality between 11 and 16 years. *Archives of Sexual Behavior*, 1976, **5**, 353–370.

Schrag, Peter, and **Divoky, Diane.** *The myth of the hyperactive child and other means of child control*. New York: Pantheon, 1975.

Schwartz, Gary, and **Merten, Don.** The language of adolescence: An anthropological approach to the youth culture. *The American Journal of Sociology*, 1967, **72**, 453–468.

Scott, Ralph, Hartson, John, and **Cunningham, Mark.** Race of examiner as a variable in test attainments of preschool children. *Perceptual and Motor Skills*, 1976, **42**, 1167–1173.

Scrimshaw, Nevin S., and **Gordon, John E.** (Eds.). *Malnutrition, learning and behavior: Proceedings*. Cambridge, Mass.: MIT Press, 1968.

Sears, Robert R., Maccoby, Eleanor E., and **Levin, Harry.** *Patterns of child rearing*. Evanston, Ill.: Row, Peterson and Company, 1957.

Sears, Robert R., Rau, Lucy, and **Alpert, Richard.** *Identification and child rearing*. Stanford, Calif.: Stanford University Press, 1965.

Seashore, Marjorie J., Leifer, Aimee Dorr, Barnett, Clifford R., and **Leiderman, P. Herbert.** The effects of denial of early mother-infant interaction on maternal self-confidence. *Journal of Personality and Social Psychology*, 1973, **26**, 369–378.

Seffrin, John R., and **Seehafer, Roger W.** A survey of drug use, beliefs, opinions, and behaviors among junior and senior high school students: Part I. group data. *Journal of School Health*, 1976a, **46**, 263–268.

Seffrin, John R., and **Seehafer, Roger W.** Multiple drug-use patterns among a group of high school students: Regular users vs. nonusers of specific drug types. *Journal of School Health*, 1976b, **46**, 413–416.

Segal, Bernard. Reasons for marijuana use and personality: A canonical analysis. *Journal of Alcohol and Drug Education*, 1977, **22**(3), 64–67.

Serafica, Felicisima C. The development of attachment behaviors: An organismic-developmental perspective. *Human Development,* 1978, **21,** 119–140.

Seymour, Dorothy. Black children, black speech. *Commonweal,* 1971, 175–178.

Shantz, Carolyn Uhlanger. The development of social cognition. In E. Mavis Hetherington (Ed.), *Review of child development research* (Vol. V). Chicago: University of Chicago Press, 1975. Pp. 257–323.

Shapira, Ariella, and **Madsen, Millard C.** Cooperative and competitive behavior of kibbutz and urban children in Israel. *Child Development,* 1969, **40,** 609–617.

Shapiro, Howard I. *The birth control book.* New York: St. Martin's Press, 1977.

Shephard, Roy J. Physiology—Comment. In J. G. Albinson and G. M. Andrew (Eds.), *Child in sport and physical activity.* Baltimore: University Park Press, 1976. Pp. 35–40.

Sherman, Lawrence W. An ecological study of glee in small groups of preschool children. *Child Development,* 1975, **46,** 53–61.

Shields, James. *Monozygotic twins, brought up apart and brought up together: An investigation into the genetic and environmental causes of variation in personality.* London: Oxford University Press, 1962.

Shinn, Marybeth. Father absence and children's cognitive development. *Psychological Bulletin,* 1978, **85,** 295–324.

Shirley, Mary M. *The first two years: A study of twenty-five babies* (Vols. II and III). Institute of child welfare monograph No. 8. Minneapolis: University of Minnesota Press, 1933.

Shneidman, Edwin S. Suicide. In Gardner Lindzey, Calvin S. Hall, and Richard F. Thompson, *Psychology* (2nd Ed.). New York: Worth, 1978.

Sieben, Robert L. Controversial medical treatments of learning disabilities. *Academic Therapy,* 1977, **13,** 133–147.

Siegler, Robert S., and **Richards, D. Dean.** Development of time, speed, and distance concepts. *Developmental Psychology,* 1979, **15,** 288–298.

Silberman, Charles. *Crisis in the classroom: The remaking of American education.* New York: Random House, 1970.

Simmons, James Q., and **Lovaas, O. Ivar.** Use of pain and punishment as treatment techniques with childhood schizophrenics. *American Journal of Psychotherapy,* 1969, **23,** 23–26.

Simmons, Roberta G., Rosenberg, Florence, and **Rosenberg, Morris.** Disturbance in the self-image at adolescence. *American Sociological Review,* 1973, **38,** 553–568.

Simon, Rita James, and **Altstein, Howard.** *Transracial adoption.* New York: Wiley, 1977.

Simpson, Joe Leigh (Ed.). *Disorders of sexual differentiation: Etiology and clinical delineation.* New York: Academic Press, 1976.

Simpson, Richard L. Parental influence, anticipatory socialization, and social mobility. *American Sociological Review,* 1962, **27,** 517–522.

Sinclair, Caroline B. *Movement of the young child: Ages two to six.* Columbus, Ohio: Merrill, 1973.

Sinclair, David. *Human growth after birth* (2nd Ed.). London: Oxford University Press, 1973.

Singer, Dorothy G., and **Singer, Jerome L.** *Partners in play: A step-by-step guide to imaginative play in children.* New York: Harper & Row, 1977.

Siqueland, Einar R., and **Lipsitt, Lewis P.** Conditioned head-turning in human newborns. *Journal of Experimental Child Psychology,* 1966, **3,** 356–376.

Skinner, B. F. *Science and human behavior.* New York: Macmillan, 1953.

Skinner, B. F. *Verbal behavior.* New York: Appleton, Century, Crofts, 1957.

Skinner, B. F. *Beyond freedom and dignity.* New York: Knopf, 1971.

Sloane, Howard N., Jr., and **MacAulay, Barbara D.** (Eds.). *Operant procedures in remedial speech and language training.* Boston: Houghton Mifflin, 1968.

Slobin, Dan I. *Psycholinguistics.* Glenview, Ill.: Scott, Foresman, 1974.

Smith, Madorah Elizabeth. An investigation of the development of the sentence and the extent of vocabulary in young children. *University of Iowa Studies in Child Welfare,* 1926, **3**(5).

Smith, Nils V. *The acquisition of phonology: A case study.* Cambridge, England: Cambridge University Press, 1973.

Smith, R. Jeffrey. Agency drags its feet on warning to pregnant women. *Science,* 1978, **199,** 748–749.

Snow, Catherine E. The development of conversation between mothers and babies. *Journal of Child Language,* 1977, **4,** 1–22.

Snow, Catherine E., and **Ferguson, Charles A.** (Eds.). *Talking to children.* Cambridge, England: Cambridge University Press, 1977.

Society for Research in Child Development. Committee on ethics in research with children. *SRCD Newsletter,* 1973 (Winter), Pp. 3–4.

Sontag, L. W., and **Wallace, Robert F.** The effect of cigarette smoking during pregnancy upon the fetal heart rate. *American Journal of Obstetrics and Gynecology,* 1935, **29,** 77–83.

Sorensen, Robert C. *Adolescent sexuality in contemporary America: Personal values and sexual behavior, ages thirteen to nineteen.* New York: World, 1973.

Soule, A. Bradley. *The pregnant couple.* Paper presented at the meeting of the American Psychological Association, New Orleans, 1974.

Spache, George D. *Investigating the issues of reading disabilities.* Boston: Allyn and Bacon, 1976.

Spelke, Elizabeth, Zelazo, Philip, Kagan, Jerome, and **Kotelchuck, Milton.** Father interaction and separation protest. *Developmental Psychology,* 1973, **9**, 83–90.

Spence, Janet T., and **Helmreich, Robert L.** *Masculinity and femininity: Their psychological dimensions, correlates, and antecedents.* Austin, Texas: University of Texas Press, 1978.

Spilton, Doreen, and **Lee, Lee C.** Some determinants of effective communication in four-year-olds. *Child Development,* 1977, **48**, 968–977.

Spitz, René Arpad. Hospitalism: An inquiry into the genesis of psychiatric conditions in early childhood. *Psychoanalytic Study of the Child,* 1945, **1**, 53–74.

Spitz, René Arpad. *The first year of life: A psychoanalytic study of normal and deviant object relations.* New York: International Universities Press, 1965.

Spock, Benjamin. *Baby and child care.* New York: Pocket Books, 1976.

Spring, Carl, and **Sandoval, Jonathan.** Food additives and hyperkinesis: A critical evaluation of the evidence. *Journal of Learning Disabilities,* 1976, **9**, 560–569.

Sroufe, L. Alan. A methodological and philosophical critique of intervention-oriented research. *Developmental Psychology,* 1970, **2**, 140–145.

Sroufe, L. Alan. Drug treatment of child with behavior problems. In Frances Degan Horowitz (Ed.), *Review of child development research* (Vol. IV). Chicago: University of Chicago Press, 1975.

Sroufe, L. Alan. Attachment and the roots of competence. *Human Nature,* 1978, **1**, 50–57.

Sroufe, L. Alan, and **Waters, Everett.** The ontogenesis of smiling and laughter: A perspective on the organization of development in infancy. *Psychological Review,* 1976, **83**, 173–189.

Staffieri, J. Robert. A study of social stereotype of body image in children. *Journal of Personality and Social Psychology,* 1967, **7**, 101–104.

Standley, Kay, Soule, A. Bradley, Copans, Stuart A., and **Duchowny, Michael S.** Local-regional anesthesia during childbirth: Effect on newborn behaviors. *Science,* 1974, **186**(4164), 634–635.

Stein, Aletha Huston, and **Friedrich, Lynette Kohn.** Impact of television on children and youth. In E. Mavis Hetherington (Ed.), *Review of child development research* (Vol. V). Chicago: University of Chicago Press, 1975.

Stein, Zena A., and **Susser, Mervyn W.** Prenatal nutrition and mental competence. In J. D. Lloyd-Still (Ed.), *Malnutrition and intellectual development.* Littleton, Mass.: Publishing Sciences Group, 1976. Pp. 39–79.

Stein, Zena A., Susser, Mervyn W., Saenger, Gerhart, and **Marolla, Francis.** *Famine and human development: The Dutch hunger winter 1944–1945.* New York: Oxford University Press, 1975.

Steinberg, L. D. *A longitudinal study of physical growth, intellectual development, and family interaction in early adolescence.* Unpublished doctoral dissertation, Cornell University, 1977.

Stengel, Erwin. *Suicide and attempted suicide.* New York: Penguin, 1964.

Stern, Daniel. *The first relationship: Mother and infant.* Cambridge, Mass.: Harvard University Press, 1977.

Stewart, Ann L., and **Reynolds, E. O. R.** Improved prognosis for infants of very low birthweight. *Pediatrics,* 1974, **54**, 724–735.

Stockton, William. Death in the family. *The New York Times Magazine,* August 12, 1979, p. 28–39.

Stolzenberg, Ross M., and **Waite, Linda J.** Age, fertility expectations and plans for employment. *American Sociological Review,* 1977, **42**, 769–783.

Stone, L. Joseph, and **Church, Joseph.** *Childhood and adolescence: A psychology of the growing person.* (3rd Ed.). New York: Random House, 1973.

Streissguth, Ann P., Herman, Cynthia S., and **Smith, David W.** Intelligence, behavior, and dysmorphogenesis in the fetal alcohol syndrome: A report on 20 patients. *Pediatrics,* 1978, **92**, 363–367.

Streitfeld, Pamela Port. Congenital malformation: Teratogenic foods and additives. *Birth and the Family Journal,* 1978, **5**, 7–19.

Sugarman, Muriel. Paranatal influences on maternal-infant attachment. *American Journal of Orthopsychiatry,* 1977, **47**, 407–421.

Sullivan, Edmund V. A study of Kohlberg's structural theory of moral development: A critique of liberal social science ideology. *Human Development,* 1977, **20**, 352–376.

Suomi, Stephen J., and **Harlow, Harry F.** Monkeys without play. In Jerome S. Bruner, Alison Jolly, and Kathy Sylva (Eds.), *Play.* New York: Basic Books, 1976. Pp. 490–495.

Super, Charles M. Environmental effects on motor development: The case of 'African infant precocity.' *Developmental Medicine and Child Neurology,* 1976, **18**, 561–567.

Super, Donald E., and **Hall, Douglas T.** Career development: Exploration and planning. *Annual Review of Psychology,* 1978, **29**, 333–372.

Swain, Helen L. Childhood views of death. *Death Education,* 1979, **2**, 341–358.

Szalai, Alexander, Converse, Philip E., Feldheim, P., Scheuch, E. K., and **Stone, P. J.** (Eds.). *The use of time: Daily activities of urban and suburban populations in twelve countries.* The Hague, The Netherlands: Mouton, 1972.

Tanner, James M. The regulation of human growth. *Child Development,* 1963, **34,** 817–847.

Tanner, James M. Physical growth. In Paul H. Mussen (Ed.), *Carmichael's manual of child psychology* (3rd Ed.), (Vol. I). New York: Wiley, 1970, Pp. 77–155.

Tanner, James M. Sequence, tempo, and individual variation in the growth and development of boys and girls aged twelve to sixteen. *Daedalus,* 1971, **100,** 907–930.

Tanner, James M. Variability of growth and maturity in newborn infants. In Michael Lewis and Leonard A. Rosenblum (Eds.), *The effect of the infant on its caregiver.* New York: Wiley, 1974. Pp. 77–103.

Tanzer, Deborah, and **Block, Jean Libman.** *Why natural childbirth?: A psychologist's report on the benefits to mothers, fathers and babies.* New York: Schocken Books, 1976.

Tec, Nechema. Some aspects of high school status and differential involvement with marijuana: A study of suburban teenagers. *Adolescence,* 1972, **7,** 1–28.

Terman, Lewis M., and **Oden, Melita H.** *Genetic studies of genius* (Vol. 5), *The gifted group at mid-life: Thirty-five years' follow-up of the superior child.* Stanford, Calif.: Stanford University Press, 1959.

Tew, B., and **Lawrence, K. M.** Matrimonial relationships following the death or continued survival of a congenitally handicapped child. *Bulletin of the British Psychological Society,* 1975, **28.**

Thomas, Alexander, and **Chess, Stella.** *Temperament and development.* New York: Brunner/Mazel, 1977.

Thomas, Alexander, Chess, Stella, and **Birch, Herbert G.** *Behavioral individuality in early childhood.* New York: New York University Press, 1963.

Thomas, Alexander, Chess, Stella, and **Birch, Herbert G.** *Temperament and behavior disorders in children.* New York: New York University Press, 1968.

Thompson, Jean R., and **Chapman, Robin S.** Who is "Daddy" revisited: The status of two-year-olds' overextended words in use and comprehension. *Journal of Child Language,* 1977, **4,** 359–375.

Thompson, Spencer K. Gender labels and early sex role development. *Child Development,* 1975, **46,** 339–347.

Thompson, William R., and **Grusec, Joan.** Studies of early experience. In Paul H. Mussen (Ed.), *Carmichael's manual of child psychology* (3rd Ed.). New York: Wiley, 1970, 565–654.

Thornburg, Hershel D. Adolescent sources of sex information. In Robert E. Grinder (Ed.), *Studies in adolescence: A book of readings in adolescent development.* New York: Macmillan, 1975.

Thornton, Arland. Children and marital stability. *Journal of Marriage and the Family,* 1977, **39,** 531–540.

Tilford, Jane A. The relationship between gestational age and adaptive behavior. *Merrill-Palmer Quarterly,* 1976, **22**(4), 319–326.

Tizard, Barbara, and **Rees, Judith.** A comparison of the effects of adoption, restoration to the natural mother, and continued institutionalization on the cognitive development of four-year-old children. *Child Development,* 1974, **45,** 92–99.

Tod, E. D. M. Puerperal depression. In Norman Morris (Ed.), *Psychosomatic medicine in obstetrics and gynecology.* Basel: Karger, 1972.

Toffler, Alvin. *Future shock.* New York: Random House, 1970.

Tonkova-Yampol'skaya, R. V. Development of speech intonation in infants during the first two years of life. In Charles A. Ferguson and Dan Isaac Slobin (Eds.), *Studies of child language development.* New York: Holt, Rinehart, and Winston, 1973, Pp. 128–138.

Torgesen, Joseph. Problems and prospects in the study of learning disabilities. In E. Mavis Hetherington (Ed.), *Review of child development research* (Vol. V). Chicago: University of Chicago Press, 1975. Pp. 385–440.

Torrence, E. Paul. Characteristics of creatively gifted children and youth. In E. Philip Trapp, and Philip Himelstein (Eds.), *The exceptional child.* New York: Appleton Century Crofts, 1972. Pp. 273–291.

Tower, Roni Beth, Singer, Dorothy G., Singer, Jerome L., and **Biggs, Ann.** Differential effects of television programming on preschoolers' cognition, imagination, and social play. *American Journal of Orthopsychiatry,* 1979, **49,** 265–281.

Trainer, F. E. A critical analysis of Kohlberg's contributions to the study of moral thought. *Journal for the Theory of Social Behavior,* 1977, **7,** 41–63.

Trethowan, W. H., and **Conlon, M. F.** The couvade syndrome. *British Journal of Psychiatry,* 1965, **111,** 57–66.

Tulkin, Steven R., and **Kagan, Jerome.** Mother-child interaction in the first year of life. *Child Development,* 1972, **43,** 31–41.

Tulkin, Steven R., and **Konner, M. J.** Alternative conceptions of intellectual functioning. *Human Development,* 1973, **16,** 33–52.

Turiel, Elliot. Conflict and transition in adolescent moral development. *Child Development,* 1974, **45,** 14–29.

United Nations. *Demographic Yearbook, 1977.* New York: United Nations, 1978.

U. S. Department of Health, Education, and Welfare. *Abortion Surveillance, 1976.* Public Health Service, Center for Disease Control, August 1978.

U.S. Department of Health, Education, and Welfare. *Smoking and health: A report of the Surgeon General,* Public Health Service, 1979.

U. S. Department of Justice. *Sourcebook of criminal justice statistics (1974–1975).* Law Enforcement Commission, February, 1978.

United States Senate. Hearing before the subcommittee on children and youth of the Committee on Labor and Public Welfare. United States Senate, 93rd Congress. First Session, on S. 1191, Child Abuse Prevention Act, U. S. Government Printing Office, Washington D. C., 1973.

Uzgiris, Ina C., and **Hunt, J. McVicker.** *Assessment in infancy: Ordinal scales of psychological development.* Urbana, Ill.: University of Illinois Press, 1975.

Vaillant, George E. *Adaptation to life.* Boston: Little, Brown, 1977.

Vandenberg, Brian. Play and development from an ethological perspective. *American Psychologist,* 1978, **33,** 724–738.

Vander Maelen, Ann L., Strauss, Milton E., and **Starr, Raymond H., Jr.** Influence of obstetric medication on auditory habituation in the newborn. *Developmental Psychology,* 1975, **11,** 711–714.

Vener, Arthur M., and **Stewart, Cyrus S.** Adolescent sexual behavior in middle America revisited: 1970–1973. *Journal of Marriage and the Family,* 1974, **36,** 728–735.

Ventura, Stephanie J. Teenage childbearing: United States, 1966–1975. *Monthly Vital Statistics Reports.* National Center for Health Statistics, **26,** No. 5 (Supp.), 1977.

Vurpillot, Elaine. The development of scanning strategies, and their relation to visual differentiation. *Journal of Experimental Child Psychology,* 1968, **6,** 632–650.

Vigotsky, Lev Semenovich. *Thought and language.* Cambridge, Mass.: MIT Press, 1962.

Wachs, Theodore D. Relation of infant performance on Piaget scales between twelve and twenty-four months and their Stanford-Binet performance at thirty-one months. *Child Development,* 1975, **46,** 929–935.

Wachs, Theodore D. Utilization of a Piagetian approach in the investigation of early experience effects: Research strategy and some illustrative data. *Merrill-Palmer Quarterly,* 1976, **22,** 11–30.

Wallach, Michael A., and **Kogan, Nathan.** *Modes of thinking in young children: A study of the creativity-intelligence distinction.* New York: Holt, Rinehart, and Winston, 1965.

Watson, John B. Experimental studies on the growth of emotions. In Carl Allanmore Murchison (Ed.), *Psychologies of 1925.* Worcester, Mass.: Clark University Press, 1926.

Watson, John B. *Psychological care of the infant and child.* New York: Norton, 1928.

Watson, John B. *Behaviorism.* (Rev. Ed.). Chicago: University of Chicago Press, 1967 (originally published in 1930).

Watson, John B., and **Rayner, Rosalie.** Conditioned emotional reactions. *Journal of Experimental Psychology,* 1920, **3,** 1–14.

Wechsler, David. *Manual for the Wechsler Intelligence Scale for Children* (Rev. Ed.). New York: Psychological Corporation, 1974.

Weideger, Paula. *Menstruation and menopause: The physiology and psychology, the myth, and the reality.* New York: Knopf, 1976.

Weil, William B., Jr. Infantile obesity. In Myron Winick (Ed.), *Childhood obesity.* New York: Wiley, 1975. Pp. 61–72.

Weisberg, Paul. Social and nonsocial conditioning of infant vocalizations. *Child Development,* 1963, **34,** 377–388.

Welds, Kathryn. *Voluntary childlessness in professional women.* Paper presented at the meeting of the American Psychological Association, San Francisco, 1977.

Wendler, Paul. *Minimal brain dysfunction in children.* New York: Wiley, 1971.

Wente, Arel S., and **Crockenberg, Susan B.** Transition to fatherhood: Lamaze preparation, adjustment difficulty and the husband-wife relationship. *Family Coordinator,* 1976, **25,** 351–357.

Werry, John S. Childhood psychosis. In Herbert C. Quay and John S. Werry (Eds.), *Psychopathological disorders of childhood.* New York: Wiley, 1972. Pp. 173–233.

Westinghouse Learning Corporation. *The impact of Head Start: An evaluation of the Head Start experience on children's cognitive and affective development.* Athens, Ohio: Ohio University Press, 1969.

Weston, James Tuthill. The pathology of child abuse. In Ray E. Helfer and C. Henry Kempe (Eds.), *The battered child* (2nd Ed.). Chicago: University of Chicago Press, 1974. Pp. 61–86.

Westphal, Raymond C. *The effects of a primary-grade level interethnic curriculum on racial prejudice.* San Francisco, Calif.: R and E Research Associates, 1977.

Whalen, Carol K., and **Henker, Barbara.** Psychostimulants and children: A review and analysis. *Psychological Bulletin,* 1976, **83,** 1113–1130.

White, Burton L. *Human infants: Experience and psychological development.* Englewood Cliffs, N. J.: Prentice-Hall, 1971.

White, Burton L. *The first three years of life.* Englewood Cliffs, N. J.: Prentice-Hall, 1975.

White, Burton L., and **Watts, Jean Carew.** *Experience and environment: Major influences on the development of the young child.* Englewood Cliffs, N. J.: Prentice-Hall, 1973.

White, Robert W. Motivation reconsidered: The concept of competence. *Psychological Review,* 1959, **66**, 297–333.

White, Robert W. Competence as an aspect of personal growth. In Martha Whalen Kent and Jon E. Rolf (Eds.), *Primary prevention of psychopathology* (Vol. III), *Social competence in children.* Hanover, N. H.: University Press of New England, 1979. Pp. 5–22.

White, Sheldon H. Evidence for a hierarchical arrangement of learning processes. In Lewis P. Lipsitt and Charles C. Spiker (Eds.), *Advances in child development and behavior* (Vol. 2). New York: Academic Press, 1965. Pp. 187–220.

Whiting, Beatrice Blyth (Ed.). *Six cultures: Studies of child rearing.* New York: Wiley, 1963.

Whiting, John W. M. Effects of climate on certain cultural practices. In Ward H. Goodenough (Ed.), *Explorations in cultural anthropology: Essays in honor of George Peter Murdock.* New York: McGraw-Hill, 1964, Pp. 511–544.

Wiggins, Jerry S., and Holzmuller, Ana. Psychological androgyny and interpersonal behavior. *Journal of Consulting and Clinical Psychology.* 1978, **46**, 40–52.

Wilson, Kenneth L., Zurcher, Louis A., McAdams, Diana Claire, and Curtis, Russell L. Stepfathers and stepchildren: An exploratory analysis from two national surveys. *Journal of Marriage and the Family,* 1975, **37**, 526–536.

Wilson, Ronald S. Twins: patterns of cognitive development as measured on the Wechsler Preschool and Primary Scale of Intelligence. *Developmental Psychology,* 1975, **11**, 126–134.

Wilson, Ronald S., and Harpring, E. B. Mental and motor development in infant twins. *Developmental Psychology,* 1972, **7**, 277–287.

Wilson, William P., Shogren, Robert E., and Witryol, Sam L. Storage in children's word recognition as a function of incentives. *Journal of Genetic Psychology,* 1978, **132**, 137–147.

Winick, Myron (Ed.). *Childhood obesity.* New York: Wiley, 1975.

Winick, Myron. *Malnutrition and brain development.* New York: Oxford University Press, 1976.

Winick, Myron, Meyer, Knarig Katchadurian, and Harris, Ruth C. Malnutrition and environmental enrichment by early adoption. *Science,* 1975, **190**(4220), 1173–1175.

Winn, Marie. *The plug-in drug.* New York: Viking, 1977.

Wolff, Peter. The natural history of crying and vocalization in early infancy. In B. M. Foss (Ed.), *Determinants of infant behavior* (IV). London: Methuen, 1969. Pp. 81–109.

Wray, Joe D. Maternal nutrition, breast-feeding and infant survival. In W. Henry Mosley (Ed.), *Nutrition and human reproduction.* New York: Plenum Press, 1978. Pp. 197–229.

Wright, John C., and Vlietstra, Alice G. The development of selective attention: From perceptual exploration to logical search. In Hayne W. Reese (Ed.), *Advances in child development and behavior* (Vol. 10). New York: Academic Press, 1975. Pp. 195–239.

Yalisove, Daniel. The effect of riddle-structure on children's comprehension and appreciation of riddles. Doctoral dissertation, New York University. *Dissertation Abstracts International,* 1975, **36**, 6.

Yalisove, Daniel. The effect of riddle structure on children's comprehension of riddles. *Developmental Psychology,* 1978, **14**, 173–180.

Yang, Raymond K., Zweig, Ann R., Douthitt, Thomas C., and Federman, Edward J. Successive relationships between maternal attitudes during pregnancy, analgesic medication during labor and delivery, and newborn behavior. *Developmental Psychology,* 1976, **12**, 6–14.

Yankelovich, Daniel. *The new morality: A profile of American youth in the 1970's.* New York: McGraw-Hill, 1974.

Yarrow, Marian Radke, Campbell, John D., and Burton, Roger V. *Child-rearing: An inquiry into research & methods.* San Francisco: Jossey-Bass, 1968.

Young, Michael and McGeeney, Patrick. *Learning begins at home: A study of a junior high school and its parents.* London: Routledge and Kegan Paul, 1968.

Yunis, Jorge J. (Ed.). *New chromosomal syndromes.* New York: Academic Press, 1977.

Zacharias, L., Rand, W. M., and Wurtman, R. J. A prospective study of sexual development and growth in American girls: The statistics of menarche. *Obstetrical and Gynecological Survey,* 1976, **31**, 325–337.

Zaporozhets, A. V., and Elkonin, D. B. (Eds.). *The psychology of preschool children.* Cambridge, Mass.: MIT Press, 1971.

Zaslow, M. *A study of social behavior.* Doctoral dissertation; Harvard University, 1977 (cited in Kagan, Kearsley, and Zelazo, 1978).

Zegiob, Leslie E., and Forehand, Rex. Maternal interactive behavior as a function of race, socioeconomic status, and sex of the child. *Child Development,* 1975, **46**, 564–568.

Zelnik, Melvin, and Kantner, John F. Sexual and contraceptive experience of young unmarried women in the United States, 1976 and 1971. *Family Planning Perspectives,* 1977, **9**, 55–71.

Zigler, Edward, Abelson, Willa D., and Seitz, Victoria. Motivational factors in the performance of economically disadvantaged children on the Peabody Picture Vocabulary Test. *Child Development,* 1973, **44**, 294–303.

Zigler, Edward F. Project Head Start: Success or failure? *Children Today,* 1973, **2**, 2–7.

Zinser, Otto, Perry, James S., Bailey, Roger C., and Lydiatt, Edward W. Racial recipients, value of donations, and sharing behavior in children. *Journal of Genetic Psychology,* 1976, **129**, 29–35.

Acknowledgments

Quote on page ix from *Horton Hears a Who* by Dr. Seuss. Copyright © 1954 by Dr. Seuss. With permission of Random House, Inc.

Part Openers
I Prenatal photographs, Landrum B. Shettles; *far right*, Martin Weaver, Woodfin Camp
II *all*, Chester Higgins, Jr., Rapho/Photo Researchers
III *all*, Ken Heyman
IV *In order from left to right*, Ken Heyman; Dan Budnik, Magnum; Elizabeth Hamlin, Stock, Boston; Charles Gatewood
V *In order from left to right*, Phiz Mezey, DPI; Bonnie Freer, Photo Researchers; Sybil Shelton, Monkmeyer Press Photo Service; Ann Hagan Griffiths, DPI; Paul Conklin, Monkmeyer Press Photo Service

Chapter 1
Opener: Raimondo Borea
1.2 Jan Lukas, Rapho/Photo Researchers
1.3 Alice Kandell, Rapho/Photo Researchers
1.5 John Rees, Black Star
1.6 The Granger Collection
1.7 The Bettmann Archive
1.9 Novosti from Sovfoto
1.10 Yves de Braine, Black Star
1.11 *both*, Jason Lauré, Woodfin Camp
1.15 Wide World Photos
1.16 New York Post photograph by Pomerantz ©1979, New York Post Corporation

Chapter 2
Opener: Thomas Höpker, Woodfin Camp
2.2 Culver Pictures
2.4 Oliver R. Pierce, Black Star
2.5 *left*, Joel Gordon; *right*, Erika Stone, Peter Arnold
2.6 Thomas Höpker, Woodfin Camp
2.7 The Bettmann Archive
2.8 Ken Heyman
2.9 Beryl Goldberg
Research Report pp. 50–51, courtesy of Albert Bandura, Stanford University
2.11 *left*, Raimondo Borea; *right*, Alice Kandell, Rapho/Photo Researchers
Chart p. 51 Bandura, A; Ross, D., and Ross, S. A., "Imitation of film-mediated aggressive models." *Journal of Abnormal and Social Psychology*, 1963, **66**, 3–11. Copyright © 1963 by the American Psychological Association. Reprinted by permission.
2.13 The Bettmann Archive
2.14 *left*, Erika Stone; *right*, Lew Merrim, Monkmeyer Press Photo Service

Chapter 3
Opener: From the book *A Child is Born* by Lennart Nilsson. English translation copyright © 1966, 1977 by Dell Publishing Co., Inc. Originally published in Swedish under the title *Ett Barn Blir Till* by Albert Bonniers Förlag, copyright © 1965 by Albert Bonniers Förlag, Stockholm (Rev. Ed.), copyright © 1976 by Lennart Nilsson, Mirjam Furuhjelm, Axel Ingelman-Sundberg, Cales Wirsén. Used by permission of DELACORTE PRESS/SEYMOUR LAWRENCE.
Closer Look p. 71, (a) Yvonne Freund, Photo Researchers; (b) Paolo Kock, Photo Researchers; (c) Bernard Pierre Wolff, Photo Researchers; (d) Paolo Kock, Photo Researchers
3.3 The Granger Collection
Closer Look p. 75, Wide World Photos
3.7 The March of Dimes
3.9 Harvey Stein
3.10 Russell Dian, Grand Projects
3.12 Charles Cocaine, Photo Researchers
3.13 Curt Gunther, Camera 5
3.15 Adapted from Wilson, R. S., "Twins: Patterns of cognitive development as measured on the Wechsler Preschool and Primary Scale of Intelligence," *Developmental Psychology*, 1975, **11**. Copyright © 1975 by the American Psychological Association. Adapted with permission.
3.16 Roy Pinney, Monkmeyer Press Photo Service
3.17 Bruce Roberts, Rapho/Photo Researchers
Closer Look p. 98, Sylvia Plachy
Closer Look (text) p. 98–99. From "Death in the Family" by William Stockton, August 12, 1979, *New York Times Magazine*. Copyright © 1979 by the New York Times Company. Reprinted by permission.
3.18 Courtesy of Victor A. McKusick
3.19 © by the New York Times Company. Reprinted by permission.
3.20 © Cutter Laboratories, Inc., courtesy of The National Hemophilia Foundation
3.21 Photo courtesy of Solomon Fox
3.22 Ira Wyman, Sygma

Chapter 4
Opener: From the book *A Child is Born* by Lennart Nilsson. English translation copyright © 1966, 1977 by Dell Publishing Co., Inc. Originally published in Swedish under the title *Ett Barn Blir Till* by Albert Bonniers

Förlag, copyright © 1965 by Albert Bonniers Förlag, Stockholm (Rev. Ed.), copyright © 1976 by Lennart Nilsson, Mirjam Furuhjelm, Axel Ingelman-Sundberg, Cales Wirsén. Used by permission of DELACORTE PRESS/SEYMOUR LAWRENCE.

4.1   National Library of Medicine

4.2   Landrum B. Shettles

4.3   Redrawn from *Biology 3/e* by Helena Curtis. Copyright © 1979 by Worth Publishers, Inc.

4.4   *all*, Landrum B. Shettles

4.5   Carolina Biological Supply Company

4.6   *both*, United Press International

4.7   *all*, Carnegie Institution of Washington, Department of Embryology, Davis Division

4.8   From *The Developing Human* by Keith L. Moore. Copyright © 1977 by W. B. Saunders Company. Adapted with permission.

4.9   Courtesy of The New York Institute for the Education of the Blind

4.10   Heggemann, Stern/Black Star

4.11   Erika Stone

4.12   "Fetal alcohol syndrome experience with 41 patients," *Journal of the American Medical Association*, **235**, No. 14, courtesy of James W. Hanson, M.D., Department of Pediatrics, College of Medicine, The University of Iowa.

4.13   Courtesy of Odyssey Institute, Inc.

4.14   Courtesy of St. Vincent's Hospital and Medical Center of New York

4.15   W. Eugene Smith, courtesy of Center for Creative Photography, University of Arizona

Chart p. 132   Adapted from Holmes, T. S., and Holmes, T. H., "Short-term intrusions into the life style routine." Reprinted with permission from *Journal of Psychosomatic Research*, 1970, **14**, 121–132.

4.16   Erika Stone

4.17   Erika Stone, Photo Researchers

4.18   Joel Gordon

4.19   Erika Stone

Chapter 5

Opener: Joel Gordon

5.1   Redrawn from *A Baby is Born* (10th Ed.). Copyright © 1964 by Maternity Center Association, New York, N.Y.

5.2   Hella Hammid, Rapho/Photo Researchers

5.3   Doug Wilson, Black Star

5.4   (a) Suva, DPI; (b) Eve Arnold, Magnum; (c) Lew Merrim, Monkmeyer Press Photo Service; (d) Beryl Goldberg

Table 5.1 p. 148   Guttmacher, A. F., *Pregnancy, Birth, and Family Planning*. Copyright © 1973 by A. F. Guttmacher, M.D. Reprinted by permission of Viking Penguin Inc., New York.

5.5   The Bettmann Archive

5.6   *both*, United Press International

5.7   Charlotte Brooks, Magnum

5.9   From *The Cesarian Birth Experience*, Copyright © 1977 by Bonnie Donovan. Reprinted by permission of Beacon Press; photographs courtesy of John and Elizabeth Caswell.

5.10   From *Birth Without Violence* by Frederick Leboyer, Copyright © 1975 by Alfred A. Knopf, Inc., Reprinted by permission of the publisher; photographs courtesy of Éditions du Seuil, Paris.

5.11   *all*, Fred Ward, Black Star

5.12   Redrawn from *Studies in Animal and Human Behavior*, by Konrad Lorenz. Copyright © 1971 by Konrad Lorenz. Courtesy of the Harvard University Press.

Research Report p. 163, Hella Hammid, Rapho/Photo Researchers

5.13   Thomas McAvoy, *Life Magazine* © 1955 Time Inc.

5.14   Reproduced from *Pediatrics*, 1970, **46**, 187. Copyright American Academy of Pediatrics, 1970. Courtesy of John H. Kennell, M.D., Department of Pediatrics, Case Western Reserve University.

Chapter 6

Opener: Phoebe Dunn/DPI

6.1   National Center for Health Statistics

6.2   From *Growth*, by W. J. Robbins et al. Copyright © 1929 by Yale University Press. Reprinted by permission.

6.3   *In order from left to right*, Martin Weaver, Woodfin Camp; Richard Frieman, Photo Researchers; Erika Stone, Peter Arnold

6.4   Adapted from C. M. Jackson (Ed.), *Morris' Human Anatomy*, 7th ed. Copyright © 1923 by P. Blakiston's Son & Co. Used by permission of McGraw-Hill Book Company.

6.5   Erika Stone

6.6   Erika Stone

6.7   Erika Stone

6.8   Russ Kinne, Photo Researchers

6.9   Erika Stone

Table 6.1 p. 180   Adapted from Frankenburg, W. K., and Dodds, J. B., "The Denver Developmental Screening Test." *Journal of Pediatrics*, 1967, **71**(2) 181–191.

6.10   Tass from Sovfoto

6.11   Martin Weaver, Woodfin Camp

6.12   Adapted from Robert L. Fantz, "The Origin of Form Perception." Copyright © 1961 by Scientific American, Inc. All rights reserved.

Research Report p. 185, courtesy of Joseph Campos, University of Denver

6.13   © Frostie, Woodfin Camp

6.14   *In order from left to right*, Beryl Goldberg; Costa Manos, Magnum; Loren McIntyre, Woodfin Camp; William Hubbell, Woodfin Camp

6.15   Edward Lettau, Peter Arnold

6.17   Mariette Pathy Allen

6.18   Erika Stone

6.19   *left*, Erika Stone, Photo Researchers; *right*, Jan Lukas, Rapho/Photo Researchers

6.20   (a) Bernard Pierre Wolff, Photo Researchers; (b) United Press International

6.22   Ira Sandler

Chapter 7

Opener: Peter Deane

7.1   Maurice Manson, Photoworld/FPG

7.2   Grete Mannheim, DPI

7.3   Lew Merrim, Monkmeyer Press Photo Service

7.4   *all*, George Zimbel, Monkmeyer Press Photo Service

7.7   Eastfoto

7.8   Betty Medsger

7.9   *both*, reprinted from *Human Infants* by Burton L. White, Prentice-Hall, Englewood Cliffs, N.J., 1971.

7.10   Lew Merrim, Monkmeyer Press Photo Service

7.11   Alice Kandell, Rapho/Photo Researchers

7.12   Suzanne Szasz, Photo Researchers

7.13   Erika Stone

7.14 Adapted from R. V. Tonkova-Yampol'skaya, "Development of speech intonation in infants during the first two years of life." In *Soviet Psychology,* 1969, **7**(3), 48–54. Reprinted with permission of M. E. Sharpe, Inc.

Table 7.1 p. 232 Kessen, W., Haith, M. M., Salapatek, P. H., "Human infancy: A bibliography and guide." In P. H. Mussen (Ed.), *Carmichael's Manual of Child Psychology* (3rd Ed.), 1970, 287–445. New York: Reproduced by permission of John Wiley & Sons, Inc.

7.15 Erika Stone

Chapter 8

Opener: Joan Menschenfreund

8.1 Solomon Fox

8.3 Suzanne Szasz, Photo Researchers

8.4 Roxanne Edwards, Woodfin Camp

8.5 Mariette Pathy Allen

8.6 From Eckerman, C.O., Whatley, J. L., and Kutz, S. L., "Growth of social play with peers during the second year of life," *Developmental Psychology,* 1975, **11**, Copyright © 1975 by the American Psychological Association. Reprinted by permission.

Research Report p. 246, from an article by Susan Goldberg and Michael Lewis entitled "Play behavior in the year-old infant: Early sex differences," *Child Development,* 1969, **40**, 21–31; photographs courtesy of Michael Lewis.

Table 8.1 p. 248 Adapted from Lewis, M., and Brooks, J., "Self-knowledge and emotional development." In M. Lewis, and L. A. Rosenblum (Eds.), *The Development of Affect.* New York: Plenum, 1978, 205–226.

8.7 *both,* Erika Stone

8.8 Erika Stone

Closer Look p. 252, Harvey Stein

Table 8.2 p. 253 Adapted from Dennis, W. "Causes of retardation among institutional children: Iran." *Journal of Genetic Psychology,* 1960, **96**, 47–59. The Journal Press.

Chart p. 259 White, Kaban, Marmor, Shapiro in White, B. L., and Watts, J. C., *Experience and Environment,* © 1973. Reprinted by permission of Prentice-Hall, Inc., Englewood Cliffs, New Jersey.

Closer Look p. 257, Joan Menschenfreund

8.9 *left,* Joel Gordon; *right,* Paul Fusco, Magnum

8.10 Beryl Goldberg

8.11 *both,* Erika Stone

8.12 Joan Menschenfreund

8.14 United Press International

8.15 John Bryson, Sygma

8.16 From *Child Abuse,* by Ruth S. Kempe and Henry C. Kempe. Copyright © 1978 by Ruth S. Kempe and Henry C. Kempe. Reprinted by permission of The Harvard University Press.

Chapter 9

Opener: David Plowden, DPI

9.1 all, Hella Hammid, Rapho/Photo Researchers

9.2 National Center for Health Statistics

9.3 Joel Gordon

9.4 The Bettmann Archive

9.5 Beryl Goldberg

9.6 Ken Heyman

9.8 Courtesy of Larry Fenson, San Diego State University

9.9 George Roos, Peter Arnold

9.10 *left,* Erich Lessing, Magnum; *right,* June Lundborg

9.12 Joel Gordon

9.13 Tass from Sovfoto

9.14 *left,* Joel Gordon; *right,* Raimondo Borea

Chapter 10

Opener: Burt Glinn, Magnum

10.1 Joseph P. Schuyler, Stock, Boston

10.2 Linda Ferrer Rogers, Woodfin Camp

Chart p. 304 Adapted from *Developmental Psychology* by Howard Gardner. Copyright © 1978 by Little, Brown and Co. With permission of the publisher.

Chart p. 307 Adapted from Denney, N. W., "A developmental study of free classification in children, *Child Development,* 1972, **43**, 1161–1170. Copyright © 1972 by The Society for Research in Child Development. Reprinted by permission.

10.4 Adapted from *Developmental Psychology* by Howard Gardner (Figure 7.3). Copyright © 1978 by Little, Brown and Co. With permission of the publisher.

Table 10.1 p. 312 Adapted from Flavell, J. H., *The Development of Role-taking and Communication Skills in Children.* Huntington, New York: R. E. Krieger Publishing Co., Inc., 1975. © 1968, John Wiley & Sons, Inc. Reproduced by permission.

Research Report p. 309, Ken Heyman

10.5 From *Smashed Potatoes* by Jane G. Martel, copyright © 1974 by Jane G. Martel. Reprinted by permission of Houghton-Mifflin Company.

p. 315 "Little stones…," "The world is so…," and "A hole is to dig" from *A Hole is to Dig,* written by Ruth Krauss, illustrated by Maurice Sendak. Copyright, 1952, as to pictures, by Maurice Sendak. By permission of Harper & Row, Publishers, Inc.

10.6 Andrew McKeever, EPA

10.7 Ken Heyman

10.8 Alice Kandell, Rapho/Photo Researchers

10.9 (a) Tass from Sovfoto; (b) Swedish Information Office; (c) Eastfoto; (d) Cary Wolinsky, Stock, Boston

Research Report p. 330, Ken Heyman

Closer Look p. 331 Chart from Miller, L. B., and Dyer, J. L. "Four preschool programs: Their dimensions and effects. *Monographs of the Society for Research in Child Development,* 1975, **40**, (5 & 6). Reprinted with permission from The Society for Research in Child Development.

10.10 Adapted from H. L. Garber & F. R. Heber, "The Milwaukee Project," a paper presented at the meeting of the International Association for the Scientific Study of Mental Deficiency, Washington, D.C., August, 1976.

Chapter 11

Opener: Erika Stone

11.1 *left,* Beryl Goldberg; *right,* Joan Menschenfreund

11.2 Sovfoto

11.3 Beryl Goldberg

Research Report pp. 344–345, *both,* University of Wisconsin, Primate Laboratory

11.5 Ken Heyman

11.7 *left,* Bruce Roberts, Rapho/Photo Researchers; *right,* Hella Hammid, Rapho/Photo Researchers

11.8 *In order from left to right,* Owen Franken, Stock, Boston; Joel Gordon; William Hubbell, Woodfin Camp

11.9 Joel Gordon

11.10 Myron Papiz, Photo Researchers

11.11 Myron Papiz, Photo Researchers

11.13 Stephen J. Potter, Stock, Boston

11.14 Joanne Leonard, Woodfin Camp

11.16 Burk Uzzle, Magnum

Chapter 12
Opener: Dan Budnik, Woodfin Camp
12.1   Peter Vandermark, Stock, Boston
12.4   Grete Mannheim, DPI
12.5   *In order from left to right,* Paul Fusco, Magnum; Fred Lombardi, Photo Researchers; David Barnes, Photo Researchers
12.6   *both,* Joan Menschenfreund
12.7   Bruce Roberts, Rapho/Photo Researchers
Closer Look pp. 384–385, *all,* Ken Heyman
12.9   *all,* Will McIntyre, Photo Researchers

Chapter 13
Opener: Tana Hoban, DPI
13.1   both, Charles Harbutt, Magnum
13.2   Doug Magee/EPA
13.3   Beryl Goldberg
13.4   Suzanne Szasz, Photo Researchers
13.5   Bruce Roberts, Rapho/Photo Researchers
Closer Look pp. 402–403, *all,* Ken Heyman
13.6   Raimondo Borea
13.7   Joel Gordon
13.10   (a) Peter Mentzel, Stock, Boston; (b) Paul Fusco, Magnum
Chart p. 413   Reprinted by permission of The MIT Press from Chomsky, C., *The Acquisition of Syntax in Children from Five to Ten,* © 1969 by The Massachusetts Institute of Technology.
13.11   Lawrence Fried, Magnum
13.12   The New York Public Library
13.13   The Bettmann Archive
13.14   *both,* George Roos, Peter Arnold
Chart p. 422   Adapted from Harrell, T. W., and Harrell, M. S. "Army General Classification Test Scores for Civilian Occupations." *Educational and Psychological Measurement,* 1945, **5,** 229–239.

Chapter 14
Opener: Leanne Schmidt, DPI
14.1   *In order from left to right,* Beryl Goldberg; Ken Heyman; Ken Heyman; Ken Heyman; Ken Heyman
14.2   Joel Gordon
14.3   Tass from Sovfoto
Closer Look p. 435, Jan Lukas/EPA
14.7   Bob Adelman, Magnum
Research Report, p. 447   Adapted from Koluchova, Jarmila, "Severe deprivation in twins: A case study," and "A report on further development of twins after severe and prolonged deprivation," *Early Experience: Myth and Evidence,* A. M. Clarke and A. D. B. Clarke (Eds.). Copyright © 1976 by The Free Press.
14.9   Jehangir Gazdar, Woodfin Camp
14.10   Chester Higgins, Jr., Rapho/Photo Researchers
14.11   Joan Menschenfreund
14.12   Kenneth Murray, Nancy Palmer Photo Agency
14.13   From Michael Rutter, "Protective factors in children's responses to stress and disadvantage." Reprinted from *Primary Prevention of Psychopathology,* Volume III: Social Competence in Children, edited by Martha Whalen Kent and Jon E. Rolf, by permission of The University Press of New England. Copyright 1970 by the Vermont Conference on the Primary Prevention of Psychopathology.

Chapter 15
Opener: Joel Gordon
15.1   The Granger Collection
15.3   James Carroll

15.4   George Ancona
Closer Look p. 467, *left,* A. J. Levin, Black Star; *right,* Charles Gatewood
15.5   Beryl Goldberg
15.6   Ann Hagen Griffiths, Omni-Photo Communications
15.7   Edward Lettau, Peter Arnold
Table 15.1 p. 471   Adapted from Koff, E., Rierdan, J., and Silverstone, E. "Changes in representation of body image as a function of menarcheal status." *Developmental Psychology,* 1978, **14,** 635–642. Reproduced by permission of the American Psychological Association.
Research Report p. 471, Nasjonalgalleriet, Oslo
15.9   David S. Strickler, Monkmeyer Press Photo Service
Closer Look p. 476, Tass from Sovfoto
15.10   James Carroll
15.11   John Running, Stock, Boston
15.12   National Center for Health Statistics

Chapter 16
Opener: Roger Malloch, Magnum
16.2   Richard Kalvar, Magnum
16.3   *left,* Roger Malloch, Magnum; *right,* Charles Harbutt, Magnum
16.5   By permission of the Estate of Norman Rockwell; photograph courtesy of Harry N. Abrams, Inc.
16.6   Mary Ellen Mark, Magnum
16.7   Courtesy of Planned Parenthood of Central Ohio, Inc.
16.8   *left,* Charles Gatewood, Stock, Boston; *right,* Owen Franken, Stock, Boston
16.9   Owen Franken, Stock, Boston

Chapter 17
Opener: James Carroll
17.1   Charles Harbutt, Magnum
Closer Look p. 510, Fritz Goro, LIFE MAGAZINE © 1951 Time Inc.
17.2   Alex Webb, Magnum
17.3   Daniel S. Brody, Stock, Boston
17.4   *both,* The Bettmann Archive
17.5   James Carroll
17.6   Paul Conklin, Monkmeyer Press Photo Service
17.7   Paul Conklin, Monkmeyer Press Photo Service
17.8   Arthur Grace, Stock, Boston
17.9   Cary Wolinsky, Stock, Boston
Chart p. 518   Adapted from Elder, G. H. "Structural variations in the childrearing relationship." *Sociometry,* 1962, **25,** 241–262. Reprinted by permission of the American Sociological Association.
Closer Look p. 520, John Running, Stock, Boston
17.10   National Center for Health Statistics
17.11   *left,* Jean-Claude Lejeune, Stock, Boston; *right,* Joel Gordon
17.12   Bureau of Labor Statistics
17.14   Russell Dian, Grand Projects

Epilogue
Opener: James H. Karales, Peter Arnold
Fig. 1   *In order from left to right,* Paul Fusco, Magnum; Wayne Miller, Magnum; Joan Menschenfreund; Hella Hammid, Rapho/Photo Researchers
Fig. 2   Joel Gordon
Fig. 3   Linda Ferrer Rogers, Woodfin Camp
Fig. 4   From *The Seasons of a Man's Life,* by Daniel J. Levinson. Copyright © 1978 by Daniel J. Levinson. Reprinted by permission of Alfred A. Knopf, Inc.
Fig. 6   Sepp Seitz, Woodfin Camp
Fig. 7   Klaus Franke, Peter Arnold

Name Index

Subject Index